Advanced Methods of Marketing Research

Advanced Methods of Marketing Research

Edited by Richard P. Bagozzi

Copyright © Basil Blackwell Ltd, 1994

First published 1994

Blackwell Publishers
238 Main Street
Cambridge, Massachusetts 02142
USA

108 Cowley Road
Oxford OX4 1JF
UK

Library of Congress Cataloging-in-Publication Data

Advanced methods of marketing research / edited by Richard P. Bagozzi.
    p. cm.
   Includes bibliographical references and index.
   ISBN 1–55786–549–3
   1. Marketing research. I. Bagozzi, Richard P.
  HF5415.2.A265 1994
  658.8'3—dc20   93–40009
                                            CIP

British Library Cataloguing in Publication Data

A CIP catalogue record for this book is available from the British Library.

Typeset in 10.5/12.5 pt Times by Pure Tech Corporation, Pondicherry, India
Printed in Great Britain by T.J. Press (Padstow) Ltd, Padstow, Cornwall.

This book is printed on acid-free paper

Contents

List of Figures

List of Tables

List of Contributors

Phipps Arabie, Graduate School of Management, Rutgers University, Newark

Ramesh V. Arjunji, Ph.D. Candidate, School of Management, University of Texas at Dallas

Richard P. Bagozzi, Dwight F. Benton Professor of Behavioral Science in Management and Marketing, School of Business Administration, University of Michigan

Jaesung Cha, Ph.D. Candidate, School of Business Administration, University of Michigan

Wayne S. DeSarbo, Sebastian S. Kresge Distinguished Professor of Marketing and Statistics, School of Business Administration, University of Michigan

William R. Dillon, Distinguished Foundation Fellow, College of Business Administration, University of South Carolina

Claes Fornell, Donald C. Cook Professor of Business Administration and Marketing, School of Business Administration, University of Michigan

Donna Hoffman, Professor, Owen Graduate School of Management, Vanderbilt University

Lawrence Hubert, Professor, Department of Psychology, University of Illinois, Champaign

Ajith Kumar, Associate Professor, College of Business, Arizona State University

Jan de Leeuw, Associate Professor, Department of Mathematics, University of California, Los Angeles

Jordan Louviere, Professor of Marketing and Park Fellow, Eccles School of Business, University of Utah

Jay Magidson, President, Statistical Innovations Inc., Belmont, Massachusetts

Ajay K. Manrai, Associate Professor, Department of Business Administration, University of Delaware

Lalita A. Manrai, Assistant Professor, Department of Business Administration, University of Delaware

Michel Wedel, Faculty of Economics, University of Groningen, the Netherlands

Youjae Yi, School of Business Administration, Seoul National University, South Korea

Acknowledgments

Appreciation is expressed to the School of Business Administration, the University of Michigan for support in preparation of this monograph and to Mrs Carolyn Maguire and Mrs Joan Walker for help in word-processing and administrative details. Special thanks go to the following scholars who reviewed at least one, and in many cases, two or more chapters: Elizabeth Edwards (Eastern Michigan University), Hans Baumgartner (Pennsylvania State University), Frank Andrews (deceased, University of Michigan), Donald Barclay (University of Western Ontario), Terry Elrod (University of Alberta), Joel Huber (Duke University), Peter Lenk (University of Michigan), Wayne De Sarbo (University of Michigan), and Clifford Clogg (Pennsylvania State University).

In addition, many authors have acknowledged the help of others in endnotes to their chapters.

Introduction

Richard P. Bagozzi

The past few years have witnessed unparalleled developments in research methods. Much of this has occurred in the fields of psychometrics and statistics, but many important contributions have been made by marketing researchers as well.

The present volume presents recent innovations in research methods found in all three fields mentioned above but with particular relevance to marketing. Virtually all the major advanced techniques are covered including structural equation modeling, partial least squares, the multivariate analysis of categorical data, chi-square automatic interaction detection (applied to market segmentation), multidimensional scaling, conjoint analysis, multiple correspondence analysis, latent structure analysis, and latent class regression.

This book is the first one to consider all these major advances. It is intended for three audiences: PhD students, faculty, and practicing researchers who desire in-depth, state-of-the-art coverage of the newest methods. It is conceivable that some instructors will find the book suitable as an assigned text in the MBA research and modeling courses. Useful background can be obtained by reading the companion volume, *Principles of Marketing Research* (Bagozzi, 1994) also published by Blackwell.

Chapter 1 by Bagozzi and Yi covers three advanced topics in structural equation models (SEMs). First, the analysis of experimental data by SEMs are considered for MANOVA designs. Second, SEM panel models are explored. Finally, canonical correlation analysis is examined from the point of view of SEMs. Each topic is illustrated with relevant examples.

In Chapter 2, Fornell and Cha give a thorough introduction to partial least squares (PLS). They begin by pointing out that PLS is based upon a stochastic concept of causality, which is the primary way that PLS differs from such traditional statistical treatments as econometric and LISREL models. They then address, in turn, the topics of predictor specification, model structure, and estimation. Finally, they discuss criteria for the evaluation of PLS models.

The multivariate statistical analysis of categorical data is presented by Magidson in Chapter 3. Focus is placed upon the analysis of categorical dependent variables as functions of categorical independent variables. The author begins with an introduction to the use of log-linear models for describing relationships in two-way tables and for analyzing standardized frequency counts (i.e. rates). Following this, the logit model is introduced and examples provided showing the use of the model for an experiment designed to increase the return rate of mail surveys and the use of the model for adjusting TV diary ratings. Next, polytomous models are considered including the case of a trichotomous dependent variable and the multinomial logit model. The chapter closes with the Y-Assocation or ordinal regression model. Many examples are given throughout.

One of the newest and most exciting techniques for market segmentation is the chi-squared automatic interaction detection technique (CHAID) which is now available with the SPSS-PC and SAS statistical packages. In Chapter 4, Magidson introduces CHAID and contrasts it with the earlier regression, AID, and clustering approaches. He also treats CHAID analyses of polytomous dependent variables (i.e. those with more than two categories). Two novel extensions of CHAID are developed as well: ordinal criteria and single-factor calibration (Y*-Association). Many examples are given for these procedures.

Arabie and Hubert provide a state of the art review of cluster analysis in Chapter 5. After reviewing substantive uses of cluster analysis in marketing, they point-out misunderstandings and misuses of clustering and related procedures. A useful taxonomy of clustering methods is then introduced. Finally, the chapter closes with a discussion of practical problems and software.

Advances in multidimensional scaling have pushed the technique in many new directions. DeSarbo, Manrai, and Manrai (Chapter 6) consider recent developments in one of these directions, latent class multidimensional scaling (LCMDS), which is especially relevant to the problem of market segmentation. The authors begin their chapter with a framework for the estimation of LCMDS models. They then discuss the use of LCMDS models for proximity, dominance, and choice data. Although the focus of the chapter is on technical aspects of this new technique, they briefly mention recent and potential applications.

In Chapter 7, Louviere examines new and emerging areas of conjoint analysis technology. After reviewing the behavioral foundations of conjoint analysis, he gives a metatheoretical overview of the technique. The heart of the chapter then analyzes recent developments. The reader will be exposed to many novel ideas that are sure to stimulate new directions and provoke debates in the years ahead.

Hoffman, de Leeuw, and Arjunji provide an overview of multiple correspondence analysis (MCA) in Chapter 8. They consider the philosophy of the approach, discuss its history, and reveal its relationships with multidimensional scaling and more generally classical multivariate analysis.

Special attention is given to the underlying theory of MCA. An interesting empirical example is given and discussion made of the use of MCA in representing brands and variables in a single map.

Latent structure and other mixture models are surveyed by Dillon and Kumar in Chapter 9. The authors begin with a detailed presentation of finite mixture models. They then consider unconstrained latent class analysis and provide an illustration. Next, constrained latent class analysis is covered. Finally, a sample of various applications from the literature are reviewed.

Wedel and DeSarbo (Chapter 10) review recent developments in latent class regression models. Special consideration is given to the foundation of the models as applied to various categories of data. An application of latent class regression is also provided to conjoint analysis in the field of service quality measurement.

The technology of marketing research has reached a stage of unusual complexity and diversification. It was a humbling experience putting together the chapters for this volume. It is hoped that marketing scholars, new and old, will be excited by the many developments and use and build upon them in their work. Answers to end of chapter questions can be obtained by writing to Richard P. Bagozzi, School of Business Administration, University of Michigan, Ann Arbor, Michigan, 48109–1234, USA.

1

Advanced Topics in Structural Equation Models

Richard P. Bagozzi
Youjae Yi

Introduction

In this chapter we consider how structural equation models can be extended to handle various research designs. Among others, we focus on three useful designs: experimental designs, panel designs, and canonical correlation analysis. For each, basic considerations in the application of structural equation analyses are presented, similarities and differences between structural equation analyses and traditional analyses are discussed, and illustrations are provided. Most of the models are estimated using LISREL (Jöreskog and Sörbom, 1989) because of its availability and ease of use, although one might employ other programs such as EQS (Bentler, 1989), EzPath (Steiger, 1989), LINEQS (a subroutine in SAS Proc CALIS), or PLS (Lohmöller, 1984). Although these topics are interrelated and overlap, we examine each category in sequence to facilitate the presentation.

Experimental Designs

Structural equation models can be used to analyze the data from experimental designs (Bagozzi and Yi, 1989; Bagozzi, Yi, and Singh, 1991; Kühnel, 1988). In this section, we will examine structural equation models for various experimental designs. We begin with a structural equation specification of a one-way MANOVA as an alternative to traditional analysis. Then we examine structural equation models extended to accommodate more complex designs such as latent variable MANOVAs, MANCOVAs, step-down analysis, and two-way MANOVAs.

Manifest variable MANOVA

The analysis of MANOVA designs can be accomplished with structural equation models by respecifying the parameters. To demonstrate the use of structural equation models for the analysis of experimental data, let us consider a basic experimental design with three dependent variables (Y_1 to Y_3) and two groups (experimental and control groups). Figure 1.1a illustrates the specification for this design. There are two parts in the specification: measurement and structural models.

(a) Measurement model

$$\text{Dummy} = \xi_1$$
$$\text{One} = \xi_2$$
$$Y_i = \eta_i \qquad \text{for } i = 1 \text{ to } 3$$

where Dummy = 0 (control group) or 1 (experimental group).

(b) Structural model

$$\eta_i = \gamma_i \xi_1 + \gamma_{i+3} \xi_2 + \zeta_i \qquad \text{for } i = 1 \text{ to } 3$$

(a) Manifest variable MANOVA

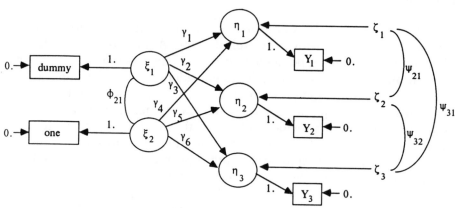

(b) Latent variable MANOVA

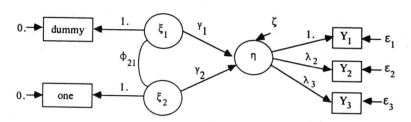

Figure 1.1 Models for MANOVA on three measures of a latent variable

Note that an exogenous latent variable (ξ_1) is a dummy variable representing two groups: control and experimental. There is a single indicator with a fixed loading of unity and no corresponding residual. Hence, the latent variable is equivalent to a manifest variable. We use a single 0, 1 dummy variable for two groups in this case, but we can use several dummy variables to represent n groups in the general case.

Note also that a pseudo-variable (i.e. "one") is used as another exogenous latent variable (ξ_2) to capture the means of dependent variables. This variable is a constant added to the sample moment matrix as another variable having 1 in the diagonal and the means of other variables as nondiagonal elements. Alternatively, this pseudo-variable could be added to the raw data as a column of 1's (Sörbom, 1974, 1982), as is needed for estimating the intercept term in multiple regression. Either specification enables one to analyze the means of observed dependent variables as a function of the independent variables. To do this, one must analyze the augmented moment matrix, not the usual correlation or covariance matrix.

To test the multivariate null hypothesis that the means of dependent variables are equal across groups, we can use the likelihood ratio chi square tests in LISREL (Jöreskog and Sörbom, 1989) or EQS (Bentler, 1989). Because the dummy variable is 0 for the control group and 1 for the experimental group, the paths from the "one" latent variable to dependent variables (i.e., $\gamma_4, \gamma_5, \gamma_6$) correspond to the means of dependent variables for the control group, and the paths from the dummy variable to dependent variables (i.e. $\gamma_1, \gamma_2, \gamma_3$) reflect the differences in their means across the two groups. For example, the means of Y_1 are γ_4 and $\gamma_1 + \gamma_4$ for the control and experimental groups, respectively, and thus γ_1 is the mean difference in Y_1 between the two groups. Thus, γ_1, γ_2 and γ_3 are the differences in the means of dependent variables between the two groups.

The full model as specified in Figure 1.1a will be exactly identified and thus will fit any data perfectly. If the means of the dependent variables are equal across groups, then $\gamma_1 = \gamma_2 = \gamma_3 = 0$. By imposing these constraints, we obtain a restricted model which is overidentified. The significance of the mean differences can be tested either individually with the critical ratios for the parameters or globally with the chi-square difference tests of the zero restrictions for these parameters.

An illustration To illustrate the use of structural equation models in MANOVA designs, we will use data from an experiment on consumer decision-making (Bagozzi, Yi, and Baumgartner, 1990). That experiment examined conditions in which choice behaviors would be influenced directly or indirectly influenced by one's preferences. Under low-impedance conditions when little planning and effort is needed, preferences were expected to affect choices directly with little or no impact of an explicit volition or decision. Under high-impedance conditions, in contrast, explicit decisions are required to overcome obstacles and thus preferences were expected to influence choices indirectly through their effect on these decisions. The three behavior measures represented alternative indicators of actual choices. Two different measures of decisions were also obtained. Preference

Table 1.1 Data used in experimental designs

Measure	High impedance group (n = 73)						Low impedance group (n = 79)					
Behavior 1	1.000						1.000					
Behavior 2	0.774	1.000					0.641	1.000				
Behavior 3	0.736	0.945	1.000				0.580	0.921	1.000			
Decision 1	0.256	0.425	0.430	1.000			0.255	0.173	0.171	1.000		
Decision 2	0.263	0.426	0.430	0.907	1.000		0.263	0.205	0.181	0.882	1.000	
Preference	0.082	0.190	0.209	0.325	0.263	1.000	0.310	0.343	0.344	0.316	0.271	1.000
Mean	0.21	0.27	0.55	4.03	3.93	14.16	4.05	1.70	4.09	4.90	4.76	14.48
SD	0.73	0.84	1.63	1.46	1.46	4.09	5.69	1.62	3.88	1.45	1.40	4.51

was measured with a single indicator. Table 1.1 reports the means, standard deviations, and within-group correlations for the data. In the current context, one hypothesis might be: Are choice behaviors different between low and high impedance groups?

First, the traditional MANOVA analysis was conducted via the SPSS[x] program. We chose to use the test for Wilks' Λ, because it is the most frequently employed statistic in the literature. The results of this analysis suggest a rejection of the null hypothesis that the means of choice behaviors are equal across the low and high impedance groups: Wilks' $\Lambda = 0.727$, $F(3, 148) = 18.56$, $p < 0.001$.

Next, the structural equation analysis of the same data was performed by using the LISREL program. The full LISREL model specified in Figure 1.1a, which allows for the differences in means, is exactly identified and gives a perfect fit to the data: $\chi^2(0) = 0.00$, $p = 1.00$. See Appendix 1.1 for the specification of this model. The restricted model with the zero constraints for the mean difference parameters (i.e. $\gamma_1 = \gamma_2 = \gamma_3 = 0$) gives the following results: $\chi^2(3) = 48.21$, $p < 0.001$.

An omnibus test of mean difference can be conducted by comparing the fit of these two models. The significant chi-square difference ($\chi^2_d(3) = 48.21$, $p < 0.001$) suggests that the means on *at least one* dependent variable are significantly different across groups. The estimates for individual mean difference parameters are examined to test whether each dependent variable is different across groups. The mean differences, denoted as γ_i's in the LISREL analysis, are $3.84(t = 5.2)$, $1.42(t = 6.7)$, and 3.54 ($t = 7.2$), respectively. They are all significant, suggesting that the means of *all* dependent variables are significantly different across groups for these particular data. Note that they are equal to the mean differences at the bottom of Table 1.1. For example, the difference in B1 is $4.05 - 0.21 = 3.84$, which is the estimate for γ_1.

Latent variable MANOVA

The structural equation approach can be extended to MANOVAs on latent variables, whereas the traditional MANOVA analysis is conducted only at the level of manifest variables. This extension is motivated by several considerations (Bagozzi and Yi, 1989). First, if individual measures of the variables show excessive random error, the traditional tests may be lacking in statistical power to detect valid experimental effects. Second, certain variables might be inherently unobservable constructs such that they can be measured only indirectly with multiple indicators. For example, measured variables might reflect variation in an underlying theoretical construct. Third, one might be concerned more with explanation and understanding of latent variables or constructs than with prediction or description of observed variables or measures, *per se*. That is, one may wish to test hypotheses implied by a theory involving latent variables as opposed to focusing on individual measures.

Figure 1.1b presents the specification for a latent variable MANOVA design. Note here that three measures are used as multiple indicators of a single latent variable. We wish to test whether the experimental manipulation affects the mean of the theoretical construct as measured by three indicators. The path (γ_1) from the dummy variable (ξ_1) to the latent dependent variable (η) reflects the difference in the means of the behavioral construct.

When the full model is fit to the behavior data in Table 1.1, the following goodness-of-fit measures are obtained: $\chi^2(4) = 5.77$, $p > 0.20$. The restricted model with the constraint (i.e. $\gamma_1 = 0$) gives the following results: $\chi^2(5) = 48.89$, $p < 0.001$. The chi-square difference between the two models is significant: $\chi^2_d(1) = 43.12$, $p < 0.001$. Also, the estimate of γ_1 is 3.21 with $t = 6.43$. These results show that the means of η are significantly different across the two groups.

MANCOVA

Researchers often need to control for the effects of covariates in examining experimental effects and wish to use multivariate analysis of covariance (MANCOVA). Structural equation models can be used to perform analyses of the general MANCOVA model. Let us consider the case for a one-way analysis with three dependent variables and a single covariate. Figure 1.2 illustrates a specification of the MANCOVA model in this case. We show the covariate with a single measure for simplicity, but multiple measures can be easily accommodated.

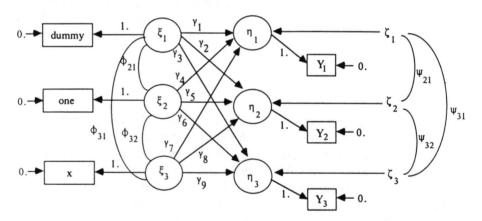

Figure 1.2 Models for MANOVA on three dependent variable and one covariate

The model in Figure 1.2 is applied to the behavior data in Table 1.1. Preference is taken as the covariate. The chi-square difference test from structural equation analysis suggests that we must reject the null hypothesis of equal means: $\chi^2_d(3) = 50.67$, $p < 0.001$. The estimates for the gammas reveal that all three dependent variables differed across groups even after variation in preferences is controlled for: $\gamma_1 = 3.77$ ($t = 5.77$), $\gamma_2 = 1.40$($t = 6.85$), $\gamma_3 = 3.48$ ($t = 7.39$). The findings from the SPSSx analysis suggest the same conclusion: Wilks' $\Lambda = 0.715$, F (3, 147) $= 19.54$, $p = 0.001$.

Homogeneity and multiple group approach

An important assumption of the MANOVA procedure is that the distributions of measures of dependent variables are equal across groups. Pillai's V has been found to be fairly robust to violations in equality of distributions but only when sample sizes are equal across groups (Olson, 1976). Within the context of traditional MANOVAs, a test of the equality of

Group 1

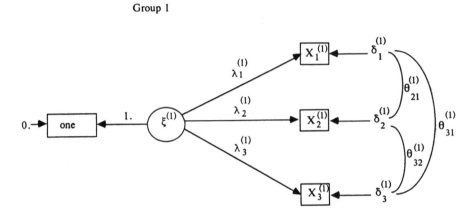

Group 2

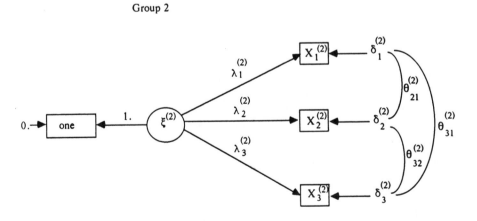

Figure 1.3 MANOVA models for homogeneity test and multiple group approach

variances and covariances can be performed with Box's M test (Norusis, 1988).

When this test is performed on the data in Table 1.1, it is found that Box's $M = 339.07$, $\chi^2(6) = 331.71$, $p < 0.001$. We therefore must reject the null hypothesis that the variance-covariance matrices for the dependent variables are equal across groups. That is, the assumption of the traditional MANOVA analysis is violated. What can we do? Shall we stop analyzing the data? The traditional procedure provides little recourse in such a case.

Fortunately, structural equation models can be used not only to test the homogeneity assumption, but also to perform a test of experimental effects even if homogeneity is rejected (Kühnel, 1988). The test is appropriate whether or not the sample sizes are equal across groups. To do this, we must reformulate the experimental design as a multiple group analysis. Figure 1.3 illustrates a specification for a MANOVA design with the three dependent variables and two groups. This procedure will be called a multiple group approach, whereas the procedure illustrated in Figure 1.1 is called a dummy variable approach.

The multiple group approach shown in Figure 1.3 can be used to test the homogeneity assumption. Because each ξ variable is defined as 1 through use of a pseudovariable in the moment matrix, it turns out that the dependent variables (X_i's) are equal to the sum of the mean for their respective group and error. Given this specification, the variance–covariance matrix for the error terms is, in fact, the variance–covariance matrix for the dependent variables. The specification for the full model in Figure 1.3 is exactly identified. To test for homogeneity, we must specify: $\Theta_\delta^{(1)} = \Theta_\delta^{(2)}$. That is, $\theta_{11}^{(1)} = \theta_{11}^{(2)}$, $\theta_{22}^{(1)} = \theta_{22}^{(2)}$, $\theta_{33}^{(1)} = \theta_{33}^{(2)}$, $\theta_{21}^{(1)} = \theta_{21}^{(2)}$, $\theta_{31}^{(1)} = \theta_{31}^{(2)}$, $\theta_{32}^{(1)} = \theta_{32}^{(2)}$. The resulting restricted model has six overidentifying restrictions, and the test of equal variances and covariances is performed by comparing chi-squares from the full and restricted models.

The multiple group approach can also be used to test the MANOVA hypotheses on the means of the dependent variables. The multiple group approach in Figure 1.3 is equivalent to the dummy variable approach in Figure 1.1a, but with one important difference. The dummy variable approach, like the traditional MANOVA analysis, assumes that variances and covariances of dependent variables are equal across groups. This homogeneity assumption is imposed because the covariance matrices among dependent variables are collapsed into one (i.e. the submatrix of the covariance matrix after dropping the dummy variable column) under the dummy variable approach. The multiple group approach can accommodate instances in which the variances and covariances are totally equal, totally unequal, or partially equal across groups. Under the multiple group approach, equality in means can be tested by fixing $\Lambda^{(1)} = \Lambda^{(2)}$: that is, $\lambda_1^{(1)} = \lambda_1^{(2)}$, $\lambda_2^{(1)} = \lambda_2^{(2)}$, $\lambda_3^{(1)} = \lambda_3^{(2)}$. This step yields three overidentifying restrictions, and again the test of equal means is performed by taking the difference in chi squares for the full and restricted models.

To illustrate, we applied the model in Figure 1.3 to the behavior data in Table 1.1. The following results were obtained:

A Full model (all parameters free): $\chi^2(0) = 0.00, p = 1.00$
B Equal variance–covariance: $\chi^2(6) = 339.23, p < 0.001$
C Equal means: $\chi^2(3) = 46.26, p < 0.001$
D Equal means and variance–covariance: $\chi^2(9) = 387.11, p < 0.001$

The assumption of homogeneity in variances and covariances can be tested by comparing Models A and B: $\chi^2_d(6) = 339.23, p < 0.001$. This is the structural equation analogue of the Box's M test. The results suggest that the homogeneity assumption must be rejected. Note that the results are quite similar to those from Box's M test: Box's $M = 339.07, \chi^2(6) = 331.71, p < 0.001$. When the homogeneity assumption holds, one can test the hypothesis of equal means across groups by comparing Models B and D. When the homogeneity assumption is violated, one can test the hypothesis of equal means by comparing Models A and C. Under the heterogeneity assumption, which is the case with the current data, the latter comparison (C – A) is used. The results indicate that means are not equal across groups: $\chi^2_d(3) = 46.26, p < 0.001$.

In general, the multiple group approach seems preferable to the dummy variable approach, because it can test the homogeneity assumption and applies to heterogeneous as well as homogeneous contexts. However, multiple group analyses are not available for programs such as PLS, and the dummy variable approach might be the only way to conduct analyses. Moreover, when the sample size is too small to be split into multiple groups, the dummy variable approach may be used.

Step-down analysis

Finding differences in the means for different groups is only the first step in MANOVA analysis. An important next step is to explain the differences. Given that an omnibus test indicates a difference in means, one may want to determine which of the dependent variables are responsible for the global significance. An inspection of the gamma parameters is useful for uncovering which variables are affected. This test for each individual parameter is equivalent to the univariate ANOVA on the dependent variables.

When there is a causal order among the dependent variables, however, step-down analyses provide useful information as to whether the mean difference in a certain variable is due to the direct effect of the experimental manipulation or its dependence on other variables (Bray and Maxwell, 1985; Roy 1958). In general, the first stage of a step-down analysis begins with a MANOVA test performed on all dependent variables. If the omnibus test points to a rejection of equal means, then the next step consists of testing the final variable in the hypothesized causal chain, while partialling out all remaining dependent variables as covariates. A significant omnibus test would indicate that the final variable differs even after controlling for its dependence on previous variables. In contrast, a non-significant test suggests that the difference in the final criterion is wholly due to the causal relation between the final variable and other variables. In this case, one moves backward to the preceding dependent variable and performs a similar test.

(a) Step 1

(b) Step 2

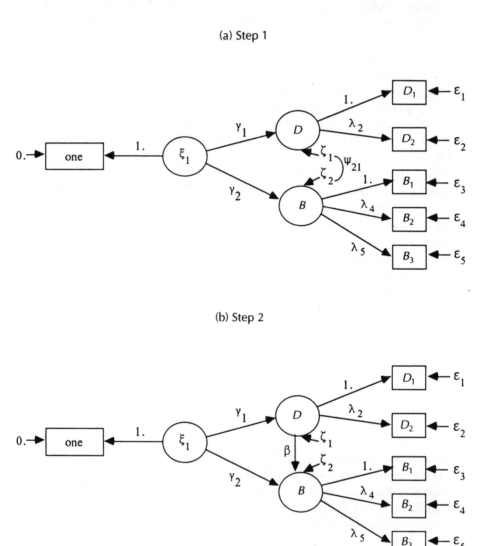

Figure 1.4 Step-down analysis with two latent variables: multiple-group approach

The structural equation approach to MANOVA can be used to perform step-down analyses (Bagozzi and Yi, 1989; Bagozzi, Yi, and Singh, 1991). Figure 1.4 shows the step-down analysis procedures for the MANOVA design which has two latent dependent variables: decision (D) and behavior (B). Note that it shows a multiple group approach to step-down analyses. In Step 1, γ_1 and γ_2 correspond to the means of latent variables D and B, respectively. Thus, the equality of means can be tested by comparing these parameters (i.e. $\gamma_i^{(1)}$ vs $\gamma_i^{(2)}$) across groups. This can be accomplished via a simultaneous analysis of both groups. In Step 2, γ_2 would correspond to the portion of the mean for B that is not due to the effect of D. Thus, a comparison of γ_2 across groups indicates whether the means of B differ between the groups when the effect of D on B is partialled out.

This approach allows one to test the two assumptions: (1) homogeneity of variances and covariances and (2) invariance of causal paths. Specifically, before conducting the first step of the analysis noted in Figure 1.4, one can test the homogeneity assumption. Then, in Step 1 the differences in D and B can be tested under either homogeneity or heterogeneity assumptions. One can also test the invariance of causal paths (i.e. $\beta^{(1)} = \beta^{(2)}$) across groups. If this test is significant, a subsequent step would be to test for the significance of the mean difference while allowing for different causal paths across groups. Thus, the multiple group approach allows for step-down analyses even when these assumptions are violated.

An illustration   The step-down analyses are illustrated with the data in Table 1.1. The two latent variables D and B are measured with two (d_1, d_2) and three indicators (b_1, b_2, b_3), respectively. See Table 1.2 for a summary of the results.

Table 1.2   Step-down analysis with a multiple group approach

Homogeneity test	
Full model	*Restricted model with equal variances*
$\chi^2(0) = 0.00, p \approx 1.00$	$\chi^2(15) = 351.96, p \approx 0.000$
	Hence: $\chi_d^2(15) = 351.96, p \approx 0.000$
First stage	
Full model	*Restricted model with $\gamma_i^{(1)} = \gamma_i^{(2)}$*
$\chi^2(14) = 7.89, p \approx 0.90$	$\chi^2(16) = 66.08, p \approx 0.000$
$\gamma_1^{(1)} = 4.03 \ (0.17)^a, \gamma_1^{(2)} = 4.90 \ (0.16)$	Hence: $\chi_d^2(2) = 58.19, p \approx 0.000$
$\gamma_2^{(1)} = 0.19 \ (0.07), \gamma_2^{(2)} = 4.01 \ (0.55)$	
Invariance of causal path test	
Full model	*Restricted model with $\beta^{(1)} = \beta^{(2)}$*
$\chi^2(14) = 7.89, p \approx 0.90$	$\chi^2(15) = 9.35, p \approx 0.86$
$\beta^{(1)} = 0.18 \ (0.05), \beta^{(2)} = 0.59 \ (0.32)$	Hence: $\chi_d^2(1) = 1.46, p > 0.10$
Second stage	
Full model	*Restricted model with $\gamma_2^{(1)} = \gamma_2^{(2)}$*
$\chi^2(15) = 9.35, p \approx 0.86$	$\chi^2(16) = 60.58, p \approx 0.000$
$\gamma_2^{(1)} = -0.58 \ (0.19), \gamma_2^{(2)} = 3.04 \ (0.59)$	Hence: $\chi_d^2(1) = 51.23, p \approx 0.000$

[a] standard errors are in parentheses.

We begin by testing the homogeneity of variance and covariances across groups. This test is conducted by comparing the model with free covariance matrices and the model with equal covariance matrices for residuals. The results indicate that the homogeneity assumption should be rejected for the data; $\chi_d^2(15) = 351.96$, $p < 0.001$. Thus, the subsequent analyses are conducted while allowing for different variances and covariances for the two groups.

When the mean parameters (γ_i's) are allowed to differ across groups, the model gives satisfactory results: $\chi^2(14) = 7.89$, $p > 0.89$. The estimates of mean parameters for both groups are 4.03 and 4.90 for D, and 0.19 and 4.01 for B, respectively. When the mean parameters are fixed to be invariant across groups, the model fit is not satisfactory; $\chi^2(16) = 66.08$, $p < 0.001$. The chi-square difference is 58.19 with 2 degrees of freedom, which is significant at the 0.001 level. Thus, the equality constraints (i.e. $\gamma_i^{(1)} = \gamma_i^{(2)}$ for $i = 1$ to 2) produce a significant increase in the chi-square values, suggesting the rejection of the null hypothesis that means are equal across groups.

Before moving to the second stage, the invariance of the causal path (i.e. $\beta^{(1)} = \beta^{(2)}$) is tested by comparing the full model without the equality constraint and the restricted model with the constraint. The full model gives the following results: $\chi^2(14) = 7.89$, $p > 0.89$. The restricted model with the constraint yields the following results: $\chi^2(15) = 9.35$, $p > 0.85$. The chi-square difference is 1.46 with 1 degree of freedom, which is not significant at the 0.10 level. One cannot reject the hypothesis that the causal path between D and B is invariant across groups. That is, the assumption of invariant causal paths is plausible for these data. Subsequent analyses are thus conducted using the invariant causal path in the model.

The next step examines the equality of means in B while controlling for the effect of D (see Step 2 in Figure 1.4). The model allowing for different means of D shows satisfactory results: $\chi^2(15) = 9.35$, $p > 0.85$, whereas the restricted model hypothesizing equal means for D reveals unsatisfactory results: $\chi^2(16) = 60.58$, $p < 0.001$. The chi-square difference is 51.23 with 1 degree of freedom, which is significant at the 0.001 level. These findings suggest that the hypothesis of equal means for behavior must be rejected even after controlling for the effect of decision.

Two-way MANOVA

In this section, we will examine the structural equation model for the two-way MANOVA design. The extension to the n-way case would follow a parallel development.

Let us consider a basic two-way design in which two levels are manipulated for each of two independent variables and two dependent variables are measured. Figure 1.5 is a structural equation representation of the two-way MANOVA design. We have four groups in total. By expressing one of the independent variables as a dummy separately for each of two groups, we have the model shown in Figure 1.5.

Group 1

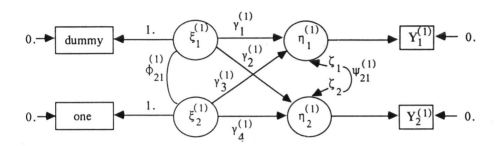

Group 2

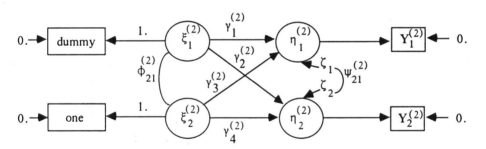

Figure 1.5 Two-way MANOVA for two dependent variables

The hypothesis of no interaction effect between the two variables would impose the following constraints: $\gamma_1^{(1)} = \gamma_1^{(2)}$, $\gamma_2^{(1)} = \gamma_2^{(2)}$. That is, the effects of one independent variable do not vary with the level of another independent variable. The interaction effect can be tested by comparing the full model in Figure 1.5 and this restricted model.

To test for main effects, we can compare the model with no interaction (i.e. $\gamma_1^{(1)} = \gamma_1^{(2)}$, $\gamma_2^{(1)} = \gamma_2^{(2)}$) and the model with no main and interaction effects (i.e. $\gamma_1^{(1)} = \gamma_1^{(2)} = \gamma_2^{(1)} = \gamma_2^{(2)} = 0$). The difference in chi square values for the two models provides a test statistic.

MANOVAs via PLS

Thus far, we have illustrated the use of structural equation models via LISREL, a popular program in marketing. However, the use of LISREL might be limited for several reasons. First, experimental data often do not satisfy the requirements of maximum likelihood estimation in LISREL such as multivariate normality, interval scaling, and large sample sizes. Also, improper or non-convergent solutions sometimes occur in LISREL analyses, which will reduce the interpretability of estimates (e.g. Boomsma, 1985; Gerbing and Anderson, 1987). It would be desirable to have an alternative procedure for analyzing such data to which LISREL is not well suited.

The structural equation analysis of MANOVA designs can be accomplished via Wold's (1985) partial least squares (PLS) approach, which avoids many of the assumptions and chances that improper solutions will occur in LISREL analyses. PLS is applicable not only to the basic design, but also to other MANOVA designs (e.g. latent variable MANOVA, step-down analysis).

General PLS model   Before we present the PLS formulation of MANOVA, we present a brief overview of the general PLS model, including specification and estimation. For more details, see Wold (1982, 1985).

Relations among latent variables are expressed in the following system of equations:

$$\boldsymbol{\eta} = \boldsymbol{\beta}_0 + \boldsymbol{\beta\eta} + \boldsymbol{v} \qquad (1.1)$$

where $\boldsymbol{\eta}$ is a vector of latent variables, $\boldsymbol{\beta}_0$ is a location parameter vector, $\boldsymbol{\beta}$ is a matrix of coefficients relating ηs among themselves, and $\boldsymbol{v}$ is a vector of residuals for the ηs. Equation (1.1) is sometimes referred to as the theoretical relations or the structural equation model. Latent variables are connected to observations through the following system of equations:

$$\mathbf{y} = \boldsymbol{\Pi}_0 + \boldsymbol{\Pi\eta} + \boldsymbol{\epsilon} \qquad (1.2)$$

where $\mathbf{y}$ is a vector of manifest variables, $\boldsymbol{\Pi}_0$ is a location parameter vector, $\boldsymbol{\Pi}$ is a matrix of loading coefficients (analogous to factor loadings), and $\boldsymbol{\epsilon}$ is a vector of residuals for the ys. Equation (1.2) is usually referred to as the measurement model. It is assumed that the cov $(\boldsymbol{v}, \boldsymbol{\epsilon}) = \mathbf{0}$.

The covariance matrix for the ηs is written as

$$\mathbf{P} = (\mathbf{I} - \boldsymbol{\beta})^{-1}\boldsymbol{\Psi}(\mathbf{I} - \boldsymbol{\beta}')^{-1} \qquad (1.3)$$

where $\mathbf{I}$ is an identity matrix and $\boldsymbol{\Psi}$ is the cov $(\boldsymbol{v})$. For the ys, the covariance matrix is

$$\boldsymbol{\Sigma} = \boldsymbol{\Pi} \, \mathbf{P} \, \boldsymbol{\Pi}' + \boldsymbol{\theta} \qquad (1.4)$$

where $\boldsymbol{\theta} = \text{cov}(\boldsymbol{\epsilon})$.

To facilitate the discussion of estimation, the following equation is added to Equations (1.1) and (1.2):

$$\eta = \Omega \, y + \delta \tag{1.5}$$

where Ω is a matrix of coefficients making latent variables dependent upon manifest variables and δ is a vector of residuals. Estimation under the PLS algorithm then proceeds in the three steps. In the first, iterative estimations of the Ω are performed. This consists of a sequence of ordinary least squares (OLS) regressions, linear operations, and square root extractions. In the second step, the βs and πs are estimated non-iteratively using the latent variables estimated in the first step. This is done assuming that the location parameters are zero. Finally, in the third step, the location parameters and generative relations are estimated. This is done non-iteratively with OLS regressions.

More intuitively, the PLS program proceeds iteratively by first estimating each latent variable from its observed indicators and then refining it by relating each latent variable to other latent variables' indicators. Once the latent variables have been estimated, they are then correlated, and the structural parameters of the model are estimated via path analysis using OLS regression. The resulting coefficients are interpreted as standardized partial regression coefficients.

Manifest variable MANOVA via PLS   Figure 1.6A shows the specification of the PLS model that is equivalent to the LISREL model in Figure 1.1a. Like the LISREL model, the PLS model has two parts:

(a) Measurement model

$$\text{Dummy} = \pi_d \, \xi_1$$
$$Y_i = \pi_i \, \eta_i \qquad \text{for i} = 1 \text{ to } 3$$

(b) Structural Model

$$\eta_i = I_i + \gamma_i^* \, \xi_1 + \zeta_i^* \qquad \text{for } i = 1 \text{ to } 3.$$

where I_i is the intercept that reflects the location of the dependent variable (η_i). To make the comparisons of our LISREL and PLS formulations of MANOVA as simple as possible, we have made several redefinitions of variables and parameters found in Wold's (1982, 1985) original exposition. Namely, $\beta_{0i} = I_i$, $\beta_{1i} = \beta_{2i} = \beta_{3i} = 0$, and $\beta_{4i} = \gamma_i^*$, $\eta_4 = \xi_1$, and $v_i = \zeta_i^*$.

We can note two differences between PLS and LISREL specifications. First, the pseudo-variable of one is not used in the PLS specification, whereas it is necessary in the LISREL specification. This is because PLS estimates the location parameters as intercepts without the need for introducing such a pseudo-variable. Second, the loadings relating latent variables to observed measures are set free and estimated in the PLS formulation, whereas they are fixed to unity in the LISREL formulation. For example, the loadings (i.e. π_i) for endogenous variables are free for PLS but fixed to 1.0 for LISREL. The path coefficients from the dummy latent variable to endogenous variables (i.e. $\gamma_1^*, \gamma_2^*, \gamma_3^*$) can be examined in order to test whether the means are significantly different across groups.

(a) Manifest variable MANOVA

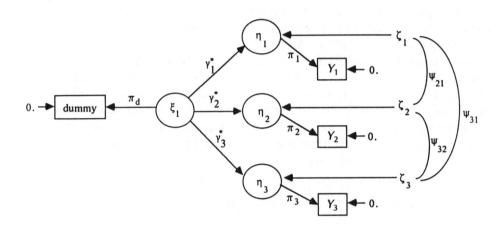

(b) Latent variable MANOVA

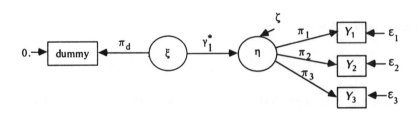

Figure 1.6 PLS models for MANOVA on three measures of a latent variable

We will now show the equivalence of the LISREL and PLS models by combining the measurement and structural parts of each model. This will permit us to compare the parameters of one model with those of the other.

LISREL Model

$$Y_i = \eta_i$$

$$= \gamma_i \, \xi_1 + \gamma_{i+3} \, \xi_2 + \zeta_i \qquad \text{since } \eta_i = \gamma_i \, \xi_1 + \gamma_{i+3} \, \xi_2 + \zeta_i$$

$$= \gamma_{i+3} + \gamma_i \, \text{Dummy} + \zeta_i \qquad \text{since } \xi_1 = \text{Dummy}, \, \xi_2 = 1.0$$

PLS Model

$$Y_i = \pi_i \, \eta_i$$

$$= \pi_i \, (I_i + \gamma_i^* \, \xi_1 + \zeta_i^*) \qquad \text{since } \eta_i = I_i + \gamma_i^* \, \xi_1 + \zeta_i^*$$

$$= \pi_i \, I_i + \pi_i \, \gamma_i^* (1/\pi_d) \, \text{Dummy} + \pi_i \, \zeta_i^* \qquad \text{since } \xi_1 = (1/\pi_d) \, \text{Dummy}$$

Then, we have the following equations:

$$\gamma_{i+3} = \pi_i \, I_i$$

$$\gamma_i = (1/\pi_d) \gamma_i^* \, \pi_i$$

$$\zeta_i = \pi_i \, \zeta_i^* \qquad \text{for } i = 1 \text{ to } 3.$$

Note that all the parameters in the LISREL model are functions of the parameters of the PLS model. For example, γ_i, the mean difference parameter for Y_i in the LISREL model, can be calculated by $(1/\pi_d) \gamma_i^* \, \pi_i$ from the PLS solutions. That is, the models are equivalent in terms of specification. However, important differences exist with respect to estimation, the properties of estimators, test statistics, and related issues which dictate the choice of the model. These issues are discussed later.

An illustration   The data in Table 1.1 are used to illustrate the equivalence of results using the PLS analysis and results from the LISREL analysis. Specifically, the three behavior measures are used as the dependent variables in MANOVA designs with two groups. The PLS model is estimated with the LVPLS 1.6 program (Lohmöller, 1984), and critical ratios for the PLS estimates are calculated by the jacknifing of parameter estimates (Efron and Gong, 1983). Specifically, LVPLX was employed because we needed to estimate location parameters, and option 4 was selected for the data metric. Appendix 1.3 provides the specification for the PLS model in Figure 1.6a. Standard errors of parameters were estimated by using the jackknife procedures which were developed by Barclay (1983) (e.g. Cooil, Winer, and Rados, 1987). Table 1.3 summarizes the key results from the LISREL and PLS analyses.

Table 1.3 MANOVA results for LISREL and PLS models

	LISREL model	PLS model
Mean differences	$\gamma_1 = 3.84\ (5.7)^a$	$\gamma_1^* = 0.424\ (10.3)$
	$\gamma_2 = 1.42\ (6.7)$	$\gamma_2^* = 0.481\ (9.0)$
	$\gamma_3 = 3.54\ (7.2)$	$\gamma_3^* = 0.508\ (9.2)$
Other parameters	$\gamma_4 = 0.20\ (0.4)$	$\pi_1 = 4.531\ (13.7)$
	$\gamma_5 = 0.27\ (1.8)$	$\pi_2 = 1.478\ (20.0)$
	$\gamma_6 = 0.55\ (1.6)$	$\pi_3 = 3.479\ (22.9)$
		$\pi_d = 0.500\ (312.7)$
		$I_1 = 0.045$
		$I_2 = 0.185$
		$I_3 = 0.157$

[a] critical ratios are in parentheses.

The PLS model in Figure 1.6a gives the following results: $\gamma_1^* = 0.424$ ($t = 10.3$), $\gamma_2^* = 0.481$ ($t = 9.0$), $\gamma_3^* = 0.508$ ($t = 8.5$). The LISREL results suggest the same conclusion: the means of the three dependent variables are significantly different between the two groups. In fact, the solutions for the LISREL analysis can be calculated from the solutions from the PLS analysis. For example, the mean difference for Y_1 can be computed as: $(1/\pi_d)\ \gamma_1^*\ \pi_1 = (2.00)\ (0.42)\ (4.53) = 3.84$. Note that this value is identical to the estimate of γ_1 in the LISREL model. Similarly, γ_2 and γ_3 can be calculated from the PLS solutions. Also, $\gamma_4 - \gamma_6$ can be obtained from the PLS solutions: $\gamma_{i+3} = \pi_i\ I_i$. For example, the mean (γ_4) of Y_1 for the control group can be obtained by $\pi_1\ I_1 = (4.53)\ (0.045) = 0.20$.

We have shown that PLS can be used to analyze experimental data with an example of the basic MANOVA design. However, PLS is applicable not only to the basic design, but also to other MANOVA designs (e.g. latent variable MANOVA, step-down analysis, MANCOVA). Because these extensions are rather straightforward, they are not discussed in this chapter. For example, Figure 1.6b provides a PLS specification of the latent variable MANOVA design (see Figure 1.1b for the corresponding LISREL specification). Interested readers should refer to Bagozzi, Yi, and Singh (1991).

LISREL or PLS? As we have seen, both LISREL and PLS models can be used to analyze experimental data. A question then arises: Under what conditions should one model be preferred to the other? A comparison of estimation methods between the two models would be useful in this regard (Fornell and Bookstein, 1982; Jöreskog and Wold, 1982). PLS, which uses fixed point estimation (e.g. Wold, 1965), differs from LISREL which uses maximum likelihood (ML) estimation in its basic assumptions and principles. The ML estimation in LISREL maximizes the probability of observing the data given the hypothesized model assuming multivariate normality of variables. However, PLS uses a series of interdependent OLS regressions to minimize residual variances without making any assumptions with respect to the population or scales of measurement. Hence, no distributional assumptions are required.

The PLS procedure is also applicable even when the sample size is small. Wold (1985) reports an analysis with a sample of 10, and Fornell and Bookstein (1982) use PLS on a sample of 24. In the former study, 28 manifest variables were included in the model. Analyses of such data sets by maximum likelihood procedures are often not feasible (Wold 1989). Sampling errors or too many parameters to estimate can yield non-convergent and improper solutions in LISREL analyses, which make it difficult to interpret the solutions (e.g. Gerbing and Anderson, 1987). In contrast, PLS does not suffer from non-convergent or improper solutions (Fornell and Bookstein, 1982).

An examination of the preceding assumptions suggests that the use of PLS is preferred over LISREL when (1) the multivariate normality assumption is violated, (2) the sample size is small, and (3) non-convergent or improper solutions are likely to occur (e.g. a complex model with many parameters).

The second situation (small sample size) would be the most important one in experimental designs. The assumption of multivariate normality can be relaxed with elliptical estimation or asymptotic distribution-free estimation (e.g. Browne, 1984), but this requires a large sample size (typically, the sample size must be 200 or more, depending on the number of variables in the model). Also, non-convergent or improper solutions are less likely to occur for large sample sizes (e.g. Anderson and Gerbing, 1984). Nevertheless, obtaining a large sample size might be difficult in typical experimental designs.

Some problems of the PLS approach also need to be mentioned. First, PLS tends to overestimate loadings and underestimate path coefficients (Dijkstra, 1983). In fact, as the proposed methodology is primarily concerned with path coefficients (which are underestimated), the significant results in a PLS analysis can be given more credence, because the test would be more conservative. Another problem with PLS concerns the interpretation of parameter estimates. The substantive interpretation of LISREL estimates is clear. In Figure 1.1a for example, $\gamma_1 - \gamma_3$ correspond to the mean differences of dependent variables across the control and experimental groups, whereas $\gamma_4 - \gamma_6$ reflect the means of dependent variables for the control group. In contrast, the parameter estimates in the PLS specification do not have such direct interpretations. Rather, they are multiplicative components of the means or mean differences, as shown earlier. Still another problem with PLS applications is that jackknife or bootstrap procedures are needed to obtain estimates for the standard errors of the parameter estimates, which are potentially subject to biases (Dijkstra, 1983; Efron and Gong, 1983). Furthermore, because it is a limited-information estimation method, PLS parameter estimates are not as efficient as full-information estimates (Fornell and Bookstein, 1982). Finally, PLS does not provide formal statistical tests or multiple sample analysis procedures, which are available for LISREL.

Comments

The structural equation approach has several advantages over traditional analyses. First, the procedure provides a natural way to correct for measurement error in the measures of variables and thus should reduce the chances of making Type II errors. Second, the procedure is more general in that it does not require the restrictive assumption of homogeneity in variances and covariances of the dependent variables. Third, the procedure allows for a more complete modeling of theoretical relations, whereas traditional analysis leaves associations among measures unanalyzed. Finally, structural equation models constitute flexible, convenient procedures.

Marketing researchers have used experimental designs over the years in consumer behavior, advertising, sales management, and other areas of research. Also, multiple dependent variables are often of interest to marketers. In this sense, the structural equation procedure has a great potential to be utilized in marketing research. Indeed, the procedure starts to see some application in substantive research (e.g. Yi, 1990).

Panel Designs

Marketing researchers are often interested in explaining changes of variables such as beliefs, attitudes, and intentions over time. For example, does consumer attitude change over time, and if so, how? What is the nature of the processes that generate attitude change or stability? Such questions can be investigated by collecting data at more than one point in time on the same individuals in panel designs. In the typical panel study, observations are collected for a number of individuals at two or more (often relatively few) points in time, and the unit of analysis is the individual (Hsiao, 1986; Kessler and Greenberg, 1981; Markus, 1979). The panel design enables researchers to investigate cross-sectional as well as longitudinal variations. Of particular interest to many researchers are the reliability and stability of key variables. It would be desirable to have a general procedure for analyzing panel data so that these properties could be assessed simultaneously.

One way of analyzing panel data is by examining observed test–retest (interwave) correlations for measures of key variables. However, this method has several limitations. First, a simple test–retest correlation is affected by random measurement errors as well as temporal instability of a variable. That is, it does not separate temporal instability from attenuation due to random measurement error (Heise, 1969). Second, a distinction is not made between observations and latent variables when one assumes, as frequently done, that variables are measured perfectly. Considering that many variables of interest to marketing researchers can be measured only imperfectly, conclusions based on observed scores can be misleading. For example, even when true scores do not change, observed scores may differ over time (perhaps due to measurement or response error). In such cases one might falsely conclude that the variable has changed. Third, few statistical tests are available for the adequacy of any hypothesized structural relationships among variables. Given these limitations of simple correlations, we need a method of analysis that can separate the reliability and stability of latent variables by explicitly modeling measurement errors. A structural equation modeling approach seems useful in this regard, because it enables researchers to introduce latent variables that cannot be observed directly (Bagozzi and Yi, 1993).

Single-indicator multiple-wave models

In some panel studies, key variables may be measured only with a single question; that is, a latent variable is measured with a single indicator repeatedly on the same people over several occasions. We can analyze such data with a so-called "single-indicator multiple-wave (SIMW) model," which is illustrated in Figure 1.7.

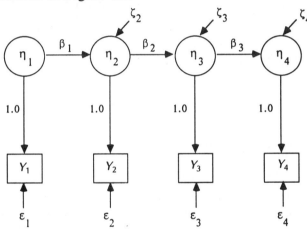

Figure 1.7 Single-indicator multiple-wave model

To demonstrate the use of structural equation models in panel designs, we will analyze the data obtained from a four-wave panel study of college students. In this study, the authors measured student's attitudes and intentions toward weight loss at four occasions (one week apart), among other variables. In total, 98 respondents completed all four waves. Intentions (I) to lose weight were measured with a 7-point item. Because intentions were measured with a single question, they will be used for the single-indicator multiple-wave models (see Table 1.4). Attitudes toward losing weight, which were measured with multiple items, will be investigated later.

Observed intention scores (Y_i) are obtained at four points in time ($i = 1$ to 4) for the true intention (η_i). The unit of measurement in the true variable (η_i) may be chosen to be the same as in the observed variable Y_i.

These intention data can be analyzed with a model depicted in Figure 1.7. This model can be specified in LISREL notation as follows:

$$Y_i = \eta_i + \varepsilon_i \qquad \text{for all } i = 1 \text{ to } 4$$
$$\eta_i = \beta_{i-1}\eta_{i-1} + \zeta_i \qquad \text{for all } i = 2 \text{ to } 4.$$

where $E(Y_i) = E(\eta_i) = E(\varepsilon_i) = E(\zeta_i) = 0$, for all $i = 1$ to 4; $E(\eta_{i-1}\zeta_i) = 0$, for all $i = 2$ to 4; $E(\eta_i\varepsilon_j) = E(\zeta_i\varepsilon_j) = 0$, for all $i, j = 1$ to 4; $E(\varepsilon_i\varepsilon_j) = 0$, for all $i \neq j$; $i, j = 1$ to 4; $E(\varepsilon_i\varepsilon_i) = \theta_i$, for all $i = 1$ to 4

If we estimate this model, we can easily assess the temporal stability and reliability of I. We can examine the corresponding path coefficient β_i for I (i.e. η_{i+1}), since it indicates the degree to which a latent variable at time $i + 1$ is a function of a latent variable at previous time i. For example, if $\beta_i = 1$ the latent variable does not change (or is perfectly stable) except for random fluctuation. Note that the stability of I is evaluated at the latent variable level rather than at the observed variable level. Thus, β_i is a parameter reflecting the stability of I after measurement errors have been taken into account. On the other hand, the reliability (ρ_i) of the observed variable (Y_i) can be obtained as the ratio of true score variance and observed variance (Lord and Novick, 1968):

$$\rho_i = \frac{\text{Var}(\eta_i)}{\text{Var}(Y_i)} = 1 - \frac{\theta_i}{S_i}$$

where S_i is the variance of the observed variable (Y_i) and θ_i is the error variance at the i-th time point.

Unfortunately, the model in Figure 1.7 is not identified without additional assumptions. The observed 4×4 variance–covariance matrix contains only 10 distinct pieces of information, whereas the number of unknown parameters is 11. For example, there is an indeterminacy associated with each of the "outer" variables Y_1 and Y_4 (Jöreskog and Sörbom, 1989).

To eliminate these indeterminacies some restrictions must be imposed on the parameters of the model. Over the years, researchers have proposed several alternative models based on different assumptions about the parameters. These alternative models are summarized in the top left-hand columns in Table 1.5.

Model 1 assumes that each of the two outer variables has the same error variance as the adjacent variable (i.e. $\theta_1 = \theta_2$, $\theta_3 = \theta_4$), as suggested by Jöreskog and Sörbom (1989). Model 2, originally introduced by Wiley and Wiley (1970), assumes that all measurement error terms have identical variance (i.e. $\theta_1 = \theta_2 = \theta_3 = \theta_4$). This model implies that the error variances remain the same, while the true score variances may change over time. Model 3 hypothesizes that the variances of measurement errors are identical and that the temporal stabilities are equal across time points: i.e.

$\theta_1 = \theta_2 = \theta_3 = \theta_4$ and $\beta_1 = \beta_2 = \beta_3$. Model 4 adds another restriction to those of Model 3 that the variances (Ψ) of residuals in equations (ζ) are identical: i.e. $\theta_1 = \theta_2 = \theta_3 = \theta_4$, $\beta_1 = \beta_2 = \beta_3$, and $\psi_2 = \psi_3 = \psi_4$.

Table 1.4 Data for single-indicator multiple-wave models ($n = 98$)

Item	Time	BI_1	BI_2	BI_3	BI_4
BI_1	1	1.000			
BI_2	2	0.639	1.000		
BI_3	3	0.657	0.722	1.000	
BI_4	4	0.536	0.646	0.701	1.000
SD		1.801	1.756	1.806	1.661

Table 1.5 Results for alternative single-indicator multiple-wave models

Model	Model description	Restrictions	Goodness-of-fit
M_1	baseline model	$\theta_1 = \theta_2, \theta_3 = \theta_4$	$\chi^2(1) = 0.74, p \approx 0.39$
M_2	equal error variance	$\theta_1 = \theta_2 = \theta_3 = \theta_4$	$\chi^2(2) = 1.31, p \approx 0.52$
M_3	equal error variance and equal stability	$\theta_1 = \theta_2 = \theta_3 = \theta_4$ $\beta_1 = \beta_2 = \beta_3$	$\chi^2(4) = 2.94, p \approx 0.57$
M_4	equal error variance, equal stability, and equal residual variance	$\theta_1 = \theta_2 = \theta_3 = \theta_4$ $\beta_1 = \beta_2 = \beta_3$ $\psi_2 = \psi_3 = \psi_4$	$\chi^2(6) = 4.93, p \approx 0.55$
M_5	equal error variance, perfect stability, and equal residual variance	$\theta_1 = \theta_2 = \theta_3 = \theta_4$ $\beta_1 = \beta_2 = \beta_3 = 1$ $\psi_2 = \psi_3 = \psi_4$	$\chi^2(7) = 8.97, p \approx 0.26$
M_6	equal error variance, equal stability, and zero residual variance	$\theta_1 = \theta_2 = \theta_3 = \theta_4$ $\beta_1 = \beta_2 = \beta_3$ $\psi_2 = \psi_3 = \psi_4 = 0$	$\chi^2(7) = 10.55, p \approx 0.16$

Comparison	Test of	χ^2_d test
$M_1 - M_2$	equal error variance	$\chi^2_d(1) = 0.57, p > 0.50$
$M_2 - M_3$	equal stability	$\chi^2_d(2) = 1.63, p > 0.25$
$M_3 - M_4$	equal residual variance	$\chi^2_d(2) = 1.99, p > 0.25$
$M_4 - M_5$	perfect stability	$\chi^2_d(1) = 4.04, p < 0.05$
$M_5 - M_6$	zero residual variance	$\chi^2_d(1) = 5.62, p < 0.05$

Model 5 has equal error variances, equal residual variances, and perfect stabilities as restrictions: $\theta_1 = \theta_2 = \theta_3 = \theta_4$, $\beta_1 = \beta_2 = \beta_3 = 1$, and $\psi_2 = \psi_3 = \psi_4$. That is, Model 5 postulates that no systematic change occurs in the latent variable except for random fluctuations. Model 6 specifies equal error variances, equal stabilities, and zero residual variances (i.e. $\theta_1 = \theta_2 = \theta_3 = \theta_4$, $\beta_1 = \beta_2 = \beta_3$, and $\psi_2 = \psi_3 = \psi_4 = 0$). In other words, no random fluctuations are predicted for equally stable intentions. The restrictions of equal stabilities and zero residual variances have been suggested by Blok and Saris (1983).

Since there are no *a priori* reasons for choosing one of the models over the others, all the models will be tested against the data to see which one is the most reasonable. Throughout this section, we have analyzed covariances of measures using the maximum likelihood procedure in LISREL (Jöreskog and Sörbom, 1989). Table 1.5 shows the results of the analyses for all six models applied to the intention data. We have evaluated the adequacy of model restrictions for these data with chi-square difference tests. Since Models 1–4 are nested within each other, the difference between the chi-square statistics is also distributed chi-square with the number of degrees of freedom equal to the difference in numbers of restrictions between the nested models. Thus, the restrictions are tested by hierarchical model comparisons, starting with Model 1 as a baseline. As shown in Table 1.5 Model 1 fits the data satisfactorily, suggesting that the outer error terms are equal to the error terms of their respective adjacent variables. To see whether the remaining restrictions are reasonable or not, we can test each in sequence.

When the restriction of identical error variances is introduced in Model 2, the chi-square statistic does not increase significantly ($\chi_d^2(1) = 0.57$, $p > 0.50$), suggesting that this assumption is tenable for these data. Model 3 has the additional restriction of equal stabilities over time, and the overall fit is still satisfactory: $\chi^2(4) = 2.94, p \approx 0.57$. The constraint of equal stabilities is also acceptable, since the chi-square difference is 1.63 with two degrees of freedom, which is not significant at the 0.25 level. Similarly, the restriction of equal residual variances has not caused a significant increase in the chi-square value: $\chi_d^2(2) = 1.99, p > 0.25$. However, the model cannot be restricted any further because extra restrictions lead to significant increases in the chi-square statistics. When perfect stabilities ($\beta_1 = \beta_2 = \beta_3 = 1$) are assumed, there is a significant drop in the goodness-of-fit ($\chi_d^2(1) = 4.04, p < 0.05$). The restriction of zero residual variances ($\psi_2 = \psi_3 = \psi_4 = 0$) also yields a significant increase in the chi-square statistic: $\chi_d^2(1) = 5.62, p < 0.05$. Overall, the restrictions of equal error variances, equal stabilities, and equal residual variances are accepted, but the hypotheses of perfect stabilities and nil residual variances in equations are rejected.

An inspection of the findings in Table 1.5 shows that all six models fit the data satisfactorily on the basis of the chi-square goodness-of-fit measures. Nevertheless, Models 5 and 6 can be rejected on the basis of chi-square difference tests. Moreover, an examination of the standardized residuals reveals that one residual each in Models 5 and 6 approaches significance. All residuals for Models 1–4 are insignificant. It is not possible to discriminate among Models 1–4 strictly on the basis of the chi-square measures, and each has approximately the same adjusted goodness-of-fit index (AGFI), ranging from 0.96 to 0.97. Model 4, however, demonstrates as a consequence of the chi-square difference tests that the assumptions of equal measurement error variances, equal stabilities, and equal errors in equations cannot be rejected. Hence, for illustrative purposes we focus upon this model.

We can examine two aspects of the model: stability and reliability of intentions. The temporal stabilities of intentions are equal across time points ($\beta_1 = \beta_2 = \beta_3$). The stability is quite high ($\beta_i = 0.90$), although it is not perfect ($\beta_i \neq 1$). It should be noted that the stability estimate ($\beta_i = 0.90$) obtained after correcting for attenuation due to measurement error is substantially higher than the observed test–retest (interwave) correlations between any two adjacent time points (i.e. $r_{1, i+1} = 0.64$, 0.72, and 0.70 for $i = 1, 2, 3$). If one were to overlook measurement error, one might seriously underestimate the stability of I. This finding illustrates the advantage of using structural equation models with measurement errors over examining simple test–retest correlations, as discussed earlier.

We can also examine the reliability estimates for all of the intention measures. In general, reliabilities are relatively high (ranging from 0.72 to 0.76). Furthermore, they do not change substantially over time; no reliability coefficients differ from their means (0.75) by more than 0.03. The reliability is lower (0.72) at the last occasion than at any other occasion.

We have shown that using single-indicator (structural equation) models with latent variables has several advantages over simple test–retest correlations. These advantages stem from the ability to represent measurement error and estimate stability coefficients corrected for attenuation, whereas test–retest correlations are parameters which reflect an amalgam of random error and true stability that cannot be separated and are individually unknown.

Nevertheless, single-indicator models are not without limitations. In general, a SIMW model is not identified. Some restrictions must be introduced to avoid indeterminacies in the model, but a number of alternatives are possible. For example, Heise (1969) assumes equal reliabilities over time, whereas Wiley and Wiley (1970) argue that the assumption of equal error variances is more plausible. Jöreskog (1977) and Blok and Saris (1983) propose still other restrictions. These restrictions are somewhat arbitrary, and they can lead to quite different conclusions under certain conditions. Also, a distinction cannot be maintained between specific and common factors, since they are not separately identified. These difficulties can be overcome when key variables are measured with multiple items. With this goal in mind, we next examine a more general case of multiple-indicator multiple-wave models.

Multiple-indicator multiple-wave models

In marketing as well as in other social sciences, many variables are measured with multiple items. In our study, respondents' attitudes toward losing weight were measured with three 7-point bipolar items (pleasant/unpleasant, good/bad, and happy/unhappy) at four occasions. Table 1.6 presents these panel data. Let us define Y_{ij} as the observed response at the i-th wave ($i = 1$ to 4) with item j ($j = 1$ to 3). For example, Y_{13} is the attitudinal response collected at the first occasion with the third item. To analyze such data, we can use a so-called "multiple-indicator multiple-wave (MIMW) model." Such a model is illustrated in Figure 1.8, where η_i is the value of latent (true) attitude at wave i and a linear relationship is assumed between latent attitude (η_i) and manifest measures (Y_{ij}). Since there are four time points, we postulate four latent variables in Figure 1.8.

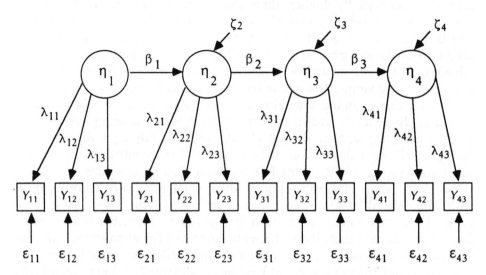

Figure 1.8 Multiple-indicator multiple-wave model

Table 1.6 Data for multiple-indicator multiple-wave models ($n = 98$)

Item	Y_{11}	Y_{12}	Y_{13}	Y_{21}	Y_{23}	Y_{31}	Y_{32}	Y_{33}	Y_{41}	Y_{42}	Y_{43}
Y_{11}	1.000										
Y_{12}	0.748	1.000									
Y_{13}	0.754	0.647	1.000								
Y_{21}	0.515	0.594	0.527	1.000							
Y_{22}	0.516	0.565	0.520	0.852	1.000						
Y_{23}	0.436	0.348	0.433	0.624	0.664	1.000					
Y_{31}	0.598	0.452	0.432	0.576	0.628	0.531	1.000				
Y_{32}	0.598	0.478	0.473	0.607	0.677	0.556	0.906	1.000			
Y_{33}	0.292	0.292	0.319	0.402	0.439	0.386	0.537	0.561	1.000		
Y_{41}	0.445	0.394	0.407	0.551	0.547	0.450	0.721	0.709	0.442	1.000	
Y_{42}	0.376	0.356	0.343	0.547	0.590	0.453	0.683	0.733	0.404	0.736	1.000
Y_{43}	0.333	0.299	0.327	0.417	0.404	0.418	0.522	0.480	0.597	0.615	0.518	1.000
SD	1.058	1.065	1.003	0.909	0.926	1.151	0.893	0.925	1.119	0.990	0.905	1.097

The MIMW model depicted in Figure 1.8 can be formulated as follows:

$$Y_{ij} = \lambda_{ij}\eta_i + \varepsilon_{ij} \qquad \text{for all } i = 1 \text{ to } 4, j = 1 \text{ to } 3$$
$$\eta_i = \beta_i\eta_{i-1} + \zeta_i \qquad \text{for all } i = 2 \text{ to } 4$$

where $E(Y_{ij}) = E(\eta_i) = E(\varepsilon_{ij}) = E(\zeta_i) = 0$, for all $i = 1$ to 4, $j = 1$ to 3; $E(\eta_{i-1}\zeta_i) = 0$, for all $i = 2$ to 4; $E(\eta_g\varepsilon_{ij}) = E(\zeta_g\varepsilon_{ij}) = 0$, for all $i, g = 1$ to 4; $j = 1$ to 3; $E(\varepsilon_{ij}\varepsilon_{gh}) = 0$, for all $ij \neq gh$; $i, g = 1$ to 4; $j, h = 1$ to 3; $E(\varepsilon_{ij}\varepsilon_{ij}) = \theta_{ij}$, for all $i = 1$ to 4; $j = 1$ to 3.

Although there are many different ways to analyze MIMW models, it seems useful to develop a systematic approach. We propose a general procedure for analyzing MIMW models by asking the following questions in sequence:

1 Which measurement model is appropriate (e.g. parallel, tau-equivalent, or congeneric)?
2 Are there serially correlated errors? If so, what is the order of auto-correlation? What are the consequences of correlated errors?
3 How can we explain the correlated errors? What processes underlie the correlations among errors?
4 Do variables change or remain stable over time? Are they equally stable across time points?

Let us now examine the specification and test of structural equation models to investigate these questions.

Measurement models One basic question about the MIMW model is: What are the epistemological relationships? Several alternatives exist for measurement models that link latent variables and observed variables. There are at least three measurement models: parallel models, tau-equivalent models, and congeneric models (Jöreskog, 1971). Parallel models, the most restrictive measurement models, assume that measures of a latent variable have identical factor loadings and error variances (i.e. $\lambda_{ij} = \lambda_{ik}$, $\theta_{ij} = \theta_{ik}$). Tau-equivalence models assume that factors loadings are equal (i.e. $\lambda_{ij} = \lambda_{ik}$), while error variances are possibly different. Congeneric models do not impose restrictions on factor loadings or error variances, except that the measurements are assumed to measure the same thing.

A question then arises: Which of these models is appropriate? These models were thus tested against the attitude data. We have chosen to test these measurement models at four time points simultaneously (cf. Figure 1.8), rather than testing them separately for each point in time for two reasons. First, a separate analysis for each wave will lead to just identified models for 3-indicator congeneric models, which cannot be tested statistically. Second, measurements should be validated within the theoretical context in which they will be used. In the present study examining the reliability and stability of attitude over time, it was necessary to include all attitude measures at the four occasions.

These alternative measurement models have been applied to the attitude data in Table 1.6. None of the models gives an acceptable fit to the data according to the usual rule-of-thumb ($p > 0.05$). The parallel model yields $\chi^2(67) = 252.78$, $p \approx 0.000$, whereas the tau-equivalent model gives

$\chi^2(59) = 96.66$, $p \approx 0.001$. Even the congeneric model does not provide a satisfactory fit to the data: $\chi^2(51) = 84.55$, $p \approx 0.002$.

The adequacy of alternative assumptions about the structure of measurement can be tested with the chi-square difference tests by comparing nested models. First, the invariance of factor loadings can be tested by comparing the congeneric model with the tau-equivalent model. When the restriction of invariant factor loadings is introduced, the fit of the model does not decrease significantly; the chi-square difference (χ^2_d) is 12.11 with 8 degrees of freedom ($p > 0.10$). It is therefore reasonable to assume that factor loadings are equal for the attitude measures. Next, we can test a hypothesis that measurement errors have equal variances. Adding this constraint yields a significant increase in the chi-square statistic ($\chi^2_d(8) = 156.1$, $p < 0.001$), suggesting the rejection of the null hypothesis that error variances are equal among measures. In sum, the tau-equivalent model fits this data set, and this measurement model is used in subsequent analyses.

Structure of autocorrelation among measurement errors   As we have seen earlier, the congeneric model did not give a satisfactory fit to the data. This finding suggests that one might need to eliminate some restrictions. One restriction is that errors at different times are uncorrelated with each other. To this point it has been assumed that the measurement error for one item is independently distributed over time (across waves). In many situations, however, measurement errors may reveal serial dependence or autocorrelation. In panel studies, measurement errors are often autocorrelated due to memory effects, shared methods, or omitted variables (e.g. Sörbom, 1975). For example, respondents may recall earlier answers and try to be consistent in their responses over time. We have thus examined the possibility that errors for the same item might be autocorrelated or serially correlated with each other (Kessler and Greenberg, 1981).

An important question about autocorrelated errors is: What is the order of autocorrelation? For example, if measurement errors are correlated between only two adjacent points in time, the autocorrelation follows a first-order process. In order to investigate the order of error correlations, we can examine several models with alternative restrictions. These restrictions range from no correlated errors, to first-order autocorrelations, to second-order autocorrelations, and to third-order autocorrelations.

The baseline model with no correlated errors gives an unsatisfactory fit: $\chi^2(59) = 96.66$, $p \approx 0.001$. When the first-order autocorrelation is introduced by allowing correlated errors for the same item across adjacent occasions, the model yields the following goodness-of-fit measures: $\chi^2(50) = 63.23$, $p \approx 0.099$. According to the chi-square difference test, relaxing the constraint of zero first-order autocorrelations improves the model fit significantly: $\chi^2_d(9) = 33.43$, $p < 0.001$. Then, the second-order autocorrelation can be introduced in the model; that is, errors (e.g. ε_{ij}, $\varepsilon_{i+1, j}$ and $\varepsilon_{i+2, j}$) for the same item (e.g. j-th item) across three waves are allowed to correlate with each other. The results are as follows: $\chi^2(44) = 49.77$, $p \approx 0.254$.

Compared with the model with first-order correlations only, the fit of the model improves significantly; the χ_d^2 is 13.46 with 6 degrees of freedom, which is significant at the 0.05 level.

Finally, the third-order autocorrelation can be examined by allowing all the error terms (i.e. ε_{1j}, ε_{2j}, ε_{3j}, and ε_{4j}) for the j-th item to be correlated across waves. The model gives a satisfactory fit to the data ($\chi^2(41) = 49.04$, $p \approx 0.182$), but the improvement in the goodness-of-fit is not significant: $\chi_d^2(3) = 0.73$, $p > 0.50$. This result suggests that an addition of third-order autocorrelations does not improve the model fit, and the model with second-order autocorrelations is the most appropriate based on the chi-square difference tests.

Processes underlying correlated errors We have found for our data that the errors are serially correlated with a second-order process. The incorporation of correlated errors permits us to examine the stability of the focal variable while controlling for omitted variables. However, correlations themselves are not very informative of underlying processes, since there are several reasons why errors might be correlated. Next, let us examine several alternative models that can be offered as explanations for serially correlated errors in general, and test which model provides the best explanation for this data set in particular. The models to be examined are as follows: (a) higher-order factor model, (b) model with an omitted background variable, (c) multiple-lag model, (d) model with a simplex error structure, (e) model with method factors.

Correlated errors across time may occur because latent variables at different time points share a *higher-order latent construct*. As illustrated in Figure 1.9, this model hypothesizes that a general, abstract latent variable underlies responses measured at different occasions. In this study, a general, stable attitude would be a second-order factor (ξ) that guides four first-order factors $\eta_1 - \eta_4$ (i.e. attitudes at different time points). The first-order factors are linear combinations of a second-order factor plus a unique variable (i.e. residual) for each first-order factor. The observed variables are linear combinations of the first-order factors, plus an error term for each observed variable. General discussions of higher-order factor models can be found elsewhere in marketing (e.g. Bagozzi, 1985; Gerbing and Anderson, 1984).

This model can be specified as follows:

$$Y_{ij} = \eta_i + \varepsilon_{ij} \qquad \text{for all } i = 1 \text{ to } 4, j = 1 \text{ to } 3$$
$$\eta_i = \gamma_i \xi + \zeta_i \qquad \text{for all } i = 2 \text{ to } 4$$

where $E(\eta_i) = E(\zeta_i) = E(\xi) = E(\xi\zeta_i) = 0$, for all $i = 1$ to 4; $E(Y_{ij}) = E(\varepsilon_{ij}) = E(\eta_i\varepsilon_{ij}) = E(\xi\varepsilon_{ij}) = E(\zeta_i\varepsilon_{ij}) = 0$, for all $i = 1$ to 4; $j = 1$ to 3; $E(\varepsilon_{ij}\varepsilon_{gh}) = 0$, for all $ij \neq gh$; $i, g = 1$ to 4; $j, h = 1$ to 3; $E(\varepsilon_{ij}\varepsilon_{ij}) = \theta_{ij}$, for all $i = 1$ to 4; $j = 1$ to 3. Before we present the empirical findings for this model, let us present the forms and logic for the other four models.

Autocorrelations among errors might arise when one omits from the analysis a variable that influences the focal variables throughout the measurement period (the *omitted background variable* case). In such a case, the error terms are likely to be correlated with each other, because they include the effects of the omitted variable. That is, omitted variables are suggested as explanations of the correlation among measurement errors. For the data under consideration in this part of the chapter, this model would ascribe the correlated errors to the omission of an exogenous variable that influences attitudes at different time points. One plausible background variable is the individuals' expectations that they would actually lose weight assuming that they try to lose weight. That is, one's attitudes toward an outcome might be affected by one's expectations that one would achieve the outcome. Expectations were measured with two indicators: likely–unlikely (1 to 7) and no chance–certain (0.0 to 1.0 in probability) items. Figure 1.10 illustrates such a model, where ξ is the omitted background variable (i.e. expectation).

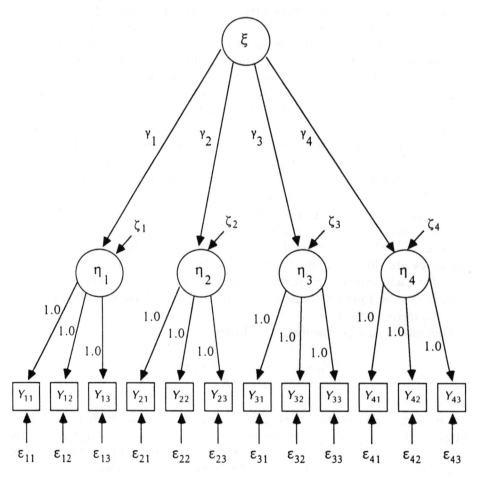

Figure 1.9 Second-order factor model

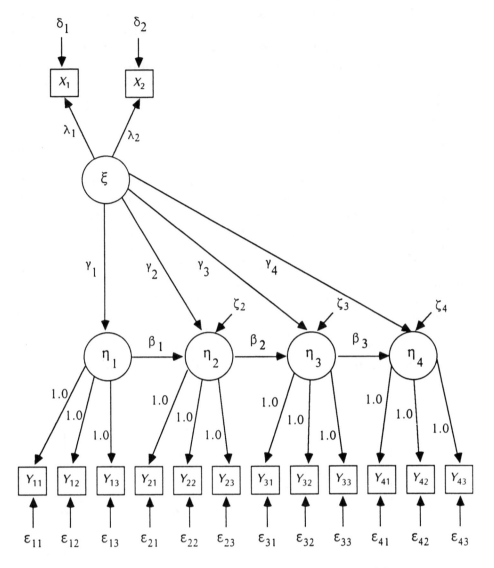

Figure 1.10 Model with a background variable

This model can be formulated as follows:

$$Y_{ij} = \eta_i + \varepsilon_{ij} \qquad \text{for all } i = 1 \text{ to } 4, j = 1 \text{ to } 3$$
$$X_k = \lambda_k \xi + \delta_k \qquad \text{for all } k = 1, 2$$
$$\eta_i = \beta_{i-1}\eta_{i-1} + \gamma_i \xi + \zeta_i \qquad \text{for all } i = 2 \text{ to } 4$$

where $E(\eta_i) = E(\zeta_i) = E(\xi) = E(\xi\zeta_i) = 0$, for all $i = 1$ to 4; $E(\eta_{i-1}\zeta_i) = 0$, for all $i = 2$ to 4; $E(Y_{ij}) = E(\varepsilon_{ij}) = E(\eta_i\varepsilon_{ij}) = E(\xi\varepsilon_{ij}) = E(\zeta_i\varepsilon_{ij}) = 0$, for all $i = 1$ to 4; $j = 1$ to 3; $E(\varepsilon_{ij}\varepsilon_{gh}) = 0$, for all $ij \neq gh$; $i, g = 1$ to 4; $j, h = 1$ to 3; $E(\varepsilon_{ij}\varepsilon_{ij}) = \theta_{ij}$, for all $i = 1$ to 4; $j = 1$ to 3.

So far, we have implicitly assumed that attitudes form a "simplex pattern" over time. That is, a true attitude score obtained at one occasion is predicted from an individual's attitude score at the immediate prior occasion, and other earlier attitude scores will not improve that prediction; that is, an attitude has lag-1 effects in subsequent periods. The simplex model has been found appropriate for many longitudinal studies in which the same variable is measured repeatedly on the same people over several occasions (e.g. Jöreskog, 1970). As a consequence, the correlation between two latent attitudes (e.g. η_i and η_j) is expected to decrease as they become distant in time (i.e. the larger $|i - j|$).

However, it is possible for a variable to have effects for more than one subsequent period (i.e. *multiple-lag effects*). In the context of the present four-wave study, the multiple lags can be either two or three. The lag-3 model is presented in Figure 1.11, where a variable at time i has effects for the subsequent three periods. For example, η_1 influences not only η_2 but also η_3 and η_4. In Figure 1.11 $\beta_4 - \beta_5$ represent the lag-2 effects, whereas β_6 represents lag-3 effects. The lag-2 model can be easily obtained by eliminating β_6 (the third-order effect) from the model in Figure 1.11. The multiple-lag models imply that the simplex hypothesis for attitudes may not be correct and that the correlated errors are due to the mis-specification of the functional relationships among latent variables; that is, omitting the relevant paths such as the second-order and third-order effects over time.

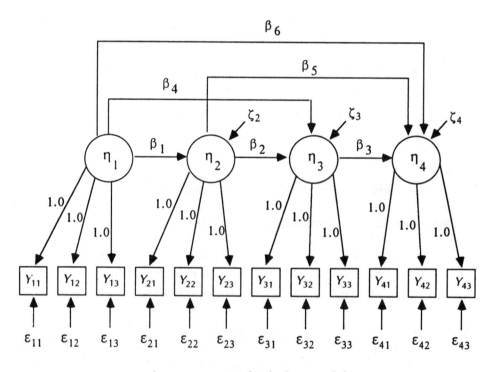

Figure 1.11   Multiple-lag model

The lag-3 model depicted in Figure 1.11 can be specified as follows:

$$Y_{ij} = \eta_i + \varepsilon_{ij}$$ for all $i = 1$ to 4, $j = 1$ to 3
$$\eta_i = \beta_i \eta_{i-1} + \beta_{i-1} \eta_{i-2} + \beta_{i-2} \eta_{i-3} + \zeta_i$$ for all $i = 2$ to 4
$$\eta_j = 0$$ if $j < 0$

with the usual assumptions for the basic MIMW model depicted in Figure 1.8.

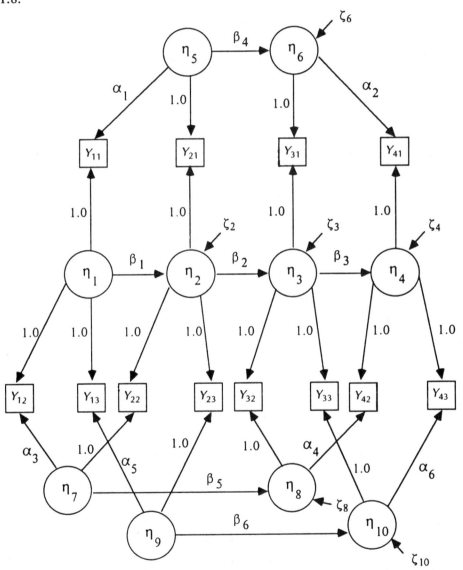

Figure 1.12 Model with a simplex error structure (measurement errors are omitted for simplicity)

Another possibility that might cause autocorrelations is illustrated in Figure 1.12 (termed, the *model with simplex errors*). In this model the measurement relations between latent variables and observed variables as well as the structural relations among latent variables are the same as in the basic MIMW model. But the model with a simplex error structure differs from the basic model in that a set of systematic errors is hypothesized for each type of item. The systematic errors, denoted as $\eta_5 - \eta_{10}$ in Figure 1.12, follow a simplex structure analogous to the structural relationships among latent variables (e.g. attitudes). Therefore, this model suggests that the errors have been correlated because they are in fact causally related to each other.

The model in Figure 1.12 can be formulated as follows:

$$Y = \begin{bmatrix} 1 & 0 & 0 & 0 & \Lambda_a \\ 0 & 1 & 0 & 0 & \Lambda_b \\ 0 & 0 & 1 & 0 & \Lambda_c \\ 0 & 0 & 0 & 1 & \Lambda_d \end{bmatrix} \eta + \varepsilon$$

$$\eta = \begin{bmatrix} \beta_a & 0 & 0 & 0 \\ 0 & \beta_b & 0 & 0 \\ 0 & 0 & \beta_c & 0 \\ 0 & 0 & 0 & \beta_d \end{bmatrix} \eta + \zeta$$

where

$$\Lambda_a = \begin{bmatrix} \alpha_1 & 0 & 0 & 0 & 0 & 0 \\ 0 & 0 & \alpha_3 & 0 & 0 & 0 \\ 0 & 0 & 0 & 0 & \alpha_5 & 0 \end{bmatrix}, \qquad \Lambda_b = \begin{bmatrix} 1 & 0 & 0 & 0 & 0 & 0 \\ 0 & 0 & 1 & 0 & 0 & 0 \\ 0 & 0 & 0 & 0 & 1 & 0 \end{bmatrix}$$

$$\Lambda_c = \begin{bmatrix} 0 & 1 & 0 & 0 & 0 & 0 \\ 0 & 0 & 0 & 1 & 0 & 0 \\ 0 & 0 & 0 & 0 & 0 & 1 \end{bmatrix}, \qquad \Lambda_d = \begin{bmatrix} 0 & \alpha_2 & 0 & 0 & 0 & 0 \\ 0 & 0 & 0 & \alpha_4 & 0 & 0 \\ 0 & 0 & 0 & 0 & 0 & \alpha_6 \end{bmatrix}$$

$$\beta_a = \begin{bmatrix} 0 & 0 & 0 & 0 \\ \beta_1 & 0 & 0 & 0 \\ 0 & \beta_2 & 0 & 0 \\ 0 & 0 & \beta_3 & 0 \end{bmatrix}, \quad \beta_b = \begin{bmatrix} 0 & 0 \\ \beta_4 & 0 \end{bmatrix}, \quad \beta_c = \begin{bmatrix} 0 & 0 \\ \beta_5 & 0 \end{bmatrix}, \quad \beta_d = \begin{bmatrix} 0 & 0 \\ \beta_6 & 0 \end{bmatrix}$$

$\eta = (\eta_1, \eta_2, \eta_3, \eta_4, \eta_5, \eta_6, \eta_7, \eta_8, \eta_9, \eta_{10})'$, $\epsilon = (\varepsilon_{11}, \varepsilon_{12}, \varepsilon_{13}, \varepsilon_{21}, \varepsilon_{22}, \varepsilon_{23}, \varepsilon_{31}, \varepsilon_{32}, \varepsilon_{33}, \varepsilon_{41}, \varepsilon_{42}, \varepsilon_{43})'$, and $\zeta = (\zeta_1, \zeta_2, \zeta_3, \zeta_4, \zeta_5, \zeta_6, \zeta_7, \zeta_8, \zeta_9, \zeta_{10})'$. The estimates of the variances of η_i's are as follows: $\mathrm{Var}(\eta_i) = \mathrm{Var}(\zeta_i) = \psi_i$, for $i = 1, 5, 7, 9$; $\mathrm{Var}(\eta_j) = \beta_{j-1}^2 \mathrm{Var}(\eta_{j-1}) + \psi_j$, for $j = 2, 3, 4, 6, 8, 10$

Since the same variables are measured repeatedly on the same people with the same instruments (i.e. the same methods or items) in panel studies, these instruments might have systematic influences on the observed variables (Jagodzinski, Kühnel, and Schmidt, 1987; Raffalovich and Bohrnstedt, 1987). In such cases, one needs to model the systematic external influences explicitly by introducing "method factors." *Method factors* are hereafter used to represent any unmeasured systematic factors influencing individual responses. Method factors may inflate or deflate the correlations among variables (Bagozzi and Yi, 1990, 1991).

In the present context, it is possible to hypothesize that all the responses are affected by sharing a common method of measurement (e.g. self-report). Figure 1.13 presents such a possibility by introducing one method factor common to all items about attitude (Bagozzi and Yi, 1990). In other words, this model would suggest that the serially correlated errors among measurements come from sharing a common method.

The model in Figure 1.13 can be specified as follows:

$$Y_{ij} = \eta_i + \lambda_{ij}\eta_m + \varepsilon_{ij} \qquad \text{for all } i = 1 \text{ to } 4, j = 1 \text{ to } 3$$
$$\eta_i = \beta_i\eta_{i-1} + \zeta_i \qquad \text{for all } i = 2 \text{ to } 4$$

where η_m is the method factor (scaled to unit variance) shared by all measures and the usual assumptions for the basic MIMW model hold.

Alternatively, it is possible that each item (e.g. good–bad) may have its own systematic influence on the individual responses, as occurs when an item has a specific meaning other than attitude. For example, a good–bad item may denote not only personal liking or disliking (i.e. overall affect) for the attitude object but also social desirability or undesirability (i.e. moral evaluations) of the attitude object. In such cases, it is necessary to postulate a method factor for each type of item. Figure 1.14 presents a model that incorporates such item-specific method factors.

This model hypothesizes that each item has a specific effect on individuals' responses. That is, responses to the same item will be affected not only by the underlying trait (attitude) but also by the specific item used. Each latent variable measured with the same item at four different occasions is hypothesized to share a method variance. It is thus possible to decompose an observed score on each item into three distinct components: (1) the latent variable common to all items at one point in time (common factor), (2) the item-specific method factor (specific factor), and (3) the random measurement error.

The model in Figure 1.14 can be formulated as follows:

$$Y_{ij} = \eta_i + \lambda_{ij}\eta_{mj} + \varepsilon_{ij} \qquad \text{for all } i = 1 \text{ to } 4, j = 1 \text{ to } 3$$
$$\eta_i = \beta_i\eta_{i-1} + \zeta_i \qquad \text{for all } i = 2 \text{ to } 4$$

where η_{mj} is the item-specific method factor for measurements with item j (1 to 3) and the usual assumptions for the basic MIMW model hold.

Results We have thus far examined five types of models that might underlie the observed autocorrelations among errors. In order to determine which is the most plausible, we have applied these models to the attitude data. Table 1.7 summarizes the findings for the alternative models.

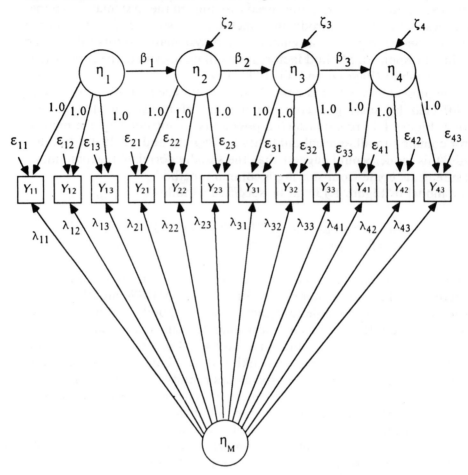

Figure 1.13 Model with one method factor

Table 1.7 Summary of findings for alternative models underlying correlated errors

Model	Goodness-of-fit
A a higher-order factor model	$\chi^2(58) = 98.30, p \approx 0.001$
B a model with a background variable	$\chi^2(78) = 106.77, p \approx 0.017$
C multiple-lag models	
(i) lag-two model	$\chi^2(57) = 89.62, p \approx 0.004$
(ii) lag-three model	$\chi^2(56) = 88.66, p \approx 0.004$
D a model with a simplex error structure	$\chi^2(44) = 62.89, p \approx 0.03$
E models with method factors	
(i) one method factor	$\chi^2(47) = 58.59, p \approx 0.12$
(ii) three item-specific factors	$\chi^2(47) = 52.62, p \approx 0.27$

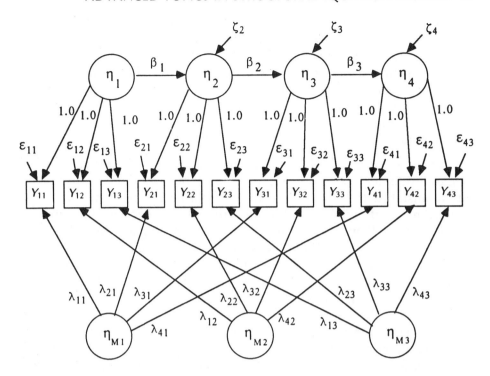

Figure 1.14 Model with three item-specific method factors

First, the higher-order factor model is found to be unsatisfactory. The chi-square statistic is 98.30 with 58 degrees of freedom, which is significant at the 0.001 level. This results suggest the rejection of the hypothesis that an abstract, general attitude might underlie responses to attitude questions at four occasions. Next, the model with an omitted background variable is examined (see Figure 1.10). The goodness-of-fit of this model is not satisfactory according to the usual rule-of-thumb: $\chi^2(78) = 106.77$, $p \approx 0.017$. This result suggests that an omission of expectations as a background variable does not fully explain the correlated errors.

Multiple-lag models are also examined as alternatives to the simplex model with lag-1 effects only. Two types of multiple-lag models are hypothesized: the lag-2 model and the lag-3 model. The model with lag-2 effects gives the following goodness-of-fit results: $\chi^2(57) = 89.62$, $p \approx 0.004$. The lag-3 model presented in Figure 1.11 gives also an unsatisfactory fit to the data. The chi-square value is 88.62 with 56 degrees of freedom, which is significant at the 0.005 level. Next, we examine a model hypothesizing that errors have a simplex structure, as illustrated in Figure 1.12. This model shows the following goodness-of-fit measures: $\chi^2(44) = 62.89$, $p \approx 0.03$. The fit of the model is still unsatisfactory, although it approaches an acceptable level.

Finally, models with method factors are examined. The model postulating one common method factor for all items (see Figure 1.13) yields the following results: $\chi^2(47) = 58.59$, $p \approx 0.12$. An alternative model with three item-specific method factors also reveals a satisfactory fit: $\chi^2(47) = 52.62$, $p \approx 0.27$. Although the overall goodness-of-fit tests indicate satisfactory fits for both models, substantial improvements in fits result for the model with three method factors over the model with one method factor; the chi-square difference is 5.97 with no difference in the degrees of freedom. Hence, the model with three method factors is chosen as a model that best accounts for the underlying structures associated with autocorrelated errors.

Stability of variables over time   The final question of interest concerns the temporal stability of attitude. Are attitudes stable over time? If attitudes are totally unstable, the stability coefficients will be insignificant (i.e. $\beta_i = 0$). The estimates of stability coefficients from the model with three method factors are as follows: $\beta_1 = 0.66(0.08)$, $\beta_2 = 0.76 \ (0.08)$, and $\beta_3 = 0.83 \ (0.07)$, with standard errors in parentheses. All are statistically significant at the 0.01 level, suggesting that they are significantly different from zero. Overall then attitudes are quite stable after correcting for attenuation due to measurement errors and possible dependencies among errors.

But what is the nature of attitude stabilities? Are they equally stable across time? Are they perfectly stable? We can test two hypotheses about stabilities of attitudes over time. One hypothesis is that stabilities are equal across four time points (i.e. $\beta_1 = \beta_2 = \beta_3$). Another hypothesis is that attitudes show perfect stabilities (i.e. $\beta_1 = \beta_2 = \beta_3 = 1$). These hypotheses can be tested by examining several nested models with respect to stability coefficients.

The baseline model with free stability coefficients gives a chi-square value of 52.62 with 47 degrees of freedom ($p \approx 0.27$). When the restriction of equal stability coefficients is imposed, the following results ensue: $\chi^2(49) = 55.07$, $p \approx 0.26$. The chi-square difference is not significant at the 0.05 level ($\chi_d^2(2) = 2.45$), suggesting the equal stability restriction is tenable. The additional restriction of perfect stability can be tested similarly. When the restriction of perfect stability is introduced into the model, the model fit becomes unsatisfactory: $\chi^2(50) = 87.31$, $p \approx 0.001$. We should note that the restriction causes a significant drop in the model fit: $\chi_d^2(1) = 32.24$, $p < 0.001$. One should therefore reject the hypothesis that attitudes have perfect stabilities. These findings suggest that the model with equal stabilities is most appropriate for these data. Therefore, the best model is the one with three item-specific factors plus equally stable attitudes.

Let us now examine key findings about the stability and reliability of attitudes. First, the temporal stability of attitudes is quite high, although not perfect. Furthermore, the stabilities are equal across four occasions. The stability estimate (0.76) is higher than any observed correlation between two adjacent time points, which ranges from 0.39 to 0.73 with an average of 0.58. Again, this result illustrates the possible attenuation in observed correlations due to random error. These findings are similar to the findings for intentions (I) in the single-indicator models.

One advantage of the model with method factors is that the variance of each observed variable can be partitioned into three parts: parts due to a latent variable (trait), a specific factor (method), and random measurement error (Bagozzi and Yi, 1991; Raffalovich and Bohmstedt, 1987):

$$\text{Var}\,(Y_{ij}) = \text{Var}\,(\eta_i) + \lambda_{ij}^2\,\text{Var}\,(\eta_{mj}) + \text{Var}\,(\varepsilon_{ij})$$

This suggests that the results can be restated in terms of explained variances. When the total variance of each measurement is partitioned into components due to trait, method, and random error, one can see that most of the attitude measures show high levels of trait variation. Specifically, more than half of the observed variance in most measurements is accounted for by the underlying trait (i.e. attitude).

Table 1.8 Reliabilities of attitude measures used in the study

Measure	Individual item reliability	Composite reliability	Average variance extracted
Time 1			
Y_{11}	0.92		
Y_{12}	0.69	0.91	0.77
Y_{13}	0.72		
Time 2			
Y_{21}	0.88		
Y_{22}	0.87	0.89	0.73
Y_{23}	0.56		
Time 3			
Y_{31}	0.94		
Y_{32}	0.90	0.91	0.81
Y_{33}	0.70		
Time 4			
Y_{41}	0.72		
Y_{42}	0.90	0.91	0.79
Y_{43}	0.76		

One can also compute reliabilities of individual attitude items, composite reliabilities of attitude scales, and the average variance extracted (AVE) (Bagozzi and Yi, 1988; Fornell and Larcker, 1981; Werts, Linn, and Jöreskog, 1974). Table 1.8 presents these reliability estimates for the measures used in this study. Overall, measures of attitudes are quite reliable; the average individual item reliability is 0.80, the average composite reliability 0.91, and the average AVE is 0.78. Although individual item reliabilities show some fluctuations over time, no systematic patterns exist. The composite reliabilities are very similar across four time points, ranging from 0.89 to 0.91. All AVE measures are higher than 0.70, indicating that more than 70 per cent of the variance in the construct is accounted for by the measures. Also, AVEs remain quite similar across four time points; no AVE measures differ from their average (0.78) by more than 0.05. Overall, these findings with respect to reliabilities are comparable to those for I in two ways: (1) reliabilities are quite high and (2) reliabilities do not change substantially over time.

Comments

We have demonstrated the applications of various structural equation models in panel analysis in order to assess reliability and stability simultaneously. It has been shown that there are many different models available for analyzing panel data. The models and test procedures are so general that they can be applied in many situations. Nevertheless, the particular findings of this study should be interpreted as specific to the data set we used.

We should mention that a number of topics and models in panel analysis have not been examined in this chapter. First, we have examined continuous (or interval level) variables by using structural equation models. In some cases, variables might be at best discrete, either dichotomies or polychotomies. Interested readers are referred to Wiggins (1973) and Coleman (1964) for analysis of discrete variables. We have also analyzed discrete-time processes where the state of units of analysis is recorded at discrete points in time. A discussion of continuous-time designs is available elsewhere (e.g. Coleman, 1964; Tuma and Hannan, 1984).

We have also ignored the first moments by analyzing covariances based on deviations from the means. Thus, a latent variable is assumed to have perfect stability if $\eta_{i+1} = \eta_i + \zeta_i$ (or $\beta_i = 1$), where η_i is the mean-centered value at time i. That is, perfect stability means that the expected value of all observed or latent variables between time i and $i + 1$ are equal to each other. We used unstandardized regression coefficients to assess the temporal stability of variables (Jöreskog, 1977; Judd and Milburn 1980). This is useful when one examines perfect stability in the sense: $\eta_{i+1} = \eta_i + \zeta_i$ (Jagodzinski and Kühnel, 1987). However, some researchers prefer standardized regression coefficients or correlation coefficients (Wheaton et al., 1977).

We have assumed homogeneity among respondents. But if responses vary across individuals, one may employ multiple-group analyses for subgroups. For this particular data set, it was not practical to do so because of the small sample size ($n = 98$), but it can be easily implemented for larger data sets (Jöreskog and Sörbom, 1989). Several questions can be raised: Are reliabilities different across subgroups? Do stabilities differ across subgroups? For example, Converse (1970) has argued that response uncertainty will vary across individuals, depending upon the centrality of the attitude object (cf. Jagodzinski and Kühnel, 1987).

A final point to note is the following. Panel data can be used to provide estimates of measure specificity, examine cross-lagged relationships, and even investigate construct validity. For discussion of these topics, see Bagozzi and Yi (1993).

Canonical Correlation Analysis

In this section we consider structural equation models to conduct canonical correlation analysis (Bagozzi, Fornell, and Larcker, 1981). First, we examine the conventional canonical correlation model. Then, we consider the structural equation approach to canonical correlation analysis and illustrate the two approaches with empirical data. After showing the equivalence of the solutions from the two approaches, we discuss the potential advantages of the structural equation approach.

Canonical correlation model

Let q denote the number of x variables and p be the number of y variables. The objective of canonical correlation analysis is to find a linear combination of the q predictors that is maximally correlated with a linear combination of the p criteria. This problem is equivalent to solving the eigenstructures:

$$R_{xx}^{-1}R_{xy}R_{yy}^{-1}R_{yx} - \lambda_j I) \, \mathbf{w} = 0$$

$$(R_{yy}^{-1}R_{yx}R_{xx}^{-1}R_{xy} - \lambda_j I) \, \mathbf{v} = 0$$

where R_{yy} is a $(p \times p)$ criterion variable correlation matrix R_{xx} is a $(q \times q)$ predictor variable correlation matrix, R_{xy} and (R_{yx}) are $(q \times p)$ and $(p \times q)$ cross correlation matrices, $\mathbf{w}$ and $\mathbf{v}$ are eigenvectors (weight vectors) for the predictor and criterion variate, respectively, λ_j is the eigenvalue (or the squared jth canonical correlation), and I is the identity matrix.

The variance of the canonical variates is constrained to equal 1, or $\mathbf{w'}R_{xx}\mathbf{w} = 1$ and $\mathbf{v'}R_{yx}\mathbf{v} = 1$. Once the eigenvectors and eigenvalues are determined, a second set of canonical variate pairs, orthogonal to the first, can be formed from the residual variance.

Figure 1.15 illustrates the canonical correlation model with $p = q = 3$. The canonical correlation (R_c) is the bivariate correlation between the two linear composites of predictor and criterion sets and reflects the strength of the overall relationship between the two composites. The eigenvalue (λ) is the squared canonical correlation and indicates the amount of shared variance between linear combinations of the variables in each set. The canonical loadings (structure correlations) are the correlations of predictor (x) or criterion (y) variables with their respective canonical variates $(x^*$ and $y^*)$. They are obtained by premultiplying the eigenvectors (weight vectors) by their associated correlation matrix: $r_{y*y} = R_{yy}\mathbf{v}$, $r_{x*x} = R_{xx}\mathbf{w}$. Cross loadings are the correlations of individual variables in one set with the canonical variate from another set. For example, r_{x*yj} is the correlation between the $x*$ variate and the observed y_i.

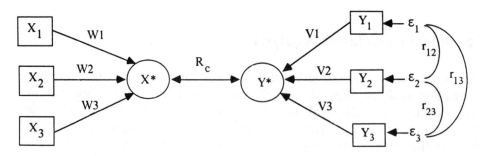

Figure 1.15   The canonical correlation model

Figure 1.16 presents a structural equation specification of the canonical correlation model in Figure 1.15 (Bagozzi, Fornell, and Larcker, 1981). Note that the paired variates ($x*$ and $y*$) are reduced to a model with a single variable. That is, the first canonical variate pair is expressed as a Multiple Indicators/Multiple Causes (MIMIC) model of a single variate (Jöreskog and Goldberger, 1975).

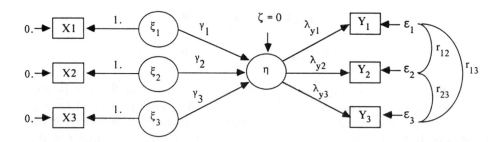

Figure 1.16   Structural equation model for canonical correlation analysis – first variate pair (The correlations among the ξ_i are omitted from the figure for simplicity.)

The measurement equations are

$$y = \Lambda_y \eta + \varepsilon$$

$$x = I \xi$$

where I is a $(q \times q)$ identity matrix. The structural equation model is $\eta = \Gamma\xi$.

Because no measurement errors are assumed for x_i's, the observed variables (x_i's) are identical to the latent variables (ξ_i's). Note that η is an exact combination of the x_i's (ξ_i's). Assuming that the x variables and y

variables are standardized, the elements in Γ are identical to the canonical weights (w) for the predictor variate. The elements in Λ_y are the correlations between the predictor variate (x^*) and the criterion variables (y_i); that is, Λ_y is the ($p \times 1$) matrix of cross loadings, r_{x*y}. The eigenvalue can be calculated as: $\lambda = R_c^2 = r'_{x*y} R_{yy}^{-1} r_{x*y} = \Lambda'_y R_{yy}^{-1} \Lambda_y$. The loadings for the criterion variate (y^*) are obtained as: $r_{y*y} = (1/R_c) \Lambda_y$.

By formulating canonical correlation analysis as a MIMIC model, the goodness of fit between the structure implied by the canonical model and the observed data can be examined and tested with the chi-square statistic. Standard errors for the estimated predictor weights and cross loadings between the predictor variate and criterion variables are also available. These standard errors can be used to calculate critical ratios and test the statistical significance of individual weights and cross-loadings. Because canonical correlation analysis is symmetric, the criterion weights and cross loadings between the criterion variate and predictor variables can be estimated by simply interchanging the x variables and y variables.

An illustration

To illustrate, we have applied the model in Figure 1.16 to the data in Bagozzi, Fornell, and Larcker (1981). Table 1.9 provides the correlation matrix for these data. There are three x variables (x_1, x_2, x_3) and three y variables (y_1, y_2, y_3).

The traditional canonical correlation analysis indicates that there are two statistically significant canonical variate pairs. For purposes of illustration, however, we will look at only the results for the first canonical variate pair. The following results are obtained: $R_c = 0.603$; λ (or R_c^2) $= 0.363$. The R_c^2 is significant at the 0.001 level via a test based on Bartlett (1941). The canonical loadings for the criterion set (y_1, y_2, y_3) and the predictor set (x_1, x_2, x_3) are obtained as follows:

$$r_{x*x} = \begin{bmatrix} r_{x*x1} \\ r_{x*x2} \\ r_{x*x3} \end{bmatrix} = \begin{bmatrix} 0.593 \\ 0.586 \\ 0.811 \end{bmatrix}.$$

$$r_{y*y} = \begin{bmatrix} r_{y*y1} \\ r_{y*y2} \\ r_{y*y3} \end{bmatrix} = \begin{bmatrix} 0.799 \\ 0.956 \\ 0.788 \end{bmatrix}.$$

The structural equation model is also used to analyze the same data. The chi square statistic associated with the first canonical pair for the MIMIC model indicates a borderline fit: $\chi^2(4) = 10.27$, $p < 0.05$. A second latent variable is introduced in the MIMIC model to improve the fit. This is accomplished by fixing the parameter estimates for the first canonical pair to the unstandardized values obtained from the MIMIC model with a single latent variable. The goodness-of-fit results are satisfactory: $\chi^2(1) = 1.72$, $p < 0.70$. Thus, we can conclude that there are two significant canonical variate pairs and that the structure imposed by the two-canonical-variate model is consistent with the data.

Table 1.9 Correlation matrix for canonical correlation analysis $n = 127$)

Measure	Y1	Y2	Y3	X1	X2	X3
Y1	1.000					
Y2	0.589	1.000				
Y3	0.806	0.640	1.000			
X1	0.292	0.330	0.372	1.000		
X2	0.354	0.300	0.340	0.170	1.000	
X3	0.349	0.494	0.293	0.140	0.252	1.000

To show the equivalence between the traditional analysis and structural equation approach, we can compare the results. The standardized parameter estimates for the MIMIC model in Figure 1.16 are as follows:

$$\Gamma = \begin{bmatrix} \gamma_1 \\ \gamma_2 \\ \gamma_3 \end{bmatrix} = \begin{bmatrix} 0.442 \\ 0.344 \\ 0.662 \end{bmatrix}$$

$$\Lambda_y = \begin{bmatrix} \lambda_{y1} \\ \lambda_{y2} \\ \lambda_{y3} \end{bmatrix} = \begin{bmatrix} 0.482 \\ 0.576 \\ 0.475 \end{bmatrix}$$

Recall that the γ_i's are equivalent to the canonical weights for the predictor variate. Thus, one can compute the associated loadings for the first variate pair as:

$$\begin{bmatrix} r_{x * x1} \\ r_{x * x2} \\ r_{x * x3} \end{bmatrix} = \begin{bmatrix} 1 & 0.170 & 0.140 \\ 0.170 & 1 & 0.252 \\ 0.140 & 0.252 & 1 \end{bmatrix} \begin{bmatrix} 0.442 \\ 0.344 \\ 0.662 \end{bmatrix} = \begin{bmatrix} 0.593 \\ 0.586 \\ 0.811 \end{bmatrix}.$$

The first eigenvalue (λ or R_c^2) can be calculated as:

$$\lambda = \Lambda'_y R_{yy}^{-1} \Lambda_y = [0.482\ 0.576\ 0.475] \begin{bmatrix} 1 & 0.589 & 0.806 \\ 0.589 & 1 & 0.640 \\ 0.806 & 0.640 & 1 \end{bmatrix} - 1 \begin{bmatrix} 0.482 \\ 0.576 \\ 0.475 \end{bmatrix} = 0.363$$

Thus, the first canonical correlation is 0.603. The criterion loadings for the first variate pair are then computed as:

$$\begin{bmatrix} r_{y*y1} \\ r_{y*y2} \\ r_{y*y3} \end{bmatrix} = (1/R_c)\, \Lambda_y = 1/0.603 \begin{bmatrix} 0.482 \\ 0.576 \\ 0.475 \end{bmatrix} = \begin{bmatrix} 0.799 \\ 0.956 \\ 0.788 \end{bmatrix}.$$

These results show that the predictor and criterion loadings and canonical correlation for the first variate pair as calculated from the structural equation model are identical to those calculated from the traditional canonical model. It may also be verified that the loadings and canonical correlation for the second pair are identical for both the structural equation and traditional canonical models.

Comments

At least two important advantages are gained by performing canonical correlation analysis via structural equation models. First, one may test for statistical significance of individual parameters in canonical correlations. The estimated standard errors can be used to calculate the critical ratios for the individual weights and cross loadings. Second, the structural equation approach is more flexible than the conventional canonical analysis. If one cannot reject the null hypothesis that canonical variates are independent, the assumption of variate orthogonality may be relaxed in structural equation analysis. Thus, the structural equation approach does not merely assume certain restraints (e.g. variate orthogonality). Rather it enables the researcher to test the plausibility of these restraints for the particular data and to examine relationships between variables by relaxing some constraints. Further, other variations can be explored with the structural equation model such as constraining to zero various covariances among error terms for the dependent variables.

Canonical correlation analysis is a general model for most parametric bivariate and multivariate statistical methods (Knapp, 1978). Because it can handle multiple predictors and multiple criteria simultaneously, canonical correlation analysis has a great deal of potential for marketing research. However, it has found more application in exploratory research than in theory testing because of several shortcomings such as lack of statistical tests. By overcoming such problems, the structural equation approach should increase the use of canonical correlation analysis in confirmatory research.

Conclusion

The topics we have considered in this chapter represent several recently developed applications of structural equation models to empirical data in the social sciences. These represent directions in which structural equation models can move beyond the conventional applications, and they require a new way of thinking about the structural equation methodology.

The scope of the topics we have covered is rather limited. To pursue other topics not covered in this chapter, one can refer to several excellent books on structural equation models (e.g. Bollen, 1989; Hayduk, 1987). For articles on up-to-date developments in structural equation models, see journals such as *Psychometrika, Psychological Bulletin, British Journal of Mathematical and Statistical Psychology, Sociological Methods and Research, Multivariate Behavioral Research*, and *Applied Psychological Measurement*.

Appendix 1.1   LISREL Specification for Figure 1.1a

MANOVA BY DUMMY VARIABLE APPROACH (*reading the raw data*)
DA NI = 4 NO = 152 MA = AM
NA
BEHAVIOR1 BEHAVIOR2 BEHAVIOR3 DUMMY
RA RE
MO NX = 2 NY = 3 BE = ZE GA = FU, FR PS = FU, FR
OU

Appendix 1.2   LISREL Specification for Figure 1.3

MANOVA BY MUTIPLE GROUP APPRAOCH
DA NI = 3 NG = 2 NO = 73 MA = AM
ME
0.206 0.274 0.548
SD
0.726 0.838 1.633
KM SY
1.000
0.774 1.000
0.736 0.945 1.000
MO NX = 4 NK = 1 LX = FU, FR TD = SY, FR PH = SY, FR
FI TD 4 1 TD 4 2 TD 4 3 TD 4 4
FI LX 4 1
VA 1.00 LX 4 1
ST 1 PH 1 1 TD 1 1 TD 2 2 TD 3 3
OU NS SS TV
MULTIPLE GROUP APPROACH
DA NI = 3 NO = 79 MA = AM
ME
4.051 1.696 4.089
SD

5.686 1.620 3.877
KM SY
1.000
0.641 1.000
0.580 0.921 1.000
MO NX = 4 NK = 1 PH = PS TD = PS LX = PS
OU NS SS TV
BEHAVIOR1 BEHAVIOR2 BEHAVIOR3 DUMMY
RA RE
MO NX = 2 NY = 3 BE = ZE GA = FU, FR PS = FU, FR
OU

Appendix 1.3   PLS Specification for Figure 1.6a

Number of blocks = 4
Number of cases = 152
Number of dimensions = 0
Output quantity = 3377
Inner weighting scheme = 1
Number of iterations = 100
Estimation accuracy = 5
Analyzed data metric = 4
*Read matrix, Unit = 0, Rewind = 0, Format = (2A4, 4F2.0)

Block	N-MV	Deflate	Direction	Model
ZAI1	1	0	Ourwards	Exogen.
ETA1	1	0	Outwards	Endogen.
ETA2	1	0	Outwards	Endogen.
ETA3	1	0	Outwards	Endogen.
	4			Mode A

Path design matrix

	ZAI1	ETA1	ETA2	ETA3
ZAI1	0.00	0.00	0.00	0.00
ETA1	1.00	0.00	0.00	0.00
ETA2	1.00	0.00	0.00	0.00
ETA3	1.00	0.00	0.00	0.00

*Read matrix, Unit = 0, Rewind = 0, Format = (2A4, F5.1, 19X, 3(F5.1, 1X))

*The matrix format is optional, because it is specific to each research design

Questions

1   The following table shows the augmented moments matrix for two experimental groups. There are three variables to measure attitude (Att1, Att2, Att3) and a dummy variable (Dummy) to denote the two groups. Run a latent variable MANOVA model in Figure 1.1b on these data. Can you conclude that there are differences in attitudes between the two groups?

Att1	18.967				
Att2	18.875	19.633			
Att3	19.517	19.942	20.933		
Dummy	2.233	2.275	2.333	0.500	
constant	4.167	4.233	4.417	0.500	

2   Draw the LISREL models via the dummy variable approach for the step-down analysis shown in Figure 1.4.

3   For the data in Table 1.4, run the four SIMW models with the following autocorrelation structures:

A   no correlated error
B   first-order correlations
C   second-order correlations
D   third-order correlations

Report the stability estimates under these models.

4   Provide the LISREL program statements to run the canonical correlation model in Figure 1.16 for the data in Table 1.9.

5   Repeat the canonical correlation analysis of the data in Table 1.9 using the MIMIC model with two latent variables. Report the predictor weights and cross loadings for the second variate pair. Show the equivalence between the solutions from the conventional and structural equation approaches.

References

Anderson, James C. and Gerbing, David W. 1984: The effect of sampling error on convergence, improper solutions, and goodness-of-fit indices for maximum likelihood confirmatory factor analysis. *Psychometrika*, 49 (2), 155–73.

Bagozzi, Richard P. 1985: Expectancy-value attitude models: an analysis of critical theoretical issues. *International Journal of Research in Marketing*, 2, 43–60.

Bagozzi, Richard P., Fornell, Claes, and Larcker, David F. 1981: Canonical correlation analysis as a special case of a structural relations model. *Multivariate Behavioral Research*, 16 (October), 437–54.

Bagozzi, Richard P. and Yi, Youjae 1988: On the evaluation of structural equation models. *Journal of the Academy of Marketing Science*, 16 (Spring), 74–94.

Bagozzi, Richard P. and Yi, Youjae 1989: On the use of structural equation models in experimental designs, *Journal of Marketing Research*, 26 (August), 271–84.

Bagozzi, Richard, P. and Yi, Youjae 1990: Assessing method variance in multitrait – multimethod matrices: the case of self-reported affect and perceptions at work. *Journal of Applied Psychology*, 75 (October), 547–60.

Bagozzi, Richard, P. and Yi, Youjae 1991: Mutlitrait–multimethod matrices in consumer research: critique and new developments. *Journal of Consumer Research*, 17 (March), 426–39.

Bagozzi, Richard P. and Yi, Youjae 1992: Multitrait–multimethod matrices in consumer research: critique and new developments. *Journal of Consumer Psychology*, 2, 143–70.

Bagozzi, Richard P. and Yi, Youjae 1993: On the use of structural equation models in panel designs. Unpublished working paper, The University of Michigan.

Bagozzi, Richard P., Yi, Youjae and Baumgartner, Johann 1990: The level of effort required for behavior as a moderator of the attitude–behavior relation. *European Journal of Social Psychology*, 20 (1), 45–59.

Bagozzi, Richard P., Yi, Youjae, and Singh, Surrendra 1991: On the use of structural equation models in experimental designs: two extensions. *International Journal of Research in Marketing*, 8, 125–40.

Barclay, Donald, W. 1983: Jackknifing in PLS. Unpublished working paper, The University of Michigan.

Barlett, M. S. 1941: The statistical significance of canonical correlation. *Biometrika*, 32, 29–38.

Bentler, Peter M. 1989: *EQS: Structural Equations Program Manual*, Los Angeles: BMDP Statistical Software.

Blok, Henk and Saris, Willem 1983: Using longitudinal data to estimate reliability. *Applied Psychological Measurement*, 7 (3), 295–301.

Bollen, Kenneth A. 1989: *Structural Equations with Latent Variables*, New York: John Wiley & Sons.

Boomsma, Anne 1985: Nonconvergence, improper solutions, and starting values in LISREL maximum likelihood estimation. *Psychometrika*, 50 (June), 229–42.

Bray, James H. and Maxwell, Scott E. 1985: *Multivariate Analysis of Variance*, Beverly Hills, CA: Sage Publications, Inc.

Browne, Michael W. 1984: Asymptotically distribution-free methods for the analysis of covariance structures. *British Journal of Mathematical and Statistical Psychology*, 32, 62–83.

Coleman, James Samuel, 1964: *Introduction to Mathematical Sociology*, New York: Free Press.

Converse, Philip. E. 1970: Attitudes and non-attitudes: continuation of a dialogue. In E. R. Tufte, (ed.), *The Quantitative Analysis of Social Problems*, Reading, MA: Addison-Wesley, 168–89.

Cooil, B., Winer, R. S., and Rados, D. L. 1987: Cross-validation for prediction. *Journal of Marketing Research*, 24, 271–9.

Dijkstra, Theo 1983: Some comments on maximum likelihood and partial least squares methods. *Journal of Econometrics*, 22, 67–90.

Efron, Bradley and Gong, Gail 1983: A leisurely look at the bootstrap, the jackknife, and cross-validation. *The American Statistician*, 34 (February), 36–48.

Fornell, Claes and Larcker, D. F. 1981: Evaluating structural equation models with unobservable variables and measurement errors. *Journal of Marketing Research*, 18 (February), 39–50.

Fornell, Claes and Bookstein, Fred L. 1982: Two structural equation models: LISREL and PLS applied to consumer exit-voice theory. *Journal of Marketing Research*, 19 (November), 440–52.

Gerbing, David W. and Anderson, James C. 1984: On the meaning of within-construct correlated errors. *Journal of Consumer Research*, 11 (June), 572–80.

Gerbing, David W. and Anderson, James C. 1987: Improper solutions in the analysis of covariance structures: their interpretability and a comparison of alternative respecifications. *Psychometrika*, 52 (1), 99–111.

Hayduk, Leslie A. 1987: *Structural Equation Modeling with LISREL: Essentials and Advances*, Baltimore, MN: Johns Hopkins University Press.

Heise, David R. 1969: Separating reliability and stability in test–retest correlations. *American Sociological Review*, 34 (1), 93–101.

Hsiao, Cheng 1986: *Analysis of Panel Data*. Cambridge, UK: Cambridge University Press.

Jagodzinski, W. and Kühnel, S. M. 1987: Estimation of reliability and stability in single-indicator multiple-wave models. *Sociological Methods and Research*, 15, 219–58.

Jagodzinski, W., Kühnel, S. M. and Schmidt, P. 1987: Is there a "Socratic Effect" in Nonexperimental Panel Studies? *Sociological Methods and Research*, 15, 259–302.

Jöreskog, Karl G. 1970: Estimation and testing of simplex models. *The British Journal of Mathematical and Statistical Psychology*, 23 (2), 121–45.

Jöreskog, Karl G. 1971: Statistical analysis of sets of congeneric tests. *Psychometrika*, 36 (June), 109–33.

Jöreskog, Karl G. 1977: Statistical models and methods for analysis of longitudinal data. In D. V. Aigner and A. S. Goldberger, (eds), *Latent Variables in Socio-Economic Models*, Amsterdam: North Holland, 285–352.

Jöreskog, Karl G. and Goldberger A. S. 1975: Estimation of a model with multiple indicators and multiple causes of a single latent variable. *Journal of the American Statistical Association*, 10, 631–9.

Jöreskog, Karl G. and Sörbom, Dag 1989: *LISREL 7: A Guide to the Program and Applications*, 2nd edn, Chicago: SPSS[X].

Jöreskog, Karl G. and Wold, Herman 1982: *Systems under Indirect Observation: Causality, Structure, Prediction*, Amsterdam: North-Holland.

Judd, Charles M. and Milburn, M. A. 1980: The structure of attitude systems in the general public: comparisons of a structural equation model. *American Sociological Review*, 45, 627–43.

Kessler, R. C. and Greenberg, D. F. 1981: *Linear Panel Analysis: Models of Quantitative Change*, New York: Academic Press.

Kanpp, Thomas R. 1978: Canonical correlation analysis: a general parametric significance-testing system. *Psychological Bulletin*, 85 (2), 410–16.

Kühnel, Steffen M. 1988: Testing MANOVA designs with LISREL. *Sociological Methods and Research*, 16 (May), 504–23.

Lord, F. M. and Novick, M. R. 1968: *Statistical Theories of Mental Test Scores*, New York: Addison-Wesley.

Lohmöller, Jan-Bernd 1984: *LVPLS 1.6 Program Manual: Latent Variables Path Analysis with Partial Least-Squares Estimation*, Köln: Zentralarchiv Fur Empirische Sozialforschung, Universitat zu Köln, Federal Republic of Germany.

Markus, Gregory Blake 1979: *Analyzing Panel Data*, Beverly Hills, CA: Sage.

Norusis, Marija J. 1988: *SPSS/PCT Advanced Statistics V2.0*, Chicago: SPSS.

Olson, Chester L. 1976: On choosing a test statistic in multivariate analysis of variance. *Psychological Bulletin*, 83 (4), 579–86.

Raffalovich, Lawrence E. and Bohrnstedt, George W. 1987: Common, specific, and error variance components of factor models. *Sociological Methods & Research*, 15 (May), 385–405.

Roy, J. 1958: Step down procedure in multivariate analysis. *Annals of Mathematical Statistics*, 29 (December), 1177–87.

Saris, Willem E. and Putte, B. V. D. 1988: True score or factor models: a secondary analysis of the ALLBUS-test–retest data. *Sociological Methods and Research*, 17 (November), 123–57.

Sörbom, Dag 1974: A general method for studying differences in factor means and factor structure between groups. *British Journal of Mathematical and Statistical Psychology*, 27, 229–39.

Sörbom, Dag 1975: Detection of correlated errors in longitudinal data. *British Journal of Mathematical and Statistical Psychology*, 28 (November), 138–51.

Sörbom, Dag 1982: Structural equation models with structured means. In Karl J. Jöreskog and Herman Wold, (eds), *Systems Under Indirect Observations*, Amsterdam: North-Holland Publishing Company, 183–95.

Steiger, J. H. 1989: *EzPATH: Causal Modeling*, Evanston, IL: SYSTAT, Inc.

Tuma, Nancy B. and Hannan, Michael T. 1984: *Social Dynamics: Models and Methods*, New York: Academic Press.

Werts, Charles E., Linn, Robert L. and Jöreskog, Karl G. 1974: Intraclass reliability estimates: testing structural assumptions. *Educational and Psychological Measurement*, 34 (1), 25–33.

Wheaton, Blair, Muthen, Bengt, Alwin, Duane F. and Summers, G. F. 1977: Assessing reliability and stability in panel models. In D. R. Heise (ed.), *Sociological Methodology*, San Francisco: Jossey-Bass, 84–136.

Wiggins, Lee Manning 1973: *Panel Analysis: Latent Probability Models for Attitude and Behavioral Processes*, San Francisco: Jossey-Bass.

Wiley, D. E. and Wiley, J. A. 1970, The estimation of measurement error in panel data, *American Sociological Review*, 35, 112–17.

Wold, Herman 1965: A fixed-point theorem with econometric background I–II. *Arkiv för Matematik*, 6, 209–40.

Wold, Herman 1982: Systems under indirect observations using PLS. In C. Fornell (ed.), *A Second Generation of Multivariate Analysis*, Vol. 2, New York: Praeger, 325–47.

Wold, Herman 1985: Partial least squares. In *Encyclopedia of Statistical Sciences*, Vol. 6, New York: Wiley, 581–91.

Wold, Herman 1989: Introduction to the second generation of multivariate analysis. In H. Wold (ed.), *Theoretical Empiricism*, VII–XL, New York: Paragon House.

Yi, Youjae 1990: Contextual priming effects in print advertisements. *Journal of Consumer Research*, 17 (September), 215–22.

2

Partial Least Squares

Claes Fornell and
Jaesung Cha

Introduction

Path or structural-equation models with latent variables combine econometric prediction with psychometric modeling of variables indirectly observed by multiple manifest variables. Karl Jöreskog provided an operative algorithm for Maximum Likelihood (ML) estimation of factor models in 1967, and the ML algorithm LISREL was developed in 1970 (Jöreskog, 1970). This became the first wide-spread statistical estimation method of general scope for path models with latent variables.

The general applicability of covariance structure models as implemented by LISREL was questioned by Herman Wold (Jöreskog's doctoral adviser), because, in practice, distributions are often either unknown or far from normal. For these situations, Wold developed an alternative approach, Partial Least Squares (PLS). Wold, already in 1966, provided two iterative algorithms for Least Squares (LS) estimation of single- and multi-component models and of the canonical correlation model, and in 1977, this was followed by the general PLS algorithm, originally called NIPALS (Nonlinear Iterative PArtial Least Squares), for LS estimation of path models with latent variables. The basic PLS algorithm has since been extended in many directions: non-linear inner structural relations (Wold, 1982), various inner weighting schemes (Lohmöller, 1981, 1989), and interdependent inner structure (Hui, 1982). As PLS has evolved, and as its basic underpinnings have become explicit, PLS should probably not simply be viewed as an alternative to LISREL with less stringent assumptions, but as an approach to empirical modeling that is quite different from covariance structure analysis. Whereas covariance structure models like LISREL focus on a causality concept based on accounting for covariances, PLS is prediction-oriented with a different notion of cause-and-effect.

In marketing, PLS has been used limitedly, for example, in cases where distributional assumptions are hardly met (e.g. Jagpal, 1981), and was formally introduced as an alternative to maximum likelihood LISREL as a way to avoid problems of improper solutions and factor indeterminacy as well as the violations of distributional assumptions (Fornell and Bookstein, 1982; Fornell, 1982). PLS estimates case values of the latent variables using *weight relations*, and therefore, the problem of factor indeterminacy is eliminated. In addition, the least squares estimation method used by PLS eliminates the problem of improper solutions. Since 1982 PLS has been applied to several marketing studies (Barclay, 1991; Bagozzi, Yi and Singh, 1991; Barclay, Higgins and Thompson, 1992; Fornell, 1992; Fornell and Bookstein, 1982; Fornell and Robinson, 1983; Fornell and Westbrook, 1984; Jain, Pinson and Malhotra, 1987; Johnson, Anderson and Fornell, 1992; Johnson and Horne, 1992; Johnson, Lehmann, Fornell and Horne, 1992; Kujala and Johnson (forthcoming); Qualls, 1987; Zinkhan, Joachimsthaler and Kinnear, 1987).

The purpose of this chapter is to provide a reasonably concise description of PLS. We begin by reviewing the philosophical underpinning of Wold's work: conditional expectations.

The Stochastic Concept of Causality

A "causal (or cause–effect) relationship" can be represented by the functional form of

$$Y = f(X) + \varepsilon, \tag{2.1}$$

where f represents some rule which maps the changes in X into changes in Y, and ε sums up the influence of all other factors that are not modeled in Eq. (2.1).

More formally, the stochastic notion of causality is a special case of conditional probability. The probability that an event y_i will take place depends on the condition that one of the events x_j or x_k has taken place:

$$Pr[Y = y_i | X = x_j] \neq Pr[Y = y_i | X = x_k], \qquad \text{for all } i, j, k \neq j \tag{2.2}$$

This definition can be directly reformulated in terms of conditional expectations:

$$E[Y = y_i | X = x_j] \neq E[Y = y_i | X = x_k] \tag{2.3}$$

When a causal relationship is hypothesized, the events Y can be expressed by the conditional expectation $E[Y|X]$. Further, the conditional expectation $E[Y|X]$ can be approximated by a polynomial of any degree:

$$E[Y|X] = f_{\text{true}}(x) = \beta_0 + \beta_1 x + \beta_2 x^2 + \beta_3 x^3 + \ldots \tag{2.4}$$

If we take up to a degree one for approximation, we have

$$E[Y|X] = f_{\text{linear}}(x) = \beta_0 + \beta_1 x \qquad (2.5)$$

Now, the true value of Y at $X = x$ is

$$
\begin{aligned}
y_{x=x} &= E[Y|X = x] + \upsilon \\
&= f_{\text{linear}}(x) + \upsilon \\
&= \hat{y} + \upsilon \\
&= \beta_0 + \beta_1 x + \upsilon
\end{aligned}
\qquad (2.6)
$$

The conditional expectation, as a representation of the causal relationship, has the following properties:

1 Expected residual is zero: $E[\upsilon] = 0$
2 Uncorrelatedness: The residual, υ, is uncorrelated with the conditional variable, x, and $\hat{y} = f_{\text{linear}}(x)$, i.e., $\text{Cov}[x, \upsilon] = \text{Cov}[\hat{y}, \upsilon] = 0$. From this, it can be derived that $\text{Cov}[y, x] = \text{Cov}[\hat{y}, x] = \beta_1 \text{Var}[x]$.
3 Least squares property: Suppose any arbitrary function, $g(x)$, to approximate Y at $X = x$. Then the variation around $g(x)$ is minimal if and only if $g(x)$ is the conditional expectation, $f_{\text{linear}}(x)$.
4 Nonreversibility: $E[Y|X] \neq E[X|Y]$.

In summary, the main implications of the linear conditional expectation are summarized as:

$$y = \beta_0 + \beta_1 x + \upsilon$$

$$
\begin{aligned}
&\hat{y} \equiv E[y|x] = \beta_0 + \beta_1 x \\
&\Rightarrow E[\upsilon] = 0 \\
&\Rightarrow \text{Cov}[x, \upsilon] = \text{Cov}[\hat{y}, \upsilon] = 0 \\
&\Rightarrow \text{Cov}[x, y] = \text{Cov}[x, \hat{y}] = \beta_1 \text{Var}[x]
\end{aligned}
\qquad (2.7)
$$

It is this property of conditional expectation as an interpretation of causality that Wold considers a main distinction in PLS models compared to traditional econometric-type structural models or LISREL models. We will elaborate on this concept in terms of predictor specification. Subsequently we will describe the model structure, estimation, algorithms, properties of the estimators, and the evaluation of PLS results. We conclude with a discussion of strengths and limitations of PLS relative to covariance structure models (e.g. LISREL).

Predictor Specification

In the basic design, PLS models are linear, and can be specified by an *arrow scheme* as illustrated in Figure 2.1. Each latent variable (LV) is indirectly observed by a block of manifest variables (MV's). The LV's and the path of *inner* relations among the LV's are the core of the model. Inner relations among LV's can have the form of a causal chain or an interdependent system. Our discussion will be limited to the case of a causal chain system. For interdependent systems, Hui (1978, 1982) reports estimation results from Wold's Fix-Point method (Wold, 1981) in the context of PLS.

While maximum likelihood models are based on assumptions of a specific joint multivariate distribution and independence of the observations (independently and identically distributed, i.e., *iid*), PLS does not impose such requirements on data. PLS applies to situations where knowledge about the distribution of the latent variables is limited and requires the estimates to be more closely tied to the data compared to covariance structure analysis. In other words, the latent variables in PLS are indirectly observed; in covariance structure analysis, they are not uniquely identified (and can therefore be said to be further from raw data).

"Predictor specification" not only leads to a key distributional assumption but also provides a general rationale for the Least Squares (LS) model specification and estimation. It can be understood as an LS version of distributional assumptions, and as a counterpart to the distributional assumptions of ML modeling. LS estimation is distribution-free (testing is another matter, to which we shall return), except for predictor specification, and does not require independence of observations.

Predictor specification can be summarized as a linear conditional expectation relationship between dependent and independent variables (Wold, 1985b). It adopts a set of statistical assumptions given in Eq. (2.7), and implies

1   that x is a predictor (cause) of y, and not the other way around (nonreversibility),
2   that $\hat{y}$ is the systematic part of y, explained by x,
3   that the systematic part, $\hat{y}$, is a linear function of x.

In order to fully understand Wold's concept of "predictor specification," let us put it in the context of multiple regression and then turn to causal chain systems.

Multiple regression

With k explanatory variables, the regression equation is

$$y = \beta_1 x_1 + \ldots + \beta_k x_k + \varepsilon \tag{2.8}$$

subject to *predictor specification*:

$$E[y|x_1, \ldots, x_k] = \beta_1 x_1 + \ldots + \beta_k x_k \tag{2.9}$$

That is, the *conditional expectation*, $E[y|x_1, \ldots, x_k]$ equals the systematic part of y as given on the righthand side of Eq. (2.9). This implies

$$E[\varepsilon] = 0$$
$$\text{Cov}[x, \varepsilon] = 0 \qquad (2.10)$$

As a result, we have the following properties:

1 The OLS (ordinary least squares) estimates of β's are consistent.
2 The prediction given by the conditional expectation in Eq. (2.9), using OLS estimates of β's, (i.e. $E[y|x_1, \ldots, x_k] = b_1 x_1 + \ldots + b_k x_k$) is consistent with minimum variance.

Causal chain systems

Consider the following structural form of a system of equations.

$$\begin{pmatrix} y_1 \\ y_2 \\ \vdots \\ y_H \end{pmatrix} = \begin{pmatrix} 0 & 0 & \ldots & 0 & 0 \\ \beta_{21} & 0 & \ldots & 0 & 0 \\ \vdots & \vdots & \ldots & \vdots & \vdots \\ \beta_{H1} & \beta_{H2} & \ldots & \beta_{H,H-1} & 0 \end{pmatrix} \begin{pmatrix} y_1 \\ y_2 \\ \vdots \\ y_H \end{pmatrix} + \begin{pmatrix} \gamma_{11} & \gamma_{12} & \ldots & \gamma_{1K} \\ \gamma_{21} & \gamma_{22} & \ldots & \gamma_{2K} \\ \vdots & \vdots & \ldots & \vdots \\ \gamma_{H1} & \gamma_{H2} & \ldots & \gamma_{HK} \end{pmatrix} \begin{pmatrix} x_1 \\ x_2 \\ \vdots \\ x_K \end{pmatrix} + \begin{pmatrix} u_1 \\ u_2 \\ \vdots \\ u_H \end{pmatrix} \qquad (2.11)$$

After appropriate arrangement of the order of equations, y_i does not appear in the equation for y_j, for all $j < i$, and the coefficient matrix of endogenous variables, **B**, is lower-triangular. This type of system is *a causal chain system* (or recursive system). Let's denote y's and x's which occupy the righthand side of the hth equation in the structural form by y_h^{SF} and x_h^{SF}, and the corresponding coefficients as β_h and γ_h, respectively. The reduced form of the system is:

$$y = (I - B)^{-1}\Gamma x + (I - B)^{-1}u$$
$$= B^* x + u^* \qquad (2.12)$$

As in the structural form, some β^*'s can be zeros. Let's denote the x's of the hth equation in the reduced form by x_h^{RF}, and the corresponding coefficients by β_h^*. Now, the predictor specification requires

$$E[y_h|y_h^{SF}, x_h^{SF}] = \sum \beta_h y_h^{SF} + \sum \gamma_h x_h^{SF} \qquad (2.13)$$

for $h = 1 \ldots H$, in the structural form, and

$$E[y_h | x_h^{RF}] = \sum \beta_h^* x_h^{RF} \qquad (2.14)$$

for $h = 1 \ldots H$, in the reduced form. To make the relations in Eq. (2.13) and Eq. (2.14) possible, we need the assumption of

$$E[u_h^* | x_h^{RF}] = 0 \qquad (2.15)$$

for $h = 1, \ldots, H$. From Eq. (2.15), we have $\text{Cov}[x_h^{RF}, u_h^*] = 0$. It is important that predictor specification for the structural form of the causal chain system in Eq. (2.13) is also valid when Eq. (2.15) is satisfied. Moreover, application of OLS to each equation in the system gives us consistent estimates.

In summary, predictor specification is the only condition imposed to assure desirable estimation properties in LS modeling. Therefore, predictor specification avoids the assumptions that the observations are jointly ruled by a specified multivariate distribution, and that the observations are independently distributed.

Note that predictor specification does not restrict the structure of the residual covariance. In LS modeling, the relevant residual variance terms are minimized. In Wold' terminology, LS modeling based upon predictor specification is *prediction-oriented*, while ML modeling is *parameter-oriented*.

Model Structure

All path models with latent variables in PLS modeling consist of three parts: (1) inner relations, (2) outer relations, and (3) weight relations. In

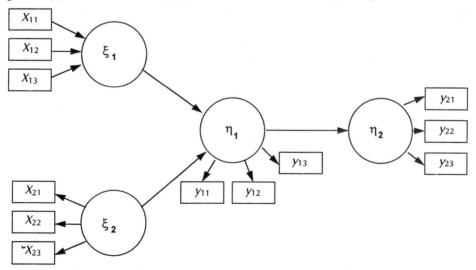

Figure 2.1 An example of PLS model

the following, we will discuss these components of the model in detail. Without loss of generality, all variables are standardized to zero means and unit variances, and constant terms (*location parameters* in PLS) are ignored.

Inner (structural) relations

The inner relations (inner model, structural model, inner structural model, core model, epistemological model, substantive part) depict the relationships among the latent variables as posited by substantive theory.

$$\boldsymbol{\eta} = \boldsymbol{B}\boldsymbol{\eta} + \boldsymbol{\Gamma}\boldsymbol{\xi} + \boldsymbol{\zeta} \tag{2.16}$$

where $\boldsymbol{\eta}$ is a vector of the endogenous latent variables, $\boldsymbol{\xi}$ is a vector of the exogenous latent variables, $\boldsymbol{\zeta}$ is a vector of residuals, and $\boldsymbol{B}$ and $\boldsymbol{\Gamma}$ are the path coefficient matrices. The reduced form of (2.16) can be obtained by substracting $\boldsymbol{B}\boldsymbol{\eta}$ from both sides of the equation and premultiplying by $(\boldsymbol{I} - \boldsymbol{B})^{-1}$:

$$\begin{aligned} \boldsymbol{\eta} &= (\boldsymbol{I} - \boldsymbol{B})^{-1}\boldsymbol{\Gamma}\boldsymbol{\xi} + (\boldsymbol{I} - \boldsymbol{B})^{-1}\boldsymbol{\zeta} \\ &= \boldsymbol{B}^{*}\boldsymbol{\xi} + \boldsymbol{\zeta}^{*} \end{aligned} \tag{2.17}$$

where $\boldsymbol{B}^{*}$ represents the total effect of the exogenous latent variables, $\boldsymbol{\xi}$.

As discussed before, when the system is a causal chain, the assumption of $E[\boldsymbol{\zeta}^{*}|\boldsymbol{\xi}] = 0$ from the reduced form makes predictor specification possible in both the structural form and reduced form.

$$E[\boldsymbol{\eta}_h | \boldsymbol{\eta}_h^{*}, \boldsymbol{\xi}_h^{*}] = \boldsymbol{\beta}_h \boldsymbol{\eta}_h^{*} + \boldsymbol{\gamma}_h \boldsymbol{\xi}_h^{*}, \qquad \text{for } h = 1, \ldots, H \tag{2.18}$$

where H is the total number of equations in the system, $\boldsymbol{\eta}_h$ is the hth endogenous latent variable, $\boldsymbol{\eta}_h^{*}$ and $\boldsymbol{\xi}_h^{*}$ are the column vectors of the endogenous predictor latent variables and exogenous latent variables for $\boldsymbol{\eta}_h$, and $\boldsymbol{\beta}_h$ and $\boldsymbol{\gamma}_h$ are the row vectors of coefficients. Thus, predictor specification implies $E[\boldsymbol{\zeta}_h | \boldsymbol{\eta}_h^{*}, \boldsymbol{\xi}_h^{*}] = 0$ and $\text{Cov}[\boldsymbol{\zeta}_h, \boldsymbol{\eta}_h^{*}] = \text{Cov}[\boldsymbol{\zeta}_h, \boldsymbol{\xi}_h^{*}] = 0$. The structural model of the example in Figure 2.1 is:

$$\begin{pmatrix} \eta_1 \\ \eta_2 \end{pmatrix} = \begin{pmatrix} 0 & 0 \\ \beta_{21} & 0 \end{pmatrix} \begin{pmatrix} \eta_1 \\ \eta_2 \end{pmatrix} + \begin{pmatrix} \gamma_{11}\gamma_{12} \\ 0 & 0 \end{pmatrix} \begin{pmatrix} \xi_1 \\ \xi_2 \end{pmatrix} + \begin{pmatrix} \zeta_1 \\ \zeta_2 \end{pmatrix} \tag{2.19}$$

This is a simple example of a causal chain system, and the model can be estimated by OLS for each equation with predictor specification.

Outer relations (measurement model)

The relationships between the manifest variables and the latent variables are defined by *outer relations*. Two kinds of measurement models can be specified: reflective and formative. The former assumes that the observed phenomena are a reflection of an underlying construct. In the latter, the MV's *form* a latent variable as a composite.

Reflective (outward) model The relationships between the latent variables and the manifest variables in the reflective mode are defined as:

$$y = \Lambda_y \eta + \epsilon_y$$
$$x = \Lambda_x \xi + \epsilon_x$$

(2.20)

where η and ξ are, as defined before, the endogenous and the exogenous LV's, respectively, and y and x are the observed measures (indicators, MV's) of η and ξ. Λ_y and Λ_x are the matrices of *loadings*, which relate the latent variables to their measures. Finally, ε's are the residuals and usually interpreted as *measurement errors* or noise. As in the inner relations, the outer relations are also ruled by predictor specification:

$$E[y|\eta] = \Lambda_y \eta$$
$$E[x|\xi] = \Lambda_x \xi$$

(2.21)

In the case of the example in Figure 2.1, ξ_2, η_1, and η_2 have the reflective indicators, and the measurement models for these LV's are:

$$\begin{pmatrix} x_{21} \\ x_{22} \\ x_{23} \end{pmatrix} = \begin{pmatrix} \lambda_{x21} \\ \lambda_{x22} \\ \lambda_{x23} \end{pmatrix} \xi_2 + \begin{pmatrix} \varepsilon_{x21} \\ \varepsilon_{x22} \\ \varepsilon_{x23} \end{pmatrix}$$

(2.22)

and

$$\begin{pmatrix} y_{11} \\ y_{12} \\ y_{13} \\ y_{21} \\ y_{22} \\ y_{23} \end{pmatrix} = \begin{pmatrix} \lambda_{y11} & 0 \\ \lambda_{y12} & 0 \\ \lambda_{y13} & 0 \\ 0 & \lambda_{y21} \\ 0 & \lambda_{y22} \\ 0 & \lambda_{y23} \end{pmatrix} \begin{pmatrix} \eta_1 \\ \eta_2 \end{pmatrix} + \begin{pmatrix} \varepsilon_{y11} \\ \varepsilon_{y12} \\ \varepsilon_{y13} \\ \varepsilon_{y21} \\ \varepsilon_{y22} \\ \varepsilon_{y23} \end{pmatrix}$$

(2.23)

When each manifest variable is influenced by only one latent variable, as in the example, the standardized loadings are correlation coefficients between the manifest variables and their corresponding latent variables.

Formative (inward) model

In the formative case, the relationships between the LV's and the MV's are defined as:

$$\eta = \pi_\eta y + \delta_\eta$$
$$\xi = \pi_\xi x + \delta_\xi \qquad (2.24)$$

where η, ξ, y, and x are same as before, and π's are the multiple regression coefficients and δ's are the residuals from regressions. Predictor specification is also applied, and reads

$$E[\eta|y] = \pi_\eta y \qquad (2.25)$$
$$E[\xi|x] = \pi_\xi x$$

This should not be confused with *weight relations* which will be discussed shortly. Whereas weight relations define the *estimated* latent variables as the weighted aggregates of the manifest variables, the formative specification describes the relationships between the manifest variables and the *true* latent variables.

Formative measurement model specifies that the MV's are multiple causes of an LV. In other words, the MV's are assumed to be a collection of variables, informative about a matter of unknown dimensionality and unknown representativeness. Therefore, the direction of the relationship between LV and MV's is opposite to that of reflective models.

One latent variable, ξ_1, in the example, has a formative relationship with its manifest variables, and its measurement model is:

$$\xi_1 = (\pi_{\xi 11}\ \pi_{\xi 12}\ \pi_{\xi 13}) \begin{pmatrix} x_{11} \\ x_{12} \\ x_{13} \end{pmatrix} + \delta_{\xi 1} \qquad (2.26)$$

Choice of measurement model

To gain further insights into the difference between formative vs. reflective specification, Fornell, Rhee and Yi (1991) compared the two formally. If O is the observed measure, T, the true score and ε an error component, the reflective specification is:

$$O = T + \varepsilon \qquad (2.27)$$

with the assumptions that

$$E[\varepsilon] = 0$$
$$\mathrm{Cov}[T, \varepsilon] = 0 \qquad (2.28)$$
$$\mathrm{Cov}[\varepsilon_i, \varepsilon_j] = 0,$$

which imply

$$\mathrm{Var}[O] = \mathrm{Var}[T] + \mathrm{Var}[\varepsilon], \text{ and}$$
$$\mathrm{Var}[T] < \mathrm{Var}[O] \qquad (2.29)$$

That is, the variance in the true scores is smaller than the variance in the measured variables. However, in the formative specification, the opposite is true. Now we have:

$$T = O + \varepsilon \tag{2.30}$$

or since $E[\varepsilon] = 0$, we can write this as

$$T = O - \varepsilon \tag{2.31}$$

which brings us back to the reflective equation

$$O = T + \varepsilon \tag{2.32}$$

But since ε represents all remaining causes of T other than O, we also have

$$\text{Cov}[T, \varepsilon] \neq 0 \tag{2.33}$$

and instead

$$\text{Cov}[O, \varepsilon] = 0 \tag{2.34}$$

which imply

$$\text{Var}[T] > \text{Var}[O]. \tag{2.35}$$

The choice of indicator model depends primarily on the substantive theory behind the model: the way in which variables are conceptualized. Constructs such as "attitude" or "personality" are typically viewed as underlying factors that give rise to something that is observed. In such a case, the reflective indicator model would be used. In contrast, when constructs are conceived as explanatory combinations of indicators, such as "marketing mix," which are determined by a combination of variables, their indicators are probably better understood as formative (Fornell and Bookstein, 1982).

In addition to conceptual issues, the choice of formative vs. reflective measurement models has implications for the predictive power as well as assessing the individual contribution of one's measures. The reflective formulation can never account for more variance in the dependent variable than the formative specification (Fornell, Rhee and Yi, 1991). This is related to the different optimization rules for these two measurement models: the reflective model minimizes the trace of the residual variances in the "outer" (measurement) equations while the formative model minimizes the trace of the residual variances in the "inner" (structural) equation, both subject to certain systematic constraints.

Weight relations

In addition to two relations above described, one more relation is required to complete the PLS model: weight relations. In PLS, each case value of the latent variables are estimated by the "weight relations" as follows:

$$\hat{\eta} = \omega_\eta y$$

$$\hat{\xi} = \omega_\xi x$$

(2.36)

where ω's are the weights. As we can see, the estimates of the latent variables are the linear aggregates of their empirical indicators.

The weights, ω_η and ω_ξ, are determined in different ways according to the mode of measurement model. When the model is reflective, the loadings are the weights after rescaling (to make the variance of LV's equal to one). In the formative model, the multiple regression coefficients between the MV's and LV's, as in Eq. (2.24), are used as the weights, that is, $\omega = \pi$. As will be discussed subsequently in detail, LV's in a reflective mode are akin to principal components, but they are formed to be the best predictands in the formative case.

Estimation

General description of PLS estimation

In PLS, a set of model parameters is divided into subsets and estimated by ordinary multiple regressions with the values of parameters in other subsets as given. An iterative method provides successive approximations for the estimates, subset by subset, of loadings and structural parameters.

Any estimation method has its own optimization rule to obtain estimates with desirable properties. For example, ML searches for parameter values which maximize the value of a maximum likelihood function derived from assumed distribution. The optimization rule of OLS is minimization of residual variance. PLS, like OLS, seeks parameter values that minimize residual variances. However, there are different kinds of residual variables (ζ, ε, and δ) to be minimized in PLS. Wold (1966) proposed treating each residual variable separately, by defining a set of partial least squares (PLS) criteria:

1   Minimize Var[ζ] for all endogenous latent variables.
2   Minimize Var[ε] for all outward directed blocks.
3   Minimize Var[δ] for all inward directed blocks.

The basic idea of PLS estimation is that one part of the parameters is considered as known and held fixed, while the other part is estimated. This means a partitioning of the parameters in estimable subsets. For one and two block models, the iterative algorithms of PLS are almost always convergent. For multi-block models, however, convergence has not been proved, but practice suggests that non-convergence is rare.

Some least squares modules for PLS algorithms

In order to simplify the description of the PLS algorithms, let us start with four simple models (Lohmöller, 1989: pp. 9–41). Later we will see these simple structures in the context of an extended PLS model, and how a full PLS model can be understood as a combination of these simple structures.

The centroid

$$Z = \sum_k w_k y_k \qquad (2.37)$$

Z is called the centroid factor of a set of variables y_k, $k = 1, \ldots, K$, if the weights, w_k, are equal to $+1$ or -1 and chosen such that $\mathrm{Var}[Z]$ is maximized. Usually, the weights are found by $w_k = sign \; \mathrm{Cov}[Z, y_k]$ (Woodward and Bentler, 1979).

The multiple regression

$$Z^* = \sum_l w_l x_l \qquad (2.38)$$

If Z is the predictand and x's are a set of predictors, Z^* is *the LS approximation to Z as the best predictand* when the weights are calculated from multiple regression.

The principal component

$$_{c+1}Z = {}_c f \sum_k {}_c p_k y_k \qquad (2.39)$$

where $_cZ$ is an approximation of the principal component of a set of target variables, y's, $_cp_k = \mathrm{Cov}[{}_cZ, y_k]$, and $_cf$ is a scale factor to make $\mathrm{Var}[{}_{c+1}Z] = 1$. The principal component is obtained by iterating the above equation until converging in p_k for all k. The principal component is *the best predictor of y's* (Bock, 1975).

The MIMIC variable

$$_{c+1}Z = {}_c f \left(\sum_l {}_c w_l x_l + \sum_k {}_c p_k y_k \right) \qquad (2.40)$$

where $_cw_l$ is a multiple regression coefficient, $_cp_k = \text{Cov}[_cZ, y_k]$, and $_cf$ is a scale factor that makes $\text{Var}[_{c+1}Z] = 1$. The MIMIC variable is the best predictor of the target variables, y's, and at the same time, the best predictand of predictors, x's (Wold, 1975).

Detailed description of PLS estimation

As described earlier, each LV is involved in two equation systems: the inner system, Eq. (2.16), and the outer system, Eq. (2.20) and Eq. (2.24). In each iteration cycle $c = 1, 2, \ldots$ both equation systems are used to find approximations to the "true" LV's. One approximation is an "outside" approximation, resulting in a weighted aggregate of the MV's. The other is an "inside" approximation, resulting in a weighted aggregate of the adjacent LV's. These two approximations serve as interlocking constraints. That is, the LV's are estimated so that they are the "best suitable" variables in the inner system (according to some criterion to be discussed shortly), and at the same time, the best suitable variables in their outer models. After convergence, LV is finally determined by a linear aggregate of the MV's, as defined in weight relations.

For purposes of explanation, we will use an illustration with four LVs, each of them connected to three MVs (Figure 2.1). Among the LV's, ξ_1 has formative indicators, and ξ_1 will be estimated as the best predictand of its indicators by taking multiple regression coefficients between ξ_1 and x_1's as the weights. On the other hand, all the other LV's in the reflective mode are estimated as the principal components of their indicators, and therefore, the best predictors of the MV's. Of course, these LV's will be determined in such a way that they are also the best suitable variables in the inner structural model. One important implication is that ξ_2, η_1, and η_2 will not be the same as the principal components from separate principal component analysis.

Initial outer approximations   Initially, the LV's are approximated by weighted aggregates of their MV's by using arbitrary values for the weights to initiate the iterations. After this initialization, PLS uses one of three different algorithms for "inside approximation."

Table 2.1   Weighting schemes for inside approximation

Inner weighting scheme	$v_{ji} = 0$, but if η_i is	
	predictor of η_j, then $v_{ji} =$	target of η_j, then $v_{ji} =$
1 Path weighting scheme	β_{ji}	ρ_{ji}
2 Centroid weighting scheme	sign (ρ_{ji})	sign (ρ_{ji})
3 Factor weighting scheme	ρ_{ji}	ρ_{ji}

where v_{ji} is inner weight, β_{ji} is regression coefficient from η_i to η_j, and ρ_{ji} is correlation coefficient between η_i and η_j.

Source: Lohmöller, 1989: p. 42.

Inside approximation   The equations of the inner relations are used to find an inside approximation, and the LV's are approximated by weighted aggregate of neighboring LV's. By this approximation, an LV is estimated to be the "most suitable neighbor" in its own vicinity in the inner structure of the model. The "neighboring LV's" of an LV are the predictor(s) and the predictand(s) in the system of equations. The weights can be estimated by (1) a path weighting scheme, (2) a centroid weighting scheme, and (3) a factor weighting scheme (Table 2.1).

1 Path weighting scheme   In this scheme, an LV is estimated to be the "best predictable" variable (predictand) of its predictors as well as the best predictor of the subsequent dependent variable(s). In calculating the weighted aggregate as an approximation, the independent variables of the LV are weighted by multiple regression coefficients, while the dependent variables of the LV are weighted by correlation coefficients. In the example, ξ_1 and ξ_2 are approximated by $\rho_{\xi_j \eta_1} \times \eta_1$, for $j = 1, 2$, where $\rho_{\xi_j \eta_1}$ is the correlation coefficient between ξ_j and η_1 . η_2 is approximated by $\beta_{21} \times \eta_1$, where β_{21} is the regression coefficient between η_2 and η_1. The implications of these two simple cases, where an LV is either purely exogenous or purely endogenous, are straightforward. If an LV is purely exogenous, it is approximated to be the principal component of its dependent LV's (as described in the LS module section). On the other hand, if an LV is purely endogenous, it is approximated to be the best predictand of its predictors.

In the case of η_1, the story is different. η_1 is the dependent variable of ξ_1 and ξ_2, and at the same time, a predictor of η_2. It is approximated by $\gamma_{11}\xi_1 + \gamma_{12}\xi_2 + \rho_{\eta_1 \eta_2}\eta_2$, where γ's are multiple regression coefficients and $\rho_{\eta_1 \rho_2}$ is the correlation coefficient between η_1 and η_2, as a MIMIC variable between the predictors and the dependent LV (so that it is the best predictor of η_2 and at the same time the best predictand of ξ_1 and ξ_2).

2 Centroid weighting scheme   This was Wold's original PLS algorithm. It utilizes the directions of LV correlations only, that is, the signs of the correlation coefficients between the LV's. The directions of causality and the strength of the relationship between LV's are ignored. LV's are approximated by the *sign weighted sum* of their neighboring LV's, and thus become similar to centroid factors.

This scheme is particularly useful if the LV correlation matrix is singular. On the other hand, if an LV correlation coefficient is close to zero and oscillates during the iteration from small positive to small negative values, then these values are magnified to -1 and $+1$ and have more impact on the results than the factor weighting scheme (Lohmöller, 1989).

3 Factor weighting scheme   In this scheme, the neighboring LV's of an LV are weighted by the correlation coefficients between a target LV and its neighboring LV's, regardless of causal order. Therefore, the LV becomes "principal component" of its neighboring LV's. In the example, η_1 is approximated by $\rho_{\xi_1 \eta_1} \times \xi_1 + \rho_{\xi_2 \eta_1} \times \xi_2 + \rho_{\eta_1 \eta_2} \times \eta_2$, and η_2 is by $\rho_{\eta_1 \eta_2} \times \eta_1$.

Outside approximations   The LV's are approximated by the weight relations which determine the LV's as weighted aggregates of MV's. The loadings are used as the weights in a reflective mode, and the multiple regression coefficients from MV's to LV are used as weights in a formative mode. These outside-approximated LV's are then fed into the inside approximation step.

The two approximations, inside and outside, are iterated until the parameter estimates converge, and LV scores are given by the weight relations. Again, if an LV has reflective indicators, it is approximated to be a principal component of its MV's, which minimizes outer residual variances, under the constraint which requires the LV to be the best neighbor of the adjacent LV's in the inner system. If an LV has formative specification, it is approximated to be the best predictand of the MV's under the same constraints. Accordingly, PLS estimation is a constrained optimization procedure.

Properties of the Estimators

Inconsistency of latent variable estimates

In PLS, the case values of the LVs are estimated as weighted aggregates of the corresponding blocks of indicators. These case values are *inconsistent* (Wold, 1982, 1985a); an inevitable property since the LVs are estimated as the aggregates of manifest variables which involve measurement error, i.e. $\hat{\eta} = \omega_{\eta} y = \omega_{\eta}(\Lambda_y \eta + \varepsilon_y) = \omega_{\eta}\Lambda_y \eta + \omega_{\eta}\varepsilon_y$, where $\hat{\eta}$ is the estimated latent variable scores, Λ_y is a loading matrix, ω_{η} is a weight matrix, and ε_y is a vector of residuals. This is the price for obtaining latent variable case values. The error, however, can be minimized from the principle of consistency-at-large. We will discuss this principle shortly.

Biasedness and inconsistency of loadings and inner structural coefficients

It is well-known property of PLS that, as in the case of principal components and canonical correlations, the estimates of loadings and structural coefficients for the latent variable relationships are biased, being overestimated and underestimated, respectively (Dijkstra, 1983; Wold, 1985a). When all the correlation coefficients across all the manifest variables are identical, the bias factor relative to ML estimates is

$$bias(\lambda) = \sqrt{\frac{s + (1 - s)/K}{s}} \qquad (2.41)$$

where s is the identical correlation coefficient across all the manifest variables, and K is the number of the manifest variables. This indicates that the higher the true loadings are, the smaller the bias, and that the more indicators we have, the closer we get to the ML estimates.

When this simple correlation structure is extended to the case of a two-block model with the same number of manifest variables, where correlations among the variables in the same block are all identical and the between-block correlations are also identical, we can show that the correlation between latent variables are biased, relative to ML estimate, by

$$bias(\rho) = \frac{s}{s + (1 - s)/K} \tag{2.42}$$

where s is the identical correlation among manifest variables and K is the number of manifest variables in each block. Note that

$$bias(\lambda) = \frac{1}{\sqrt{bias(\rho)}}.$$

Therefore, the predicted correlation between two manifest variables in different blocks is unbiased in the simple case above, since the bias factors are canceled out. Areskoug (1982) proved the general theorem that the bias of the loadings and the bias of the canonical correlation coefficient cancel each other out, even for unequal block-sizes (that is, different number of manifest variables in two blocks) and unequal weights and loading coefficients.

Consistency at large

It is obvious from the bias equations that the bias factors of loadings and latent variable correlations are reduced as the number of manifest variables increases. The estimate of the latent variable scores approaches to "true" latent variable scores as the number of indicators goes to infinity (see Wold (1982) for a formal proof of this). Further, it is known that the inaccuracy as measured by standard errors varies inversely with the square root of the block size (Lyttkens, 1966; 1973). This limiting behavior of the PLS estimator is called *consistency at large*. This asymptotic property requires a large number of manifest variables as well as a large number of cases which are required in the usual asymptotic property of *consistency*. Thus, it is based upon a double invocation of the law of large numbers. In sum, the PLS estimates approach the true values proportionally, as the number of cases in the sample increases and as the number of indicators increases.

Evaluation of a PLS Model

Since no distributional assumptions, except for predictor specification, are made in PLS, the traditional statistical testing methods based upon assumptions about statistical distributions are not well suited: PLS would then be "free of assumptions" in estimation, but not in testing. Wold has always maintained that it is more consistent with PLS modeling to apply non-parametric tests. In addition, the evaluation of PLS models should be based on prediction-oriented measures, not covariance fit. There are several fit indices such as communality and redundancy measures and Stone-Geisser's Q^2 measure, which can be used to evaluate the predictive power of the model. Let us describe this in some detail.

Fit indices

PLS models make several types of predictions, and there are different fit indices for testing the predictive relevance of the model. Figure 2.2 illustrates the different predictions: *communality*, *structural prediction*, *validity*, *redundancy*, and *operational variance* (Lohmöller, 1989).

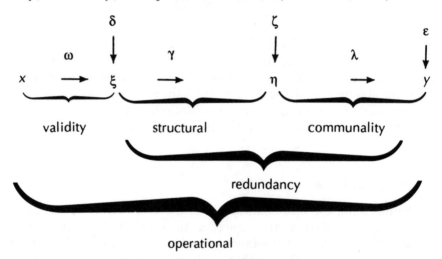

Figure 2.2   Various preditions and relevant fit measures in PLS models

Communality   The manifest variables can be predicted by their own latent variables using the relations in Eq. (2.20). Using Eq. (2.20), we can reformulate the variance–covariance of the manifest variables belonging to an LV:

$$
\begin{aligned}
y &= \Lambda_y \eta + \epsilon \\
\mathrm{Cov}[y] &= E[yy'] \\
&= E[(\Lambda_y \eta + \epsilon)(\Lambda_y \eta + \epsilon)'] \\
&= \Lambda_y \mathrm{Var}[\eta]\Lambda_y' + \mathrm{Cov}[\epsilon] \\
&= \Lambda_y \Lambda_y' + \Theta_\epsilon
\end{aligned}
\tag{2.43}
$$

where $\mathrm{Var}[\eta] = 1$ since all the latent variables are normalized to eliminate scale indeterminacy. Eq. (2.43) shows that the variances of the manifest variables can be divided into two parts: one is the part from diagonal elements of $\Lambda_y \Lambda'_y$, and the other is the diagonal parts of Θ_ϵ which is a variance–covariance matrix of the outer residuals. For example, the variance of a manifest variable, y_k, is $\text{Var}[y_k] = \lambda_k^2 + \theta_k$. The first part of the manifest variable variance, λ_k^2, is the variance which is systematically determined by its latent variable (the variance shared with its latent variable). The proportion of this shared variance to the total variance of the manifest variable, i.e. $\lambda_k^2/(\lambda_k^2 + \theta_k)$, is called the communality of the manifest variable, which is same as the reliability (convergent validity) measure in measurement error models. When the manifest variables are standardized, the communality measures of the manifest variables are simply the squared loadings. The average of the communalities in each block can be calculated as the block communalities, and the average of the communalities of all the manifest variables can also be calculated as the communality of an overall model.

Fornell and Larcker (1981) proposed a measure called Average Variance Extracted (AVE) to measure the amount of variance that is captured by the construct in relation to the amount of variance due to measurement error. AVE of a latent variable is calculated as follows:

$$
AVE = \frac{\displaystyle\sum_{k=1}^{K} \lambda_k^2}{\displaystyle\sum_{k=1}^{K} \lambda_k^2 + \sum_{k=1}^{K} \theta_k}
$$

$$
= \frac{\displaystyle\sum_{k=1}^{K} \lambda_k^2}{\displaystyle\sum_{k=1}^{K} (\lambda_k^2 + \theta_k)} \tag{2.44}
$$

When all the manifest variables are standardized, this is equivalent to the average of the communalities in each block, i.e. the block communalities. This measure can be used to evaluate the goodness of measurement model, that is, reliability of the latent variables. In addition, AVE also can be used to evaluate *discriminant validity* of the constructs. Fornell and Larcker suggest that AVE's of the latent variables should be greater than the correlations among the latent variables to fully satisfy the requirements for discriminant validity. For example, in case of two block model, $\text{AVE}[\eta_1] > \text{Cor}[\eta_1, \eta_2]$ and $\text{AVE}[\eta_2] > \text{Cor}[\eta_1, \eta_2]$.

R^2: *Explanatory power of structural models* When the case values of the latent variables are given by the weight relations, each inner structural model can be estimated by OLS with predictor specification, and the explanatory power of each model can be evaluated by OLS's standard R^2's.

Redundancy Another possible prediction in a PLS model is from pre-dictor LV's to the MV's belonging to the dependent LV. Redundancy is the average variance of the set of the MV's that is explained by the predictor LV's. Let's consider η_1 in Figure 2.1. The outer model is

$$y_1 = \begin{pmatrix} y_{11} \\ y_{12} \\ y_{13} \end{pmatrix} = \begin{pmatrix} \lambda_{11} \\ \lambda_{12} \\ \lambda_{13} \end{pmatrix} \eta_1 + \begin{pmatrix} \varepsilon_{11} \\ \varepsilon_{12} \\ \varepsilon_{13} \end{pmatrix} = \Lambda_1 \eta_1 + \varepsilon_1 \tag{2.45}$$

and has inner model

$$\eta_1 = \gamma_1 \xi_1 + \gamma_2 \xi_2 + \zeta_1 \tag{2.46}$$

By substituting η_1 with the righthand side terms of Eq. (2.46), we get

$$y_1 = \Lambda_1 (\gamma_1 \xi_1 + \gamma_2 \xi_2 + \zeta_1) + \varepsilon_1$$
$$= \Lambda_1 \gamma \xi + \Lambda_1 \zeta_1 + \varepsilon_1 \tag{2.47}$$

where $\gamma = (\gamma_1 \ \gamma_2)$ and $\xi' = (\xi_1 \ \xi_2)$. Eq. (2.47) shows the common part, $\Lambda_1 \eta_1$, in Eq. (2.45) which determines the communalities is again split up into the unique part of $\Lambda_1 \zeta_1$ and the *redundant* part of $\Lambda_1 \gamma \xi$. The unique part can be reproduced only by the latent variable, η_1, which is directly connected to y_1, never by ξ's. However, the redundant part is represented twice in the latent variables: it can be predicted either by η_1 or by the predictor latent variables of η_1, that is, ξ's. The redundancy coefficient of a manifest variable y_k, F_k^2, is defined as the proportion of the MV variance which is explained by the redundant part of the variable. For example, the redundancy coefficient of y_{11}, F_{11}^2, is:

$$F_{11}^2 = \frac{Var[\lambda_{11} \ \gamma \xi]}{Var[y_{11}]}$$

$$= \frac{\lambda_{11}^2 \gamma \Phi \gamma'}{Var[y_{11}]} \tag{2.48}$$

This measure represents the explanatory power with which the predictor latent variables, ξ's in the example, can explain the manifest variables, y_{11}, belonging to η_1.

As in the case of communality, the redundancy coefficients of the manifest variables in a block can be averaged to obtain a block redundancy coefficient, and all the redundancy coefficients of the manifest variables can be averaged to obtain a redundancy coefficient of overall model.

Validity A latent variable can be predicted by its own manifest variables:

$$\eta = \Pi y + \delta \tag{2.49}$$

where δ represents the unmeasured part of the latent variable, η, and a validity coefficient can be defined as the multiple correlation coefficient from Eq. (2.49). However, since PLS estimates the latent variables by the weights relations, this type of validity cannot be evaluated in PLS.

Operational variance (Fornell and Bookstein, 1982; Fornell and Larcker, 1981) If we substitute ξ's in Eq. (2.47) with their relationships with their manifest variables in Eq. (2.49), then we can eliminate all the latent variables in Eq. (2.47) and trace the effects all the way back to the manifest variables in the predictor latent variables. For purposes of illustration, let's consider the prediction relations from the manifest variables, x's, to their latent variables, ξ's in Figure 2.1, as in Eq. (2.49):

$$\xi = \begin{pmatrix} \xi_1 \\ \xi_2 \end{pmatrix}$$

$$= \begin{pmatrix} \pi_{11} & \pi_{12} & \pi_{13} & 0 & 0 & 0 \\ 0 & 0 & 0 & \pi_{21} & \pi_{22} & \pi_{23} \end{pmatrix} \begin{pmatrix} x_{11} \\ x_{12} \\ x_{13} \\ x_{21} \\ x_{22} \\ x_{23} \end{pmatrix} + \begin{pmatrix} \delta_1 \\ \delta_2 \end{pmatrix} \tag{2.50}$$

$$= \Pi x + \delta$$

If we substitute Eq. (2.50) into Eq. (2.47), we get

$$\begin{aligned} y_1 &= \Lambda_1 \gamma \xi + \Lambda_1 \zeta_1 + \epsilon_1 \\ &= \Lambda_1 \gamma (\Pi x + \delta) + \Lambda_1 \zeta_1 + \epsilon_1 \\ &= \Lambda_1 \gamma \Pi x + \Lambda_1 \gamma \delta + \Lambda_1 \zeta_1 + \epsilon_1 \end{aligned} \tag{2.51}$$

The operational variance of the endogenous manifest variables which is explained by the manifest variables of the predictor latent variables is $\text{Var}[\Lambda_1 \gamma \Pi x] = \Lambda_1 \gamma \Pi(E[xx'])\Pi'\gamma'\Lambda_1' = \Lambda_1 \gamma \Pi(\text{Cov}[x])\Pi'\gamma'\Lambda_1'$.

Since the validity residual, δ, is deliberately set to zero by weight relation in PLS, the second term, $\Lambda_1 \gamma \delta$, disappears, and as a result, the operational variance is same as redundancy.

Stone-Geisser test and jackknifing standard deviations by blindfolding

The Stone-Geisser test (Stone, 1974; Geisser, 1974) follows a blindfolding procedure that involves omission of a part of the data matrix while estimating parameters, and then reconstructing the omitted part by the estimated parameters. This procedure of omitting and reconstructing is repeated until each and every data point is omitted and reconstructed once.

The blindfolding technique provides two types of results: the generalized cross-validation measures and the jackknifing standard deviations of parameter estimates. Both results are helpful in deciding on the quality and relevance of a model.

Blindfolding Even with missing data, it is possible to estimate parameters and latent variable scores.[1] For crossvalidation, we need two data sets: one for estimation, and the other for validation. Blindfolding splits up the data set at hand into these two groups by taking out some data points from the data set and treating them as missing in estimation.

Stone-Geisser's Q^2 Briefly speaking, the Stone-Geisser test criterion, Q^2, is evaluated as an R^2 in OLS without loss of degrees of freedom. It indicates how well the observed values can be reconstructed by the model and its parameters. The general form of the Q^2 is

$$Q^2 = 1 - \frac{E}{O} \tag{2.52}$$

where E is the sum of the squares of the prediction errors and O is the sum of the squares of the errors from the trivial predication given by the mean of the remaining data points. More specifically, the prediction errors in E are calculated as the differences between the true values of the omitted data points and the predicted values using the parameter estimates from the remaining data points. Suppose the nth case data point of the kth manifest variable in block j, y_{jkn}, is omitted, and denote the predicted value of that data point from the model estimated by the remaining data points by $\hat{y}_{jkn}$. Then the E for the manifest variable is

$$E_{jk} = \sum_{n=1}^{N} (y_{jkn} - \hat{y}_{jkn})^2 \tag{2.53}$$

and

$$O_{jk} = \sum_{n=1}^{N} (y_{jkn} - \bar{y}_{jkn})^2 \tag{2.54}$$

where $\bar{y}_{jkn}$ is the mean of the kth manifest variable with y_{jkn} omitted. Now, the Q^2 for the kth manifest variable is calculated as

$$Q_{jk}^2 = 1 - \frac{E_{jk}}{O_{jk}} \tag{2.55}$$

Q^2 for the block is calculated as

$$Q_j^2 = 1 - \frac{\sum_k E_{jk}}{\sum_k O_{jk}} \qquad (2.56)$$

Depending on what kind of prediction is used, we can construct different kinds of Q^2 measures. For example, the blindfolding communality measure is constructed by the prediction from the latent variables to their own manifest variables, and the blindfolding redundancy measure is constructed by the redundancy prediction.

Q^2 can be used to evaluate the predictive relevance of the model and parameters, and also to compare different specifications of the model. If the relations in the model have predictive relevance, then $Q^2 > 0$. Lack of the predictive relevance is suggested by $Q^2 < 0$.

Jackknifing standard deviations As a by-product, it is simple to obtain jackknifing standard deviations of the parameter estimates. For each blindfolded sample, a set of parameter estimates including weights, loadings, inner structural path coefficients, latent variable scores and the correlations of the latent variables, are estimated. This information can be used for jackknifing estimates of standard errors or standard deviations. While Q^2 gives information about predictive relevance, the jackknifing measures provide information about the precision of the parameter estimates.

Discussion

Since structural equation models with latent variables were introduced to marketing, covariance structure analysis (such as LISREL) has been the dominant protocol of the modeling efforts. To understand the benefits and limitations of PLS, it may be helpful to compare variance-based methods (e.g. PLS) to covariance structure analysis (e.g. LISREL).

Table 2.2 Comparisons of PLS and LISREL

PLS	LISREL
• Variance structure	• Covariance structure
• Predictor Specification	• Multivariate normal distribution and independence of the observations
• Prediction oriented	• Parameter oriented
• Consistency-at-large	• Consistency
• Optimal prediction accuracy	• Optimal parameter accuracy
• Case values of latent variables are estimated	• Factor indeterminacy
• Any combination of outward and inward measurement models	• Typically outward measurement model

The objective of covariance structure analysis is to find parameters which provide the best fit to theoretical covariance matrix (from the empirical covariance matrix). On the other hand, PLS aims at minimizing the residual variances involved in the predictive relations. Therefore, it uses a very different optimization criterion: all residual variances are iteratively minimized until the parameter estimates stabilize.

Further, the two methods are based upon different assumptions. Covariance structure analysis requires distributional assumptions and *iid* conditions. PLS does not require distributional assumptions (except for the predictor specifications).

If the assumptions are met, LISREL provides consistent estimates; PLS estimates are consistent-at-large. Both consistency and consistency-at-large are asymptotic properties. Consistency requires a large sample size, but as the number of observations increases, the probability that the model is rejected (based on covariance fit) also increases. This is not the case with Q^2 which tends to stabilize with sample size (Wold, 1982).

According to Wold, ML methods are parameter oriented, and give optimal parameter accuracy; PLS is prediction oriented, and gives optimal prediction accuracy. Wold further maintains that there is a choice between parameter accuracy and prediction accuracy. We cannot have both, except for the special case when LISREL and PLS produce the same parameter estimates.

Both LISREL and PLS deal with latent variables that are not directly observed. The resulting problem of *scale indeterminacy* is solved in PLS by normalizing the LVs in the process of estimation. However, for predictive purposes, the normalized variables must be rescaled back to their original metric.

Covariance structure analysis suffers from identification deficiencies. Particularly, there is the problem of factor indeterminacy. This is avoided in PLS by defining the unobservables by weight relations. The price for this, however, is bias and inconsistency. If factor scores are indeterminate, specific case predictions are not possible, and the ability to predict and control is limited.

Parameter identification is not a problem in most PLS specifications. Since covariance structure analysis decomposes the manifest variable covariance matrix by theory, and tries to find the parameter values which give the best match between the theoretical (expected) covariance structure and the empirical covariance structure, the number of identifiable parameters is restricted. Therefore, some constraints on parameters are always applied. As PLS aims only to minimize the variance terms, that is, the trace of the covariance matrix, the off-diagonal elements are not among the unknowns of the model. Obviously, the identification of structural parameters is an issue if the system is nonrecursive. This is the case for PLS as well.

Finally, a note on the sample size for PLS may be in order. Among some users of PLS, it is sometimes taken as "mysterious" that PLS can use fewer cases than manifest variables. However, the estimation procedure is such that only a part of the model is involved in each step of the estimation. The measurement models are estimated separately from block to block. Moreover, if the measurement model is reflective, it is estimated by simple regressions. The minimum required number of cases is determined by the number of parameters estimated simultaneously. For example, if the measurement model is reflective, the only concern is the largest number of parameters to be estimated in each structural equation. If the measurement model is formative, the number of cases should be determined by the largest measurement equation and the largest structural equation.

Questions

1 In classical true-score theory, the measurement equation can be written:

$$O = T + e$$

where T = true score, O = observed score, and e = measurement error.

(a) If there are minor coding errors, lapses of memory on the part of respondents, rounding errors, and other errors that have about the same aggregate effect on the measured variables as if e in the equation above had been generated from a table of normally distributed random numbers, what type of measurement error is e? What is the formal implication of this type of measurement error in terms of expected values for the terms (and their covariances) in the equation above?

(b) If $E(e) = \kappa$ where $\kappa \neq 0$ what type of measurement error do we have? What is the effect of this error if it is ignored?

(c) What is the effect of random measurement error in a purely endogenous variable? Demonstrate.

(d) What is the effect of random measurement error in an exogenous variable? Demonstrate.

2 Again, consider the true score

(a) Equation

$$O = T + e$$

In the case of formative indicators, what would the corresponding equation look like? What would be included in the error term e? Will $Cov(T, e) = 0$? Develop "a theory" for formative indicators by specifying the conditions in terms of expected values and variances for all terms.

(b) In PLS, we can write the reflective indicator model as

$$y = \Lambda_y \, \eta + \epsilon$$

where $y' = (y_1, y_2, \ldots, y_p)$ observed variables, Λ_y $(p \times m)$ regression coefficients, $\eta' = (\eta_1, \eta_2, \ldots, \eta_m)$ latent variables, ϵ a residual vector. The formative indicator model is

$$\eta = \pi_\eta y$$

where $\pi_\eta(pxm)$ regression coefficients

Does this mean that there is no measurement error? Explain in the context of your suggestions under (a).

3 How would you interpret the following assumptions $E(\eta) = E(\xi) = 0$? What is your interpretation of a model in which Ψ (the covariance matrix of residuals from structural equations) contains non-zero off-diagonal terms?

4 There are several ways in which a structural model with unobservables can be evaluated. Below are some of these (measures) criteria. For each, discuss the *underlying rationale* (including what *exactly* is being tested), under what *circumstances* it should be used as well as the assumptions necessary.

(a) The chi-square likelihood ratio
(b) The trace of a matrix of a block of residual manifest variables
(c) $\Sigma = S$, if Σ is the parameter matrix and S is the covariance matrix
(d) Root mean square residual of $\Sigma = S$
(e) The covariance matrix of measurement residuals
(f) The Bentler–Bonett Index
(g) Redundancy
(h) Communality
(i) R^2 of the latent variables

Notes

1 We can do this by using pairwise deletion of the missing values to construct moment matrix or by substituting means. However, if a column of a data matrix is missing, obviously one cannot estimate the parameters for that variable. On the other hand, if a row of the data matrix for a block is missing, we can still estimate all the parameters *except the latent variable score for that particular case*.

References

Areskoug, B. 1982: The first canonical correlation: theoretical PLS analysis and simulation experiments. In K. G. Jöreskog and Herman Wold (eds), *Systems under Indirect Observation: Causality, Structure, Prediction*, Amsterdam: North Holland, Vol. 2, 95–118.

Bagozzi, Richard P., Yi, Youjae and Singh, Surrendra 1991: On the use of structural equation models in experimental designs: two extensions. *International Journal of Research in Marketing*, 8, 125–40.

Barclay, Donald W. 1991: Interdepartmental conflict in organizational buying: the impact of the organizational context. *Journal of Marketing Research*, 28 (May), 145–59.

Barclay, Donald W., Higgins, Christopher and Thompson, Ronald 1992: The partial least squares (PLS) approach to causal modeling: personal computer adoption and use as an illustration. Paper submitted to *Technology Studies*.

Bock, R. D. 1975: *Multivariate Statistical Methods in Behavioral Research*, New York: McGraw-Hill.

Dijkstra, Theo 1983: Some comments on maximum likelihood and partial least squares methods. *Journal of Econometrics*, 22, 67–90.

Fornell, Claes (ed.) 1982: *A Second Generation of Multivariate Analysis*, vols I and II, New York: Praeger.

Fornell, Claes 1992: A national customer satisfaction barometer: the Swedish experience. *Journal of Marketing*, 56 (Jan), 6–21.

Fornell, Claes and Bookstein, Fred 1982: Two structural equation models: LISREL and PLS applied to consumer exit-voice theory. *Journal of Marketing Research*, 19 (Nov), 440–52.

Fornell, Claes and Larcker, David F. 1981: Evaluating structural equation models with unobservable variables and measurement error. *Journal of Marketing Research*, 18 (Feb), 39–50.

Fornell, Claes, Rhee, Byong-Duk and Yi, Youjae 1991: Direct regression, reverse regression, and covariance structure analysis. *Marketing Letters*, 2, (3), 309–20.

Fornell, Claes and Robinson, William T. 1983: Industrial organization and consumer satisfaction/dissatisfaction. *Journal of Consumer Research*, 9 (March), 403–12.

Fornell, Claes and Westbrook, Robert A. 1984: The vicious circle of consumer complaints. *Journal of Marketing*, 48 (Summer), 68–78.

Geisser, S. 1974: A predictive approach to the random effect model. *Biometrika*, 61, 101–7.

Hui, B. S. 1978: The partial least squares approach to path models of indirectly observed variables with multiple indicators. Doctoral thesis (University of Pennsylvania, Philadelphia, PA).

Hui, B. S. 1982: On building partial least squares models with interdependent inner relations. In K. G. Jöreskog and H. Wold (eds), *Systems under Indirect Observation: Causality, Structure, Prediction*, Amsterdam: North-Holland, Part II, 249–72.

Jain, A. K., Pinson, C. and Malhotra, N. K. 1987: *A Partial Least Squares (PLS) Causal Investigation of Customers' Shopping Behavior*, Fontainebleau Cedex, France: INSEAD.

Jagpal, Harsharanjeet S. 1981: Measuring joint advertising effects in multiproduct firms. *Journal of Advertising Research*, 21 (Feb), 65–9.

Johnson, Michael D. and Anderson, Eugene W. and Fornell, Claes 1992: A model of market level expectations, performance, and customer satisfaction. Working Paper, University of Michigan.

Johnson, Michael D. and Fornell, Claes 1987: The nature and methodological implications of the cognitive representation of products. *Journal of Consumer Research*, 14 (Sept), 214–28.

Johnson, Michael D. and Horne, David A. 1992: An examination of the validity of direct product perceptions. *Psychology and Marketing*, 9 (3), 221–35.

Johnson, Michael D., Lehmann, Donald R., Fornell, Claes and Horne, Daniel R. 1992: Attribute abstraction, feature-dimensionality, and the scaling of product similarities. *International Journal of Research in Marketing*, 9, 131–47.

Jöreskog, K. G. 1967: Some contributions to maximum likelihood factor analysis. *Psychometrika*, 32, 443–82.

Jöreskog, K. G. 1970: A general method for analysis of covariance structures. *Biometrika*, 57, 239–51.

Kujala, Jouni T. and Johnson, Michael D. (forthcoming): Price knowledge and search behavior for habitual, low involvement food purchases. *Journal of Economic Psychology.*

Lohmöller, Jan-Bernd 1981: *LVPLS 1.6 Program Manual: Latent Variables Path Analysis with Partial Least Squares Estimation*, München: Hochschule der Bundeswehr.

Lohmöller, Jan-Bernd 1989: *Latent Variable Path Modeling with Partial Least Squares*, Heidelberg: Physica-Verlag.

Lyttkens, E. 1966: On the fix-point property of Wold's iterative estimation method for principal components. In P. R. Krishnaiah (ed.), *Multivariate Analysis* (Academic Press, New York) 335–50.

Lyttkens, E. 1973: Fixed-point method for estimating interdependent systems with the underlying model specification. *Journal of the Royal Statistical Society*, Series A, 136: 353–94.

Qualls, William J. 1987: Household decision behavior: the impact of husbands' and wives' sex role orientation. *Journal of Consumer Research*, 14 (Sept.), 264–79.

Stone, M. 1974: Cross-validatory choice and assessment of statistical predictions. *Journal of the Royal Statistical Society*, Series B 36, 111–33.

Wold, H. 1966: Nonlinear estimation by iterative least squares procedures. In F. N. David (ed.), *Festschrift for J. Neyman: Research Papers in Statistics*, London: Wiley, 411–44.

Wold, H. 1975: Path models with latent variables: the NIPALS approach. In H. M. Blalock *et al.* (eds), *Quantitative Sociology: International Perspectives on Mathematical and Statistical Modeling*, New York: Academic.

Wold, H. (ed.) 1981: *The Fix-Point Approach to Interdependent Systems*, Amsterdam: North-Holland.

Wold, H. 1982: Soft modeling: the basic design and some extensions. In K. G. Jöreskog and H. Wold (eds), *Systems under Indirect Observation: Causality, Structure, Prediction*, Vol. 2, Amsterdam: North-Holland, 1–54.

Wold, H. 1985a: Partial least squares. In S. Kotz and N. L. Johnson (eds), *Encyclopedia of Statistical Sciences*, Vol. 6, New York: Wiley, 481–91.

Wold, H. 1985b: Predictor specification. In S. Kotz and N. L. Johnson (eds), *Encyclopedia of Statistical Sciences*, Vol. 8, New York: Wiley, 587–99.

Woodword, J. A. and Bentler, P. M. 1979: Application of optimal sign-vectors to reliability and cluster analysis. *Psychometrika*, 44, 337–41.

Zinkhan, George M., Joachimsthaler, Erich and Kinnear, Thomas C. 1987: Individual differences and marketing decision support system usage and satisfaction. *Journal of Marketing Research*, 24 (May), 208–14.

3

Multivariate Statistical Models for Categorical Data

Jay Magidson

Regression analysis was developed over 100 years ago for the statistical analysis of a continuous dependent variable. On the other hand, multivariate models for the analysis of categorical variables have been developed much more recently, and continue to evolve at a rapid pace. Goodman (1991) refers to the past two decades as an "Age of Progress in the Analysis of Categorical Data." (See also Clogg (1992) for a historical perspective on the development of these newer techniques.) As of this date, however, simple cross-tabulation summaries of categorical variables still predominate over the use of these multivariate methods.

One reason for the lag time between the development and application of new multivariate methods is that researchers have become accustomed to "linear" thinking, while the proper analysis of categorical data turns out to be log-linear (or log-bilinear, multiplicative, etc). The attempt to force categorical data into a linear mode has delayed the understanding and acceptance of the new methods.

Linear thinking is appropriate under normal distribution theory for continuous variables. If the distribution of two variables follows the bivariate normal, it can be shown that the regression of one on the other is linear. However, normally distributed variables are rare in social science data, especially data obtained from surveys. Moreover, categorical variables, whether qualitative or quantitative, can *never* be normally distributed. Even when bivariate normal variables are discretized, the relationship between the resulting categorical variables turns out *not* to be linear.

Linear thinking is related to our preference for using percentages to summarize cross tabulations. While the percentage provides a meaningful way of describing relationships between two categorical variables, as summarized in a two-way cross tabulation, it does not foster the development of analytic tools for the multi-way table. Rather, it is frequency counts themselves, ratios of frequencies (i.e. odds), ratios of odds, and ratios of odds ratios, etc., that provide the natural statistics for analyzing the multi-way table.

The new models derive from maximum likelihood theory based on the binomial, multinomial, Poisson and similar sampling distributions that are appropriate for categorical data. They include log-linear models (such as the logit model) and log-bilinear models (such as certain association models).

Overview

Our focus throughout this chapter will be on the analysis of a dependent variable as a function of predictor variables, where all variables are categorical. As such, we will draw on analogies to statistical models developed for the analysis of a continuous dependent variable; namely, regression and analysis of variance (ANOVA) models. In addition, readers familiar with structural equation models for continuous variables (e.g. see Bagozzi, 1994) will notice various similarities with respect to the use of a chi-square statistic to assess the fit of the hypothesized model.

In introducing the new multivariate models, we will begin with the analysis of dichotomous dependent variables (i.e. dependent variables having only two categories). (Actually, we begin by analyzing a multi-way table of frequency counts formed using only one category of a dichotomous dependent variable.) Applications for four real world data sets will be used throughout this chapter to introduce several log-linear and logit models and we will interpret the results from these analyses.

We will then consider the analysis of dependent variables having three or more categories (polytomous variables). We distinguish between models which attempt to explain all associations between the predictors and the dependent variable and models which attempt to explain only associations with respect to a single set of dependent variable scores. The former models, known as multinomial logit models, are appropriate for the analysis of nominal dependent variables, i.e. those for which no natural ordering exists between any of its categories. The latter models, known as Y-Association (Magidson, 1992), are directly analogous to traditional regression models. A fifth real world data set is used to introduce the models for polytomous dependent variables.

BASICS: Categorical Variables and Models

Categorical variables differ from continuous variables in that they are classified into a relatively small number of mutually exclusive and exhaustive groupings or intervals called categories, as opposed to being measurable more and more finely, on some continuous scale. For example, survey variables such as marital status, income level, age, attitudes, purchase behavior, etc. are typically obtained in the categorical form. Alternatively, many exogenous variables, such as the outdoor temperature at the time of the survey, are *not* categorical since they are quantified on a continuous scale (e.g. the Fahrenheit scale).

The simplest categorical variable, known as a *dichotomous* (or binary) variable, has only two categories, which denote the presence and absence of some attribute. Examples of dichotomous variables are ATTITUDE-A: (Present, Absent), PURCH: Purchase Intent (Yes, No), and RESP2: (Responder, Non-responder). Some examples of *polytomous* variables (i.e. those having more than two categories) are RATING (Favorable, Neutral, Unfavorable), RESP3: (Paid responder, Unpaid responder, Non-responder), MARSTAT: (Married, Single, Widowed, Divorced), and AGE: (18–24, 25–34, 35–44, 45–54, 55–64, 65+).

A frequency distribution summarizes the number of observations that fall into each category of a variable. Cross-tabulations provide summaries of the joint frequency counts associated with any combination of two or more categorical variables. By convention, when we present a cross-tabulation, the rows of the table will be formed jointly by the categories of the predictor variables, and the columns will represent the categories of the dependent variable.

Incomplete tables are ones where some of the frequency counts are missing for certain row-column combinations for reasons other than a small sample. For example, the two-way table GENDER (Male, Female) by type of operation (appendectomy, hysterectomy, other) would be incomplete because the male-hysterectomy cell will always be zero regardless of the size of the sample. Statistical models for incomplete tables differ from those for complete tables in important ways. (See discussion problem 1b.)

Just as a structural equation model hypothesizes a structure for the relationships among continuous variables, each model that we will present for categorical variables hypothesizes a structure for the relationships among categorical variables. However, unlike covariance structure models, for which the hypothesized structures involve one-way (means) and two-way (covariances) but not higher order moments, the structures hypothesized by the categorical models may not be so limited. While some of the log-linear models impose structures on the frequency counts in one-way and two-way tables, others impose structures on the counts in three-way as well as higher order tables.

The categorical models can be used to generate estimated expected counts for each cell of the full multi-way table. By using a chi-squared statistic to compare the estimated expected counts to the corresponding observed counts, the goodness of model fit can be tested. Such a test is similar to the use of the chi-squared statistic to test the goodness of fit of overidentified structural equation models.

Logit and Association Models

The various log-linear models that we describe in this chapter will be written in the form of a regression-type model where the conditional probability distribution (and/or frequency distribution) of a designated dependent variable is expressed as a function of the predictor variables. In the case that the dependent variable is dichotomous, a single regression-type equation is sufficient, because only one conditional probability is needed to determine the entire conditional distribution. For example, with the dichotomous dependent variable RESP2, if the probability of response (the first category of RESP2) is estimated to be 2 percent for a particular group, then the corresponding probability of *non-response* (the second category of RESP2) is necessarily $100\% - 2\% = 98\%$. It would be redundant to attempt to estimate a separate function of the predictor variables for each category of RESP2.

In the case that the dependent variable contains $K > 2$ categories, the models may be $K - 1$ dimensional. In this case, a vector of $K - 1$ conditional probabilities (or $K - 1$ probability contrasts) may be estimated as separate functions of the predictor variables, similar to simultaneous equation econometric models. Again, as with a dichotomous dependent variable, if the vector of conditional probabilities for any group are estimated for say the first $K - 1$ categories of the dependent variable, the probability estimate for the Kth category is determined using the fact that the sum of all K of these conditional probabilities must equal one. For $K = 3$, for example, the model is analogous to a bivariate regression model, where there are two dependent variables, and hence $K - 1 = 2$ regression-type equations.

The model used to analyze a dichotomous dependent variable as a function of one or more predictor variables is known as the *logit* model. The $K - 1$ dimensional model that is used to express the entire probability distribution of a polytomous dependent variable as a function of predictor variables is known as the *multinomial logit* model. As mentioned earlier, the multinomial logit model is generally used with a nominal dependent variable.

For some applications, it may be desired to scale a polytomous dependent variable by assigning explicit quantitative scores $Y = (y_1, y_2, \ldots, y_K)$ to its categories, and to formulate a single regression-type model which expresses the conditional expectation of Y as a function of the predictor variables. The resulting model, referred to as the *Y-Association* model, Magidson (1992), is a type of ordinal regression model. Like the simple logit model and the ordinary regression model, the Y-Association model is one-dimensional because only one set of dependent variable scores are hypothesized.

The general log-linear model

The logit, multinomial logit and Y-Association models mentioned above are all special cases of the general *log-linear* model which expresses the expected distribution of the multi-way frequency counts as a function of all the variables (dependent and predictors). We will show how this general model may be re-expressed in a form analogous to a regression model, with the dependent variable on the left side of the equation and the predictor variables on the right. We will also describe several different kinds of regression analogues and discuss when each should be used.

To begin, we will specify a particular log-linear model which we will use to analyze traffic fatalities based on a complete and an incomplete table of counts. We then show how this model may be extended to analyze fatality *rates*. We follow these analyses with some further examples of the analyses of a dichotomous dependent variable, before considering examples for a dependent variable containing more than two categories.

A Log-linear Model for Traffic Fatalities

In some instances, data may be available for only one category of a dependent variable. For example, one may have collected counts, on a monthly basis, of new customers. It may not be possible or feasible to collect data on non customers. While it is not possible to analyze the factors that determine who becomes a customer and who doesn't without including both customers and non-customers in the analysis, it is possible to use a log-linear model to *describe* the data. Such a model can also be used to identify time points that show significantly higher or lower than

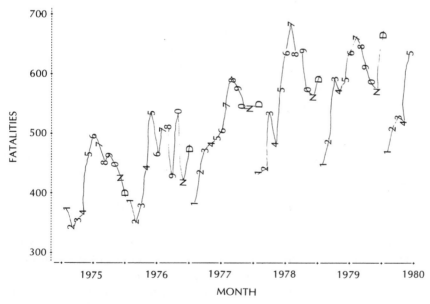

Legend: 1 = January, 2 = February, 3 = March, 4 = April, 5 = May 6 = June, 7 = July, 8 = August,
9 = September, O = October, N = November D = December.

Figure 3.1 Plot of the five-year trend in traffic fatalities for Region 9 (Southwestern US) during January 1975 through May 1980

the expected number of sales after adjusting for seasonality and annual trend, as well as to forecast future sales.

For our first example, we will utilize a log-linear model to describe the annual trend factor (YEAR effect) and the seasonality factor (MONTH effect) for a monthly time series of five years of traffic fatalities in the southwestern region of the US from January 1975 through December 1979. A time series plot of the data in Figure 3.1 shows the obvious seasonal nature of the data, as well as the overall increasing trend.

A residual analysis of these data can serve to identify particular "outlier" time points where the actual observed count is significantly below or above the count that was expected, perhaps coincident with extreme weather conditions (or some intervention) which may have occurred in one or more of those time points.

We will also add an additional five months of data for January–May 1980, and illustrate the use of the log-linear model for an incomplete table. In particular, we will use this incomplete table to forecast the counts that would be expected during the balance of 1980.

Both the analysis of the complete 12×5 table of counts of 12 months by 5 years as well as the analysis of the incomplete 12×6 table (where the counts for June–December 1980 are missing) are performed using the following log-linear model expressed in its additive form:

$$\log_e(F_{ij}) = \lambda + \lambda_i^M + \lambda_j^Y \qquad i = 1, 2, \ldots, I; \; j = 1, 2, \ldots, J \qquad (3.1)$$

where F_{ij} = Expected frequency count for month i of year j
  λ^M = Parameter vector for the MONTH effects (read "lambda")
  λ^Y = Parameter vector for the YEAR effects
  λ = the intercept constant
  I = 12 and J = 5 (for the complete table) or 6 (for the incomplete table)

Note that model (3.1) hypothesizes only main effects associated with the categorical variables MONTH and YEAR. It is used to estimate those fatalities that would be expected *without* the effects of a MONTH × YEAR interaction; i.e. without the effects of, say, unusual weather that may have occurred during a particular month of a particular year.

In the case of the complete table, model (3.1) expresses the hypothesis of independence in the two-way table of observed counts given in columns 1–5 of Table 3.1. In the case of the incomplete table, model 3.1 expresses the hypothesis of quasi-independence.[1] In this case, the missing counts of fatalities for June–December 1980 are treated as "structural" as opposed to sampling zeroes and are "ignored" by the model. It is incorrect (see discussion question 1b) to replace the missing cells in an incomplete table with zeroes and analyze the table as if it were a complete table, treating the zeroes as if they were sampling zeroes (i.e. due to a small sample).

Table 3.1 Observed counts of traffic fatalities in Region 9 (Southwestern US) during January 1975 through May 1980

Month	1975	1976	Year 1977	1978	1979	1980
Jan.	378	393	386	441	453	473
Feb.	346	355	440	442	490	511
Mar.	362	383	480	540	597	532
Apr.	371	447	487	487	580	524
May	470	541	496	577	595	637
June	501	468	507	638	641	–
July	487	513	552	685	665	–
Aug.	458	519	595	638	653	–
Sept.	467	433	582	644	616	–
Oct.	451	538	547	577	591	–
Nov.	429	427	546	571	580	–
Dec.	404	480	554	596	669	–

Model (3.1) is analogous to the usual ANOVA formulation. Since only $I - 1$ components of the λ^M-vector are identified, the I components of λ^M are standardized so that they sum to zero. Thus, there will be only $I - 1 = 11$ degrees of freedom associated with the λ^M-parameters. The components of the λ^Y-parameters are similarly standardized. These standardizations are identical to the identification conditions used in ANOVA (see e.g. Goodman, 1970, for more specifics).

In general, we will use the likelihood ratio chi-squared statistic (L^2) to assess the goodness of fit (actually, the lack of fit) of a given model. Specifically, the expected frequencies F_{ij}, as estimated under some model by the method of maximum likelihood, are compared to the observed frequency counts, f_{ij} using the following formula:

$$L^2 = 2 \sum_i \sum_j f_{ij} \log_e (f_{ij}/\hat{F}_{ij}) \qquad (3.2)$$

The lower the value for L^2, the better the fit of the model. A value for L^2 of 0 is indicative of a perfect fit, i.e. all of the estimated expected counts are identical to the corresponding observed counts.

The number of degrees of freedom used in testing the fit of a model is equal to the number of distinct structural restrictions that the model makes on the data. For the main-effects-only model (3.1), the degrees of freedom may be counted by observing that the model implicitly excludes all interaction terms. For the complete table, such exclusions are equivalent to the following structural restrictions:

$$\lambda_{ij}^{MY} = 0 \qquad \text{for } i = 1, \ldots, 12; j = 1, 2 \ldots, 5; \qquad (3.3)$$

where the λ_{ij}^{MY} parameters, if included in the model, would also have been subject to the standard ANOVA-like identification restrictions.

For the incomplete table, five more interactions exist, corresponding to the first five months of 1980:

$$\lambda_{ij}^{MY} = 0 \qquad \text{for } (i, j) = (1, 6), (2, 6), (3, 6), (4, 6), (5, 6) \qquad (3.4)$$

Hence, there are a total of $(12 - 1) * (5 - 1) = 44$ distinct interaction terms for the analysis of the complete table plus $5 - 1 = 4$ additional distinct interactions for the analysis of the incomplete table. Thus, there are 44 degrees of freedom for testing the fit of model (3.1) when applied to the complete table, and 48 when applied to the incomplete table. This test of fit is a test of how closely the estimated expected counts generated from model (3.1) fit the data, or equivalently, the truth of the restrictions given in eq. (3.3) (or, eq. (3.1)).

The test of fit for the incomplete table yields $L^2 = 96.81$ with 48 degrees of freedom, a highly significant result ($p < 0.0001$). Thus, we must conclude that at least one of the MONTH × YEAR interactions, as quantified by the λ_{ij}^{MY} parameters, is significantly different from 0.

If the λ_{ij}^{MY} parameters were included in eq. (3.1), the model would change from a main-effects-only log-linear model to what is called a *saturated* log-linear model, which would fit the data perfectly ($L^2 = 0$; $p = 1$). Since these interaction parameters were *not* included, model (3.1) is an example of an *unsaturated* model.

By taking the antilog of both sides of eq. (3.1), the additive log-linear model can be re-expressed equivalently in the simpler multiplicative form in terms of τ-parameters (read, "tau"):

$$F_{ij} = (\tau)(\tau_i^M)(\tau_j^Y) \qquad i = 1, 2, \ldots, 12; j = 1, 2, \ldots, J \qquad (3.5)$$
$$\text{where } \tau = \exp(\lambda), \tau_i^M = \exp(\lambda_i^M), \text{ and } \tau_j^Y = \exp(\lambda_j^Y)$$

As we shall see, the above multiplicative parameters have a straightforward interpretation.

The results of fitting model (3.1) (or, the equivalent model (3.5)) to the incomplete table are summarized in Tables 3.2, 3.3 and 3.4. In Table 3.2, column B contains the estimated expected counts under model (3.1), and column C contains the corresponding residuals. An examination of these residuals identifies several cells that may be associated with significant interactions. In order to determine which residuals are significantly different from 0, the residuals are adjusted[2] in column D to standard normal deviates. Those adjusted residuals having an absolute value of 1.96 or larger indicate those several time points which have a significantly higher or lower than expected number of fatalities. Presumably, many of the significant interactions are explainable by extreme weather patterns.

Table 3.2 Results from Model 3.1/3.5: observed, expected
frequencies and residuals

	(A) OBS count	(B) EXP count	(C) Residual	(D) Adj Resid
1975				
January	378.00	341.27	36.726	2.218
February	346.00	349.39	− 3.386	− 0.202
March	362.00	391.30	− 29.302	− 1.662
April	371.00	391.57	− 20.572	− 1.166
May	470.00	448.36	21.639	1.154
June	501.00	458.94	42.057	2.254
July	487.00	483.43	3.569	0.187
August	458.00	476.93	− 18.934	− 0.997
September	467.00	456.78	10.223	0.549
October	451.00	450.45	0.553	0.030
November	429.00	425.29	3.708	0.206
December	404.00	450.28	− 46.280	− 2.501
1976				
January	393.00	366.12	26.883	1.576
February	355.00	374.82	− 19.820	− 1.150
March	383.00	419.79	− 36.787	− 2.026
April	447.00	420.08	26.923	1.482
May	541.00	481.00	60.000	3.107
June	468.00	492.35	− 24.351	− 1.269
July	513.00	518.62	− 5.622	− 0.286
August	519.00	511.65	7.348	0.376
September	433.00	490.03	− 57.028	− 2.979
October	538.00	483.24	54.763	2.878
November	427.00	456.25	− 29.252	− 1.578
December	480.00	483.06	− 3.058	− 0.161
1977				
January	386.00	411.07	− 25.074	− 1.403
February	440.00	420.85	19.154	1.060
March	480.00	471.33	8.666	0.455
April	487.00	471.66	15.340	0.806
May	496.00	540.06	− 44.063	− 2.177
June	507.00	552.81	− 45.809	− 2.284
July	552.00	582.31	− 30.306	− 1.476
August	595.00	574.48	20.520	1.006
September	582.00	550.20	31.799	1.589
October	547.00	542.58	4.424	0.222
November	546.00	512.28	33.723	1.740
December	554.00	542.38	11.625	0.585
1978				
January	441.00	455.30	− 14.298	− 0.768
February	442.00	466.12	− 24.121	− 1.282
March	540.00	522.04	17.959	0.907

Table 3.2 *(Contd.)*

	(A) OBS count	(B) EXP count	(C) Residual	(D) Adj Resid
April	487.00	522.40	− 35.402	− 1.787
May	577.00	598.16	− 21.165	− 1.005
June	638.00	612.28	25.718	1.235
July	685.00	644.95	40.048	1.879
August	638.00	636.28	1.716	0.081
September	644.00	609.39	34.607	1.666
October	577.00	600.95	− 23.947	− 1.160
November	571.00	567.39	3.611	0.180
December	596.00	600.73	− 4.725	− 0.229
1979				
January	453.00	474.88	− 21.879	− 1.157
February	490.00	486.17	3.832	0.200
March	597.00	544.49	52.507	2.608
April	580.00	544.87	35.131	1.745
May	595.00	623.89	− 28.891	− 1.350
June	641.00	638.61	2.385	0.113
July	665.00	672.69	− 7.690	− 0.355
August	653.00	663.65	− 10.649	− 0.495
September	616.00	635.60	− 19.601	− 0.929
October	591.00	626.79	− 35.793	− 1.708
November	580.00	591.79	− 11.791	− 0.577
December	669.00	626.56	42.439	2.025
1980				
January	473.00	475.36	− 2.359	− 0.132
February	511.00	486.66	24.341	1.354
March	532.00	545.04	− 13.043	− 0.695
April	524.00	545.42	− 21.419	− 1.141
May	637.00	624.52	12.480	0.633
June	—	639.26	—	—
July	—	673.37	—	—
August	—	664.32	—	—
September	—	636.24	—	—
October	—	627.42	—	—
November	—	592.39	—	—
December	—	627.19	—	—

Table 3.3 presents the estimates for the seasonality parameters, i.e. the MONTH effects, as expressed in the additive and multiplicative forms, respectively. These effects quantify what is obvious in Figure 3.1 – that fatalities tend to increase each month from January through July and August and then decline through the winter months, except in December, where there is a small increase in fatalities over November. It is clear that fatalities are higher during the vacation months, as the amount of travel increases.

Table 3.3 Additive and multiplicative estimates of month effects for Model 3.1/3.5

Month	(A) Additive (Model 3.1)	(B) Multiplicative (Model 3.5)
January	− 0.218	0.804
February	− 0.195	0.823
March	− 0.081	0.922
April	− 0.081	0.923
May	0.055	1.056
June	0.078	1.081
July	0.130	1.139
August	0.117	1.124
September	0.073	1.076
October	0.060	1.061
November	0.002	1.002
December	0.059	1.061

Table 3.4 Additive and multiplicative estimates of year effects for Model 3.1/3.5

Month	(A) Additive (Model 3.1)	(B) Multiplicative (Model 3.5)
1975	− 0.201	0.818
1976	− 0.131	0.877
1977	− 0.015	0.985
1978	0.087	1.091
1979	0.129	1.138
1980	0.130	1.139

As mentioned above, the interpretation of the multiplicative parameters is straightforward. Selecting $i = 1$ (January) as the base, the ratio of the parameter for any month i to January is equal to the ratio of expected fatalities for month i to January's expected fatalities, within each year j. Formally, from model (3.5), it follows that:

$$F_{ij}/F_{1j} = \tau_i^M/\tau_1^M \tag{3.6}$$

Thus, according to the MONTH effect estimates in Table 3.3, the number of traffic fatalities for July is expected to be 48 percent higher (i.e. $\tau_i^M/\tau_1^M = 1.48$ times as high) as in January of the same year.

Table 3.4 presents the estimates for the YEAR effects which show an upward trend in the data. Similar to eq. (3.6), taking 1975 as the base year, the increase in fatalities from year 1975 to year $1975 + j - 1$ can be obtained by examining the following parameter ratios:

$$F_{ij}/F_{i1} = \tau_j^Y/\tau_1^Y \qquad \text{for } i = 1, 2, \ldots, 12 \qquad (3.7)$$

Alternatively, to examine the annual increase from the previous year, we would use different parameter ratios:

$$F_{ij}/F_{ij-1} = \tau_j^Y/\tau_{j-1}^Y \qquad \text{for } i = 1, 2, \ldots, 12 \qquad (3.8)$$

Thus, for example, taking $j = 5$, the relevant estimates from Table 3.4 can be used to determine that fatalities during 1980 are expected to be only slightly higher than during 1979. The parameter estimates in Tables 3.3 and 3.4 were used to project the fatality counts for the remainder of 1980. These projections, listed under the column marked "EXP Count" in Table 3.2, were found to be close to the actual counts.

We conclude this initial example by noting that the models and methods described herein utilize maximum likelihood methods based on the Poisson, binomial, multinomial and related sampling distributions. Thus, for example, a log-linear model like model (3.1)–(3.5) may be used when the expected counts are assumed to follow a Poisson distribution with mean F_{ij}, an assumption which is often made for counts of rare events. The log-linear model may also be used with other than rare events, in which case the binomial distribution may be assumed to hold.

A Log-linear Model for Rates

In our first example, we have shown how one of the simplest log-linear models can be used to describe the relationships in a two-way table. This model, which is equivalent to the well-known model of independence, was chosen primarily to introduce and interpret the model parameters and to describe the chi-square test of model fit. The remaining examples will illustrate how log-linear models can be useful in more complex applications.

For our second example, we will consider the analysis of *rates*. Rates are frequency counts which are standardized by division by some measure of "exposure", as expressed by a quantitative variable. For example, instead of modeling customer counts or counts of traffic fatalities, one might wish instead to model rates of customer penetration or traffic fatality rates. Customer penetration might be operationalized as the number of customers in a given geographic area, divided by the total number of households in that area. Fatality rates might be defined as the number of traffic fatalities over a period of time divided by the number of vehicle miles traveled during that period.

To illustrate the log-linear model for rates, we will re-analyze the data in Table 3.1, adjusting for the fact that some months have more days than others. Dividing the monthly fatality counts by the number of days in the month, we will convert from a model for estimating the number of monthly traffic fatalities to a model for predicting the average *daily* rate of traffic fatalities.

The log-linear model for rates, as expressed in the multiplicative form, is:

$$\frac{F_{ij}}{Z_{ij}} = (\tau)(\tau_i^M)(\tau_j^Y) \qquad i = 1, 2, \ldots, 12; \, j = 1, 2, \ldots, J \qquad (3.9)$$

where the z_{ij} (which are treated as fixed values) denote the number of days in month i of year j.

Table 3.5 Additive and multiplicative estimates of month effects for Model 3.9

Month	(A) Additive	(B) Multiplicative
January	− 0.236	0.790
February	− 0.122	0.885
March	− 0.099	0.906
April	− 0.066	0.937
May	0.037	1.038
June	0.092	1.097
July	0.111	1.118
August	0.098	1.103
September	0.087	1.091
October	0.041	1.042
November	0.016	1.016
December	0.040	1.041

Table 3.6 Additive and multiplicative estimates of year effects for Model 3.9

Month	(A) Additive	(B) Multiplicative
1975	− 0.200	0.819
1976	− 0.132	0.876
1977	− 0.014	0.986
1978	0.089	1.093
1979	0.131	1.140
1980	0.126	1.134

Tables 3.5 and 3.6 present the parameter estimates under model (3.9). Comparing these estimates to the corresponding estimates in Tables 3.3

and 3.4, we see several differences. For example, the estimate for the MONTH effect in February is higher (-0.12 vs. -0.19) under the rate model (3.9), than under the corresponding log-linear model (3.5). Since model (3.5) did not take into account that February has fewer days than the other months, the effect estimate under model (3.5) understates the average daily fatality rate for February relative to the other months. Note also that the estimates for March and April are no longer identical to each other.

The Z-table is used as starting values for the iterative proportional fitting (IPF) algorithm, a maximum likelihood algorithm used to estimate the expected cell counts (see discussion question 1d). For the usual log-linear model, all of the Z-values are fixed at 1, so that Z does not appear in the model formulation at all. In addition to being used to convert counts to rates, the Z-values can also be used to incorporate sampling weights into an analysis, or to specify certain cells in incomplete tables as "structural zeroes" (see discussion question 1b). (As mentioned earlier, a structural zero is a frequency count of zero which is due to structural design rather than a small sample size.)

In the case that sampling weights are used, the Z value for a particular cell is taken as the inverse of the average sampling weight for that cell (see e.g. Magidson, 1987, and Clogg and Eliasin, 1987). In the case of an incomplete table, the Z-values which correspond to the structural zeroes are set to 0. Thus, in models (3.1), (3.5) and (3.9) the Z values corresponding to June–December 1980 were set to zero.[3]

Model (3.9) can be estimated by any log-linear modeling computer program that employs the IPF algorithm and that allows the user to input starting values. In addition, model (3.9) can be estimated by the SPSS LOGLINEAR program which utilizes an alternative maximum likelihood algorithm and also calculates the adjusted residuals which were described earlier. For further information on the IPF algorithm, including an example, see Goodman (1972). For further information on using IPF with sampling weights, see Magidson (1987) and Clogg and Eliasin (1987). For further applications of the log-linear rate model, see Haberman (1978).

An Experiment Designed to Increase the Return Rate to a Mail Survey

Next we introduce the logit model, which is used to analyze a dichotomous dependent variable as a function of one or more categorical predictor variables. The logit model is the analog to the regression model when the dependent variable has only two categories (see e.g. Magidson, 1978). The logit model is a special case of the general log-linear model.

To illustrate this important model, we analyze the three-way table of counts given in Table 3.7a. The data in this table was obtained from an experiment to test the effects of a reminder call (C) and of monetary payments (M) on the likelihood of completing and returning (R) a mail survey.

To derive the main-effects-only logit model for this example, we first form the following unsaturated log-linear model:

$$\log_e (F_{ijk}) = \lambda + \lambda_i^C + \lambda_j^M + \lambda_k^R + \lambda_{ij}^{CM} + \lambda_{ik}^{CR} + \lambda_{jk}^{MR} \tag{3.10}$$

where $i = 1, 2$; $j = 1, 2, 3, 4$; and $k = 1, 2$
and, as in the earlier models, the usual ANOVA-like standardizations are used to identify the parameters:

$$\sum_i \lambda_i^C = \sum_j \lambda_j^M = \sum_k \lambda_k^R = 0 \tag{3.11}$$

$$\sum_i \lambda_{ij}^{CM} = \sum_j \lambda_{ij}^{CM} = 0 \tag{3.12}$$

Table 3.7a Observed counts and associated summary statistics for responders and non-responders based on the main-effects-only logit model

(C) Reminder call	(M) Monetary payment	(R) Response		Observed % response	Observed odds	Observed logit
		Yes	No			
Yes	$1	2,407	1,954	55.2%	1.23	0.21
	$2	1,265	881	58.9%	1.44	0.36
	$3	1,340	809	62.4%	1.66	0.50
	$4	1,306	779	62.6%	1.68	0.52
No	$1	2,133	2,176	49.5%	0.98	−0.02
	$2	1,156	942	55.1%	1.23	0.20
	$3	1,262	897	58.5%	1.41	0.34
	$4	1,248	839	59.8%	1.49	0.40

$$\sum_i \lambda_{ik}^{CR} = \sum_k \lambda_{ik}^{CR} = 0 \tag{3.13}$$

$$\sum_i \lambda_{jk}^{MR} = \sum_k \lambda_{jk}^{MR} = 0 \tag{3.14}$$

For example, eq. (3.11) implies that $\lambda_2^R = -\lambda_1^R$ and eq. (3.13) implies that $\lambda_{12}^{CR} = -\lambda_{11}^{CR}$ and that $\lambda_{22}^{CR} = -\lambda_{21}^{CR}$.

Note that model (3.10) excludes the three-factor interactions. These exclusions are equivalent to the following restrictions on the λ^{CMR}-parameters:

Table 3.7b Expected counts and associated summary statistics for responders and non-responders based on the main-effects-only logit model

(C) Reminder call	(M) Monetary payment	(R) Response		Expected % response	Expected odds	Expected logit
		Yes	No			
Yes	$1	2381.26	1979.74	54.6%	1.20	0.18
	$2	1271.14	874.86	59.2%	1.45	0.37
	$3	1344.50	804.50	62.6%	1.67	0.51
	$4	1321.10	763.90	63.4%	1.73	0.55
No	$1	2158.74	2150.26	50.1%	1.00	0.00
	$2	1149.86	948.14	54.8%	1.21	0.19
	$3	1257.50	901.50	58.2%	1.39	0.33
	$4	1232.90	854.10	59.1%	1.44	0.37

$$\lambda_{i\,j\,k}^{CMR} = 0 \tag{3.15}$$

where these parameters would also be subject to the usual identification conditions:

$$\sum_i \lambda_{i\,j\,k}^{CMR} = \sum_j \lambda_{i\,j\,k}^{CMR} = \sum_k \lambda_{i\,j\,k}^{CMR} = 0 \tag{3.16}$$

The number of degrees of freedom for testing the fit of this model is 3, corresponding to the $(2-1) * (4-1) * (2-1)$ distinct λ^{CMR}-parameters which are set to zero in eq. (3.15).

While the regression model predicts the conditional expectation of the dependent variable, the logit model predicts the conditional logit. For the dependent variable R, the conditional logit is defined as the logarithm of the ratio of the expected number of responders (i.e. $k = 1$) to the expected number of nonresponders (i.e. $k = 2$), given categories of C and M. As we will show, model (3.10) can be re-expressed in the equivalent form of the main-effects-only logit model.

Form equations (3.10)–(3.14) it follows that the conditional logit is:

$$\log_e(F_{ij1}/F_{ij2}) = \log_e(F_{ij1}) - \log_e(F_{ij2})$$

$$= (\lambda_1^R - \lambda_2^R) + (\lambda_{i\,1}^{CR} - \lambda_{i\,2}^{CR}) + (\lambda_{i\,1}^{MR} - \lambda_{i\,2}^{MR}) \tag{3.17}$$

$$= 2\lambda_1^R + 2\lambda_{i\,1}^{CR} + 2\lambda_{i\,1}^{MR}$$

$$\alpha + \beta_i^C + \beta_j^M$$

where $\alpha \equiv 2\lambda_1^R$; $\beta_i^C \equiv 2\lambda_{i\,1}^{CR}$; and $\beta_j^M \equiv 2\lambda_{i\,1}^{MR}$

The third equality in (3.17) follows from equations (3.11), (3.13), and (3.14). Hence, it is seen that the effect of the reminder call (C) is assessed by the *main* effect $\beta^C \equiv \beta_1^C = -\beta_2^C$ in logit model (3.17) or equivalently by the *interaction* effect $\lambda^{CR} \equiv \lambda_{11}^{CR} = -\lambda_{21}^{CR}$ in log-linear model (3.10). The assessment of whether β^C is significantly different from zero is equivalent to the assessment of whether λ^{CR} is significantly different from zero. The β^C and λ^{CR} parameters differ only by a factor of 2.

Similarly, the effect of the monetary payment (M) is assessed by the four-component parameter $\beta^M = (\beta_1^M, \beta_2^M, \beta_3^M, \beta_4^M)$, (read "beta"). Since these four components sum to zero (recall eq. (3.14)), only three of these components are needed to describe the effect of M.

As we did with eq. (3.1), we may re-express eq. (3.17) in the equivalent multiplicative form in terms of γ-parameters (read, "gamma"), which yields the following multiplicative form of the logit model, more simply known as the *odds* model:

$$\Omega_{ij} \equiv F_{ij1}/F_{ij2} = \gamma(\gamma_i^C)(\gamma_j^M) \tag{3.18}$$

where $\gamma = \exp(\alpha)$, $\gamma_i^C = \exp(\beta_i^C)$, $\gamma_j^M = \exp(\beta_j^M)$ and

$$\Omega_{ij} = \text{Conditional odds of a response given } C = i \text{ and } M = j \tag{3.19}$$

Notice that equations (3.11)–(3.14) imply the following equalities among the γ-parameters:

$$\gamma_2^C = 1/\gamma_1^C \text{ and } \prod_{j=1}^{J}(\gamma_j^M) = 1 \tag{3.20}$$

Note that F_{ij1}/F_{ij2} expresses the conditional odds of responding as a function of the explanatory factors C and M. Since there is a 1:1 monotonic relationship between odds and probabilities, the conditional odds model (3.18) is equivalent to a conditional probability model. The equations relating probabilities to odds and vice versa are:

$$P_{ij} = \Omega_{ij}/(1 + \Omega_{ij}) \tag{3.21}$$

and

$$\Omega_{ij} = P_{ij}/(1 - P_{ij})$$

$$= F_{ij1}/F_{ij2} \tag{3.22}$$

where $P_{ij} = $ Conditional probability of a response given $C = i$ and $M = j$
The rightmost columns in Table 3.7a contain the observed proportions, odds, and logits for these data, respectively.

Before presenting the results of fitting this model, we will further pursue the analog between the logit model and the regression model by using indicator variables for the predictors to re-express the main-effects-only logit model described in eq. (3.17) from the ANOVA formulation to the following equivalent regression formulation:

$$Log_e(\Omega) = \alpha + \beta^C * X_C + \beta_1^M * X_1 + \beta_2^M * X_2 + \beta_3^M * X_3 \qquad (3.23)$$

where Ω denotes the 8×1 vector of expected odds, β_j^M denotes the jth component of the β^M parameter vector, and the Xs are indicator variables that are "effects coded" (as in the traditional regression formulation of the ANOVA model):

$$X_C = 1 \text{ if reminder call is made,}$$
$$-1 \text{ otherwise;}$$
$$\text{and for } j = 1, 2, 3:$$
$$X_j = 1 \text{ if monetary payment} = j \text{ dollars,}$$
$$-1 \text{ if monetary payment} = \$4,$$
$$0, \text{ otherwise.}$$

The estimated expected counts are provided in Table 3.7b and the parameter estimates and goodness of fit are summarized in Table 3.8.

Table 3.8 Results from estimation of Model (3.23) Model fit: $L^2 = 2.37$, degrees of freedom $= 3$ ($p = 0.50$)

Parameter	α	β^C	β_1^M	β_2^M	β_3^M	β_4^M
Estimate	0.31^a	0.09^a	-0.22^a	-0.03	0.11^a	0.14^a
Standard error	0.01	0.01	0.02	0.03	0.03	0.03

[a] indicates statistically significant at 0.05 level

Note first that the model fit statistic indicates an acceptable fit to these data (i.e. $p > 0.05$). That is, the observed counts (Table 3.7a) are sufficiently close to those counts expected (Table 3.7b) under the main-effects-only logit model, as assessed by the usual 0.05 significance level. Thus, we accept the non-existence of any interactions, and may conclude that the (main) effect of the reminder call is the same regardless of the amount of monetary payment.

Next, notice that the effect of the reminder call is statistically significant. Dividing the estimate for β^C by its estimated standard error yields 6.2, a highly significant result. Under the assumption that the model is correct, the additive parameter estimate divided by its standard deviation can be used to test whether the parameter equals 0. Under the null hypothesis of zero effect, this ratio has a standard normal distribution. (Note that the ratio has been calculated to more decimal places than given in Table 3.8.)

Using eq. (3.18) to transform the parameter estimate to the multiplicative form and squaring the result, we can interpret the estimate directly:

$$(\hat{\gamma}^C)^2 = [\text{Exp}(0.09)]^2 = 1.20$$

As we did in equations (3.6)–(3.8) we may interpret the multiplicative parameter estimate in terms of percentage increase. Specifically, we may say that the effect of the reminder call is to increase the odds of response by 20 percent. (See discussion question 2.)

The effect of monetary payment is somewhat more difficult to assess because the parameters are defined as in the ANOVA model (i.e. by effects coding), and hence they are interpretable as the difference between the current monetary payment and the *average* payment. For example, we note that estimate for β_2 is not significant because it reflects an assessment of the effect of a $2 payment vs the average payment (where the average payment is approximately $2).

A more meaningful parameterization would assess the incremental effect of an additional dollar. Such an assessment can be performed by examining $\beta_j^{M'} = \beta_j^M - \beta_{j-1}^M$, or equivalently by examining $\gamma_j^{M'} = \gamma_j^M / \gamma_{j-1}^M$. (The assessment of whether $\beta_j^{M'}$ is significantly different from zero is equivalent to the assessment of whether $\gamma_j^{M'}$ is significantly different from one.)

Similar to eq. (3.6), the interpretation of $\gamma_j^{M'}$ can be found from model (3.18) to be as follows:

$$\gamma_j^{M'} \equiv \gamma_j^M / \gamma_{(j-1)}^M = (F_{ij1}/F_{ij2})/(F_{i(j-1)1}/F_{i(j-1)2}) \tag{3.24}$$

While estimates for the ratio of the gamma parameters in eq. (3.24) can be obtained by substituting the corresponding estimates for the gamma parameters in eq. (3.24), this approach would not yield an estimate for the standard error. An alternative approach, is to estimate model (3.25) instead of (3.23), using the $\beta^{M'}$ parameterization in place of β^M.

$$\text{Log}_e(\Omega) = \alpha + \beta^C * X_C + \beta_1^{M'} * X_1' + \beta_2^{M'} * X_2' + \beta_3^{M'} * X_3' \tag{3.25}$$

In order to accomplish this reparameterization, we use the following coding for the x-variables in place of effects coding:[4]

M	X_1'	X_2'	X_3'
$1	− 0.75	− 0.5	− 0.25
$2	0.25	− 0.5	− 0.25
$3	0.25	0.5	− 0.25
$4	0.25	0.5	0.75

Model (3.23) or (3.25) can be estimated using a general log-linear modeling program such as SAS CATMOD or SPSS LOGLINEAR which allows the model to be specified by a design matrix or by using a "contrast" statement. Use of model (3.25) instead of (3.23) does not alter the

estimated expected counts or the associated fit statistic; only the parameter estimates. The resulting multiplicative and additive effect estimates for
the M-parameters and the associated standard errors are given in Table 3.9.

Dividing the additive effect estimate by its standard error, we can see
that the $2 monetary payment results in a significantly higher response rate
than a $1 payment (i.e. $0.19/0.04 > 1.96$), and a $3 payment results in a
significantly higher response rate still (i.e. $0.14/0.04 > 1.96$), but a further
increase to $4 results in a nonsignificant increase in response (i.e.
$0.03/0.04 < 1.96$).

Table 3.9 Multiplicative and additive effect estimates and
associated standard errors for the M-parameters in Model (3.25)

	$(J=1)$ $2 vs. $1	$(J=2)$ $3 vs. $2	$(J=3)$ $4 vs. $3
$\gamma_j^{M'}$	1.20^a	1.15^a	1.03
$\beta_j^{M'}$	0.19^a	0.14^a	0.03
standard error of $\beta^{M'}{}_j$	0.04	0.04	0.04

[a] indicates statistically significant at 0.05 level

Since we are no longer using effects coding we can interpret the
multiplicative parameters directly. From eq. (3.24) it follows that the effect
of increasing the monetary payment from $1 to $2 is to increase the odds
of response by 20 percent ($1.20 - 1 = 20\%$); a further $1 increment in-
creases response by an additional 15 percent ($1.15 - 1 = 15\%$) and an
additional $1 increment possibly increases response by an additional 3
percent ($1.03 - 1 = 3\%$), the latter estimated increase not being significantly
different from 0.

Next, we will formulate and estimate the linear logit model (3.26), which
hypothesizes that an additional $1 payment would be expected to increase
the odds of response by the same amount regardless of whether it is used
to increase the payment from a base of $1, $2 or $3. We will see that this
model will be rejected because it is not consistent with the data.

The linear logit model is directly analogous to the linear regression
model. It may be specified as follows:

$$\text{Log}_e(\Omega) = \alpha + \beta^C * X_C + \beta^{M'} * j \tag{3.26}$$

Note that model (3.26) is a distinctly different model than (3.23) or
(3.25). While the latter models only hypothesize that the 3-degree-of-
freedom interaction terms are nil, model (3.26) also hypotheses the additional 2-degree-of-freedom restriction that the monetary effect is linear.
Model (3.26) is equivalent to model (3.25) with the following restrictions:

$$\beta_1^{M'} = \beta_2^{M'} = \beta_3^{M'} \tag{3.27}$$

The results from estimation of model (3.26) are given in Table 3.10.

Since model (3.26) is equivalent to model (3.25) plus the linearity restriction (3.27), the restrictions in eq. (3.27) may be tested separately by subtracting the likelihood chi-square measure of fit for both models, and assessing this difference with $5 - 3 = 2$ degrees of freedom. We have $9.45 - 2.37 = 7.08$ with 2 degrees of freedom ($p < 0.05$). Hence, the linearity restriction is rejected, and we accept model (3.25) over model (3.26). In traditional regression analysis, the linearity assumption is rarely put to a test; it is usually accepted without question.

Table 3.10 Results from estimation of Model (3.26)
Model fit: $L^2 = 9.45$ with 5 degrees of freedom

Parameter	α	β^C	$\beta^{M'}$
Estimate	0.016	0.090[a]	0.130[a]
Standard error	0.029	0.014	0.012

[a] indicates statistically significant at 0.05 level.

Unlike models (3.23) and (3.25), model (3.26) requires a non-standard log-linear modeling program such as SPSS LOGLINEAR or SAS PROC CATMOD that allows the use of a design matrix for model specification (or a logistic regression program like SPSS Logistic Regression or SAS PROC LOGISTIC).

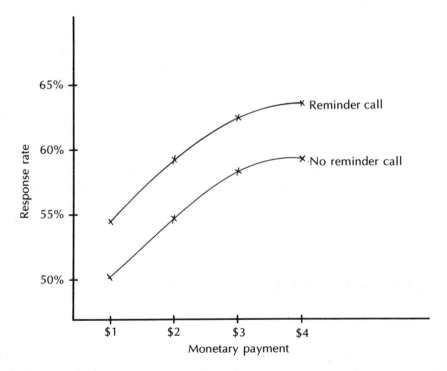

Figure 3.2 Plot of expected response rates under the main-effects only logit model

Such programs are similar to regression in that the variable M takes on the quantitative values $j = 1, 2, 3, 4$ as specified by eq. (3.26). One interpretation for the lack of fit for this model is that the integer scores given by j are incorrect to assign to the variable M with model (3.26).

We will leave it as an exercise to show that if the β_j^M were used as values instead of j in eq. (3.26), the new model would fit the data. In general, the use of incorrect scores can provide extremely misleading results and can alter drastically the effects of other variables, changing a positive effect to negative and vice versa (see discussion question 2).

The estimated percentage response expected under model (3.25) is plotted in Figure 3.2. In this diagram, the effect of the reminder call shows up as the constant difference between the two curves, and the effect of the monetary payment shows up as the increase in the curve as the payment level increases in $1 increments from $1 to $4. As was noted earlier, the final $1 increment is not statistically significant. (The difference between the two curves in Figure 3.2 is constant when the vertical scale is measured in logits. When measured in percentages, it is approximately constant.)

In our first two examples, we focused primarily on the main-effects in the model. We saw that the main-effects-only log-linear model did not fit the data because of certain significant MONTH × YEAR interactions that were not included in the model. We hypothesized that these interactions may have been due to some unusual weather conditions.

In model 3.10 and its derivatives and extensions (models 3.17, 3.18, 3.23, 3.25, and 3.26), we again focused on the main effects and a main-effects-only logit model was found to fit the data. In each of these examples, we focused on the interpretation of the main effects. For example, we concluded that the main effect of the reminder call was to increase the expected odds of returning the survey by 20 percent regardless of the amount of the monetary payment. We also estimated the main effect of an additional dollar payment at different payment levels (and concluded that the effect of an additional dollar is to increase the likelihood of response by the same amount regardless of whether a reminder call was made).

For our next example, our focus will be on the interpretation, measurement and assessment of the interaction parameter. Again, we will see that the parameter in the multiplicative model has a straightforward interpretation.

A Logit Model for Adjusting TV Diary Ratings

Prior to the "People-Meter", the A.C. Nielsen Co. selected approximately 400 households in a given market who agreed to have their television hooked up to a passive meter to record all of their television viewing. The resulting viewing counts were used to estimate household-level program ratings within the market. In order to determine *who* was viewing within the household, Nielsen also selected a similar number of additional households to keep a diary of their viewing, identifying the particular household member(s) who were viewing in addition to the station and time viewed.

The data obtained from the meter sample accurately reported household-level viewing but did not identify the viewer. On the other hand, the diary data *did* identify the viewer but was not always complete, and in some cases contained inaccurate information. Nielson used the diary data to estimate disaggregated ratings by demographic categories, but adjusted the overall viewing rate to agree with the meter sample.

Table 3.11 compares counts of New York meter and diary sample households according to recorded viewing of WPIX during the 4:00–4:15 p.m. time slot on Thursday, February 3, 1983. These counts are provided separately for households with and without children (i.e. household members under 18 years of age).

Table 3.11 Observed counts of meter and diary sample viewing and non-viewing households by presence of children

	Households with children				Households without children		
	Viewers	Non viewers	% Viewers		Viewers	Non viewers	% Viewers
Diary	9	161	5.3%	Diary	13	239	5.2%
Meter	16	128	11.1%	Meter	38	269	12.4%

A comparison of the overall viewing suggests a substantial amount of under-reporting by the diary sample – while 12.0 percent of all meter households were tuned to WPIX at this time, only 5.2 percent of the diary households reported such viewing. In terms of odds, the likelihood of viewing this particular station quarter-hour is .11 according to the household meter and 0.05 according to the diary. Table 3.11 shows that the apparent under-reporting occurs in households with children as well as in those without children.

Our analysis will address the following questions:

1 Is the observed amount of diary under-reporting statistically significant? and
2 Are diary households in which nonadults are present more likely to under-report viewing?

In terms of odds, the amount of under-reporting can be assessed by the following odds-ratio:

$$\theta = \frac{\text{Odds of viewing according to the diary}}{\text{Odds of viewing according to the meter}} \tag{3.28}$$

To the extent to which $\theta < 1$, the diary *under*-reports viewing. To the extent to which $\theta > 1$, the diary *over*-reports viewing.

We will first address question 2.

The conditional odds of viewing, by sample (S) and presence of non-adults (K), may be expressed by the following saturated model:

$$\Omega_{ij} \equiv F_{ij1}/F_{ij2} = \gamma(\gamma_i^S)\,(\gamma_j^K)\,(\gamma_{ij}^{SK}) \tag{3.29}$$

where the γ-parameters are subject to the usual identification restrictions (e.g. recall eq. (3.20)).

Translation of the odds model (3.29) to an odds ratio model, is similar to the translation from a log-linear model to a logit model. From eq. (3.29) we have:

$$\theta_j \equiv \frac{F_{1j1}/F_{1j2}}{F_{2j1}/F_{2j2}} = \frac{\gamma(\gamma_1^S)\,(\gamma_j^K)\,(\gamma_{1j}^{SK})}{\gamma(\gamma_2^S)\,(\gamma_j^K)\,(\gamma_{2j}^{SK})} = (\gamma_1^S)^2(\gamma_{1j}^{SK})^2 \tag{3.30}$$

where the second equality follows from the identification restrictions.

If the amount of diary mis-reporting does not depend upon the presence of nonadults, $\theta_1 = \theta_2$, in which case $\gamma_{1j}^{SK} = 1$ in eq. (3.30). This hypothesis can be expressed by the following 1 degree of freedom unsaturated model:

$$\theta_j \equiv \frac{F_{1j1}/F_{1j2}}{F_{2j1}/F_{2j2}} = (\gamma_1^S)^2 \tag{3.31}$$

By applying the restriction $\gamma_{1j}^{SK} = 1$ to the saturated logit model (3.29), model (3.31) can be re-expressed in the form of the following 1 degree of freedom logit model:

$$\Omega_{ij} \equiv F_{ij1}/F_{ij2} = \gamma(\gamma_i^S)(\gamma_j^K) \tag{3.32}$$

Or, by applying the equivalent restriction $\tau_{ijk}^{SKV} = 1$ to the saturated log-linear model, it can be alternatively be re-expressed in the form of the following 1 degree of freedom log-linear model:

$$F_{ij} = (\tau)\,(\tau_i^S)\,(\tau_j^K)\,(\tau_k^V)\,(\tau_{ij}^{SK})\,(\tau_{ik}^{SV})\,(\tau_{jk}^{KV}) \tag{3.33}$$

The chi-square test of fit for model (3.31), which is equivalent the test of fit for model (3.32) or model (3.33), yields $L^2 = 0.07$ with 1 degree of freedom, an excellent fit. Thus, we accept the hypothesis that $\theta_1 = \theta_2$, (which is equivalent to the hypothesis that $\gamma_{1j}^{SK} = 1$ in model (3.32), and is also equivalent to the hypothesis that $\tau_{ijk}^{SKV} = 1$ in model (3.33). The answer to question 2 is no. The expected rate of diary misreporting is identical for households where non-adults are present or not present.

Note that model (3.31) is expressed in terms of *odds ratios*, model (3.32) is expressed in terms of *odds*, and model (3.33) is expressed in terms of *expected frequencies*. While these models are equivalent, model (3.33) contains some parameters that do not appear in model (3.32) or model (3.31) and model (3.32) contains some parameters that do not appear in model (3.31). The parameters that appear in model (3.33) but not model (3.32) (or model (3.31)) are required to estimate the expected frequencies but are not needed to estimate the odds (or odds ratios). Similarly, the parameters that are included in model (3.32) but not (3.31) are required to estimate the odds but are not needed to estimate the odds ratios.

Next, we focus on question 1. There is no mis-reporting if $\theta_j = 1$. That is, if $\theta_1 = \theta_2 = 1$.

Table 3.12 provides the estimated expected counts under model (3.33). The common odds ratio, θ, as estimated from these counts (from either the diary sample or from the meter sample), is 0.407. This estimate could have alternatively been obtained as the square of the estimate of the γ_i^S-parameter in the unsaturated logit model (3.32). Or, it could be calculated by raising to the fourth power the estimate for the τ_{11}^{SV}-parameter in the unsaturated log-linear model (3.33).

In order to assess the significance of this estimate, we formulate an unsaturated model with 2 degrees of freedom. One way to obtain such a model, is by imposing the additional 1 degree of freedom restriction on model (3.32) that the parameters $\gamma_i^S = 1$, which yields the following 2 degree of freedom unsaturated odds model:

$$\Omega_{ij} \equiv F_{ij1}/F_{ij2} = \gamma(\gamma_j^K) \tag{3.34}$$

Alternatively, we could obtain the desired model by imposing the restriction that the parameters $\tau_{ik}^{SV} = 1$ in model (3.33), which yields the equivalent to model (3.34) expressed in the form of the following unsaturated log-linear model:

Table 3.12 Estimated expected counts of meter and diary sample viewing and non-viewing households by presence of children

	Households with children				Households without children		
	Viewers	Non viewers	% Viewers		Viewers	Non viewers	% Viewers
Diary	8.5	161.5	5.0%	Diary	13.5	238.5	5.4%
Meter	16.5	127.5	11.5%	Meter	37.5	269.5	12.2%

$$F_{ijk} = (\tau)\,(\tau_i^S)\,(\tau_j^K)\,(\tau_k^V)(\tau_{ij}^{SK})\,(\tau_{jk}^{KV}) \tag{3.35}$$

The chi-squared test of fit for model (3.34) (or model (3.35)) is $L^2 = 12.76$ with 2 degrees of freedom, a highly significant result ($p = 0.002$). Assuming that the answer to question 2 is no, the answer to question 1 can be addressed by subtracting the above chi-square fit statistic from that obtained from model (3.33), and testing the result with only 1 degree of freedom. We have $12.76 - 0.07 = 12.69$ with 1 degree of freedom, which is an extremely significant result. Thus, we conclude that the estimated common odds ratio is significantly different from 1, and the amount of under-reporting implied by the data in Table 3.11 is statistically significant.

Models for Polytomous Variables

Each of the four examples considered thus far featured either a dichotomous dependent variable or a degenerate dependent variable containing only a single category. For these examples, the general log-linear models were shown to be unidimensional. That is, the relationships between the dependent variable and the predictors were expressed by a single equation (recall equations (3.5), (3.9), (3.18) and (3.29).

In this section, we will consider the analysis of a polytomous dependent variable having $k > 2$ categories. Unlike the case of a dichotomous dependent variable where the conditional distribution is described by a single quantity (i.e. the conditional odds F_1/F_2 or conditional probability P_1), there are $K - 1$ distinct conditional odds (and $K - 1$ conditional probabilities) that must be estimated. Thus, the log-linear model induces $K - 1$ equations that describe the associated $K - 1$ dimensional multinomial logit model.

In this section, we will use the trichotomous dependent variable RESP3 to introduce the two-dimensional multinomial logit model and the associated analyses. As we will see, the model for the expected cell counts (with subscript notation) is identical to the earlier one-dimensional log-linear models. We will then re-express the log-linear model in the form of a logit model and show that we now obtain two logit equations. Finally, we will show that these two logit equations are not unique and introduce the general multinomial logit scaling model which can generate various other "logit-type" equations.

In general, when the dependent variable has K categories, the general multinomial logit scaling model allows a researcher to specify up to $K - 1$ contrasts that define the $K - 1$ logit-type equations. When all $K - 1$ equations are allowed, the dependent variable is treated as being measured on a nominal scale.

Next, we introduce the Y-Association model. This model is used to analyze a polytomous dependent variable for which only a single set of category scores are used. These scores define an interval scale for the dependent variable. Analogous to the usual regression model, we show how the Y-Association model may be used to perform an ordinal regression analysis of RESP3 as a function of two predictor variables.

Analysis of a Trichotomous Dependent Variable

To illustrate the multidimensional nature of the analysis of a polytomous variable, in this section we analyze the response to a promotional mailing for a magazine subscription (RESP3) as a function of known presence of children (KIDS) and known presence of a bank card (BANKCARD).

There are three categories for the dependent variable RESP3: paid responders, unpaid responders and non-responders. Paid responders are those who returned the order form, checked off that they would like to subscribe to the magazine and after receiving a free issue, became paid subscribers to the magazine. Unpaid responders are those who returned the order form, checked off that they would like to subscribe to the magazine and receive a free issue, but canceled their subscription order prior to paying. Non-responders are all others (i.e. those households who never requested a subscription).

The multiplicative form of the saturated log-linear model for this example can be expressed as:

$$F_{ijk}^{KCR} = (\tau)\,(\tau_i^K)\,(\tau_j^C)\,(\tau_k^R)\,(\tau_{ij}^{KC})\,(\tau_{ik}^{KR})\,(\tau_{jk}^{CR})\,(\tau_{ijk}^{KCR}) \qquad (3.36)$$

where the superscripts K, C, and R refer to the variables KIDS, BANKCARD and RESP3 respectively. The 3-way table of observed counts is provided in Table 3.13.

The Multinomial Logit Model

Table 3.13 Observed counts for the 2 × 2 × 3 table of KIDS by BANKCARD by RESP3

Known presence of KIDS	Presence of BANKCARD	Response		
		Paid	Unpaid	Non-response
Yes	Yes	10	11	917
Yes	No	31	64	5,278
No	Yes	56	22	5,067
No	No	381	356	68,847

Earlier, for a dichotomous dependent variable, we showed how the log-linear model could be re-expressed in the form of a single equation odds model which contrasts category 1 with category 2. For example, eq. (3.34) is an expression of that contrast which is equivalent to log-linear model (3.35). In the case of a polytomous dependent variable, $K - 1$ distinct contrasts are required, each being expressed as an equation.

For example, with regard to the dependent variable RESP3, the first such equation might contrast paid responders with non-responders (the category 1: category 3 odds), and the second might contrast unpaid responders with non responders (the category 2: category 3 odds):

$$\Omega_{ij}(1) \equiv F_{ij1}/F_{ij3} = \gamma(1) \, (\gamma_i^K(1)) \, (\gamma_j^C(1)) \, (\gamma_{ij}^{KC}(1)) \tag{3.37}$$

$$\Omega_{ij}(2) \equiv F_{ij2}/F_{ij3} = \gamma(2) \, (\gamma_i^K(2)) \, (\gamma_j^C(2)) \, (\gamma_{ij}^{KC}(2)) \tag{3.38}$$

Equation (3.37)–(3.38) are the equivalent to eq. (3.36), expressed in the form of the multinomial logit model.

Equations (3.37)–(3.38) are not the only way that the multinomial logit model may be expressed. In fact, we may use *any* two distinct score vectors $Y(1)$ and $Y(2)$ to designate the contrasts. Without loss of generality, the following substitutions can be made in model (3.36):

$$\tau_{ik}^{KR} = \gamma_i^K(1)^{Y_k(1)} \gamma_i^K(2)^{Y_k(2)} \tag{3.39}$$

$$\tau_{ik}^{CR} = \gamma_i^C(1)^{Y_k(1)} \gamma_i^C(2)^{Y_k(2)} \tag{3.40}$$

and

$$\tau_{iik}^{KCR} = \gamma_i^K(1)_i^C(1)^{Y_k(1)} \, \gamma_{ii}^{KC}(2)^{Y_k(2)} \tag{3.41}$$

where $Y_k(s)$ denotes the kth component of score vector s.

For example, model (3.37)–(3.38) implicitly assumes the score vectors $Y(1) = (1, 0, 0)$ and $Y(2) = (0, 1, 0)$. (This is left to the reader to verify as question 4.) Generally, $K - 1$ linearly independent score vectors are required, where K = the number of categories in the dependent variable. The model given by eq. (3.36) together with equations (3.39)–(3.41) may be referred to as the multinomial logit scaling model for a trichotomous dependent variable. (The generalization to a K-category dependent variable is direct.) When $M = K - 1$ distinct score vectors are used, the model will always be saturated.[5]

While the estimated expected counts F_{ijk}^{KCR} equal the *observed* counts under any saturated model regardless which score vectors are used, different sets of score vectors will yield different estimates for the τ-parameters (and γ-parameters). In general, one should use those score vectors that specify the two most meaningful contrasts for the dependent variable categories.

For the purpose of illustration, we will select as our first score vector, the profitability contrast $Y'(1) = (35, -7, -0.15)$, which corresponds to the fact that a paid responder is valued at \$35, an unpaid responder, $-\$7$, (the cost associated with several mailings including the free issue), and a non-responder, $-\$0.15$ (the cost of mailing). This selection will allow us to assess the effect of each of the predictor variables K and C (and their interaction) on the profitability of the promotion.

The effects associated with the profitability contrast $Y'(1)$, will be denoted by the $\gamma'(1)$-parameter vector, consisting of $\gamma_i'^K(1)$, $\gamma_j'^C(1)$ and

$\gamma_j'^K(1)_f^C(1)$, respectively. Since both the K and C variables are dichotomous, we will provide only the estimate associated with the first category ($i = 1$ or $j = 1$), and simplify the notation by dropping the subscript altogether. (The estimates associated with the second category, as determined by the identifying restrictions, can be obtained by inverting the corresponding estimate for the first category.)

While we can select any other distinct score vector (i.e. one that is not an exact linear function of the above profitability score vector) to complete the specification of the multinomial logit scaling model, for purposes of illustration, we will select the second score vector $Y'(2) = (0, 1, 0)$, which would generally be used to model the probability of an unpaid response. (Some additional interpretational benefits would be obtained if the score vectors were selected to be orthogonal to each other, but we will not pursue those benefits here.)

The $\gamma'(1)$ and $\gamma'(2)$ (multiplicative) effect estimates are given under the column designated "gamma" in Table 3.15. These estimates are converted to the additive form (by taking the natural logarithm of the gamma-parameter) in the column marked "beta". The rightmost columns in Table 3.14 contain the standard error for beta and the standardized value (beta divided by its standard error). Standardized values having a magnitude larger than 1.96 indicate that the beta is significantly different from 0 (a null effect) at the 0.05 level.

Note first that the KIDS × BANKCARD interaction effects are not statistically significant for either the first or second score vector. Thus, we will eliminate these effects from the model, and consider the main-effects-only model, which still fits the data well ($L^2 = 0.206$ with 2 degrees of freedom; $p = 0.9$). Tables 3.14 and 3.15 present the results from estimating the main-effects-only model.

Table 3.14 Expected counts for the 2 × 2 × 3 table of KIDS by BANKCARD by RESP 3

Known presence of KIDS	Presence of BANKCARD	Response		
		Paid	Unpaid	Non response
Yes	Yes	8.6	4.8	924.6
Yes	No	24.8	31.4	5,316.8
No	Yes	56.8	25.2	5,063.0
No	No	387.8	391.6	68,804.6

The effect estimates in Table 3.15 show that the KIDS-effect is significant for component 2 but not component 1; and the BANKCARD-effect is significant for component 1 but not 2. Hence equations (3.39)–(3.41) simplify to $\tau^{KR} = \gamma^K(2)^{Y_k(2)}$ and $\tau^{CR} = \gamma^C(1)^{Y_k(1)}$. Since our primary focus is the profitability contrast (i.e. component 1), we conclude that households who are known to own a bankcard are more profitable to mail, regardless of whether children are known to be present. However, the KIDS effect for contrast 2 must also be taken into account if one's goal is to predict more than the profitability.

Table 3.15 Parameter estimates and standard errors for the saturated and main-effects-only multinomial logit model

(a) Component-1 effects ("profitability" contrast)

	Gamma	Beta	Standard error	Standardized value
KIDS: $\gamma'^K(1)$				
Saturated model	1.0007	0.00071	0.00274	0.26
Main-effects-model	1.0006	0.00060	0.00234	0.26
BANKCARD: $\gamma'^C(1)$				
Saturated model	1.0096	0.00960	0.00274	3.50
Main-effects-model	1.0097	0.00970	0.00191	5.09
KIDS × BANKCARD: $\gamma'^{KC}(1)$				
Saturated model	0.9997	− 0.00034	0.00274	− 0.12

(b) Component-2 effects ("probability of unpaid response" contrast)

	Gamma	Beta	Standard error	Standardized value
KIDS: $\gamma'^K(2)$				
Saturated model	1.6144	0.47897	0.09919	4.83
Main-effects-model	1.55237	0.43978	0.06600	6.66
BANKCARD: $\gamma'^C(2)$				
Saturated model	1.0343	0.03370	0.09919	0.34
Main-effects-model	1.0035	0.00347	0.09219	0.04
KIDS × BANKCARD: $\gamma'^{KC}(2)$				
Saturated model	1.0434	0.04246	0.09919	0.43

The Concept of Y-Association

The multinomial logit model is used to investigate all of the associations between the predictor variables and a dependent variable with $K > 2$ categories. The usual measure of goodness of model fit is used to determine the extent to which the model can explain all of these associations.

Often, however, the goal may be to analyze and explain only a single contrast of the dependent variable. In this "regression" context, only a single set of dependent variable scores – such as the profitability scores – is considered to be relevant. In the regression context, we focus our analysis on "Y-Association", where Y, as in regression analysis, denotes the relevant scores for the dependent variable.

As in regression, it is the conditional expectation rather than the entire conditional distribution of the dependent variable that is explained as a function of the predictors. Because of this similarity to regression, the Y-Association model (which can be expressed as a log-linear model) may be referred to as an "ordinal regression" model.

The Y-Association model may be used when the dependent variable scores are all known and it can also be employed when one or more scores are unknown. When some of the scores are not known, they are estimated simultaneously with the other model parameters by maximum likelihood methods, using a log-bilinear model referred to as the Y^*-Association model (Magidson, 1992). In the remainder of this chapter, we will only deal with the case where all scores are known.

Prior to presenting the results of the Y-Association model for the three-way table, we will first introduce the simpler Y-Association model for the 2×3 table of KIDS by RESP3. The simpler model with help to shed light on the results of analysis for the three-way table.

Table 3.16 Analysis of the 2×3 table KIDS by RESP3

Known presence of KIDS	Model	RESP3			Average score
		Paid	Unpaid	Non-response	
Yes	Saturated	41	75	6,195	– 0.003
	Y-Association	33.4	36.0	6,241.5	– 0.003
	Independence	37.2	35.3	6,238.5	0.019
No	Saturated	437	378	73,914	0.021
	Y-Association	444.6	417.0	73,867.4	0.021
	Independence	440.7	417.7	73,870.5	0.019

Analysis of association for table of KIDS by RESP3

Model	Chi – square L^2	d. f.	p - value
Independence	38.3	2	< 0.001
Due to			
Y-Association	0.4	1	> 0.05
Residual	37.9	1	< 0.0001

Table 3.16 summarizes the results of the analysis of the KIDS by RESP3 table. Notice that the conditional expectation obtained for each household in which children under 18 are present is – \$0.003 compared to \$0.021 for those households in which children are not known to be present, a small

difference. Nevertheless, note that the test for independence is strongly rejected ($L^2(0) = 38.3$ with 2 d.f.; $p < 0.0001$).

In order to better understand this result, let P_{11} and P_{21} denote the conditional probability of a paid subscription among households with children and other households respectively. Similarly, let P_{12} and P_{22} denote the corresponding probabilities of an unpaid subscription.

The test for independence may be expressed by the following two 1-degree-of-freedom restrictions:

$$H_0: P_{11} = P_{21} \text{ and } P_{12} = P_{22} \tag{3.42}$$

Independence is equivalent to the occurrence of both of these restrictions.

If we examine the sample proportions we find that the proportion within each household group who obtain a *paid* subscription is approximately the same ($P_{11} = P_{21} = 0.6\%$, but households with children are substantially more likely to result in an *unpaid* subscription ($P_{21} = 1.2\%$ while $P_{22} = 0.5\%$). Although the first difference in proportions is negligible, the latter difference is large enough to reject independence based on the usual test with 2 degrees of freedom.

Next, we shall focus only on that part of the non-independence which is due to Y-Association, where Y is taken as the profitability scores $(35, -7, -0.15)$. The null hypothesis now becomes:

$$H_Y: \mu_1 = \mu_2 \tag{3.43}$$

where μ_i denotes the conditional expectation of Y:

$$\mu_i = P_{i1} * (\$35) + P_{i2} * (-\$7) + P_{i3} * (-\$0.15)$$

and P_{ij} = the conditional probability of observing the score Y_j given that children are known to be present ($i = 1$) in the household or not ($i = 2$).

The test of eq. (3.43), summarized in Table 3.16, yields $L^2(0|Y) = 0.4$ with 1-degree-of-freedom, an extremely *non*-significant result. Thus, the degree of Y-Association in the KIDS × RESP3 table is weak as suggested by the small difference between the means which we observed earlier.

Table 3.16 also presents the maximum likelihood estimates for the expected counts under independence and under Y-Association. Note that the estimates under the Y-Association model preserve the observed mean scores while those estimated under the independence model do not. The maximum likelihood estimates under the Y-Association model (or under the Y^*-Association model) will always preserve the observed mean scores for Y (see questions 4c and 4d).

We conclude that known presence of children (i.e. the variable KIDS) is *not* important for predicting the expected Y-value of a response (i.e. the difference between the observed mean values between the two groups is found *not* to be significant). The test for independence however, suggests that there are some strong differences between households with and without children regarding their likelihood to result in an *unpaid* response, but these differences are largely judged to be irrelevant since these groups do not differ with respect to their mean value for Y.[6]

Since some of the associations are considered to be irrelevant and thus are not addressed by the Y-Association model, the model fit chi-square for a Y-Association model must be interpreted differently than the fit of the multinomial logit model. As shown in the analysis of association table of Table 3.16, only about 1 percent of the non-independence (as measured by the independence chi-square) is due to Y-Association (i.e. $0.4/38.3 = 1\%$); 99 percent of the non-independence remains unexplained.

An Ordinal Regression Model

Ordinal regression may be used when the polytomous dependent variable is measured on an interval scale with known category scores. In this case, the conditional expectation of the dependent variable is analyzed as a function of the predictors, as it is in the usual regression model. However, unlike regression, there is no assumption of the normal distribution, an assumption which is violated for categorical dependent variables. (For further insights into this model see question 5c.)

For the trichotomous dependent variable R (RESP3) and predictors K and C, the main-effects-only ordinal regression model, expressed in the form of a log-linear model, is described as the main-effects-only multinomial logit model (3.44) subject to the structural restrictions (3.45)–(3.46):

$$F_{ijk}^{KCR} = (\tau)(\tau_i^K)(\tau_j^C)(\tau_k^R)(\tau_{ij}^{KC})(\tau_{ik}^{KR})(\tau_{jk}^{CR}) \tag{3.44}$$

$$\tau_{ik}^{KR} = (\gamma_i^K)_k^Y \tag{3.45}$$

$$\tau_{jk}^{CR} = (\gamma_j^C)_k^Y \tag{3.46}$$

for $i = 1, 2$ $j = 1, 2$ $k = 1, 2, 3$; where the Y_k represent the category scores $35, -7$ and -0.15. Note that equations (3.45)–(3.46) are structural restrictions while eqs. (3.39)–(3.41) simply re-parametrize the model without imposing any restrictions.

The results from an ordinal regression model are summarized in Table 3.17. Note that the effect of BANKCARD is statistically significant, while the effect of KIDS is not. These results are similar to the results associated with the profitability scores (contrast 1) presented in Table 3.15.

In conclusion, we note that the above model as expressed in eq. (3.44) in conjunction with restrictions (3.45)–(3.46) can also be used for other applications where some or all of the Y-scores are *not* known. In this case, the Y-scores are estimated simultaneously along with the τ and γ-parameters. A test of model fit is available to determine whether a single equation is sufficient to explain the observed data.

Table 3.17 Results from the ordinal regression model
Model fit[a]: $L^2 = 37.79$ with 4 d.f.

	Gamma	Beta	Standard error	Standardized value
KIDS: γ^K	0.9973	−0.00267	0.00252	−1.06
BANKCARD: γ^C	1.0098	0.00980	0.00189	5.18

[a] Model fit represents the goodness of fit of the model. Programs for Logistic Regression also contain an overall statistic which some programs label "Model Fit". This statistic is not a measure of goodness of model fit but rather represents the overall significance of the parameters (i.e. the test of $H_0: \gamma^K = \gamma^C = 1$), and is analogous to the overall F-test in regression.

This latter model of ordinal regression with unknown scores is especially important in marketing where so many dependent variables are rating scales of one type or another. Rather than assuming a Likert scale, or utilizing multiple rating indicators in conjunction with a structural equation model, it is now possible to obtain maximum likelihood scores for each of the rating categories and to use these scores in a regression type model without relying on the normal distribution. For further discussion of this type of application in marketing and an example with a single predictor variable, see Magidson (1994) and the references cited there.

Finally, we note that at the time of this writing, the mainstream statistical packages are (1) without a program to perform maximum likelihood ordinal regression with unknown scores, and (2) contain no examples in the manuals of how current programs (such as SPSS LOGLINEAR and SAS CATMOD) may be used to perform ordinal regression with known scores.[7] We expect considerable program development in these areas in the near future.

Summary and Conclusion

Least squares regression analysis, which has its origin with Galton in 1888, remains today the most widely used multivariate statistical technique. On the other hand, multivariate statistical techniques for categorical data have been developed more recently and tend not to be used as often as they should because they have not been well understood.

In this chapter we have introduced and illustrated the use of a variety of log-linear models for analyzing a categorical dependent variable as a function of categorical predictor variables. When present, we showed how quantitative scores for the predictor variable(s) and the dependent variable may be taken into account in the model.

When scores for the K categories of the dependent variable are not present, we showed that a dependent variable having more than two categories will generally require a $K-1$ dimensional multinomial logit model which might be expressed in the form of $K-1$ regression-like equations. When scores do exist or are estimated from the data, we showed how the single equation Y-Association can be formulated and estimated. In addition, there are many M-equation models ($1 < M < K-1$) that can be formulated, but these are beyond the scope of this chapter.

A significant limitation of traditional regression analysis is that it relies heavily on the normal distribution, an assumption that is typically violated with social science (especially survey) data. The methods described in this chapter make no assumptions about the existence of a normal distribution. They provide maximum likelihood estimates under the Poisson, multinomial and related sampling distributions, based on saturated and unsaturated parametric models which have been shown to fit real data extremely well (Goodman, 1991).

New developments in ordinal regression, such as the Y^*-Association model (Magidson, 1992, 1993) allow the ability to estimate unknown scores for one or more categories of the dependent variable simultaneously with the estimation of the regression coefficients, all by maximum likelihood. As these methods become part of the mainstream statistical packages, they are likely to significantly alter the way that categorical data is analyzed as well as the way that regression analysis of quantitative variables will be performed in the near future.[8]

Questions

1   Traffic fatality analyses

   (a)   Use the SPSS LOGLINEAR or similar program to fit model (3.1) to the complete table given by the first 5 columns of Table 3.1. Does the model fit the data? How do you interpret this result. How do the parameter estimates compare to those in Tables 3.3 and 3.4? What is the year effect parameter estimate for 1980? (Hint: The SPSS LOGLINEAR, SAS CATMOD and similar programs do not print out the parameter estimates that correspond to the last category of each variable. Use the fact that the λ^Y parameters are standardized so that they sum to zero.) The SPSS LOGLINEAR program does not print out the parameter estimate for λ. Can you determine this estimate from the remainder of the output? If so, how?

   (b)   Use the SPSS LOGLINEAR program to fit model (3.1) to the incomplete table given in Table 3.1. Compare the value for L^2, the degrees of freedom and the parameter estimates to the corresponding quantities given in this chapter to make sure that you have done this correctly. (Hint: You must use the CWEIGHT statement to specify that you wish to ignore the cells corresponding to June–December 1980.) Now, fit the model again without specifying that the table is incomplete (i.e. omit the CWEIGHT statement). Does the model now fit better or worse? Are the degrees of freedom the same as before? Why or why not? (Hint: examine the adjusted residuals to see which cells fit poorly.) Were there truly no traffic fatalities during the last 7 months of 1980? Explain. How does the year effect parameter estimate for 1980 differ from before? Why?

(c) Use the parameter estimates from model (3.1) (fit to the incomplete table) to obtain predicted monthly fatality counts for June–December 1980. Check to make sure that they agree with the counts given in Table 3.2.

(d) Use the SPSS LOGLINEAR model to fit model (3.9). (Hint: Specify the number of days in a month using the CWEIGHT statement.)

2. Mail survey return rate experiment.

(a) Use the SPSS LOGLINEAR program to fit model (3.23) to the data in table 3.7a. (Hint: Use the BY command.)

(b) Fit model (3.25). (Hint: Use the special contrast command.)

(c) Fit model (3.26), and then re-estimate using the scores β_j^M for the categories of Monetary Payment (M). Is it "fair" to use these scores? (discuss with regards to the statistical tests and degrees of freedom.)

(d) Suppose that a new test yields the following hypothetical data below: Estimate the effect of the Reminder Call (C) when the Monetary Payment levels are scored 1, 2, and 10. Re-estimate, using the scores 1, 5, and 10. Does the Reminder Call have a positive or negative effect? Are the results similar when a regression model is used? Why do the scores assigned to M affect the coefficient estimate for C? What are the implications regarding how values are chosen for ordinal variables? If you are uncertain about the relative difference between the categories, is it safe to use consecutive integer scores which assumes that the categories are equally spaced?

			Returned:	
Monetary payment	Reminder call:	Yes	No	Total
$1	Yes	246	754	1000
	No	22	78	100
$2	Yes	276	224	500
	No	258	242	500
$10	Yes	82	18	100
	No	801	199	1000

3. TV ratings data

(a) Fit model (3.31) to obtain an estimate for γ_1^S. (Hint: Fit the equivalent model (3.32))

(b) Use the results from question 3a to test $\gamma_1^S = 1$.

(c) Can we conclusively state that households with children do not under-report viewing of WPIX at the designated time? How about viewing of children's programs? How about households with small children? Is it possible that households with children under 13 under-report viewing and households with teens over-report viewing? How could this be detected using log-linear modeling?

4. Analysis of the trichotomous dependent variable RESP3.

(a) Show that the multinomial logit model as expressed by equations (3.37)–(3.38) is obtainable from the general multinomial logit scaling model with the scores $Y(1) = (1, 0, 0)$ and $Y(2) = (0, 1, 0)$. Hint: Use equations (3.39)–(3.41).

(b) Use SAS CATMOD to fit model (3.37)–(3.38) using the scores given in question 4a.

(c) Use SPSS LOGLINEAR to fit the Y-Association model to table 3.16. Compare the results from a 1-way ANOVA, where the dependent variable is Y (taking on the 3 values 35, -7, and -0.15). Do the two approaches give the same conclusion? What assumptions are made by the ANOVA? Are these assumptions warranted? Would you expect the results from these two approaches to always be similar?

(d) Fit the ordinal regression model (3.44) using the score vector $Y = (35, -7, -0.15)$. Show that the estimated expected counts from this model preserve the mean Y-score for each predictor. (Hint: Aggregate the estimated counts to form the 2-way table KIDS by RESP3. Compute the mean score for households with and without kids and show that they agree with the corresponding mean scores obtained using the observed counts. Repeat using the BANKCARD by RESP3 table.)

(e) Estimate the ordinary least squares (OLS) regression equation:

$$SCORE = a + b1 * KIDS + b2 * BANKCARD$$

Are the t statistics for $b1$ and $b2$ similar to the standardized values in the ordinal regression model? Which represents the "better" tests of significance. How do the assumptions differ between the two approaches? Would you expect the results from the OLS and ML approaches to always be similar?

Notes

1 Quasi-independence is a generalization of independence (Goodman, 1968) that is applicable to an incomplete table or a complete table where some of the cells are ignored. Table 3.1 is incomplete in that data is not available for all months in 1980. See also note 3.

2 Adjusted residuals (Haberman, 1978) are residuals divided by their standard error.

3 Model (3.5) was used in example 1 together with the specification that the missing cell entries were to be treated as structural zeroes, not as sampling zeroes. Such a specification can be made with certain computer programs which utilize the IPF algorithm. An equivalent way to specify this model is to use the general model (3.9), where the Z-table would contain entries of 1 and 0, with the 0 entries being used to designate the structural zeroes. See question 1b.

4 In order to obtain this design matrix, first express the coefficients associated with the predictor M as the desired function of the logits (for simplicity, ignore the other predictor, C):

$$B = WL$$

where $B = (\alpha \ \beta_1^{M'} \ \beta_2^{M'} \ \beta^{M'})'$ $L = (L_1 \ L_2 \ L_3 \ L_4)'$ and

$$W = \begin{pmatrix} 0.25 & 0.25 & 0.25 & 0.25 \\ -1 & 1 & 0 & 0 \\ 0 & -1 & 1 & 0 \\ 0 & 0 & -1 & 1 \end{pmatrix}$$

and $L_{ij} = \log_e(F_{j1}/F_{j2})$.
Then solve for the design matrix X, where $L = XB$.
The solution is $X = W^{-1}$.

5 A saturated model may also result with fewer score vectors ($M = R - 1$) if the number of rows (R) in the associated multi-way table (where the predictor variables form the rows and the dependent variable, the K columns) is less than K. This will occur for example, when the score vectors are estimated from Goodman's RC (M) model; see Goodman (1991).

6 For further interpretations of these data see Magidson (1992, 1993a, 1993b, 1994).

7 Some programs estimate a different ordinal regression model known as the cumulative logit or proportional odds model. For comparisons with the models presented here, see Agresti (1990), Koch and Edwards (1988) and Magidson (1993c).

8 A computer program EXL (Extended Logit Analysis) is currently under development with NIH support (SBIR # 1 R43 CA61507–01). For information, write to Statistical Innovations, 375 Concord Ave., Belmont MA, 02178.

References

Agresti, Alan 1990: *Categorical Data Analysis*, New York: Wiley.

Bagozzi, Richard P. 1994: Structural equation models in Marketing Research: Basic Principles. Chapter 9 in Richard P. Bagozzi (ed.), *Principles of Marketing Research*, Oxford: Blackwell.

Clogg, Clifford C. 1992: The impact of sociological methodology on statistical methodology. *Statistical Science*, 7 (2), 183–207.

Clogg, Clifford C. and Eliasin, Scott R. 1987. Some common problems in log-linear analysis. *Sociological Methods and Research*, 16 (1), 8–44.

Goodman, Leo A. 1968: The analysis of cross-classified data: independence, quasi-independence, and interactions in contingency tables with or without missing entries. *Journal of the American Statistical Association*, 63, 1091–1131.

Goodman, Leo A. 1970: The multivariate analysis of qualitative data: interactions among multiple classifications. *Journal of the American Statistical Association*, 65, 226–56. Reprinted in Leo A. Goodman with Jay Magidson (ed.) 1978: *Analyzing Qualitative/Categorical Data*, Cambridge: Abt Books.

Goodman, Leo A. 1972: A general model for the analysis of surveys, *American Journal of Sociology*, 77, May, 1035–86.

Goodman, Leo A. with Jay Magidson (ed.) 1978: *Analyzing Qualitative/Categorical Data*, Cambridge: Abt Books.

Goodman, Leo A. 1979: Simple models for the analysis of associations in cross-classifications having ordered categories. *Journal of the American Statistical Association*, 74, 537–52. Reprinted in *The Analysis of Cross-Classified Data Having Ordered Categories*, 1984, Harvard University Press.

Goodman, Leo A. 1983: The analysis of dependence in cross-classifications having ordered categories: using log-linear models for frequencies and log-linear models for odds. *Biometrics*, 39, 149–60. Reprinted in *The Analysis of Cross-Classified Data Having Ordered Categories*, 1984, Harvard University Press.

Goodman, Leo A. 1985: The analysis of cross-classified data having ordered and/or unordered categories: association models, correlation models, and asymmetry models for contingency tables with or without missing entries. *The Annals of Statistics*, 13 (1), 10–69.

Goodman, Leo A. 1991: Measures, models and graphic displays in the analysis of cross-classified data. *Journal of the American Statistical Association*, 86, 1085–1138 (includes invited comments and a reply by Goodman).

Haberman, Shelby 1978: *Analysis of Qualitative Data, Volume 1: Introductory Topics*, New York: Academic Press.

Koch, Gary and S. Edwards 1988: Clinical efficacy trials with categorical data, chapter 9 in Peace, Karl, *Biopharmaceutical Statistics for Drug Development*, New York: Marcel Dekker, Inc.

Magidson, Jay 1978: An illustrative comparison of Goodman's approach to logit analysis with dummy variable regression analysis, Chap. 2 in *Analyzing Qualitative/Categorical Data*, Cambridge: Abt Books.

Magidson, Jay 1981: Qualitative variance, entropy and correlation ratios for nominal dependent variables, *Social Science Research*, (August).

Magidson, Jay 1987: Weighted log-linear modeling. American Statistical Association, 1987 Proceedings of the Social Statistics Division, 171–74.

Magidson, Jay 1992: Chi-squared analysis of a scalable dependent variable, Proceedings of the 1992 annual meeting of the American Statistical Association, section on Statistical Education, 242–7.

Magidson, Jay 1993a: *SPSS for Windows CHAID Release 6,0*, Chicago: SPSS, Inc.

—— 1993b: The use of the new ordinal algorithm in CHAID to target profitable segments, *Journal of Database Marketing*, Vol. 1, Number 1, 29–48.

—— 1993c: Maximum likelihood assessment of clinical trials based on an ordered categorical response variable, paper presented at the Drug Information Association Workshop "Statistical Issues in the Pharmaceutical Industry", March 30, 1993.

Magidson, Jay 1994: The CHAID approach to segmentation modeling: Chi-squared automatic interaction detection, chapter 4 in Richard Bagozzi (ed.), *Advanced Methods of Marketing Research*, Oxford: Blackwell.

4

The CHAID Approach to Segmentation Modeling: CHi-squared Automatic Interaction Detection

Jay Magidson

It is difficult to think of a topic in marketing that is more pervasive than market segmentation. The overall goal of segmentation modeling is to divide a population into mutually exclusive and exhaustive subgroups (called segments) which differ with respect to some criterion, and to identify those segments which are "best" from a marketing perspective so that they can be targeted.

Segmentation models may be classified into criterion-based models and non-criterion-based (cluster type) models. Non-criterion-based models are developed using cluster analysis alone or in conjunction with other multivariate techniques. These models identify clusters of households (or businesses, or other observational unit) which tend to be homogeneous with respect to certain defining variables, which may be demographic variables, ratings of benefits sought, or some other kinds of variables. While cluster type models are not derived to be predictive of any single criterion, they represent the traditional descriptive approach to segmentation modeling. They are most often used in benefit segmentation studies to classify observations into groups who seek similar benefits.

Criterion-based models differ from cluster type models in that they make use of a criterion as a dependent variable to derive the household groupings. The resulting groups, referred to as segments, are defined explicitly in terms of independent variables which are found to be predictive of the criterion. That is, segments derived using criterion-based models are defined as explicit combinations of (i.e. interactions between) predictor variables. For example, the segment

> two or three person households where the occupation of the head of household is classified as white collar

is defined as a combination of the variables household size (HHSIZE) and occupation (OCCUP). (Later, we will see that this segment is most likely to subscribe to a particular magazine.)

Segments obtained from a criterion-based model differ from clusters obtained from a non-criterion based model in that (1) they are derived to be predictive of a criterion variable, and (2) they are defined by combinations of predictor variable(s).

In this chapter we focus on criterion-based segmentation modeling and the related problem of interaction detection – how to identify and detect the relevant combinations of the predictor variables that define the segments. Specifically, we will focus on the solution offered by the CHAID (CHi-squared Automatic Interaction Detector) approach to interaction detection and criterion-based segmentation modeling, as developed by Kass (1980) and extended by Magidson (1992, 1993).

Early Criterion-Based Approaches: Regression and AID

The most widely used criterion-based modeling technique is linear regression analysis. Modern regression theory relies heavily on the assumption that the conditional distribution of the dependent variable follows a normal distribution. This assumption is often violated in segmentation modeling where the criterion is often dichotomous (i.e. has only two categories, such as User or Non-user). Moreover, while traditional applications of regression include main-effects but not interactions, the definition of good segments often requires interaction terms. While interactions can be included in the regression model, regression theory itself offers little assistance in finding the appropriate terms to include and interpretation of higher order interactions is often difficult.

As an alternative to the traditional regression approach, an *ad hoc* technique known as Automatic Interaction Detection (AID) was developed in 1963 at the University of Michigan's Institute for Social Research. AID, which is also called "binary tree analysis," employs a hierarchical, binary splitting algorithm. The approach assumes that the population represents a heterogeneous grouping with respect to some continuous or dichotomous dependent variable criterion, and segments the population into mutually exclusive and exhaustive groups based on selected combinations of dichotomized predictor variables.

AID begins by splitting the population into two distinct groups based on the categories of the "best" predictor variable. It then further dichotomizes each of these groups and successively continues the splitting process on each of the resulting subgroups in turn until no predictor can be found which meets the selection condition or some other stopping rule is met.

AID was widely used in marketing research during the late 1960s and early '70s, but fell into disrepute because by ignoring the issue of simultaneous inference, its searching process was shown to capitalize on chance. As a result, segments identified by AID often did not validate on other samples.

The AID algorithm searches for the most significant way to dichotomize a predictor, but does not adjust for the fact that there are many ways to do this (unless the predictor only has two original categories). By ignoring the fact that it selected the way that appears to be most statistically significant, the AID algorithm has an inherent bias which overstates the probability value (p-value) of polytomous predictors (i.e. predictors having more than two categories). In general, the bias is greater for predictors having the most categories. Hence, variables originally having many categories are more likely to be selected by the AID algorithm as being the best predictor because they have artifactually low p-values.

In order to illustrate the problem of improper significance levels and the related issue of simultaneous inference, suppose that two variables, A and B, are candidates for the best predictor of some dependent variable, R, where A is dichotomous and B has 5 categories. Suppose further that the predictive relationship between A and R is found to be marginally significant at the 0.05 level.

Note that there are $(2^4) - 1 = 15$ different ways of dichotomizing B[1]. Even if B were in fact statistically independent of R, by chance alone, at least one of these 15 different ways might appear to be more significant than A. Hence, if the most significant of these 15 tests has a conditional p-value of 0.04, in this case, it would not be correct to conclude that B is more predictive than A. In order to determine whether predictor A or B is more significant, one needs to assess the likelihood of observing a spurious relationship.

The CHAID alternative

In 1978, Kass developed a statistical algorithm called CHi-squared Automatic Interaction Detection (CHAID) which improved over AID in several respects. CHAID will merge those categories of a predictor that are homogeneous with respect to the dependent variable, but will maintain all categories that are heterogeneous. That is, CHAID combines categories that do not differ significantly from each other, but separates those that are different. Since several categories may differ statistically, unlike AID, the result of the CHAID merging process will not necessarily be a dichotomy. In addition, CHAID applies the Bonferroni multiplier to adjust for simultaneous inference. Finally, only variables that are statistically significant are eligible to split a group.

CHAID, unlike AID, is limited to nominal and ordinal categorical variables. It utilizes the chi-square test for independence (in conjunction with the Bonferroni adjustment) to assess statistical significance. CHAID makes no assumption of normality.

Before outlining the algorithm and interpreting the results from several CHAID analyses, we will briefly describe how the CHAID technique utilizes the Bonferroni adjustment. For simplicity, we will again consider the example where a 5-category variable is dichotomized.

Let α denote the desired type 1 error rate associated with the test of independence in a 2-way table formed by cross tabulating B and R. (That is, α denotes the desired probability of rejecting the null hypothesis of independence when in fact independence holds; say, $\alpha = 0.05$.) Consider performing 15 tests for independence, testing each of the 15 possible dichotomized forms for B. If these 15 tests were independent of each other, the probability of making a type 1 error (in one or more of these tests), would be equal to 1 minus the probability of not making a type 1 error in any of these tests, which would be substantially greater than α:

$$1 - (1 - \alpha)^{15} > \alpha \qquad (4.1)$$

In the above example, the number 15 is called the Bonferroni multiplier because the probability in (4.1) above turns out to be approximately 15α when α is small. More generally, let M equal the number of ways of ending up with $K < I$ categories, where I is the original number of categories. Then we have:

$$1 - (1 - \alpha)^M = M\alpha \qquad \text{for } \alpha \text{ small} \qquad (4.2)$$

There is only one way to dichotomize a variable for which $I = 2$ (i.e. it is already dichotomous), thus the probability of making a type 1 error with variable A is simply α.

The CHAID approach is to compare the p-value associated with the test for independence for variable A with the Bonferroni adjusted p-value for B. For the above example, the adjusted p-value is the conditional p-value (calculated after the categories have been merged) times 15. More generally, the adjusted p-value is the conditional p-value times the Bonferroni multiplier M.

Since the 15 tests are *not* independent, it should be noted that the above Bonferroni adjustment is somewhat conservative. It can be improved upon by noting that the adjusted p-value can never be higher than the p-value obtained *before* merging the categories. Hence, the p-value obtained prior to merging categories will serve as an upper bound on the adjusted p-value.[2]

Of course, in the case that CHAID does not merge any categories of the predictor, the Bonferroni multiplier will equal 1 and the adjusted p-value equals the unadjusted p-value. For more information on AID see Sonnquist, and Morgan (1964). Further details on CHAID are provided in the following sections and in Kass (1980).

The Subscribe Dataset

In order to illustrate the CHAID technique, we will be using a dataset called SUBSCRIBE. This dataset involves the response to a promotion that was used to encourage people to subcribe to a particular magazine. Households are classified into three categories of the dependent variable RESP3: paid responders, unpaid responders and non-responders. Paid responders are households who returned an order form, checking off that they would like to subscribe to the magazine, and later paid for the subscription. Unpaid responders are those who checked off that they would like to subscribe to the magazine, but then cancelled their subscriptions prior to paying. Non-responders are all others (i.e. those who never requested a subscription).

For our initial example, the dependent variable will be treated as a simple dichotomy, which distinguishes between responders (the combination of paid and unpaid responders) and non-responders:

RESP2 – Response to a subscription offer

Y	Responder (paid and unpaid)
N	Non-responder

CHAID distinguishes between three types of predictors – free, monotonic, and float, a choice that affects CHAID's category merging algorithm.

Categories of monotonic variables may only be combined by CHAID if they are adjacent to each other. Generally, researchers will treat ordinal variables (i.e. those whose categories contain a natural ordering) as monotonic, such as the INCOME variable below.

Categories of free variables may be combined whether or not they are adjacent to each other. Variables whose categories contain no natural ordering should always be treated as free.

Floating variables are treated as monotonic, except for the last category (often one which reflects a type of "missing value"), which is allowed to combine with any other category. For example, the predictor HHSIZE, below, would normally be treated as ordinal except that the final category is "Unknown," and thus it is treated as floating. The float option is somewhat analogous to imputation, since the float category is merged with (and hence, takes on the characteristics of) that category to which it is most similar with regard to the distribution of the dependent variable.

A brief description of each predictor in the SUBSCRIBE dataset, including the type of variable and its categories is given in Figure 4.1.

Introduction to CHAID Modeling

The basic components of a CHAID analysis are the following:

1   a categorical dependent variable;
2   a set of categorical predictor variables, combinations of which are used to define the segments; and
3   settings for the various CHAID parameters.

At any point in the CHAID analysis, some subgroup is being analyzed and the "best" predictor is identified. The best predictor is defined as that predictor variable having the lowest adjusted p-value. Since the p-value represents the probability that the observed sample relationship between a predictor and the dependent variable would occur if in fact the two

variables were statistically independent, that predictor with the lowest
p-value is the one that is least likely to be unrelated to and thus has the
most predictive power.

---

1   AGE – Age of household head – Float
    1   18–24
    2   25–34
    3   35–44
    4   45–54
    5   55–64
    6   65 years or more
    ?   Unknown

2   GENDER – Sex of household head – Monotonic[a]
    M   Male
    F   Female

3   KIDS – Known presence of children – Monotonic[a]
    Y   Yes
    N   No

4   INCOME – Household income – Monotonic
    1   Under $8,000
    2        $ 8,000–$ 9,999
    3        $10,000–$14,999
    4        $15,000–$19,999
    5        $20,000–$24,999
    6        $25,000–$34,999
    7        $35,000–$49,999
    8        $50,000 or more

5   BANKCARD – Known presence of bankcard – Monotonic[a]
    Y   Yes
    N   No

6   HHSIZE – Number of persons in household – Float
    1   One person
    2   Two
    3   Three
    4   Four
    5   Five or more
    ?   Unknown

7   OCCUP – Occupation of household head – Free
    W   White collar
    B   Blue collar
    O   Other
    ?   Unknown

---

[a] Dichotomous variables will be treated the same regardless of whether
they are classified as Free, Monotonic or Float.

Figure 4.1   Predictor variables in the SUBSCRIBE dataset

The CHAID algorithm

The algorithm consists of three stages – merging, splitting and applying the stopping rule. It may be formally described as follows:

Stage 1: Merging   For each predictor, $X_1, X_2, \ldots, X_K$

1   Form the full two-way cross-tabulation with the dependent variable.
2   For each pair of categories that is eligible to be merged together, compute chi-square statistics (which will be referred to as "pairwise chi-squares") to test for independence in the $2 \times J$ subtable formed by that pair of categories and the dependent variable which has J categories.
3   For each pairwise chi-square, compute the corresponding "pairwise *p*-value." Among those pairs that are found to be non-significant merge the most similar pair (i.e. that pair having the smallest pairwise chi-square value) into a single joint category, and go to step 4. If all remaining pairs are significant, go to step 5.
4   For any joint category containing three or more categories, test to see if any predictor category should be unmerged by testing the significance associated with that category vs. the others in that joint category. If a significant chi-square obtains, unmerge that category from the others. If more than one category is eligible to be unmerged, unmerge the one having the highest chi-square. Return to step 3.
5   Optionally, merge any category having unacceptably few observations with the most similar other category k', as measured by the smallest pairwise chi-square; i.e. $X^2(i', k') = \min X^2(i', k)$ where $k = 1, 2, \ldots, I, k \neq i'$.
6   Compute the Bonferroni adjusted *p*-value based on the after-merged table.

Stage 2: Splitting

7   Select as best that predictor with the lowest significant adjusted *p*-value and split the group on this predictor (i.e. use each of the optimally merged categories of that predictor to define a subdivision of the parent group into a new subgroup). If no predictor has a significant *p*-value, do not split the group.

Stage 3: Stopping

8   Return to step 1 to analyze the *next* subgroup. Stop when all subgroups have either been analyzed or contain too few observations.

Comparison with cluster analysis

The segments attained from a CHAID analysis of the dependent variable RESP2 in the SUBSCRIBE dataset are given in Figure 4.2 and graphically presented in the form of a tree diagram in Figure 4.3.

Segment 1	One person households
Segment 2	Two or three person households where the occupation of the head of household is classified as white collar
Segment 3	Two or three person households where the occupation of the head of household is other than white collar
Segment 4	Households containing four or more persons
Segment 5	Number of persons in household is unknown and head of household is assumed to be male
Segment 6	Number of persons in household is unknown and head of household is assumed to be female

Figure 4.2 Segments resulting from a CHAID analysis of RESP2

Prior to interpreting these results, it is useful to distinguish CHAID segments from clusters which are obtained from a traditional cluster analysis. While both CHAID and cluster analysis are techniques which divide a population into subgroups, as mentioned earlier, only CHAID makes use of an explicit dependent variable criterion in forming the subgroups. In particular, CHAID uses statistical significance between the dependent variable and predictors to drive its segmentation algorithm. Thus, unlike clusters, which may or may not be predictive of some dependent variable, CHAID segments are derived to be predictive.

According to the CHAID analysis, that segment that is most likely to respond is Segment 2 (we will see why later). It is defined as follows based on the predictors HHSIZE and OCCUP:

$$HHSIZE = 2 \text{ or } 3 \text{ person households}$$
and
$$OCCUP = W \text{ (White collar)}$$

This segment will tend to have a higher rate of response than any equal sized cluster which is derived using a traditional cluster analysis technique.

A second difference mentioned earlier is that segments are defined as explicit functions of the predictors. Hence, the definitions can be applied easily to classify a new sample into these segments. Alternatively, the results of a cluster analysis can not be used to classify a new sample into clusters. (Often a discriminant or similar analysis is performed to predict the cluster group based on certain "predictor-type" variables in order to classify additional samples.)

Interpreting results from a CHAID analysis

Notice that in the definition of Segment 2 above, CHAID has combined (merged) together the 2nd and 3rd categories of the predictor HHSIZE. As discussed above, an integral part of the CHAID technique is to merge together categories of a predictor variable that are homogeneous with respect to the dependent variable. This category merging procedure, combined with the splitting algorithm, serve to ensure that observations which are grouped into the same segment are homogeneous with respect to the dependent variable criterion, while those which fall into different segments will tend to be heterogeneous with respect to the dependent variable criterion.

Table 4.1 below shows the percentage of responders (i.e. category 1 of the dependent variable RESP2) by the overall best predictor, HHSIZE, before and after the categories of HHSIZE were merged together.

Table 4.1 Comparison of response rates by HHSIZE, before and after merging categories

| HHSIZE | n | Percent response | |
		Before merging	After merging
1	25,384	1.09	1.09
2	11,240	1.49[a]	1.52
3	4,892	1.59[a]	1.52
4	3,187	1.79[b]	1.92
5+	3,011	2.06[b]	1.92
unknown	33,326	0.87	0.87

[a] These percentages are not significantly different from each other and thus were merged by CHAID.

[b] These percentages are not significantly different from each other and thus were merged by CHAID.

Table 4.2 Ranking of CHAID segments by response rate

Rank	No.	Description	Percent response
1	Segment 2	Two or three person households where the occupation of the head of household is classified as white collar	2.39
2	Segment 4	Households containing four or more persons	1.92
3	Segment 3	Two or three person households where the occupation of the head of household is other than white collar	1.42
4	Segment 1	One person households	1.09
5	Segment 6	Number of persons in household is unknown and head of household is assumed to be female	1.08
6	Segment 5	Number of persons in household is unknown and head of household is assumed to be male	0.81

As can be seen from Table 4.1, the response rate for 2-person and 3-person households are similar (1.49% vs. 1.59%), and after being merged together, the combined group responds at 1.52 percent. As mentioned above, these two merged groups are considered to be homogeneous with respect to response (because their response rates are not significantly different), and hence the combined response rate after merging is assigned to each of these groups separately. Similarly, CHAID assigns the response rate of 1.92 percent to 4-person households and households with 5+ persons, since these categories are also homogeneous with respect to the RESP2 criterion.

The basic CHAID approach has maximum power and its results are simplest to interpret when the dependent variable is dichotomous. In this case, the resulting segments may be ranked from high to low according to the prevalence of the desirable trait (e.g. the likelihood of response). For example, the segments in Figure 4.2 are ranked in Table 4.2.

The tree diagram

In this section we will describe the tree diagram display which is the heart of a CHAID analysis. We will then describe two gains charts which rank the segments and summarize their performance individually and in the form of a quantile array.

For a dichotomous dependent variable, only one percentage is needed to characterize its distribution – the percentage who are responders. Since the percentage of non-responders will always equal 100 percent minus the percentage who are responders, it is not necessary to include that percentage in the tree diagram.

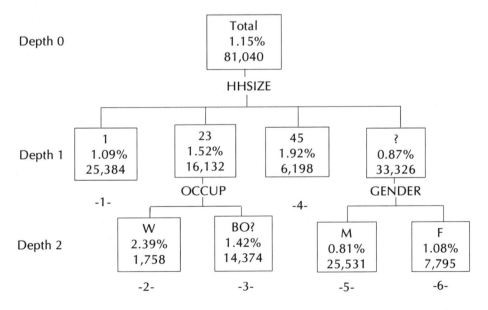

Figure 4.3 Results of CHAID based on dichotomous dependent variable RESP2 and original algorithm: display = % distribution

At level 1 of the tree in Figure 4.3, the root node gives rise to four subnodes that are formed by the categories of the best predictor. For this analysis, the best predictor is the Household Size variable, which is designated by the variable name "HHSIZE" appearing directly beneath the root node.

HHSIZE classifies each household into one of six groups according to the number of persons residing in that household (one, two, three, four, five or more, unknown). However, as we noted earlier (recall Table 4.1), some of these groups were found by CHAID to be statistically indistinguishable with respect to their rate of response, and thus have been merged together. Thus, after merging categories, HHSIZE contains the following four categories (1, 2–3, 4+, unknown).

As in the root node, three elements are also displayed in each of the derivative nodes (or "child nodes") of the tree:

1 a symbol(s) identifying the particular category (or merged categories) that define the associated group;
2 a dependent variable summary statistic for that group (e.g. percent response);
3 the sample size for the group. Sample sizes are preceeded by "$n =$".

Thus, the left-most level 1 node of the above tree contains the HHSIZE category symbol "1", representing 1-person households. Of the 25,384 1-person households who were mailed the subscription promotion ($n = 25, 384$), 1.09 percent of them responded.

Moving over one node to the right, the symbol "23" denotes households that contain 2 or 3 persons, of which 1.52 percent of the 6,132 households mailed responded, etc.

Note that each child node is a derivative of the "parent" node that precedes it. For example, the four group sample sizes in the HHSIZE nodes will equal the total sample size in the root node (25,384 + 16,132 + + 6,198 + 33,326 = 81,040), just as adding up the two sample sizes of the OCCUP nodes will equal the sample size for HHSIZE = 2–3 node (1,758 + 14,374 = 16,132).

The terminal or end nodes of the tree represent the final subgroups, which are referred to as segments. These segments are ranked from high to low and summarized with respect to their response rate in the gains charts which are described next.

Note that overall, the results displayed in the tree diagram suggest that larger households tend to have a higher response rate than smaller ones. The single best segment to mail is segment 2 – households with 2 or 3 persons where the head of the household has a white collar occupation (2.39 percent response rate). The lowest responding is segment 5 – households of unknown size where the head of household is assumed to be male. This segment responded at just 0.81 percent, significantly below the overall response rate of 1.15 percent.

Table 4.3 Gains charts based on percentage distribution

(a) Selection array of response by market segment

Segment	Segment id	Individual segments				Sample size	% of total (%)	Cumulative			
		Sample size	Resps	Resp rate (%)	Index			Resps	Resp rate (%)	% of resps (%)	Index
1	2	1,758	42	2.4	208	1,758	2.2	42	2.4	4.5	208
2	4	6,198	119	1.9	167	7,956	9.8	161	2.0	17.3	176
3	3	14,374	204	1.4	124	22,330	27.6	365	1.6	39.2	142
4	1	25,384	276	1.1	95	47,714	58.9	641	1.3	68.9	117
5	6	7,795	84	1.1	94	55,509	68.5	725	1.3	77.9	114
6	5	25,531	206	0.8	70	81,040	100.0	931	1.1	100.0	100

The gains chart summary

Since the CHAID analysis was based on a dichotomous dependent variable, RESP2, it is possible to summarize the results with respect to the percentage falling in category 1, i.e. the percentage of households who requested a subscription (responders). Such summaries, in the form of gains charts, are shown in Tables 4.3a and 4.3b.

Table 4.3 (*Contd.*)

(b) Performance of model at different depths of selection

Depth of selection (%)	Sample size	Responses	Response rate (%)	% of resps (%)	Index
5	4,052	86	2.1	9.2	185
10	8,104	163	2.0	17.5	175
15	12,156	221	1.8	23.7	158
20	16,208	278	1.7	29.9	149
25	20,260	336	1.7	36.0	144
30	24,312	387	1.6	41.5	138
35	28,364	431	1.5	46.3	132
40	32,416	475	1.5	51.0	127
45	36,468	519	1.4	55.7	124
50	40,520	563	1.4	60.4	121
55	44,572	607	1.4	65.2	119
60	48,624	651	1.3	69.9	117
65	52,676	694	1.3	74.6	115
70	56,728	735	1.3	78.9	113
75	60,780	768	1.3	82.4	110
80	64,832	800	1.2	86.0	107
85	68,884	833	1.2	89.5	105
90	72,936	866	1.2	93.0	103
95	76,988	898	1.2	96.5	102
100	81,040	931	1.1	100.0	100

The gains chart in Table 4.3a is known as the detailed gains chart since it contains a row for each segment. It rank orders these six CHAID segments from best to worst by response rate. The ID number corresponds to the numbered segment on the tree diagram as given in Figure 4.3. For example, ID#2 corresponds to HHSIZE = 2–3 and OCCUP = white collar.

From the cumulative response row it can be seen that the three best segments, which comprise 27.6 percent of the sample, account for 39.2 percent of all respondents. An index score gives reference to the response rate of each segment in relation to the overall response rate. For example, Segment 1 has an index of 208, calculated as $100 \times 2.39\%/1.15\% = 208$.

The gains chart in Table 4.3b is known as the summary chart, also referred to as the quantile gains chart. The quantile chart displays cumulative results at fixed percentage points of the running segment size total. It describes the results that would have been obtained if only the highest responding x% of households were mailed. Observations are grouped into 20 5% quantile groupings associated with the highest scoring 5%, 10%, . . ., 80%, etc. of the sample.

Gains charts can be helpful for determining how deep into a file one can profitably mail. For example, if the breakeven response level were 1.5%, the quantile chart shows that the best 40% can be profitably mailed. Segments below this level respond below the breakeven point.

Examining the Profitability of CHAID Segments

In order to better assess the profitability of these segments, instead of evaluating them with respect to their likelihood of responding, we will use explicit profitability scores. Specifically, a paid responder is valued at $y_1 = \$35$, a non-responder at $y_2 = -\$0.15$ (the cost of mailing), and an unpaid responder at $y_3 = -\$7$, (the cost associated with several mailings including the trial issue). If we let the variable RESP3 form the three columns, and the I categories for some predictor A form the rows in a two-way cross tabulation of A and RESP3, then for the ith row of A, the mean value of $Y = (y_j)$ provides a measure of profitability as follows:

$$\bar{y}_i = p_{i1} * (\$35) + p_{i2} * (-\$7) + p_{i3} * (-\$0.15) \tag{4.3}$$

where p_{ij} is the proportion of the ith category of A for whom $Y = Y_j$.

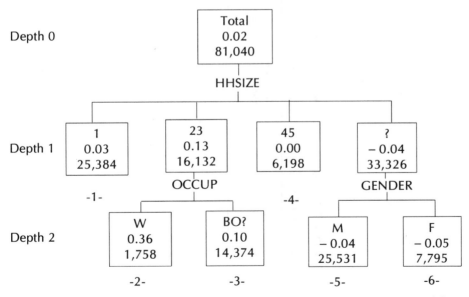

Figure 4.4 Results of CHAID based on dichotomous dependent variable RESP2 and original algorithm: display = average scores

Table 4.4 Gains charts based on average scores (I)

(a) Selection array of response by market segment

Segment	Segment id	Individual segments				Sample size	Cumulative		
		Sample size	% of total	Expected gain	Index		% of total	Avg. score	Index
1	2	1,758	2.17	0.36	1866	1,758	2.17	0.36	1866
2	3	14,374	17.74	0.10	528	16,132	19.91	0.13	674
3	1	25,384	31.32	0.03	168	41,516	51.23	0.07	365
4	4	6,198	7.65	−0.00	−18	47,714	58.88	0.06	315
5	5	25,531	31.50	−0.04	−187	73,245	90.38	0.03	139
6	6	7,795	9.62	−0.05	−269	81,040	100.00	0.02	100

Notice that we must distinguish between paid and unpaid responders in calculating the measure of average gain (profitability) in eq. (4.3). Figure 4.4 and Table 4.4 present the alternative tree diagram and gains charts respectively, based on average gain rather than the percentage response.

Table 4.4 (*Contd.*)

(b): Performance of model at different depths of selection

Depth of selection (%)	Sample size	Expected gain	Index
5	4,052	0.21	1109
10	8,104	0.16	818
15	12,156	0.14	722
20	16,208	0.13	671
25	20,260	0.11	571
30	24,312	0.10	504
35	28,364	0.09	456
40	32,416	0.08	420
45	36,468	0.07	392
50	40,520	0.07	369
55	44,572	0.06	338
60	48,624	0.06	305
65	52,676	0.05	267
70	56,728	0.04	235
75	60,780	0.04	207
80	64,832	0.03	182
85	68,884	0.03	160
90	72,936	0.03	141
95	76,988	0.02	119
100	81,040	0.02	100

Overall, as indicated in the root node at "depth 0" of the tree diagram, the average gain for households that were mailed is $0.02. In depth 1 of the tree we see that not all segments have the same expected gain. In particular, 2–3 person households are valued at $0.13 while households containing an unknown number of persons have a negative value or expected loss.

Notice at depth 2 of the tree that the splitting of the HHSIZE = unknown group by GENDER provided little improvement with regard to average value. This extraneous split is due to the fact the original CHAID analysis did not take into account the differential value of a paid and unpaid responder.

In Table 4.4a, the segments for the gains charts are now ranked from high to low based on average gain rather than response. The highest ranking segments are the ones that would generally be targeted for additional promotions.

Comparing these gains charts with those based on the response rate, it can be seen how distinguishing between the value of a paid and unpaid responder can help to improve the selection of profitable segments. For example, the scores in Table 4.4a suggest that mailing to those people in

Table 4.5 Gains charts based on average scores (II)

(a) Selection array of response by market segment

Segment	Segment id	Individual Segments					Cumulative			
		Sample size	% of total	Expected gain	Index	Sample size	% of total	Avg. score	Index
1	3	3,249	4.01	0.16	851	3,249	4.01	0.16	851
2	2	7,991	9.86	0.16	826	11,240	13.87	0.16	833
3	4	8,079	9.97	0.05	277	19,319	23.84	0.11	601
4	1	25,384	31.32	0.03	168	44,703	55.16	0.07	355
5	6	25,531	31.50	−0.04	−187	70,234	86.67	0.03	157
6	7	7,795	9.62	−0.05	−269	78,029	96.28	0.02	115
7	5	3,011	3.72	−0.05	−282	81,040	100.00	0.02	100

segment #4 would result in a breakeven proposition (average score = 0.00), even though this segment has the second highest overall gross response rate at 1.9 percent (See Table 4.3a). In addition, rather than relying on an indirect measure of profitability, the breakeven response rate, one can use direct measures of profitability as given by the dependent variable category scores.

Table 4.5 (*Contd.*)

(b): Performance of model at different depths of selection

Depth of selection (%)	Sample size	Expected gain	Index
5	4,052	0.16	846
10	8,104	0.16	836
15	12,156	0.15	791
20	16,208	0.13	663
25	20,260	0.11	580
30	24,312	0.10	512
35	28,364	0.09	463
40	32,416	0.08	426
45	36,468	0.08	397
50	40,520	0.07	374
55	44,572	0.07	355
60	48,624	0.06	311
65	52,676	0.05	273
70	56,728	0.05	240
75	60,780	0.04	211
80	64,832	0.04	186
85	68,884	0.03	164
90	72,936	0.03	142
95	76,988	0.02	120
100	81,040	0.02	100

CHAID Analysis of Polytomous Dependent Variables

The CHAID algorithm presented earlier is applicable for dependent variables that are polytomous (i.e. those that have more than two categories) as well as ones that are dichotomous. For example, the responder category of the RESP2 variable may be split into two groups: those responders who subsequently became Paid Responders and those who canceled prior to paying. The trichotomous variable RESP3 (Paid Responder, Unpaid Responder, Non-Responder) contains two categories of responders plus the non-responder category.

Implicit in the use of the chi-squared test for independence which drives the CHAID algorithm is the notion that the dependent variable is qualitative/categorical (nominal). While CHAID can still be used to analyze an ordinal dependent variable (i.e. a categorical dependent variable measured on an interval scale), there is a substantial loss of statistical power in this case for reasons which are explained in the next section.

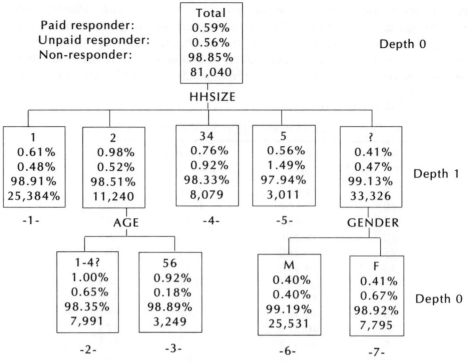

Figure 4.5   Results of CHAID based on trichotomous dependent variable
RESP2 and original algorithm: display = % distribution

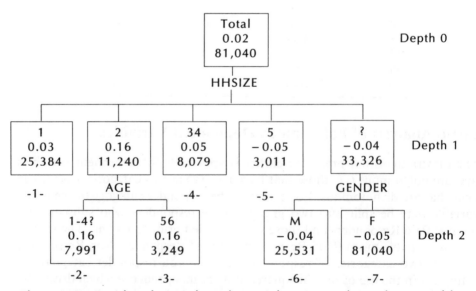

Figure 4.6   Results of CHAID based on trichotomous dependent variable
RESP2 and original algorithm: display = average scores

In this section, we will describe the results of an analysis of RESP3 using
the CHAID algorithm, as documented earlier. In the next section, we will

describe an extension of the CHAID algorithm for ordinal dependent variables that does not involve any loss of power. We will then re-analyze RESP3 using the new algorithm and compare the results from these two different approaches. The new algorithm is due to Magidson (1992) and has been implemented in the SI-CHAID® computer programs.[3]

The tree diagrams resulting from the traditional CHAID analysis of RESP3 are presented in Figures 4.5 and 4.6. The tree in Figure 4.5 displays percentages for each of the three dependent variable categories. The tree in Figure 4.6 displays the expected gain.

By comparing Figures 4.5 and 4.6 with corresponding Figures 4.3 and 4.4, it can be seen that the segments have only changed slightly based on the analysis of RESP3 rather than RESP2. The variable HHSIZE is now split into five categories (1, 2, 3–4, 5+, unknown) instead of four and AGE is now used to subdivide 2-person households (i.e. HHSIZE = "2"). Also, OCCUP no longer shows up as a significant predictor.

Notice that at depth 2 of the tree in Figure 4.6, the splitting of 2-person households into two segments based on AGE does not provide any improvement in average value. These segments are equally valued at $0.16. Similarly, the splitting of the HHSIZE = unknown group by GENDER provided little improvement with regard to average value.

Overall, the results displayed in the tree diagrams thus far suggest that 2–3 person households tend to be the best segments for future subscription promotions for this magazine. It also suggests that the segments having the lowest value are those containing households of unknown size. However, this CHAID analysis, like the first, has provided extraneous segments, and as will soon be seen, it has also failed to discover other segments that have a high average value.

For the trichotomous dependent variable RESP3, the gains charts provided in Table 4.5 are based on the average score. Despite the fact that we have analyzed RESP3 rather than RESP2, the quantile gains chart remains virtually the same, (or possibly suggests a somewhat *less* powerful segmentation) than the earlier gains chart in Table 4.4.

An Extension of the CHAID Algorithm

Conceptually, category scores for an ordinal dependent variable provide a way to account for differential utilities or value. For example, the RESP3 scores specified earlier (35, − 7, − 0.15) were used to assign a positive value of $35 to each paid responder, − $0.15 to each non-responder and − $7 to the more costly responder category who respond but then cancel prior to paying. However, these scores were not utilized by CHAID during the analysis – they were only applied after the CHAID segments were identified.

In this section we introduce the Magidson (1992) approach for segmentation based on a quantitative/categorical (ordinal) criterion. Specifically, the chi-squared test for independence used in CHAID is replaced by an alternative chi-squared test for Y-Association (actually, the lack of Y-Association). The test for Y-Association focuses on how well a variable can predict the scores of a quantitative dependent variable, denoted as Y.

The new chi-squared test may be applied in the case where some or all of the scores for the categories of the dependent variable are known and it may also be applied when all of the scores are unknown. In the case that not all scores are known, a maximum likelihood calibration technique is used to estimate the unknown scores based on some designated predictor variable (i.e. the "instrument"). The test is based on Goodman's (1969, 1970) calculus for partitioning the likelihood ratio chi-square statistic, and involves a new model which is closely related to Goodman's R and RC association models (Goodman, 1979, 1985).

The new algorithm has been implemented in the SPSS CHAID 5.0/6.0 computer program. To utilize it, the user would select METHOD = ORDINAL, as opposed to the default METHOD = NOMINAL, which employs the original algorithm. When the ORDINAL method is selected, distinct quantitative scores or values must be associated with each of the different categories of the dependent variable. (If two or more categories are assigned the same score, they are automatically merged into a single joint category.)

It is possible to obtain different segmentations depending upon which scores are used. Thus, if one is unsure of the scores to use, separate analyses can be performed, each with different scores, and the resulting segmentations can be compared to determine what differences (if any) result from using the different scores.

If there is no theoretical basis to select scores, the new CHAID algorithm will estimate the scores using a predictor variable as an "instrument" to calibrate the dependent variable. This case will be discussed further later.

We will utilize several examples from the SUBSCRIBE dataset to introduce and illustrate the new methods and contrast them with the original algorithm. Prior to comparing the CHAID results based on the new algorithm with those from the original algorithm, we describe the new chi-squared test in some detail. For more technical details, readers are referred to Magidson (1992).

Testing for nonassociation vs. independence

In the test for independence in an $I \times J$ table (between a predictor with I categories and a dependent variable with J categories), a large chi-squared value is indicative of some type of non-independence being present. In particular, the test for independence may be specified as $(I-1)(J-1)$ distinctly different 1-degree-of-freedom restrictions, each of which specifies that a particular kind of nonindependence is nil. The specific formulation of such restrictions is not unique – there are numerous ways that they can be specified.

The test for independence is usually expressed by the following restrictions:

the conditional probability for the dependent response j is the same for each category i of the predictor

However, as mentioned above, there are many alternative ways of defining independence, each of which is equivalent. Following Magidson (1992), we will define independence by specifying an initial set of I–1 1-degree-of-freedom restrictions as in eq. (4.4), which state that the conditional expectation of Y, denoted μ, is identical for each row:

$$\mu_1 = \mu_2 = \ldots = \mu_I \qquad (4.4)$$

where
$$\mu_i \equiv P_{i1} * y_1 + P_{i2} * y_2 + \ldots + P_{iJ} * y_J \qquad (4.5)$$
$$\text{for } i = 1, 2, \ldots, I$$

and an additional $J - 2$ sets of $(I - 1)$ 1-degree-of-freedom restrictions that state that the conditional expectation based on each of the score vectors $V^{(1)}, V^{(2)}, \ldots, V^{(J-2)}$ is identical for each row, where the score vectors $V^{(k)}$, are each linearly independent of each other and of the Y-score vector. Thus, independence can be interpreted as meaning that the conditional expectations based on any set of column scores are equal for each row (see Magidson, 1992). Under independence, we may say that there is zero association between the rows and any set of column scores. There is zero Y-Association and there is zero $V^{(k)}$-Association, for each $k = 1, 2, , \ldots, J - 2$.

(Note that eq. (4.5) is a generalization of eq. (4.3).)

When the restrictions given in eq. (4.4) hold, we will say that "Y-Association" is nil. The truth of eq. (4.4) can be tested by partitioning the independence chi-squared statistic into an $I - 1$ degrees-of-freedom component which is due to Y-Association and a $(I - 1) * (J - 2)$ degree of freedom residual component which is associated with the $V^{(k)}$-Associations. The I–1 degrees-of-freedom chi-squared test for (the lack of) Y-Association is a more focused test than the test for independence in that a high chi-squared value attained in the former case assesses only a particular type of non-independence – that which we refer to as Y-Association. Any residual amount of non-independence, as assessed by the $(I - 1)(J - 2)$ degrees-of-freedom chi-squared residual component, can be ignored as being irrelevant to the dependent variable Y, because it is associated with the $V^{(k)}$-score vectors which are linearly independent of the Y-scores.

In summary, the test for Y-Association focuses only on the relationship between the row variable and the particular column variable Y, having specific scores $y_1, y_2, \ldots, y_J$. The test for independence, on the other hand, can be viewed as the test of whether there is non-association between the rows and columns under any possible column scores. When a dependent variable does have known column scores as given by y, the test for Y-Association is a more focused and therefore more powerful test than that of independence; i.e. the test that Y-Association is nil involves only $(I - 1) * 1 = I - 1$ degrees of freedom while the test for independence involves $(I - 1)(J - 1)$ degrees of freedom.

In some cases, the test for independence will be significant, but the test for Y-Association will *not* be significant. Alternatively, the reverse is also possible – the test for Y-Association may be significant, but the test for independence is not. Next, we will examine an example of each situation.

Partitioning the independence chi-squared statistic

In this section we assume that the scores for all categories of the dependent variable are known in advance. They may represent profitability or some other meaningful construct. We will now formalize the process of partitioning the independence chi-squared statistic into an I–1 degree-of-freedom component, $X^2(0|Y)$, measuring the degree of Y-Association in the table, and an $(I - 1)(J - 2)$ degree-of-freedom residual component, $X^2(Y)$, measuring all other kinds of non-independence.

Taking "0" to denote the independence model (i.e. the zero association model), and "Y" for the model of Y-Association, we have:

$$X^2(0) = X^2(0|Y) + X^2(Y) \qquad (4.7)$$

or, X^2 (independence) $= X^2$ (Due to Y-Association) $+ X^2$(residual)

Note that the $X^2(0|Y)$ component assesses the extent to which the Y-Association in the table is statistically significant. Note also that since $X^2(Y) = X^2(0) - X^2(0|Y)$ if the $X^2(Y)$ residual chi-square is found to be *not* significant, we may conclude that the Y-score alone is sufficient to explain all of the non-independence in the table. In this case, we may say that the Y-Association model fits the data. Thus, eq. (4.7) partitions the independence chi-square statistic into a component associated with the significance and a residual component associated with the fit of the Y-Association model:

$$X^2 \text{ (independence)} = X^2 \text{ (significance of } Y\text{-Model)} + X^2 \text{ (fit of } Y\text{-Model)}$$

The examples discussed below, will serve to contrast the test for independence with the test for (the lack of) Y-Association. For each of these examples we analyze a specific table in depth. For the first example, we will see that the former test is highly significant but the latter is *not* significant. For our second example, the reverse is true.

Following these examples, we then perform an ordinal CHAID analysis of RESP3 utilizing all of the predictors in the SUBSCRIBE dataset and contrast the results with those from the traditional CHAID analysis described earlier, where the dependent variable was treated as if it were nominal.

Example 1 KIDS *by* RESPONSE

Table 4.6 Analysis of the 2 × 3 table KIDS by RESPONSE

(a) Observed and expected frequency counts under Y-Association and Independence

Known presence of kids	Model	Paid	*RESPONSE* Unpaid	Non-response	Average score	Total n
Yes	Saturated	41	75	6,195	– $0.003	6,311
	Y-Association	33.4	36.0	6,241.5	– 0.003	6,311
	Independence	37.2	35.3	6,238.5	0.019	6,311
No	Saturated	437	378	73,914	$0.021	74,729
	Y-Association	444.6	417.0	73,867.4	0.021	74,729
	Independence	440.7	417.7	73,870.5	0.019	74,729
Total		478	453	80,109	0.019	81,040

(b) Observed and expected row percents under Y-Association and Independence

Known presence of kids	Model	*RESPONSE* Paid (%)	Unpaid (%)	Non-response (%)	Total %
Yes	Saturated	0.65	1.19	98.16	100
	Y-Association	0.53	0.57	98.90	100
	Independence	0.59	0.56	98.85	100
No	Saturated	0.58	0.51	98.91	100
	Y-Association	0.59	0.56	98.85	100
	Independence	0.59	0.56	98.85	100

(c) Analysis of association for table of KIDS by RESPONSE

Model	Likelihood X^2	d.f.	p-value
Independence	38.33	2	< 0.001
Due to Y-Association	0.46	1	> 0.05
Residual	37.87	1	< 0.0001

For this example, we consider the 2 × 3 table of KIDS by RESPONSE in Table 4.6. The conditional expectation obtained for each household in which children under 18 are present is – $0.003, compared to $0.019 for those households in which children are not known to be present. We may take the difference in average values between these two household groups as a measure of the Y-Association in the table (– 0.003 – 0.019 = – 0.022). Despite the small amount of Y-Association that is evident in the table, the test for independence is strongly rejected ($X^2(0) = 38.3$ with 2 d.f.; $p < 0.001$).

Let P_{11} and P_{21} denote the conditional probability of a paid subscription among households with children and other households respectively. Similarly, let P_{12} and P_{22} denote the corresponding probabilities of an unpaid subscription.

The test for independence may be expressed by the following two 1-degree-of-freedom restrictions:

$$H_0 : P_{11} = P_{21} \quad \text{and} \quad P_{12} = P_{22} \tag{4.8}$$

If we examine the sample proportions we find that the proportion within each household group who obtain a *paid* subscription is approximately the same ($p_{11} = p_{21} = 0.6\%$) but households with children are substantially more likely to result in an *unpaid* subscription ($p_{21} = 1.2\%$ while $p_{22} = 0.5\%$. Although the first difference in proportions is negligible, the latter difference is large enough to reject independence based on the 2 degrees-of-freedom test.

As mentioned earlier, there are many equivalent ways to formulate the test for independence. In eq. (4.8), we formulated it in terms of the two 1-degree-of-freedom-tests. Alternatively, we could have formulated it in terms of the following 1-degree-of-freedom-tests:

$$H_0: P_{11} + P_{12} = P_{21} + P_{22} \tag{4.9}$$

and
$$P_{11}/(P_{11} + P_{12}) = P_{21}/(P_{21} + P_{22}) \tag{4.10}$$

Equation (4.9) above specifies that the conditional probability of requesting a subscription is the same for households with and without children. Equation (4.10) states that among those households who request a subscription, the probability of paying is identical for those with and without children. The test for independence is equivalent to the occurrence of both of these restrictions.

Examining the sample proportions which correspond to the terms in equations (4.9) and (4.10), we see that households with children are *more* likely than those without children to request a subscription (1.8% vs. 1.1%), and among those who do, *less* likely to pay for it (45% vs. 67%). Thus, again it should not be surprising that the hypothesis of independence is rejected.

Next, we shall focus only on that part of the non-independence which is due to Y-Association. The null hypothesis states that the Y-Association is nil; that is, the conditional expectation (profitability) is the same among households with and without children:

$$H_Y: \mu_1 = \mu_2 \tag{4.11}$$

The test of eq. (4.11), summarized in Table 4.6c, yields $X^2(0|y) = 0.46$ with 1-degree-of-freedom, an extremely *non*-significant result. Thus, the degree of Y-Association in the KIDS × RESPONSE table is weak as suggested by the small difference between the means which we observed earlier. (For the details on how this chi-square test was performed, see Magidson, 1993.)

Table 4.6 also presents the maximum likelihood estimates for the expected counts under independence and under Y-Association. Note that the estimates under the Y-Association model preserve the observed mean scores while those estimated under the independence model do not. It turns out that maximum likelihood estimates under the Y-Association model will always preserve the observed mean scores for Y.

We conclude that known presence of children (i.e. the variable KIDS) is *not* important for predicting the expected Y-value of a response (i.e. the difference between the observed mean values between the two groups is found *not* to be significant). The test for independence, however, suggests that there are some strong differences between households with and without children regarding their likelihood to result in an *unpaid* response, but these differences are largely judged to be irrelevant since these groups do not differ with respect to their mean value for Y.

As shown in the Analysis of association table (Table 4.6c), only about 1 percent of the non-independence (as measured by the independence chi-square) is due to Y-Association (i.e. $0.46/38.33 = 1\%$).

Example 2: BANKCARD *by* RESPONSE   For the next example, we examine the relationship between known presence of a bank card (BANKCARD) and RESPONSE, for 2-person households. The data are summarized in Table 4.7.

Examining the observed sample proportions, we find that 2-person households who are known to own a bank card are more likely than other 2-person households to result in a *paid* subscription (1.5% vs. 0.9%) and about equally likely to result in an *unpaid* subscription (0.5% for each). Overall, however, as shown in the Analysis of association table (Table 4.7c), these differences are not sufficiently large to enable rejection of the independence hypothesis based on these data ($p = 0.056$).

Under the "Average score" column in Table 4.7a for the Y-Association model, we see that the value for the conditional expectation for 2-person households with bank cards is three times that of similar households *without* bank cards (i.e. $0.36 vs. $0.12). Thus, it is not surprising to find that the test of significance for (the lack of) Y-Association *is* rejected ($p = 0.018$).

Recall, from eq. (4.7), that while it is always the case that the chi-squared value for the test of Y-Association can not exceed the chi-squared value for independence, the number of degrees of freedom will always be $(I - 1)$ $(J - 2)$ fewer. From Table 4.7c we see that $X^2(0) = 5.75$, but with 2 degrees of freedom for testing independence is not significant. On the other hand, $X^2(0|Y) = 5.57$ with 1 degree of freedom for testing (the lack of) Y-Association, a statistically significant result. Approximately 97 percent of the non-independence here is due to Y-Association (i.e. $5.57/5.75 = 97\%$).

Table 4.7 Analysis of the 2 × 3 table BANKCARD by RESPONSE (for two-person households)

(a) Observed and expected counts under Y-Association and Independence

Known presence of BANKCARD	Model	Paid	Unpaid	RESPONSE Non-response	Average score	Total n
Yes	Saturated	26	9	1,649	$0.356	1,684
	Y-Association	25.8	7.9	1,650.3	0.356	1,684
	Independence	16.5	8.7	1,658.8	0.159	1,684
No	Saturated	84	49	9,423	$0.124	9,556
	Y-Association	84.2	50.1	9,421.7	0.124	9,556
	Independence	93.5	49.3	9,413.2	0.159	9,556

(b) Observed and expected row percents under Y-Association and Independence

Known presence of BANKCARD	Model	Paid (%)	Unpaid (%)	RESPONSE Non-response (%)	Total (%)
Yes	Saturated	1.54	0.53	97.92	100
	Y-Association	1.53	0.47	98.00	100
	Independence	0.98	0.52	98.50	100
No	Saturated	0.88	0.51	98.61	100
	Y-Association	0.88	0.52	98.59	100
	Independence	0.98	0.52	98.50	100

(c) Analysis of association for table of BANKCARD card by RESPONSE (for 2-person households)

Model	Likelihood X^2	d.f.	p-value
Independence	5.75	2	0.056
Due to Y-Association	5.57	1	0.018
Residual	0.18	1	> 0.05

Comparison of Results from Ordinal and Nominal CHAID Analyses

Next, we provide the comparison of CHAID analyses of the SUBSCRIBE data conducted using the standard test for independence and the test for *Y*-Association.

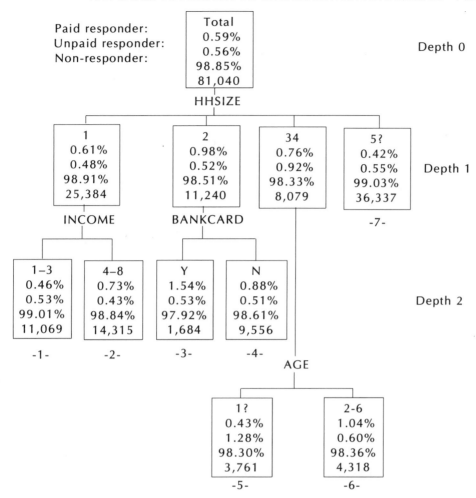

Figure 4.7 Results of CHAID based on trichotomous dependent variable
RESP2 and association algorithm: display = % distribution

Tree results from the ordinal CHAID analysis

Figures 4.7 and 4.8 provide the resulting tree diagrams from a CHAID
analysis of the SUBSCRIBE data analyzed earlier, but using the test for
Y-Association in place of the test for independence. The analysis was
performed using the SPSS PC+ CHAID 5.0 program using the METHOD =
ORDINAL option with the explicit scores ($35, − $7, − $0.15). We used the
program's option to display the tree diagram with average scores (the
default option under the ORDINAL method) as well as the option to display
the percentage distribution.

The resulting tree diagrams differ substantially from the results of the
earlier analyses. First, at depth 1, HHSIZE still turned out to be the most
significant predictor, but the categories of HHSIZE were merged to form
four rather than five subgroups. In particular, note that HHSIZE = "5" and

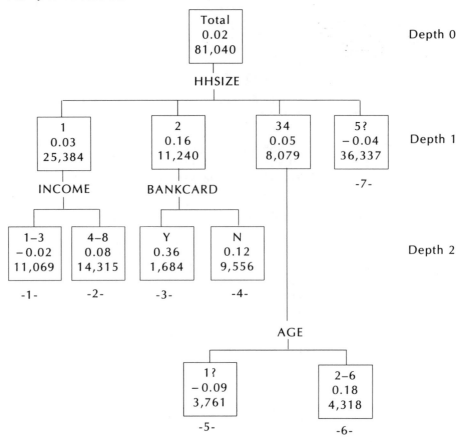

Figure 4.8 Results of CHAID based on trichotomous dependent variable RESP2 and association algorithm: display = average scores

HHSIZE = "?" are now merged. These groups have average scores of – $0.05 and – $0.04 respectively (see Figure 4.8).

Next, at depth 2 we again see very different results from those provided by the traditional CHAID analysis. Particularly noteworthy is that 2-person households were split into two segments based on whether or not they are known to own a bank card. The expected value for 2-person households who own a bank card is three times that of other 2-person households ($0.36 vs. $0.12). Note that this significant split ($p = 0.018$) was not identified by the traditional CHAID analyses.

Note also that HHSIZE = "1", which was not split on in the previous examples, is now split by INCOME. While the earlier analyses suggested that 1-person households are a homogeneous segment, having an expected gain of $0.03 per household, the current analysis now weeds out the bad performing part of this group. Specifically, the current analysis separates those 1-person households with lower incomes (< $15K), from higher income groups. The expected gain (actually, a loss) for the former is – $0.02, compared with $0.08 for the latter.

Table 4.8 Gains charts based on average scores (III)

(a) Selection array of response by market segment

Segment	Segment id	Individual segments		Expected gain	Index	Sample size	Cumulative		
		Sample size	% of total				% of total	Avg. score	Index
1	3	1,684	2.08	0.36	1871	1,684	2.08	0.36	1871
2	6	4,318	5.33	0.18	920	6,002	7.41	0.23	1186
3	4	9,556	11.79	0.12	651	15,558	19.20	0.16	857
4	2	14,315	17.66	0.08	398	29,873	36.86	0.12	637
5	1	11,069	13.66	-0.02	-128	40,942	50.52	0.08	430
6	7	36,337	44.84	-0.04	-213	77,279	95.36	0.02	127
7	5	3,761	4.64	-0.09	-461	81,040	100.00	0.02	100

Table 4.8   (*Contd.*)

(b)   Performance of model at different depths of selection

Depth of Selection (%)	Sample size	Expected gain	Index
5	4,052	0.25	1315
10	8,104	0.20	1186
15	12,156	0.17	915
20	16,208	0.16	839
25	20,260	0.14	751
30	24,312	0.13	692
35	28,364	0.12	650
40	32,416	0.11	577
45	36,468	0.09	499
50	40,520	0.08	436
55	44,572	0.07	378
60	48,624	0.06	328
65	52,676	0.05	287
70	56,728	0.05	251
75	60,780	0.04	220
80	64,832	0.04	193
85	68,884	0.03	169
90	72,936	0.03	148
95	76,988	0.02	129
100	81,040	0.02	100

Finally, note that a similar result occurs in the HHSIZE = "34" group which is now split by AGE. Younger people (< 25) and those where age is unknown have an expected gain (loss) of − $0.09 per household while all other ages are the second highest average score group at $0.18.

Overall, the results displayed in the tree diagram suggest that 2-person households along with those 3–4 person households in which the head of the household is older than 24 tend to be the best segments for future subscription promotions for this magazine. Segments having the lowest value are those containing households of unknown size and 3–4 person households where the head of the household is under 25 or the age is unknown.

Gains chart summary of the ordinal CHAID analysis

Comparing the new gains charts in Table 4.8 with the ones produced earlier show the increased gain, or lift in response, that would be produced. For the quantile chart in Figure 4.8b, we can see that the best 5 percent have an average gain of $0.25, compared to $0.21 and $0.16 obtained in the earlier analyses.

In summary, the tree diagrams and gains charts provide clear summaries of the best performing and the worst performing segments based on a nominal or ordinal CHAID analysis. Tree diagrams display the conditional distribution of the dependent variable or the average expected gain. The gains chart can be used to determine how deep into one's file one can profitably mail.

For the analysis of RESP3, the traditional nominal analysis of the trichotomous variable RESP3 provided similar results as the analysis of RESP2 which ignored the important distinction between paid and unpaid responders. The ordinal analysis of RESP3, on the other hand, provided an improved segmentation.

In a response analysis where there are different categories of responders (e.g. paid vs. unpaid responders), who are differentially valued, the new ordinal algorithm will generally provide a much improved segmentation, which will allow one to achieve, on average, larger gains from one's marketing efforts.

Introducing Single-Factor Calibration (Y^*-Association)

In our earlier examples, we knew what scores should be used. In some cases, however, we may still wish to test for nonassociation (rather than independence), but may not know the scores to specify for the dependent variable.

For example, suppose we wish to predict whether the head of household is employed in a "white collar," "blue collar" or "other" occupation category (where "other" includes retired, student, farmer, military and unemployed). We believe that the score for blue collar should lie somewhere between the scores for white collar and other, but we do not know the actual scores to use. This example is considered further later.

As a second example, suppose we wish to assess the impact of an advertisement on consumers' attitudes toward a brand, as measured on a 5-point ordinal scale. If a score can be assigned to each of the $J = 5$ categories, the ad can be assessed by calculating a mean attitude score for the exposed and unexposed groups, and testing the difference. (Pre-treatment score differences can also be examined.)

In this second example, we might use the 5-point scale pre- measurement as an *instrument* to *calibrate* the post-measurement, and then use the resulting category scores to quantify both the pre- and post-scales. The tests for significance between the treatment and control groups in this case would be based on the $I - 1$ degrees of freedom for Y-Association plus an additional $J - 2$ degrees of freedom to take into account the fact that the outcome scores are derived from the baseline variable.

The calibration technique, implemented in SPSS CHAID 5.0/6.0, may be used to estimate one or more category scores for the dependent variable, by the method of maximum likelihood. In the case that all of the y-scores are unknown, estimation in CHAID is performed using Goodman's (1979) maximum likelihood algorithm for estimating his row and column effects model (the RC model). In the more general case where some of the y-scores are known but at least one is unknown, a new maximum likelihood algorithm, provided by Magidson (1992) may be used.

For notational clarity, we will utilize the asterisk superscript "*" to denote those scores which are estimated, and we will refer to the situation where at least one score is estimated as Y^*-Association. Thus, if the score for category j is free to be estimated, it will be denoted as y^*j.

The Y^*-Association model, may also be referred to as the single factor calibration model. In order to use this method, one needs to specify a second categorical variable, known as the "instrument," which is associated with the dependent variable whose scores are to be estimated. The maximum likelihood methods provide a test of whether the model fits the data, i.e. whether the scores and implied relative distances (between the categories) are consistent with the observed data.

As noted earlier, the chi-squared test of significance for Y-Association is assessed with $I - 1$ degrees of freedom. The test of significance for Y^*-Association is based on $I - 1 + M$ degrees of freedom where M is the minimum of J^* and $J - 2$, and J^* denotes the number of scores that are estimated.

Finally, we note that the significance tests for Y-Association and Y^*-Association, unlike the traditional test for correlation, require no assumption of normality. Rather, they employ maximum likelihood methods, based on the Poisson, multinomial or related distributions.

An alternative partitioning of the independence chi-square

As in eq. (4.7), the independence chi-square can be partitioned into a component due to Y^*-Association and a residual component:

$$X^2(0) = X^2(0 \mid Y^*) + X^2(Y^*) \tag{4.12}$$

The Y^*-Association model specifies that there is a single score vector which accounts for all of the non-independence in the $I \times J$ table formed by the I-category instrument and the J-category dependent variable. If the resulting score vector does not account for all of the non-independence (within the usual statistical limits), $X^2(Y^*)$ should be large. On the other hand, if the Y^*-Association model fits the data, $X^2(Y^*)$ should be small. The model fit is testable with $(I - 1)(J - 2) - M$ degrees of freedom.

Issues in dimensionality

Accounting for all of the non-independence in an $I \times J$ table may require up to $J - 1$ distinctly different (linearly independent) score vectors. The actual number of potential score vectors is the minimum of $J - 1$ and $I - 1$. When $J = 2$, the Y^*-Association model becomes saturated and the category scores will be completely determined by the standardizing constants which must be employed to identify the model. Since no scores are free to be estimated in this case, the model reduces to the Y-Association analysis, which in this case further reduces to the traditional analysis where the dependent variable is treated as nominal.

When $J > 2$ but $I = 2$, as in the case where $J = 2$, the Y^*-Association model becomes saturated. However, unlike the first case, the category scores are not determined by the standardizing constants. Rather, as long as each cell contains at least one observation, the scores are determined by a simple formula without the need to apply the iterative algorithm. (However, the maximum likelihood algorithm can still be used to obtain the correct scores.)

In either of these degenerate cases where the non-independence in the table is necessarily 100 percent explainable by a single (unique) score vector, the test for model fit will always show that the model fits the data perfectly (i.e. $X^2(Y^*) = 0$ with 0 d.f.).

It is useful to digress briefly in order to elaborate on the results from our earlier analysis of the KIDS by RESPONSE, and BANKCARD by RESPONSE tables, each of which utilized a dichotomous predictor variable. As noted above, since in both of these examples the table contains just 2 rows, there exists a *unique* set of RESPONSE scores that can account for all of the non-independence in the tables. These unique score vectors, say Y^* attainable from the KIDS by RESPONSE table, and Y^{**} for BANKCARD by RESPONSE, would be attained by the calibration technique.

Recall from Table 4.6 that in the KIDS by RESPONSE table, only about 1 percent of the independence chi-square (which measures the extent of non-independence) was accounted for by the score vector $Y = (\$35, -\$7, -\$0.15)$. Thus, it must be the case that the Y^*-scores (which must account for 100 percent of the independence chi-square) are very different from the Y-scores. Also recall from Table 4.7 that in the BANKCARD by RESPONSE table, about 97 percent of the independence chi-square was explained by the Y-scores. Hence, it must be that the Y-scores and Y^{**}-scores are very similar.

For the purpose of our earlier examples, we did not concern ourselves with the Y^* and Y^{**} scores because we wished to test hypotheses concerning our known Y-scores. The issue of calibration only comes up when one or more of the specific Y-scores are unknown.

Smoothed and unsmoothed calibration

Calibration in SPSS PC+ CHAID 5.0 may be performed in either a smoothed or unsmoothed form. In the smoothed form, the given ordering of the dependent variable categories is always preserved by equating scores from adjacent categories of the dependent variable that are out of order.[4] (Equating the scores for two or more categories of a dependent variable is formally equivalent to merging these categories into a single joint category; i.e. the distance between two categories having the same score, as measured by the difference between the scores, is zero.)

In the unsmoothed form, the given ordering may or may not be preserved. The unsmoothed form should be used when one believes that the dependent variable categories may be ordered in a meaningful way but is unsure about the ordering of one or more categories. In an exploratory analysis, a researcher may wish to examine the resulting scores (and the implied category ordering) from both forms of calibration (as well as the corresponding fit statistics), and either accept one or use them to determine how to modify some initial hypothesized set of scores.

When the dependent variable scores are obtained by the calibration process, the SPSS PC+ CHAID 5.0 program adjusts the degrees of freedom used with the chi-square test, taking into account the fact that the scores have been estimated based on a predictor variable. Thus, rather than $I - 1$ degrees of freedom, $(I - 1) + M$ degrees of freedom are used in the test for Y^*-Association. Similarly, when a smoothed calibration requires that categories of the dependent variable be merged, the number of degrees of freedom will be $(I - 1) + M'$, where M' is the minimum of the number of calibrated categories for which distinctly different scores have been estimated, and $J^* - 2$.

It should be noted that the above-mentioned adjustment in the number of degrees of freedom is theoretically correct when testing for association (non-association) between the dependent variable and the instrument. When testing for association (non-association) between the dependent variable and some other predictor variable, the adjustment is conservative.

To illustrate the calibration approach, three examples will be considered. In the first example, the dependent variable OCCUPATION (obtained from the SUBSCRIBE dataset) is calibrated based on AGE as the instrument. In the second example, data from a comparative assessment of four treatments for duodenal ulcer patients (Grizzle, Starmer and Koch, 1969) is reanalyzed, where OUTCOME is calibrated using TREATMENT as the instrument. In the final example, data from a discretized bivariate normal distribution is used to show how to estimate the endpoints when it is known that the inner categories are equally spaced.

Calibration of occupation

Table 4.9 Results of calibration of OCC and OCCUP

| Dependent variable | Category scores | | | | Model fit | |
	White collar	Blue collar	Other	Unknown	Chi-square	Degrees of freedom
OCC	100[a]	75	0[a]	N/A	6.4	5
OCCUP	100[a]	79	26	0[a]	858.5	10

[a] denotes that score is fixed for purposes of identification.

Table 4.9 presents the results of a smoothed calibration of the variable OCC (white collar, blue collar, other) using AGE as the instrument. For this example, the score for the blue-collar category does turn out to fall *between* white collar and other. If the scores did not preserve the category order, the smoothed calibration option would have automatically combined certain adjacent categories and equated the score. Note that the score for the "blue collar" category is 3 times closer to "white collar" category than the "other" category. The model fit indicates that the model *does* fit the data, so we accept these scores as unique (i.e. we accept the single factor calibration model; see e.g. Magidson, 1992, 1993).

Table 4.10a Table of TREATMENT by OUTCOME

TREATMENT	OUTCOME	(Side effects)		
(Operation)	Moderate	Slight	None	Total
GR (3/4)	16	38	53	107
HV (1/2)	12	40	58	110
AV (1/4)	13	23	68	104
DV (0)	7	28	61	96
Total	48	129	240	417

Source: Duodenal ulcer data: Grizzle, Starmer and Koch, 1969.

Table 4.10b Comparison of fitting various models to the duodenal ulcer data presented in Exhibit G1

Dependent variable	Model	Category scores			Tests of significance		
		Moderate	Slight	None	Chi-square	Degrees of freedom	p-value
OUTCOME	0	n/a	n/a	n/a	10.88	6	0.088
OUTCOME	$Y^*_{(unsmoothed)}$	77	100	0	8.02	4	0.091
OUTCOME	$Y^*_{(smoothed)}$	100	100	0	7.92	3	0.048
OUTCOME	CHAID	100	100	0	7.62	1	0.040[a]

[a] Bonferroni-adjusted p-value.

In general, the choice of the variable to be used as the instrument is important as different intruments will typically yield different score estimates. One should select a variable which is known to be related to (and hence predictive of) the dependent variable, and ideally, should be one that provides an acceptable model fit.

Table 4.9 also presents calibration results for the 4-category occupation variable OCCUP, defined earlier. In addition to the three categories of OCC, the OCCUP variable contains a fourth category, "unknown". The example with OCCUP was chosen to illustrate the situation where the smoothing feature would *not* be used, since one is unsure about the placement of the "unknown" category relative to the other categories.

For OCCUP, Table 4.9 shows the model fit is poor, which means that there may exist at least one additional set of relevant category scores for OCCUP which are linearly independent of those that are given in Table 4.9. Note that for the scores displayed in Table 4.9, again "blue collar" lies between "white collar" and "other", while the "unknown" category follows the "other" category.

Calibration of outcome of treatments for duodenal ulcer

Our next example is the 4×3 table of TREATMENT for duodenal ulcer patients by OUTCOME, given in Table 4.10a. The treatments differ with respect to the amount of the stomach that is surgically removed – GR: 3/4 resection, HV: 1/2 resection and vagotomy, AV: 1/4 resection and vagotomy, or DV: drainage and vagotomy only (Grizzle, Starmer and Koch, 1969).

Table 4.10b presents the results of various statistical tests to assess the efficacy of thee alternative treatments. The first row of that table shows that the test for independence could not be rejected at the 0.05 level. Row 2 of Table 4.10b shows that the test for Y^*-Association (unsmoothed) also finds no significant association. However, when the smoothed Y^*-Association model is estimated (see row 3 in Table 4.10b) we conclude that there *is* a significant difference among the different treatments ($p = 0.048$). (For a similar analysis of these data see Agresti, 1984, pp. 12–13.)

The result of a CHAID analysis which utilizes the smoothed calibration is summarized in row 4 of Table 4.10b. CHAID merged treatments GR and HV together, and also merged AV and DV together. The CHAID model concludes that surgical removal of 1/2 or 3/4 of the stomach is significantly more likely to result in side effects than removal of 1/4 or none of the stomach ($p = 0.040$), when performed together with the other medical procedures (drainage and vagotomy). The CHAID tree diagram is given in Figure 4.9.

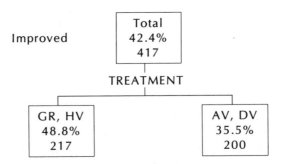

Figure 4.9 Results of CHAID analysis of the duodenal ulcer data

Estimation of endpoints

Finally, we consider the often occurring situation in marketing research where continuous variables are discretized. For example, a continuous latent construct may be measured in a survey on say a 5-point rating scale. Often, the distances between the first and second categories and/or between the last and next-to-last categories of discretized variables may be found to be greater than the distances between the inner categories. This phenomenon, known as a floor effect or a ceiling effect is due to the fact that the average score based on a tail of the distribution may contain extreme scores. In such a case, the commonly used Likert scale which assumes equal distances between categories may provide misleading results.

As a second example, INCOME on a survey may be categorized within $5,000 intervals beginning with $15,000 and continuing up to $50,000. The seven inner categories may be considered as equally spaced from each other, (i.e. the distance from the $15,000–$19,999 category, to the $20,000–$24,999 category, is the same as the distance from $25,000–$29,999 to $30,000–$34,999, etc.). But, the distance between $45,000–$49,999 and $50,000 + may be considerably larger, because the $50,000 + end category contains households whose income is extremely high. Thus, we may wish to estimate the relative distance between the last two categories relative to some constant hypothesized distance between the other adjacent categories.

As a further example, suppose persons are categorized according to their score on an exam. If the exam was exceptionally easy, there may be a number of people who received a perfect score. Thus, some persons would be included in the highest category who would have been included in a *much* higher category had there not been a "ceiling" effect. In this case, the distance between the two highest categories may be expected to be greater than that between other adjacent categories.

In this section we will show how the Y^*-Association model can be used to estimate the endpoints in a situation where it is believed that the middle categories are equally spaced from each other. It might also be used in more general situations to impute missing scores for any number of categories.

Table 4.11 Cross-tabulation of discretized bivariate normal variables X and Y with $\rho = 0.5$ and $N = 10,000$

X/Y	< 0	0–0.5	0.5–1	1–1.5	1.5–2	2+	Total[a]
< 0	3,335	850	505	221	71	20	5,002
0–1	1,355	765	645	396	178	75	3,414
1+	310	299	350	301	192	134	1,586
Total	5,000	1,914	1,500	918	441	229	10,002

[a] Cell entries are probabilities $\times 10^4$ rounded to nearest whole number. (Total differs from 10^4 because of rounding.) X and Y each have mean zero and variance one.

Table 4.11 cross tabulates two variables from a bivariate normal distribution where $\rho = 0.5$. For this cross-tabulation, variable $X = N(0, 1)$ has been discretized into 3 categories based on the cutoff points of 0 and 1. The second variable, $Y = N(0, 1)$, forms the 6 columns of the table, based on the cutoffs 0, 0.5, 1, 1.5, and 2. The cell entries are the actual probabilities multiplied by 10,000.

We begin by fitting the Y-Association model to these data, (i.e. $J^* = 0$) under the hypothesis that the categories of Y are equally spaced. Without any loss of generality, the standardization constants a and c were selected to scale Y so that the scores for the inner categories coincide with the midpoint of the ranges for these categories. The scores are summarized in Table 4.12 along with the model fit chi-square under this model, which turns out to be 49.6.

Table 4.12   Results from fitting various association models to the rounded expected counts presented in Exhibit H1

Model	< 0	0–0.5	0.5–1	1–1.5	1.5–2	2+	Chi-square	d.f.
			Category scores				*Model fit[a]*	
Y^*	− 0.77	0.25^b	0.74	1.23	1.75^b	2.48	2.25	4
$Y^*(1,6)$	− 0.77	0.25^b	0.75	1.25^b	1.75^b	2.50	2.29	6
Y	$− 0.25^b$	0.25^b	0.75	1.25^b	1.75^b	2.25^b	49.6	8

[a] The chi-square statistic is presented here as a *descriptive* measure of how closely the estimated expected counts under the hypothesized model fits the rounded expected counts given in Table 4.11.
[b] Denotes a fixed score. For the Y^* model, two scores were prespecified in order to fix the scale.

We next fit the Y^*-Association model where all scores for Y are estimated (i.e. $J^* = J = 6$). In this case, (again, without any loss of generality), we selected the standardization constants so that the scores for categories 2 and 5 were fixed at 0.25 and 1.75, respectively. This model fits much better than the Y-Association model, as evidenced by the chi-square of 2.25.

Our final model fixes the scores for the four inner categories in such a manner that they are equally spaced from each other, but the model allows the end category scores to be more (or less) distant than the inner categories. This model is denoted $Y^*(1, 6)$ in Table 4.12 to make it clear that category scores #1 and #6 were estimated. For this model, $J^* = 2$, since only the end scores are free to be estimated. For expository purposes (and without any loss of generality) we selected scores for the inner categories to be the same as those chosen for the Y-Association model.

The chi-square in Table 4.12 shows that model $Y^*(1, 6)$ fits the data almost as well as the unrestricted Y^*-Association model where all the scores were free to be estimated. We conclude that the inner categories, and only the inner categories, are equally spaced. The scores for the endpoints exhibit both a floor effect and a ceiling effect.

The results from Goodman (1985, 1991) show that such results will always occur when the data being analyzed obtains from a discretized bivariate normal distribution, with $\rho \neq 0$. This extremely important result suggests that the proposed models may be useful in analyzing not only true categorical variables, but also continuous variables that have been discretized.

Conclusion

The CHAID segmentation algorithm (Kass, 1980) may be viewed as a criterion-based approach to cluster analysis where all of the predictor variables are categorical. It represents an advance over its predecessor AID, as well as traditional clustering algorithms, when the resulting clusters are desired to differ with respect to a designated criterion.

The CHAID algorithm was recently extended by Magidson (1992) to handle a categorical dependent variable scaled by quantitative scores, Y. Some or all of the Y-scores may be pre-specified, the remainder being estimated by a maximum likelihood (ML) calibration technique. The approach involves replacing the chi-square test for independence with a more focused chi-square test for Y-association (or lack of Y-association).

The results of a CHAID analysis are summarized in the form of a tree diagram and gains charts which provide individual and quantile summaries of the best performing and the worst performing segments. Tree diagrams displaying both the conditional distribution of the dependent variable and the average score were shown to provide complementary information. The quantile gains chart can be used to compare different segmentations, as well as estimate the performance of the best $x\%$ of the segments.

Several applications utilizing the SUBSCRIBE dataset were used to illustrate various models and compare the results. We concluded that the traditional nominal analysis of the trichotomous variable RESP3 provided similar results as the analysis of RESP2, which ignored the important distinction between paid and unpaid responders. The ordinal analysis of RESP3, on the other hand, provided an improved segmentation. In general, a response analysis where there are different categories of responders (e.g. paid vs. unpaid responders), who are differentially valued, the new ordinal algorithm (as implemented for example in SPSS PC+ CHAID 5.0 or in SAS PROC SICHAID) should provide a much improved segmentation, which will allow researchers to perform more focused analyses.

Questions

1 Use Table 4.1 to reconstruct the observed counts in the cross-tabulation of RESP2 by HHSIZE. Use the likelihood ratio chi-square statistic to show that categories 2 and 3 are not significantly different and that categories 4 and 5 are not significantly different. Do you get the same results when you use the Pearson chi-square? Are categories 1 and 6 significantly different? The likelihood statistic is:

$$X^2 = 2\sum_i \sum_j f_{ij} \log_e(f_{ij}/\hat{F}_{ij})$$

2 Use the SPSS PC+ CHAID 5.0 program (or the SPSS 6.0 CHAID for WINDOWS program) to reproduce the result for the duodenal ulcer data. What happens if you make the treatment variable MONOTONIC instead of FREE? In general, how should you determine whether to specify a predictor to be free or monotonic?

3a   Suppose predictor B has I categories. Show that the number of ways it can be dichotomized is $(2^{I-1})^{-1}$

b   Suppose that only adjacent categories were eligible to be combined. Show that the number of ways that B can be dichotomized is $I - 1$.

c   How many ways can B be trichotomized if all categories were free to be merged?

d   How many ways can B be trichotomized if only adjacent categories can be merged?

4   Suppose predictor B has I categories. Now answer questions 3a–3d.

Notes

1   For example, any 4 categories could be merged together; or, any 3 categories could be merged together, and the remaining 2 categories could be merged, etc. See discussion problem #3.

2   The upper bound for the Bonferroni adjusted p-value has been implemented in the SPSS CHAID 5.0/6.0 computer program. See note 3.

3   SI-CHAID is a registered trademark of Statistical Innovations Inc., Belmont MA. The computer program is available as a stand alone package on the IBM PC and compatible computers, marketed and distributed by SPSS Inc. (SPSS CHAID 5.0/6.0) and on IBM mainframes (running under MVS, CMS or TSO operating systems) as a SAS Procedure, marketed and distributed directly by Statistical Innovations Inc. (PROC SICHAID).

4   If the dependent variable category scores are found not to be strictly monotonic, there are two different approaches for forming new categories that are properly ordered by combining an "out-of-order" category with the previous category – the "high to low" method and the "low to high" method.

The high to low method assumes that the correct ordering of scores is from high to low, and beginning with the first two categories, checks to see if the order is correct. If not, these categories are merged and a new score for the merged category is computed as the weighted average of the original scores. If the order of the original categories is found to be ordered correctly, scores for the second and third categories are compared to determine if their order is correct. If not, they are merged and again the score for the merged category is computed as the weighted average of the two scores that were out of order. The resulting score is then compared to the score of the previous category, and if it is found to be out of order, it is again merged. The procedure continues in this manner until all category scores are properly ordered.

The low-to-high method works similarly, except that a category is merged with the preceding category if and only if its score is lower. Estimated expected counts are then derived separately from the high-to-low and low-to-high solutions and chi-squared statistics are computed to determine which provides the better fit to the original observed counts. The SPSS CHAID 5.0/6.0 program will select the one having the closest fit to the observed data.

References

Agresti, Alan 1984: *Analysis of Ordinal Categorical Data*, New York: John Wiley & Sons.

Goodman, Leo A. 1969: On partitioning X^2 and detecting partial association in three-way contingency tables. *Journal of the Royal Statistical Society*, Series B, 31.

Goodman, Leo A. 1970: The multivariate analysis of qualitative data: interactions among multiple classifications. *Journal of the American Statistical Association*, 65, 226–56. Reprinted in L. Goodman (1978), *Analyzing Qualitative/Categorical Data*, ed. J. Magidson, Cambridge, Massachusetts: Abt Books.

Goodman, Leo A. 1979: Simple models for the analysis of associations in cross-classifications having ordered categories. *Journal of the American Statistical Association*, 74, 537–52. Reprinted in *The Analysis of Cross-Classified Data Having Ordered Categories*, 1984, Harvard University Press.

Goodman, Leo A. 1985: The analysis of cross-classified data having ordered and/or unordered categories: association models, correlation models, and asymmetry models for contingency tables with or without missing entries. *The Annals of Statistics*, 13(1), 10–69.

Goodman, Leo A. 1991: Measures, models and graphic displays in the analysis of cross-classified data. *Journal of the American Statistical Association*, 86, 1085–1138.

Grizzle, J. E., Starmer, C. F. and Koch, G. G. 1969: Analysis of categorical data by linear models. *Biometrics*, 25, 489–504.

Kass, Gordon 1980: An exploratory technique for investigating large quantities of categorical data. *Applied Statistics*, 29 (2), 119–27.

Magidson, Jay 1992: Chi-squared analysis of a scalable dependent variable, *Proceedings of the 1992 annual meeting of the American Statistical Association, Section on Statistical Education*.

Magidson, Jay 1993a: Multivariate statistical models for categorical data. Chapter 4 in R. P. Bagozzi (ed.), *Advanced Methods of Marketing Research*, Oxford: Blackwell.

Magidson, Jay 1993b: SPSS for Windows CHAID Release 6.0, Chicago: SPSS, Inc.

Sonnquest, J. A. and Morgan, J. N. 1964: The detection of interaction effects. Ann Arbor: Institute for Social Research, University of Michigan.

5

Cluster Analysis in Marketing Research

Phipps Arabie and Lawrence Hubert

Introduction

According to Hartigan (1975, p. 1), "Clustering is the *grouping of similar objects* [emphasis in original] . . . The word clustering is almost synonymous with classification." There is no *single* problem or purpose in the development and usage of cluster analysis, but whenever one encounters the phrases "homogeneous groups," "equivalence classes," or "multimodal data," clustering should be among the first of multivariate data analysis techniques used in attempting to identify such structures.

In this chapter, we will seek to update and extend the comprehensive review provided by Punj and Stewart (1983) and will even follow their outline at times. Limitations on length preclude our discussing or even citing all the relevant and meritorious literature. Whenever possible, we will simply refer the reader to other, current review chapters.

Substantive uses of cluster analysis in marketing

Punj and Stewart (1983) listed the most common applications of cluster analysis as: market segmentation, identifying homogeneous groups of buyers, development of potential new product opportunities, test market selection, and as a general data reduction technique. We consider these topics in turn before getting to some more recent patterns of usage.

Wind (1978a, b) presciently laid out the problems of market segmentation for decades to follow and noted that as an alternative to *a priori* segmentation (in which management or some other expert decides on a basis for segmentation, generally unassisted by data analysis), clustering is the principal recourse for identifying homogeneous subgroups of markets, consumers, or organizations. The variety of applicable methods of clustering and sophistication of their underlying assumptions has increased enormously (e.g. Mahajan and Jain, 1978) in response to the problems chronicled by Wind (1978a, b). Among the more noteworthy advances are segmentation based on price sensitivity (Elrod and Winer, 1982; Blozan and Prabhaker, 1984), a simultaneous approach to segmentation and market structuring by Grover and Srinivasan (1987), and a simultaneous approach to segmentation and estimation in the framework of conjoint analysis (Ogawa, 1987). (Many more references are given in a useful review by Beane and Ennis, 1987.) Researchers in industrial marketing have also shown increased interest in segmentation (Doyle and Saunders, 1985; Robles and Sarathy, 1986; de Kluyver and Whitlark, 1986). But to date, there has been insufficient progress on Nicosia and Wind's (1977, p. 102) call for industrial firms to pursue segmentation of buying centers (cf. Arabie and Wind, 1994), despite innovative work by Choffray and Lilien (1978, 1980a, 1980b).

A rather closely related area of applications of cluster analysis in marketing research concerns the identification of homogeneous groups of buyers, particularly according to benefit segmentation (Punj and Stewart, 1983). Noteworthy substantive bases toward which such strategies have been applied include: external information search patterns among purchasers of new automobiles (Furse, Punj, and Stewart, 1984), reactions to advertising copy schemes, flavor assortments, and other responses to heterogeneous benefit/feature preferences (Green, Krieger, and Schaffer, 1985), inferred choice routes and strategies (Currim and Schneider, 1991), human values systems (Kamakura and Mazzon, 1991), and brand loyal versus brand switching consumers (Grover and Srinivasan, 1992).

A third area of applications in Punj and Stewart's (1983) taxonomy, the development of potential new product opportunities, has seen Choffray and Lilien's (1980a, 1980b) efforts to bring industrial marketing up to par methodologically with its consumer counterpart. But the latter domain has in recent years seen such a shift of emphasis that its use of clustering in new product development will be discussed below under the heading of "market structure analysis."

Punj and Stewart's (1983) fourth area of applications seeks identification of relatively homogeneous and comparable test markets. It is assumed that management requires such test markets to be matched, so that inferences about the population can be attempted. In spite of a highly promising start (e.g. Green, Frank, and Robinson, 1967; G. S. Day and Heeler, 1971; Murphy and Tatham, 1979), this area has seen very little development in recent years. Also, few papers now fall in the miscellaneous, fifth category of using cluster analysis as a "general data reduction technique" (Punj and Stewart, 1983, p. 136). This decline probably attests to increasing sophistication in the marketing research community, the realization of what clustering can and cannot do well, and journal editors' refusal to publish straightforward applications.

Explicitly excluded from Punj and Stewart's (1983, p. 135) review were such applications of clustering and closely related techniques as "an alternative to multidimensional scaling (MDS) and factor analytic approaches to representing similarity data" (see chapters in this volume on these respective topics by DeSarbo, Manrai, and Manrai, and in the companion volume, *Principles of Marketing Research*, by Iacobucci). In the last decade, this area of applications has competed with market segmentation as the focus of heaviest usage and development of techniques tailored for marketing applications. For many of the stimulus domains whose mental representations have been intensively studied by experimental psychologists (e.g. perception of rectangles, similarities of animals, etc.), there is no counterpart to managerial significance or immediate practical implications. The choice of such stimulus domains typically reflects *a priori* theorizing about category structure, underlying dimensions, and embedding metrics, as well as the practical and easy presentation to the subjects making judgments (e.g. see Pruzansky, Tversky, and Carroll, 1982). In contrast, the majority of product domains to which marketing researchers apply clustering have significance, at least in principle, to management.

To the extent that such academically oriented explorations of stimulus domains have supplied answers, hypotheses, or more refined questions to experimental psychologists, the same relevant techniques might offer marketing researchers a better understanding of how consumers perceive, remember, judge, compare, and select among members of a product domain of managerial significance. Noteworthy papers in the marketing literature resulting from this strategy include Johnson and Fornell (1987), Glazer and Nakamoto (1991), and Hutchinson and Mungalé (1993).

In addition to such papers, a related tradition, even more distinctly marketing-oriented, falls under the rubric "competitive market structure analysis." The structure being studied is that of competing brands that can be regarded by consumers as substitutes for each other. Aspects of this process for which structure is sought include customer segments, products/brands, and usage/purchase situations. Managerial implications drawn from the portrayal of such structure include sales promotion and sales force allocation, price discounts, advertising, the design and development of new products, and even antitrust considerations. Because an excellent and comprehensive review (covering both substantive and methodological details) is given by DeSarbo, Manrai, and Manrai (1993; also see Rao, Sabavala, and Zahorik, 1982), we will give only a brief sketch here.

The tradition of research in market structure analysis that has led to so many developments in and applications of clustering effectively begins with Butler (1976) and the Hendry Corporation's scheme for analyzing consumer behavior for frequently purchased products. While seeking to depict patterns of brand switching and market partitioning inherent in aggregate data, this scheme results in a set of alternative *a priori* hierarchical structures[2] for the product domain, such as those found in Figure 1 (taken from Wind, 1982, p. 77). In this idealized representation of the margarine market, the top panel suggests that marketing strategy should give more emphasis to the form of the product than to competing brands, whereas the lower panel implies the opposite strategy. That is, the top panel implies that the form of the product is of primary concern to the consumer, while the lower panel implies a primary concern instead with the brand. As Wind

(1982, p. 77) notes, consumers in a brand-primary market should exhibit higher brand loyalty than those in a form-primary market. Introduction of a new product in a form-primary market should lead to less "cannibaliza-tion" than would be found in a brand-primary market.

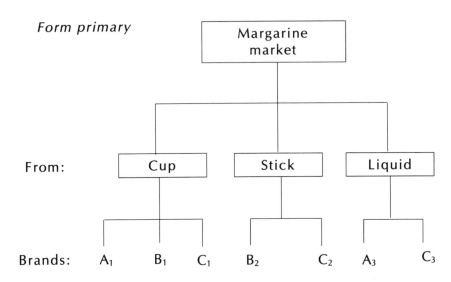

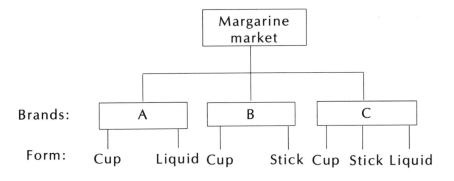

Figure 5.1 Form primary versus brand primary market structure
Source: Wind, 1982, p. 77

Rao and Sabavala (1981) made a major contribution by logically embedding the substantive questions underlying market structure analysis in the context of clustering. Those authors began with panel data and extracted from them a matrix, designated here as $S = \{s_{ij}\}$ $(i, j = 1, \ldots N,$ the number of products being considered), where s_{ij} denotes the number of panelists who purchased product i on the first choice occasion but switched to product j on the next occasion. Most forms of clustering ignore the diagonal entries (s_{ji}) in a matrix like S, but departures from symmetry (i.e., the fact that in general $s_{ij} \neq s_{ji}$, $i \neq j$) are a more persistent problem for most methods of clustering and of multidimensional scaling (see Appendix of Arabie and Soli, 1982, for a survey). Another problem of using the raw entries of S is undue influence of differential market shares among the N products. Rao and Sabavala (1981) therefore devised a transformation of the data that normalizes the entries in S and is interpreted as a "flow measure":

$$f_{ij} = \frac{s_{ij} \, s_{..}}{s_{i.} \, s_{j.}},$$

where $s_{i.}$ is the number of panelists who selected product i on the
first choice occasion,
$s_{j.}$ is the number of panelists who selected product j on the
second choice occasion, and
$s_{..}$ is the number of panelists in the homogeneous population.

Rao and Sabavala interpreted their measure as the ratio of the actual number of panelists switching from product i to j to the number expected under the traditional but arguable hypothesis of independence, both between the two consecutive choice occasions and by choice probabilities given by the marginals.

Rao and Sabavala (1981, pp. 85–6) then provided a tightly reasoned argument for why aggregate choice processes could be described using hierarchical clustering (considered below at length) applied to the F matrix.[3] A noteworthy point made by the authors is that brand switching between clusters should be least at the highest levels in a tree like that in Figure 5.1 and greatest at the lowest levels.

After the compelling work by Rao and Sabavala, the next logical steps were (a) dealing more adroitly with problems of nonsymmetry and normalization and (b) using types of clustering better suited than traditional hierarchical ones to the data at hand to reveal market structure. DeSarbo and De Soete (1984) used a different normalization[4] (dividing each entry by the product of the row and column arithmetic means, as suggested earlier by Rao, Sabavala, and Langfeld, 1977) and, more importantly, devised clustering methods explicitly designed to accommodate non-symmetric data quite elegantly (for a more recent approach, see DeSarbo, Manrai, and Burke, 1990).

In an impressive program of research, Shocker and Srivastava and their collaborators have made monumental contributions to objective (b). Srivastava (1981) emphasized the importance of usage-situational influences on consumers' perceptions of markets. Taking this point further, Srivastava and Alpert (1982) argued that multiple uses of a product, influenced by situational variables, cannot be faithfully represented by hierarchical clustering. Srivastava, Alpert, and Shocker (1984) used the ADCLUS model (Shepard and Arabie, 1979; see also Arabie and Carroll, 1980, and Arabie, Carroll, DeSarbo, and Wind, 1981) to portray market structure using *overlapping* clustering. Such clustering allows products to appear in more than one submarket, rather than being confined to exactly one cluster, as in Figure 5.2. Srivastava *et al.* (1984, p. 43) concluded:

> While hierarchical market structures may be developed based on measures of substitution-in-use, these structures may be misleading because products can be assigned to one and only one branch of a tree (each branch may be viewed as a submarket). This exclusivity requirement is incompatible with the basic reason for examining usage-situational influences. When products (within a set being examined) have multiple uses, each product may be competitive with different subsets of products, depending on the use (usage situation). Accordingly, overlapping clusters become more relevant. As illustrated in the previous section, the discrepancies between hierarchical and overlapping structures were salient in that the latter offered managerial insights – with attendant potential actions – which would not have been apparent otherwise.

In seeking a tighter logical connection between market structure analysis and the types of clustering employed to depict those structures, Shocker, Stewart, and Zahorik (1990, p. 128) noted: "Several papers reviewing the characteristics of various [clustering] algorithms and the issues related to their use already exist . . . Missing from these prior works is explicit discussion of the assumptions that various methods and techniques imply about the phenomena being represented, i.e., market structure." Shocker *et al.* (1990) discussed at the managerial level "options, conceptual issues, and problems that exist in dealing with MSA [market structure analysis]." A more technical and comprehensive discussion of the many techniques that have been developed for such analyses is given by DeSarbo, Manrai, and Manrai (1993). These two papers are strongly recommended.

Green and Srinivasan (1978) opened a new arena for clustering when they advocated segmentation of consumers by clustering them according to vectors of part-worth utilities derived from conjoint analyses. This recommendation led to a series of papers in which clustering methods (usually either partitioning or hierarchical) were used in further developments of conjoint analysis (Moore, 1980; Currim, 1981; Ogawa, 1987; Kamakura, 1988; Green and Krieger, 1991). Some of the methodological issues entailed in this development are considered by Green and Krieger (1985), Green and Helsen (1989), and Green and Srinivasan (1990, p. 8).

As the role of social network analysis becomes more conspicuous in marketing research (especially applied to buying centers; see Wind and Robertson, 1982), it is likely that cluster analysis will be used for many applications in this area (see Iacobucci and Hopkins, 1992, and Arabie and Wind, 1994, for overviews).

Readers seeking a bibliography of applications of clustering in marketing research should consult Dickinson (1990, pp. 784–796). An annual bibliography, not limited to the marketing literature, is published annually by the Classification Society of North America (W. H. E. Day, 1991) and often contains over 1,000 references relevant to clustering and related techniques of data analysis (e.g. MDS).

Misunderstandings of Clustering and Misuses of (Sometimes) Related Methods

Performing a cluster analysis requires using a method that explicitly and objectively seeks clusters. The data analyst should *not* try visually or manually to "define" clusters on the basis of a spatial representation of the products derived from such continuous models as principal components analysis (PCA), factor analysis, correspondence analysis, or spatial MDS (cf. Stewart, 1981, p. 53). Of course, one may refer to groupings and other spatial patterns in such a configuration of products, but it is misleading to elevate such groupings to the status of "clusters" and suggest that they have any reality other than visual. Such subjective clustering dates back to the early days of factor analysis and has empirically been undermined by Ling (1971) and by Baker and Hubert (1976, p. 877).

Another regrettable legacy from factor analysis, and practiced all too often in marketing research, consists of "tandem" cluster analyses. Concretely, a data analyst wanting to get a clustering of a set of products is faced with a products (rows) by attributes (columns) data matrix[5] and becomes concerned with either (a) non-independence of the columns (i.e. intercorrelations generally not equal to zero) and/or (b) an "excessive" number of columns. An all too common response is to run PCA or a related technique on the matrix, extract a few of the eigenvectors having the largest eigenvalues, and use this "reduced" matrix of components as input for clustering.

Concerning (a), it is difficult to imagine empirical data arising in the behavioral sciences that would have all columns mutually independent, and if one did encounter them, why consider running PCA, cluster analysis, or any other technique that by its very nature assumes that interdependencies are exactly what are to be portrayed? Apropos concern (b), if the cluster analysis is to be given a chance to reveal structure, why should that structure first be "filtered" through an incompatible, spatial model? Using both actual and simulated data, W.-C. Chang (1983) showed that using PCA to "reduce" data prior to running a cluster analysis discards relevant "distance" information. Still other statistical arguments are given by Gnanadesikan and Kettenring (1972) and by Dillon, Mulani, and Frederick (1989). DeSarbo, Jedidi, Cool, and Schendel (1990, p. 130) have also noted the number of fairly arbitrary decisions that must be made in the PCA stage of "tandem" cluster analyses. Each of these decisions can have an impact on what ultimately goes into and emerges from the cluster analysis.

The conclusion is straightforward: *"tandem" clustering is an outmoded and statistically insupportable practice.*

Relationships between some methods of clustering and some spatial models

In a classic result, Holman (1972) showed that error-free proximities data[6] corresponding to products in a low-dimensional Euclidean space are incompatible with the geometric structure (i.e., the ultrametric inequality; see below) characterizing most commonly used methods of hierarchical clustering. That is, such data can satisfy either the Euclidean spatial model without error in a low dimensionality or the ultrametric clustering model without error, but *not* both models simultaneously. But because empirical data rarely ever fit either model without error, the folklore of compatibility between relevant discrete and spatial models is still empirically useful; see Kruskal (1977) for an excellent discussion of the *complementary* interpretations often afforded by using both clustering and MDS on the same data sets. Such interpretations often show convex contours enveloping each cluster's constituent objects, which are also embedded in an MDS spatial solution. To date, there is no analytical demonstration to support the common expectation of convex clusters for either hierarchical or overlapping clustering. Some interesting but highly formal relationships between hierarchical clustering and Euclidean spaces have been revealed by Critchley (1986, 1988) and Critchley and Heiser (1988). Pruzansky *et al.* (1982) carried out a more empirically based program that sought diagnostics to determine whether a given proximities matrix was more suited toward certain types of discrete clustering models versus Euclidean spatial models. Two properties of the data sets those authors studied emerged as having predictive value: the skewness of the distribution of dissimilarities and the proportion of elongated triangles implicit in triads of interproduct dissimilarities.

A Taxonomy of Clustering Methods, Based on Admissible Overlap

The literature on the methodology of clustering is enormous, and the foci here will be on relevance to marketing and steering the reader toward current sources. For comprehensive overviews, see Hartigan (1975), Jain and Dubes (1988), Arabie and Hubert (1992, 1994), as well as other chapters in Arabie, Hubert, and De Soete (1994). While there are many ways to organize that literature, the one proposed here takes its inception from the substantive emphasis Srivastava, Shocker, and their colleagues placed on patterns of *overlap* in market structure analysis.

But a digression is first necessary to introduce some terminology to describe types of data. We will make extensive use of Tucker's (1964) terminology, distinguishing between "ways" and "modes". Consider two matrices, one of which has N rows and the same number of columns, with entries depicting direct judgments of pairwise similarities for all distinct pairs of the N products, and the other matrix with N rows of products and M columns of attributes of the products. Although both matrices have two *ways* (viz., rows and columns), the former is said to have one mode because both its ways correspond to the same set of entities (i.e., the N products). But the matrix of products by their attributes has two disjoint sets (and thus two *modes*) of entities corresponding to the ways; usually a clustering representation is sought for only one of the two ways. For a one-mode two-way matrix (e.g., for brand switching), an additional consideration is whether conjugate off-diagonal entries (s_{ij} and s_{ji}) are always equal, in which case the matrix is symmetric; otherwise it is non-symmetric. One-mode two-way data often take the form of "proximities" (Shepard, 1962), "similarities" or "dissimilarities" data. The frequently encountered problem of converting a two-way two-mode to a two-way one-mode matrix, as required for input by many forms of clustering, will be considered below.

Clustering by partitioning methods

For many substantively motivated users of clustering, the idea of maximal homogeneity within subgroups (clusters) of products and maximal heterogeneity between or across clusters suggests partitioning. Informally speaking, a partition is a clustering in which each of the N products belongs to exactly one of the m clusters ($m \leq N$), so that there is no overlap between any pair of clusters, and null clusters are not allowed. (Recall that each horizontal cross-section of Figure 5.1 is a partition.) The user is required to specify m (or its range) at the start of the analysis. Because the number of distinct partitions of N objects into m clusters increases approximately as $m^N/m!$, attempting to find a globally optimum solution (regardless of the measure of goodness-of-fit employed) is usually not computationally feasible. Thus, a wide variety of heuristic approaches (capably reviewed both by Belbin, 1987 and by Jain and Dubes, 1988, pp. 89–117) have been developed to find local optima.

Hartigan (1975, p. 102) summarized differences among approaches as stemming from "(i) the starting clusters, (ii) the movement rule [i.e. transferring objects among clusters], and (iii) the updating [of goodness-of-fit] rule." Within marketing research, the most commonly used method of partitioning is the Howard–Harris (1966) method, applicable to two-way two-mode interval scale data. This method enjoys greatest usage in the Marketing Department at Wharton and by researchers trained there. The most readily available description of it is given by Carroll (1973), and the program is not included in any widely distributed software package. Another heavily used (e.g. Grover and Srinivasan, 1992) partitioning approach is given by numerous variants of MacQueen's (1967) k-means method,[7] which is implemented in widely available software packages (e.g. SYSTAT[8]: Wilkinson, 1992).

Because the results of partitioning methods tend to be extremely dependent on initial configurations (cf. Hartigan's point (i) above), Punj and Stewart (1983, p. 145) recommended using such hierarchical methods as Ward's (1963) or average-link to get an initial configuration for a partitioning method. Nearly a decade later, that recommendation still seems like a good one, but we would advise additionally using configurations from other clustering methods and/or random configurations.

Hierarchical clustering

In this approach to clustering, if A and B are two distinct clusters, then exactly one of the following must hold: $A \subset B$, $B \subset A$, or $A \cap B = \emptyset$. That is, if there is any overlap at all between any pair of clusters, one must be entirely nested within the other. Except for Ward's (1963) method, these methods assume one-mode two-way data, typically, measures of similarity or dissimilarity. Most implementations do not allow for non-symmetric data, and the scale type assumed is usually interval, but single- and complete-link only use ordinal properties of an input matrix. As noted in the section immediately preceding this one, an inverted tree representation of an hierarchical structure consists of a succession of partitions, bounded at the top by the trivial partition in which all products are lumped together and at the bottom by the equally trivial cluster in which each product is its own (singleton) cluster. Some algorithms (called "divisive") start with the lumper cluster and work down to the finest partition consisting of all singletons, while others (called "agglomerative") work in the reverse direction. Although the distinction between agglomerative versus divisive was once regarded as fundamental (with the latter in disfavor), Jardine and Sibson's (1971; also see Hubert, 1973) observation that some methods of hierarchical clustering could be implemented by *either* agglomerative or divisive algorithms relegated that dichotomy to an almost metaphysical status from most users' perspectives and led to the realization that the really important distinction is between a given *method* and possible varieties of *algorithms* for producing (identical) output. While most algorithms suitable for pencil and paper approaches are agglomerative, computer-oriented ones for large data sets tend not to be.

Consider the one-mode two-way matrix $\Delta = \{\delta_{ij}\}$ of (derived) dissimilarities among fifteen breakfast foods, as shown in Table 5.1 (the source of these data[9] gives further background details: Green and Rao, 1972, p. 26). Taking an agglomerative approach to finding the first cluster is easy. The smallest dissimilarity in the matrix is 5.52, corresponding to the row for buttered toast and jelly and the column for toast and marmalade. As soon as we consider that dyad of products as one entity, the next question is to redefine the numerical dissimilarities between $\{BTJ, TMd\}$ and each of the

Table 5.1 Dissimilarity data for breakfast food items

	TP	BT	EMM	JD	CT	BMM	HRB	TMd	BTJ	TMn	CB	DP	GD	CC
BT	59.13													
EMM	62.42	30.79												
JD	43.64	83.89	82.37											
CT	36.01	44.15	57.76	65.46										
BMM	60.21	60.94	23.80	53.33	64.11									
HRB	78.01	27.02	26.85	93.71	72.92	50.49								
TMd	34.57	36.36	52.44	55.35	32.87	59.96	64.23							
BTJ	32.10	32.29	50.18	49.11	36.29	55.83	61.55	5.52						
TMn	61.52	8.49	25.29	85.64	48.96	58.73	31.52	37.94	38.32					
CB	51.26	78.35	72.21	32.68	21.65	47.42	78.21	64.23	61.30	80.14				
DP	46.65	84.55	76.14	21.40	49.30	46.98	83.70	59.80	57.48	86.42	20.31			
GD	55.17	83.82	78.07	7.83	55.70	55.00	88.85	60.38	65.85	83.86	23.33	20.54		
CC	53.67	83.01	70.68	30.56	49.87	47.08	78.13	63.77	65.56	84.24	23.10	10.70	24.76	
CMB	72.17	48.13	21.87	73.62	62.49	15.25	33.37	63.52	64.49	52.93	58.26	62.46	66.77	54.17
	TP	BT	EMM	JD	CT	BMM	HRB	TMd	BTJ	TMn	CB	DP	GD	CC

Food item	Plotting code used in figures
1. Toast pop-up	TP
2. Buttered toast	BT
3. English muffin and margarine	EMM
4. Jelly donut	JD
5. Cinnamon toast	CT
6. Blueberry muffin and margarine	BMM
7. Hard rolls and butter	HRB
8. Toast and marmalade	TMd
9. Buttered toast and jelly	BTJ
10. Toast and margarine	TMn
11. Cinnamon bun	CB
12. Danish pastry	DP
13. Glazed donut	GD
14. Coffee cake	CC
15. Corn muffin and butter	CMB

Source: Green and Rao (1972, p. 26).

remaining thirteen products. Let $d_{(ij),k}$ be the new measure between a newly formed cluster (consisting in the present case of $\{BTJ, TMd\}$, more generally of the products/clusters subsumed in the new cluster) and any other entity external to that cluster (either a singleton or another cluster; in the present case, any of the thirteen products not in the only cluster formed to date). For the first cluster of the Green–Rao data, the newly defined distance may be written as:

$$d_{\{BTJ, TDd\}, k} = f(\delta_{BTJ,k}, \delta_{TMd, k}). \tag{5.1}$$

If the data in Δ are regarded as ordinal, then min or max is an obvious choice for the function f. In the former case, the implication is that distance between the cluster and all external entities is given by the (single) smallest dissimilarity value, and the method of clustering is called single-link.[10] If f is declared to be the maximum, then all entities with the newly formed cluster are linked to the external entity at a threshold defined by the maximal numerical value represented by the right side of (5.1). The method is thus called complete-link.[11] The rows and columns corresponding to the subscripts in (5.1) are then updated according to (5.1) and the user's implicit selection of the function f. Regardless of the function chosen, the next cluster is then identified by finding the smallest dissimilarity (or largest similarity[12]) in the iteratively updated matrix. The process is continued iteratively until every product is in the same (lumper) cluster, and the entire matrix Δ has been transformed into a matrix $\mathbf{D} = \{d_{ij}\}$ defined completely according to the $N - 1$ values (if no ties occur) that identify the successive clusters formed by the iterative process.

In marketing and other behavioral sciences, the most popular choices for f tend to be max (i.e. complete-link) and arithmetic average (possibly weighted), and numerous evaluations have supported their usage (e.g. Baker, 1974; Baker and Hubert, 1975; Milligan, 1981). For a wide range of choices of the updating rule given in simplified form in (5.1), the sequence of $N - 1$ values (if no ties occur) will be monotone increasing for dissimilarities or decreasing for similarities data (see Ohsumi and Nakamura, 1994). In such cases, it can be shown that these values (in the matrix $\mathbf{D}$) obey the ultrametric inequality:

$$d_{ij} \leq \max (d_{ik}, d_{jk}) \text{ for all } k,$$

where i, j, and k are members of the set of N products, and d_{ij} is the distance between products i and j. This inequality is strictly stronger than the triangle inequality, and the $N - 1$ numerical values like 5.520 that result from choosing the successive clusters to be formed and the iterative application of (5.1) qualify as (ultrametric) distances. Just as MDS iteratively transforms Δ to satisfy the triangle inequality, hierarchical clustering transforms Δ to $\mathbf{D}$, with the latter satisfying the ultrametric inequality. The dendrogram and ultrametric values resulting from applying complete-link (as implemented in

SYSTAT; Wilkinson, 1992) to the Green–Rao data are given in Figure 5.2 (see Green & Rao, 1972, p. 35, for a different formatting of the same result). Note that, characteristic of hierarchical clustering, all "internal" nodes in the dendrogram correspond to clusters and not to products.

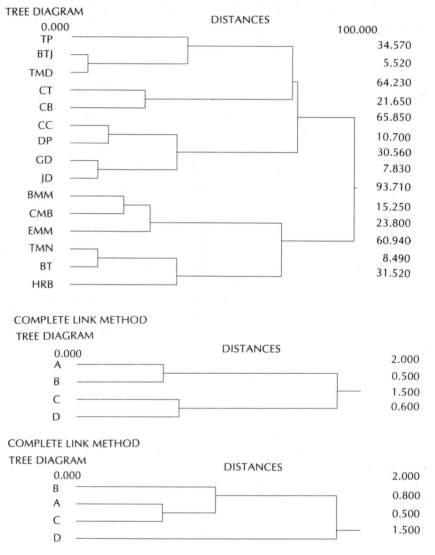

Figure 5.2 Complete-link clustering solution for the Green-Rao (1972, p. 26) data

As presented here, hierarchical clustering is characterized by algorithms; nothing has been said about either underlying models or optimization of objective functions. The latter can and have been "contrived for the occasion" (Hartigan, 1975, p. 199), and much the same can be said for models. Consideration of these topics goes beyond the scope of this chapter; see Gordon (1987, 1994) for excellent and comprehensive reviews of such issues in hierarchical clustering.

As a more intuitive alternative to the ultrametric, the path length or "additive" metric entails fitting numerical values to all the links or arcs connecting pairs of products. The distance between a pair of products is found by taking the shortest path from the node representing one product to that for the other. In such dendrograms, internal nodes can correspond either to products or to clusters, and fitting the model leads to no preferred root for the resulting tree. Developments using this metric have been so numerous that they could claim a chapter of their own (e.g. Carroll, 1976; Carroll, Clark, and DeSarbo, 1984; De Soete, Carroll, and DeSarbo, 1986, 1987; De Soete, DeSarbo, Furnas, and Carroll, 1984a, 1984b; see Carroll and De Soete, 1994, for an overview).

For data sets of the type typically encountered in market structure analysis (but not for survey data like those commonly used in market segmentation), hierarchical clustering tends to be inexpensive to run. This claim may seem surprising since a sequence of as many as $N - 1$ partitions are being formed, and for most of these, the number of possibilities is immense. What must be noted is that hierarchical clustering, like other stepwise multivariate techniques, is seeking only a *local* optimum as it considers a very small subset (viz., those conforming to a nesting pattern) of all possible solutions. Another common oversight is the possibility of non-uniqueness. With the exception of single-link, most methods of hierarchical clustering break ties arbitrarily when they occur, so that the solution the user sees is only one of a class of possibly equally good fitting solutions. To our knowledge, only NT-SYS[13] (Rohlf, 1992) warns users of such non-uniqueness when it arises. We have noted these two concerns with hierarchical clustering because they are most easily understood in that context, but the two problems arise in fitting a wide class of discrete models (cf. Arabie and Carroll, 1980, pp. 226–7).

With the exception of some of the references on path length approaches to hierarchical clustering, the discussion in this section has generally assumed that the input data at hand are one-mode two-way or can be converted to that form to meet the requirements of hierarchical clustering algorithms. A very important exception, especially in marketing research, is Ward's (1963) method. It assumes as input a two-mode two-way matrix of interval scale data, and that the user seeks a clustering representation for only one of the modes (e.g. products in a products × attributes matrix). (A user seeking clustering solutions for each of the modes in two-or higher-mode matrix should see De Soete, DeSarbo, Furnas, and Carroll, 1984a, 1984b, and Arabie, Hubert, and Schleutermann, 1990). Typically programmed as an agglomerative algorithm (e.g., Wishart, 1969), Ward's method seeks at each step to form a new cluster leading to the least "error sum of squares". As such, the method enjoys an optimization-based history from its inception and is especially useful in marketing research because it ostensibly obviates the step of preliminary computation to obtain a one-mode matrix. Ward's method is available in numerous statistical software packages (e.g. SYSTAT), but the preprocessing normalization empirically found to be most appropriate (Milligan and Cooper, 1988; see discussion below) for the mode not clustered generally requires extra effort from the data analyst. Reassurances about the comparative performance of Ward's (1963) method are given by Klastorin (1985), and Ogawa (1987) has innovatively provided an extension, tailored to use with conjoint analysis.

Overlapping clustering

As the name suggests, this type of clustering allows more general patterns of overlap than the nesting that is characteristic of hierarchical clustering. The model most commonly used for two-way one-mode interval scale data is ADCLUS (Shepard and Arabie, 1979; also see Arabie et al. 1981) and for three-way two-mode data (as in subjects × products × products) the INDCLUS[14] (Carroll and Arabie, 1983) generalization. Those models, corresponding algorithms, and their applications have been reviewed elsewhere (Arabie et al., 1987; Arabie and Hubert, 1992, 1993) and will thus not be considered here. For substantive developments, the papers cited earlier by Shocker, Srivastava, and their collaborators should be consulted, as well as Wind (1982, pp. 103–4). Important methodological developments include DeSarbo (1982) and Grover and Srinivasan (1987, 1989); Price (in press) gives a caveat on software.

Mixture models

The patterns of overlap considered thus far can be discretely characterized: none for partitions, all-or-none for hierarchical clustering, and for overlapping clustering, the number of products in the intersection of any pair of clusters is an integer (including zero, for ADCLUS). In contrast, mixture models allow continuous degrees of overlap because an underlying continuum is assumed to give rise to distinct but continuous clusters or subpopulations, corresponding to different distributions. Sampling from such a space produces a "mixture" from the clusters and the problem of estimating parameters characterizing those clusters/distributions. Since the seminal paper of Wolfe (1970), interest in this approach has steadily increased (e.g. Kamakura and Mazzon, 1991; Rust, Kamakura, and Alpert, 1992), and McLachlan and Basford's (1988) laudable *Mixture Models: Inference and Applications to Clustering* attests to the strength of this research tradition. Because many recent developments in marketing are framed in the context of latent class models (e.g. Carroll, De Soete, and Pruzansky, 1989), Dillon's chapter in this volume should be consulted for background.

Other approaches to and aspects of clustering

The concept of overlap has no meaning when one considers network approaches to clustering (Hutchinson, 1989; Klauer and Carroll, 1989,

1991), which fit path length distances to ordinal one-mode two-way matrices. Unfortunately, software is not generally available for these approaches. The same problem exists for another highly promising and general method, Carroll and Pruzansky's (1980) "hybrid" approaches, which use alternating least squares techniques to fit one or more trees as well as a spatial (MDS) model simultaneously to a one-mode two-way interval scale matrix.

As marketing researchers have become more acquainted with newer approaches to clustering, methodologists have increased the flexibility and versatility of earlier models and associated algorithms. For example, the substantive emphasis on "usage situations" that Srivastava and Shocker and their collaborators have so profitably pursued translates directly into a call for "higher-way" (i.e. three or more, so that usage situations can be accommodated as one or more ways of the design) models and algorithms, as provided, for example, by Carroll, Clark, and DeSarbo (1984) and De Soete and Carroll (1988, 1989).

Marketing methodologists have also devised new statistical procedures that incorporate clustering to answer traditionally important practical problems that applied statisticians have ostensibly overlooked. An example is clusterwise linear regression, which simultaneously clusters observations into a user-specified number of groups and estimates the corresponding regression functions' coefficients, while optimizing a common objective function (DeSarbo and Cron, 1988; Kamakura, 1988; DeSarbo, Oliver, and Rangaswamy, 1989; Wedel and Steenkamp, 1991). Another such development is Kamakura's clusterwise multinomial logit models (Kamakura and Agrawal, 1990; Kamakura, 1992).

The most protracted methodological effort in clustering during the last decade has been in the development of Stochastic Tree UNfolding (STUN) models, fitted to paired comparisons (i.e. dominance or preference, rather than dis/similarities) data, and using either ultrametric or path length distances (Carroll, DeSarbo, and De Soete, 1987, 1988, 1989; DeSarbo, De Soete, Carroll, and Ramaswamy, 1988, Carroll and De Soete, 1990, 1991).

Researchers seeking to be *au courant* in methodological developments in clustering, with emphasis on marketing research, should regularly consult the *Journal of Classification, Journal of Marketing Research*, and *Marketing Science*.

Practical Problems and Issues

Normalization of variables for hierarchical clustering

Whether a two-mode two-way matrix (e.g. products × attributes or variables) is being analyzed with Ward's (1963) technique or first converted to a one-mode matrix, using Euclidean distances between all pairs of columns and then is analyzed with a different hierarchical method, the question arises of whether and how to normalize the columns (variables) to make them more commensurable (cf. Morrison, 1967). The option most readily available in most statistical software is standardization of each column to have a mean of zero and variance of unity. But a very important result by Milligan and Cooper (1988) shows empirically that, according to ability to recover known clustering structure, the best of a considerable variety of normalization strategies is instead to divide each variable by its range (possibly after first subtracting the minimum value occurring prior to normalization). This finding held for complete- and single-link, average-link (UPGMA: Sokal and Michener, 1958), and Ward's (1963) methods.

Choosing a dis/similarity measure

For many two-mode matrices, using Ward's (1963) technique to obtain a clustering representation of one of the modes ostensibly sidesteps the problem of selecting a measure of dis/similarity such as Euclidean distance (however, a squared Euclidean distance is implicitly used by Ward's method; see Wishart, 1969) or some measure of correlation to convert the data at hand to a one-mode matrix (Green and Rao, 1969). But if the data are binary, that strategy is not a good one. The two most popular measures in this case are Jaccard's and the "simple matching coefficient" (see Heltshe, 1988; Snijders, Dormaar, van Schuur, Dijkman-Caes, and Driessen, 1990), both of which are available in NT-SYS. (See Arabie and Hubert, 1992, pp. 175–7, for an overview of this topic.) For the user burdened with mixed data (i.e. arising from different scale types), Gower (1971) provided a valuable if under-utilized coefficient, which Rohlf has said (personal communication) will be included in a future version of NT-SYS.

Cluster validity

Even if one only considers using hierarchical clustering, different methods will generally produce different solutions based on the same input data. The question naturally arises as to whether the clusters have "reality" or validity vis-à-vis the data (cf. Hartigan, 1975, pp. 202–3; Dubes and Jain, 1979). According to Wind (1978b, p. 328), "The validity of segmentation research is by far the most crucial question facing management." Jain and Dubes (1988, Ch. 4) provide a useful summary of strategies for validation: "*External criteria* measure performance by matching a clustering structure to a priori information... *Internal criteria* assess the fit between the structure and the data, using only the data themselves... *Relative criteria* decide which of two structures is better in some sense, such as being more stable or appropriate for the data" (emphasis in the original, p. 161).

Among the issues most commonly investigated in studies of cluster validation are (a) selection of indices of cluster structure and their distributions and (b) determining the appropriate number of clusters. The first problem appears to have been solved. Concluding a comparative study of the coefficients regarded for either theoretical or empirical reasons to be forerunners for measures of relatedness between partitions in cluster validation, Milligan and Cooper (1986, p. 457) stated: "it would appear that of the five indices the Hubert and Arabie [1985] adjusted Rand measure seems to be the index of choice for clustering validation research."

Milligan and Cooper (1985, 1988; also see Milligan, 1994) have also studied the problem of choosing the "correct" number of clusters extensively. When we asked Glenn Milligan for a summary of the current status of research on this problem, we received the following response (Milligan, 1992, personal communication):

> My current advice is to try two or three of the top-rated methods from Milligan and Cooper (1985; Cooper and Milligan, 1988). When consistent results are found, they provide substantial support for the selection of the number of clusters. This situation has occurred for a few of my correspondents. If there is partial agreement, opt for the larger number of clusters. Future research will help confirm whether clusters should be merged. If there is no consistency, then I stress that any selected solution should be clearly interpretable within the context of the area of research. If not, I strongly encourage individuals to consider the hypothesis of no clustering in the data.

An alternative, solution by fiat, is suggested by de Kluyver and Whitlark (1986, p. 280), who note that "To be managerially relevant, the number of clusters must be small enough to allow complete strategy development. At the same time, each cluster or segment should be large enough to warrant such strategic attention and to be reachable, and defensible against competitors." While this argument is limited to market segmentation, it does have an analogue in Shepard's (personal communication, 1972) recommendation that solutions for nonmetric two-way MDS should be limited to at most three dimensions, so that the spaces can be easily visualized.

An exemplary study of cluster validation in marketing research is given by Helsen and Green (1991).

Although the vast majority of applications of cluster analysis are exploratory, inferential procedures *are* available for testing significance for bimodality (Giacomelli, Wiener, Kruskal, Pomeranz, and Loud, 1971) as well as for multimodality (Hartigan and Hartigan, 1985; Hartigan, 1988; Hartigan and Mohanty, 1992). See Bock (1994) for an overview of the difficulties of devising inferential tests for problems arising in cluster analysis.

Permutation tests (Hubert, 1978, 1979, 1987, Ch. 2, 4–6) could be used, for example, to assess the significance of the relatedness of a pair of independently generated dendrograms on the same set of products, but it is often the two input matrices that should instead be compared directly. To date, the only general-purpose software available for carrying out such analyses is in NT-SYS (Rohlf, 1992), through the matrix comparison routine MXCOMP.

Variable selection and weighting

Because marketing researchers are often faced with data having an excessive number of variables (e.g. in survey research), approaches to selection and weighting of variables are very important to segmentation research. Accordingly, DeSarbo, Carroll, Clark, and Green (1984) devised an approach for "synthesized clustering" in which the variables in a two-mode (products × variables) matrix were iteratively and differentially weighted according to their relative importance to the emergent k-means (MacQueen, 1967) cluster structure. This procedure was extended from partitions to ultrametric trees by De Soete, DeSarbo, and Carroll (1985), who also sketched details for further extensions to path-length, multiple, and three-way trees, some of which were implemented later by De Soete and Carroll (1988; also see De Soete, 1994). De Soete provided both an algorithm (1986) and software (1988) for optimal variable weighting in fitting either an ultrametric or path-length tree to a single two-mode matrix. Fowlkes, Gnanadesikan, and Kettenring (1987, 1988) devised a forward selection procedure for variables in a two-mode matrix intended for complete-link hierarchical clustering as well as other methods. For a summary of the (mixed) results of evaluations of these approaches, see Arabie and Hubert (1992, p. 181).

Constrained clustering

Mahajan and Jain (1978, p. 341) stressed the importance of being able to impose constraints on partitioning approaches to market segmentation. In the clustering literature, the constraint most commonly considered is contiguity in a plane (see Gordon, 1980, 1981, pp. 61–9; Finden and Gordon, 1985; Murtagh, 1985; Legendre, 1987; Legendre and Legendre, 1993). DeSarbo and Mahajan (1984) contributed an algorithm allowing constraints for either a partition or overlapping clusters and applied it to the problem of defining sales territories. Similarly, DeSarbo (1982) in generalizing the ADCLUS (Shepard and Arabie, 1979) model also provided an algorithm allowing some very useful constraints in fitting (possibly) overlapping clusters. Other types of constraints for ultrametric and additive tree representations are given by De Soete et al. (1987).

Software

The current status of software for clustering is far less advanced than that for the related field of MDS, where "industry leaders" for portability and accuracy are readily identified and available[15] for two-way (KYST2A: Kruskal, Young, and Seery, 1977) and three-way (SINDSCAL: Pruzansky, 1975; Carroll and J.-J. Chang, 1970) analyses. For example, such desirable options as constraints and selection and weighting of variables (as discussed above) are not included in *any* readily available and implemented clustering software. Data analysts willing to study and implement FORTRAN code will find some useful routines in books by Hartigan (1975) and Späth (1980, 1985, 1991). Also, Degerman (1982) has provided useful software for permuting the nodes of one dendrogram to bring the two dendrograms into maximal congruity. For users seeking to run cluster analyses from an integrated statistical software package, we recommend SYSTAT (Wilkinson, 1992) and the more specialized NT-SYS (Rohlf, 1992). Our criteria for this recommendation include: integrity and accuracy of algorithms, accuracy of documentation, and the expertise and scholarly contributions of the staff responsible for producing the software. Our reasons for *not* recommending some other well-known and general-purpose packages include: omission of important basic techniques (e.g. complete-link), misleading and/or deliberately cryptic documentation, and dendrograms that surely result from high-stakes in-house competitions to produce ever more *un*intelligible output.

Questions

1 Below are setups for running a small dissimilarity matrix in SYSTAT. The data matrix is:

	A	B	C
B	0.5		
C	0.8	0.5	
D	1.0	1.5	0.6

In the first of the two files below, the order of the four variables is A, B, C, D. But in the second file, the variables' order of being entered and the corresponding data have been permuted. That is, the same data are being entered two different ways. Verify that either matrix gives the same dendrogram for single-link clustering, but not for complete-link. (Note: programs other than SYSTAT may require a different permutation of the matrix to get the discrepant dendrograms.)

```
SAVE TIES1
INPUT A,B,C,D
TYPE = DISSIMILARITY
DIAGONAL = ABSENT
RUN
0.5
0.8, 0.5
1.0, 1.5,0.6
~
SAVE TIES3
INPUT C,A,B,D
```

```
TYPE = DISSIMILARITY
DIAGONAL = ABSENT
RUN
0.5
0.8, 0.5
0.6, 1.5, 1.0
~
```

2 Run the Green–Rao (1972) data, as given in Table 5.1, through SYSTAT or some other clustering program, and obtain a solution using average- and single-link clustering. Compare the results to Figure 5.2.

Notes

1 For comments on an early draft of this chapter, we are indebted to Rick Bagozzi, Doug Carroll, Geert De Soete, Wayne DeSarbo, and Dave Stewart. Authors' addresses: Phipps Arabie, Graduate School of Management, Rutgers University, 92 New Street, Newark NJ 07102–1895, USA; Lawrence J. Hubert, Department of Psychology, University of Illinois, 603 E. Daniel St., Champaign IL 61820, USA.

2 Each horizontal level within such structures constitutes a *partition* of the products, as considered later in greater detail. These inverted tree diagrams are also called dendrograms.

3 Actually, only an arbitrarily chosen half of the **F** matrix was used. DeSarbo and De Soete (1984) circumvented this problem with their approach.

4 A third method of normalization, used by Slater (1984, pp. 121–3) iteratively converts the input matrix to have constant marginals (Deming and Stephan, 1940; Fienberg, 1970), possibly after zeroing the diagonal entries. It should be noted that none of the three methods symmetrizes the matrix.

5 More generally, using terminology defined below, a two-mode matrix.

6 Specifically, two-way one-mode data, as resulting from direct judgments of dis/similarity of all distinct pairs of a set of products.

7 The Howard–Harris approach can also be regarded as such a variant.

8 Available from SYSTAT, 1800 Sherman Avenue, Evanston, Illinois 60201–3793.

9 Only a halfmatrix is presented because these data are symmetric.

10 Because this method has been reinvented numerous times in different disciplines, it has several synonymous names: min, connectedness, or nearest neighbor.

11 Synonyms include max, diameter, compactness, and furthest neighbor.

12 If the data are similarities, then references in the text to minima should be replaced with maxima and vice versa.

13 Available from Exeter Software, 100 North Country Rd. Bldg. B, Setauket, New York 11753.

14 Available from: Software Distribution Service, Room 3D-588, AT&T Bell Laboratories, 600 Mountain Avenue, Murray Hill, NJ 07974.

15 From: Software Distribution Service, Room 3D-588, AT&T Bell Laboratories, 600 Mountain Avenue, Murray Hill, NJ 07974.

References

Arabie, P. and Carroll, J. D. 1980: MAPCLUS: A mathematical programming approach to fighting the ADCLUS model. *Psychometrika*, 45, 211–35.

Arabie, P., Carroll, J. D., and DeSarbo, W. S. 1987. *Three-way scaling and clustering*, Newbury Park, CA: Sage. Translated into Japanese by A. Okada and T. Imaizumi, 1990, Tokyo: Kyoritsu Shuppan.

Arabie, P., Carroll, J. D., DeSarbo, W., and Wind, J. 1981: Overlapping clustering: a new method for product positioning. *Journal of Marketing Research*, 18, 310–17.

Arabie, P., and Hubert, L. 1992: Combinatorial data analysis. *Annual Review of Psychology*, 43, 169–203.

Arabie, P. and Hubert, L. 1994: An overview of combinatorial data analysis. In P. Arabie, L. Hubert, and G. De Soete (eds), *Clustering and classification*, River Edge, New Jersey: World Scientific.

Arabie, P., Hubert, L., and De Soete, G. (eds), 1994: *Clustering and Classification*, River Edge, New Jersey: World Scientific.

Arabie, P., Hubert, L., and Schleutermann, S. 1990: Blockmodels from the bond energy algorithm. *Social Networks*, 12, 99–126.

Arabie, P. and Soli, S. D. 1982: The interface between the types of regression and methods of collecting proximity data. In R. G. Golledge and J. N. Rayner (eds), *Proximity and Preference: Problems in the Multidimensional Analysis of Large Data Sets*, 90–115. Minneapolis, MN: University of Minnesota Press.

Arabie, P. and Wind, J. 1994: Marketing and social networks. In J. Galaskiewicz and S. S. Wasserman (eds), *Advances in Social and Behavioral Sciences from Social Network Analysis*, Newbury Park, CA: Sage.

Baker, F. B. 1974: Stability of two hierarchial grouping techniques, Case I: Sensitivity to data errors. *Journal of the American Statistical Association*, 69, 440–5.

Baker, F. B. and Hubert, L. J. 1975: Measuring the power of hierarchical cluster analysis. *Journal of the American Statistical Association*, 70, 31–8.

Baker, F. B. and Hubert, L. J. 1976: A graph-theoretic approach to goodness-of-fit in complete-link hierarchical clustering. *Journal of the American Statistical Association*, 71, 870–8.

Beane, T. P. and Ennis, D. M. 1987: Market segmentation: A review. *European Journal of Marketing*, 21, 20–42.

Belbin, L. 1987: The use of non-hierarchical allocation methods for clustering large sets of data. *Australian Computer Journal*, 19, 32–41.

Blozan, W. and Prabhaker, P. 1984: Notes on aggregation criteria in market segmentation. *Journal of Marketing Research*, 21, 332–5.

Bock, H. H. 1994: Significance tests in cluster analysis. In P. Arabie, L. Hubert and G. De Soete (eds), *Clustering and Classification*, River Edge, New Jersey: World Scientific.

Butler, D. H. 1976: Development of statistical marketing models. In *Speaking of Hendry*, Croton-on-Hudson, NY: Hendry Corporation.

Carroll, J. D. 1973: Models and algorithms for multidimensional scaling, conjoint measurement, and related techniques (Appendix B). In P. E. Green and Y. Wind, *Multiattribute Decisions in Marketing*. Hinsdale, IL: Dryden Press, 299–387.

Carroll, J. D. 1976: Spatial, non-spatial and hybrid models for scaling. *Psychometrika*, 41, 439–63.

Carroll, J. D. and Arabie, P. 1983: INDCLUS: An individual differences generalization of the ADCLUS model and the MAPCLUS algorithm. *Psychometrika*, 48, 157–69.

Carroll, J. D. and Chang, J. J. 1970: Analysis of individual differences in multidimensional scaling via an *N*-way generalization of "Eckart-Young" decomposition. *Psychometrika*, 35, 283–319.

Carroll, J. D., Clark, L. A., and DeSarbo, W. S. 1984: The representation of three-way proximities data by single and multiple tree structure models. *Journal of Classification*, 1, 25–74.

Carroll, J. D. and De Soete, G. 1990: Fitting a quasi-Poisson case of the GSTUN (General Stochastic Tree Unfolding) model and some extensions. In M. Schader and W. Gaul (eds), *Knowledge, Data and Computer-assisted Decisions*, Berlin: Springer-Verlag.

Carroll, J. D. and De Soete, G. 1991: Toward a new paradigm for the study of multiattribute choice behavior. *American Psychologist*, 46, 342–51.

Carroll, J. D. and De Soete, G. 1994: Spatial, non-spatial and hybrid models for scaling. In P. Arabie, L. Hubert, and G. De Soete (eds), *Clustering and Classification*, River Edge, New Jersey: World Scientific.

Carroll, J. D., De Soete, G. and Pruzansky, S. 1989: Fitting of the latent class model via iteratively reweighted least squares CANDECOMP with nonnegativity constraints. In R. Coppi and S. Bolasco (eds), *Multiway Data Analysis*, Amsterdam: North-Holland, 463–72.

Carroll, J. D., DeSarbo, W. S., and De Soete, G. 1987: Stochastic tree unfolding (STUN) models. *Communication and Cognition*, 20, 63–76.

Carroll, J. D., DeSarbo, W., and De Soete, G. 1988: Stochastic tree unfolding (STUN) models: Theory and application. In H. H. Bock (ed.), *Classification and Related Methods of Data Analysis*, Amsterdam: North-Holland, 421–30.

Carroll, J. D., DeSarbo, W., & De Soete, G. (1989). Two classes of stochastic tree unfolding models. In G. De Soete, H. Feger, and C. Klauer (eds.), *New Developments in Psychological Choice Modeling*. Amsterdam: North-Holland, 161–76.

Carroll, J. D. and Pruzansky, S. 1980: Discrete and hybrid scaling models. In E. D. Lantermann and H. Feger (eds), *Similarity and Choice*, Bern: Hans Huber, 108–39.

Chang, W.-C. 1983: On using principal components before separating a mixture of two multivariate normal distributions. *Applied Statistics*, 32, 267–75.

Choffray, J.-M. and Lilien, G. L. 1978: A new approach to industrial market segmentation. *Sloan Management Review*, Spring, 17–29.

Choffray, J.-M. and Lilien, G. L. 1980a: *Market Planning for New Industrial Products*, New York: Wiley.

Choffray, J.-M. and Lilien, G. L. 1980b: Industrial market segmentation by the structure of the purchasing process. *Industrial Marketing Management*, 9, 331-42.

Cooper, M. C. and Milligan, G. W. 1988: The effect of measurement error on determining the number of clusters in cluster analysis. In W. Gaul and M. Schader (eds), *Data, Expert Knowledge and Decisions*, Berlin: Springer-Verlag, 319–28.

Critchley, F. 1986: Some observations on distance matrices. In J. de Leeuw, W. Heiser, J. Meulman, and F. Critchley (eds), *Multidimensional Data Analysis*, Leiden: DSWO, 53–60.

Critchley, F. 1988: The Euclidean structure of a dendrogram, the variance of a node and the question: "How many clusters really are there?" In H. H. Bock (ed.), *Classification and Related Methods of Data Analysis*, Amsterdam: North-Holland, 75–84.

Critchley, F. and Heiser, W. 1988: Hierarchical trees can be perfectly scaled in one dimension. *Journal of Classification*, 5, 5–20.

Currim, I. S. 1981: Using segmentation approaches for better prediction and understanding from consumer mode choice models. *Journal of Marketing Research*, 18, 301–9.

Currim, I. S. and Schneider, L. G. 1991: A taxonomy of consumer purchase strategies in a promotion intensive environment. *Marketing Science*, 10, 91–110.

Day, G. S. and Heeler, R. M. 1971: Using cluster analysis to improve marketing experiments. *Journal of Marketing Research*, 8, 340–7.

Day, W. H. E. (ed.), 1991: *Classification Literature Automated Search Service*, 20.

de Kluyver, C. A. and Whitlark, D. B. 1986: Benefit segmentation for industrial products. *Industrial Marketing Management*, 15, 273–86.

De Soete, G. 1986. Optimal variable weighting for ultrametric and additive tree clustering. *Quality and Quantity*, 20, 169–80.

De Soete, G. 1988: OVWTRE: A program for optimal variable weighting for ultrametric and additive tree fitting. *Journal of Classification*, 5, 101–4.

De Soete. G. 1994: Variable selection and weighting in cluster analysis. In P. Arabie, L. Hubert, and G. De Soete (eds), *Clustering and Classification*, River Edge, New Jersey: World Scientific.

De Soete, G., and Carroll, J. D. 1988: Optimal weighting for one-mode and two-mode ultrametric tree representations of three-way three-mode data. In M. G. H. Jansen and W. H. van Schuur (eds), *The Many Faces of Multivariate Data Analysis*, Groningen: RION, 16–29.

De Soete, G. and Carroll, J. D. 1989: Ultrametric tree representations of three-way three-mode data. In R. Coppi and S. Bolasco (eds), *Analysis of Multiway Data Matrices*, Amsterdam: North-Holland, 415–26.

De Soete, G., Carroll, J. D., and DeSarbo, W. S. 1987: Least squares algorithms for constructing constrained ultrametric and additive tree representations of symmetric proximity data. *Journal of Classification*, 4, 155–73.

De Soete, G., DeSarbo, W. S., and Carroll, J. D. 1985: Optimal variable weighting for hierarchical clustering: An alternating least-squares algorithm. *Journal of Classification*, 2, 173–92.

De Soete, G., Carroll, J. D., and DeSarbo, W. S. 1986: Alternating least squares optimal variable weighting algorithms for ultrametric and additive tree representations. In W. Gaul and M. Schader (eds), *Classification as a Tool of Research*, Amsterdam: North-Holland, 97–103.

De Soete, G., Carroll, J. D. and DeSarbo, W. S. 1987: Least squares algorithms for constructing constrained ultrametric and additive tree representations of symmetric proximity data. *Journal of Classification*, 4, 155–73.

De Soete, G., DeSarbo, W. S., Furnas, G. W., and Carroll, J. D. 1984a: The estimation of ultrametric and path length trees from rectangular proximity data. *Psychometrika*, 49, 289–310.

De Soete, G., DeSarbo, W. S., Furnas, G. W., and Carroll, J. D. 1984b: Tree representations of rectangular proximity matrices. In E. Degreef and J. Van Buggenhaut (eds), *Trends in Mathematical Psychology*, Amsterdam: North-Holland, 377–92.

Degerman, R. 1982: Ordered binary trees constructed through an application of Kendall's tau. *Psychometrika*, 47, 523–7.

Deming, W. E. and Stephan, F. F. 1940: On a least squares adjustment of a sampled frequency table when the expected marginal totals are known. *Annals of Mathematical Statistics*, 11, 427–44.

DeSarbo, W. S. 1982: GENNCLUS: New models for general nonhierarchical clustering analysis. *Psychometrika*, 47, 446–9.

DeSarbo, W. S., Carroll, J. D., Clark, L. A., and Green, P. E. 1984: Synthesized clustering: A method for amalgamating alternative clustering bases with differential weighting of variables. *Psychometrika*, 49, 57–78.

DeSarbo, W. S. and Cron, W. L. 1988: A conditional mixture maximum likelihood methodology for clusterwise linear regression. *Journal of Classification*, 5, 249–89.

DeSarbo, W. S. and De Soete, G. 1984: On the use of hierarchical clustering for the analysis of nonsymmetric proximities. *Journal of Consumer Research*, 11, 601–10.

DeSarbo, W. S. and De Soete, G., Carroll, J. D. and Ramaswamy, V. 1988: A new stochastic ultrametric tree unfolding methodology for assessing competitive market structure and deriving market segments. *Applied Stochastic Models and Data Analysis*, 4, 185–204.

DeSarbo, W. S., Jedidi, K., Cool, K., and Schendel, D. 1990: Simultaneous multidimensional unfolding and cluster analysis: An investigation of strategic groups. *Marketing Letters*, 2, 129–46.

DeSarbo, W. S. and Mahajan, V. 1984: Constrained classification: The use of a priori information in cluster analysis. *Psychometrika*, 49, 187–216.

DeSarbo, W. S., Manrai, A., and Burke, R. 1990: A nonspatial methodology incorporating the distance-density hypothesis. *Psychometrika*, 55, 229–53.

DeSarbo, W. S., A. K. Manrai, and L. A. Manrai (1993). Non-spatial tree models for the assessment of competitive market structure: an integrated review of the marketing and psychometric literature. In J. Eliashberg and G. Lilien (eds), *Handbook in Operations Research and Management Science: Marketing*. New York: Elsevier, 193–257.

DeSarbo, W. S., Oliver, R. L., and Rangaswamy, A. 1989: A simulated annealing methodology for clusterwise linear regression. *Psychometrika*, 4, 707–36.

Dickinson, J. R. 1990: *The Bibliography of Marketing Research methods*, 3rd edn, Lexington, MA: Lexington.

Dillon, W. R., Mulani, N., and Frederick, D. G. 1989: On the use of component scores in the presence of group structure. *Journal of Consumer Research*, 16, 106–12.

Doyle, P. and Saunders, J. 1985: Market segmentation and positioning in specialized industrial markets. *Journal of Marketing*, 49, 24–32.

Dubes, R. and Jain, A. K. 1979: Validity studies in clustering methodologies. *Pattern Recognition*, 11, 235–54.

Elrod, T. and Winer, R. S. 1982: An empirical evaluation of aggregation approaches for developing market segments. *Journal of Marketing*, 46 (Fall), 65–74.

Fienberg, S. E. 1970: An iterative procedure for estimation in contingency tables. *Annals of Mathematical Statistics*, 41, 907–17 (Erratum, p. 1778).

Finden, C. R. and Gordon, A. D. 1985: Obtaining common pruned trees. *Journal of Classification*, 2, 255–76.

Fowlkes, E. B., Gnanadesikan, R., and Kettenring, J. R. 1987: Variable selection in clustering and other contexts. In C. L. Mallows (ed.), *Design, Data, and Analysis*, New York: Wiley, 13–34.

Fowlkes, E. B., Gnanadesikan, R. and Kettenring, J. R. 1988: Variable selection in clustering. *Journal of Classification*, 5, 205–28.

Furse, D. H., Punj, G. N., and Stewart, D. W. 1984: A typology of individual search strategies among purchasers of new automobiles. *Journal of Consumer Research*, 10, 417–31.

Giacomelli, F., Wiener, J., Kruskal, J. B., Pomeranz, J. V., and Loud, A. V. 1971: Subpopulations of blood lymphocytes demonstrated by quantitative cytochemistry. *Journal of Histochemistry and Cytochemistry*, 19, 426–33.

Glazer, R. and Nakamoto, K. 1991: Cognitive geometry: An analysis of structure underlying representations of similarity. *Marketing Science*, 10, 205–28.

Gnanadesikan, R. and Kettenring, J. R. 1972: Robust estimates, residuals, and outlier detection with multiresponse data. *Biometrics*, 28, 81–124.

Gordon, A. D. 1980: Methods of constrained classification. In R. Tomassone (ed.), *Analyse de Données et Informatique*, Le Chesnay: INRIA, 161–71.

Gordon, A. D. 1981: *Classification*. London: Chapman & Hall.

Gordon, A. D. 1987: A review of hierarchical classification. *Journal of the Royal Statistical Society Series A*, 150, 119–37.

Gordon, A. D. 1994: Hierarchical classification. In P. Arabie, L. Hubert, and G. De Soete (eds), *Clustering and Classification*. River Edge, New Jersey: World Scientific.

Gower, J. C. 1971: A general coefficient of similarity and some of its properties. *Biometrics*, 27, 857–71.

Green, P. E., Frank, R. E., and Robinson, P. J. 1967: Cluster analysis in test market selection. *Management Science*, 13, B387–B400.

Green, P. E. and Helsen, K. 1989: Cross-validation assessment of alternatives to individual-level conjoint analysis: A case study. *Journal of Marketing Research*, 26, 346–50.

Green, P. E. and Krieger, A. M. 1985: Buyer similarity measures in conjoint analysis: Some alternative proposals. *Journal of Classification*, 2, 41–61.

Green, P. E. and Krieger, A. M. 1991: Segmenting markets with conjoint analysis. *Journal of Marketing*, 55 (October), 20–31.

Green, P. E., Krieger, A. M., and Schaffer, C. M. 1985: Quick and simple benefit segmentation. *Journal of Advertising Research*, 25, 9–17.

Green, P. E. and Rao, V. R. 1969: A note on proximity measures and cluster analysis. *Journal of Marketing Research*, 6, 359–64.

Green, P. E. and Rao, V. R. 1972: *Applied Multidimensional Scaling: A Comparison of Approaches and Algorithms*, New York: Holt, Rinehart, & Winston.

Green, P. E. and Srinivasan, V. 1978: Conjoint analysis in consumer research: Issues and outlook. *Journal of Consumer Research*, 5, 103–23.

Green, P. E. and Srinivasan, V. 1990: Conjoint analysis in marketing: New developments with implications for research and practice. *Journal of Marketing*, 54 (October), 3–19.

Grover, R. and Srinivasan, V. 1987: A simultaneous approach to market segmentation and market structuring. *Journal of Marketing Research*, 24, 139–53.

Grover, R. and Srinivasan, V. 1989: An approach for tracking within-segment shifts in market shares. *Journal of Marketing Research*, 26, 230–6.

Grover, R. and Srinivasan, V. 1992: Evaluating the multiple effects of retail promotions on brand loyal and brand switching segments. *Journal of Marketing Research*, 29, 76–89.

Hartigan, J. A. 1975: *Clustering Algorithms*, New York: Wiley. Translated into Japanese by H. Nishida, M. Yoshida, H. Hiramatsu, and K. Tanaka, 1983. Tokyo: Micro Software.

Hartigan, J. A. 1988: The span test for unimodality. In H. H. Bock (ed.), *Classification and Related Methods of Data Analysis* Amsterdam: North-Holland, 229–36.

Hartigan, J. A. and Hartigan, P. M. 1985: The dip test of unimodality. *Annals of Statistics*, 13, 70–84.

Hartigan, J. A. and Mohanty, S. 1992: The runt test for multimodality. *Journal of Classification*, 9, 63–70.

Helsen, K. and Green, P. E. 1991: A computational study of replicated clustering with an application to market segmentation. *Decision Sciences*, 22, 1124–41.

Heltshe, J. F. 1988: Jackknife estimate of the matching coefficient of similarity. *Biometrics*, 44, 447–60.

Holman, E. W. 1972: The relation between hierarchical and Euclidean models for psychological distances. *Psychometrika*, 37, 417–23.

Howard, N. and Harris, B. 1966: *A Hierarchical Grouping Routine (IBM 360/65 FORTRAN IV Program)*. Unpublished documentation, University of Pennsylvania Computer Center, Philadelphia.

Hubert, L. J. 1973: Monotone invariant clustering procedures. *Psychometrika*, 38, 47–62.

Hubert, L. J. 1978: Generalized proximity function comparisons. *British Journal of Mathematical and Statistical Psychology*, 31, 179–92.

Hubert, L. J. 1979: Generalized concordance. *Psychometrika*, 44, 135–42.

Hubert, L. J. 1987: *Assignment Methods in Combinatorial Data Analysis*, New York: Marcel Dekker.

Hubert, L. J. and Arabie, P. 1985: Comparing partitions. *Journal of Classification*, 2, 193–218.

Hutchinson, J. W. 1989: NETSCAL: A network scaling algorithm for nonsymmetric proximity data. *Psychometrika*, 54, 25–51.

Hutchinson, J. W. and Mungalé, A. 1993: *Pairwise Partitioning: A Nonmetric Algorithm for Identifying Feature-based Similarity Measures*. Manuscript submitted for publication.

Iacobucci, D. and Hopkins, N. 1992: Modeling dyadic interactions and networks in marketing. *Journal of Marketing Research*, 29, 5–17.

Jain, A. K. and Dubes, R. C. 1988: *Algorithms for Clustering Data*, Englewood Cliffs, NJ: Prentice-Hall.

Jardine, N. and Sibson, R. 1971: *Mathematical Taxonomy*, London: Wiley.

Johnson, M. D. and Fornell, C. 1987: The nature and methodological implications of the cognitive representation of products. *Journal of Consumer Research*, 14, 214–28.

Kamakura, W. A. 1988: A least squares procedure for benefit segmentation with conjoint experiments. *Journal of Marketing Research*, 25, 157–67.

Kamakura, W. A. 1992: *A Clusterwise Multinomial Logit Model for Multiple Locally-independent Choice Sets*. Unpublished manuscript, Owen Graduate School of Management, Vanderbilt University, Nashville.

Kamakura, W. A. and Agrawal, J. 1990: *A Clusterwise Multinomial Logit Model for Benefit Segmentation*. Unpublished manuscript, Owen Graduate School of Management, Vanderbilt University, Nashville.

Kamakura, W. A. and Mazzon, J. A. 1991: Value segmentation: A model for the measurement of values and value systems. *Journal of Consumer Research*, 18, 208–18.

Klastorin, T. D. 1985: The p-median problem for cluster analysis: A comparative test using the mixture model approach. *Management Science*, 31, 84–95.

Klauer, K. C. and Carroll, J. D. 1989: A mathematical programming approach to fitting general graphs. *Journal of Classification*, 6, 247–70.

Klauer, K. C. and Carroll, J. D. 1991: A mathematical programming approach to fitting directed graphs to nonsymmetric proximity measures. *Journal of Classification*, 8, 251–68.

Kruskal, J. B. 1977: The relationship between multidimensional scaling and clustering. In J. Van Ryzin (ed.), *Classification and Clustering*, New York: Academic Press, 17–44.

Kruskal, J. B. Young, F. W. and Seery, J. B. 1977: *How to Use KYST2, a Very Flexible Program to do Multidimensional Scaling and Unfolding*. Murray Hill, NJ: AT & T Bell Laboratories.

Legendre, P. 1987: Constrained clustering. In P. Legendre and L. Legendre (eds), *Developments in Numerical Ecology* (NATO Advanced Study Institute Series G (Ecological Sciences)), Berlin: Springer-Verlag, 289–307.

Legendre, L. and Legendre, P. 1993: *Numerical Ecology*, 2nd edn, Amsterdam: Elsevier.

Ling, R. F. 1971: *Cluster Analysis*, Ann Arbor, MI: University Microfilms. No. 71-22356.

MacQueen, J. 1967: Some methods for classification and analysis of multivariate observations. In L. M. Le Cam and J. Neyman (eds), *Proceedings of the Fifth Berkeley Symposium on Mathematical Statistics and Probability*, Vol. 1, Berkeley: University of California Press, 281–97.

Mahajan, V. and Jain, A. K. 1978: An approach to normative segmentation. *Journal of Marketing Research*, 15, 338–45.

McLachlan, G. J. and Basford, K. E. 1988: *Mixture Models: Inference and Applications to Clustering*, New York: Marcel Dekker.

Milligan, G. W. 1981: A Monte Carlo study of thirty internal criterion measures for cluster analysis. *Psychometrika*, 46, 187–99.

Milligan, G. W. 1994: Clustering validation: Results and implications for applied analyses. In P. Arabie, L. Hubert, and G. De Soete (eds), *Clustering and Classification*. River Edge, New Jersey: World Scientific.

Milligan, G. W. and Cooper, M. C. 1985: An examination of procedures for determination of clusters in a data set. *Psychometrika*, 50, 159–79.

Milligan, G. W. and Cooper, M. C. 1986: A study of the comparability of external criteria for hierarchical cluster analysis. *Multivariate Behavioral Research*, 21, 441–58.

Milligan, G. W. and Cooper, M. C. 1988: A study of standardization of variables in cluster analysis. *Journal of Classification*, 5, 181–204.

Moore, W. L. 1980: Levels of aggregation in conjoint analysis: An empirical comparison. *Journal of Marketing Research*, 17, 516–23.

Morrison, D. G. 1967: Measurement problems in cluster analysis. *Management Science*, 13, B774–B780.

Murphy, R. A. and Tatham, R. L. 1979: Optimal construction of experimental clusters. *Management Science*, 25, 182–90.

Murtagh, F. 1985: A survey of algorithms for contiguity-constrained clustering and related problems. *Computer Journal*, 28, 82–8.

Nicosia, F. M. and Wind, Y. 1977: Behavioral models of organizational buying processes. In F. M. Nicosia and Y. Wind (eds), *Behavioral Models for Market Analysis: Foundations for Marketing Action*, Hinsdale, IL: Dryden, 96–120.

Ogawa, K. 1987: An approach to simultaneous estimation and segmentation in conjoint analysis. *Marketing Science*, 6, 66–81.

Ohsumi, N. and Nakamura, N. 1994: Comparison of hierarchical clustering algorithms based on space-distorting properties. In P. Arabie, L. Hubert, and G. De Soete (eds), *Clustering and Classification*, River Edge, New Jersey: World Scientific.

Price, L. J. (in press): Identifying Cluster Overlap with NORMIX Population Membership Probabilities. *Multivariate Behavioral Research*.

Pruzansky, S. 1975: *How to Use SINDSCAL: A Computer Program for Individual Differences in Multidimensional Scaling*, Murray Hill, NJ: AT & T Bell Laboratories.

Pruzansky, S., Tversky, A. and Carroll, J. D. 1982: Spatial versus tree representations of proximity data. *Psychometrika*, 47, 3–24.

Punj, G. and Stewart, D. W. 1983: Cluster analysis in marketing research: Review and suggestions for application. *Journal of Marketing Research*, 20, 134–48.

Rao, V. R. and Sabavala, D. J. 1981: Inference of hierarchical choice processes from panel data. *Journal of Consumer Research*, 8, 85–96.

Rao, V. R., Sabavala, D. J. and Langfeld, P. A. 1977: *Alternative Measures for Partitioning Analysis Based on Brand Switching Data*. Unpublished manuscript, Johnson Graduate School of Cornell University, Ithaca NY.

Rao, V. R., Sabavala, D. J., and Zahorick, A. J. 1982: Market structure analysis using brand switching data: A comparison of clustering techniques. In R. K. Srivastava and A. Shocker (eds), *Analytical Approaches to Product and Marketing Planning: The Second Conference*, Cambridge, MA.: Marketing Science Institute, 17–25.

Robles, F. and Sarathy, R. 1986: Segmenting the commuter aircraft market with cluster analysis. *Industrial Marketing Management*, 15, 1–12.

Rohlf, F. J. 1992: *NTSYS-pc Numerical Taxonomy and Multivariate Analysis System* (version 1.70), Setauket, NY: Exeter Software.

Rust, R. T., Kamakura, W. A., and Alpert, M. I. 1992: Viewer preference segmentation and viewing choice models for network television. *Journal of Advertising*, 21, 1–18.

Shepard, R. N. 1962: The analysis of proximities: Multidimensional scaling with an unknown distance function. I. *Psychometrika*, 27, 125–40.

Shepard, R. N. and Arabie, P. 1979: Additive clustering: Representation of similarities as combinations of discrete overlapping properties. *Psychological Review*, 86, 87–123.

Shocker, A. D., Stewart, D. W., and Zahorik, A. J. 1990: Determining the competitive structure of product-markets: Practices, issues, and suggestions. *Journal of Managerial Issues*, 2, (2) 127–59.

Slater, P. 1984: *Tree Representations of Internal Migration Flows and Related Topics*. Santa Barbara: Community and Organization Research Institute, University of California.

Snijders T. A. B., Dormaar, M., van Schuur, W. H., Dijkman-Caes, C., and Driessen, G. 1990: Distribution of some similarity coefficients for dyadic binary data in the case of associated attributes. *Journal of Classification*, 7, 5–31.

Sokal, R. R. and Michener, C. D. 1958: A statistical method for evaluating systematic relationships. *University of Kansas Science Bulletin*, 38, 1409–38.

Späth, H. 1980: *Cluster Analysis Algorithms* (U. Bull, trans.), Chichester, England: Ellis Horwood (original work published 1977).

Späth, H. 1985: *Cluster Dissection and Analysis: Theory, FORTRAN Programs, Examples*. (J. Goldschmidt, trans.), Chichester: Ellis Horwood (original work published 1983).

Späth, H. 1991: *Mathematical Software for Linear Regression*, San Diego: Academic Press.

Srivastava, R. K. 1981: Usage-situational influences on perceptions of product-markets: Theoretical and empirical issues. In K. B. Monroe (ed.), *Advances in Consumer Research, Vol. 8*, Ann Arbor, MI: Association for Consumer Research, 106–11.

Srivastava, R. K. and Alpert, M. I. 1982: A customer-oriented approach for determining market structures. In R. K. Srivastava and A. D. Shocker (eds). *Proceedings of the Second Conference on Analytic Approaches to Product and Marketing Planning*, Cambridge, MA: Marketing Science Institute, 26–57.

Srivastava, R. K., Alpert, M. I., and Shocker, A. D. 1984: A customer-oriented approach for determining market structures. *Journal of Marketing*, 48 (Spring), 32–45.

Stewart, D. W. 1981: The application and misapplication of factor analysis in marketing research. *Journal of Marketing Research*, 18, 51–62.

Tucker, L. R 1964: The extension of factor analysis to three-dimensional matrices. In N. Frederiksen and H. Gulliksen (eds.), *Contributions to Mathematical Psychology*, New York: Holt, Rinehart, & Winston, 109–27.

Ward, J. H., Jr. 1963: Hierarchical grouping to optimize an objective function. *Journal of the American Statistical Association*, 58, 236–44.

Wedel, M. and Steenkamp, J.-B. E. M. 1991: A clusterwise regression method for simultaneous fuzzy market structuring and benefit segmentation. *Journal of Marketing Research*, 28, 385–96.

Wilkinson, L. 1992: *SYSTAT: The System for Statistics*, Evanston, IL: Systat, Inc.

Wind, Y. 1978a: Introduction to special section on market segmentation research. *Journal of Marketing Research*, 15, 315–16.

Wind, Y. 1978b: Issues and advances in segmentation research. *Journal of Marketing Research*, 15, 317–37.

Wind, Y. J. 1982: *Product Policy: Concepts, Methods, and Strategy*, Reading, MA: Addison-Wesley.

Wind, Y. and Robertson, T. S. 1982: The linking pin role in organizational buying centers. *Journal of Business Research*, 10, 169–84.

Wishart, D. (1969). An algorithm for hierarchical classifications. *Biometrics*, 22, 165–70.

Wolfe, J. H. 1970: Pattern clustering by multivariate mixture analysis. *Multivariate Behavioral Research*, 5, 329–50.

6

Latent Class Multidimensional Scaling: A Review of Recent Developments in the Marketing and Psychometric Literature

Wayne S. DeSarbo,
Ajay K. Manrai and
Lalita A. Manrai

Abstract

We present a description of current, state-of-the-art methods for performing latent class multidimensional scaling (LCMDS). The organizing framework utilized to present these various methods revolves around the types of data collected and the associated spatial representation desired from such approaches. As such, methods for proximity, paired comparisons, preference, choice, and profile or ratings data are described. A general form of the *E-M* maximum likelihood estimation procedure typically utilized for the vast majority of these methods is also presented. Finally, the potential application of these methods in marketing, as well as directions for future research, are discussed.

1 Introduction

Multidimensional Scaling (MDS) has been defined (cf. Kruskal and Wish, 1978) as a set of spatial models and associated estimation procedures utilized to obtain a multidimensional spatial representation of the structure in various types of data including proximity (similarity or dissimilarity), dominance (preferences, ratings), or discrete choice (e.g. "pick any") data. Multidimensional scaling can assist marketing managers and researchers in depicting market structure (Wind, 1980; DeSarbo, Manrai, and Manrai, 1993), market segmentation (Cooper, 1983), product design and positioning (DeSarbo and Manrai, 1992; Eliashberg and Manrai, 1993; DeSarbo and Rao, 1984, 1986), competitive influences and patterns (Cooper, 1988), and relationships between consumer perceptions and choice (Manrai and

Sinha, 1989; Manrai and Manrai, 1993). Carroll and Arabie (1981) provide an excellent taxonomy of the various MDS methods based on the types of data collected and the associated form of the spatial display of the structure derived from such data. For example, simple unfolding MDS models typically provide a joint space representation of both subjects (e.g. consumers) and stimuli (e.g. brands) in a common dimensional representation for dominance data (e.g. consumers rating their preference for various brands in a specified product class).

One of the obvious limitations of such MDS procedures stems from their inability to represent the structure in such data collected from a representative sample of consumers in a particular market. Marketing research suppliers often collect samples from thousands of consumers, and the ability of MDS procedures to fully portray the structure in such volumes of data is indeed limited. The resulting joint spaces or individual weight spaces become saturated with points/vectors, often rendering interpretation impossible. In addition, most MDS programs are tailored to small samples ($N < 100$) given the complexity of many of the numerical computing schemes utilized. For example, most of the commercially available versions of MDPREF (Carroll, 1980) are limited to samples of $N \leqslant 50$. Yet, marketers are rarely interested in the particular responses of consumers at the individual level because of the impracticality of developing marketing strategy for each consumer. Given the traditional role of market segmentation in marketing strategy (cf. Wind, 1980), marketers are more concerned with identifying and targeting market segments – homogeneous groups of consumers who share some designated set of characteristics (e.g. demographics, psychographics, consumption patterns, etc.) – that are relevant to the purchase of the brand under study. And this interest in market segmentation is the fundamental motivation for using latent class multidimensional scaling (LCMDS) methods in marketing. LCMDS performs MDS and segmentation/cluster analysis simultaneously. That is, in a marketing context, LCMDS can portray the structure in the same types of data as traditional MDS procedures, with the difference being that market segments are represented in the resulting maps in place of the individual consumers. Furthermore, a classification of each consumer into the derived market segments is simultaneously estimated. Thus, the fundamental motivation that drives LCMDS is the belief that the consumers belong to different market segments and the observed individual level data is sampled from a finite mixture of several stochastic distributions, one for each market segment. A LCMDS procedure can be viewed as a "data unmixing" procedure in the latent class tradition introduced by Lazarsfeld and Henry (1968). It simultaneously estimates market segments as well as perceptual or preference structures of consumers in each segment from data obtained from N consumers ($i = 1, 2, \ldots, N$) rendering judgments on J brands ($j = 1, 2, \ldots, J$). It assumes that N consumers belong to S segments ($s = 1, 2, \ldots, S$) and the individual consumer membership to a particular segment is not known *a priori*.

This review chapter is organized as follows. Section 2 describes, in general terms, the *E-M* framework for estimating most LCMDS models. The next section describes the set of LCMDS models used for proximity data (e.g. similarity, dissimilarity data). Section 4 describes LCMDS models used for metric and non-metric dominance data (e.g. preferences, ratings). Section 5 presents a collection of LCMDS models for the analysis of choice data (e.g. pick-any/*J*, paired comparisons). We conclude this review by discussing potential marketing applications, as well as some directions for future research.

2 A Generalized *E-M* Framework for the Estimation of LCMDS Models

Let:

$i = 1, \ldots, N$ consumers;
$j = 1, \ldots, J$ brands;
$t = 1, \ldots, T$ dimensions;
$s = 1, \ldots, S$ latent classes;
Δ_i = a one or two-way data array collected from consumer i, where $\Delta = ((\Delta_i))$;
θ_{ts} = a concatenated vector of LCMDS parameters where $\theta = ((\theta_{ts}))$
λ_s = the latent class mixing parameter where $\lambda = ((\lambda_s))$.

In the general case, it is assumed that:

$$\Delta_i \sim G_i(\Delta_i; \lambda, \theta) = \sum_{s=1}^{S} \lambda_s f_{its}(\Delta_i | \theta_{ts}), \qquad (6.1)$$

where $f_{its}(\Delta_i | \theta_{ts})$ is specified depending upon the type of data collected and LCMDS model to be fitted, and the $S - 1$ independent mixing proportions $\lambda = (\lambda_1, \ldots, \lambda_{S-1})$ are such that:

$$0 < \lambda_s < 1 \qquad (6.2)$$

and

$$\lambda_S = 1 - \sum_{s=1}^{S-1} \lambda_s. \qquad (6.3)$$

The condition specified in (6.1) implies that if a consumer belongs to segment s, then the structure, in the data can be represented by θ_{st} for $t = 1, \ldots, T$ dimensions. The mixing proportions, λ_s, can be construed as the prior probability, *Prob(s)*, that any consumer belongs to segment s. Once estimates of θ_{st}, for $t = 1, \ldots, T$, are obtained, the posterior probability of membership for consumer i in segment s can be computed using Bayes' rule as:

$$P_{is} = Prob(s; \theta_{st}|\Delta_i)$$
$$= \lambda_s f_{its} (\Delta_i|\theta_{st}) / \left(\sum_s \lambda_s f_{its} (\Delta_i|\theta_{st}) \right). \tag{6.4}$$

Hence, upon estimation of the parameters θ_{st}, the posterior probabilities provide a "fuzzy" segmentation of the N consumers into S segments. These posterior probabilities can later be related to relevant background consumer characteristics for prediction and/or targeting purposes.

For a sample of N consumers, we can form the general *ln* likelihood expression:

$$ln\ L = \sum_{i=1}^{N} ln \left[\sum_{s=1}^{S} \lambda_s f_{its} (\Delta_i|\theta_{st}) \right]. \tag{6.5}$$

Given Δ, and values of S and T, one needs to estimate the mixing proportions $\lambda = (\lambda_1, \ldots, \lambda_{S-1})$ and the parameters θ_{st} so as to maximize the likelihood L (or equivalently *ln* L), subject to the conditions specified in (6.2) and (6.3).

LCMDS models typically utilize an *E-M* algorithm (cf. Dempster, Laird, and Rubin, 1977) for estimation. To do so, we introduce non-observed data via the indicator function:

$$z_{is} = \begin{bmatrix} 1\ iff\ \text{consumer}\ i\ \text{belongs to segment}\ s; \\ 0\ \text{otherwise.} \end{bmatrix} \tag{6.6}$$

The column vector z_i is defined as $(z_{i1}, \ldots, z_{is})'$, and the matrix $Z = (z_1, \ldots, z_N)'$. We assume that for consumer i, the non-observed data z_i are independently and identically multinomially distributed with probabilities λ. The joint likelihood of Δ_i and z_i (i.e. the "complete" data) is then:

$$L_i (\Delta_i, z_i; \theta, \lambda) = \sum_{s=1}^{S} [\lambda_s f_{its} (\Delta_i|\theta_{st})]^{z_{is}} \tag{6.7}$$

and the *complete ln* likelihood over all customers is:

$$ln\ L_c = \sum_{i=1}^{N} \sum_{s=1}^{S} z_{is}\ ln(f_{its} (\Delta_i|\theta_{st})) + \sum_{i=1}^{N} \sum_{s=1}^{S} z_{is}\ ln\ \lambda_s. \tag{6.8}$$

With the matrix $\mathbf{Z}$ considered as missing data, the E-M algorithm here amounts to iteratively alternating between an E-step (a conditional expectation step) and a M-step (a maximization step). In the E-step, the expectation of $ln\ L_c$ is evaluated over the conditional distribution of the non-observed data $\mathbf{Z}$, given the observed data $\mathbf{\Delta}$, and provisional estimates $(\mathbf{\theta}_{st}^*)$ of the parameters $\mathbf{\theta}_{st}$ for specified values of S and T. The conditional expectation of z_{is} can be computed as:

$$E(z_{is};\ \mathbf{\theta}_{st}^*|\mathbf{\Delta}_i) = \lambda_s^*\, f_{its}\, (\mathbf{\Delta}_i|\mathbf{\theta}_{st})/\left(\sum_{s=1}^{S} \lambda_s^*\, f_{its}(\mathbf{\Delta}_i|\mathbf{\theta}_{st}^*)\right), \qquad (6.9)$$

which is equivalent to the posterior probability, P_{is}, defined earlier in (6.4). Consequently,

$$E(z_{is};\ \mathbf{\theta}_{st}^*|\mathbf{\Delta}_i) = P_{is}^*, \qquad (6.10)$$

where P_{is}^* denotes the posterior probability evaluated with provisional estimates λ_s^* and $\mathbf{\theta}_{st}^*$. Thus, in the E-step, the non-observed discrete data $\mathbf{Z}$ are replaced by the posterior probabilities computed on the basis of provisional parameter estimates, and the conditional expectation becomes:

$$E_z\ (ln\ L_c;\ \mathbf{\theta}_{st} = \mathbf{\theta}_{st}^*) = \sum_{i=1}^{N}\sum_{s=1}^{S} P_{is}^*\, ln(f_{its}(\mathbf{\Delta}_i|\mathbf{\theta}_{is}^*))$$

$$+ \sum_{i=1}^{N}\sum_{s=1}^{S} P_{is}^*\, ln\ \lambda_s^*. \qquad (6.11)$$

In the M-step, $E_z(ln\ L_c;\ \lambda_s = \lambda_s^*, \mathbf{\theta}_{st} = \mathbf{\theta}_{st}^*)$ is maximized with respect to λ_s and $\mathbf{\theta}_{st}$, $\supset_{s,t}$ (subject to constraints (6.2) and (6.3) in order to obtain revised parameter estimates. These revised estimates are then used in the subsequent E-step to compute new estimates of the non-observed data $\mathbf{Z}$. The new estimate of $\mathbf{Z}$ is used in the subsequent M-step to arrive at new estimates of the parameters λ and θ. The E-step and the M-step are successively iterated until no further significant improvement in the ln-likelihood function occurs based on a specified convergence criterion. Dempster, Laird, and Rubin (1977) provide a proof based on Jensen's inequality that $L_c^{(h+1)} \geqslant L_c^{(h)}$ (monotonic increasing) so that convergence to at least a locally optimum solution can be proven using a limiting sums argument (where h is the iteration counter). Boyles (1983) and Wu (1983) provide a discussion of the convergence properties of the E-M algorithm.

Schematically, the E-M algorithm proposed above may be described as follows:

1 Initialize the iteration index h; $h \leftarrow 0$. Input Δ, S and T values. Specify initial estimates $\lambda^{(0)}$ and $\theta^{(0)}$.
2 Compute $Z^{(h)}$ with $z_{is}^{(h)} = P_{is}^{(h)}$.
3 Obtain revised estimates $\theta^{(h)}$ for the S groups and T dimensions.
4 Compute new estimates $\lambda^{(h)}$ of λ.
5 Test for convergence. If change in the ln likelihood from iteration (h) to $(h + 1)$ is smaller than some positive constant, stop.
6 Increment iteration index h: $h \leftarrow h + 1$; return to step (1).

Note, the specific estimation sub-routine employed in step (3) above is dependent upon the structure of the LCMDS model and the specification of $f_{its}(\bullet)$. Estimates of λ_s can typically be obtained as $\sum_{i=1}^{N} P_{is}/N$. Hence, upon convergence, one obtains estimates of the group proportions λ and the group-specific spatial coordinates θ. An asymptotic estimate of the variance–covariance matrix of the parameters can be obtained using the (generalized) inverse of the estimated Hessian matrix.

Since the number of dimensions and latent classes or groups is rarely known in practice, the estimation algorithm must be run for a varying number of latent classes (S) and number of dimensions (T). (For most LCMDS models, solutions with $T > S$ are not identifiable.) Note that the regularity conditions for the likelihood ratio test typically do not hold for this class of models (see McLachlan and Basford, 1988). As such, a number of alternative heuristics have been suggested for selecting S and T values. Bozdogan and Sclove (1984) propose using Akaike's (1974) information criterion (AIC) for choosing the number of latent classes (and dimensions) in mixture models. Accordingly, the values of S and T are the solution which minimizes:

$$\text{AIC}_{S,T} = - 2 \ln L + 2 N_{S,T}, \tag{6.12}$$

where $N_{S,T}$ is the number of free parameters in the full model being estimated given no additional restrictions on any of the parameters. More recently however, Bozdogan (1987) proposed that researchers use the CAIC (Consistent AIC) as a heuristic since it penalizes overparameterization more strongly than the AIC. This CAIC statistic is computed as:

$$\text{CAIC}_{S,T} = - 2 \ln L + N_{S,T} (\ln n + 1), \tag{6.13}$$

where n is the number of independent data observations. Note that the CAIC is more conservative than the AIC. The CAIC is recommended when the data entail a large number of observations (Bozdogan, 1987).

Note that both the AIC and CAIC measures have their theoretical basis grounded on asymptotic expansions assuming the same regularity conditions as the likelihood ratio test which we previously mentioned as not legitimately holding in such LCMDS situations. Researchers like Aitkin,

Anderson, and Hinde (1981) and De Soete and DeSarbo (1991) have recommended the use of Monte Carlo methods for determining S (and T). However, this class of heuristics involves extensive and burdensome computer computations, and is not feasible for larger data sets often encountered in marketing research practice. Recent work underway by Windham and Cutler (1991) using the estimated information matrix and rates of convergence looks quite promising in this regard.

While these heuristics account for over-parameterization as larger numbers of latent classes and dimension are derived, one must also ensure that the group centroids of $f_{its}(\bullet)$ are sufficiently separated for the solution that is chosen. To assess the separation of the latent classes (when $S > 1$), an entropy-based measure is often utilized (see DeSarbo, Wedel, Vriens, and Ramaswamy, 1992) to examine the degree of fuzziness in latent class membership based on the estimated posterior probabilities:

$$E_{S,T} = 1 - \left[\sum_{i=1}^{N} \sum_{s=1}^{S} - P_{is} \ln P_{is} \right] / n \ln S. \qquad (6.14)$$

$E_{S,T}$ is a relative measure that is bounded between 0 and 1. Given S latent classes, $E_{S,T} = 0$ when all the posterior probabilities are equal for each consumer (maximum entropy). A value of $E_{S,T}$ very close to zero is cause for concern as it implies that the centroids of the conditional parametric distributions are not sufficiently well separated for the particular number of latent classes that have been derived.

3 LCMDS for the Analysis of Proximity Data

In marketing, a classical approach to measure customer perceptions is through the multidimensional scaling of proximity data (cf. DeSarbo and Manrai, 1992; DeSarbo, Johnson, Manrai, Manrai, and Edwards, 1992; Manrai 1990; Manrai and Manrai, 1989). Typically, this involves asking consumers to give judgments of overall proximity between $J(J - 1)/2$ distinct pairs of brands and then use this data to estimate a geometric map in which the J brands are designated as points in a multidimensional space. The traditional MDS model (Torgersen, 1958; Gower, 1966) is given below in equation (6.15) and a weighted Euclidean distance model (Carroll and Chang, 1970) is given in equation (6.16):

$$\delta_{ijk} \cong d_{ijk} = \left[\sum_{t=1}^{T} \left(x_{jt} - x_{kt} \right)^2 \right]^{1/2} \qquad (6.15)$$

and

$$\delta_{ijk} \cong d_{ijk} = \left[\sum_{t=1}^{T} w_{it}\left(x_{jt} - x_{kt}\right)^2 \right]^{1/2}, \qquad (6.16)$$

where δ_{ijk} is the proximity judgment given by the i-th consumer for a pair
of brands $\{j, k\}$, x_{jt} is the coordinate of the j-th brand on the t-th dimension
($t = 1, \ldots, T$), w_{it} is the weight for the t-th dimension for the i-th customer;
and d_{ijk} is the model distance between the j-th and the k-th brands from the
i-th consumer ($j, k = 1, 2, \ldots, J; j \neq k$). The weights w_{it} in equation (6.16)
are typically required to be non-negative: $w_{it} \geq 0$. In contrast to the
traditional MDS model in equation (6.15), the INDSCAL or Euclidean
weighted distance model proposed by Carroll and Chang (1970) in equation (6.16) produces a multidimensional representation of the J brands that
is not invariant to rotation, thus providing marketers with dimensions
that are potentially interpretable in terms of their underlying psychological
meaning. This INDSCAL model, however, involves a large number of
parameters which increase with the number of consumers providing the
proximity judgments. Typically, the additional individual level w_{it} parameters
are rarely interpreted for individual consumers and the improvement in
goodness-of-fit measures seldom seems to justify the additional parameters.

Winsberg and De Soete (1992) attempt to resolve this excessive parameter problem associated with the INDSCAL model by proposing a latent
class approach to this framework. Their CLASCAL model, like INDSCAL,
removes the rotational indeterminancies in the brand space and thereby aids in obtaining psychologically meaningful dimensions; but, unlike
INDSCAL, CLASCAL requires far fewer parameters to be estimated. Let
$\mathbf{\Delta}_i = (\delta_{i12}, \delta_{i13}, \ldots, \delta_{iJ(J-1)/2})'$ be a column vector of pair-wise dissimilarities
between $J(J-1)/2$ distinct pairs brands obtained from consumer i. The
complete data set is a $N \times M$ matrix, where $M = J(J-1)/2$, designated by
$\mathbf{\Delta} = (\mathbf{\Delta}_1, \mathbf{\Delta}_1, \ldots, \mathbf{\Delta}_N)'$. The unconditional probability that any customer
belongs to latent class s will be denoted as λ_s, where λ_s obeys (6.2) and (6.3).
Winsberg and De Soete's (1992) CLASCAL deals with metric or continuous
proximity data with the assumption of independent normal distributions
that have a common variance; i.e. CLASCAL assumes $\mathbf{\Delta}_i$ to be normally
distributed:

$$\mathbf{\Delta}_i \sim N(\mathbf{m}_s, \sigma^2 \mathbf{I}), \qquad \text{for consumer } i \text{ in latent class } s. \qquad (6.17)$$

Note that the column vector of means is designated as $\mathbf{m}_s = (m_{s12}, m_{s13}, \ldots, m_{sJ(J-1)/2})$. In this latent class Euclidean weighted distance model, the
elements m_{sjk} of the M-component vector of means $\mathbf{m}_s$ are defined as:

$$m_{sjk} = \left[\sum_{t=1}^{T} w_{st}\left(x_{jt} - x_{kt}\right)^2 \right]^{1/2}, \qquad (6.18)$$

where $W_s = (w_{s1}, w_{s2}, \ldots, w_{sT})''$ denotes the INDSCAL-like weights for latent class s. Thus, the CLASCAL model estimates a separate set of weights (W_s) for each class s. Here, the matrix of location coordinates of the J brands, X, and the variance parameter, σ^2, are assumed to be the same for all S latent classes. The weights for the S latent classes are denoted by the $S \times T$ matrix $W = (W_1, W_2, \ldots, W_S)'$. The following two constraints are imposed on the weight parameters of the latent classes and location coordinates of the J brands by Winsberg and De Soete (1992) to fully identify the CLASCAL latent class model:

$$\sum_{s=1}^{S} w_{st} = S \qquad \text{for } t = 1, 2, \ldots, T, \qquad (6.19)$$

$$\sum_{j=1}^{J} x_{jt} = 0 \qquad \text{for } t = 1, 2, \ldots, T. \qquad (6.20)$$

The degrees of freedom of CLASCAL are $S + (S + J - 2)T$. Note that CLASCAL reduces to the classical unweighted Euclidean distance model in equation (6.15) when $S = 1$. It is also equivalent to INDSCAL, the weighted Euclidean distance model in equation (6.16), when $S = N$.

The probability density function of the data of consumer i belonging to latent class s can be written as:

$$G_i(\Delta_i | X, W_s, \sigma^2) = (\sigma\{2\pi\}^{1/2})^{-M} \exp[-\{(\Delta_i - m_s)' (\Delta_i - m_s)/2\sigma^2]. \quad (6.21)$$

Since a consumer's membership to a particular latent class is not known in advance, the density function of Δ_i becomes a finite mixture of multivariate normal densities. The maximum likelihood estimates of parameters X, W, σ^2, λ are obtained by maximizing the likelihood function based on the finite mixture of these multivariate densities subject to (6.2), (6.3), (6.19), (6.20), and $w_{st} \geq 0$. Winsberg and De Soete (1992) employ an E-M algorithm similar to the general form described in Section 2 to obtain the parameter estimates. Once the parameters are estimated, Bayes' theorem may be used to compute the posterior probability that consumer i belongs to class s via expression (6.4), and a consumer can be assigned to the class for which the posterior membership probability is the largest.

De Soete, Meulman, and Heiser (1992) proposed a different LCMDS approach to analyze three-way, two-mode proximity data. Here, unlike CLASCAL, both the matrix of location coordinates of the multidimensional configuration of the J brands and the variance parameters can vary from one latent class to another. The distance between brands j and k in latent class s is given as:

$$d_{sjk} = d(X_{sj}, X_{sk})' = [(X_{sj} - X_{sk})' (X_{sj} - X_{sk})]^{1/2}, \qquad (6.22)$$

where X_{sj} denotes the jth row of X_s written as a column vector and $X = \{X_1, X_2, \ldots, X_S\}$. These authors propose two models: (1) a constant variance model (DMH 1) in which the variance parameter is same for all latent classes as in CLASCAL, and (2) a proportional variance model (DMH 2) in which, unlike CLASCAL, the variance parameters are allowed to vary by latent class. Specifically, in DMH 2, the variance parameters are assumed to be proportional to the square of the inter-brand distances within a latent class. Thus, the dissimilarity judgment of consumer i for a pair of brands $\{j, k\}$ is assumed to follow the following normal distributions:

$$\delta_{ijk} \sim N(\alpha_s + d_{sjk}, \sigma^2) \qquad \text{in Model DMH 1} \qquad (6.23)$$

or

$$\delta_{ijk} \sim N(\alpha_s + d_{sjk}, \beta_s\, d_{sjk}^2) \qquad \text{in Model DMH 2.} \qquad (6.24)$$

The degrees of freedom of these models are:

$$\text{DMH 1 model: } 2S + S[JT - T(T + 1)/2],$$

and

$$\text{DMH 2 model: } 3S + S[JT - T(T + 1)/2] - 1.$$

The probability density function of the dissimilarity judgment Δ_i of consumer i belonging to class s for these models are given as:

DMH 1 model:

$$G_i(\Delta_i|X, \alpha_s, \sigma^2) = (\sigma\{2\pi\}^{1/2})^{-M} \exp\left[-\{1/2\sigma^2\}\sum_{j>k}^{J}\left(\delta_{ijk} - \alpha_s - d_{sjk}\right)^2\right] \quad (6.25)$$

DMH 2 model:

$$G_i(\Delta_i|X_s, \alpha_s, \beta_s) = (2\pi\beta_s)^{-M/2}\left(1/\prod_{j>k}^{J} d_{sjk}\right)\exp\left[-\left\{1/2\,\beta_s\right\}\right.$$

$$\left.\sum_{j>k}^{J}\left\{\left(\delta_{ijk} - \alpha_s - d_{sjk}\right)^2 / d_{sjk}^2\right\}\right]. \qquad (6.26)$$

In these models, the probability distribution functions of the data of any consumer i (who is not known in advance to belong to any particular latent class) becomes a finite mixture of multivariate normal densities, and maximizing the corresponding likelihood functions yields a vector of parameters: $(\lambda, X, \alpha, \sigma^2)$ in case of the DMH 1 model or $(\lambda, X, \alpha, \beta)$ in case of the DMH 2 model. After estimating the parameters using a generalized expectation maximizing (GEM) algorithm similar to that described in Section 2, De Soete, Meulman, and Heiser (1992) use Bayes' theorem to obtain posterior probabilities of consumer i belonging to class s as in equation (6.4), and assign a consumer to the class for which the posterior membership probability is the highest.

4 LCMDS for the Analysis of Dominance Data

DeSarbo, Howard, and Jedidi (1990) develop a maximum likelihood based method for performing LCMDS with a scalar products or vector model on a given set of two-way dominance/preference or profile data. This procedure, which they call MULTICLUS, utilizes mixtures of multivariate conditional normal distributions to estimate a joint space of brand coordinates and S vectors, one for each latent class, in a T-dimensional space. Define:

$\delta_{ij} =$ the observed profile/dominance value of brand j for consumer i, where $\Delta_i = (\delta_{ij})$;

$x_{jt} =$ the t-th coordinate value for brand j, where $X = ((x_{jt}))$;

$y_{st} =$ the t-th coordinate for the vector terminus for latent class s, where $Y_s = (y_{st})$ and $Y = ((y_{st}))$;

$\Sigma_s =$ the $J \times J$ variance–covariance matrix for latent class s.

The authors assume that the probability density function for the $1 \times J$ random vector $\Delta_i = (\delta_{i1}, \ldots, \delta_{iJ})$ is a finite mixture of conditional distributions:

$$G_i (\Delta_i; \lambda, Y, X, \Sigma) = \sum_{s=1}^{S} \lambda_s f_{its} (\Delta_i | Y_s, X, \Sigma_s), \qquad (6.27)$$

where λ obeys the restrictions in (6.2) and (6.3). Here, $\Sigma = (\Sigma_1, \Sigma_2, \ldots, \Sigma_S)$ is a $S \times J \times J$ array and Y_s is the $1 \times T$ row vector of coordinates for the s-th row of Y. The distribution of each f_{its} is specified as a conditional multivariate normal:

$$f_{its} (\Delta_i | Y_s, X, \Sigma_s) = (2\pi)^{-J/2} |\Sigma_s|^{-1/2}$$

$$\exp\{-1/2(\Delta_i - Y_s X') \Sigma_s^{-1} (\Delta_i - Y_s X')'\}, \qquad (6.28)$$

where $Y_s X'$ represents the scalar products or linear projection of the brand points onto latent class s's vector. That is, the authors assume a random sample of Δ_i drawn from a mixture of conditional multivariate normal densities of S underlying groups or clusters in unknown proportions $\lambda_1, \lambda_2, \ldots, \lambda_S$ (see McLachlan and Basford, 1988, concerning the use of such mixtures in previous approaches to pattern clustering, as well as Goodman, 1974, and Takane, 1976, for model similarities with latent structure analysis and latent profile models).

Given a sample of independent consumers, the likelihood has the form:

$$L = \prod_{i=1}^{N} \left[\sum_{s=1}^{S} \lambda_s (2\pi)^{-J/2} |\Sigma_s|^{-1/2} \right. \tag{6.29}$$

$$\left. \exp\left\{ -1/2(\Delta_i - Y_s X') \Sigma_s^{-1} (\Delta_i - Y_s X')' \right\} \right],$$

or

$$\ln L = \sum_{i=1}^{N} \ln \left[\sum_{s=1}^{S} \lambda_s f_{its} (\Delta_i | \Sigma_s, Y_s, X) \right]. \tag{6.30}$$

Given Δ, T, and S, the task is to estimate λ, Σ, Y, and X so as to maximize expressions (6.29) or (6.30), given the conditions specified in (6.2) and (6.3). DeSarbo, Howard, and Jedidi (1990) use the first derivative conditions to derive analytical expressions for parameter estimates as opposed to the explicit E-M framework discussed in Section 2. We summarize their approach to illustrate the similarities of their approach to the E-M framework.

The maximum likelihood estimates of λ, Y, X and Σ, and $P = ((P_{is}))$ are found by initially forming an augmented Lagrangean to reflect the constraints on λ_s:

$$\Phi = \sum_{i=1}^{N} \ln \left[\sum_{s=1}^{S} \lambda_s f_{its} (\Delta_i | Y_s, X, \Sigma_s) \right] - u \left(\sum_{s=1}^{S} \lambda_s - 1 \right), \tag{6.31}$$

where u is the corresponding multiplier. The resulting maximum likelihood stationary equations are obtained by equating the first order partial derivatives of the augmented log-likelihood function in (6.31) to zero:

$$\frac{\partial \Phi}{\partial u} = \sum_{s=1}^{S} \lambda_s - 1 = 0; \tag{6.32}$$

$$\frac{\partial \Phi}{\partial \lambda_s} = \sum_{i=1}^{N} \frac{1}{\sum_s \lambda_s f_{its}(\bullet)} f_{its}(\bullet) - u = 0; \tag{6.33}$$

$$\frac{\partial \Phi}{\partial \mathbf{Y}_s} = \sum_{i=1}^{N} \frac{1}{\sum_s \lambda_s f_{its}(\bullet)} \lambda_s f_{its}(\bullet)\,(\mathbf{X}' \Sigma_s^{-1} \Delta_i' - \mathbf{X}' \Sigma_s^{-1} \mathbf{X} \mathbf{Y}_s') = 0; \tag{6.34}$$

$$\frac{\partial \Phi}{\partial \mathbf{X}} = \sum_{i=1}^{N} \frac{1}{\sum_s \lambda_s f_{its}(\bullet)} \sum_{s=1}^{S} \lambda_s f_{its}(\bullet)\, \Sigma_s^{-1}\,(\Delta_i - \mathbf{Y}_s \mathbf{X}')' \mathbf{Y}_s = 0; \tag{6.35}$$

$$\frac{\partial \Phi}{\partial \Sigma_s^{-1}(r, n)} = \sum_{i=1}^{N} \frac{\lambda_s f_{its}(\bullet)}{\sum_s \lambda_s f_{its}(\bullet)} (1 - h_{rn}/2)$$

$$\left[\left(\sum_s (r, n) - (\Delta_i - \mathbf{Y}_s \mathbf{X}')\,(\Delta_i - \mathbf{Y}\mathbf{X})' \right)_i \right] = 0; \tag{6.36}$$

or if all covariance matrices are assumed equal,

$$\frac{\partial \Phi}{\partial \Sigma^{-1}(r, n)} = \sum_{i=1}^{N} \frac{1}{\sum_s \lambda_s f_{its}(\bullet)} \sum_{s=1}^{S} \lambda_s f_{its}(\bullet)$$

$$(1 - h_{rn}/2) \left[(\sum(r, n) - (\Delta_i - \mathbf{Y}_s \mathbf{X}'))\,(\Delta_i - \mathbf{Y}_s \mathbf{X}')' \right] = 0 \tag{6.37}$$

where $\sum_s^{-1}(r, n)$ denotes the *rn*-th element of Σ_s^{-1}, $\sum_s (r, n)$ denotes the *rn*-th element of Σ_s, and h_{rn} is the Kronecker delta. To estimate u, one multiplies both sides of (6.33) by λ_s and sums over s:

$$\sum_{i=1}^{N} \frac{\sum_s \lambda_s f_{its}(\bullet)}{\sum_s \lambda_s f_{its}(\bullet)} - u \sum_s \lambda_s = 0,$$

or

$$\hat{u} = N. \tag{6.38}$$

To estimate λ_s, one multiplies both sides of (6.33) by λ_s and simplifies:

$$\sum_{i=1}^{N} \frac{\lambda_s f_{its}(\bullet)}{\sum_s \lambda_s f_{its}(\bullet)} - \lambda_s u = 0, \tag{6.39}$$

or

$$\sum_{i=1}^{N} \hat{P}_{is} - \lambda_s N = 0, \tag{6.40}$$

and

$$\hat{\lambda}_s = \frac{\sum_{i=1}^{N} \hat{P}_{is}}{N}. \tag{6.41}$$

To solve for $\hat{Y}_s$, one expands (6.34) and substitutes for $\hat{P}_{is}$:

$$\sum_{i=1}^{N} \hat{P}_{is}(\mathbf{X}'\boldsymbol{\Sigma}_s^{-1} \boldsymbol{\Delta}_i' - \mathbf{X}'\boldsymbol{\Sigma}_s^{-1} \mathbf{X}\mathbf{Y}_s') = \mathbf{0}, \tag{6.42}$$

or

$$\hat{Y}_s' = \left(\sum_{i=1}^{N} \hat{P}_{is}\mathbf{X}'\boldsymbol{\Sigma}_s^{-1}\mathbf{X} \right)^{-1} \left(\sum_{i=1}^{N} \hat{P}_{is}\mathbf{X}'\boldsymbol{\Sigma}_s^{-1} \boldsymbol{\Delta}_i' \right). \tag{6.43}$$

By expanding and substituting in (6.36) and (6.37), analytical expressions for $\hat{\boldsymbol{\Sigma}}_s$ or $\hat{\boldsymbol{\Sigma}}$ can be obtained using:

$$\hat{\boldsymbol{\Sigma}}_s = \frac{1}{N\hat{\lambda}_s} \sum_{i=1}^{N} \hat{P}_{is} (\boldsymbol{\Delta}_i - \mathbf{Y}_s\mathbf{X}')' (\boldsymbol{\Delta}_i - \mathbf{Y}_s\mathbf{X}'), \tag{6.44}$$

or

$$\hat{\boldsymbol{\Sigma}} = \frac{1}{N} \sum_{i=1}^{N} \sum_{s=1}^{S} \hat{P}_{is} (\boldsymbol{\Delta}_i - \mathbf{Y}_s\mathbf{X}')' (\boldsymbol{\Delta}_i - \mathbf{Y}_s\mathbf{X}'). \tag{6.45}$$

To solve for $\hat{\mathbf{X}}$, the following stationary equation is derived from (35):

$$\sum_{i=1}^{N} \sum_{s=1}^{S} \hat{P}_{is} \boldsymbol{\Sigma}_s^{-1} (\boldsymbol{\Delta}_i' - \mathbf{X}\mathbf{Y}_s')\mathbf{Y}_s = \mathbf{0}, \tag{6.46}$$

or

$$\sum_{i=1}^{N} \sum_{s=1}^{S} \hat{P}_{is} \Sigma_s^{-1} \Delta_i' \, Y_s = \sum_{i=1}^{N} \sum_{s=1}^{S} \hat{P}_{is} \Sigma_s^{-1} XY_s' \, Y_s. \tag{6.47}$$

Taking the transpose of both sides and post multiplying by Σ_s yields:

$$\sum_{i=1}^{N} \sum_{s=1}^{S} \hat{P}_{is} \, Y_s' \Delta_i = \sum_{i=1}^{N} \sum_{s=1}^{S} \hat{P}_{is} \, Y_s' \, Y_s X', \tag{6.48}$$

and

$$\hat{X} = \left(\sum_{i=1}^{N} \sum_{s=1}^{S} \hat{P}_{is} \, Y_s' \, Y_s \right)^{-1} \left(\sum_{i=1}^{N} \sum_{s=1}^{S} \hat{P}_{is} \, Y_s' \, \Delta_i \right). \tag{6.49}$$

The unique inverse exists for $S \geq T$ with $\lambda_s \neq 0$ for all s; otherwise, a generalized inverse in (6.49) must be used. Note, since S vectors can always be perfectly fitted in a S dimensional space, solutions with $T > S$ will not improve the log likelihood over corresponding $T = S$ solutions and can thus be ignored. Thus, in this formulation, the maximum likelihood equation for estimating Σ_s (or Σ), Y_s, and X are weighted averages of the maximum likelihood equations:

$$\frac{\partial \log f_{its}(\bullet)}{\partial M} = 0,$$

where M denotes the parameter of interest, arising from each component separately, and the weights are the posterior probabilities of membership of the objects in each cluster. This specific structure is equivalent to the application of a two stage E-M algorithm (Dempster, Laird, and Rubin, 1977) described in general terms earlier in Section 2 for the iterative estimation of these parameters. In the E stage, one estimates λ_s and P_{is}. In the M stage, one estimate Y, Σ_s (Σ), and X. For specified initial values of these parameters, the expectation (E phase) and maximization (M phase) steps of this algorithm are alternated until convergence of a sequence of log-likelihood values is obtained. DeSarbo, Howard, and Jedidi (1990) use an AIC (or CAIC) heuristic for selection of the appropriate values of S and T. De Soete and Winsberg (1993) later generalize this MULTICLUS procedure to incorporate linear restrictions on X.

DeSarbo, Jedidi, Cool, and Schendel (1991) later extended this MULTI-CLUS LCMDS framework to multidimensional unfolding for profile data in their application of finding strategic groups (i.e. latent classes) of firms or

SBUs from PIMS strategy and performance data. For their application, they define:

$i = 1, \ldots, N$ firms or SBUs;

$j = 1, \ldots, J$ strategy and performance attributes;

$s = 1, \ldots, S$ strategic groups;

δ_{ij} = the value of strategy/performance variable j for firm i, where
   $\mathbf{\Delta}_i = (\delta_{ij})$;

x_{jt} = the t-th coordinate for variable j;

y_{st} = the t-th coordinate for strategic group s;

w_{st} = the importance or salience of dimension t for strategic group s;

c_s = an additive constant for strategic group s;

$\mathbf{\Sigma}_s$ = a $J \times J$ variance–covariance matrix for strategic group s.

It is assumed that the row vector $\mathbf{\Delta}_i$ of dimension J has a probability density function which can be modeled as a finite mixture of the following conditional distributions:

$$G_i (\mathbf{\Delta}_i; \mathbf{\lambda}, \mathbf{X}, \mathbf{Y}, \mathbf{\Sigma}, \mathbf{c}, \mathbf{W}) = \sum_{s=1}^{S} \lambda_s f_{its} ((\mathbf{\Delta}_i | \mathbf{X}, \mathbf{Y}_s, c_s, \mathbf{W}_s, \mathbf{\Sigma}_s), \qquad (6.50)$$

where:

$\mathbf{X} = ((x_{jt})),$

$\mathbf{Y} = ((y_{jt}))$

$\mathbf{Y}_s$ = the $1 \times T$ row vector of coordinates of the s-th row (strategic group) of $\mathbf{Y}$,

$\mathbf{W} = ((w_{st}))$

$\mathbf{W}_s$ = the $1 \times T$ row vector of salience weights of the s-th row (strategic group) of $\mathbf{W}$,

$\mathbf{c} = (c_1, c_2, \ldots, c_s)$

$\mathbf{\Sigma} = (\mathbf{\Sigma}_1, \mathbf{\Sigma}_2, \ldots, \mathbf{\Sigma}_s)$

The distribution for each f_{its} is specified as a conditional (nonlinear) multivariate normal:

$$f_{its} (\mathbf{\Delta}_i | \mathbf{X}, \mathbf{Y}_s, c_s, \mathbf{W}_s, \mathbf{\Sigma}_s) = (2\pi)^{-J/2} |\mathbf{\Sigma}_s|^{-1/2}$$
$$\exp [- 1/2 (\mathbf{\Delta}_i - \mathbf{R}_s) \mathbf{\Sigma}_s^{-1} (\mathbf{\Delta}_i - \mathbf{R}_s)'], \qquad (6.51)$$

where:

$$\mathbf{R}_s = (R_{1s}, R_{2s}, \ldots, R_{Js}),$$

$$R_{js} = \sum_{t=1}^{T} w_{st}(x_{jt} - y_{st})^2 + c_s. \tag{6.52}$$

Expression (6.52) represents a weighted Euclidean distance formulation (see Carroll, 1980) between strategic group s and (strategy or performance) variable j in the derived Euclidean space. This approach models the data via a joint space of strategy and performance variables on the one hand, and strategic group locations on the other. More specifically, the "closer" a particular strategy and/or performance variable is to a strategic group location, the higher the value of that variable predicted for that strategic group. This is equivalent to the notion of distance in the strategy map concept of Day, DeSarbo, and Oliva (1987) in their application of the DeSarbo and Rao (1984, 1986) GENFOLD2 procedure. However, this methodology determines the locations and behavior for strategic groups, and not that of individual firms. (Note, De Soete and Heiser (1993) have generalized this latent class unfolding model to accommodate linear restrictions on $\mathbf{X}$.)

The "full" model thus provides the coordinates of the J strategy and performance variables ($\mathbf{X}$), the coordinates of the strategic groups ($\mathbf{Y}$), the coordinates of the strategic group weights ($\mathbf{W}$), the covariance matrices ($\mathbf{\Sigma}_s$), and the additive constants (c_s). The $\mathbf{X}$ and $\mathbf{Y}$ are plotted in a joint T-dimensional space indicating (by these distance notions) the relationships between the derived strategic groups and the strategy and performance variables. The $\mathbf{W}_s$ indicate which dimensions are more salient for the s-th strategic group. The $\mathbf{\Sigma}_s$ gives the estimated covariance structure among the strategy and performance variables for strategic group s.

Given a sample of N independent firms, one can thus form a likelihood expression:

$$L = \prod_{i=1}^{N} \left[\sum_{s=1}^{S} \lambda_s (2\pi)^{-J/2} |\mathbf{\Sigma}_s|^{-1/2} \exp[-1/2 (\mathbf{\Delta}_i - \mathbf{R}_s)\mathbf{\Sigma}_s^{-1} (\mathbf{\Delta}_i - \mathbf{R}_s)'] \right] \tag{6.53}$$

or,

$$\ln L = \sum_{i=1}^{N} \ln \left[\sum_{s=1}^{S} \lambda_s f_{its} (\mathbf{\Delta}_i | \mathbf{X}, \mathbf{Y}_s, \mathbf{W}_s, \mathbf{\Sigma}_s) \right]. \tag{6.54}$$

Given $\mathbf{\Delta}$, T, and S, one wishes to estimate λ, $\mathbf{\Sigma}$, $\mathbf{X}$, $\mathbf{Y}$, c, and $\mathbf{W}$, in the "full model" so as to maximize expressions (6.53) or (6.54), given the conditions specified in equation (6.2) and (6.3). Strategic group memberships are given by the posterior probabilities. Again, the first derivative stationary equations are utilized for parameter estimation. However, analytical expressions are not obtainable for $\hat{X}, \hat{Y}$, or c, and a conjugate gradient search procedure is used iteratively.

Bockenholt and Gaul (1991) generalize these two previous DeSarbo *et al.* (1990, 1991) approaches to the analysis of ordinal or rank-ordered data using a successive categories scaling approach (Schonemann and Tucker, 1967; Takane, 1981). Due to restricted space in this chapter, we only consider the case of J ordered categorical variables (usually collected on rating scales), which describe the preference or buying intention of consumers with respect to various choice alternatives (e.g. brands). To accommodate this kind of data, Bockenholt and Gaul (1991) assume a latent response scale for brand j consisting of ordered, mutually exclusive and exhaustive intervals, i.e.

$$- \infty = b_{j0} < b_{j1} < \ldots < b_{jg_j} < \ldots < b_{jk_{j-1}} < b_{jk_j} = \infty \qquad (6.55)$$

where b_{jg_j} denotes the upper boundary of the g_j^{th} interval. In order to provide a graphical representation of latent class specific response probabilities $p_{jg_j|s}$, these authors represent each latent class K_s ($s = 1, \ldots, S$) either by an ideal point $\mathbf{Y}_s = (y_{s1}, \ldots, y_{sT})$ or a preference vector $\mathbf{V}_s = (v_{s1}, \ldots, v_{st})$ in a T-dimensional space, where $\mathbf{X}_j = (x_{j1}, \ldots, x_{jT})$ are the coordinates of the j-th brand under study, with:

$$D_{sj} = \left(\sum_{t=1}^{T} w_{st} \left(y_{st} - x_{jt} \right)^2 \right)^{1/2} + \epsilon_{sj}, \qquad w_{st} > 0 \qquad (6.56)$$

and
$$U_{sj} = \sum_{t=1}^{T} v_{st} x_{jt} + \varepsilon_{sj}, \qquad (6.57)$$

where: $\epsilon_{sj} \sim N\left(0, \sigma_{sj}^2\right)$,

$$\text{cov}\left(\epsilon_{s'j'}, \epsilon_{s''j''}\right) = \begin{cases} \sigma_{sj}^2 & \text{if } s = s' = s'', j = j' = j'' \\ 0 & \text{else.} \end{cases}$$

Note, equation (6.56) corresponds to an ideal point model (w_{st} is a latent class specific positive weight assigned to dimension t of the joint space), while (6.57) represents a scalar products or vector approach. The probability $p_{jg_j|s}$ can be expressed as:

$$p_{jg_j|s} = \text{Prob}\left(b_{j(k_j - g_j)} < D_{sj} \leq b_{j(k_j - g_{j+1})}\right)$$

$$= \int_{a_j(k_j - g_j)}^{a_j(k_j - g_{j+1})} \varphi(z)dz, \qquad (6.58)$$

$$\text{where: } a_j\left(k_j - g_{j+1}\right) = \frac{b_j\left(k_j - g_{j+1}\right) - \left(\sum_{t=1}^{T} w_{st}\left(y_{st} - x_{jt}\right)^2\right)^{\frac{1}{2}}}{\sigma_{sj}},$$

or

$$p_{jg_j|s} = \text{Prob}\left(b_{j(g_{j-1})} < U_{sj} \leq b_{jg_j}\right)$$

$$= \int_{a_{jg_j-1}}^{a_{jg_j}} \varphi(z)\, dz, \tag{6.59}$$

$$\text{where: } \quad a_{jg_j} = \frac{b_{jg_j} - V_s X_j'}{\sigma_{sj}}, \tag{6.60}$$

and φ denotes the standard normal distribution function. In the most general case, the parameters to be estimated are the coordinates of the latent class specific ideal points Y_s (respectively the coordinates of the latent class specific preferences vectors V_s), the coordinates of the brands X_j (these parameters might be *a priori* specified in terms of background variables which characterize the J choice alternatives under study), the weighting factors w_{st}, the variance components σ_{sj} (these parameters provide information about the heterogeneity in each latent class K_s), and the interval boundaries b_{jg_j}. For further extensions concerning a reparameterization of X_j or interval boundaries b_{jg_j}, as well as for a modified *E-M* algorithm which allows for the estimation of the parameters mentioned above, we refer to Bockenholt (1989). If we restrict (6.58) by $S = 1$ and $k_j = 2$ for $j = 1, \ldots, J$, we obtain the threshold ideal point model proposed by DeSarbo and Hoffmann (1986) as a special case of this generalized LCA approach. The corresponding likelihood function kernal for this Bockenholt and Gaul (1991) LCMDS model is:

$$L = \prod_{g_1 \cdots g_j} \left(\sum_{s=1}^{S} \lambda_s \left(\prod_{j=1}^{J} p_{jg_g|s}\right)\right)^{n_{g_1, \ldots, g_j}} \tag{6.61}$$

and an *E-M* maximum-likelihood based estimation procedure is utilized for estimation.

DeSarbo, Ramaswamy, and Lenk (1992) develop a scalar products vector LCMDS methodology for compositional data (e.g. constant sum ratings that sum to 1.0) using reparameterized mixtures of Dirichlet distributions. Let:

δ_{ij} = the observed proportional value of brand j for consumer i, where
$\quad \Delta_i = (\delta_{ij})$;
α_{js} = the value of the j-th parameter for the Dirichlet distribution for
latent class s;
x_{jt} = the t-th coordinate value for brand j;
y_{st} = the t-th coordinate value for the vector terminus for latent class s,

DeSarbo, Ramaswamy, and Lenk (1992) assume that the observed row vector Δ_i of dimension J has a probability density function, $G_i(\bullet)$, which can be modeled as a finite mixture of S conditional distributions:

$$G_i(\Delta_i; \lambda, \mathbf{Y}, \mathbf{X}) = \sum_{s} \lambda_s f_{its} (\Delta_i | \mathbf{Y}_s, \mathbf{X}), \qquad (6.62)$$

where each conditional distribution is specified as Dirichlet conditional upon class s:

$$f_{its} (\Delta_i; \mathbf{Y}_s, \mathbf{X}) = \left[\Gamma \left(\prod_{j=1}^{J} \alpha_{js} \right) / \prod_{j=1}^{J} \Gamma(\alpha_{js}) \right] \prod_{j=1}^{J} X_{hj}^{\alpha_{js} - 1}, \qquad (6.63)$$

and they impose (as a model option) the reparameterization $\alpha_{js} = \exp(\sum_t y_{st} x_{jt})$ given the need for α_{js} to be greater than zero (see also Maddala, 1990, for the use of the exponential function for such reparameterization in Poisson regression models). The expression $(\sum_t y_{st} x_{jt})$ represents the scalar product or linear projection of the brand point j onto the vector for class s. These authors have thus reparameterized the within-cluster parameters of the Dirichlet distribution $(\alpha_{ls}, \ldots, \alpha_{js})$ using the underlying multidimensional structure of the compositional data. The likelihood of observing the row vector Δ_i is now conditional upon the membership of consumer i in class s. One can also assess the extent of within-class heterogeneity via the parameter $\rho_s = 1/((\sum_j \alpha_{js}) + 1)$, for each class $s = 1, \ldots, S$. The authors also provide a proof for the identifiability of Dirichlet mixtures.

Given a sample of N consumers, the likelihood can be computed as:

$$L(\Delta_i; \lambda, \mathbf{Y}, \mathbf{X}) = \Phi \sum_{i=1}^{N} \sum_{s} \lambda_s \left[\Gamma \left(\sum_j \exp \left(\sum_t y_{st} x_{jt} \right) \right) \right/ $$

$$\prod_j \Gamma \left(\exp \left(\sum_t y_{st} x_{jt} \right) \right) \right] \times \prod_j \delta_{ij} \exp \left(\sum_t y_{st} x_{jt} \right) - 1, \qquad (6.64)$$

or

$$ln\ L = \sum_i ln\ G_i(\mathbf{\Delta}_i;\ \mathbf{\lambda},\ \mathbf{Y},\ \mathbf{X}). \tag{6.65}$$

Again, an *E-M* maximum likelihood based procedure is utilized to maximize (6.65) in obtaining parameter estimates.

5. Lᴄᴍᴅs for the Analysis of Choice Data

Two particular methods of data collection are quite prevalent in marketing research for measuring consumer choice behavior (cf. DeSarbo and Hoffman, 1986, 1987; DeSarbo and Cho, 1989; Manrai and Sinha, 1989). In the paired comparison method (David, 1988), a consumer is required to compare a pair of brands and to choose the most preferred one. In the second procedure, consumers select their preferred brand from a set of brands. The choice set could be constrained, i.e. "pick-any/J," or unconstrained, i.e. "pick-any" (see Coombs, 1964). The second data collection method is quick and simple. It also resembles the natural process of consumer choice behavior. The paired comparison task, on the other hand, is more time-consuming, but has the potential to provide more complete data regarding consumers' choices (Manrai and Manrai, 1993). For example, consider a consumer making an automobile choice. S/he may pick a Mercedes from a large set of luxury automobiles, i.e. "pick-any," or from a more limited choice set of say, seven luxury automobiles, e.g. {Acura, BMW, Cadillac, Corvette, Lexus, Mercedes, Porsche}, i.e. "pick-any/J," where $J = 7$. The paired comparison task in this latter case would involve a consumer stating her/his preference or choice of an automobile from each distinct possible set of pairs of automobiles, e.g. {Acura, BMW}, {Acura, Cadillac}, . . . , {Mercedes, Porsche}, a total of 21 pairs. The data obtained in this way may be coded as a binary variable where $z_{ijk} = 1$ *iff* consumer i prefers brand j over k, and 0 otherwise. The data of consumer i is denoted by a $J(J-1)/2$ component vector, $\mathbf{z}_i = (z_{i12}, z_{i13}, \ldots, z_{iJ(J-1)/2})'$, and the total data set is denoted by the matrix $\mathbf{Z} = (\mathbf{z}_1, \mathbf{z}_2, \ldots, \mathbf{z}_N)'$.

Traditionally, choice model defines the probability that consumer i prefers brand j over brand k as a function of some vector of model parameters $\mathbf{\theta}_i$. Assuming the data for $J(J-1)/2$ pairs of brands given by a consumer are independent of each other, the process can be represented by a multivariate Bernoulli distribution as:

$$f(\mathbf{z}_i|\mathbf{\theta}_i) = \prod_{j>k}\ p_{jk}\ (\mathbf{\theta}_i)^{z_{ijk}}[1 - p_{jk}\ (\mathbf{\theta}_i)]^{1-z_{ijk}}, \tag{6.66}$$

where $p_{jk}(\mathbf{\theta}_i)$ denotes the probability that consumer i prefers brand j to k. There are three ways to analyze a data set $\mathbf{Z}$ consisting of unreplicated paired comparison data from N customers: (1) the consumers are considered to be all different and individual parameters are estimated for each customer; (2) the N consumers may be considered as replications of each other and two-way replicated paired comparisons are derived from Z; and (3) Z is transformed to a three-way replicated $J \times J \times S$ paired comparison array by some *a priori* grouping of the N customers into $S (S << I)$ homogeneous segments.

Examples of the approach listed under (1) above are developed in DeSarbo, Oliver, and De Soete (1986), and DeSarbo, De Soete, and Eliashberg (1987). These models tend to have larger numbers of parameters whose order varies with the size of N and J. Individual level vectors or ideal points are estimated for each consumer. This limits the complexity of the structural component of these models. In addition, both the models by DeSarbo *et al.* referred to above are strong utility models. It may not be feasible to extend these models to allow for violations of the strong stochastic transitivity condition while still modeling unreplicated individual level data.

The other extreme is the approach in (2) above where the data are treated as replicated paired comparisons from a single consumer. Examples of choice models employing analysis of such three-way replicated paired comparison data are the wandering vector model of De Soete and Carroll (1983) and wandering ideal point model due to De Soete, Carroll, and DeSarbo (1986). Here, one aggregate vector or ideal point is typically estimated across the entire sample. These approaches are somewhat untenable from a marketing perspective as the consumers are typically heterogeneous in their tastes and preferences (Kotler, 1991). Furthermore, violation of this homogeneity assumption may lead to this particular approach yielding a rather incomplete or distorted description of the data.

A third approach that lies between these two extremes is to treat the N consumers belonging to $S (S << N)$ homogeneous segments. Consumers within each segment are treated as replications of each other and the choice models incorporate parameters to account for heterogeneity across different segments. However, this approach is of limited value because it has heretofore required an *a priori* classification of consumers into S market segments. De Soete (1990) proposes a latent class procedure that, on the basis of the choice data matrix Z, simultaneously classifies N customers in S segments, and models the preference structures of these segments. Each consumer i belongs to one and only one latent class s $(1 \leq s \leq S)$, but it is not known in advance to which specific class a particular consumer belongs. In addition to a set of parameters, τ, that are common across the S latent classes, the choice model also incorporates a set of class specific parameters, μ_s. The probability that a particular consumer i belongs to latent class s is λ_s. Hence, the distribution of the data of consumer i is a finite mixture of multivariate Bernoulli distributions:

$$G_i(z_i|\theta, \lambda) = \sum_{s=1}^{S} \lambda_s f_{its}(z_i|\tau, \mu_s), \quad (6.66)$$

with $\theta = \{\tau, \mu\}$, and

$$f_{its}(z_i|\tau, \mu_s) = \prod_{j<k} p_{sjk}^{z_{ijk}} (1 - p_{sjk})^{(1 - z_{ijk})}, \tag{6.67}$$

where $p_{sjk} = p_{jk}(\tau, \mu_s)$.

De Soete (1990) presents two latent class choice models based on the wandering vector and ideal point models. In the LCMDS model based on the wandering vector model (De Soete and Carroll, 1983), the J brands are represented as points, $X_1, X_2, \ldots, X_J$, in a multidimensional Euclidean space. Each latent class (segment) is represented by a vector in the same space, emanating from the origin. The endpoint of this vector follows a multivariate normal distribution with mean v_s and covariance matrix Σ_s. It can be shown that this model predicts the following choice probabilities:

$$p_{sjk} = \Phi((X_j - X_k)' \, v_s / \sigma_{sjk}), \tag{6.68}$$

with Φ defined as the standard normal cumulative distribution function, and

$$\sigma_{sjk}^2 = (X_j - X_k)' \, \Sigma_s \, (X_j - X_k) \tag{6.69}$$

In this case, τ and μ_s are defined as

$$\tau = \{X_1, X_2, \ldots, X_J\} \text{ and } \mu_s = \{v_s, \Sigma_s\}. \tag{6.70}$$

In the LCMDS model based on the wandering ideal point model (De Soete, Carroll, and DeSarbo, 1986), each brand j is also represented by X_j in a multidimensional Euclidean space. However, a latent class is represented by a point in the same space instead of a vector. This point is assumed to be multivariate normally distributed with mean v_s and covariance Σ_s. The choice probability predicted by this model is:

$$p_{sjk} = \Phi[\{(X_k' X_k - X_j' X_j) - 2(X_k - X_j)' v_s\} / 2\sigma_{sjk}], \tag{6.71}$$

where σ_{sjk}, and parameters τ and μ_s are as defined above in (6.69) and (6.70) in the case of wandering vector model.

In a typical application of these two LCMDS models, one needs to estimate the parameter vectors, θ and λ, on the basis of the observed data matrix, Z. Once parameter estimates are obtained, the posterior probability that a consumer i belongs to latent class s can be computed using Bayes' theorem as discussed previously. A consumer can then be assigned to a segment (latent class) for which the posterior membership probability is the largest. Maximum likelihood estimates of θ and λ can be obtained by maximizing the following likelihood function subject to the constraints in (6.2) and (6.3):

$$L(\mathbf{Z}|\boldsymbol{\theta}, \boldsymbol{\lambda}) = \prod_{i=1}^{N} G_i(z_i|\boldsymbol{\theta}, \boldsymbol{\lambda}) \tag{6.72}$$

with respect to $\boldsymbol{\theta}$ and $\boldsymbol{\lambda}$. The estimation problem is resolved by use of the *E-M* algorithm (Dempster, Laird, and Rubin, 1977) presented earlier.

Bockenholt and Bockenholt (1990a) present a restricted latent class (RLC) approach (cf. Formann, 1985, 1989) to model individual differences for describing "pick-any/*J*" and paired comparison data. Their approach complements the latent trait unfolding model introduced by Andrich (1988, 1989). DeSarbo and Hoffman (1986, 1987) had earlier specified a multidimensional, non-latent class version of this model. Bockenholt and Bockenholt (1990a) combine the restricted latent class analysis with an unfolding model (Coombs, 1950, Bennett and Hays, 1960). They provide empirical evidence to show that the model(s) and proposed estimation scheme can produce a meaningful classification of the consumers as well as a parsimonious representation of the unfolding structure in the data. Specifically, Bockenholt and Bockenholt (1990a) propose four undimensional unfolding models. We begin with a brief summary of basic assumptions of RLC (cf. Formann, 1985) before presenting the four models combining RLC with unfolding models introduced by Bockenholt and Bockenholt (1990a). Let $p_{j|s}$ be the probability that a consumer i in latent class s $(s = 1, \ldots S)$ selects brand j from a finite set of J brands – that is,

$$P(R_{ij} = 1|i \in K_s) = P_{j|s}, \tag{6.73}$$

where $R_{ij} = \{0, 1\}$ is a random variable. Let λ_s denotes the prior probability of a consumer belonging to a latent class s. The unconditional probability that a consumer i selects brand j is:

$$P(R_{ij} = 1) = \sum_{s=1}^{S} \lambda_s p_{j|s} = P_j, \tag{6.74}$$

where $\sum_{s=1}^{S} \lambda_s = 1$. Consumers are assumed to be conditionally independent within each latent class. Thus, the probability of a consumer selecting pattern $\mathbf{R}_i = \{R_{i1}, \ldots, R_{it}\}$ is:

$$P(R_i|i \in K_s) = \prod_{j=1}^{J} p_{j|s}^{R_{ij}}(1 - p_{j|s})^{1 - R_{ij}}, \tag{6.75}$$

and the corresponding unconditional probability of observing a choice pattern $\mathbf{R}_i$ is:

$$P(\mathbf{R}_i) = \sum_{s=1}^{S} \lambda_s P(R_i | i \in K_s).$$ (6.76)

Both sets of parameters, λ_s and $p_{j|s}$, are obtained by maximizing the kernel of the likelihood function:

$$L = \prod_{i=1}^{N} \left\{ \sum_{s=1}^{S} \lambda_s \left[\prod_{j=1}^{J} p_{j|s}^{R_{ij}} (1 - p_{j|s})^{1 - R_{ij}} \right] \right\}^{n_i},$$ (6.77)

where n_i denotes the observed frequency for a response pattern R_i. The parameters are estimated using the *E-M* algorithm (c.f. Dempster, Laird, and Rubin, 1977; Goodman, 1978, 1979; Takane and DeLeeuw, 1987) described in general form earlier.

The class specific probabilities of the RLC framework are defined by Bockenholt and Bockenholt (1990a) in their model 1, as a function of the distance between the ideal point of a latent class, Y_s, and brand coordinate, X_j:

$$P_{j|s} = 1 / \{1 + \exp[- c_s + (Y_s - X_j)^2]\}.$$ (6.78)

A latent class formulation of Hoijtink's (1990) model is captured in Bockenholt and Bockenholt's (1990a) model 2, where:

$$p_{j|s} = 1 / \{1 + (Y_s - X_j)^{2\gamma}\},$$ (6.79)

where γ is positive. Note that in model 1, $p_{j|s}$ approaches 1 only when $(Y_s - X_j) = 0$ and $c_s \to \infty$. In model 2, however, the class specific probability is 1 when $(Y_s - X_j) = 0$. Hence, a brand is always chosen by the consumers in a latent class when the brand location coincides with the ideal point of that latent class.

Based on Andrich's (1989) derivation of model 1 in equation (6.78) for pick any/J data, Bockenholt and Bockenholt (1990a) present the following RLC model 3 for paired comparison data:

$$p_{jk|s} = 1 / \{1 + \exp[(X_j^2 - X_k^2 - 2Y_s(X_j - X_k)]\}, \qquad \text{for } (X_j < X_k).$$ (6.80)

Similarly, corresponding to model 2 in equation (6.79), model 4 for paired comparison data is:

$$p_{jk|s} = (Y_s - X_k)^{2\gamma} / [(Y_s - X_j)^{2\gamma} + (Y_s - X_k)^{2\gamma}]$$ (6.81)

Note that while the four models are somewhat different in structure, these models are virtually indistinguishable on the basis of fit statistics as shown in an empirical study presented by Bockenholt and Bockenholt (1990a). Therefore, one advantage of the combined RLC and unfolding models is that the RLC probabilities for the qualitative characteristics can be inspected before a particular model is specified and tested, and this may provide a more concise representation of the paired comparison or "pick-any/J" data. One disadvantage of these models is their *unidimensional* nature which fails to capture the multidimensional nature of the preference data. (Bockenholt and Bockenholt (1990b) later apply constrained latent class analysis to *multidimensional* preference data which are ordinal in nature.)

De Soete and Winsberg (1992) present a latent class extension of the Thurstone's Case V model with spline transformations based on the latent class approach to the modeling of paired comparison data developed by Bockenholt and Bockenholt (1990a), De Soete (1990), and Formann (1989). Instead of a single dimension they assume that the utility of each brand is modeled in terms of its values on several (though usually a small number) attributes or dimensions. For example, the utility of a luxury automobile may be modeled in terms of its ratings on attributes such as body style, country of origin, and brand name. De Soete and Winsberg (1992) employ either an additive univariate spline model or a multivariate spline model to construct the utility function in terms of such attributes or dimensions. A separate univariate spline transformation is estimated for each attribute in the additive univariate spline model; and the utility of a brand is assumed to be an additive combination of transformed values. In the multivariate case, the utility of a brand is assumed to be a general multivariate spline function in the attributes. The De Soete and Winsberg (1992) model also assumes the existence of S latent classes ($s = 1, \ldots, S$) and that each consumer i ($i = 1, 2, \ldots, N$) belongs to one and only one (unknown) latent class s ($1 \leqslant s \leqslant S$). In accordance with Lazarsfeld and Henry's (1968) formulation, it is assumed that all consumers belonging to the same latent class utilize the same transformation function $f_{(s)}(\bullet)$ to arrive at a utility scale where a separate transformation function is estimated for each latent class s. As before, the vector of parameters required to characterize a transformation function in latent class s will be denoted by θ_s. Assuming there are T dimensions or attributes, in the case of univariate spline model, θ_s contains the coefficients of the T univariate polynomial spline transformations for latent class s; whereas, in the case of multivariate spline model, θ_s contains the weight coefficients for the tensor product basis function.

It may be appropriate at this juncture to introduce additional notation to familiarize the reader with further details regarding spline transformations. In the additive univariate spline model for $f(x)$, it is assumed that a separte univariate spline transformation $g_t(x_t)$ exists for each attribute or dimension t, $t = 1, 2, \ldots, T$. The utility of a brand j is an additive combination of the transformed values on the T attributes or dimensions:

$$f(x) = \sum_{t=1}^{T} g_t(x_t),$$

(6.82)

where:

$$g_t(x_t) = \sum_{q=1}^{\psi^{(t)}} C_q^{(t)} B_{q^{(t)}, K^{(t)}, r^{(t)}}(x_t),$$

(6.83)

and $B_{q^{(t)}, K^{(t)}, r^{(t)}}(x_t)$, the basis function, is defined as the K-th divided difference at $r_q^{(t)}, \ldots, r_{q+K}^{(t)}$ multiplied by $(r_{q+K}^{(t)} - r_q^{(t)})$.

$K^{(t)}$ is the maximum order, and $K^{(t)} - 1$ is the degree of the polynomial for attribute or dimension t. The notation $r^{(t)}$ refers to a knot sequence $\{r_1^{(t)}, \ldots, r_{m+K}^{(t)}\}$, and the number $\psi^{(t)}$ is determined by the equation:

$$\psi^{(t)} = L^{(t)} K^{(t)} - \sum_{q=2}^{L^{(t)}} \gamma_q^{(t)},$$

(6.84)

where $L^{(t)}$ represents polynomial segments each of order $K^{(t)}$ subject to the $\sum_{g=2}^{L^{(t)}} \gamma_g^{(t)}$ constraints. The location of a strictly increasing sequence $\{\xi_g^{(r)}\}$ of junction points satisfies: lower bound $1^{(r)} = \xi_1^{(r)} < \ldots < \xi_{L+1}^{(r)} = u^{(r)}$ upper bound, on which the function for the t-th attribute is defined.

In the multivariate spline model, $f(x)$ is assumed to be a general multivariate spline function of x. In this case, the basis function, $\Psi = \prod_{t=1}^{T} \Psi^{(t)}$ form the tensor products of the univariate spline bases. The multivariate spline transformation of a T-dimensional variable x can be written as a linear combination of the Ψ basis functions:

$$f(x) = \sum_{q^{(1)}=1}^{\psi^{(1)}} \cdots \sum_{q^{(R)}=1}^{\psi^{(T)}} C_{q^{(1)} \ldots q^{(T)}} \prod_{t=1}^{T} B_{q^{(t)}, K^{(t)}, r^{(t)}}(x_t).$$

(6.85)

The unconditional probability that a customer i belongs to latent class s will again be denoted λ_s, satisfying conditions (6.2) and (6.3) as before. The data for consumer i indicating a preference judgment about a pair of brands $\{j, k\}$ is again coded as $z_{ijk} = 1$ *iff* customer i prefers brand j over k, 0 otherwise, and $z_i = (z_{i12}, z_{i13}, \ldots, z_{i(J-i)J/2})'$ is data for consumer i, and $Z = (z_1, \ldots, z_N)$. is the entire data set for all consumers. Assuming local independence, the distribution of the data of consumer i, z_i, becomes a finite mixture $G_i(\mathbf{z}_i|\boldsymbol{\theta}_1, \ldots, \boldsymbol{\theta}_S, \boldsymbol{\lambda})$ of multivariate Bernoulli distributions $f_{is}(\mathbf{z}_i|\boldsymbol{\theta}_s)$:

$$G_i(\mathbf{z}_i|\boldsymbol{\theta}_1, \ldots, \boldsymbol{\theta}_S, \boldsymbol{\lambda}) = \sum_{s=1}^{S} \lambda_s f_{is}(\mathbf{z}_i|\boldsymbol{\theta}_s), \qquad (6.86)$$

with:

$$f_{is}(\mathbf{z}_i|\boldsymbol{\theta}_s) = \prod_{j>k} [p_{jk|s}]^{z_{ijk}} [(1 - p_{jk|s}]^{(1 - z_{ijk})}, \qquad (6.87)$$

where $p_{jk|s}$ denotes the probability that a consumer belonging to latent class s prefers brand j to k (see De Soete, 1990). Maximum likelihood estimates of the model parameters $\boldsymbol{\theta}_1, \ldots, \boldsymbol{\theta}_S$ and $\boldsymbol{\lambda}$ can be obtained by maximizing the likelihood function:

$$L*(\mathbf{Z}|\boldsymbol{\theta}_1, \ldots, \boldsymbol{\theta}_S, \boldsymbol{\lambda}) = \prod_{i=1}^{N} G_i(\mathbf{z}_i|\boldsymbol{\theta}_1, \ldots, \boldsymbol{\theta}_S, \boldsymbol{\lambda}) \qquad (6.87)$$

with respect to $\boldsymbol{\theta}_1, \ldots, \boldsymbol{\theta}_S, \boldsymbol{\lambda}$ subject to (6.2) and (6.3). This estimation problem is solvable by the *E-M* algorithm described earlier (McLachlan and Basford, 1988). De Soete and Winsberg's (1992) latent class approach based on the Thurstone Case V model with spline transformations gives an estimate of the transformation function $f_{(s)}(\bullet)$ for each latent class s, and also a probabilistic clustering of the N customers into S homogeneous segments.

6 Conclusion

We have provided a thorough review of the latest developments in LCMDS models for potential application in marketing. As discussed, this recent literature has been classified by type of data collected: proximity, dominance, and choice. The data requirements, model structure, and estimation procedures have been examined for each of the many LCMDS models presented. In light of the importance of market segmentation, such recently developed techniques should prove useful for many empirical marketing research studies, once the computer software for LCMDS becomes readily available.

Because of manuscript length restrictions, we have concentrated primarily on the technical aspects of the various models, as opposed to the many marketing applications presented in these papers (as well as other potential applications). The majority of the applications presented in many of these manuscripts entail the spatial modeling of market structure and segmentation, where the derived latent classes are composed of individual consumers. Given the importance of market segmentation in most product/service classes, LCMDS models provide a parsimonious display of brands/services and/or latent classes, and the particular interaction or relationships between the two. Another application discussed in this review manuscript concerned the DeSarbo, Jedidi, Cool, and Schendel (1991) latent class unfolding model applied to the definition of strategic groups derived from an analysis of PIMS data. Other applications are indeed plausible from the use of such models. For example, LCMDS models can be utilized for deriving market segments from the analysis of scanner/panel data. Or, country segments can be derived from the spatial analysis of international macro-economic data available from the World Bank. Similar types of analyses can be conducted with export/import data available for different nations. Industrial segmentation schemes can also be developed with LCMDS given appropriate data characterizing business-to-business marketing. Latent class conjoint analysis (DeSarbo, Wedel, Vriens, and Ramaswamy, 1992) can be performed in a spatial manner using many of the LCMDS procedures with dominance data that allow for linear restrictions on **X**. Here, benefit segments can be derived on the basis of structural differences in the latent class part-worth functions. A host of other potential applications are indeed possible. Typically, LCMDS can be gainfully employed wherever three-way MDS procedures are sought.

While this area of research is quite recent, a number of future avenues of research are recommended. One, the development of finite mixtures for latent class analyses with the ability to include prior information in a Bayesian framework would be quite useful. Two, finite mixtures involving smoothing functions that do not require rigid distributional specifications need to be devised for non-parametric LCMDS analyses. Three, further research on statistical tests for the selection of S and T is recommended given the heuristics currently used in practice and their shortcomings as discussed in this manuscript. Finally, future research is needed in the area of more closely relating individual level information to the posterior probabilities of membership derived in equation (6.4) for targeting specific market segments.

Questions

1   You are given a data set consisting of unreplicated paired comparison data set from N customers for J brands. There are several ways of analyzing this data set as discussed in (i) De Sarbo, Oliver, and De Soete in *Applied Psychological Measurement* (1986), and De Sarbo, De Soete, and Eliashberg in *Journal of Economic Psychology* (1987), (ii) De Soete and Carroll in *Psychometrika* (1983), and De Soete, Carroll, and De Sarbo in *Journal of Mathematical Psychology* (1986), and (iii) De Soete in *Knowledge, Data, and Computer-Assisted Decisions* (1990). Compare and contrast these approaches.

2 Discuss the major advantages of LCMDS over traditional multidimensional scaling methodologies, such as MDPREF, PREFMAP, INDSCAL, etc.

3 Derive equation (6.4) in the text using the properties of conditional probability.

References

Aitkin, M., Anderson, D. and Hinde J. 1981: Statistical modeling of data on teaching styles. *Journal of the Royal Statistical Society*, A144, 419–61.

Akaike, H. 1974. A new look at statistical model identification. *IEEE Transactions on Automatic Control*, 6, 716–23.

Andrich, D. 1988: The application of an unfolding model of the PIRT type to the measurement of attitude. *Applied Psychological Measurement*, 12, 33–51.

Andrich, D. 1989: A probabilistic IRT model for unfolding preference data. *Applied Psychological Measurement*, 13, 193–216.

Bennett, J. F. and Hays, W. L. 1960: Multidimensional unfolding: determining the dimensionality of ranked preference data. *Psychometrika*, 25, 27–43.

Bockenholt, U. 1989: *The multidimensional scaling of qualitative data*. Ph.D Thesis, Lang, Frankfurt.

Bockenholt, U. and Bockenholt, I. 1990a: Modeling individual differences in unfolding preference data: a restricted latent class approach. *Applied Psychological Measurement*, 14 (3), 257–69.

Bockenholt, U. and Bockenholt, I. 1990b: Constrained latent class analysis: simultaneous classification and scaling of discrete data. Unpublished manuscript, University of Illinois, Champaign.

Bockenholt, I. and Gaul, W. 1991: Generalized latent class analysis: a new methodology for market structure analysis. In O. Opitz (ed.), *Conceptual and Numerical Analysis of Data*, Springer-Verlag; West Germany, 367–76.

Boyles, R. A. 1983: On the convergence properties of the EM algorithm, *Journal of the Royal Statistical Society*. B45, 47–50.

Bozdogan, H. 1987: Model selection and Akaike's Information Criterion (AIC): the general theory and its analytical extensions. *Psychometrika*, 52, 345–70.

Bozdogan, H. and Sclove, S. L. 1984: Multi-sample cluster analysis using Akaike's Information Criterion. *Annals of the Institute of Statistical Mathematics*, 36, 163–80.

Carroll, J. D. 1980: Models and methods for multidimensional analysis of preferential choice data. In E. D. Lantermann and H. Feger (eds), *Similarity and Choice*, Bern: Hans Huber.

Carroll, J. D. and Arabie, P. 1981: Multidimensional scaling. *Annual Review of Psychology*, 31, 607–49.

Carroll, J. D. and Chang, J. J. 1970: Analysis of individual differences in multidimensional scaling via an N-way generalization of Eckart–Young decomposition. *Psychometrika*, 35, 283–319.

Coombs, C. H. 1950: Psychological scaling without a unit of measurement. *Psychological Review*, 57, 148–58.

Coombs, C. H. 1964: *A Theory of Data*, New York: Wiley.

Cooper, L. G. 1983: A review of multidimensional scaling in marketing research. *Applied Psychological Measurement*, 7, 427–50.

Cooper, L. G. 1988: Competitive maps: the structure underlying asymmetric cross elasticities. *Management Science*, 34, 707–23.

David, H. A. 1988: *The Method of Paired Comparisons*, 2nd revised edn, London, Griffin.

Day, D. L., DeSarbo, W. S. and Oliva, J. A. 1987: Strategy maps: a spatial representation of intra-industry competitive strategy. *Management Science*, 33, 1534–51.

Dempster, A. P., Laird, N. M. and Rubin, D. B. 1977: Maximum likelihood estimation from incomplete data via the EM algorithm. *Journal of Royal Statistical Society*, B, 39, 1–22.

DeSarbo, W. S. and Cho, J. 1989: A stochastic multidimensional scaling vector threshold model for the spatial representation of "Pick Any/N" Data. *Psychometrika*, 54, 105–30.

DeSarbo, W. S., De Soete, G. and Eliashberg, J. 1987: A new stochastic multidimensional unfolding model for the investigation of paired comparison consumer preference/choice data. *Journal of Economic Psychology*, 8, 357–84.

DeSarbo, W. S. and Hoffman, D. L. 1986: A new unfolding threshold model for the spatial representation of the binary choice data. *Applied Psychological Measurement*, 10, 247–64.

DeSarbo, W. S. and Hoffman, D. L. 1987: Constructing MDS joint spaces from binary choice data: a multidimensional unfolding threshold model for marketing research. *Journal of Marketing Research*, 24, 40–54.

DeSarbo, W. S., Howard, D. J. and Jedidi, K. 1990: MULTICLUS: a new method for simultaneously performing multidimensional scaling and cluster analysis. *Psychometrika*, 56, 121–36.

DeSarbo, W. S., Jedidi, K. J., Cool, K. and Schendel, P. 1991: Simultaneous multidimensional unfolding and clusters analysis: an investigation of strategic groups. *Marketing Letters*, 2, 129–46.

DeSarbo, W. S., Johnson, M., Manrai, A. K., Manrai, L. A. and Edwards, E. 1992: TSCALE: a new multidimensional scaling procedure based on Tversky's contrast model. *Psychometrika*, 57, (1), 43–69.

DeSarbo, W. S. and Manrai, A. K. 1992: A new multidimensional scaling methodology for the analysis of asymmetric proximity data in marketing research. *Marketing Science*, 11 (1), 1–20.

DeSarbo, W., Manrai, A. K. and Manrai, L. A. 1993: Non-Spatial tree models for the assessment of competitive market structure: an integrated review of the marketing and psychometric literature. In Eliashberg and Lilien (eds), *Handbooks in Operations Research and Management Science: Marketing*, Amsterdam, Netherlands: Elsevier Science (accepted for publication).

DeSarbo, W. S., Oliver, R. L. and De Soete, G. 1986: A probabilistic multidimensional scaling vector model. *Applied Psychological Measurement*, 10, 78–98.

DeSarbo, W. S., Ramaswamy, V. and Lenk, P. 1992: A latent class procedure for the structural analysis of two-way compositional data. *Journal of Classification*, forthcoming.

DeSarbo, W. S. and Rao, V. R. 1984: GENFOLD2: a set of models and algorithms for the general unfolding analysis of preference/dominance data. *Journal of Classification*, 1, 146–85.

DeSarbo, W. S. and Rao, V. R. 1986: A new constrained unfolding model for product positioning. *Marketing Science*, 5, 1–19.

Desarbo, W. S., Wedel, M., Vriens, M. and Ramaswamy, V. 1992: Latent class metric conjoint analysis. *Marketing Letters*, 3, 273–88.

De Soete, G. 1990: A latent class approach to modeling pair wise preferential choice data. In M. Schader and W. Gaul (eds), *Knowledge, Data, and Computer-Assisted Decisions*, Berlin: Springer-Verlag, 103–13.

De Soete, G., and Carroll, J. D. 1983: A maximum likelihood method for fitting the wandering vector model. *Psychometrika*, 48, 621–6.

De Soete, G. Carroll, J. D. and DeSarbo, W. S. 1986: The wandering ideal point model: a probabilistic multidimensional unfolding model for paired comparison data. *Journal of Mathematical Psychology*, 30, 28–41.

De Soete G. and DeSarbo, W. S. 1991: A latent class probit model for analyzing Pick Any/*N* Data: *Journal of Classification*, 8, 45–64.

De Soete, G. and Heiser, W. 1993: A latent class unfolding model for analyzing single stimulus preference ratings. Unpublished Manuscript, University of Ghent, Belgium.

De Soete, G., Meulman J. and Heiser, W. 1992: *A Mixture Distribution Approach to Points of View of Analysis*, a paper presented at the Annual Meeting of the Classification Society of North America, Michigan State University, East Lansing, Michigan.

De Soete, G. and Winsberg, S. 1992: A Thurstonian pair wise choice model with univariate and multivariate spline transformations. *Unpublished manuscript*, University of Ghent, Belgium.

De Soete, G. and Winsberg, S. 1993: A latent class vector model for preference ratings. Unpublished manuscript, University of Ghent, Belgium.

Eliashberg, J. And Manrai, A. K. 1993: Optimal positioning of new product-concepts: some analytical implications and empirical results. *European Journal of Operational Research* (in press).

Formann, A. K. 1985: Constrained latent class models: theory and applications. *British Journal of Mathematical and Statistical Psychology*, 38, 87–111.

Formann, A. K. 1989: Constrained latent class models: some further applications. *British Journal of Mathematical and Statistical Psychology*, 42, 37–54.

Goodman, L. A. 1974: Exploratory latent structure analysis using both identifiable and unidentifiable models. *Biometrika*, 61, 215–31.

Goodman, L. A. 1978: *Analyzing Qualitative/Categorical Data: Log-linear Models and Latent Class Structure Analysis*, Cambridge, Abt Books.

Goodman, L. A. 1979: On the estimation of parameters in latent class analysis. *Psychometrika*, 44, 123–8.

Gower, J. C. 1966: Some distance properties of latent root and vector methods using multivariate analysis. *Biometrika*, 53, 325–38.

Hoijtink, H. 1990: A latent trait model for dichotomous choice data. *Psychometrika*, 55, 641–56.

Kotler, P. 1991: *Marketing Management: Analysis, Planning, Implementation, and Control*, 7th edn, Englewood-Cliffs, NJ: Prentice Hall.

Kruskal, J. B. and Wish, M. 1978: *Multidimensional Scaling*, Beverly Hills: Sage Publications.

Lazarsfeld, P. F. and Henry, N. W. 1968: *Latent Structure Analysis*, New York: Houghton-Mifflin.

Maddala, G. S. 1990: *Limited Dependent and Qualitative Variables in Econometrics*, 3rd edn, Cambridge: Cambridge University Press.

Manrai, A. K. 1990: Multidimensional scaling models for asymmetric proximity data. In Muhlbacher *et al.* (eds), *Advanced Research in Marketing*, Vol. II, European Marketing Academy, University of Innsbruck, Austria, 1185–203.

Manrai, A. K. and Manrai, L. A. 1989: Mathematical models for relating proximity to multidimensional scaling. In Avlontis *et al.* (eds), *Marketing Thought and Practice in the 1990s*, Vol. 1, European Marketing Academy, Athens School of Economics and Business, Greece, 853–68.

Manrai, A. K. and Sinha, P. K. 1989: Elimination-by-cutoffs. *Marketing Science*, 8 (2), 133–52.

Manrai, L. A. and Manrai, A. K. 1993: Positioning European countries as brands in a perceptual map: an empirical study of determinants of consumer perceptions and preferences. *Journal of Euromarketing*, 2 (3) (in press).

McLachlan, G. J. and Basford, K. E. 1988: *Mixture Models*, New York: Marcel Dekker.

Schönemann, P. H. and Tucker, L. R. 1967: A maximum likelihood solution for the method of successive intervals allowing for unequal stimulus dispersions. *Psychometrika*, 32, 403–17.

Takane, Y. 1976: A statistical procedure for the latent profile model. *Japanese Psychological Research*, 18, 82–90.

Takane, Y. 1981: Multidimensional successive categories scaling: a maximum likelihood method. *Psychometrika*, 46, 9–28.

Takane, Y. and DeLeeuw, J. 1987: On the relationship between item response theory and factor analysis of discretized variables. *Psychometrika*, 52, 393–408.

Torgerson, W. S. 1958: *Theory and Methods of Scaling*, New York: Wiley.

Tucker, L. R. 1960: Intra-individual and inter-individual multidimensionality. In H. Gulliksen and S. Messick (eds), *Psychological Scaling: Theory and Applications*, New York: Wiley, 155–67.

Wind, Y. 1980: *Product Policy: Concepts, Methods, and Strategy*, Reading, MA: Addison-Wesley.

Windham, M. P. and Cutler, A. 1991: Information ratios for validating Cluster analyses. Conference Paper, presented at the 1991 Joint Meetings of the Classification and Psychometric Societies, Rutgers University, N. J.

Winsberg, S. and De Soete, G. 1992: A latent class approach to fitting the Euclidean weighted Euclidean model, CLASCAL. Unpublished manuscript, IRCAM, Paris, France.

Wu, C. F. J. 1983: On the convergence properties of the EM algorithm. *Annals of Statistics*, 11, 95–103.

7

Conjoint Analysis

Jordan J. Louviere

1 Introduction

Since its introduction in the marketing research literature in the early 1970s (e.g. Green and Rao, 1971; Green and Wind, 1973), conjoint analysis has become one of the most widely applied marketing research methods for understanding and predicting consumer and customer tradeoffs, decisions and choices. Although conjoint analysis techniques were well-known and applied in psychology prior to their introduction into marketing (e.g. Anderson 1962; 1970; Hoffman, 1960; Hoffman, Slovic and Rorer, 1968), and are now used in geography, transportation, urban planning, sociology and many other areas, nowhere have they been so widely embraced and applied as in marketing. In fact, conjoint analysis as practiced by a majority of academics and practitioners is now a mature technology. The rate of innovation in traditional conjoint analysis has slowed markedly in recent years, and research and applications attention has begun to shift to other, newer areas during the past decade.

As a consequence of the mature state of traditional conjoint technology, this chapter will focus more on new and emerging areas of conjoint technology rather than review what is already well-known and well-worn. This focus strikes me as particularly relevant insofar as there was an excellent recent review of traditional technology published by Green and Srinivasan (1990). Thus, my objectives are to (a) provide a brief and succinct overview of the general area of conjoint analysis and its role in the overall objective of understanding and predicting consumer decision-making and choice behavior; (b) discuss random utility theory as a behavioral and theoretical basis for conjoint analysis; and (c) concentrate on describing recent advances in conjoint technology associated with random utility theory. The organization of this chapter follows these objectives.

Conjoint analysis is a generic term coined by Green and Srinivasan (1978) to refer to a number of paradigms in psychology, economics and marketing that are concerned with the quantitative description of consumer preferences or value tradeoffs. The conceptual foundation of conjoint analysis as applied in marketing arises from the theory of consumer demand, especially the work of Lancaster (1966), who assumed that a consumer's utility for an economic good could be decomposed into separate utilities for characteristics or benefits provided by that good. This decompositional view of the consumer's utility formation process has come to be widely accepted as a reasonable approximation to the market behavior of consumers, although there is still debate over the process(es) involved in the decomposition. The behavioral foundation of conjoint analysis has always been weak, despite appeals to paradigms in information integration for descriptive models of information processing in judgment (e.g. Louviere 1988a,b).

In contrast, the methodological foundations of conjoint analysis are firmly rooted in axiomatic or statistical grounds, although the particular basis depends on which of several flavors of the overall paradigm one chooses to implement. In fact, there is really no "plain vanilla" conjoint approach practiced by marketers, which in part explains the paucity of comparative academic research and validity tests. That is, to a large extent conjoint analysis is what conjoint analysts do, and each analyst seems to do something somewhat differently than others. Because marketers have traditionally positioned conjoint analysis as a research method and not a theory of consumer behavior, it is important to consider its behavioral links, which have been largely ignored in the published literature. Hence, I concentrate on providing a rationale for the decomposition of preferences based on random utility theory, and emphasize the random utility view of conjoint in this chapter, including recasting some well-known approaches to be consistent with this view.

2 Behavioral Foundations of Conjoint Analysis

Conjoint analysis' behavioral foundations rest on the following primary sources: (a) Lancastrian consumer theory (e.g. Lancaster 1966), which views economic goods as bundles of characteristics or attributes, and suggests that preferences for economic goods can be decomposed into separable preferences for their constituent characteristics or benefits, (b) behavioral decision theory in psychology, particularly the area of information processing in judgment (e.g. Hammond, 1955; Slovic and Lichtenstein, 1971; Anderson, 1970, 1981, 1982), particularly paradigms dealing with the process(es) by which consumers process information, or form preferences for certain categories of goods, (c) random utility theory (e.g. Thurstone, 1927; McFadden, 1974; Manski, 1977; Yellott, 1977), which forms the basis of several models and theories of consumer judgment and decision-making in psychology and economics.

At the risk of oversimplification, one can summarize the conceptual issues addressed by the above foundation areas as a series of relationships outlined in Figure 7.1. Consumers/customers perceive that they need to solve particular problems or can benefit from particular features of

1. Actionable, measurable variables that affect perception of product i's position(s) on key decision dimensions		2. Perceived positions of product i on key decision dimensions		3. Valuation of product i's positions on each key decision dimension		4. Holistic evaluation of product i based on valuation of all decision dimensions		5. Probability of choosing product i conditional on product i's holistic evaluation
	⇒		⇒		⇒		⇒	
X1 (e.g. warranty in months) X2 (e.g. mean time to failure in days) X3 (e.g. # of defects per 1000 items)	⇒	Product i's position on Key decision dimension 1, e.g. Product quality	⇒	Value of position on dimension 1				
X4 (e.g. refund or replace no questions) X5 (e.g. 800 no. for questions/problems) X6 (e.g. follow-up call to assess satisfaction)	⇒	Product i's position on Key decision dimension 2, e.g. Post-sale service	⇒	Value of position on dimension 2	⇒	overall utility of product i	⇒	Probability of choosing product i
X7 (e.g. initial total price) X8 (e.g. long-term maintenance costs)	⇒	Product i's position on Key decision dimension 3, e.g. Total cost	⇒	Value of position on dimension 3				

Figure 7.1 Conceptual framework for decision-making and choice behavior

products/services, which initiates search and learning on their part to learn about and identify what's available in the market. In a real sense, these consumer needs are initiated and/or influenced by the actions of managers. We use managers to mean broadly those who control the production and marketing of goods and services, and attempt to launch new or make changes in existing products/services in response to past and anticipated actions of consumers. These managerial actions impact consumer perceptions of the positions of goods and services on some set of key decision dimensions which consumers use to evaluate and compare offerings. The positions that products/services occupy on key decision dimensions are themselves evaluated in terms of "how good" is it to be positioned at thus and such on product quality, as opposed to positioned in a particular way on total cost. These latter valuations lead consumers to form impressions of and preferences for particular offerings, ultimately choosing whether to purchase any of the offerings available, and if so which one.

The domain of application of conjoint analysis lies primarily in providing insights into stages 3, 4 and 5 of the conceptual scheme. That is, given descriptions of product offerings on key decision dimensions (Stage 2), or perhaps, in the case of "expert" or at least knowledgeable decision-makers, given the actual actions taken to "engineer" particular product outcomes (Stage 1), conjoint analysis techniques allow analysts to study and model how consumers evaluate product characteristics and choose among competing products. However, strictly speaking, conjoint analysis is not limited to this domain. For example, conjoint analysis techniques can be used to shed light on links between the actions of Stage 1 and the product perceptions of Stage 2 (e.g. Anderson 1970; Louviere, 1984), although such applications have been rare in marketing. Nor is it necessarily the case that the relational system implied by Figure 7.1 is the sole province of conjoint analysis. Rather, many other paradigms in the social and behavioral sciences can be used to gain insight into the behavioral system implied by Figure 7.1.

For example, much of economic theory deals with direct (rather than indirect cognitive links) between actions and behavior (choices). Thus, in applied econometrics it is common for analysts to observe choices made by consumers in real product markets together with various managerial actions (i.e. explanatory variables) associated with the choice outcomes of interest. Random utility theory provides a logical way to link observed choices to actions, and develop statistical choice models that explain the observed choices conditional on the managerial actions. Suffice it to say that conjoint analysis is not the only way to model decision-making and choice behavior, but conjoint techniques have provided many useful insights into the behavior of consumers in specific contexts and will certainly continue to do so in the future.

Figure 7.1 implies that managerial actions provide informational or stimulus cues which consumers use to evaluate and compare products. Some informational cues are easy to observe and learn, such as prices marked on items. Others may be printed on the product package in the form of ingredient lists, performance specs, warranties and the like. Still others such as taste, convenience and quality are more subjective and often must be experienced to be evaluated. Consumers typically learn about a particular product category by examining products and/or product-related literature or demonstrations. During this process, consumers not only learn about different products, but also about the relative advantages of product attributes or features. In this way, consumers develop evaluation rules that emphasize certain attributes and de-emphasize others. They also form beliefs or perceptions about which products occupy which attribute positions.

Once product position beliefs are formed, consumers can compare products holistically relative to their evaluation rules. These evaluation rules are what we term "utility functions". These rules and the attribute information on which they are conditional are what is studied and modeled by conjoint analysts.

Consumers therefore form preferences for products based on beliefs about characteristics or attributes. These preferences are the basis for choice decisions. Choice decisions likely differ in new and emerging product categories compared with mature categories, and depend on financial and/or other risks involved in purchasing products. For example, even if evaluated by consumers, expensive new technologies usually experience a large number of non-choice or delay of choice decisions relative to actual purchase decisions. In contrast, mature inexpensive household goods categories tend to be characterized by relatively stable preference and purchase patterns, leading to correspondingly stable non-choice and delay of choice decisions. Although simplistic, the preceding discussion suggests that how one applies conjoint analysis to model decisions and forecast choices depends heavily on the type of product category and its stage in the product life-cycle.

The random utility view

Random utility theory was first proposed by Thurstone (1927) as a way to model dominance judgments in a paired comparison context. Thurstone's basic idea, although extended in many ways, has remained relatively unchanged. Essentially, random utility theory suggests that consumers try to choose (buy, etc.) those alternatives that they like the best subject to constraints, such as income and time. Of course, viewed from the researcher's perspective, consumers do not always appear to choose what they like best, but rather at least some of their choices fluctuate over purchase occasions. We can explain these fluctuations in behavior by recognizing that there is a random component to the consumer's utility function. Thus,

$$U_i = V_i + e_i, \qquad (7.1)$$

where U_i is the unobservable, but true utility of alternative i; V_i is the observable or systematic component of utility; and e_i is the random component. Put another way, V_i is the proportion of the variance in choice that can be explained, and ε_i is the portion that cannot. Because there is always some proportion of the variation in choice behavior that cannot be explained when viewed from the standpoint of the analyst, one typically is interested in modeling or predicting the probability that a consumer will choose a particular product, say the i-th brand, from some set of competing product offerings, say set C. This can be expressed as follows:

$$P(i|C) = P[(V_i + e_i) > (V_j + e_j)], \forall_j \in C, \qquad (7.2)$$

where all terms are as previously defined, except $P(i|C)$ which is the probability of choosing product or brand i from a set of competing product offerings, C.

The so-called systematic or "explainable" component of choice behavior is predicated on the analyst or researcher's ability to identify, measure and include as many sources of influence on choice behavior as possible. That is, it is incumbent on the researcher to spend sufficient time before beginning a modeling effort to insure that they've identified as many of the key decision variables and/or other influences on choice (e.g. variables that account for differences in individual decision-makers) as possible. Once, the researcher has identified as exhaustive a set of decision variables as possible, s/he must specify how these explanatory variables combine to influence choice. That is, based on theory, educated guesses and/or previous empirical evidence, the researcher must specify a decision heuristic or "combination rule" (more generally, a utility function) which is a formal expression of the relationship between the explanatory variables and choice behavior. Without loss of generality, we can express the relationship between the systematic component and the explanators as a linear in the parameters and variables function:

$$V_i = \beta x_i' + \varepsilon_i \tag{7.3}$$

where β is a $k \times 1$ vector of utility coefficients associated with a vector of k explanatory variables, x'.

Thus, we can rewrite equation 2 as follows:

$$P(i|C) = P[(\beta x_i' + \varepsilon_i) > (\beta x_j' + \varepsilon_j)], \ \forall_j \in C, \tag{7.4}$$

where all terms are as previously defined. Equation (7.4) implies that the probability that the consumer will choose product or brand i is equal to the probability that the systematic component and its associated error for alternative i is higher than the systematic and associated error components for all other competing offerings. Moreover, equation (7.4) tells us that the object of our analysis is to identify and estimate the β vector associated with the variables that we hypothesize to underlie choice behavior.

As currently formulated, our model specifies that choice behavior is a function of variables that describe differences in competing products or brands. However, as previously mentioned, choices also differ from individual to individual, and we would like to account for as many of these individual differences as possible in any choice modeling exercise as well. Thus, we broaden our set of explanatory variables to include those that describe differences in individual consumers or customers. Such variables can include constraints like money and time, or can be sociodemographic or psychographic measures. Let the vector of such measures be z' and the associated 1×1 vector of coefficients be γ. Then we can re express equation (7.4) as follows:

$$P(i|C) = P[\boldsymbol{\beta}x_i' + \boldsymbol{\gamma}z' + \varepsilon_i) > (\boldsymbol{\beta}x_j' + \boldsymbol{\gamma}z' + \varepsilon_j)], \forall_j \in C, \qquad (7.5)$$

where all terms are as previously defined. This relatively general model assumes that different individuals may differ in their utilities for different product features, problem solutions, benefits or, more generally, attributes. The consumers decision rule is to optimize the function implied by equation (7.5), but to solve the optimization problem we have to impose more structure (make more assumptions) on the problem.

In particular, a variety of probabilistic discrete choice models can be formulated by making different assumptions about the distribution of the random component. For example, Thurstone (1927) assumed a normal distribution, which yields the binary probit model; while McFadden (1974) assumed a Gumbel distribution, which gives rise to the conditional or Multinomial Logit (MNL) model. Randomness is inherent in the process because one rarely if ever can specify all the possible antecedents associated with a particular choice; and variation in individual choices occur because of errors, inattention, idiosyncratic circumstances and a variety of other sources. Thus, however consistent and deterministic a particular individual might be, choice behavior is stochastic when viewed from the vantage point of the analyst. Of course, marketing researchers are rarely interested in individuals *per se*, but rather are more interested in segments or groups of individuals who tend to behave alike or whose patterns of choice behavior are highly similar. Of course, this introduces yet another source of variation in choice, namely variation between individuals. Similar to the case with individuals, the randomness inherent in individual choices must necessarily also be manifest in segment-level choices for the reasons previously stated, plus the additional observation that no analyst can fully account for differences in individuals. As well, it is at least worth noting at this point that modeling variation within individuals requires multiple observations of choice for the same individual over choice occasions. This is a difficult and formidable task in most circumstances likely to be of practical interest. Thus, henceforth in this chapter we concentrate on applying the theory and methods to groups (segments) of individuals.

Of particular interest to conjoint analysis is the explainable or observable (mean) component of utility. This component can be identified from an appropriately designed study in which one or more individuals judge or choose among products whose positions on a set of key decision variables (attributes) vary systematically in such a way that the "effect" or utility of each attribute position can be estimated from the judgments or choices. In essence, individuals reveal their utilities by the judgments or choices that they make in response to a stated preference experiment. By "stated preference" I mean that individuals express their preferences in a hypothetical market in which neither corresponding actual choices nor their consequences necessarily occur. Even though the market may be hypothetical, random utility theory nonetheless suggests that consumers should try to maximize their utility subject to constraints. Hence, as equation (7.2) indicates, they should seek to choose that product or brand with the highest systematic and random component sum.

Utility maximization is therefore the basis of our behavioral view of conjoint analysis, which provides a very general framework for understanding and modeling market behavior in many circumstances. Common sense suggests that consumers ought to choose those things that they like the best, subject to constraints. My experience is that those who object to the notion of utility maximization invariably fail to take into account attributes or contextual effects that explain differences in utility. For example, it is sometimes suggested that consumers cannot possibly know about or evaluate all alternatives in a particular product category, and hence adopt some simplifying decision rule that is inconsistent with utility maximization. Such a view fails to account for the fact that time and search effort also have utility or disutility; hence, the utility function must take these factors into account to fully explain individual behavior.

In the next section we provide an overview of traditional "full profile" conjoint analysis with special emphasis given to its links to random utility theory. Following that, we discuss conjoint analysis approaches that are consistent with random utility theory.

Overview of Traditional Conjoint Analysis

Conjoint analysis is the generic name applied to a family of paradigms that can be used to model the links implied by Stages 3 to 5 in Figure 7.1. Different paradigms arise from different disciplinary traditions and interests. For example, Information Integration Theory (Anderson, 1962, 1970, 1981, 1982) and Social Judgment Theory (Brunswick, 1952; Hammond 1955; Hammond, Hursch and Todd, 1964) give rise, respectively to Functional Measurement and Judgment Policy Capturing. These latter terms refer to the methods by which one specifies utility functions and measures utilities. Both paradigms are concerned with understanding and describing the behavioral and cognitive processes involved in information processing in judgment and decision-making. However, their theoretical and methodological bases differ, which gives rise to different applications procedures. For example, Functional Measurement relies on orthogonal attribute arrays and has a well-developed theory of response errors. Policy Capturing, on the other hand often disdains orthogonal arrays for "representative designs", in which inter attribute correlations are deliberately constructed to closely match the corresponding correlations in the particular environment under study.

In contrast to these two cognitive theories of behavior, there are a variety of axiomatic conjoint paradigms whose basis is not the behavior of humans, but the behavior of numerical responses to orthogonal or other attribute arrays. The best known and most widely applied of these approaches include axiomatic utility theory (e.g. Keeney and Raiffa, 1976) and axiomatic conjoint measurement (e.g. Krantz, *et al*. 1969; Krantz and Tversky, 1971; Barron, 1977). Both paradigms deal with the algebraic basis for representing ordinal response data in a manner that is consistent with a variety of utility specifications. Thus, neither paradigm is concerned with behavioral theory *per se*, but rather with methods that can be used to test aspects of behavioral theory or model particular behavioral processes. In other words, both paradigms are theories of the behavior of numbers and not people. However, if the numbers supplied by humans in a decision-making experiment are approximately consistent with the proposed algebraic models of decision-making, one can use the rich theory associated with these paradigms to make inferences about behavior based on the numerical responses of people. Of course, if the responses of individuals to conjoint experiments are inconsistent with models postulated by these paradigms, it is not clear whether or how useful insights based on their application might be in any particular situation. Furthermore, without an error theory to falsify particular decision models, one must rely on notoriously inaccurate and potentially misleading goodness-of-fit "tests" like *r*-squared or 'stress' (see, e.g. Anderson and Shanteau, 1977). Until and unless a theoretically acceptable statistical basis is provided for these paradigms, it is not clear what advantage if any they provide over their more cognitively appealing competitors.

Each conjoint paradigm is associated with particular experimental approaches, types of response modes and analytical methods. These aspects distinguish each paradigm, despite their common interest in understanding preference and value tradeoffs (as well as other issues of interest in cognitive information processing or utility theory). For example, early applications in marketing emphasized axiomatic conjoint measurement and ordinal preference responses (Green and Srinivasan, 1978; Cattin and Wittink, 1982). This approach required special purpose monotonic regression or analysis of variance software to estimate (measure) respondent utilities from their responses to stated preference experiments. More recently, however, academic and commercial applications have been dominated by approaches more akin to Functional Measurement or Judgment Policy Capturing, emphasizing ratings responses and regression analysis (Cattin and Wittink, 1982). Even more recently, new paradigms have emerged which rely on random utility theory, discrete or qualitative responses and discrete multivariate statistical analysis techniques. These new paradigms have been referred to as experimental choice analysis (Batsell and Louviere, 1991) or choice-based conjoint (Oliphant *et al.*, 1992).

Thus, the nature and measurement level of the types of preference responses required of consumers differs substantially between paradigms. At one extreme are category ratings scales, or possibly magnitude estimation or production scales (Anderson, 1970; Louviere, 1988a; Stevens, 1951, 1957). Such scales are assumed to be at least interval in measurement level, meaning that utility differences between levels of the same attribute are meaningful; although, similar to the Fahrenheit temperature scale, the origin of the scale is arbitrary. If consumer responses to conjoint profiles are consistent with these metric scale assumptions, one can apply traditional parametric statistical methods like OLS regression to estimate models and measure attribute level utilities. At the other extreme lie nominal or qualitative responses, such as "yes/no" (attractive, unattractive) or discrete choices of one or more items from a set of competing items. The latter data are nominal or qualitative, hence, it is not always possible or even desirable to use traditional parametric methods to estimate models and measure the utilities of attribute levels. Thus, qualitative response paradigms tend to rely on discrete multivariate statistical methods, which only recently have become widely available. It is worth noting, however, that a major difference in qualitative and metric responses is that one imposes stronger assumptions on responses and cognitive requirements on respondents with the latter than with the former.

Thus, assuming that consumers can identify the one attribute bundle they prefer most in a set of such bundles is less demanding axiomatically and cognitively than assuming that consumers can rank bundles from most to least preferred, or associate an interval scale of preference with the bundles such that differences (or ratios) between bundles on the scale are empirically meaningful. In this way each conjoint paradigm places different cognitive demands on respondents and makes rather different statistical assumptions about the response data that they provide. Researchers therefore should carefully consider the assumptions of each paradigm, the demands placed on respondents that must be satisfied to obtain unbiased estimates of utilities and the realism of the task relative to the behavior they wish to model before deciding which approach is best for a particular application.

Currently, all conjoint paradigms, with the exception of choice-based conjoint and Policy Capturing, rely on consumer responses to sets of orthogonal arrays of attribute values or levels to measure utilities. Thus, conjoint analysts must first decide which attributes influence consumer decisions in a particular research context. Such attributes usually are identified from prior academic or exploratory research, or the dictates of particular research problems. In the latter case, attributes might include both those already known to influence consumer preferences plus one or more additional attributes of particular managerial interest. Methods of attribute identification have been discussed by Green and Srinivasan (1978, 1990) and Louviere (1988a). Once attributes are identified, one assigns values or *levels* to each to represent the relevant range of variation in the present or future market of interest.

Given a set of attributes and associated levels, conjoint analysts normally use some type of orthogonal array to generate different combinations of attribute levels, which are called "profiles" (e.g. Green 1974; Louviere, 1988a). Profiles are samples of attribute bundles drawn from the complete factorial combination of attribute levels. Each such sample has a particular set of statistical properties which determine what utility specification(s) can be estimated (identified) from the response data with what level of statistical precision (efficiency). Virtually all applications of traditional conjoint technology have used samples of attribute level combinations (orthogonal arrays) called "main effects plans". Main effects plans are orthogonal arrays sampled from the complete factorial such that a strictly additive, "main effects only" utility specification can be estimated if one is willing or able to assume that all other possible effects (i.e. two-way and higher-order interactions between attributes) are not significant (Green, 1974; Louviere 1988a).

The catch-22 in the use of main effects plans is that one can estimate or test only strictly additive utility specifications. Thus, if consumers' responses are more accurately described by a utility model that involves interactions among some or all attributes, not only can one not determine this from a main effects plan, but one cannot even falsify (reject) the assumption that the response process is additive. Consequently, if the process that a consumer uses to respond to the profiles is not strictly additive, the utility estimates will be biased, and the extent of the bias cannot be determined from the data because only strictly additive specifications can be estimated.

Overemphasis on main effects plans appears to be associated with a corresponding overemphasis on modeling individual utility functions. In fact, conjoint analysis traditionally has been used to measure individual consumer utilities for attribute levels (Figure 7.1, Stage 3). Estimation of individual-specific utilities places restrictions on the size of orthogonal arrays (i.e. the number of profiles respondents judge) in real commerical settings. In turn, this limits design and analysis possibilities, usually precluding estimation of any but a small number of attribute interactions at the individual respondent level.

Some compromise schemes have been proposed (Green and Srinivasan, 1978; Louviere 1988a, b) that involve use of different statistically equivalent main effects designs for individual respondents that aggregate over blocks of respondents to permit estimation of interactions. In this context, however, the individual-level estimation doesn't make much sense because one assumes simultaneously that individual main effects can differ but interactions are constant across individuals. These two assumptions are logically inconsistent; hence, it makes more sense in this case to conduct all analyses at a segment-or sample-level of aggregation (Haggerty, 1985).

Emphasis on individual-level analyses seems to stem from (a) the emphasis of conjoint theory and methods, which is individual-level in nature, (b) healthy skepticism about aggregating over disparate individual preferences in the absence of a well-developed theory about how to aggregate them in particular contexts, and (c) belief that individual-level measures provide a logical and actionable basis for segmenting samples of consumers. Although these issues are certainly pertinent to the level of analysis if consumers use error-free, additive utility functions, if there are errors in individual-level responses due to whatever source, it is not clear that this is the most appropriate level of analysis for every application.

For example, consider individual-level utility specification errors. It has been well-known for almost two decades that additive conjoint models almost always fit the preference data from which they are estimated well, and also predict holdout sets of preference data well in many (if not most) applied circumstances. For example, Dawes and Corrigan (1974) demonstrated that additive linear models fit well when the following types of conditions are met: (a) Attributes are monotonically related to preference responses, a condition met in virtually all conjoint studies, although a small minority of studies may involve one or more non-monotonic attributes or attributes whose directionality may vary from consumer to consumer; (b) Attributes are measured with error, a condition not applicable to conjoint experiments *per se*, but which arises whenever one uses conjoint models to predict to real markets because the correct predictive metric for attributes is the perceptual (Figure 7.1, Stage 2), not objective metric (Louviere, 1988a, b). That is, perceptions are measured with error, or if one assumes that objective actions have a one-to-one relationship with perceptions and they do not, then objective measures have error, (c) Ordinary least squares estimation insures that very large and very small preference responses will be well-fit, which tends to minimize the largest residuals, thereby making residuals smaller on average than they otherwise might be. Finally, although not mentioned by Dawes and Corrigan, (d) whatever a consumer's real decision rule, additive models tend to perform well when more good attribute levels imply higher preference and more bad attribute levels imply lower preference, a condition almost always satisfied in applications.

Furthermore, Dawes and Corrigan (1974) suggested and Wainer (1976) proved that even equally weighted attributes will produce predicted values that will correlate highly with typical conjoint response data. Worse yet, Anderson and Shanteau (1977) empirically verified that even drastically incorrect additive models fit non-additive data amazingly well. Thus, reliance on traditional measures of fit like R-Square or Stress may be not only be extremely misleading for individual-level data, but fits may be high even when utility measures are seriously biased. The latter results are a double-edged sword because they suggest that conjoint models will predict rank order well, even when the models are grossly misspecified. Prediction of rank order matters because only rank order counts in most conjoint choice simulators.

These latter results raise important and rarely discussed issues that call into question whether using individual-level attribute utility measures to identify segments is, in fact, a major advantage of traditional conjoint analysis. First, if individual utility functions are not additive, it is unclear what benefits arise from segmenting individuals on biased utility measures because the resulting segment-level utilities also will be biased. Second, one might argue that it would be better to segment on the *raw response data* because they do not require the analyst to assume a particular (possibly incorrect) model. Rather, individual-level raw responses constitute a model-free source of segmentation information. Thus, a more cautious analyst might suggest segmenting respondents based on similarities in raw responses. Third, both the responses and estimated utilities contain sampling (and, in the case of utilities, likely specification) errors, but most methods of segmenting respondents like cluster analysis assume error-free data. Thus, it is not clear what results are obtained when one violates the errorless assumption. Fourth, category rating scale responses to profiles pose additional problems. For example, category rating scales are at best interval in measurement level, hence, scale units and origins of both responses and estimated utilities may differ from respondent to respondent.

In the latter case, I am aware of only one reasonably theoretical basis for determining the unit of different respondent utility scales, although the response scale origins can be set to be the same for all respondents by standardizing on a particular profile (or particular attribute levels in the case of utilities). I discuss this approach to standardizing and comparing utility scales in Section 3. Thus, before applying clustering or other segmentation methods, one might (arbitrarily) choose one profile to be the zero point or origin of the response scale and rescale all respondents' data relative to that value. It should be noted that this is not the same as mean centering each respondent's data. Now having said that, there is little to no available empirical research supporting either method. Indeed, segmenting on the basis of partworth utilities at least has the appeal that the estimated utilities are means, which should be more stable than the raw data. On the other hand, Levin, Meyer and Louviere (1978) provide evidence that respondent grand means alone are highly predictive of choice behavior; hence, not accounting for scale usage differences may produce less useful results than might otherwise be the case. In any case, it appears that the field could benefit from rigorous theoretical and empirical research that addresses these issues.

The problem of accounting for individual differences in scale units and origins in rating scale applications suggests a potential advantage for rank order and qualitative response scales: respondents can be compared without accounting for scale unit differences. For example, a variety of associative measures are available to compare pairs of respondents' rank order and qualitative responses. Most such measures can be used in standard cluster analysis algorithms to represent distances between respondents. Such measures impose no *a priori* utility model specification requirement; hence, are also model-free. Of course, as previously mentioned, most popular cluster analytic procedures assume error-free data; hence, ordinal and qualitative responses provide no advantage in that regard.

The previous discussion suggests that conjoint analysis techniques are a double-edged sword: They will fit preference data from conjoint studies very well, and under the right circumstances will predict discrete or first choices well. However, predictive power may come at the expense of real understanding. That is, although individual conjoint models may fit response data well, they may be quite incorrect and misleading. Yet, they will still predict well in a variety of practical situations. Thus, it is not clear what has been learned from previous academic studies of predictive validity, because *a priori* we expect conjoint models to perform well under the typical conjoint research conditions outlined by Dawes and Corrigan (1974). Similarly, the rather common academic and commercial practice of assessing internal validity by comparing responses to holdout sets of profiles with model predicted responses also may be relatively meaningless because an incorrect model of a process that fits a designed set of data well also should cross-validate well to holdout samples of profiles drawn from the same profile population to which the model was originally fit.

To sum up, therefore, despite more than two decades of academic and commercial experience with conjoint analysis, it is not clear whether or when additive utility functions are correct representations of real decision processes. However, it is clear that even if quite incorrect, strictly additive conjoint models fit conjoint response data extraordinarily well and predict choices well in a variety of situations in which it is relatively easy to predict the highest ranked alternative (see Louviere, 1988b; Johnson, Meyer and Ghose, 1989; Green, Helsen and Shandler, 1988; Elrod, Louviere and Davey, 1992; Oliphant, Eagle, Louviere and Anderson, 1992). The latter condition will obtain when alternatives are reasonably well differentiated and/or the utility differences are sufficiently large to offset errors in predicted utilities.

Let us turn our attention now to some recent developments in conjoint analysis based on random utility theory and their pros and cons.

3 Recent developments

In addition to the widespread applications interest in using individual-level conjoint results as a basis for segmentation, there is considerable interest in using individual-level model results to simulate choices among competing products or services. In its simplest form a "conjoint simulator" consists of (1) a computer file of individual-level estimated partworth utilities, (2) a set of profile or product descriptions for which choice predictions are to be made, and (3) a rule for transforming the utilities predicted for each product profile into choices. The estimated individual level partworth utilities are derived from the judgments made by the individual in response to some experiment designed by the researcher. Depending on the 'flavor" of conjoint used, the responses might have been observed on category rating scales or rank ordering. The analytical technique used to estimate the utilities would depend on the type of response observed. The set of product profiles for which predictions are to be made are usually determined by the research objectives, and consist of at least two profiles. The transformation rule is determined by the researcher, but I am unaware of any rules used in academic or commercial applications that are not *ad hoc*. That is, rules like "the highest predicted utility equals first choice" may be reasonable, but one would like to see a well-developed and empirically sound theoretical justification for any of the rules that have been reported in the research literature. Until such time as an appropriate justification is forthcoming, one should be cautious about forecasts based on *ad hoc* rules.

Additionally, there is a serious caveat which has received relatively little attention in the conjoint literature in marketing (although, see Louviere, 1988a, b). In particular, the likely number and proportion of consumers who are non-purchasers of a category at a particular point in time depends on the expense and risk of the category as well as its stage in the product life-cycle. Hence, expensive and risky new technological developments typically are associated with high levels of non-purchase during introduction and early market expansion phases of the life-cycle. All conjoint analysis choice simulators of which I am aware forecast shares of choice or probabilities given that consumers will choose something. It is not clear why one would want to include individuals with low or zero purchase probabilities in such simulations, but almost all simulations and computerized simulators of which I am aware typically use all individuals in the sample in the simulations. Of course, it could be argued that one could segment individuals based on some external measures of purchase likelihood and only simulate the choices of those who are likely to be purchasers. However, one would presumably like to incorporate non-choice directly into conjoint simulators because it's such an important element of real market behavior. Most commercially available conjoint simulation software permits analysts to weight respondents differentially; hence, if a theoretically justifiable way of weighting respondents to account for non-purchase could be found, there is no reason why it cannot be incorporated in existing technology.

Of course, *ad hoc* "rules" or measures can be used to try to identify non-choosers or predict non-choice. Indeed, Oliphant, *et al.* (1992) recently developed and applied a measure of non-choice that predicted very well to hold-out choices that included the option not to choose. While encouraging, this study of non-choice has little to say about whether such measures of non-choice will accurately capture non-choice in a real market, as opposed to holdout profiles in a survey. To date no one has yet proposed a theoretically acceptable way to observe non-choice in a traditional conjoint context, much less a way to predict it. For example, anecdotal reports suggest that in some applications researchers assume that non-choice equals a predicted response less than a particular, arbitrarily chosen "top box" score. For example, if consumers respond to a conjoint task on a zero to ten category rating scale, predicted responses of less than eight might be assumed to be non-choices. Oliphant, *et al.* (1992) compared such a rule to their individual-level non-choice measure, and found that it predicted non-choice significantly worse than chance. Indeed, even when Oliphant, *et al.* used the mean of their highly predictive individual-level measures as a sample-wide cutoff for non-choice, they could not predict non-choice better than chance. Thus, sample-wide *ad hoc* rules or thresholds are unlikely to represent real non-choice decisions. What is needed is a way to measure and predict non-choice in a theoretically acceptable way.

Fortunately, a theoretically acceptable way to measure and predict non-choice has been available for some time. The basis for non-choice lies in the theory of consumer demand, and in particular in the random utility approach to modeling discrete demand. Discrete choice theory (McFadden, 1974) recognizes that many elemental goods and services are indivisible. That is, one cannot purchase one-third of a car or ten percent of a can of beans. Rather, one purchases (chooses) these objects in discrete units. Louviere and Woodworth (1983) provided the conceptual and methodological foundation for conducting conjoint experiments involving choices among discrete goods. In this framework non-choice is simply another discrete option faced by consumers.

Indeed, within the larger option of non-choice or purchase, one can recognize a variety of mutually exclusive and (possibly) exhaustive sub-categories of non-choice. For example, non-choice might comprise the following sub-choices: (a) non-choice of the entire category, (b) non-choice of the category because an acceptable non-category substitute exists, (c) non-choice of the category because (i) category is too new and risky or (ii) one expects category prices to fall and features improve if one waits. The first two non-choice responses represent true non-choice from a manager's perspective, while the second two may be of considerable strategic importance from a product development as well as a segmentation, targeting and positioning standpoint. Total market potential includes current choosers plus consumers in response category (c), but the two types of consumers in category (c) may require different marketing strategies and tactics.

The approach originally proposed by Louviere and Woodworth (1983) and since extended in a wide variety of ways as noted by Louviere (1988b) and Batsell and Louviere (1991), allows one to directly measure and model choice and non-choice. As well, one can subdivide the non-choice response option into as many strategically interesting sub-categories as required. Random utility theory is the basis for formulating probabilistic discrete choice models that can be estimated directly from the conjoint choice experiments proposed by Louviere and Woodworth (1983). That is, the objective is to predict the probability that an individual will choose a particular bundle, not the exact bundle that the individual will choose. Similarly, non-choice or any of its relevant sub-categories are discrete outcomes, and once a choice model is formulated for these and the profile outcomes of interest, it is a simple matter to predict the relevant choice probabilities or shares.

In this way, Louviere and Woodworth (1983) proposed that one could design choice experiments consistent with probabilistic discrete choice models in which two or more attribute bundles or products plus one or more non-choice options compete for consumers' choices. Louviere and Woodworth noted that rather than simulate choice from individual-level conjoint models, one could design conjoint *choice* studies in which individuals have to make purchase decisions like they do in real markets, and estimate models directly from their choices. As the object of many conjoint studies is to simulate choices in real markets, Louviere and Woodworth argued that one could avoid unnecessary and possibly incorrect assumptions required to transform predicted utilities into choices in traditional conjoint simulators by studying and modeling choices directly in choice experiments that simulate real market conditions as closely as possible. Since their original proposal, this approach has been applied in many contexts, and shown to predict aggregate shares of choice in holdout and predictive validity sets equal to or better than traditional individual-level conjoint choice simulators (e.g. Elrod, Louviere and Davey, 1992; Oliphant *et al.*, 1992). Hence, there is no basis for claiming predictive superiority for individual-level conjoint choice simulators.

However, one criticism that can be made of the original approach proposed by Louviere and Woodworth (1983) is that aggregation of individuals with heterogeneous preferences can provide misleading aggregate results. In this view, one might be better advised to estimate individual-level conjoint models, and use these separate models in a choice simulator to predict each individual's choices, aggregating by summing over all the predicted individual choices. Of course, if individual-level conjoint models are reliable and unbiased and there is little error in the choice process, one would expect individual-level conjoint simulators to be a viable alternative to the aggregate Louviere and Woodworth approach. Unfortunately, as previously mentioned, the empirical record does not support this expectation.

In fact, the counter argument to this criticism is that individual-level conjoint choice simulators rarely take into account the stochastic nature of choice behavior. That is, individual-level utilities estimated from conjoint response data with OLS regression or any other estimation procedure contain sampling errors, and if the model itself is not correctly specified, the utilities also contain specification errors. Presumably one wants to take these errors into account in choice simulations. To my knowledge, only the CONSURV conjoint software (Williams, 1991) allows an analyst to take errors into account, and currently CONSURV only takes test-retest errors into account. A more likely state of affairs is that the utilities themselves also have error. That is, from profile to profile or choice set to choice set, individuals may vary the amount of emphasis they place on each attribute; hence, utilities also are subject to random errors.

Some individual-level conjoint choice simulators make use of so-called probabilistic choice rules. But, such rules are simply *ad hoc* ways of transforming predicted utilities into probabilities and (with the possible exception of the CONSURV approach) do not take errors in responses or utilities into account. One exception is the approach described by Louviere (1987) in which one uses an individual's regression standard error as a measure of the unknown variance of a Gumbel distribution (Ben-Akiva and Lerman, 1985, pp. 104–6) to calculate a scale parameter with which to "adjust" or scale the individual's utilities.

The Gumbel distribution is a three parameter distribution in which the scale or location parameter is inversely proportional to the variance. This scale parameter sets the unit of the utility scale; hence, if the error variability is large, the scale is small and vice versa. Thus, highly variable individuals will have small utilities, which predict uniformly equal probabilities in the limit; while less variable individuals have relatively large utilities, which predict deterministic choices in the limit. In any event, this provides a simple way to identify the unit of the response scale for different individuals, and permit logical comparisons between individuals if the Gumbel assumption is approximately correct. Moreover, it explicitly incorporates error variability into choice forecasts, hence, is a true stochastic approach to individual-level probabilistic choice simulation. It is also consistent with random utility theory.

Despite the appeal of individual-level analysis as a way to avoid aggregation bias and identify potential segments, the work of Dawes and Corrigan (1974), Wainer (1976), Anderson and Shanteau (1977) and others strongly suggests that utilities estimated from additive, individual-level conjoint models may be highly unreliable and biased. Thus, it is worth considering whether the approach proposed by Louviere and Woodworth (1983) can take into account aggregation and other bias in choice experiments. Fortunately, the answer to this question also is "yes". As noted by Louviere and Woodworth (1983), Louviere (1988a, b), Batsell and Louviere (1991) and others, it is possible to handle both aggregation and other sources of bias in theoretically acceptable and practical ways, as we now discuss.

Segmentation in conjoint choice experiments

Let us consider the segmentation issue first. There are two general ways to use individual data from conjoint choice experiments to identify potential segments: (a) if a problem is sufficiently small, individuals can respond to a complete set of designed choice sets (i.e. a designed experiment), or (b) a common subset of choice sets can be administered to all respondents. In the first case, one can calculate marginal (and possibly joint) totals for each attribute level for each individual. These totals are analogous to marginal means or regression estimates of attribute partworth utilities. These totals or some transformation of them, e.g. a reduced space based on multiple correspondence analysis (Kaciak and Louviere, 1990), can be used to identify segments in the usual ways (e.g. cluster analytic techniques). Of course, the caveat about using cluster analytic techniques on errorful data applies in this case as well as the individual-level conjoint case.

In the second case, one can use some measure of relatedness appropriate to discrete data to compare respondents, such as the percent agreement in choice responses, or convert the choice responses into a multiple indicator matrix and use multiple correspondence analysis to develop a reduced set of coordinates. Both methods can be used to identify segments using cluster analytic techniques, subject to the caveat of sampling and (possibly) other errors in the measures. Thus, there is nothing inherently different about using individual-level measures derived from choice experiments that suggests they are any less useful for segment identification.

What is different about the choice-based conjoint approach is its design and analysis technology. In particular, the design requirements can be significantly more complicated than traditional individual-level conjoint practice, although the analytical requirements seem only marginally more difficult, especially now that analytical software has become widely available. Hence, the barrier to entry is expertise in experimental design and random utility theory choice models. There is not any inherent individual-level limitation of the approach *per se*. Once segments are identified, it is a simple matter to estimate separate choice models for each segment.

Despite the fact that choice experiments can produce individual-level measures that permit one to identify segments in a manner analogous to traditional conjoint practice, cluster analytic segmentation is not very satisfactory from a theoretical standpoint. That is, one would like an approach which is not only less *ad hoc*, but less subject to capitalization on chance. One approach that meets this condition is to incorporate individual difference measures directly in choice models to explain differences in individual utilities. This approach is common in applications of choice models in econometrics and transportation planning and research (see, e.g. Ben-Akiva and Lerman, 1985).

An example of this approach is provided by Gaudagni and Little (1983) for scanner panel data and by Louviere, Swait, Erdem-Oncu and Dubelaar (1992) or Louviere, Fox and Moore (1992) for choice experiments. For example, in the choice experiment case, Louviere, Swait, Erdem-Oncu and Dubelaar incorporate both socioeconomic and psychographic measures into sample-level choice models to explain differences in individuals' choices between, respectively, brands of deodorants, jeans and casual athletic shoes. They hypothesized that sociodemographic effects would be less significant for frequently purchased, low-involvement deodorants, and more significant for less frequently purchased, high-involvement athletic shoes, jeans being intermediate. This hypothesis was strongly supported by their results. Louviere, Fox and Moore included a variety of sociodemographic and travel related factors in a series of choice models that predicted the choice of particular vacation destinations relative to the Province of Alberta, and found many were significant and of the expected sign.

Incorporation of individual difference measures into aggregate-level choice models is one way to take into account heterogeneity in preferences that can lead to violations of a key property of stochastic choice models, known as the Independence of Irrelevant Alternatives (IIA) property (Ben-Akiva and Lerman, 1985; Louviere and Woodworth, 1983; Louviere, 1988a, b; Batsell and Louviere, 1991). Even if IIA is satisfied at an individual-level (and it generally is not), a sample of heterogeneous (with respect to utilities) individuals who each individually satisfy IIA generally will not satisfy IIA in aggregate. IIA is a property of some probabilistic discrete choice models that requires shifts in choices to be proportional to changes in utilities. Hence, if in a sample of 100 consumers, 80 choose brand A and 20 choose brand B, we expect the same relative odds of choice for A and B (i.e. 80/20 = 4) if they choose between brands A, B and C (e.g. 60%, 15%, 25%). Violations of this property in aggregate choice data are likely to arise from aggregation over heterogeneous utility functions. Hence, a way to test for violations of IIA and rule out alternative explanations is required.

As noted by Louviere and Woodworth (1983), McFadden (1986) and Batsell and Louviere (1991) it is relatively straightforward to design conjoint choice experiments not only to test for violations of IIA but also to estimate models that take the violations into account. Louviere (1988a, b) notes that a sufficient condition to test IIA is to design a choice experiment such that all attributes of all choice alternatives are orthogonal to one another. This design approach is also consistent with a very general stochastic choice model developed by McFadden (1975) called Mother Logit.

McFadden's (1975) Mother Logit model not only provides a powerful approach to testing IIA violations in designed choice experiments, but also allows one to incorporate cross-alternative effects that take the violations into account. In this approach one simultaneously estimates a system of equations for all choice alternatives that takes into account not only how changes in the attributes of a particular alternative affect its own choices, but also how changes in its attributes affect choices of other alternatives. This model does not necessarily need to capture individual differences because the cross-alternative effects account for IIA violations from whatever source.

On the other hand, if heterogeneity in preferences is the primary source of the IIA violations observed in a particular set of data, one expects that a model with appropriately specified individual difference effects not only would eliminate the IIA violations, but also would permit insights into segmentation and targeting. Experience with a large number of practical applications using this approach suggests that it consistently eliminates the IIA violations. For example, Louviere, Swait, Erdem-Oncu and Dubelaar (1992) found highly significant violations of IIA as revealed by statistically significant cross-alternative effects terms in the Mother Logit models they fit to their three sets of brand choice data. After incorporating a variety of individual difference measures in their models, no terms corresponding to IIA violations were found to be significant in any of the three product categories.

Segmentation insights with these disaggregated, aggregate choice models are relatively straightforward, and in some respects richer, than traditional segmentation based on clustering individual-level utilities. For example, the Louviere, Swait, Erdem-Oncu and Dubelaar models contain terms in income, age, and the like; and their models predict the expected shares for individuals with any sociodemographic profile expressed as a combination of these variables. For example, one can forecast brand choice probabilities for males who earn $50,000 to $60,000 per year, aged 40–45 with three kids; and obtain another forecast for the same profile but aged 45–55. Thus, rather than the few segments typically identified by clustering individual-level conjoint results, these models allow one to forecast individual differences in choices for many demographic (and/or other) profiles. Thus, this approach allows for more detailed targeting than with traditional a priori or a posteriori segmentation because one can identify particular types of consumers who are likely to respond positively to particular offerings.

Specification and other bias in conjoint choice experiments

The Mother Logit model introduced in the previous section provides a quite general approach to handling a wide variety of sources of bias in choice models. Although Mother Logit lacks theoretical appeal, it has the advantage of being able to capture violations due to attribute omissions and other misspecifications, complex decision and choice processes, preference heterogeneity, and the like. Unfortunately, this generality comes at the expense of inconsistency with utility maximization in particular choice contexts, and a (potentially) large number of additional model parameters. Thus, a more theoretically appealing approach is to estimate and test models nested within this more general form that are consistent with utility maximization.

One straightforward and appealing approach is to incorporate individual difference effects into simple multinomial logit (MNL) models (McFadden, 1975). As previously noted, our empirical results provide consistent support for the conclusion that this approach eliminates IIA violations in a wide variety of choice contexts, which suggests that the primary source of IIA violations in sample-level choice data may be preference heterogeneity. Of course, more academic work is needed to rule out alternative possibilities and/or identify the circumstances under which we can expect heterogeneity to account for the violations, but our results are nevertheless quite encouraging. If for example, IIA violations are due to decision or choice processes inconsistent with IIA, such as elimination or nested choice strategies (e.g. Gensch, 1985; Moore and Lehmann, 1990), these processes can be accommodated by choice models nested within the more general Mother Logit model. Hence, there is nothing inherently limiting about conjoint choice experiments in terms of their ability to test for various sources of specification and other errors and account for them if necessary.

Another advantage of conjoint choice experiments is that the choice models that one estimates from them are consistent with random utility theory. This is important because traditional conjoint analysis experiments and models are not based on random utility theory and are generally inconsistent with real behavioral data in the sense that we cannot directly observe rating, "preference", or like behaviors in real markets. Thus, there is no obvious parallel real market behavior that corresponds to what is studied in traditional conjoint experiments. In contrast, it is now well known that the choices that individuals make in real markets can "reveal" their preferences; similarly, choices made by consumers in conjoint choice experiments also reveal preferences. In this way, choices made in real markets and choices made in experiments can be directly compared because both are assumed to be the outcome of processes consistent with random utility theory. Probabilistic discrete choice models based on random utility theory therefore provide basic behavioral and statistical theory for analyzing choices from whatever source. However, whether choice models derived from conjoint choice experiments will predict choice more accurately than choices predicted from traditional individual-level conjoint simultators in real markets is an empirical issue deserving of more research attention.

Thus, not surprisingly Ben-Akiva and Morikawa (1991), Adamowicz, Louviere and Williams (1992), Swait and Louviere (1992) and Louviere, Fox and Moore (1992) demonstrate that one can jointly and simultaneously estimate choice models from choice experiments and marketplace choices. In this case, however, one must take into account differences in the random component of utility in the two sources of choice data. That is, the unit of the utility scale in MNL choice models is inversely proportional to the error variability in the choice data. It is unlikely that real market and experimental choices have the same variability; but if both sets of choices arise from the same choice process, utilities estimated from MNL choice models in the two sets should be proportional. Recently, Swait and Louviere (1992) provided a simple method for estimating the ratio of the scale units in two or more data sets using widely available MNL estimation software. They also proposed a simple method for rescaling one set of data (say experimental choices) against a second (say marketplace choices) and testing whether the two sets of choices reflect the same choice process.

Louviere (1992) applied the Swait and Louviere (1992) ideas to a study of ski area choices and found that the size of the error component for his respondents' most recent ski trip to one of eight ski areas differed from the error component for their reported numbers of trips to each ski area during the most recent ski season. Similarly, utilities for ski area attributes estimated from several different conjoint tasks (i.e. ratings, "yes/no" responses and "choose the most and least attractive features of each profile") were shown to differ only in the size of their error components. After accounting for differences in scale due to differences in variability, the utilities estimated from each conjoint task predicted both most recent choice and the proportion of last season's trips quite well. However, without rescaling to account for differences in variability, one would have concluded that no models predicted the number of trips well.

As discussed by Swait and Louviere (1992), the strategy for the joint estimation of experimental and marketplace choice data (e.g. survey reported choices, diary or scanner panel choices, etc.) is as follows: (a) Insure that attributes common to both sets of data are measured and coded alike in both sets of data. (b) Determine whether some effects, like alternative-specific intercepts, are unique to one or the other data set. If so, they need not be subject to the proportionality constraint. (c) Concatenate the two data sets into one large data set. (d) Reweight one of the two data sets to account for differences in the total number of choice sets by multiplying the design matrix columns corresponding to the common set of effects that are assumed to be proportional by an initial constant within the range (usually at one end) expected for the ratio of scale units. (e) Estimate the joint model and its associated log likelihood value. (h) Repeat (d) to (e) by doing a grid search over the region in which one expects to find the true scale ratio. The log likelihood value will be maximized at that constant multiplier that is the best estimate of the scale ratio. The resulting utilities for that scale ratio are the utilities that correspond to the joint model, and these utilities will be scaled relative to the units of the reference data set.

Normally, one rescales experimental utilities to the same units as marketplace choices because one wants to predict marketplace and not experimental choices. Swait and Louviere (1992) also outline a hypothesis testing procedure for this approach which allows one to reject the hypothesis of parameter proportionality and thereby reject scalability. In any case, the scale ratio value found by this method can be interpreted as an optimal rescaling value for transforming utilities from one data set into the units of the other even if the proportionality hypothesis is rejected. Thus, it constitutes a potentially useful procedure for calibrating the results of conjoint choice experiments to real marketplace choices even if the proportionality hypothesis is not exactly satisfied.

Often one only has aggregate choice shares from the real market, and one wants to test whether the predictions of an experimental (or some other conjoint choice model) are consistent with them. Recently, Horowitz and Louviere (1993) proposed and applied an adjusted regression test of the hypothesis that the observed and predicted choices are generated by the same choice process. This test takes into account the sampling errors in the estimated parameters, which are not accounted for by a simple regression of predicted against observed. Although formulated to test probabilistic predictions against discrete choices observations, it also can be used to test predicted choices probabilities against observed aggregate shares. As well, the Swait and Louviere (1992) procedure can be applied to this case to develop an optimal rescaling of the experimental utilities to correspond to the observed choices.

The latter can be accomplished as described in a recent ski area study (Louviere, 1992). Louviere systematically multiplied the vector of experimentally estimated utilities by constants in the region 0.25 to 1.25 in steps of 0.05, and examined the chi-square values between predicted and observed associated with each. He stopped the search at that ratio that produced the lowest total chi-square value. In this way he succeeded in decrementing the unadjusted chi-square value for the experimental model from 20.57 to 3.62. The final model fit the observed ski area trip choice shares very well, whereas the non-rescaled model predicted no better than chance.

A similar approach can be used to transform traditional conjoint data into a form that can be jointly estimated with marketplace data. First, as suggested by Louviere and Woodworth (1983) and elaborated by Louviere (1987), if one has individual conjoint models, one can use them to simulate the sampled individuals' expected choices in a designed choice experiment. In particular, the approach to designing choice experiments suggested by Louviere and Woodworth (1983) can be used to design as many choice sets as required to estimate a particular probabilistic choice model specification. Thus, such a design can be quite large because one uses the conjoint equations and not individuals to simulate choices. In any case, this approach requires one to design an appropriate choice experiment and use individual conjoint equations estimated from a conjoint experiment to simulate choices. Leaving aside the issue of how to simulate (e.g. "highest predicted utility equals first choice", or the probability of choosing option i in set C equals the predicted utility of i divided by the sum of the predicted utilities for all options in C, etc.), the simulation should produce the expected aggregate choices for the profiles in each choice set.

Given the simulated choice data, one again operates within the random utility framework to estimate stochastic choice models from the data. For example, given a single aggregate choice model estimated from the simulated choice data, one wishes to rescale the parameters of that model to correspond as closely as possible to the marketplace parameters. One proceeds exactly as above by following steps (a) to (f) to obtain the rescaling ratio, multiply the simulated data set design matrix columns that one assumes to be proportional by the obtained scale ratio and jointly estimate the implied parameters. As previously mentioned, Swait and Louviere (1992) provide an approach to test the hypothesis that the parameters are proportional. Otherwise, the obtained scale ratio is only an optimal rescaling constant that maximizes the fit of the two data sets.

Other new random utility related developments in conjoint

Rank order explosion and related procedures for ranking data Chapman and Staelin (1982) outlined a procedure for taking rank order response data and exploding it in a manner consistent with the MNL model and random utility theory. The procedure is based on the ranking theorem of

Luce and Suppes (1965), which demonstrates that rank order explosion is consistent with the Luce (1959) choice axiom. The MNL and Luce models are mathematically similar and share many of the same properties like IIA, hence, the theorem also applies to the MNL model. Chapman (1984) later examined the relative parameter efficiency of various numbers of profiles (ranking depths) for individual-level analysis based on MNL estimation of the partworth parameters. Chapman's (1984) and related results by Bunch and Batsell (1989) on the numbers of observations required to satisfy asymptotic statistical properties in MNL models make it clear that one would need to have an individual rank a (very) large number of profiles in order to be able to estimate individual-level MNL parameters with any relative efficiency. Thus, individual-level analysis is probably not practical with rank order data.

More troublesome, however, is the fact that Ben-Akiva, Morikawa and Shiroishi (1992) recently found that not only were response data from different ranking depths unequally reliable, but different ranks produced statistically significantly different estimates of the utilities. To understand this problem, recall that the scale of the utilities in MNL models in inversely proportional to the error variability in the data. For ranking data to satisfy the properties of the MNL model, ranks can be differentially reliable, but utilities estimated from different ranking depths must be proportional.

For example, if one observes a complete ranking of N profiles one can create $N - 1$ "choice sets" by the following "explosion" process: (a) The first choice set consists of all N profiles, and the "choice" is equal to the first ranked profile; (b) The second choice set consists of $N - 1$ profiles from which the 1st ranked has been removed, and the "choice" is assumed to be the second ranked profile. One continues to "explode" the rankings in this fashion until only the N-th and $(Nth) - 1$ pair of profiles remain. To be consistent with the MNL model, the utilities one estimates from the first choice set with all N profiles (calculated over all respondents) should be proportional to the utilities estimated from any other set that represents a particular ranking depth, such as the second set with $N - 1$ profiles. Ben-Akiva, Morikawa and Shiroishi (1992) rejected this hypothesis for several of the depth comparisons they made in their data.

This finding suggests considerable caution in estimating MNL models from ranking data. At the least, one might want to conduct the scale comparison tests discussed by Swait and Louviere (1992) and illustrated by Ben-Akiva, Morikawa and Shiroishi (1992). One could begin with the set representing rank one and do systematic comparisons with adjacent ranking depths, etc. Stop combining ranking depths at whatever depth one first rejects the hypothesis of parameter proportionality. Of course, one might use only the first set, but this defeats the purpose of the ranking task, and calls into question the wisdom of observing ranks other than most preferred. In any case, that there is now reason to question the value and validity of ranking tasks for use in MNL models. Given so many other available options, common sense suggests little gain from use of a potentially flawed procedure.

Before leaving the topic of exploded rankings, I would like to suggest another possibility which to my knowledge has not been pursued by conjoint analysts. A rather common finding in conjoint studies is that if one graphs the mean rating (or ranking) for each of N profiles against the variance in the ratings (or rankings) for that profile calculated over respondents, the relationship often resembles an inverted-U. This suggests that samples of consumers tend to agree on the most and least preferred profiles, with the degree of agreement decreasing towards the region of the middle of the preference scale, then increasing again.

If this observation is satisfied for a particular set of ranking data, it suggests several possible ways of treating the data: (a) Try to combine the top and bottom ranks because their variances should be similar, and it may be more likely that their utilities are proportional (although inverted). Of course, as previously discussed, one might wish to conduct statistical tests to insure that these ranks can be combined. (b) An inverted-U relationship is consistent with a binomial distribution of responses. Thus, one might consider estimating a binary logit model by coding profiles rated above the highest variance rating value a one and profiles below a zero. This suggestion requires one to curve fit the data with a quadratic or similar function, and solve for the rating value associated with the highest variance. One uses this value as the cutoff for "yes/no" in the binary logit.

(c) Zahoric and Rao (1990) recently proposed an interesting way to aggregate ratings data, which could be applied to ranking data. If the distribution of responses to each profile follows a beta distribution, one can calculate the parameters of the beta for each profile, and regress these parameters against the design matrix to estimate the distribution of responses for any particular profile. They illustrate this approach with the apartment profile rating data of Elrod, Louviere and Davey (1992), and provide strong evidence that the model captures the aggregate distribution of responses very well. Recently, Jennings (1992) applied their idea in her doctoral thesis to model experts' judgments of the potential future value of engineered wood products in British Columbia. Her model also recovered the response distribution of each profile quite well.

One way to extend Zahoric and Rao's approach would be to use the regression results for the beta parameters to simulate the likely choice proportions for various competing profiles by repeated sampling. That is, use the empirical results to model the expected mean and variance for each profile in a set of competing profiles. Randomly sample a beta value from this empirical distribution and add it to the predicted mean for each profile in the set for which choices are to be simulated. Assign the "choice" to the profile with the highest predicted value of mean + random error. Repetition of this process 100 or more times should provide an estimate of the proportion of times that each profile has the highest utility, which is an estimate of its likely choice share. This should work reasonably well because all the statistical information about the distribution is captured in the empirical relationships estimated from the data.

Finally, (d) Hensher and Louviere (1982) proposed a way to transform ranking responses into expected choice frequencies, which can be analyzed in the random utility framework. They suggested that if respondents choose profiles from choice sets in a manner perfectly consistent with their profile ranking, one can simulate their behavior in a designed choice experiment, and use the results to estimate the utilities. The particular case considered by Hensher and Louviere involved a ranking of N airline profiles by a sample of individuals.

Louviere and Hensher applied the rankings to calculate each respondent's expected choice outcomes in all possible sets of the N profiles. This set is given by a 2^N factorial in which each profile is treated as a factor with levels "present" or "absent". Each profile appears in the set of all sets exactly half the time and its appearance with other profiles is exactly balanced. Thus, a simple formula relates the rankings to the expected total choices if the respondent behaves perfectly consistently. The expected proportion of choices for profile i is equal to 2^{-r_i} times one-half the number of total choices sets (r_i is the rank of the i-th profile). Thus, if the i-th profile is ranked first, it will be chosen every time it's available, which is equal to exactly half the number of choice sets. If the j-th profile is ranked second, it will be chosen every time it's available and the i-th profile is not present, which is exactly one fourth of the choice sets. The formula simply recognizes this progression.

Hensher and Louviere use the formula to calculate the total expected choices of each profile for each individual across all sets. Variability between individual totals provides variability in the data because the formula precludes variance within individuals. The totals for all profiles sum to a constant equal to the number of possible sets minus one (one set is null). One uses the totals as choice frequencies for a complete set of N profiles, and estimates the utility parameters of the corresponding MNL model conditional on the design matrix using maximum likelihood. As previously described, one can also introduce individual difference measures into the model to account for differences in individuals.

Maximum difference conjoint scaling model Recently, Finn and Louviere (1992) suggested a new univariate scaling model that can be used to measure brand-by-attribute positions, develop univariate scales from multiple measures, measure concern for issues in polling situations, and a variety of other possibilities. Their model and approach is based on a multinomial extension of Thurstone's (1927) model for paired comparisons in which individuals select the two objects in a set of three or more objects which are, respectively, the most or least attractive (or preferred, etc.). We will now discuss how this model can be recast as a choice model, in which the choice involves the identification of the two attribute levels in a conjoint profile which are, respectively, the most or least attractive (or any other two extremes on a response dimension of interest).

It is straightforward to adapt this model to measure attribute level utilities in a conjoint experiment. Not only is the model a member of the family of random utility models, but it has two important advantages over existing conjoint models: (a) All attribute levels are measured on a common utility scale in which one level of one attribute serves as the zero point or origin of the scale, and (b) one can separately estimate an overall effect for each attribute independently of its attribute level scale values. As discussed by Lynch (1985), additive conjoint models (a) do not permit separation of effect (weight) and scale value, hence effect and scale position are confounded in all additive conjoint models (except the one described below); (b) the utilities of the levels of each attribute are measured on separate interval scales with different origins, hence, only ratios of differences of attribute levels on their separate scales can be compared. Thus, an approach that separates effect and scale, as well as measures attribute level utilities on a single common, interval scale is of academic and practical interest.

A Best-Worst (BW) Conjoint model can be formulated as follows: (a) For each profile, respondents report the attribute levels which are, respectively, the most and least attractive. (b) Assume that this joint choice is a report of the two attribute levels which lie farthest apart on the underlying continuum (e.g. utility) of measurement interest, and (c) that this report is subject to error. Hence,

$$D_{ij} = \delta_{ij} + \varepsilon_{ij}, \tag{7.3}$$

where D_{ij} is the true but unobservable difference between attribute levels i and j; δ_{ij} is a systematic or observable (mean) difference revealed by the choices that the respondents make; and ε_{ij} is the random component of choice.

We are interested in the largest difference, and because of the error component, we cannot know that with certainty. However, if we make assumptions about the distribution of the random component we can calculate the probability that any particular pair of attribute levels exhibits the largest difference. For example, if we assume that the errors are distributed according to the Gumbel distribution (Ben-Akiva and Lerman, 1985, p. 104–6), the resulting model has the simple closed form of the MNL model. That is, we can calculate both attribute effects and attribute level utilities simultaneously from the respondents' choices based on the MNL model.

The MNL model for this process can be expressed as follows:

$$P(ij|C) = \exp(\delta_{ij})/\sum_{kl} \exp(\delta_{kl}), \ \supset kl \in C, \tag{7.4}$$

Attribute (Levels)	Raw	Total	MNL	Model	Results		
	Most totals	Least otals	Part worths	Standard errors	T-ratios	Slopes	Overall effects (T-stats)
Airfare (return)							0.079
$799	21	90					(0.185)
$599	12	44	See	0.045	− 2.285	− 0.1018L	
$399	28	45	Slopes	0.002	6.157	0.0122Q	
Hotel (5 nights)							− 0.862
$749	8	78					(− 2.605)
$549	12	61	See	0.069	− 1.369	− 0.0945L	
$349	10	33	Slopes	0.009	2.263	0.0122Q	
Car (5 days)							0.068
$299	19	24					(0.170)
$199	31	5	See	0.113	0225	0.0253L	
$99	9	16	Slopes	0.018	− 0.016	− 0.0003Q	
Climate						See	− 0.630
Warm days, cool nights	19	61	− 0.296	0.110	− 2.699	Partworths	(− 1.930)
Hot and humid	12	78	− 0.657	0.104	− 6.306		
Hot days, warm nights*	25	12	0.954	0.107	8.911		
Scenery						See	2.058
Mtns, ocean beaches	152	3	− 0.019	0.066	− 0.287	Partworths	(6.366)
Ocean beaches, forests	160	1	0.044	0.065	0.684		
Mountains, forests*	148	0	0.025	0.065	− 0.389		
Development level						See	− 0.603
Mainly urban	10	38	− 0.057	0.118	− 0.483	Partworths	(− 1.837)
Rural with small cities	16	43	− 0.036	0.0119	− 0.307		
Mainly rural*	13	34	0.094	0.119	0.790		
Local language						See	− 0.320
English is native	15	25	0.069	0.127	0.543	Partworths	(− 0.972)
Most speak English	4	26	− 0.212	0.124	− 1.709		
Few speak English*	9	16	0.143	0.126	1.141		
Missing data	5	5	0.000				
Possible number of choices per level	258	258					

Model statistics:
$−2[L(0) − L(\beta)] = 1401.5$, 22 df

$\rho^2 = 0.83$

* Computed from table

Figure 7.2 Attributes and levels varied in BW holiday destination study, together with MNL BW estimation results

where $P(ij|C)$ is the probability of choosing i best and j worst from a set or profile of attribute levels C; and δ_{ij}, δ_{kl} are the distance values associated with the respective best, worst pairs. The model can be estimated by treating each profile as a choice set and each implied best, worst pair in that profile as a discrete outcome. Thus, one either can use the discrete choices of each individual respondent to estimate a disaggregate, aggregate model in which one can introduce individual difference effects, or one can aggregate the choices to a segment or sample level and estimate the model from the aggregate data.

If the respondents' choice behavior is reasonably consistent, then utilities estimated from best choices should be the inverse of those estimated from worst choices. In this situation, which may occur frequently in practice, the estimation problem is especially simple: (a) Calculate the best and worst totals for each attribute level by summing across all profiles. (b) Create two "choice sets", one for best and a second for worst totals. Each row in these two sets represents a particular attribute level ("Missing data" also can be included as an additional row in each set to systematically exhaust the response possibilities). (c) Develop a dummy-coded design matrix to represent each effect of interest. For example, each attribute can be represented by a column to capture its total overall effect. These columns are coded exactly one for all levels of a particular attribute in the best set, minus one in the worst set, and zero elsewhere. To capture attribute level effects (i.e. scale the partworth utilities), create effects codes for qualitative attributes or mean center quantitative attributes such that the codes are reversed for best and worst, and zero elsewhere (similar to the dummy codes for overall attribute effects).

Consider an example of BW conjoint applied to holiday destination profiles. Based on an 18 profile main effects plan sampled from the 3^7 factorial, I obtained BW choices for all 18 profiles from a sample of 43 research practitioners who attended a workshop at the 1991 AMA ART Forum. The attributes and levels are listed in Figure 7.2. Respondents simply identified which levels in each profile were, respectively, the most and least attractive. For simplicity, I employed the two set estimation procedure described earlier, assembling the most attractive totals into one set and the least attractive totals into a second set. Figure 7.2 also contains the results of the simultaneous estimation of overall attribute effects and attribute utilities. As can be seen in Figure 7.2, the model does a good job of accounting for the choice data, explaining over 80 percent of the choice totals. In terms of the attribute effects, scenery clearly dominated the choices, with hotel costs, climate and the level of development (urban/rural) next. Air fare and car rental costs played a minor role in choice. Note also that the model tells us whether the overall effect of each attribute was positive or negative, which tells us about the distribution of most and least attractive totals over the ranges of each attribute. Scenery levels were uniformly positive, hotel costs, climate and level of development were mostly negative.

Attribute utilities were estimated by coding the columns in dollar units (divided by ten), reversing codes for most and least sets. Thus, slopes for airfare, hotel and rental car are in (dollars/10) units, whereas all other estimates are based on effects coding. The estimates in Figure 7.2 can be used to predict the overall utility of a destination by calculating the differences in attribute levels between a particular holiday profile and a reference profile, multiplying each attribute difference by its respective estimate and summing the resulting products to obtain the overall utility for that destination. Of course, the utility of the reference destination is equal to zero. In this way, one can forecast choice probabilities for any combination of holiday destination profiles if IIA is satisfied.

The BW approach also can be used to develop individual-level estimates by (a) calculating an individual's best and worst totals for each attribute level; (b) assembling these totals into two "choice sets" as described above; (c) adding 0.5 to each frequency as suggested by Cox (1970) and Domencich and McFadden (1975) to adjust for zero totals; (d) calculating the natural log of the odds ratio of best totals divided by worst totals, or using maximum likelihood procedures to estimate the utilities assuming the MNL model applies. Even simpler is to calculate best minus worst differences-in-totals and use these differences as individual utility estimates. Experience with a number of BW data sets suggests that the BW differences are usually linearly related to odds ratios or MNL estimates. In any case, the best and worst totals, odds ratios or differences-in-totals can be used for segmentation purposes in cluster analytic algorithms, or analyzed with multiple correspondence analysis procedures.

4 Discussion and Conclusions

Traditional ratings- and ranking-based conjoint analysis is now a relatively mature marketing research technology. The behavioral basis for these traditional approaches to conjoint analysis has never been clear, although their use as measurement models has a sound theoretical foundation. Thus, the theoretical basis of traditional conjoint analysis pertains more to the behavior of numbers than the behavior of people. However, if numbers supplied by people satisfy the axioms and assumptions of conjoint models, one can derive rich insights into the behavior of people.

This chapter sought to place conjoint analysis on a more behavioral basis by emphasizing the random utility framework for some models and measurement procedures. Random utility theory views a consumer as trying to maximize a utility function that contains a random component. In this view, therefore, choice is inherently stochastic from the standpoint of the researcher. More importantly, this view of conjoint analysis allows us to place it within mainstream microeconomic theory, linking conjoint models to the larger family of probabilistic discrete choice models in econometrics.

The latter link is important because there is no corresponding market behavior to that which is observed in rating and ranking tasks. In the case of choice tasks, however, the links to real market behavior not only become clear, but one can simultaneously and jointly estimate models based on experimental and real market choices. In this way choice simulations or calibrations no longer becomes isolated and *ad hoc* exercises, but rather logical approaches to testing the correspondence of experimental models with real data.

The continuing appeal of traditional conjoint analysis appears to be due in large part to inertia and barriers to entry created by the newer choice-based design and analysis techniques. It also has been frequently and incorrectly argued that only traditional conjoint can provide a logical, individual-level basis for segmentation. As noted in this chapter, the latter arguments are not only specious, but possibly counterproductive. Equally unfortunate is the fact that one of the initial papers in marketing that introduced the idea of conjoint choice experiments based on random utility theory positioned the technique as "aggregate" (Louviere and Woodworth, 1983). Despite numerous academic papers since that time, choice-based conjoint appears to be firmly positioned as an aggregate technique. Hopefully this chapter will help to clarify the issues and make it obvious that this is an incorrect interpretation of its full domain of application.

Questions

1 Review the behavioral foundations of traditional conjoint analysis and compare them to newer approaches rooted in random utility theory. For example, review conjoint work based on Social Judgment Theory and Information Integration Theory in psychology, which are associated, respectively with Judgment Policy Capturing and Functional Measurement methods. Also review the behavioral foundations of axiomatic utility theory and axiomatic conjoint measurement. How do these conjoint and conjoint-related measurement methods differ from random utility theory based methods? How are they similar? Do the differences matter academically or practically?

2 Conduct your own empirical comparison of traditional ranking, or rating-based conjoint with choice-based or maximum difference scaling-based conjoint. What differences and similarities do you find in assumptions, design of experiments, analysis and interpretation of data. What advantages and disadvantages are associated with each approach. Do you obtain similar insights about tradeoffs and decisions made by segments of consumers?

3 Conduct an analysis of the power of each conjoint approach to reliably detect interactions and non-linearities in utility functions. Determine whether such effects can be reliably estimated for individual consumers, and if so, how many profiles would be required to do so.

4 Review design approaches that might be used to obtain more reliable estimates of interactions and non-linearities in utility functions. What are the design and

task requirments associated with these strategies. How might they be modified if needed to be used in field research situations.

5 Choose a particular type of consumer choice behavior that interests you and spend time observing real consumers making these types of choices in a real market. Talk to some of the consumers you observe about their decision criteria and choice strategies. Design a survey that resembles as closely as possible the actual decision situation faced by the individuals you studied. Test the survey on a sample of individuals and determine whether you can make useful inferences about their tradeoffs and choices from the data you collect.

References

Adamowicz, Louviere, W., Williams, J. J. and Williams, M. 1992: Combining revealed and stated preference methods for valuing environmental amenities. Unpublished working paper, Department of Rural Economy, University of Alberta, Edmonton. September.

Anderson, N. H. 1962: Application of an additive model to impression formation. *Science*, 138, 817–18.

Anderson, N. H. 1970: Functional measurement and psychophysical judgment. *Psychological Review*, 77, 153–70.

Anderson, N. H. 1981: *Foundations of Information Integration Theory*, New York: Academic Press.

Anderson, N. H. 1982: *Methods of Information Integration Theory*, New York: Academic Press.

Anderson, N. H. and Shanteau, J. 1977: Weak inference with linear models. *Psychological Bulletin*, 84, 1155–70.

Barron, F. H. 1977: Axiomatic conjoint measurement. *Decision Sciences*, 8, 548–59.

Batsell, R. R. and Louviere, J. J. 1991: Experimental analysis of choice. *Marketing Letters*, 2, 199–214.

Ben-Akiva, M. and Lerman, S. R. 1985: *Discrete Choice Analysis: Theory and Application to Travel Demand*, Cambridge, MA: MIT Press.

Ben-Akiva, M. and Morikawa, T. 1991: Estimation of switching models from revealed preferences and stated intentions, Transportation Research B.

Ben-Akiva, Morikawa, T. and Shiroishi, F. 1992: Analysis of the reliability of preference ranking data. *Journal of Business Research: Special Issue on Experimental Choice Analysis*, 24, 149–64.

Brunswick, E. 1952: *The Conceptual Framework of Psychology*, Chicago: University of Chicago Press.

Bunch, D. S. and Batsell, R. R. 1989: How many choices are enough?: the effect of the number of observations on maximum likelihood estimator performance in the analysis of discrete choice repeated-measures data sets with the multinomial logit model. Unpublished Working Paper, Graduate School of Management, University of California, Davis.

Cattin, P. and Wittink, D. R. 1982: Commercial use of conjoint analysis: a survey. *Journal of Marketing*, 46, 44–53.

Chapman, R. G. 1984: An approach to estimating logit models of a single decision marker's choice behavior. *Advances in Consumer Research*, 11, 656–61.

Chapman, R. G. and Staelin, R. 1982: Exploiting rank ordered choice set data within the stochastic utility model. *Journal of Marketing Research*, 19, 288–301.

Cox, D. R. 1970: *Analysis of Binary Data*, London: Methuen.

Dawes, R. M. and Corrigan, B. 1974: Linear models in decision making. *Psychological Bulletin*, 81, 95–106.

Domencich, T. G. and McFadden, D. 1975: *Urban Travel Demand: A Behavioral Analysis*, Amsterdam: North-Holland.

Elrod, T. S. and Kumar, S. K. 1989: Bias in the first choice rule for predicting share. *Proceedings of the Sawtooth Software Conference*, Ketchum, ID: Sawtooth Software, 259–71.

Elrod, T. S., Louviere, J. J. and Davey, K. S. 1992: An empirical comparison of ratings-based and choice-based conjoint models. *Journal of Marketing Research*, 29, 368–77.

Finn, A. and Louviere, J. J. 1992: Determining the appropriate response to evidence of public concern: the case of food safety. *Journal of Marketing and Public Policy*, Forthcoming.

Finn, A. Louviere, J. J. and Timmermans, H. 1992: Retail research. In M. Houston (ed.), *Handbook of Marketing Research*, New York: McGraw-Hill. Forthcoming.

Gaudagni, P. M. and Little, J. D. C. 1983: A logit model of brand choice calibrated on scanner data. *Marketing Science*, 2, 203–38.

Gensch, D. 1985: Empirically testing a disaggregate choice model for segments. *Journal of Marketing Research*, 22, 462–7.

Green, P. E. 1974: On the design of choice experiments involving multifactor alternatives. *Journal of Consumer Research*, 1, 61–8.

Green, P. E. and Rao, V. R. 1971: Conjoint measurement for quantifying judgmental data. *Journal of Marketing Research*, 8, 355–63.

Green, P. E. and Wind, Y. 1973: *Multiattribute Decisions in Marketing: A Measurement Approach*, Hinsdale, IL: Dryden Press.

Green, P. E. and Srinivasan, V. 1978: Conjoint analysis in consumer research: issues and outlook. *Journal of Consumer Research*, 5, 103–23.

Green, P. E. and Srinivasan, V. 1990: Conjoint analysis in marketing research: new developments and directions. *Journal of Marketing*, 54, (4), 3–19.

Green, Helsen and Shandler 1988: Conjoint validity under alternative profile presentations. *Journal of Consumer Research*, 15, 392–7.

Haggerty, M. R. 1985: Improving the predictive power of conjoint analysis: the use of factor analysis and cluster analysis. *Journal of Marketing Research*, 22, 168–84.

Hammond, K. R. 1955: Probabilistic functioning and the clinical method. *Psychological Review*, 62, 255–62.

Hammond, K. R., Hursch, C. J. and Todd, F. J. 1964: Analyzing the components of clinical inference. *Psychological Review*, 71, 438–56.

Hensher, D. A. and Louviere, J. J. 1982: Identifying individual preferences for international air travel: an application of functional measurement theory. *Journal of Transport Economics and Policy*, 17, 225–45.

Hoffman, P. J. 1960: The paramorphic representation of clinical judgment. *Psychological Bulletin*, 57, 116–31.

Hoffman, P. J., Slovic, P. and Rorer, L. G. 1968: An analysis-of-variance model for the assessment of configural cue utilization in clinical judgment. *Psychological Bulletin*, 69, 338–49.

Horowitz, J. L. and Louviere, J. J. 1993: Testing predicted probabilities against observed discrete choices in probabilistic discrete choice models. *Marketing Science*, Forthcoming.

Jennings, S. M. 1992: *Wood Quality Management in British Columbia*. Unpublished doctoral dissertation, Department of Rural Economy, University of Alberta, Edmonton.

Johnson, E., Meyer, R. J. and Ghose, S. 1989: When choice models fail: compensatory models in negatively correlated environments. *Journal of Marketing Research*, 26, 255–70.

Kaciak, E. and Louviere, J. J. 1990: Multiple correspondence analysis of multiple choice data. *Journal of Marketing Research*, 27, 455–65.

Kamakura, W. A. 1988: A least squares procedure for benefit segmentation with conjoint experiments. *Journal of Marketing Research*, 25, 157–67.

Keeney, R. L. and Raiffa, H. 1976: *Decisions with multiple objectives: preferences and value tradeoffs*. New York: John Wiley.

Krantz, D. H., Luce, R. D., Suppes, P. and Tversky, A. 1969: *Foundations of Measurement*, New York: Academic Press.

Krantz, D. H. and Tversky, A. 1971: Conjoint measurement analysis of composition rules in psychology. *Psychological Review*, 78, 151–69.

Lancaster, K. 1966: A new approach to consumer theory. *Journal of Political Economy*, 74, 132–57.

Levin, I. P., Meyer, R. J. and Louviere, J. J. 1978: Functional analysis of mode choice, *Transportation Research Record*, 673, 1–7.

Liebetrau, A. M. 1983: Measures of association. Sage University Papers Series on Quantitative Applications in the Social Sciences. Newbury Park, Ca: Sage Publications, Inc.

Louviere, J. J. 1984: Hierarchical information integration: a new approach for the design and analysis of complex multiattribute problems. *Advances in Consumer Research*, 11, 148–55.

Louviere, J. J. 1987: An experimental design approach to the development of conjoint based simulation systems with an application to forecasting future retirement choices. In R. J. G. Golledge and H. G. Timmermans. (eds), *Behavioral Modeling in Geography and Planning*, London: Croom-Helm.

Louviere, J. J. 1988a: *Analyzing Individual Decision Making: Metric Conjoint Analysis*, Sage University Series on Quantitative Applications in the Social Sciences, Series No. 67. Newbury Park, Ca: Sage Publications, Inc.

Louviere, J. J. 1988b: Conjoint analysis modeling of stated preferences: a review of theory, methods, recent developments and external validity. *Journal of Transport Economics and Policy*, 10, 93–119.

Louviere, J. J. 1992: Maximum difference conjoint: theory, methods and cross-task comparisons with ratings-based and yes/no full profile conjoint. Unpublished working paper, Department of Marketing, Eccles School of Business, University of Utah, Salt Lake City, September.

Louviere, J. J., Fox, M. and Moore, W. 1992: Cross-task comparison of logit models estimated from different sources of stated preference data. Unpublished working paper, Department of Marketing, Eccles School of Business, University of Utah, Salt Lake City, July.

Louviere, J. J., Swait, J., Erdem-Oncu, T., and Dubelaar, C. 1992: Measuring consumer-perceived brand equity: a test of transferability. Unpublished working paper, Department of Marketing, Eccles School of Business, University of Utah, Salt Lake City, June.

Louviere, J. J. and Timmermans, H. J. P. 1990: Stated preference and choice models applied in recreation research: a review. *Leisure Sciences*, 12, 9–32.

Louviere, J. J. and Woodworth, G. G. 1983: Design and analysis of simulated consumer choice or allocation experiments: an approach based on aggregate data. *Journal of Marketing Research*, 20, 350–67.

Luce, R. D. 1959: *Individual Choice Behavior: A Theoretical Analysis*, New York: John Wiley & Sons.

Luce and Suppes 1965: Preference, utility and subjective probability. In R. D., Luce, R. R., Bush and E. Galanter, (eds.), *Handbook of Mathematical Psychology*, New York: John Wiley & Sons, 249–410.

Lynch, J. G., Jr. 1985: Uniqueness issues in the decompositional modeling of multiattribute overall evaluations: an information perspective. *Journal of Marketing Research*, 22, 1–19.

Manski, C. 1977: The structure of random utility models. *Theory and Decision*, 8, 229–54.

McFadden, D. 1974: Conditional logit analysis of qualitative choice behavior. In P. Zarembka (ed.), *Frontiers in Econometrics*, New York: Academic Press, 105–42.

McFadden, D. 1975: On independence, structure and simultaneity in transportation demand analysis. *Working Paper No. 7511*, Urban Travel Demand Forecasting Project, Institute of Transportation Studies, University of California, Berkeley.

McFadden, D. 1986: The choice theory approach to market research. *Marketing Science*, 5, 275–97.

Moore, W. L. and Lehmann, D. R. 1990: A paired comparison nested logit model of individual preference structures. *Journal of Marketing Research*, 26, 420–8.

Oliphant, K., Eagle, T., Louviere, J. J. and Anderson, D. A. 1992: Cross-task comparison of ratings-based and choice-based conjoint. Paper presented to the American Marketing Association's Advanced Research Techniques Forum, Lake Tahoe, June. Also paper presented to the Joint Sawtooth Software, SYSTAT Conference, Sun Valley, ID, July.

Slovic, P. and Lichtenstein, S. 1971: Comparison of Bayesian and regression approaches to the study of information processing in judgment. *Organizational Behavior and Human Performance*, 6, 649–744.

Stevens, S. S. 1951: Mathematics, measurement and psychophysics. In S.S. Stevens (ed.), *Handbook of Experimental Psychology*, New York: John Wiley & Sons.

Stevens, S. S. 1957: On the psychophysical law. *Psychological Review*, 64, 153–81.

Swait, J. and Louviere, J. J. 1992: The role of the scale parameter in the estimation and use of generalized extreme value models. Paper presented to the annual TIMS Marketing Science Conference, Wilmington, DL, March. Also (1992) unpublished working paper, Department of Marketing, Eccles School of Business, University of Utah, Salt Lake City, September.

Thurstone, L. L. 1927: A law of comparative judgment. *Psychological Review*, 4, 273–86.

Wainer, H. 1976: Estimating coefficients in linear models: it don't make no nevermind. *Psychological Bulletin*, 83, 213–17.

Williams, M. 1991: *CONSURV: Conjoint Analysis Software*, Edmonton, Canada: Intelligent Marketing Systems, Inc.

Yellott, J. I. 1977: The relationship between Luce's choice axiom, Thurstone's theory of comparative judgment, and the double exponential distribution. *Journal of Mathematical Psychology*, 15, 109–44.

Zahoric, A. and Rao, V. R. 1990: An application of the beta-distribution in aggregate conjoint analysis. Paper presented to the TIMS Marketing Science Conference, Durham, NC, March.

8

Multiple Correspondence Analysis

Donna L. Hoffman, Jan de Leeuw, and
Ramesh V. Arjunji

Introduction

Multiple correspondence analysis (MCA) is a popular tool in marketing
research (Green, Krieger, and Carroll, 1987; Hoffman and Batra, 1991;
Hoffman and Franke, 1986; Kaciak and Louviere, 1990; Valette-Florence
and Rapacchi, 1991). In this chapter, we introduce MCA as a nonlinear
multivariate analysis method which integrates ideas from both classical multivariate analysis and multidimensional scaling (MVA and MDS,
from now on, respectively).

In MDS models, a geometrical representation of the brands, say, is
derived from information about the *dissimilarities* among these brands.
The brands are represented in a metric map in such a way that dissimilar
brands are relatively far apart, while similar brands are relatively close. In
most MDS approaches, the map is a low-dimensional Euclidean space
(Cooper, 1983; Green, 1975). Compare this with cluster analysis, which can
be interpreted as an MDS technique. However, the metric map in which
we display the brands is now a tree or some other combinatorial structure
(Aldenderfer and Blashfield, 1984). Nevertheless, it is clear that MDS has
a very strong geometrical orientation and that the key notion is one of
distance.

In these respects, MDS is quite different from MVA, at least in its usual
formulations. The traditional MVA approaches proceed either by constructing *linear* combinations of variables with optimality properties defined
in terms of *correlation coefficients*, or by specifying structural models
for correlated variables, which are usually assumed to be *multinormally
distributed*. In these classical formulations, the geometrical notions play
a relatively minor role, with the emphasis shifted to linear algebra in
the form of matrix calculus. Distance in low-dimensional Euclidean space,
the key concept in MDS, is replaced by the vector inner product in
high-dimensional space. Nevertheless, it is critical to realize that the
basic mathematical structure used in most forms of MVA and MDS is

identical. It is none other than the familiar Euclidean space with the inner product defining the angle, and the accompanying Pythagorean distance measure.

We draw this comparison because the basic similarity between MVA and MDS can be impressively exploited. Gifi (1981, 1990), for example, organizes the better known MVA methods into a system which takes *multiple correspondence analysis* (MCA) as the basic technique from which all others are derived as special cases. MCA, as defined there, and as we shall develop it in this chapter (see also Hoffman and de Leeuw, 1992), is an MDS method for categorical variables in which the focus is on the distance among the points in a low-dimensional map.

In MCA, our concern is primarily with the following: (1) What are the similarities and differences among the brands, say, with respect to the various variables describing them?; (2) What are the similarities and differences among the variables with respect to the brands?; (3) What is the interrelationship among the brands and the variables?; and (4) Can these relationships be represented graphically in a joint low-dimensional space?

As we shall develop it, MCA is an MDS method that answers these questions in terms of the notion of closeness. This means that between brands, two brands are close together if they share similar variables, and between each variable category, two categories are close if they occur in the same brands to the same degree; it also implies that a brand is close to a variable category if the brand falls into that category.

We organize our chapter as follows. First, we offer some philosophy, which serves to fix ideas. We then present the theory underlying this philosophy, discussing in turn the homogeneity loss function and computational aspects of our approach. Next, we focus on the geometry of the loss function, which emphasizes interpretation through the links between MCA and some of the better known MVA techniques. An empirical example is then presented which illustrates the primary geometric features of MCA. The chapter concludes with a discussion of the issues involved in representing brands and variable categories in the same map.

Some philosophy by way of history

The French literature (see, for example, Benzécri *et al.*, 1973) discusses MCA in the context of metric MDS suitable for frequency matrices, contingency tables or cross-tables. Others formulate MCA as factorial analysis of qualitative data using scale analysis (Bock, 1960; Guttman, 1941; Nishisato, 1980) or principal component analysis (Burt, 1950; de Leeuw, 1973; Greenacre, 1984; Hayashi, 1950) perspectives.

Key papers in the history of simple correspondence analysis (CA) are Pearson (1904) and Hirschfeld (1935). The history is complicated and somewhat confused because the early papers dealt with theoretical questions and not with actual data analysis. The first paper applying CA in actual data analysis was Fisher (1940).

For multiple correspondence analysis, the situation is somewhat simpler. The technique was introduced, from the start, as a data analysis method, and the first paper was undoubtedly the one by Guttman (1941). Nevertheless, there are some predecessors. In the very early days of psychometrics, Edgerton and Kolbe (1936), Horst, (1936), Richardson and Kuder (1933), and Wilks (1938) derived principal components as a form of regression in which the predictor is missing.

In a sequence of papers in the 1970s de Leeuw, Young, and Takane constructed a series of multivariate ALSOS techniques for mixed measurement level data sets based on optimal scaling (OS) and alternating least squares (ALS). These techniques were systematized by Gifi (1981, 1990), who showed that all of classical multivariate analysis (including the ALSOS techniques) can be thought of as MCA with additivity and measurement level restrictions. In this chapter we present a geometrically inspired introduction to MCA, the fundamental building block of the Gifi system. Space limitations prevent us from discussing the many additional results dealing with measurement restrictions within variables, equality restrictions between variables, partitioning of the variables into sets, and statistical and numerical stability of the results.

MCA is the analysis of *interdependence* among a set of categorical variables, as distinct from the analysis of dependence (with pre-defined sets of dependent and independent variables). The approach we present in this chapter is particularly intuitive and should appeal to marketing researchers, borrowing, as it does, concepts and terminology from discriminant analysis and analysis of variance. We emphasize construction of not only an aesthetically pleasing map, but also one that is easy to interpret, and hence, managerially relevant.

Theory

The data are m categorical variables on n objects, with the jth variable taking on k_j different values, its categories. Consider the example in Table 8.1, with $m = 7$, $n = 31$, $k_1 = 4$, $k_2 = 4$, $k_3 = 4$, $k_4 = 5$, $k_5 = 4$, $k_6 = 4$, and $k_7 = 4$. Here, the objects are 31 Swedish industries which groups of customers rated in 1990 on seven variables tapping different aspects of satisfaction. The data we present are aggregated over hundreds of customer responses in each service or product category to provide an average view of the levels of each variable in each industry. As shown in Table 8.1, except for the *Price increase tolerance* variable, which was scaled using five categories, all variables were scaled using four categories.

Price measures the perceived price level relative to quality, ranging from very unreasonable to very reasonable. *Quality* measures the perceived quality level relative to price ranging from very low quality to very high quality. *Repurchase intention* evaluates how likely it is that the next time the customer purchases in the category, from very unlikely to very likely,

Table 8.1 Customer judgments on seven satisfaction variables for 31 Swedish industries

Industry[a]	Price[b]	Quality[c]	Repurchase intention[d]	Price increase tolerance[e]	Satisfaction[f]	Expectation of Quality[g]	Ideal[h]
Airline 1	Unreasonable	High quality	Very unlikely	Very unlikely to switch	Satisfied	High	Far away
Airline 2	Unreasonable	High quality	Unlikely	Neither likely nor unlikely to switch	Satisfied	Very high	Very close
Bank (B)	Unreasonable	Very high quality	Very likely	Likely to switch	Very satisfied	High	Close
Insurance (B)	Reasonable	Low quality	Unlikely	Likely to switch	Dissatisfied	High	Far away
PC (B)	Reasonable	Very high quality	Unlikely	Unlikely to switch	Very satisfied	High	Far away
Postl (B)	Unreasonable	Low quality	Unlikely	Very unlikely to switch	Dissatisfied	Very high	Far away
Postp (B)	Very unreasonable	Very low quality	Very unlikely	Unlikely to switch	Dissatisfied	Very high	Far away
Telecommunication (B)	Very unreasonable	Very low quality	Very unlikely	Unlikely to switch	Very Dissatisfied	High	Very far away
Cars	Very unreasonable	Very high quality	Likely	Neither likely nor unlikely to switch	Very satisfied	Very high	Very close

Table 8.1 (Contd.)

Industry[a]	Price[b]	Quality[c]	Repurchase intention[d]	Price increase tolerance[e]	Satisfaction[f]	Expectation of Quality[g]	Ideal[h]
Charter-travel	Very reasonable	Very high quality	Unlikely	Likely to switch	Very satisfied	Low	Close
Cloth	Very reasonable	Low quality	Very likley	Neither likely nor unlikely to switch	Dissatisfied	Very low	Very far away
Department stores	Reasonable	Low quality	Unlikely	Neither likely nor unlikely to switch	Dissatisfied	Low	Very far away
Food	Reasonable	Very high quality	Likely	Unlikely to switch	Very satisfied	—	Very close
Food TR	Reasonable	High quality	Likely	Likely to switch	Satisfied	High	Close
Furniture	Very reasonable	Low quality	Unlikely	Very unlikely to switch	Satisfied	Very low	Far away
Mail	Very reasonable	High quality	Likely	Unlikely to switch	Satisfied	Very low	Close
Mainframe computers	Reasonable	Very high quality	Very likely	Unlikely to switch	Very dissatisfied	Very high	Far away
Bank (P)	Unreasonable	High quality	Very likely	Likely to switch	Very satisfied	Low	Close

Table 8.1 (*Contd.*)

Industry[a]	Price[b]	Quality[c]	Repurchase intention[d]	Price increase tolerance[e]	Satisfaction[f]	Expectation of Quality[g]	Ideal[h]
Insurance (P)	Unreasonable	Low quality	Likely	Unlikely to switch	Dissatisfied	Low	Far away
Gasoline	Unreasonable	High quality	Very likely	Likely to switch	Satisfied	Low	Close
Pharmacy	Very reasonable	Very high quality	Very unlikely	Very unlikely to switch	Very satisfied	Very high	Very close
Life insurance (P)	Very reasonable	High quality	Likely	Unlikely to switch	Satisfied	Low	Close
Police	Very reasonable	Low quality	Very likely	Likely to switch	Very dissatisfied	Very low	Very far away
Postl (P)	Very unreasonable	Low quality	Very likely	Very unlikely to switch	Dissatisfied	High	Very close
Postp (P)	Very unreasonable	Very low quality	Likely	Neither likely nor unlikely to switch	Very dissatisfied	High	Very close
Telecommunication (P)	Very unreasonable	Very low quality	Unlikely	Neither likely nor unlikely to switch	Dissatisfied	Low	Far away
Rail	Very unreasonable	Very low quality	Very unlikely	Very unlikely to switch	Very dissatisfied	Very low	Very far away

Table 8.1 (Contd.)

Industry[a]	Price[b]	Quality[c]	Repurchase intention[d]	Price increase tolerance[e]	Satisfaction[f]	Expectation of Quality[g]	Ideal[h]
Ship	Reasonable	High quality	Likely	Unlikely to switch	Satisfied	Very high	Close
TV station 1	Very unreasonable	Very low quality	Very unlikely	Very likely to switch	Very dissatisfied	Very low	Very far away
TV station 2	Very unreasonable	Very low quality	Very unlikely	Very likely to switch	Very dissatisfied	Very low	Very far away
TV station 3	Reasonable	Very low quality	Very unlikely	Very likely to switch	Very dissatisfied	Low	Very far away

[a] Some industries are divided into two different customer types: (B) = business clients, (P) = public clients.

[b] Measured on the four-point scale: very unreasonable, unreasonable, reasonable, very reasonable.

[c] Measured on the four-point scale: very low quality, low quality, high quality, very high quality.

[d] Measured on the four-point scale: very unlikely, unlikely, likely, very likely.

[e] Measured on the five-point scale: very likely to switch, likely, neither likely or unlikely, unlikely, very unlikely to switch.

[f] Measured on the four-point scale: very dissatisfied, dissatisfied, satisfied, very satisfied.

[g] Measured on the four-point scale: very low, low, high, very high.

[h] Measured on the four-point scale: very far away, far away, close, very close

the purchase will be for the same manufacturer or brand again. *Price increase tolerance* assesses the tolerable price increase given quality before the customer is likely to switch, ranging from very likely to switch to very unlikely to switch. *Satisfaction* measures the customer's overall satisfaction with the product or service from very dissatisfied to very satisfied. *Expectation of quality* measures the customer's prior expectations of the quality of the product or service from very low to very high. Finally, *Ideal* measures how close the product or service comes to the ideal in the category, from very far away to very close.

Sets of variables are hypothesized to measure different aspects relating to customer satisfaction. Thus, quality and price represent performance aspects of satisfaction. Satisfaction, expectations, and closeness to the ideal indicate the satisfaction construct and price increase tolerance and repurchase tap aspects of customer loyalty. Fornell (1992) provides a fuller discussion of these data in the context of his Customer Satisfaction Barometer project.[1]

We code the variables using indicator matrices, which allow for easy expression in matrix notation. An indicator matrix is a binary matrix (exactly one element equal to one in each row) which indicates the category that an industry is in for a particular variable. Thus, if variable j has k_j categories, the indicator matrix G_j for this variable is $n \times k_j$. The rows of G_j add up to one. The seven indicator matrices for our example appear in Table 8.2. Notice that the variable *Expectation of quality* is missing for the industry FOOD, as indicated by the zeros for every category of that variable. The indicator matrix for this variable is thus *incomplete*.

The purpose of multiple correspondence analysis is to construct a joint map of the industries and satisfaction variable categories in such a way that an industry will be relatively close to a category it is in, and relatively far from the categories it is not in. By the triangle inequality, this implies that industries mostly occurring in the same categories tend to be close, while categories sharing mostly the same industries tend to be close, as well.

Imagine for a moment an arbitrary map that we could construct from Table 8.2 by connecting industries with categories of the variables they are in. We might locate industries randomly in the map, while variable categories could be positioned at the centroid or average of all the industries in that category. We could draw lines that show the connections between the industries and the variable categories. Such a map would contain the same information as the data matrix in Table 8.2, but would be rather unappealing to the eye and difficult to interpret. There would be many lines in the map and they would cross every which way. Our rule for constructing such a map thus means that the map would give the impression that industries are as far from the categories they occur in as they are from the categories they do not occur in. We would deem such an arbitrary representation of the data highly unsatisfactory.

Now suppose we think of this map as a multivariable representation, i.e. as a joint map of the industries and the variable categories, in two-dimensional

Table 8.2 The seven indicator matrices constructed from the data in table 8.1

Industry	Price	Quality	Repurchase intention	Attributes: Price increase tolerance	Satisfaction	Expectation of quality	Ideal
Airline 1	0 1 0 0	0 0 1 0	1 0 0 0	0 0 0 1	0 0 1 0	0 0 1 0	0 1 0 0
Airline 2	0 1 0 0	0 0 1 0	0 1 0 0	0 0 1 0	0 0 1 0	0 0 0 1	0 0 0 1
Bank (B)	0 1 0 0	0 0 0 1	0 0 0 1	0 1 0 0	0 0 0 1	0 0 1 0	0 0 1 0
Insurance (B)	0 0 1 0	0 1 0 0	0 1 0 0	0 1 0 0	0 1 0 0	0 0 1 0	0 1 0 0
PC (B)	0 0 1 0	0 0 0 1	0 1 0 0	0 0 0 1	0 0 1 0	0 0 1 0	0 1 0 0
Postl (B)	0 1 0 0	0 1 0 0	0 1 0 0	0 0 0 1	0 1 0 0	0 0 0 1	0 1 0 0
Postp (B)	1 0 0 0	1 0 0 0	1 0 0 0	0 0 1 0	0 1 0 0	0 0 1 0	1 0 0 0
Telecommunication(B)	1 0 0 0	1 0 0 0	1 0 0 0	0 0 0 1	1 0 0 0	0 0 1 0	1 0 0 0
Cars	0 0 0 1	0 0 0 1	0 0 1 0	0 1 0 0	0 0 0 1	0 0 0 1	0 0 0 1
Charter-travel	0 0 0 1	0 0 0 1	0 1 0 0	0 0 1 0	0 0 1 0	0 1 0 0	0 1 0 0
Cloth	0 0 0 1	0 1 0 0	0 0 0 1	0 0 1 0	0 1 0 0	1 0 0 0	0 0 0 1
Department Stores	0 0 1 0	0 0 1 0	0 1 0 0	0 0 0 1	0 1 0 0	0 1 0 0	0 0 0 1
Food	0 0 1 0	0 0 0 1	0 0 1 0	0 0 0 1	0 0 1 0	0 0 0 1	0 0 0 1
Food TR	0 0 1 0	0 0 1 0	0 0 1 0	0 1 0 0	0 0 1 0	0 0 1 0	0 1 0 0
Furniture	0 0 0 1	0 1 0 0	0 1 0 0	0 0 0 1	0 0 1 0	1 0 0 0	0 0 0 1
Mail	0 0 0 1	0 0 1 0	0 0 1 0	1 0 0 0	0 0 1 0	1 0 0 0	0 0 1 0
Mainframe computers	0 0 1 0	0 0 0 1	0 0 0 1	0 0 1 0	1 0 0 0	0 0 0 1	0 0 0 1
Bank (P)	0 1 0 0	0 0 1 0	0 0 0 1	0 0 1 0	0 0 0 1	0 1 0 0	0 1 0 0
Insurance (P)	0 1 0 0	0 1 0 0	0 0 1 0	0 0 1 0	0 1 0 0	0 1 0 0	0 1 0 0
Gasoline	0 1 0 0	0 0 1 0	1 0 0 0	0 0 1 0	0 1 0 0	0 0 1 0	0 0 1 0
Pharmacy	0 0 0 1	0 0 0 1	0 0 0 1	0 0 0 1	0 0 0 1	0 0 0 1	0 0 0 1
Life insurance (P)	0 0 0 1	0 0 1 0	0 0 1 0	0 0 1 0	0 0 1 0	0 1 0 0	0 1 0 0

Table 8.2 (Contd.)

Industry	Price				Quality				Repurchase intention				Attributes Price increase tolerance				Satisfaction				Expectation of quality				Ideal			
Police	0	0	0	1	0	1	0	0	0	0	0	1	0	1	0	0	1	0	0	0	1	0	0	0	1	0	0	0
Postl (P)	1	0	0	0	0	1	0	0	0	0	0	1	0	0	0	1	0	1	0	0	0	0	1	0	0	0	0	1
Postp (P)	1	0	0	0	1	0	0	0	0	0	1	0	0	0	1	0	1	0	0	0	0	0	1	0	0	0	0	1
Telecommunication(P)	1	0	0	0	1	0	0	0	0	1	0	0	0	0	1	0	0	1	0	0	0	1	0	0	0	1	0	0
Rail	1	0	0	0	1	0	0	0	1	0	0	0	0	0	0	1	1	0	0	0	1	0	0	0	1	0	0	0
Ship	0	0	1	0	0	0	1	0	0	0	1	0	0	0	1	0	0	0	1	0	0	0	0	1	0	0	1	0
TV station 1	1	0	0	0	1	0	0	0	1	0	0	0	1	0	0	0	1	0	0	0	1	0	0	0	1	0	0	0
TV station 2	1	0	0	0	1	0	0	0	1	0	0	0	1	0	0	0	1	0	0	0	1	0	0	0	1	0	0	0
TV station 3	0	0	1	0	1	0	0	0	1	0	0	0	1	0	0	0	1	0	0	0	0	1	0	0	1	0	0	0
	G_1				G_2				G_3				G_4				G_5				G_6				G_7			

Euclidean space. How can we improve upon the map? The map will be much more useful to us if industries are close to the categories of the variables that they occur in. This is, in words, the basic premise of multiple correspondence analysis. We desire a map of the data in low-dimensional Euclidean space such that the points connected by a line are relatively close together (and the points not connected by lines are relatively far apart). By the triangle inequality this implies that industries with similar profiles (i.e. industries that are often in the same categories) will be close, and categories containing roughly the same industries will be close, as well. The resultant map will capture the essence of our original idea for a map, but in a way that yields easier and better interpretation. We now formalize these ideas by defining a suitable loss function to be minimized.

The homogeneity loss function

The concept of *homogeneity* serves as the basis for our theoretical development of multiple correspondence analysis. We use homogeneity in a data theoretical sense as being closely related to the concept of data reduction. That is, homogeneity refers to the extent to which different variables measure the same characteristic or characteristics (Gifi, 1981, 1990). Homogeneity thus specifies a type of similarity. In order to measure homogeneity, we need a measure for the difference or the similarity of the variables. There are different measures of homogeneity and different approaches to find maps with some distances smaller than others. The particular choice of loss function defines the former and the specific algorithm employed determines the latter. Note that when the variables measure more than one property or characteristic, we may wish to proceed in order to find another, orthogonal, solution. This is in keeping with the principle of data reduction which advocates that a small number of dimensions should be used to explain a maximum amount of information contained in the data.

The extent to which a particular representation $\mathbf{X}$ of the industries and particular representations $\mathbf{Y}_j$ of the categories, satisfy the axioms of multiple correspondence analysis is quantified by the *loss of homogeneity*, a least squares loss function:

$$\sigma(\mathbf{X}; \mathbf{Y}_1, \ldots, \mathbf{Y}_m) = \sum_j SSQ(\mathbf{X} - \mathbf{G}_j \mathbf{Y}_j) \tag{8.1}$$

where $SSQ(.)$ is shorthand for the sum of squares of the elements of a matrix or vector. The loss function in (1), giving the sum of squares of the distances between industries and the variable categories they occur in, measures departure from perfect fit. In words, Loss = Dist^2(Airline 1, unreasonable) + Dist^2(Airline 2, unreasonable) + ... + Dist^2(TV station 2, very far away) + Dist^2(TV station 3, very far away). A total of $n * m = 31 * 7 = 217$ squared distances are summed and these squared distances correspond exactly to the lines connecting industries and variable categories in our original messy map. Quite simply, multiple correspondence analysis produces the map with the smallest possible loss.

There are two sets of unknowns in the MCA problem: the $n \times p$ matrix of industry coordinates $\mathbf{X}$ and the m matrices of variable category coordinates $\mathbf{Y}_j$, each of order $k_j \times p$, where p is the number of dimensions. We could say that multiple correspondence analysis is a method that minimizes (1) over $\mathbf{X}$ and the $\mathbf{Y}_j$, but this would not be sufficient. In the first place, we can set $\mathbf{X} = 0$ and $\mathbf{Y}_j = 0$, for all j. This gives loss equal to zero (i.e. the map is a single point) and consequently, perfect homogeneity. In fact, more generally, taking all elements of $\mathbf{X}$ equal to a constant c, and taking all elements of $\mathbf{Y}_j$ equal to c as well, gives loss zero. These trivial solutions are excluded by imposing suitable normalizations. As we discuss subsequently, it is these normalizations which define a particular coordinate scaling. For now, we choose to minimize over all $\mathbf{Y}_j$ and all *normalized* $\mathbf{X}$, which means we require $\mathbf{X}'\mathbf{u} = 0$ and $\mathbf{X}'\mathbf{X} = n\mathbf{I}$, where $\mathbf{u}$ is a unit vector (all elements equal to one) and $\mathbf{I}$ is the identity matrix. A matrix $\mathbf{X}$ satisfying these restrictions is said to be *normalized*. We now define multiple correspondence analysis more precisely as minimization of the loss function (8.1) over all $\mathbf{Y}_j$ and over all normalized $\mathbf{X}$ (or equivalently over all normalized $\mathbf{Y}_j$ and all $\mathbf{X}$).[2]

Computational aspects: reciprocal averaging

Our algorithm, which is exceedingly simple, uses alternating least squares (or, equivalently, reciprocal averaging (Hirschfeld, 1935; Horst, 1935)). This means that we start with an arbitrarily normalized $\mathbf{X}$ and then compute the *optimal* $\mathbf{Y}_j$,

$$\mathbf{Y}_j = \mathbf{D}_j^{-1}\mathbf{G}_j'\mathbf{X} \qquad (8.2)$$

with $\mathbf{G}_j$ defined as above, and $\mathbf{D}_j = \mathbf{G}_j'\mathbf{G}_j$ the $k_j \times k_j$ diagonal matrix containing the univariate marginals of variable j.[3] In words, the optimal coordinate for a variable category is the average or *centroid* of the (optimal) coordinates of the industries in that category. Using these new $\mathbf{Y}_j$ we now compute new *optimal* $\mathbf{X}$,

$$\mathbf{X} = m^{-1}\sum_j \mathbf{G}_j\mathbf{Y}_j \qquad (8.3)$$

In words, the optimal coordinate for an industry is the centroid of the (optimal) coordinates of the categories containing that industry. We now normalize $\mathbf{X}$ by Gram-Schmidt orthogonalization and go back to (8.2) until convergence. If the pth eigenvalue is greater than the $p + 1^{th}$ eigenvalue, then convergence is guaranteed. The algorithm is implemented in the SPSS-X program CATEGORIES (SPSS Inc. 1989). Equations (8.2) and (8.3) make clear the centroid principle.

Geometric Aspects of MCA

To highlight interpretation we focus on the geometry of the loss function. Our development proceeds from initially assuming that the industry coordinates, X, are normalized and the satisfaction variable category coordinates, Y_j, are free. Loss function (8.1) has a natural lower bound, because obviously $\sigma(X; Y_1, \ldots, Y_m) \geq 0$, but no natural upper bound. The Y_j can be arbitrarily far from X, and thus σ is really unbounded. This means that we have no standard to compare loss with, and no factor to normalize it with. In order to remedy this, we define the loss function

$$\sigma(X; *, \ldots, *) = \min_{Y} \sigma(X; Y_1, \ldots, Y_m) \tag{8.4}$$

which is the minimum of the homogeneity loss function (8.1) over the variable category coordinates. It is now easy to derive an upper bound for (8.4), because $\sigma(X; *, \ldots, *) \leq \sigma(X; 0, \ldots, 0) = m \, tr(X'X) = mnp$.

MCA as discriminant analysis and ANOVA

We can restate the MCA problem in discriminant analysis or ANOVA terms. Suppose we knew the industry coordinates, X. Each variable defines a partitioning of these industries. This means we can compute the total variance of X, which is just the sum of the between and within group (variable) variance. In matrix notation, this is simply $T = B + W$. We now wish to scale the industries, that is, solve for optimal X, in such a way that W will be as small as possible while keeping T equal to a constant; I, for example.

This leads to a trivial solution: all industries in the first category of the variable are a single point, all industries in the second category are another point, and so on. The location of the points in the map is arbitrary, although $W = 0$ and $B = T = I$. But in MCA we have more than one variable, so a trivial solution for one variable will not be a trivial solution for another. This leads us to seek a compromise solution to the problem. For a given X, let us define T_*, W_*, and B_*, which are averages over variables. Clearly, for all variables, T, the total variance of X, is the same, and now we search for the smallest W_* with $T = T_* = I$. This defines MCA.

Substituting the optimal category coordinates from (8.2) gives

$$\sigma(X; *, \ldots, *) = \sum_j tr \, X' \, (I - P_j) \, X,$$
$$= mn(p - trX'P_* X/n) \tag{8.5}$$

with $P_j = G_j D_j^{-1} G_j'$ an $n \times n$ orthogonal projector matrix and P_* equal to the average of the P_j. Now, from equation (8.5) $X'P_jX$ is the *variance* *between categories* of X for variable j, and $X'(I - P_j)X$ is the *variance within categories*. Then $X'X$, which we fix at nI, is the *total variance*.

Thus, MCA maximizes the average between-category variance, while keeping the total variance fixed (or, equivalently, minimizes the average within-category variance). Consequently, the main difference between discriminant analysis and MCA is that with the former we have one categorical variable and X must be of the form ZA, with Z known and weights A unknown. In MCA, the number of variables m is greater than one and X is completely unknown (or $Z = I$).

MCA as a dual eigenproblem

This development shows that multiple correspondence analysis of X normalized and the Y_j free solves the eigenvalue problem:

$$P_*X = X\Lambda. \tag{8.6}$$

where $\lambda_1(P_*) \geqslant \ldots \geqslant \lambda_p(P_*)$ are the p largest non-trivial eigenvalues of the average projector P_*. We use "non-trivial" because P_* always has a largest trivial eigenvalue $\lambda_0(P_*) = 1$, corresponding with the trivial eigenvector $u = 1$. All other eigenvectors can consequently be chosen such that $X'u = 0$. The optimal coordinates for the industries in p dimensions are given by the p eigenvectors, with corresponding eigenvalues, of P_*. The corresponding optimal coordinates for the categories of variable j are then $Y_j = D_j^{-1}G_j'X$, as in equation (8.2) and follow from the centroid principle.

MCA as categorical PCA

MCA is also identical to a form of principal component analysis of categorical data outlined by Guttman (1941) and Burt (1950). To show this clearly, suppose that we normalize Y by $\sum_j Y_j'D_jY_j = nI$ and $\sum_j Y_j'D_ju = 0$ with the condition that X is free. Thus, we alternatively define the MCA problem as minimizing (8.1) over free X and normalized Y_j. As a first step, we examine the loss function:

$$\sigma(*; Y_1, \ldots, Y_m) = \min_X \sigma(X; Y_1, \ldots, Y_m) \tag{8.7}$$

Then we find, after substituting the optimal industry coordinates from (8.3), that MCA amounts to solving the eigenvalue problem:

$$CY = mDY\Lambda \tag{8.8}$$

with $C = G'G$ the $\sum k_j \times \sum k_j$ "Burt matrix," so-called by the French; it contains the bivariate marginals (cross-tables), where $G = [G_1|\ldots|G_m]$ is the super-indicator matrix. The Burt matrix has a block structure, wherein each off-diagonal submatrix $G_{jl} = G_j'G_l$, $j \neq 1$, is the cross-table of variables j and l containing the bivariate marginals across the n industries. Each diagonal submatrix $D_j = G_j'G_j$ is the $k_j \times k_j$ diagonal matrix with the univariate marginals of variable j. Then $D = \text{diag}(C)$ is the diagonal super-matrix of univariate marginals. The optimal coordinates for the variable categories in p dimensions are given by the p eigenvectors with corresponding eigenvalues of C. The corresponding optimal industry coordinates are then $X = m^{-1}\sum_j G_j Y_j$, as in equation (8.3), and follow from the centroid principle.

The dual eigenproblems in equations (8.6) and (8.8) amount to a singular value decomposition (SVD) of the matrix $m^{-1/2}GD^{-1/2}$. It can be shown (van Rijckevorsel and de Leeuw, 1988) that both problems have the same eigenvalues; the eigenvectors of interest are then the left and right singular vectors of $m^{-1/2}GD^{-1/2}$. Moreover, the SVD of this matrix also solves the problem of minimizing the loss function (8.1) over all normalized X and all normalized Y. Computing this SVD effectively performs a correspondence analysis on G.

Correspondence analysis as a special case of MCA

Our approach allows us to *specialize* MCA to the situation in which there are just two variables; it then becomes identical to simple or two-way correspondence analysis (Benzecri, *et al.*, 1973; Greenacre, 1984; Lebart, Morineau, and Warwick, 1984). See also Carroll, Green, and Schaffer (1986). We have already shown above that, in general, MCA can be formulated as a type of categorical PCA.

Now, suppose we have only two variables, i.e. $m = 2$. Then, $[G_1|G_2]$ and $G_1'G_2 = F$, the contingency table for these two variables. We write the univariate marginals for variables 1 and 2 along the diagonals of D_1 and D_2 respectively. For two variables, the Burt matrix C now has the very special form:

$$C = \begin{bmatrix} D_1 & F \\ F' & D_2 \end{bmatrix}$$

Since two-way correspondence analysis is given by the SVD of $D_1^{-1/2} FD_2^{-1/2}$ (cf. Hoffman and Franke, 1986, equation (11)), it is immediately seen that the SVD of $D^{-1/2} CD^{-1/2}$, with D containing D_1 followed by D_2 on the diagonal, equal to the SVD of

$$\begin{bmatrix} I & D_1^{-1/2} FD_2^{-1/2} \\ D_1^{-1/2} FD_2^{-1/2} & I \end{bmatrix}$$

gives the same solution.

MCA as an MDS method

We can also link MCA to multidimensional scaling through the notion of distance. Suppose we were to perform a multidimensional unfolding on $\mathbf{G}$, the super-indicator matrix. The MDS solution for unfolding requires a representation where the distance between an industry point and a variable category it occurs in is always smaller than the distance from that industry to a "non-chosen" variable category point. The relation with MCA is obvious. MCA plots a category point in the center of gravity of the industry points for those industries which "choose" that category, with the consequence that, overall, industry points will be closer to the chosen variable categories than to the non-chosen variable categories.

Interpretation of the industry points is guided by the fact that we solve for $\mathbf{X}$ (with unit total sum of squared distances, $\mathbf{X}'\mathbf{X}$) such that the within-category squared Euclidean distances, $\mathbf{X}'(\mathbf{I} - \mathbf{P}_j)\mathbf{X}$, are as small as possible (or, equivalently, that the between-category squared Euclidean distances, $\mathbf{X}'\mathbf{P}_j\mathbf{X}$, are as large as possible). The primary difference between MCA and MDS is that the MCA solution is obtained at the expense of stronger normalization conditions and a metric interpretation of the data. That is, MCA approaches perfect fit, i.e. distance $d_{ij}(\mathbf{X}, \mathbf{Y})$ between industry point i and variable category point j equals zero, if g_{ij} in the indicator matrix, equals one. This is a stricter requirement than in MDS, which requires that if $g_{ij} = 0$ and $g_{il} = 1$ then $d_{ij}(\mathbf{X}, \mathbf{Y}) \geqslant \mathbf{d}_{il}(\mathbf{X}, \mathbf{Y})$. However, MDS methods for unfolding make weaker assumptions, but also tend to produce degenerate solutions.[4]

Our MDS interpretation repeats the multivariate analysis development, which is in terms of variance, and reformulates it in terms of distance. The variance interpretation has appeal for those researchers familiar with discriminant analysis, analysis of variance, and principal component analysis, while the distance interpretation should appeal to those more comfortable with multidimensional unfolding. Both interpretations, however, are correct.

Handling missing data

A distinct advantage of nonlinear multivariate analysis in general, and multiple correspondence analysis in particular, is the treatment of missing data. Because all variables are treated as categorical, missing data may always be considered as a separate and bona fide category: the "missing category." Thus, there is no need to impute, estimate, or otherwise insert substitute information for the missing datum. This also means there is no need to discard observations with missing data.

In the context of multiple correspondence analysis, there are three general approaches to handle missing data. In the first place, we may leave the indicator matrix incomplete and proceed with analysis. Gifi (1990) refers to this as *missing data passive*. For our example, this means that we do not alter the four zeros in Table 8.2 for the variable *Expectation of quality* for industry FOOD. If we choose this option for missing data, the missing values are not quantified.

A second treatment for missing data completes the indicator matrix with a single additional column for each variable with missing data. This is called *missing data single* (Gifi 1990). Missing data single has the effect of treating missing data as if they are in a category by themselves. If we were to choose this option for our example, we would add a single column to the indicator matrix in Table 8.2 and enter a single 1 for the industry FOOD, to reflect that it had a missing datum for one of the variables. If further industries had missing data for that variable, they too would have 1's entered in that additional single column. This option therefore treats industries as if they are in the same category with respect to what generated the missing data. Put another way, the process assumed to underlie the occurrence of missing data is assumed to be homogeneous (across industries) for each variable. Such a treatment produces a scaling for the missing data that is the average industry score for industries with missing data on a variable.

The third option requires the indicator matrix to be completed by adding to G_j as many additional columns as there are missing data for the jth variable. Gifi (1990) refers to this as *missing data multiple*. In this case, as many extra columns as there are industries with missing data on the jth variable are added to G^j to complete it, and each such column has only a single 1. The treatment of missing data with the missing data multiple option assumes that whatever process generated the missing data differs for different industries. Each missing value receives the scaling of the associated industry.

Not surprisingly, if there are not too much missing data and they are randomly distributed over row objects and variable categories, the differences among the three treatments will be minor, with highly similar interpretation of the resulting solutions. However, if missing data seem to collect at some objects or variables, the results can be highly different. Treating missing data as a category in its own right allows special study of those objects with missing values.

Statistical stability of the results

Gifi (1990, ch. 12), studies various forms of stability of MCA results. The most important form is, perhaps, statistical stability. The basic statistics computed by MCA (category centroids, eigenvalues, discrimination measures) can be easily expanded using the delta method, which gives formulas for standard errors. The bootstrap and the jackknife are also discussed in considerable detail, and it is shown that these techniques give essentially the same information. The SPSS program ANACOR (SPSS Inc. 1989) actually computes delta method standard errors directly, and makes it possible to replace the points in the CA and MCA plots by 95 percent confidence ellipses. Van der Burg and de Leeuw (1983) discuss simple (although computer-intensive) methods to test significance of dimensions in generalized canonical analysis (of which MCA is an exceedingly special case). Finally, de Leeuw (1988) compares MCA with the type of multivariate normal analysis done by techniques such as LISREL or EQS. By using the results in his paper, we can easily combine the two classes of techniques to a fruitful hybrid, with superior statistical properties.

It is clear, however, that statistical stability depends on the assumption of random sampling, and that in many data analysis situations the idea of a simple random sample does not apply. Other forms of stability analysis, which are more appropriate under those circumstances, are discussed by Gifi (1990).

Example

In this section, we offer a detailed example based on the multivariate indicator matrix of customer satisfaction variables presented in Table 8.2. The reader is referred to Anderson and Sullivan (1993) for an insightful substantive treatment of these data. We use this example to illustrate the most important geometrical aspects of MCA maps, but remind the reader that the rules apply in general to objects (rows) and variable categories (columns) of the scaled multivariate data matrix.

Customer satisfaction across 31 Swedish industries

Remember that the purpose of MCA is to produce a map with loss as small as possible and where the distances between industries and the variable categories they occur in are as small as possible. Our original idea for an "arbitrary" map discussed earlier actually represents the initial (i.e. iteration 0) MCA solution, based on Y_j estimated according to the centroid principle and X arbitrarily normalized. Thus, this solution is already a half-step in the right direction. The loss for this solution is 0.9650.

The initial solution is highly unsatisfactory, however, as the map (not shown in the interests of space) is very cluttered. Since loss (i.e. fit) is simply the sum of squares of the line lengths in the plot, the optimal solution, in keeping with the principles of MCA, is the one where the distances connecting points are minimized. After ten iterations, the solution is much more satisfactory as the lines connecting industries to their categories are as short as possible, and the fit is improved considerably (loss = 0.2354). Although both solutions represent the super-indicator matrix G, the final solution in two-dimensional Euclidean space is the more appealing.

The MCA of the data in Table 8.2 produces dominant eigenvalues of 0.60 and 0.38. Since the singular values from an MCA are canonical correlations, we interpret the eigenvalues (squared singular values) as squared canonical correlation coefficients. Industries and variable categories are represented as points in a joint low-dimensional map. This joint map appears in Figure 8.1. Industries are represented by open circles and satisfaction variable categories by closed circles. In this figure, we leave the variable categories unlabeled for ease of presentation.

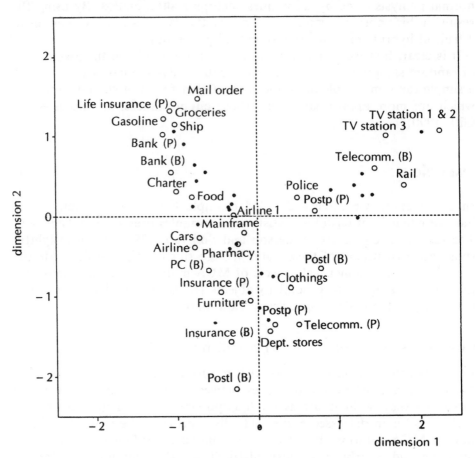

Figure 8.1   Joint map of Swedish industries and customer satisfaction variables

MCA requires industries corresponding to a certain category of a variable to have a position in the map in the direction of the associated category; other industry points will have a position in the opposite direction. Stated differently, industries are relatively close to categories they are in and relatively far from categories they are not in. Further, industries mostly occurring in the same category tend to be close to each other and categories sharing mostly the same industries tend to be close, as well.[5] Interpretation of category points is guided by the centroid principle: category coordinates are the center of gravity, or centroid, of industry coordinates occurring in that category.

The variable category points are plotted in Figure 8.2. In this figure, we have omitted the industries for ease of interpretation. Clear regions of customer satisfaction are revealed in this plot. We can see that in the upper right quadrant are the variable categories associated with the most extreme levels of dissatisfaction, price increase intolerance, unreasonable price, negative repurchase intentions, low quality, low expectations of that quality, and far distance from the ideal product or service in the category. Thus, industries in this area of the map are associated with these categories. Looking back at Figure 8.1, we can see that this includes the TV stations, telecommunications businesses with business clients, rail, police and the post office packet service with public clients. Customers of these services and products are decidedly unhappy! Perhaps not surprisingly, these services represent state-owned monopolies.

To a large extent, the analysis separates the extremely disenchanted (the upper right portion of the figure) from the rest of the customers. We can examine Figure 8.2 further and identify the region of extreme satisfaction

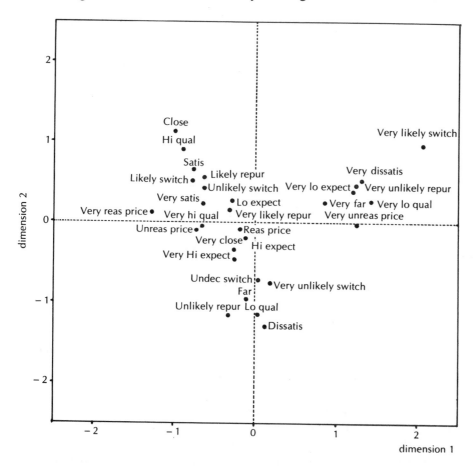

Figure 8.2 Map of category quantifications for customer satisfaction variables

slightly below and to the left of the origin. Industries here include the airlines, mainframe computers, pharmacies, automobiles, and food. Moving up in the figure we identify another region of satisfaction, with the corresponding industries of charter travel, both public and business banking, shipping, groceries, gasoline, public life insurance and mail order. In the lower center region of the map, we find those variable categories indicating dissatisfaction. The industries associated with these judgments include public and business insurance, furniture, business post office packets, clothing, public and business post office letters, department stores, and public telecommunications.

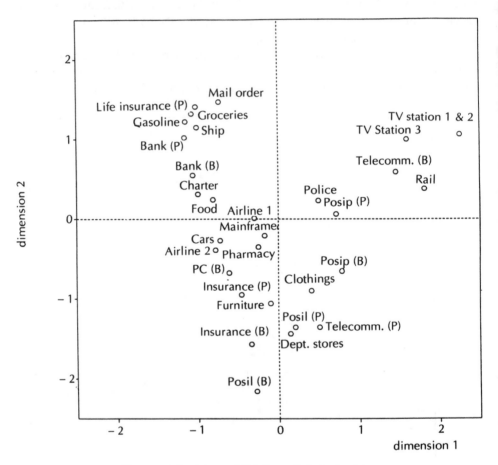

Figure 8.3 Map of 31 Swedish industries

Thus, the multiple correspondence analysis of Table 8.2 has clearly identified four distinct regions relating to customer satisfaction. Notice also that the analysis has revealed distinctly non-linear patterns of satisfaction. That is, variable categories are not linear with the dimensions of the space. This illustrates yet another advantage of non-linear multivariate analysis. By treating all variables as categorical, we may discover patterns in the data that would be hidden by conventional linear multivariate analysis. For example, the horseshoe reflects a deviation from the "correct" order, which would have been obliterated had we imposed order restrictions.

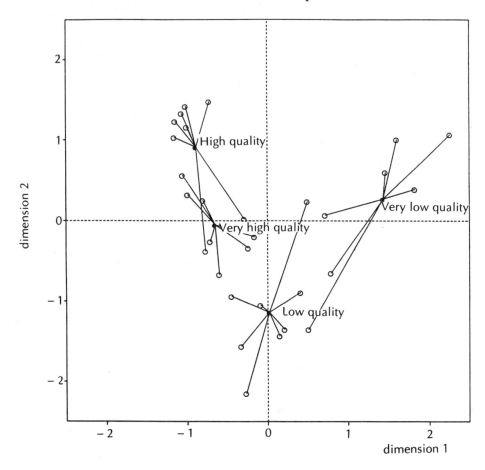

Figure 8.4   Star plot for quality

The "object plot" in Figure 8.3, simply the plot of industry points only, makes it easy to see relationships among the industries. The distance between two industry points is related to the homogeneity of their profiles, or more generally, their response-patterns.[6] Industries with identical patterns are plotted as identical points. This is illustrated in Figure 8.3 for TV stations 1 and 2 in the upper right, which as may be verified in Table 8.2, are identical in profile. Industries which are very similar include the group in the upper left, comprising mail order, public life insurance, groceries, gasoline, shipping, and public banking. If a category applies uniquely to only one industry, then the industry point and this category point will coincide. The same is true when a category applies uniquely to a group of industries with identical response patterns. For example, the price increase tolerance category "very likely to switch" applies uniquely to the three TV stations, and their similar profiles mean these points are very close to each other in the two-dimensional map.

Along the same lines, the position of "very likely to switch" indicates that a category point with low marginal frequency will be plotted farther towards the periphery of the map, while a category with high marginal frequency will be plotted nearer to the origin of the map (" 'very reasonable" and "reasonable" price). As a corollary, industries with response patterns similar to the "average" response pattern will be plotted more towards the origin (mainframe computers, airline 1), while industries with "unique" patterns (for example, post office letter service for businesses and TV stations 1, 2, and 3) appear in the periphery. These statements, however, are only precisely true when considering all dimensions, and not necessarily the map for the first two dimensions only.

Star plots

The star plots displayed in Figures 8.4, 8.5, and 8.6 for the variables quality, satisfaction and distance to ideal, respectively, illustrate a number

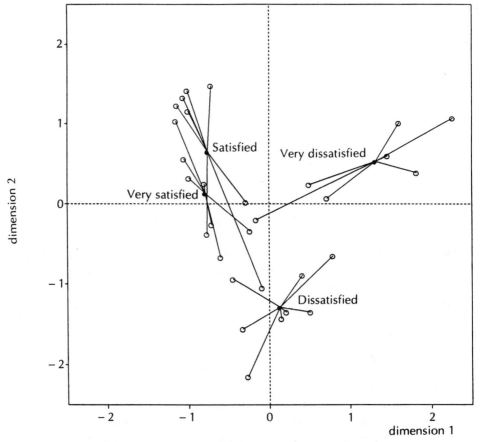

Figure 8.5 Star plot for customer satisfaction

of important properties of MCA. Each star plot maps a particular variable's categories with all the industry points and shows loss for each variable. Relative loss in the two-dimensional solution is the sum of the squared distances between industry points in a cluster and their average, the category point.[7] We have drawn lines in the star plots to illustrate this. The star plots also illustrate the centroid principle: that the optimal category coordinates are centroids of industry points in those categories.

Since category points are the average of the industry points that share the category, for each variable, categories of that variable divide the industry points into clusters, and the category points are the means of the clusters. For example, Figure 8.4 depicts clearly the four different clusters of product or service quality, Figure 8.5 reveals the corresponding levels of satisfaction with these industries, and Figure 8.6 displays the groups of industries classified according to how far away customers viewed them in relation to the ideal in that industry.

A variable *discriminates* better to the extent that its category points are further apart. The discrimination measures, shown in Table 8.3, are

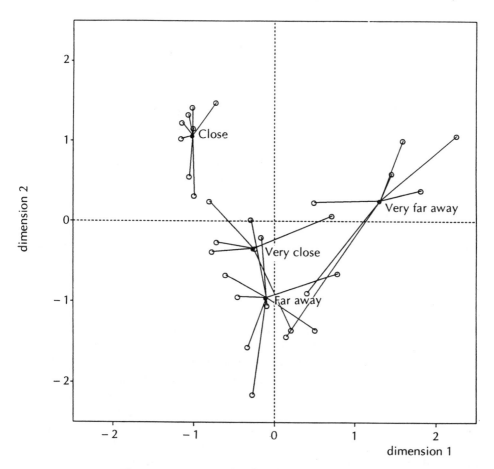

Figure 8.6 Star plot for distance to ideal

quantified as the squared correlations between the industry coordinates $\mathbf{X}$ and the optimally transformed variables, $\mathbf{G}_j \mathbf{Y}_j$, and are interpreted as squared factor loadings. Quality (Figure 8.4), Satisfaction (Figure 8.5) and Ideal (Figure 8.6) discriminate best among industries on both dimensions.

Table 8.3 The discrimination measures per variable per dimension

Variable	Dimension	
	One	Two
Price given quality	0.58	0.01
Quality given price	0.83	0.57
Repurchase intention	0.53	0.40
Price increase tolerance	0.56	0.38
Satisfaction	0.74	0.61
Expectation of quality	0.25	0.07
Ideal (distance from)	0.72	0.60
λ	0.60	0.38

To better understand the discrimination measures, we begin by noting that the covariances between the industry coordinates and the optimally transformed variables are simply $\mathbf{X}' \mathbf{G}_j \mathbf{Y}_j/n$, but, using equation (8.2), the optimally transformed variables $\mathbf{G}_j \mathbf{Y}_j$ can be expressed as $\mathbf{G}_j \mathbf{D}_j^{-1} \mathbf{G}_j' \mathbf{X}$ and this equals $\mathbf{P}_j \mathbf{X}$, where $\mathbf{P}_j$ is the orthogonal projector matrix from equation (8.5). Thus, the covariances can be written as $\mathbf{X}' \mathbf{P}_j \mathbf{X}/n$ and these are the covariances of the optimally transformed variables, as well, since $\mathbf{Y}_j' \mathbf{D}_j \mathbf{Y}_j/n = \mathbf{X}' \mathbf{P}_j \mathbf{X}/n$. Of course, our normalization fixes $\mathbf{X}'\mathbf{X}/n$ at $\mathbf{I}$. Thus, for corresponding dimensions, the squared correlations between the industry coordinates and the variables are written on the diagonals of $\mathbf{X}' \mathbf{P}_j \mathbf{X}/n$. It follows directly that the average over variables of the discrimination measures are the diagonals of $\mathbf{X}' \mathbf{P}_* \mathbf{X}/n$ which is equal to Λ. For each dimension, MCA thus maximizes the sum total of the discrimination measures.

Horseshoes

It turns out that the map in Figure 8.1 exhibits what is called the "horseshoe" effect. It has a quadratic structure, in the sense that industries are on or close to a second degree polynomial in two-dimensions. That is, the second dimension is a quadratic function of the first dimension, in this case contrasting satisfied and very dissatisfied groups of customers with those very satisfied and dissatisfied. Because industries are on a horseshoe, and category points are close to the industries occurring in them, the category points will tend to be on a horseshoe, as well. In this case, the star plots will tend to be (pieces of) horseshoes, and the stars will be elongated along the structure.

In order to explain the idea of horseshoes, we use a technique described by Gifi (1990) as *gauging*. In gauging, we use a mathematically defined data structure (that is, a model which we call a gauge), apply the technique to the model, and observe how the known properties of the model are reproduced by the technique. In our case, the technique is MCA and there are various gauges we can select which lead to horseshoes.

The first gauge that is relevant is the multivariate normal distribution. If data are a sample from a multivariate normal, classified into a discrete number of categories, then an MCA of these data (on a large enough sample), will show components which are linear, components which are quadratic, components which are cubic, and so on. The horseshoe corresponds with the case in which the first component (the one corresponding with the largest eigenvalue) is linear and the second component is quadratic (the one corresponding with the second largest eigenvalue). Multi-normal data do not necessarily give horseshoes: it is also possible that both the first and second components are linear with the original category values. An example of this is given in Gifi (1990, pp. 382–4).

Another famous gauge leading to horseshoes is the Guttman scale (Guttman, 1950). If individuals and categories can be jointly ordered in such a way that the indicator matrices have a banded or parallelogram structure (each individual only gives positive responses to a number of adjacent categories in the order), then again the first two dimensions will form a horseshoe. This generalizes to various item-response models such as the Rasch model (Rasch, 1966), the unidimensional unfolding model (Coombs, 1964) unimodal structures used in ecology (Ter Braak, 1986), and so on. All such gauges will give horseshoes when MCA is applied.

It is somewhat of a problem to decide if a horseshoe is desirable or undesirable. In one sense, we should be happy with one, because it shows a strong underlying order structure in our data. In effect, the horseshoe in multiple correspondence analysis is equivalent to the general factor in principal component analysis. In this example, that underlying variable is satisfaction. The first dimension dominates and the industries are ordered according to the ordering in the data. On the other hand, we could also be unhappy, because the horseshoe uses two linear dimensions to present this ordering. Basically, we use two dimensions to present a one-dimensional structure, and any higher-dimensional information remains hidden. For ways of dealing with this problem, we refer the reader to Bekker and de Leeuw (1988, pp. 29–30).

In some cases, horseshoe type structures can be decomposed, basically by collecting all linear transformations in one solution (which then corresponds to the ordinary linear PCA solutions), by collecting all quadratic components in another solution, and so on. In other cases, we require the transformations to be linear (or monotonic), which forces the MCA solutions away from the horseshoe. This is implemented, for example, in programs such as PRINCALS (SPSS Inc. 1989) or PRINQUAL (SAS® Institute Inc., 1988).

Discussion

For MCA maps to be useful in marketing, rules for representation and interpretation must be explicit and unambiguous. Consider our example. There we had a data matrix indicating which categories of various variables measuring satisfaction a series of Swedish industries falls into. We observed from Table 8.1, for example, that each industry fell into one of the following categories for the price variable: very unreasonable, unreasonable, reasonable, and very reasonable. As we saw in Table 8.2, the data matrix had a 1 whenever an industry fell into its category of the variable and a 0 otherwise.

The joint map produced from the MCA in Figure 8.1 has points for each industry and for each variable category. A dimensional interpretation (as is typically done in factor analysis) is problematic because we must identify constructs which can simultaneously describe both industries and variables, and it is somewhat difficult to find constructs which can convincingly do that job. On the other hand, interpretations in terms of closeness of the within-set distances, i.e. between each industry and each variable category, are quite natural and compelling. This illustrates one of the problems in graphically representing rectangular categorical data matrices: how to construct an interpretable joint map of the row and column points. The fundamental issue concerns the appropriate way to represent both the objects corresponding with the rows and variables corresponding with the columns of the matrix in the same map.

This problem is more important than ever, as the three major statistical packages have MCA programs in which the choice of scaling of row and column coordinates is left largely to the user (BMDP, 1988; SAS® Institute Inc., 1988; SPSS Inc., 1989). In addition, the variety of commercially available PC-based programs offer numerous options but little guidance to the user (BMDP, 1988; Greenacre, 1986; Nishisato and Nishisato, 1986; SAS® Institute Inc., 1988; Smith, 1988; see also Hoffman, 1991 for a review).

Recently, this debate has raged in the marketing literature. Carroll, Green and Schaffer (1986, 1987, 1989) and Greenacre (1989) provide an interesting and rather heated discussion of this seemingly innocuous topic of scaling row and column points. It seems to us that the points of view of CGS on the one side and Greenacre on the other reflect to some extent the bias that each of these researchers brings to marketing.

Greenacre was trained in the "French" school, which appears to correspond nicely with the fact that he takes simple correspondence analysis (CA) to be a more fundamental and satisfactory technique than MCA. It also means that he tends to emphasize the so-called "chi-square distance" interpretation of the within-set distances.[8] CGS have their starting point in multidimensional scaling and unfolding theory, which naturally leads them to emphasize between-set distance relations.

Although our "psychological" interpretation of the debate may be interesting, it does little to resolve any practical or theoretical problems. Marketing researchers still wish to know what is "best", or at least what they should do in any particular situation. Our geometrical approach to MCA leads directly to a set of unambiguous rules for representation and interpretation of MCA maps.

MCA as a "model"

Let us consider distance models for a moment. In multidimensional unfolding, we start explicitly with a model formulated in terms of fitting between-set distances to data. It is possible to formulate MCA as a particular, although somewhat peculiar, approximate solution to the unfolding problem (Heiser, 1981), but in general, MCA is not thought of in this way. Rather, many marketing researchers think of MCA "merely" as a technique for graphically representing a data matrix. Unfortunately, it is precisely this lack of explicitness that can lead to problems with interpretation.

Selecting a specific model implies, at the same time, choosing a framework for interpretation of the results. The results are interpreted within the model and are related to its assumptions. The interpretations use the terminology in which the model is formulated. MDS models, for instance, are formulated in terms of (dis)similarity and distance, and thus MDS results are also interpreted naturally in these terms. Factor analysis is formulated in terms of unobserved variables called factors, and consequently we can interpret a factor analysis solution as soon as we can interpret the factors. This imposed framework can be a very positive aspect of the analysis: interpretation is unambiguous, key concepts are known to many researchers in the field, and communication is made easy. But it can also be a great hindrance to communication with other fields, as the history of factor analysis amply shows. A model, like any cognitive map of the world, is a filter of reality. In many cases, such a filter is needed in order to proceed; in other cases, some of the more important, stable, and interesting aspects of the data may be filtered out or distorted by the imbedding in a rigid framework.

In the case of MCA, it seems natural for marketing researchers, perhaps owing to the popularity of multidimensional unfolding, to concentrate on simple geometrical aspects of the MCA map (e.g. interpoint distances), and observe what aspects of the data matrix they are trying to represent. This means, of course, that we look at MCA as if it is, in some devious way, still trying to fit a model to the interpoint distances. It merely does not make its loss function explicit, and thus it is inferior (at least in this sense) to unfolding techniques.

In our framework, distances corresponding to 1's in the indicator matrix must be small, but this requirement alone is not sufficient to produce a map, since the trivial solution satisfies it. Hence, we need a normalization. A natural normalization would be to examine all the distances and simply minimize the between-set distances (i.e. the sum of squares) keeping all other distances fixed. However, this always leads to a one-dimensional solution. Thus, we require something stricter, and so impose dimension orthogonality and normalization constraints. Which way we choose to normalize (i.e. normalize the objects X and leave the variables Y_j free, or the reverse) is immaterial geometrically, since the problem is formulated in a joint space. However, the choice affects the interpretation. Therefore, substantive considerations will almost always guide the researcher's choice of normalization.

Choosing the "best" normalization

Case I   The first approach is to normalize the set of object coordinates X and leave the variable category coordinates Y_j free. Normalizing X means that the Y_j are found by the centroid principle. In this case, the optimal scaling of a variable category (equation (8.2)) satisfies $Y_j' D_j Y_j = X' P_j X$ and thus $Y'DY = mX'P_*X = m\Lambda$. Quite simply, in words, a variable category coordinate is the centroid of the coordinates of the objects in that category. Gifi (1981, 1990) calls this the *first centroid principle*.

Case II   The second approach is to normalize the set of variables and leave the objects free. Normalizing the Y_j means that X is found by the centroid principle. Here, the optimal scaling of the objects (equation (8.3)) satisfies $X'X = m^{-1}Y'DY\Lambda = \Lambda$. In words, the optimal coordinate of an object is the centroid of the coordinates of the variable categories the object occurs in. This is the *second centroid principle* (Gifi, 1981, 1990).

Case III   Finally, we may choose to normalize *both* the objects and the variable categories. This is usually referred to as the "French scaling." This option treats rows and columns symmetrically and drops the centroid principle. Within-set relations are interpretable as chi-square distances, but no between-set interpretation is possible.

Cases I and II, the centroid principles, *define* graphical representation and interpretation of the MCA map. We adopt Case I as convention, but note that which case the researcher chooses is completely arbitrary, *from a geometrical standpoint*, as we can switch from one to the other without changing anything essential. MCA is an elegant multivariate method because these two normalizations can be translated into each other, through the transition formulae.

The rationale for choosing the centroid principle to guide normalization, as opposed to Case III or any other normalization that one could devise, lies in the inherent asymmetry of multivariate data. All applications of MCA, and consequently all interpretations, are inherently asymmetric as multivariate data are, by definition, row or column conditional. In other words, we treat rows and columns differently since each represents distinct entities we wish to characterize graphically. Thus, we define our data matrix as row or column conditional and proceed from there.

Row conditionality implies that we primarily wish to emphasize rows and scale them such that in the map, row points are closer together to the extent that rows are more similar with respect to the variables making up the columns. This suggests that it is logical to think of ordering objects by variables. Columns, i.e. variables, are the center of gravity of the rows. Practically speaking, choosing the Case I normalization, implied by row conditional data, means that objects will be equally spread in all directions in the map, with category points indicating the averages of subgroups of objects. In other words, objects are sorted into their respective categories of a variable. If our concern is primarily with the objects, as it would be when objects are brands, for example, then objects are normalized and the centroid interpretation applies with respect to the variable categories as weighted averages of the brands in that category. This leads, as in our industry data example, to a joint map for the industries and variable categories and a set of star plots for each separate variable.

Column conditionality implies that we primarily wish to represent the columns as points in a map and scale them such that columns close together are more similar with respect to the objects in the matrix. In situations where the objects represent individuals, for example in the Q-technique, then the Case II normalization of MCA orders variables by these individuals. In this case, variables are normalized and the individuals are free. Then, we obtain a single map for all the variable categories and a set of star plots for each individual with categories of all variables in the plots.

These arguments make clear why Case III, with symmetric treatment of rows and columns, is the least defensible normalization, both from the geometric and substantive points of view. It will almost always be the case that primary focus is on either the objects or the variables, but not both equally. *The aims of the investigation guides the researcher's choice of normalization.*

Greenacre (1989) prefers to normalize according to Case III (symmetrically scaling both sets of points in "principal" coordinates) and emphasize the within-set "chi-square" distances at the expense of any between-set interpretation. Carroll, Green and Schaffer (1989) recommend a variant of Case III, which despite their arguments to the contrary, does *not* allow for between-set interpretations. Quite simply, this is because the correspondence analysis of the two-way contingency table and the MCA of the superindicator matrix (what CGS call the "pseudo-contingency table") are well known to give equivalent parameter estimates. As the researcher loses the centroid principle, fundamental to MCA and a critical aspect of interpretability, in the symmetric Case III normalization or its variant, we do not recommend it.

Summary

In this chapter, we introduced multiple correspondence analysis as a non-linear multivariate analysis method which integrates ideas from both classical multivariate analysis and multidimensional scaling. We formulated MCA as a graphical method which seeks to connect brands, say, with all the variable categories they are in and uses a least squares loss function as the rule to do this. Our approach emphasized the geometrical aspects of multiple correspondence analysis. Considering MCA in this light leads directly to a set of unambiguous rules for representation and interpretation of MCA maps.

As we saw, interpretation of the joint map stems not from terms of "chi-square distance" or "profiles," but rather, follows from *le principe barycentrique*, the centroid principle, which says that brands close together are similar to each other. In keeping with this view, we developed simple correspondence analysis as a special case of MCA with the number of variables equal to two, rather than as a method to approximate within-set chi-square distance.

We also showed how MCA is related to a number of familiar MVA techniques, including analysis of variance, discriminant analysis, principal component analysis and multidimensional scaling. Our detailed example illustrated the most important geometrical properties of MCA maps. We hope this chapter has demonstrated how MCA, a powerful multivariate methodology, may suit many and varied applications in marketing research.

Questions

1 (a) For the data in Table 8.2, examine the effect of the three missing data options discussed in the chapter. You will need to create additional missing values. What are the differences among the "passive" and two "active" options? Do the positions of the industries change in the map? Do the positions of the variable categories change? Why?

(b) Create one industry with missing values on all variables and examine the scalings produced from each of the missing data options. Verify that missing data passive will scale the objects as 0 on all dimensions. Missing data single will scale the object as the average of all other objects with missing data and missing data multiple will scale this particular object on its own dimension.

(c) Under what different circumstances is each missing data option appropriate?

2 Consider the following 18 × 4 contingency table containing the frequencies of individuals most important terminal values. The respondents represent four different European countries. The data are adapted from Kamakura, Novak and Steenkamp (1992).

(a) Do an MCA (with your choice of normalization). What happens if you do another MCA, this time with the terminal value of "accomplishment" removed? Is the solution changed very much? Why not?

(b) Now do an MCA with each of the centroid scalings and the French scalings. What are the differences among the scalings and why?

Terminal value	Germany	Italy	Netherlands	UK
Self-respect	15	56	9	19
A world of beauty	12	3	5	1
Happiness	116	26	80	108
Wisdom	1	17	15	8
Equality	3	24	14	1
Inner Harmony	15	43	23	10
National Security	4	4	6	4
Freedom	13	49	13	15
Accomplishment	1	0	3	2
Exciting Life	0	7	5	3
A Comfortable Life	27	32	10	16
Pleasure	1	5	6	2
Salvation	10	27	27	25
True Friendship	12	14	20	14
Social Recognition	2	2	2	0
A world of peace	177	64	100	58
Family Security	170	163	47	149
Mature Love	12	10	3	2
Total	591	546	388	437

Notes

1 We thank Claes Fornell, Professor of Business Administration and Director of the Office for Customer Satisfaction Research, School of Business Administration, the University of Michigan, for graciously providing us with these data.

2 The equivalence means that loss is identical in both solutions and that the solutions are identical up to scale factors. In other words, the dimensions in the two solutions are proportional.

3 If some of the categories are empty, then D_j^{-1} becomes D_j^{+1}, where + denotes the Moore–Penrose inverse.

4 But see DeSarbo and Hoffman (1987) for a multidimensional unfolding solution for G, incorporating reparameterization, which avoids the degeneracy problem.

5 This will only be true approximately in reduced dimensionalities.

6 Note that the reverse will not necessarily be true. Two industry points that are close together in a map of the first two-dimensions may be far apart in higher dimensionalities.

7 In the perfect solution (loss equal zero), all industry points will coincide with their category points, but there must be at least as many categories as industries for this to happen.

8 The "chi-square" distance between two row points, say, is equal to the weighted sum of squared differences between row "profile" values, with weights equal to the inverse of the relative frequencies of the columns. A similar definition holds for column points. These within-set distances are denoted chi-square because if the data are a contingency table, then the numerator creates squared differences between conditional row probabilities (the profiles), while the denominator

weights the squared differences by inverse relative column marginals; thus, as Novak and Hoffman (1990) show, distances can be interpreted in terms of (a) standardized residuals (components of chi-square), (b) $O - E^1/E^1$, observed minus expected counts under the log-linear model of independence as a proportion of expected counts under independence, and (c) "profiles" (conditional probabilities).

References

Aldenderfer, M. S. and Blashfield, R. K. 1984: *Cluster Analysis*, Beverly Hills, CA: Sage.

Anderson, Eugene W. and Sullivan, Mary W. 1993: The antecedents and consequences of customer satisfaction for firms. *Marketing Science*, forthcoming.

Bekker, P. and Leeuw, de Jan 1988: Relations between variants of non-linear principal component analysis. In J. L. A. van Rijckevorsel and J. de Leeuw (eds), *Component and Correspondence Analysis: Dimension Reduction by Functional Approximation*, New York: John Wiley & Sons, 1–31.

Benzecri, J.-P., *et al.* 1973: *Analyse des Donnees* 2 vols, Paris: Dunod.

BMDP Statistical Software, Inc. 1988: CA: correspondence analysis. Technical Report No. 87. Los Angeles, CA.

Bock, R. Darrell 1960: Methods and applications of optimal scaling, Laboratory Report No. 25, L.L. Thurstone Psychometric Laboratory, University of North Carolina, Chapel Hill.

Burt, Cyril 1950: The factorial analysis of qualitative data, *British Journal of Psychology* (*Statistical Section*), 3 (November), 166–85.

Carroll, J. Douglas, Green, Paul E., and Schaffer, Catherine M. 1986: Interpoint distance comparisons in correspondence analysis. *Journal of Marketing Research*, 23 (August), 271–80.

Carroll, J. Douglas, Green, Paul E., and Schaffer, Catherine M. 1987: Comparing interpoint distances in correspondence analysis: a clarification. *Journal of Marketing Research*, 24 (November), 445–50.

Carroll, J. Douglas, Green, Paul E., and Schaffer, Catherine M. 1989: Reply to Greenacre's commentary on the Carroll-Green-Schaffer scaling of two-way correspondence analysis solutions. *Journal of Marketing Research*, 26 (August), 366–8.

Coombs, Clyde 1964: *A Theory of Data*, New York: Wiley.

Cooper, Lee 1983: A review of multidimensional scaling in marketing research. *Applied Psychological Measurement*, 7 (Fall), 427–50.

de Leeuw, Jan 1973: Canonical analysis of categorical data. Unpublished doctoral dissertation, Psychological Institute, University of Leiden, The Netherlands. Reissued DSWO-Press, Leiden, 1984.

de Leeuw, Jan 1988: Multivariate analysis with linearizable regressions. *Psychometrika*, 53, 437–54.

DeSarbo, Wayne S. and Hoffman, Donna L. 1987: constructing MDS joint spaces from binary choice data: a new multidimensional unfolding model for marketing research. *Journal of Marketing Research*, 24 (February), 40–54.

Edgerton, H. A. and Kolbe, L. E. 1936: The method of minimum variation for the combination of criteria. *Psychometrika*, 1, 183–7.

Fisher, Ronald A. 1940: The precision of discriminant functions. *Annals of Eugenics*, 10, 422–9.

Fornell, Claes 1992: A national customer satisfaction barometer: the Swedish experience. *Journal of Marketing*, 56 (January), 1–18.

Gifi, Albert 1981: *Non-linear Multivariate Analysis*, Leiden: Department of Data Theory.

Gifi, Albert 1990: *Nonlinear Multivariate Analysis*, New York: John Wiley & Sons.

Green, Paul E. 1975: Marketing applications of MDS: assessment and outlook. *Journal of Marketing*, 39 (January), 24–31.

Green, Paul E., Krieger, Abba M., and Carroll, J. Douglas 1987: Multidimensional scaling: a complementary approach. *Journal of Advertising Research*, October/November, 21–27.

Greenacre, Michael J. 1984: *Theory and Applications of Correspondence Analysis*, London: Academic Press.

Greenacre, Michael J. 1986: SIMCA: A program to perform simple correspondence analysis. *American Statistician*, 51, 230–1.

Greenacre, Michael J. 1989: The Carroll-Green Schaffer scaling in correspondence analysis: a theoretical and empirical appraisal. *Journal of Marketing Research*, 26 (August), 358–65.

Guttman, Louis 1941: The quantification of a class of attributes: a theory and method of scale construction. In Paul Horst, (ed.), *The Prediction of Personal Adjustment*, New York: Social Science Research Council, 319–48.

Guttman, Louis 1950: The basis for scalogram analysis. In S.A. Stouffer *et al.* (eds), *Measurement and Prediction*. Princeton: Princeton University Press.

Hayashi, Chikio 1950: On the quantification of qualitative data from the mathematico-statistical point of view. *Annals of the Institute of Statistical Mathematics*, 2 (1), 35–47.

Heiser, Willem J. 1981: *Unfolding Analysis of Proximity Data*, Department of Data Theory, University of Leiden, The Netherlands.

Hirschfeld, H. O. 1935: A connection between correlation and contingency. *Proceedings of the Cambridge Philosophical Society*, 31 (October), 520–4.

Hoffman, Donna L. 1991: Review of four correspondence analysis programs for the IBM PC. *American Statistician*, 45 (4), November, 305–11.

Hoffman, Donna L. and Batra, Rajeev 1991: Viewer response to programs: dimensionality and concurrent behavior. *Journal of Advertising Research*, August/September, 46–56.

Hoffman, Donna L. and Franke, George R. 1986: Correspondence analysis: graphical representation of categorical data in marketing research. *Journal of Marketing Research*, 23 (August), 213–27.

Hoffman, Donna L. and de Leeuw, Jan 1992: Interpreting multiple correspondence analysis as a multidimensional scaling method. *Marketing Letters*, 3(3), 259–72.

Horst, Paul 1935: Measuring complex attitudes. *Journal of Social Psychology*, 6 (3), 369–74.

Horst, Paul 1936: Obtaining a composite measure from a number of different measures of the same attribute. *Psychometrika*, 1, 53–60.

Kaciak, Eugene and Louviere, Jordan 1990: Multiple correspondence analysis of multiple choice data. *Journal of Marketing Research*, 27 (November), 455–65.

Kamakura, Wagner, Novak, Thomas and Steenkamp, Jan-Benedict 1992: Identifying cross-national value systems with a clusterwise rank-logit model. Paper presented at the TIMS Marketing Science Conference, July, London: UK.

Lebart, Ludovic, Morineau, Alain, and Warwick, Kenneth M. 1984: *Multivariate Descriptive Statistical Analysis*, New York: John Wiley & Sons, Inc.

Nishisato, Shizuhiko 1980: *The Analysis of Categorical Data. Dual Scaling and its Application*, Toronto: University of Toronto Press.

Nishisato, Shizuhiko and Nishisato, Ira 1986: *DUAL3 Users' Guide*, MicroStats. Toronto, Canada.

Novak, Thomas P. and Hoffman, Donna L. 1990: Residual scaling: an alternative to correspondence analysis for the graphical representation of residuals from log-linear models. *Multivariate Behavioral Research*, 25(3), 351–70.

Pearson, Karl 1904: On the theory of contingency and its relation to association and normal correlation. *Drapers Company Research Memoirs (Biometric Series)*, no. 1.

Rasch, G. 1966: An item analysis which takes individual differences into account. *British Journal of Statistical Psychology*, 19, 49–57.

Richardson, Marion and G.F. Kuder, 1933: Making a rating scale that measures. *Personnel Journal*, 12, 36–40.

SAS® Institute Inc. 1988: SAS® Technical Report: P-179 Additional SAS/STAT™ procedures Release 6.03, Cary, NC.

Smith, Scott M. 1988: *PC-MDS: Multidimensional Statistics Package*, Institute of Business Management, Brigham Young University, Provo, Utah.

SPSS Inc. (1989), SPSS-X: CATEGORIES, Chicago, IL.

Ter Braak, Cajo J.F. 1986: Canonical correspondence analysis: a new eigenvector technique for multivariate direct gradient analysis. *Ecology*, 67, 1167–79.

Valette-Florence, Pierre and Rapacchi, Bernard 1991: Improvement in means-end chain analysis using graph theory and correspondence analysis. *Journal of Advertising Research*, February/March, 30–45.

van der Burg, Eeke, and de Leeuw, Jan 1983: Non-linear canonical correlation. *British Journal of Mathematical and Statistical Psychology*, 36, 54–80.

van Rijckevorsel, Jan L. A. and de Leeuw, Jan 1988: *Component and Correspondence Analysis: Dimension Reduction by Functional Approximation*, New York: John Wiley & Sons.

Wilks, Samuel S. 1938: Weighting systems for linear functions of correlated variables when there is no independent variable. *Psychometrika*, 3, 23–40.

9

Latent Structure and Other Mixture Models in Marketing: An Integrative Survey and Overview

William R. Dillon and Ajith Kumar

1 Perspective and Organization

Since the early 1980s marketing analysts and scholars have applied latent structure and other types of finite mixture models with increasing frequency. One variant of finite mixture models, the latent class model, has been perhaps the most popular. The purpose of this chapter is to provide an integrative survey and overview of latent structure models, with particular emphasis on latent class models. Using the framework of mixture models, we discuss a variety of extremely voluble latent structure models. The models to be discussed have been applied in an enormously diverse set of psychological and behavioral arenas. The specific form of the latent structure models used vary from the relatively simple to the recondite. And though their choice as the preferred method of analysis has been justified for different reasons, latent structure models have, at the most basic level, allowed marketing analysts to account for individual heterogeneity when estimating model parameters. As such they provide a class of theory and methods for forging a bridge that connects procedures for clustering individuals on the one hand and conventional methods of estimation on the other.

In section 2 finite mixture models are introduced. The discussion focuses on the component parameters of mixture distributions, maximum likelihood estimation, general approaches for finding maximum likelihood solutions, heuristics for deciding on how many components to retain and, finally, the relation of finite mixture models to conventional clustering procedures. Next we turn attention to latent class models. In sections 3 and 4 we discuss and illustrate a wide variety of constrained and unconstrained latent class models. Among the constrained latent class models considered in section 4 are included scaling models, latent agreement models, simultaneous analysis across groups, analogs of factor analytic and covariance structure models, and linear logistic latent class models. Section 5 is devoted to discussing other varieties of finite mixture models that have appeared in the marketing literature. There we discuss two mixture models for the analysis of brand choice data, a mixture model for the analysis of paired comparisons, and a mixture model for normal densities. In section 6 we return to issues in estimation and discuss several nagging problems that continue to provide a source of consternation to those who apply finite mixture models in practice.

2 Finite Mixture Models

To varying degrees, conventional methods and procedures for analyzing marketing research data assume that the sample is homogeneous with respect to the measures and phenomenon being investigated. In other words, conventional multivariate procedures treat all individuals alike and no underlying group structure is explicitly recognized. In such cases, the tacit assumption in place is that the parameters obtained apply to each individual equally well. For example, when calibrating choice models on the basis of a given sample, the utility coefficients obtained are presumed to adequately reflect the value placed on specific attributes by all individuals in the population from which the sample was drawn.

One does not, however, have to stretch the imagination far to come up with potential sources of heterogenity in marketing and consumer behavior research. Brand awareness, product class knowledge, usage rates and context, preferences, desire for specific end benefits, along with standard demographic differences are, just to name a few, potential reasons why individuals may be different. Such differences are important since if individuals are not homogeneous then it may mean that more than a single set of parameter estimates is needed in order to adequately characterize the phenomenon being investigated.

Mixture models refer to a class of procedures that provide a simple and effective approach to modeling population heterogeneity. The term "mixture" is used because the population is assumed to consist of homogeneous subgroups. These subgroups are frequently referred to as the *components of the mixture*, or simply as *components*. To illustrate, let us introduce a simple application, which presents data from a recent branded "hard-candy" new product and concept test. Respondents were selected on the basis of age and gender quotas. In one cell of the study respondents were screened on the basis of past seven-day category usage (hereafter referred to as cell 2), whereas in the other cell (hereafter referred to as cell 1) no requirements on category usage were established. Table 9.1 presents cell 1 data on the number of individual packs of hard-candy purchased within the past seven days. Let y_i denote the number of units (packs) purchased by cell 1 respondents in the past seven days, where $y_i \geq 0$. To model such data one possibility is to use the Poisson density

$$f(y_i, \varphi) = \frac{\exp(-\varphi)\varphi^{y_i}}{y_i!} \quad y_i \in \{0, 1, \ldots,\}, \qquad (9.1)$$

where $\varphi > 0$ is an estimate of the mean purchase propensity, i.e. $E(y_i) \equiv \varphi$. If we assume a homogeneous one-parameter model, the maximum likelihood estimator of φ is

$$\hat{\varphi} = \sum_i^N y_i/N = 3.991$$

Figure 9.1 shows the distribution of packs purchased (denoted by clear dots in the figure). As can be seen by the shaded squares in the figure, which denote the fitted or predicted values, i.e. $f(y_i, \bar{y})$, the single Poisson distribution does not fit the empirical distribution very well.

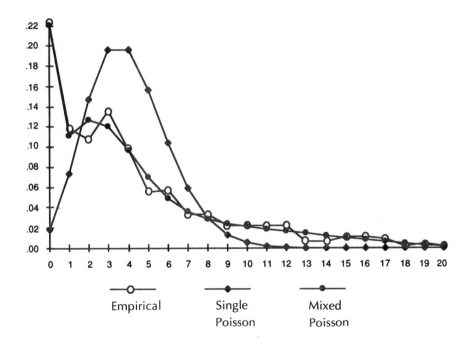

Figure 9.1   Empirical distribution, single and mixed poisson distribution of packs of hard-candy purchased in the last seven days for cell 1 respondents

Table 9.1   Distribution of packs of hard-candy purchased in the last seven days for cell 1 respondents

Packs	0	1	2	3	4	5	6	7	8	9	10	11	12	13	14	15	16	17	18	19	20
Frequency	102	54	49	62	44	25	26	15	15	10	10	10	10	3	3	5	5	4	1	2	1

The pronounced lack of fit of the data to the model is a signal that the sample may be too heterogeneous for the one-parameter Poisson model. In essence, the one-parameter Poisson model "forces" too much structure on the data. The overly restrictive structure that is imposed by this simple parameterization can also cause other problems, for example, *overdispersion*. Overdispersion refers to the violation of the mean-variance property of the Poisson distribution, that is, the restriction implicit in equation (9.1) that $E(y) = Var(y)$.[1] The mean and variance of the discrete count data shown in Table 9.1 are 3.991 and 17.689, respectively, which clearly shows these data to be overdispersed.

The heterogeneity in these data can be potentially captured by turning to a "mixed Poisson" model. The tacit assumption underlying the mixed Poisson model is that the population consists of a discrete number of homogeneous subgroups or component populations and a simple Poisson model is assumed to hold in each component, where each component of the mixture may have a different parameter value. The mixed Poisson model falls under the umbrella of statistical modeling called *finite mixture analysis*. Interested readers can consult Everitt and Hand (1981), McLachlan and Basford (1988), and Titterington, Smith and Makov (1985) for unified treatments of this class of data analysis models.

Let us now outline mixture models in more formal terms. Let $f(y, \varphi_s)$ be the probability density for observation Y, when sampled from the sth component. Assume further that the sth component is a fraction θ_s of the total population, with

$$\theta_1 + \ldots + \theta_S = 1.$$

If samples from the entire population are taken without knowledge of the component membership of each observation then Y has the mixture density

$$f(y, \mathcal{P}) = \sum_{s=1}^{S} \theta_s f(y, \varphi_s) \tag{9.2}$$

where the unknown parameter vector $\mathcal{P}$ consists of S component parameters $\varphi_1, \ldots, \varphi_S$ and S component proportions, often referred to as *mixing proportions* or *mixing weights*, $\theta_1, \ldots, \theta_S$, so that

$$\mathcal{P} = \begin{bmatrix} \theta_1 & \cdots & \theta_S \\ \varphi_1 & \cdots & \varphi_S \end{bmatrix}$$

The number of components, S, can also be viewed as giving the *support size* of the discrete distribution, that is, the number of φ_s that have strictly positive mass θ_s.

Depending on the form of the density function that is assumed to characterize each component of the mixture, different mixture model formulations can be realized. For example, as we will discuss shortly, if the within-component densities are assumed to be binomial then, with one additional assumption, the resulting mixture model is consistent with the latent class model. In the case of the "mixed Poisson" model we have

$$f(y_i, \mathcal{P}_s) = \sum_{s=1}^{S} \theta_s \frac{\exp(-\varphi_s) \varphi_s^{y_i}}{y_i!} \quad y_i \in \{0, 1, \dots,\}, \qquad (9.3)$$

where φ_s is, in this context, an estimate of the mean purchase propensities for the sth component.

Returning to the data of Table 9.1, a mixture analysis (the details of which will be discussed later) suggests that the population can be characterized in terms of six components with parameter estimates shown below.

$$\hat{\mathcal{P}} = \begin{bmatrix} 0.1555 & 0.1342 & 0.4737 & 0.1277 & 0.0300 & 0.0789 \\ 0.000 & 1.079 & 3.209 & 7.534 & 11.127 & 13.600 \end{bmatrix}$$

The estimates suggest that there are two groups of individuals who are relatively light users; one group, component 1, representing about 16 percent of the population, did not purchase any packs of hard-candy in the past seven days, the other group, component 2, representing about 13 percent of the population, purchased about 1 pack on the average. Component 3, the largest group consisting of almost one-half of the population, purchased a little over 3 packs during the last seven days on the average; component 4, a group consisting of about 13 percent of the population, are heavier users, purchasing on average over 7 packs of hard-candy during the past seven days; the remaining two groups, components 5 and 6, are relatively small, representing what must be viewed as extremely heavy users. Inspecting Figure 9.1 we see that the six-component mixed Poisson model (solid dots) provides what appears to be a much better fit to the data.

Estimation methods

Titterington, Smith and Makov (1985) provide an excellent discussion of the various approaches for estimating $\mathcal{P}$, the vector of component parameters of the mixture distribution. For our purposes, it is sufficient to concentrate on maximum likelihood (ML) estimation, for several reasons. First, of all the methods that have seen use, ML estimation is undoubtedly the most frequently used. Second, as applied in the context of estimating the component parameters of mixture distributions, ML estimation is appealing on intuitive grounds. And third, ML estimation yields estimators which are consistent (i.e. converge in probability to the true parameter values) and are asymptotically normally distributed.

ML estimation Let us begin by giving a brief and informal account of ML estimation. Assume that $Y_1, \ldots, Y_N$ are independent observations from a density $f(Y, \mathcal{P})$ where, as before, $\mathcal{P}$ is the parameter vector to be estimated. The objective in ML estimation is to find $\mathcal{P}_0$ such that the observed Y is more likely to have come from $f(Y, \mathcal{P}_0)$ than $f(Y, \mathcal{P})$ for any value of $\mathcal{P}$. In many instances, this maximization can be approached in the traditional manner. The likelihood function, denoted by $\mathcal{L}$, which measures the relative likelihood that different $\mathcal{P}$ will have given rise to the observed Y, is differentiated with respect to the components of $\mathcal{P}$. The system of equations that result, and which must be solved, are called the *normal equations*.

Let us now sketch the ML method in the context of mixture distributions. For mixture distributions the likelihood function assumes the following general form:

$$\mathcal{L}(Y, \mathcal{P}) = \prod_{i=1}^{N} \left(\sum_{s=1}^{S} \theta_s f(y_i, \mathcal{P}_s) \right),$$
(9.4)

where $\mathcal{P}_s$ denotes the parameter vector associated with the sth component. It is generally easier to effect a logarithmic transformation before taking the derivatives of $\mathcal{L}$. Letting $\mathcal{L}^*$ denote the loglikelihood, we can express equation (9.4) as follows:

$$\mathcal{L}^* = \sum_{i=1}^{N} ln \left[\sum_{s=1}^{S} \theta_s f(y_i, \mathcal{P}_s) \right] - \lambda \left(\sum_{s=1}^{S} \theta_s - 1 \right).$$
(9.5)

Note the constraint $\sum \theta_s = 1$ is introduced via the Lagrange multiplier λ. This gives the following normal equations:

$$\frac{\delta \mathcal{L}^*}{\delta \theta_s} = \sum_{i=1}^{N} \frac{f(y_i, \mathcal{P}_s)}{f(y_i)} - \lambda = 0$$
(9.6)

and

$$\frac{\delta \mathcal{L}^*}{\delta \varphi_s} = \sum_{i=1}^{N} \theta_s \frac{\partial f(y_i, \mathcal{P}_s)/\partial \varphi_s}{f(y_i, \mathcal{P})} = 0$$
(9.7)

The Lagrange multiplier λ can be found by multiplying equation (9.6) by θ_s and summing over s to give

$$N - \lambda = 0$$

so that $\lambda = N$. The maximum likelihood estimate of the mixing proportions can be found by noting that by Bayes theorem the probability that a given y_i comes from component s is

$$Pr(s|y_i) = \frac{\theta_s f(y_i, \mathcal{P}_s)}{f(y_i, \mathcal{P})}. \qquad (9.8)$$

Multiplying equation (9.6) by $\hat{\theta}_s$, and summing over s yields, after rearranging terms, the ML estimate of θ_s:

$$\hat{\theta}_s = \frac{1}{N} \sum_{i=1}^{N} Pr(s|y_i). \qquad (9.9)$$

Interestingly, we see that the maximum likelihood estimate of the mixing proportion associated with component s is given by the sample mean of the posterior probabilities that y_i comes from that component of the mixture.

In a similar fashion, it can be shown that equation (9.7) can be expressed as

$$\sum_{i=1}^{N} Pr(s|y_i) \frac{\partial \ln f(y_i, \mathcal{P}_s)}{\partial \varphi_s} = 0. \qquad (9.10)$$

Thus, the ML estimates of the φ_s parameters can be also shown to be weighted averages of the maximum likelihood equations, where the weights are the posterior probabilities of component membership.

Algorithms for finding ML solutions

A variety of algorithms can be used to find maximum likelihood solutions. In the context of mixture models and its many variants two general approaches are most frequently used to obtain ML solutions.

One approach is to apply standard numerical optimization methods to the normal equations shown in equations (9.6) and (9.7). Numerical methods for obtaining ML estimates involve the use of gradient methods. Newton-Raphson, quasi-Newton, simplex, and Fisher's scoring are some of the gradient methods that can be used. However, it is important to note that while the performance of these methods has been extensively studied in the context of estimating the parameters of single-component densities, little is known about their relative performance in the context of mixture distributions. An excellent introduction to these methods is provided by Everitt (1987), while more advanced and comprehensive treatments are provided by Dennis and Schnabel (1983) and Gill, Murray and Wright (1989).

Solving the likelihood function for mixture models represents a *constrained* optimization problem due to the restriction that $\sum \theta_s = 1$. It is possible, however, to transform the constrained maximization problem to an *unconstrained* maximization problem by enforcing this constraint through the following reparameterization

$$\theta_s = \frac{\exp(\alpha_s)}{\sum\limits_{s'=1}^{S} \exp(\alpha_{s'})}$$

The loglikelihood now assumes the following general form

$$\mathcal{L}^* = \sum_{i=1}^{N} \ln\left[\sum_{s=1}^{S} \exp(\alpha_s) f(y_i, \mathcal{P}_s)\right] - \lambda \ln\left[\sum_{s'=2}^{S} \exp(\alpha_{s'})\right], \qquad (9.11)$$

and α_1 is fixed at zero through out the iterative process.

Another approach relies on the so-called EM algorithm. In 1977 Dempster, Laid and Rubin published a seminal paper describing an algorithm which could be used to obtain ML estimates in a variety of situations. The EM algorithm derives its name from the two basic steps in the algorithm. In the E-step (expectation step) new provisional estimates of the component membership probabilities (i.e. the posterior probabilities) are obtained based upon provisional estimates of θ_s and φ_s. In the M-step (maximization step) new estimates of θ_s and φ_s are obtained on the basis of these provisional estimates of the component membership probabilities. These two steps are repeated iteratively.

To illustrate how the EM algorithm works let us return to the mixed Poisson model introduced earlier. The loglikelihood for this model is

$$\mathcal{L}^* = \sum_{i=1}^{N}\left[-\varphi_s + y_i \ln\varphi_s - \ln(y_i!) - \lambda\left(\sum_{s=1}^{S}\theta_s - 1\right)\right]. \qquad (9.12)$$

As discussed earlier, the ML estimate of θ_s is given by the sample mean of the posterior probabilities that y_i comes from each component of the mixture (see equation (9.9)). For this form of the mixed Poisson model we can obtain an explicit solution for $\hat{\varphi}_s$ by substituting equation (9.3) into equation (9.10). Solving yields the following estimate for φ_s:

$$\hat{\varphi}_s = \frac{\sum\limits_{i=1}^{N} y_i \, Pr(s|y_i)}{N\hat{\theta}_s} \qquad (9.13)$$

Schematically, the EM algorithm to obtain ML estimates of $\hat{\theta}_s$ and $\hat{\varphi}_s$ can be described as follows:

1   Initialize the iteration index $c:c \leftarrow 0$.
2   Determine initial estimates (i.e. starting values) for $\hat{\theta}_s^{(0)}$ and $\hat{\phi}_s^{(0)}$.
3   Compute the posterior probabilities $Pr(s|y_i)$ (see equation (9.8)).
4   Compute new estimates of $\hat{\theta}_s^{(c+1)}$ and $\hat{\phi}_s^{(c+1)}$ using equation (9.9) and equation (9.13) on the basis of the posterior probabilities computed in step (3).
5   If $\mathcal{L}^*(\mathbf{Y}, \mathcal{P}^{(c+1)}) - \mathcal{L}^*(\mathbf{Y}, \mathcal{P}^{(c)})$ is smaller than some positive constant, stop. Otherwise:
6   Increment $c:c \leftarrow c + 1$.
7   Go to step (3).

The EM algorithm has been also applied in cases where certain of the normal equations do not have an explicit solution (cf. Dillon, Kumar and de Borrero, 1993). To give a specific illustration let us consider a variant of the simple mixed Poisson model, called the *truncated* mixed Poisson model. The truncated mixed Poisson model is appropriate in applications where y_i assumes values strictly greater than zero. For example, to qualify for inclusion in cell 2 of the hard-candy concept and product test introduced earlier, an individual must have consumed at least one pack of hard-candy in the last seven days. Table 9.2 shows the distribution of packs purchased for cell 2 respondents.

Table 9.2   Distribution of packs of hard-candy purchased in the last seven days for cell 2 respondents

Packs	1	2	3	4	5	6	7	8	9	10	11	12	13	14	15
Frequency	80	55	45	30	20	20	15	15	10	11	9	9	3	1	2

The truncated mixed Poisson model takes the following form:

$$f(y_i, \mathcal{P}) = \sum_{s=1}^{S} \theta_s \frac{\exp(-\phi_s)\phi_s^{y_i}}{y_i![1 - \exp(-\phi_s)]} \qquad y_i = \{1, 2, \ldots,\}. \qquad (9.14)$$

In this case the normal equations for the ϕ_s parameters do not have explicit solutions and hence numerical techniques must be used. To use the EM algorithm we would modify step (4) described above as follows:

4a   Obtain a new estimate $\hat{\phi}_s^{(c+1)}$ through use of equation (9.10) and an appropriate gradient method.
4b   Compute new estimate of $\hat{\theta}_s^{(c+1)}$ using equation (9.9) on the basis of the posterior probabilities computed in step (3).

In essence, at each M-step gradient methods are applied to obtain updated estimates of those parameters which do not have explicit solutions. We could have use gradient methods to estimate the θ_s parameters as well. It is important to note that since the likelihood is separable in terms of the θ_s and φ_s parameters, gradient methods can be applied to each set of parameters separately, with considerable savings in computational effort especially when the dimensionality of the problem is large.

A modified EM algorithm for the truncated Poisson mixture problem was written and applied to the data of Table 9.2. Using nonparametric maximum likelihood estimates as starting values (see section 6), the algorithm took 75 iterations to converge and suggested that the population can be characterized in terms of four components with parameter estimates shown below.

$$\hat{\mathcal{P}} = \begin{bmatrix} 0.3891 & 0.3078 & 0.1979 & 0.1052 \\ 1.997 & 3.003 & 7.996 & 9.007 \end{bmatrix}$$

The four-component mixed truncated Poisson model provides a very good fit to these data compared to the fit of the single truncated Poisson model (see Table 9.3).

Relative performance comparisons Although as we indicated earlier more information on the relative performance of gradient methods and the EM algorithm is needed in the context of obtaining ML estimates for the component parameters of mixture distributions, some general conclusions can be stated. Wu (1983), for instance, summarizes the properties of the EM algorithm, among which are the following:

Table 9.3 Fit of the single and four-component mixed truncated Poisson models

Packs	Frequency	Percent	Single	Mixed
1	80	0.2462	0.0599	0.1354
2	55	0.1692	0.1272	0.1591
3	45	0.1385	0.1801	0.1334
4	30	0.0923	0.1912	0.0943
5	20	0.0615	0.1624	0.0662
6	20	0.0615	0.1149	0.0526
7	15	0.0462	0.0697	0.0474
8	15	0.0462	0.0370	0.0441
9	10	0.0308	0.0175	0.0393
10	11	0.0338	0.0074	0.0324
11	9	0.0277	0.0029	0.0245
12	9	0.0277	0.0010	0.0172
13	3	0.0092	0.0003	0.0112
14	1	0.0031	0.0001	0.0068
15	2	0.0062	0.0000	0.0038

1   The sequence of estimates obtained from the EM algorithm increases
    the likelihood; in other words, at each stage in the iterative process the
    likelihood is monotonically increasing.
2   The sequence of likelihood values, if bounded above, converge to some
    value $\mathcal{L}^*$.
3   Under certain regularity conditions, $\mathcal{L}^*$ will be a local maximum of the
    likelihood function.

Compared to such optimization algorithms as Newton-Raphson, quasi
Newton, or Fisher Scoring, the convergence of the EM algorithm may be
very slow, requiring several hundred EM-step iterations, since the former
approaches converge quadratically. Also, it is important to note that EM
algorithms do not directly provide standard errors for parameter estimates.
However, a number of methods for computing standard errors with the
EM algorithm have been proposed. Among these are included: (i) resamp-
ling/bootstrap operations (cf. Efron, 1982), (ii) computing the observed
information matrix (cf. Hartley, 1958, Hartley and Hocking, 1971, Kass,
1987, Louis, 1982), and (iii) computing the expected information matrix
(cf. Meilijson, 1989, Baker, 1992). Methods based on the computing the
observed or expected information matrix can also be used to significantly
speed up the convergence properties. Gradient methods, on the other hand,
do not have the property of increasing the likelihood. A problem plaguing
both of these approaches relates to the undesirable property that in some
instances the algorithm may terminate at a local maximum. Finally, the
EM algorithm is in many problem settings extremely easy to implement
since it involves two rather simple to program steps.
    Both approaches require the researcher to find reasonably "good"
starting values for solving the ML equations. Unfortunately, there is no
straightforward method for finding start values, and the common practice
has been either to generate start values randomly, or to set the initial
values assigned to parameters equal to zero. The choice of reasonably
"bad" starting values can acutely affect, in an adverse way, algorithmic
performance, leading to nonconvergence and identification problems. We
will discuss these and related issues in more detail in section 6.

Determining the number of components

In addition to the issue of finding starting values for solving the ML
equations, there is also the problem of deciding on the number of
components to retain. The typical procedure followed when fitting mixture
models is to obtain ML solutions under different values of S, the number
of components of the mixture, where in each case initial values for
parameters are set at zero or randomly generated. After obtaining solutions for models having, say, $S = 1$, $S = 2$, $S = 3$, . . ., components the
problem is to determine, based upon some criterion, which solution is best.
In essence, the question is whether a solution with $S + 1$ components gives
a significantly better fit than a solution with S components.

The overwhelming temptation in deciding how many components to retain is to compute the likelihood ratio statistic

$$U = 2[\mathcal{L}^*_{M_{s+1}} - \mathcal{L}^*_{M_s}]$$

Typically one expects U to have asymptotically a χ^2-distribution with degrees of freedom equal to the difference in the number of parameters estimated under the null hypothesis that there are S components and the number of parameters estimated under the alternative hypothesis that there are $S + 1$ components (cf. Cox and Hinkley, 1974, p. 323). Unfortunately, this is not true in the case of mixtures. U is not asymptotically χ^2-distributed with known degrees of freedom given by the difference in the number of parameters estimated under the null and alternative hypotheses, since in the case of mixtures the parameter value specified by the null hypothesis lies on the boundary of the parameter space (cf. Everitt, 1988, McLachlan and Basford, 1988, p. 21–31).

Because of the limitations of the likelihood ratio statistic other alternatives have been used. One approach has been to rely on *information-theoretic* based model selection criteria to assess goodness-of-fit. With this approach the decision on the number of components to retain proceeds by minimizing a particular information-theoretic criterion. These measures can be justified in a variety of ways, but, in essence, they attempt to balance the effects of fitting models with more components against the precision with which parameters are estimated. As S is increased goodness-of-fit improves, but since more parameters are being estimated the precision of the estimates will be adversely affected. The oldest of these information criteria measures is Akaike's AIC. Akaike (1974) suggested choosing S to make

$$AIC = -2\mathcal{L}^*_{M_m} + 2p$$

a minimum, where p is the number of parameters estimated under model M_m. Alternative versions of the AIC measure attempt to penalize over-parameterization more severely. For example, a version due to Schwarz (1978), called the BIC, is given by

$$BIC = -2\mathcal{L}^*_{M_m} + p \ln N$$

where N denotes the sample size. A more recent version suggested by Bozdogan (1987), which he calls the consistent AIC (CAIC), penalizes overfitting even more severely, is given by

$$CAIC = -2\mathcal{L}^*_{M_m} + p(\ln N + 1)$$

Note that, in principle, information-theoretic based model selection criteria can be used to compare nonnested models as well as nested models.[2]

Hope (1968) provides a parametric bootstrap approach for selecting the number of components to retain. This approach involves a Monte Carlo significance testing procedure, and was apparently first applied by Aitkin, Anderson, and Hinde (1981) in the context of latent class analysis and more recently by Dillon and Mulani (1989) in the context of a latent discriminant model. The procedure involves drawing $T - 1$ random Monte Carlo samples of size N from a population having S-components and density $f(y, \mathcal{P}_s)$. The mixture model under consideration is then fit with S and $S + 1$ components to each of the generated samples and the likelihood ratio statistic U is computed. The null hypothesis is that model M_S fits as well as model M_{S+1}. If the value of U obtained from the observed data exceeds $T(1 - \alpha)$ of the values of U obtained in the Monte Carlo samples, then the null hypothesis is rejected at the desired significance level α. A minimal value of T when using a significance level of $\alpha = 0.05$ is 20.

Relation to conventional clustering procedures

If we view the components of the mixture as "clusters" then the connection to conventional clustering procedures is immediately apparent. In principle, mixture models represent a form of non-hierarchical clustering. There is, however, an important difference between mixture models and conventional non-hierarchical clustering procedures. Conventional non-hierarchical clustering procedures are in essence "allocation methods" where the likelihood of the allocation is defined by

$$\prod_{i=1}^{N} \left\{ \sum_{s=1}^{S} \gamma_{is} f(y_i, Q_s) \right\}$$

In contrast to mixture models, however, the weights γ_{is} are defined as

$$\gamma_{is} = \begin{cases} 1 & \text{if } y_i \text{ is in cluster } s \\ 0 & \text{otherwise} \end{cases}$$

An optimal non-hierarchical allocation rule is one that which maximizes the likelihood above by trying different allocations, stepping from one trial allocation to another. In each trial allocation, however, the weight for each individual is either zero or one. In contrast, with mixture models the weights are probabilities so that "fuzzy-set" clusters are formed. The result is that unlike mixture models, allocation methods usually produce inconsistent estimates of the parameters of the component densities (i.e. the parameters characterizing the mixture). A well-known simple example can illustrate this point. Suppose one has a sample of data coming from two-component mixtures of normal distributions with $\mathcal{N}(0, 1)$ and $\mathcal{N}(1, 1)$. It can be shown that a optimal allocation rule based on $\mathrm{tr}W$ (or equivalently, $|W|$), where W, is the pooled within-component covariance matrix, would put all observations less than 0.5 in one cluster, and all greater than 0.5 in the other. For large N the means in the two clusters will tend to -0.55 and 1.55, while the pooled variance will tend to 0.7; in addition, the Mahalanobis distance between the clusters will tend to 6, instead of 1, the correct value. In general, allocation methods will always underestimate the within-cluster variability and overestimate the separation between clusters, with inconsistent estimates of the parameters of the mixture distribution.

Unconstrained Latent Class Analysis

As we indicated earlier, latent class models have been applied in a wide variety of diverse applications. Readers interested in previously published reviews are referred to Anderson (1982), Bergan (1983), Clogg (1981a), Clogg and Sawyer (1981), and Langeheine (1988). The latent class model can be motivated from several different perspectives. For example, we can view the latent class model simply as another clustering method, having unique properties that distinguish it from other conventional clustering methods; or alternatively, we can view latent class models as a latent variable modeling technique much the way we view the factor analytic model – the manifest categorical variables are viewed as being (imperfect) indicators of a construct that is itself unobservable and knowledge of the construct explains the association between the manifest categorical variables. In this section we present the basic unconstrained latent class model and present a simple illustrative example.

The latent class model

Basically, latent class models have been developed to explain the structure of a set of multivariate categorical data. In developing the latent class model we will attempt to maintain consistency in notation to the extent possible.

Let $\mathbf{y}_i = \{y_{ij}\}$ be the response vector for the ith individual, where the y_{ij} are polytomous responses, $r = 1, \ldots, R_j$ for $j = 1, \ldots, J$, random categorical variables. Further let $c_s \in C$, $s = 1, \ldots, S$, denote the S latent classes. A general latent class model is defined by

$$f(\mathbf{Y}_i, c_s) = \prod_{j=1}^{J} \prod_{r=1}^{R_j} [\varphi_{jrs}]^{\delta_{ij}} \qquad (9.15)$$

and

$$f(\mathbf{Y}_i, \mathcal{P}) = \sum_{s=1}^{S} \theta_s f(\mathbf{Y}_i, c_s), \qquad (9.16)$$

where δ_{ij} is the Kronecker delta

$$\delta_{ij} = \begin{cases} 1 & \text{iff } y_{ij} = r \\ 0 & \text{otherwise} \end{cases}$$

In order to satisfy basic laws of probabilities the implicit constraints on the model are that

$$\sum_{r=1}^{R_j} \varphi_{jrs} = 1 \qquad (9.17)$$

for all j, s and

$$\sum_{s=1}^{S} \theta_s = 1. \qquad (9.18)$$

Because of the constraints implied by equation (9.17) only $(R_j - 1)$ within-class probabilities φ_{jrs} need to be estimated for each categorical variable, and because of the constraint shown in equation (9.18) only $S - 1$ mixing proportions need to be estimated. Thus, the number of independent parameters in the model is

$$S\left(\sum_{j=1}^{J} R_j - J\right) + (S - 1)$$

Letting V denote the number of unique response patterns formed by the levels of the categorical variables, then the degrees of freedom associated with the general latent class model is

$$(V - 1) - \left[S\left(\sum_{j}^{J} R_j - J\right) + (S - 1) \right] \qquad (9.19)$$

As noted by Everitt and Hand (1981), from a purely mathematical point of view, the latent class model defined by equations (9.15) to (9.18) is a mixture of product-multinomial processes, with mixing parameters θ_s and multinomial processes characterized by the probabilities φ_{jrs}. There is, however, one important difference. The difference relates to the property that within a latent class the variables are assumed to be statistically independent. Thus, within a latent class, the joint densities can be expressed in terms of the product of independent marginal densities. This property is referred to as the *axiom of local independence*. Though the concept of conditional independence is used in other latent modeling techniques (cf. Bartholomew, 1987), it is not necessarily invoked in all varieties of mixture models.

There are two basic sets of parameters to estimate. The θ_s give the class sizes. In the parlence of mixture models, these are the mixing proportions. Because the latent classes are postulated to be mutually exclusive and exhaustive $\sum_s \theta_s = 1$. The second basic set of parameters are the φ_{jrs} which give the probability of response r to categorical variable j, conditional on membership in latent class c_s. ML estimates of the basic sets of parameters can be undertaken by gradient methods or by employing the EM algorithm. The ML equations for the basic latent class model have closed-formed solutions, which makes the EM algorithm particularly well-suited for this problem. Solutions to the ML equations yield the following estimators of θ_s and φ_{jrs}:

$$\hat{\theta}_s = \frac{1}{N} \sum_{i=1}^{N} Pr(c_s|\mathbf{Y}_i) \qquad (9.20)$$

and

$$\hat{\varphi}_{jrs} = \frac{\sum_{i=1}^{N} Pr(c_s|\mathbf{y}_i)y_{ijr}}{\sum_{s=1}^{S} Pr(c_s|\mathbf{Y}_i)} \qquad (9.21)$$

Computer programs Though the theory underlying latent class analysis was developed by Paul Lazarsfeld over forty years ago (cf. Lazarsfeld, 1950; also Lazarsfeld and Henry, 1968), early attempts to apply latent class models were thwarted by problems related to parameter estimation. The situation was remedied, however, when Goodman (1974a, b) showed how latent class parameters could be estimated according to the ML method via the EM algorithm. In 1977 the computer program MLLSA (Clogg, 1977) for latent class analysis began to be distributed. The general availability of this program contributed enormously to the use of latent class analysis in applied studies throughout the 1980s.

Today there are a variety of latent class programs available. Clogg's MLLSA program is still available, and in addition there is a PC-based version MLLSAPC (Eliason, 1987). Haberman's LAT program has been available since 1979 (see Haberman, 1979, vol. 2, appendix 2, pp. 586–96). Recently, Van de Pol, Langeheine and de Jong (1989) have provided the PANMARK program, which runs on IBM-compatible machines. Though a comprehensive review of these programs is not possible, several general observations are in order. First, the LAT program is the most flexible in the sense of allowing the user to test a seemingly unlimited variety of latent class models, and is the most rigorous in testing for local identifiability of the model parameters. It also provides standard errors of the parameters.

However, the LAT program is not "user friendly" and in fact it seems that researchers have began to work with it only recently. The MLLSA program, compared to LAT, is much easier to use. However, it does not provide standard errors, and the identification tests performed can provide misleading results in the sense that one can be fooled into assuming that everything is okay, when in fact it is not. The PANMARK program is menu-driven and as such is especially easy to use. Standard errors are provided and the program can be used to estimate a variety of latent markov models as well (cf. Van de Pol and Langeheine, 1989).

An illustrative application

Dash, Schiffman, and Berenson (1975) present data on the shopping behavior of 412 audio equipment buyers in terms of five categorical descriptors:

1 Store in which the merchandise was purchased: full line department store (DEPT = 1) or specialty merchandiser (SPEC = 2).
2 Catalog experience: individual had sought information from manufacturers catalogs (YES = 1); individual had not sought information from manufacturers catalogs (NO = 2).
3 Prior shopping experience: individual had shopped for audio equipment prior to making their final decision (YES = 1); individual had not shopped for audio equipment prior to make their final decision (NO = 2).
4 Information seeking: individual had sought information from friends and/or neighbors prior to purchase (YES = 1); individual had not sought information from friends and neighbors prior to purchase (NO = 2).
5 Information transmitting: individual had recently been asked for an opinion about buying any audio-related product (YES = 1); individual had not been asked for an opinion about buying any audio-related product (NO = 2).

These five categorical variables having two levels each, generate 32 unique response patterns. Response pattern incidences are shown in Table 9.4.

Table 9.5 provides summary goodness-of-fit heuristics for the two, three and four latent class models. Columns two and three in the table give conventional Pearson (X^2) and likelihood ratio (G^2) chi-square goodness-of-fit statistics which involve comparing the expected frequencies obtained under a specified model to the observed frequencies. Expected frequencies under the latent two- and three-class models are given in Table 9.4. The BIC and CAIC measures point to the latent two-class model, although this model does not provide an adequate fit to the observed frequencies using conventional significance levels. The latent three-class model does provide an adequate fit using conventional significance levels, yet the AIC and BIC suggest that more than 3 classes (components) may be needed.

Table 9.4 Store choice data: observed, expected and posterior probabilities

Y1	Y2	Y3	Y4	Y5	Observed frequency	2 Class expected frequency	3 Class expected frequency	Class 1	Class 2	Posterior probabilities Class 1	Class 2	Class 3
1	1	1	1	1	5.000	5.887	7.300	0.42219	0.57781	0.00000	0.00000	1.00000
1	1	1	1	2	3.000	2.961	3.195	0.04264	0.95736	0.00000	0.00000	1.00000
1	1	1	2	1	14.000	11.401	12.435	0.07412	0.92588	0.00000	0.00000	1.00000
1	1	1	2	2	2.000	8.838	5.442	0.00486	0.99514	0.00000	0.00000	1.00000
1	1	2	1	1	15.000	10.046	10.566	0.06873	0.93127	0.00000	0.04517	0.95483
1	1	2	1	2	3.000	7.830	5.826	0.00448	0.99552	0.00000	0.24215	0.75785
1	1	2	2	1	26.000	29.265	25.347	0.00802	60.99198	0.00000	0.32195	0.67805
1	1	2	2	2	32.000	24.200	31.641	0.00049	0.99951	0.00000	0.76228	0.23772
1	2	1	1	1	2.000	2.492	3.580	0.25416	0.74584	0.00000	0.00000	1.00000
1	2	1	1	2	3.000	1.581	1.567	0.02035	0.97965	0.00000	0.00000	1.00000
1	2	1	2	1	8.000	5.984	6.099	0.03599	0.96401	0.00000	0.00000	1.00000
1	2	1	2	2	3.000	4.817	2.669	0.00227	0.99773	0.00000	0.00000	1.00000
1	2	2	1	1	4.000	5.288	5.215	0.03327	0.96673	0.00000	0.05117	0.94883
1	2	2	1	2	5.000	4.268	2.954	0.00209	0.99791	0.00000	0.26699	0.73301
1	2	2	2	1	12.000	15.923	12.991	0.00376	0.99624	0.00000	0.35117	0.64883
1	2	2	2	2	17.000	13.220	17.173	0.00023	0.99977	0.00000	0.78520	0.21480
2	1	1	1	1	86.000	83.446	86.860	0.97983	0.02017	0.89165	0.00000	0.10835
2	1	1	1	2	3.000	5.554	4.119	0.74756	0.25244	0.00000	0.00000	1.00000
2	1	1	2	1	33.000	33.020	30.672	0.84184	0.15816	0.47729	0.00000	0.52271
2	1	1	2	2	8.000	5.763	7.016	0.24496	0.75504	0.00000	0.00000	1.00000
2	1	2	1	1	23.000	27.339	24.802	0.83071	0.16929	0.47554	0.00000	0.52446
2	1	2	1	2	4.000	5.009	5.693	0.23024	0.76976	0.00000	0.00000	1.00000
2	1	2	2	1	30.000	22.083	24.389	0.34964	0.65036	0.09141	0.00000	0.90859
2	1	2	2	2	8.000	12.358	9.697	0.03173	0.96827	0.00000	0.00000	1.00000
2	2	1	1	1	22.000	21.756	20.685	0.95773	0.04227	0.77685	0.00000	0.22315

Table 9.4 (Contd.)

Y1	Y2	Y3	Y4	Y5	Observed frequency	2 Class expected frequency	3 Class expected frequency	Class 1	Class 2	Posterior probabilities Class 1	Class 2	Class 3
2	2	1	1	2	4.000	1.824	2.020	0.58002	0.41998	0.00000	0.00000	1.00000
2	2	1	2	1	6.000	9.938	10.901	0.71284	0.28716	0.27865	0.00000	0.72135
2	2	1	2	2	6.000	2.737	3.441	0.13142	0.86858	0.00000	0.00000	1.00000
2	2	2	1	1	11.000	8.317	8.827	0.69692	0.30408	0.27724	0.00000	0.72276
2	2	2	1	2	3.000	2.401	2.792	0.12242	0.87758	0.00000	0.00000	1.00000
2	2	2	2	1	5.000	9.815	11.330	0.20047	0.79953	0.04082	0.00000	0.95918
2	2	2	2	2	6.000	6.639	4.756	0.01505	0.98495	0.00000	0.00000	1.00000

Table 9.5 Store choice data: goodness-of-fit measures

Number of latent classes	X^2	G^2	df	$£^*$	U	AIC	BIC	CAIC
2	38.42	40.17	20	−1237.11	−	2496.2	2540.5	2551.50
3	24.17[a]	25.126[a]	18[b]	−1229.60	15.02	2493.21	2561.57	2578.60
4	11.77[a]	11.76[a]	14[c]	−1222.90	13.4	2491.81	2584.29	2607.29

[a] $p > 0.10$

[b] Actually degrees of freedom equal 14 = [(32 − 1) − (10 − 5)3 − (3 − 1)]; parameters assumed boundary values.

[c] Actually degrees of freedom equal 8 = [(32 − 1) − (10 − 5)3 − (4 − 1)]; parameters assumed boundary values.

Table 9.6 Store choice data: parameter estimates

	2-class model		3-class model		
	1	2	1	2	3
Class size θ_s	0.4617 (0.055)	0.5383 (fixed)	0.3110 (0.053)	0.1293 (0.045)	0.5597 (fixed)
Conditional probabilities φ_{jrs}					
store department	0.0295 (0.037)	0.6690 (0.053)	0.000 (bounded)	1.000 (bounded)	0.4368 (0.076)
Specialty	0.4706 (fixed)	0.3310 (fixed)	1.000 (bounded)	0.0000 (bounded)	0.5032 (fixed)
Catalog experience					
Yes	0.7969 (0.034)	0.6466 (0.036)	0.8282 (0.043)	0.6414 (0.089)	0.6709 (0.041)
No	0.2031 (fixed)	0.3534 (fixed)	0.1718 (fixed)	0.3580 (fixed)	0.3291 (fixed)
Prior shopping					
Yes	0.7826 (0.047)	0.2667 (0.042)	0.8678 (0.063)	0.0000 (bounded)	0.4198 (0.061)
No	0.2174 (fixed)	0.7533 (fixed)	0.1372 (fixed)	1.0000 (bounded)	0.5802 (fixed)
Information seeking					
Yes	0.7463 (0.049)	0.2437 (0.039)	0.8410 (0.071)	0.0553 (0.101)	0.3699 (0.047)
No	0.2537 (fixed)	0.7563 (fixed)	0.1590 (fixed)	0.9447 (fixed)	0.6301 (fixed)
Information transmitting					
Yes	0.9517 (0.030)	0.5455 (0.045)	1.000 (bounded)	0.2528 (0.142)	0.6956 (0.049)
No	0.0483 (fixed)	0.4545 (fixed)	0.0000 (bounded)	0.7472 (fixed)	0.3044 (bounded)

Standard deviations parameters assure boundary value – treated as if fixed, and degrees of freedom adjusted accordingly.

Successive applications of the likelihood ratio statistic (U) suggests that more than four latent classes are needed; however, a latent five-class model requires an additional six parameters (one mixing proportion and 5 conditional within-segment probabilities) and therefore has only two degrees of freedom (see equation (9.19)). The fact that alternative goodness-of-fit measures will frequently point to different models underscores the element of subjectivity that is undoubtedly involved with these approaches.

For illustrative purposes Table 9.6 presents parameter estimates and corresponding standard deviations for the latent two- and three-class models.[3] In the latent two-class model, class 1, representing a little over 46 percent of the population, contains almost exclusively, specialty store shoppers. These shoppers, compared to class 2, exhibit more catalog experience, shop in stores prior to purchase and both seek and transmit information prior to purchase. In the latent three-class model, the classes have an interesting structure with respect to department and specialty store shoppers. Notice that class 1 is exclusively made up of specialty store shoppers, whereas class 2 is exclusively made up of department store shoppers. Class 3, is made up of both types of shoppers, with the odds favoring specialty store shoppers slightly. Whenever a latent class parameter assumes a value of 0.0 or 1.0, a *boundary solutions* has been obtained. Notice that four parameters in the latent three-class model hit boundary values. When boundary values are encountered, the sampling distributions of X^2 and G^2 are not known. The convention in such cases is to act as if these parameters had been set *a priori* to 0.0 or 1.0, in which case the large sampling theory underlying the X^2 and G^2 would apply (Clogg, 1979; Goodman, 1975). Thus, in the case of the latent three-class model, the degrees of freedom reported in the table is 18 instead of 14, reflecting the fact that four fewer parameters were estimated. The contrast between class 1 and class 2 is apparent. Class 1 specialty store shoppers initiate and engage in all of the pre-purchase activities with greater probability than their class 2 department store shopper counterparts.

It is also informative to compute the posterior probabilities. In the latent class literature posterior probabilities are frequently referred to as *recruitment* probabilities, reflecting the fact that the posterior probabilities give the probability that a particular profile is "recruited" from a given latent class. Table 9.4 provides the posterior probabilities for each of the 32 unique response profiles generated by the five categorical variables. To the extent that the latent classes are well separated, the posterior probabilities should be close to zero or one.

Constrained Latent Class Analysis

In many substantive applications the researcher wishes to test specific hypotheses concerning the structure of the data. Structural hypotheses can frequently be expressed in terms of the values that parameters are expected to assume, either by setting one or more parameters equal to prespecified values (typically zero), or by constraining two or more parameters to be equal. In essence, the ability to constrain latent class parameters enables the empirical researcher to test a panoply of hypotheses concerning the structure of ones data, and in effect allows latent class analysis to be used in a confirmatory fashion, much in the same way as in covariance structure analysis.

All of the popular computer programs for estimating latent class models permit constraints to be imposed.[4] The type of constraints permitted are summarized below.

(1) Restrictions that set the latent class mixing proportions to fixed constants; for example

$$\theta_s = \frac{1}{C} \ \forall s$$

where $C > 0$ is consistent with the hypothesis that the classes of latent variable are equiprobable. Similarily, restricting

$$\varphi_{jrs} = \frac{1}{R_j} \ \forall s$$

corresponds to the hypothesis that the manifest variable j is equivprobable within each latent class s.

(2) Restrictions that equate the conditional probabilities; for example restricting

$$\varphi_{jrs} = \varphi_{jrs'}$$

is consistent with the hypothesis that the probability of observing an individual on the rth level of the jth manifest variable is equally likely within latent class s and latent class s'.

The number of degrees of freedom associated with a restricted or constrained latent class model that is identified are equal to that for the unrestricted model, if identified, plus the number of nonredundant (i.e. implicit) restrictions imposed on the model. With dichotomous variables, for example, the restriction that, say, $\varphi_{i1s} = 1$ implies that $\varphi_{j2s} = 0$, and thus there is actually only one restriction to be accounted for when adjusting the degrees of freedom.

Not surprisingly, the majority of latent class applications have employed constraints on parameters. In the following sections, we will attempt to review, albeit briefly, those areas of applications where constraints have been used to test explicit structural hypotheses.

Scaling models

Over the past two decades, several articles have suggested various models for analyzing dichotomous response items constructed to reflect an assumed underlying structure (cf. Dayton and Macready, 1976, 1980; Goodman, 1975; Macready and Dayton, 1977; Owston, 1979; Proctor, 1970, 1971; White and Clark, 1973). Basically these models can be divided into two categories according to whether they are purely deterministic – that is, nonstatistical, which precludes the presence of errors in measurement – or probabilistic, which recognizes the presence of response errors explicitly in the model.

All of the scaling models to be described can be expressed as special cases of latent class models. In fact, many latent class models for hierarchies can be constructed (cf. Feick, 1987). The only requirement for a pure hierarchy with k items, which vary in difficulty, is that we define $k + 1$ latent classes. Essentially, the latent classes define the permissible scale types for a given hierarchy. As we will see, the vehicle for fitting latent class scaling models is through the judicious use of equality constraints on the conditional probabilities.

Deterministic scaling models   Purely deterministic scaling modes are best exemplified by the Guttman pure scale model (Guttman, 1950). In Guttman scaling, items are presumed to form a hierarchy of difficulty of agreeing with the item, and it is assumed that all items measure the same trait. Guttman models only recognize certain patterns of responses. Let us use an example from the work of Dillon, Madden and Mulani (1983). As part of the 1980 Evaluation of the Section 8 Housing Assistance Program, information was collected on three neighborhood quality indicators per-taining to (1) the presence of abandoned structures, (2) the presence of inadequate street lighting, and (3) the presence of poor street conditions. The presence of abandoned buildings is the most unfavorable feature, whereas the presence of poor street conditions – which could simply mean the presence of potholes – is the least unfavorable. With $k = 3$ items varying in severity, there are $k + 1 = 4$ scale types. That is, out of the $2^3 = 8$ possible combinations of the response items, the Guttman pure scale model posits a strict heirarchy which recognizes only four response pat-terns: (1, 1, 1), (2, 1, 1), (2, 2, 1), and (2, 2, 2), where a "1" denotes a yes response and a "2" denotes a no response for each item, respectively. These response patterns are called "scale types." All of the remaining $8 - 4 = 4$ response patterns are presumed to be empty. This scaling model implies a $k + 1$ latent class model where each latent class is isomorphic with one of so-called scale types; viz:

$$\varphi_{111} = \varphi_{211} = \varphi_{311} = 1.0$$
$$\varphi_{122} = \varphi_{212} = \varphi_{312} = 1.0$$
$$\varphi_{123} = \varphi_{223} = \varphi_{313} = 1.0$$
$$\varphi_{124} = \varphi_{224} = \varphi_{324} = 1.0$$

The Guttman model is extremely restrictive since it allows no response errors, and, not surprisingly, rarely provides adequate fits, which justifiably diminishes its practical usefulness.

Probabilistic scaling models

Probabilistic scaling models differ fundamentally from the Guttman pure scale model in that response errors are explicitly recognized and incorporated into the model. There are various ways to account for response errors within the basic Guttman scale model framework.

Goodman's model   Goodman (1975) incorporates an "intrinsically unscalable class" (IUS) to account for response errors in the Guttman scale model. Thus, in this formulation the respondents are divided into two groups: the scale-type respondents whose responses to the k items always conform to their true scale type, and the nonscale-type respondents whose response to the k items follow according to the relationship of mutual independence. In other words, we can say that the Guttman scale model holds only for part of the entire population – namely, the intrinsically scalable part – and that departures from the true scale types expected under the Guttman model are attributable to the response of an intrinsically unscalable part of the population.

The Goodman model can be viewed as a quasi-independence latent class model (Goodman, 1968, 1975). There are two equivalent methods of constructing and conceptualizing quasi-independence models. Such models can be viewed as a form of ordinary loglinear models in which structural zeros are used. The structural zeros indicate the observed response patterns to be ignored, and the test is one of independence among the remaining cells. In the context of scaling models, the cells ignored would be those that correspond to the particular response patterns hypothesized by the model; the remaining cells are tested for independence. Such models can be formed within the latent class framework by adding an extra latent class on which there are no restrictions and making the Guttman pure scale restrictions on the other $k + 1$ classes. The $k + 1$ classes with the restrictions are what Goodman (1975) calls "perfect scale types," while those in the unrestricted class are called "nonscale types."

Uniform error   The simplest model that incorporates measurement error is Proctor's (1970, 1971) uniform error model. Response patterns other than those consistent with the true $(k + 1)$ scale types are accounted for by the constant error rate parameter, denoted here by r which governs the expected frequency of response errors for all k items and all $k + 1$ scale types. The response error probability r is assumed to be statistically independent of the probability of response error on any of the other items, so that a respondent in the tth scale type can make j response errors (for $0 \leqslant j \leqslant k$) with probability $(1 - r)^{k-j} r^j$. The parameter r is an overall index of item scalability. When r is low, the items are said to be scalable, whereas when it is high the scalability of the items can be called into question.

The latent class model that is consistent with the uniform error specification restricts all of the conditional probabilities equal to one another, and thus their common value can be taken to be $1 - r$. In the context of the three neighborhood quality indicators the restrictions are as follows:

$$\varphi_{111} = \varphi_{211} = \varphi_{311}$$
$$\varphi_{122} = \varphi_{212} = \varphi_{312}$$
$$\varphi_{123} = \varphi_{223} = \varphi_{313}$$
$$\varphi_{124} = \varphi_{224} = \varphi_{324}$$

$$= 1 - r$$

Equal item-specific error model Instead of assuming a uniform error rate across items, the equal item-specific model – originally suggested by Proctor (1970) and discussed in greater detail by Dayton and Macready (1976) – assumes that error rates r_j dictate the response errors for the jth item ($1 \leqslant j \leqslant k$) and these r_j's do not vary across true scale types. The assumption that responses to the items are independent of one another for members of each true type is made once again, implying that the probability of any true type of individual being observed in any response pattern can be readily calculated. For an individual whose true type is scale type 3 with expected response pattern (1,1,2), the response pattern (2,1,1) would occur with probability:

$$r_1(1 - r_2)r_3$$

It is easy to see that if $r_1 = r_2 = \ldots = r_k = r$, the equal item-specific error model reduces to Proctor's uniform error model.

The item-specific error model postulates a constant error rate, r_j, for the jth item. Its latent class respresentation has the following restrictions:

$$\varphi_{111} = \varphi_{122} = \varphi_{123} = \varphi_{124} = 1 - r_1$$
$$\varphi_{211} = \varphi_{212} = \varphi_{223} = \varphi_{224} = 1 - r_2$$
$$\varphi_{311} = \varphi_{312} = \varphi_{313} = \varphi_{324} = 1 - r_3$$

Equal scale-type specific error model This reponse error model is essentially the converse of the equal item-specific error model. The equal scale-type specific error model assumes that the true scale types have different response error rates that do not depend on the particular item for which a response error is made. Thus, with k items, there are $r_1, r_2, \ldots, r_{k+1}$ of these error rates that govern the expected occurence of response errors.

In the context of the three neighborhood quality indicators, this response error model, there are r_1, r_2, r_3, and r_4, error rates, which govern the expected occurrence of response errors. The latent class representation of this model has the following restirictions:

$$\varphi_{111} = \varphi_{211} = \varphi_{311} = 1 - r_1$$
$$\varphi_{122} = \varphi_{212} = \varphi_{312} = 1 - r_2$$
$$\varphi_{123} = \varphi_{223} = \varphi_{313} = 1 - r_3$$
$$\varphi_{124} = \varphi_{224} = \varphi_{324} = 1 - r_4$$

These four scaling models do not exhaust the list of definable response error models. For example, Clogg and Sawyer (1981) discuss the latent distant model (cf. Goodman, 1975; Hays and Borgatta, 1954; Lazarsfeld and Henry, 1968) and the the modified Goodman–Proctor model.

Latent agreement models

Latent agreement models attempt to investigate the extent to which two or more observers agree in their assessment (or rating) of some phenomena. Clogg (1979, 1981a) has applied latent class models in this context and has argued that latent class agreement models have three compelling advantages related to their ability to (i) take account of chance agreement, (ii) afford coefficients which have clear interpretation, and (iii) identify sources of (dis)agreement.

To illustrate let us consider the application presented in Dillon and Mulani (1984). Three judges rated 164 individuals according to whether each individual was positive, neutral or negative toward some object. Table 9.7a presents the data. In the $3 \times 3 \times 3$ table some cells reflect perfect agreement among the judges (e.g. cell 111), some cells reveal partial agreement (e.g. cell 112), while other cells reflect no agreement at all (e.g. cell 123). An unconstrained latent three-class model tells us much about these data. This model fits the data very well ($G^2 = 5.73$, $df = 6$) with parameters as shown in Table 9.7b. The parameter estimates suggest that judge 2 does best in the positive category, but has relatively high errors in the neutral category. The overall latent reliability of the judges can be assessed by computing the judge's overall error rate, equal to the weighted sum of the individual errors; for example, for judge 3 the error rate is equal to

$$0.41(0.06 + 0.01) + 0.36(0.14 + 0.11) + 0.23(0.01 + 0.21) = 0.169$$

The model also provides a means of estimating probability of making an error within each latent agreement class; for example, the probability of a negative error in the positive agreement class is relatively small

$$0.41(0.02 + 0.01 + 0.01) = 0.016$$

Dillon and Mulani investigate a variety of other hypotheses by fitting restricted latent class models to these data.

Table 9.7 Dillon and Mulani (1984) data and parameters for the unconstrained three-class model (cf. text)

(a) Data

Judge 1	Judge 2	Positive	Judge 3 Neutral	Negative
	positive	56	12	1
Positive	neutral	1	2	1
	negative	0	1	0
	positive	5	14	2
Neutral	neutral	3	20	1
	negative	0	4	7
	positive	0	0	2
Negative	neutral	0	4	1
	negative	1	2	24

(b) Parameters for unconstrained three-class models

Judge	Category[a]	Agreement classes Positive (1)	Neutral (2)	Negative (3)
1	1	0.88	0.12	0.05
	2	0.15	0.79	0.06
	3	0.02	0.09	0.89
2	1	0.98	0.33	0.08
	2	0.01	0.55	0.04
	3	0.01	0.12	0.88
3	1	0.93	0.14	0.01
	2	0.06	0.75	0.21
	3	0.01	0.11	0.78
Size		0.41	0.36	0.23

[a] 1 = positive; 2 = neutral; 3 = negative.

Simultaneous analysis of several groups

The ability to impose constraints on the parameters of the latent class model provides a vehicle for performing what is referred to as *simultaneous latent class analysis* which allows the researcher to formulate and test latent class models across levels of a grouping variable, where the grouping relates to any one of a number of respondent characteristics (e.g. gender, age) or possibly to different points in time. Historically, when faced with such data the researcher would fit separate latent class models to each group of respondents separately and then through some informal mechanism compare the various solutions.

Extending the notation used in defining the basic latent class model let $Y_{ig} = y_{ijg}$ be the response vector for the ith individual who is in the gth group, $O_g \in O$, $g = 1, \ldots, G$. The basis latent class model can be rewritten to include the fact that each individual is a member of one and only one group:

$$f(Y_{ig}, c_s) = \prod_{j=1}^{J} \prod_{r=1}^{Rj} [\varphi_{jrgs}]^{\delta_{ijg}} \qquad (9.22)$$

and

$$f(Y_{ig}, \mathcal{P}) = \sum_{s=1}^{S} \theta_{gs} f(Y_{ig}, c_s), \qquad (9.23)$$

where all parameters are now written conditional on the group g, including equations (9.17) to (9.18) which must be appropriately modified. Notice that this model is simply the basic latent class model expressed at each level of the grouping. It does have the advantage, however, that it can accommodate a variety of interesting hypotheses concerning the structure of the data across the levels of the grouping by imposing specific kinds of constraints. For example, the hypothesis of equality of latent class proportions can be tested by imposing the constraint that

$$\theta_{gs} = \theta_s \forall_g$$

Imposing constraints of the form

$$\varphi_{irgs} = \varphi_{jrg's'}$$

allows the researcher to test whether the complexion of the latent classes are invariant across the levels g and g' within latent classes s and s'. The so-called simultaneous latent class model is due to the work of Clogg and Goodman (1985) and the interested reader is referred to this paper for examples of extensive analyses involving constraints across groups. Other applications of simultaneous latent class analysis can be found in Bergen (1983) and Dillon, Madden and Kumar (1983).

All of the available computer programs for performing latent class analysis permit across group hypotheses to be tested, but the researcher must perform the analysis somewhat differently depending on the program used. For example, the PANMARK program has a built-in facility for analyzing grouped data. In contrast, the MILLSA program must be "tricked" in order to perform simultaneous latent class analysis. In the latter case, the trick is rather simple to implement – all one need do is to include the grouping variable when defining the observed cross-classified table of counts and to fix the conditional probabilities φ_{jrgs} associated with the grouping variable deterministically. For a two level grouping variable and a latent two-class model this would involve specifying a total of four latent classes where the first two classes are deterministically associated with the first level of the grouping and the last two classes are deterministically associated with the second level of the grouping. Table 9.8 illustrates the nature of the constraints that have to be imposed. The illustration is couched in terms of the three neighborhood indicators previously introduced, where a fourth manifest indicator has been added relating to whether the ratings collected were respondent based or collected via independent inspection. This latter variable is viewed as the grouping factor. In Table 9.8a no constraints are placed on the across group conditional probabilities, except those necessary to trick the program. The constraints shown in Table 9.8b are consistent with the hypothesis that the two groups are homogeneous with respect to the structure underlying the responses to the three categorical variables.

There have been other approaches to incorporating grouping factors into latent class models. These alternative approaches view the grouping variable as a *concommitant variable* in the sense that latent class membership is functionally related to which group a respondent is in. For example, Dillon and Mulani (1989) incorporate a grouping variable in the context of their *latent discriminant model*. Dayton and Macready (1988) have also discussed concomitant-variable latent class models. Interestingly, they have shown that in principle the concomitant variable does not have to be categorical and that it is possible to adopt a parameterization for the latent mixing proportion θ_{gs}; in other words, it is possible to define a submodel in which the conditional relationship between the concomitant variable and the latent class proportion is based on a specific parameterization, for example,

$$\theta_{gs} = \varphi(y_{ig}; \beta)$$

More recently, Dillon, Kumar and de Borrero (1993) incorporate this type of specification in the context of the mixture model for paired comparisons (see section 5).

Analogs of factor analytic and covariance structure models

Consider Figure 9.2 which shows several path diagrams, reminiscent of sorts of diagrams that are routinely used to summary factor analytic and covariance structure models. In Figure 9.2a the models involve antecedent latent variables. Note that the model on the left-hand side (panel i.) is in the parlance of the factor analytic model a single factor (unidimensional) model. In the context of latent class analysis, this diagram is consistent with the unconstrained latent class model. The right-hand side (panel ii.)

of Figure 9.2a presents a model which is consistent with a latent class analysis in which there are two latent variables, denoted as $\mathscr{F}_1$ and $\mathscr{F}_2$. Goodman (1974a) shows how to fit this model by introducing a single latent variable, which we will denoted by $\mathscr{F}^*$. If the original latent variables $\mathscr{F}_1$ and $\mathscr{F}_2$ are posited to have two levels each, then $\mathscr{F}^*$ would have four levels, where

Table 9.8 Across group equality constraints

(a) Constraints on groups factor

Variables		Latent Classes			
		1	2	3	4
Abandoned structures					
	Yes	0	0	0	0
	No	0[a]	0	0	0
Inadequate street lights					
	Yes	0	0	0	0
	No	0	0	0	0
Poor street conditions					
	Yes	0	0	0	0
	No	0	0	0	0
Groups					
	Direct question	1.0[b]	1.0[b]	0	0
	Inspection	0	0	1.0[b]	1.0[b]

[a]Across-group equality restriction.
[b]A free parameter.
[c]Fixed restriction.

(b) Testing across group homogeneity

Variables		Latent classes			
		1	2	3	4
Abandoned structures					
	Yes	2	3	2	3
	No	0[a]	0	0	0
Inadequate street lights					
	Yes	4[c]	5[c]	4[c]	5[c]
	No	0	0	0	0
Poor street conditions					
	Yes	6[c]	7[c]	6[c]	7[c]
	No	0	0	0	0
Groups					
	Direct question	1.0[b]	1.0[b]	0	0
	Inspection	0	0	1.0[b]	1.0[b]

[a]Across-group equality restriction.
[b]A free parameter
[c]Fixed restriction.

(b) Intervening latent variables

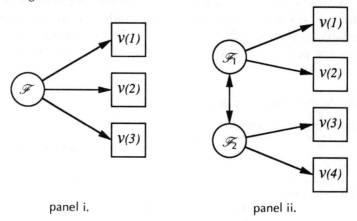

panel i.   panel ii.

(a) Antecedent latent variables

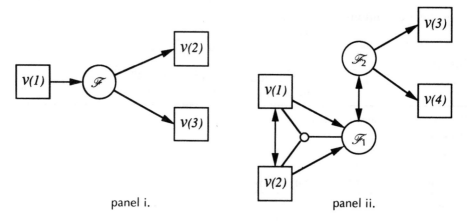

panel i.   panel ii.

Figure 9.2   Path diagrams

$$(\mathscr{F}_1, \mathscr{F}_2) \rightarrow \mathscr{F}^*$$

$(\mathscr{F}_1, \mathscr{F}_2)$	$\mathscr{F}^*$
(1,1)	1
(1,2)	2
(2,1)	3
(2,2)	4

The double-headed arrow between $\mathscr{F}_1$ and $\mathscr{F}_2$ indicates that the latent variables are posited to be associated. The other single-headed arrows in the figure indicate that $\mathscr{F}_1$ affects variables $v(1)$ and $v(2)$, but not variables $v(3)$ and $v(4)$, whereas $\mathscr{F}_2$ affects variables $v(3)$ and $v(4)$, but not variables $v(1)$ and $v(2)$. The following shows the set of equality constraints consistent with this model, where we have assumed that each manifest variable has two-levels each.

$$\varphi_{111} = \varphi_{112} \; ; \; \varphi_{113} = \varphi_{114}$$
$$\varphi_{211} = \varphi_{212} \; ; \; \varphi_{213} = \varphi_{214}$$
$$\varphi_{311} = \varphi_{313} \; ; \; \varphi_{312} = \varphi_{314}$$
$$\varphi_{411} = \varphi_{413} \; ; \; \varphi_{412} = \varphi_{414}$$

The coefficients associated with each arrow head in the figure give the "main-effect" of each latent variable on its corresponding manifest variable. Goodman (1974a) shows how to calculate these effects. In essence, these effects are related to the expected odds ratio which are used in log-linear analysis. For example, (in panel ii) the effect of $\mathcal{F}_1$ on variable $v(1)$ is computed as

$$ln\left(\frac{\varphi_{111} \; \varphi_{123}}{\varphi_{121} \; \varphi_{113}}\right)^{1/2}$$

Figure 9.2b shows other path diagrams which can be estimated with restricted latent class models. The left-hand side path diagram (panel i.) is consistent with a model that treats the latent variable as an intervening variable – variable $v(1)$ is an observed cause of $\mathcal{F}$, whereas variables $v(2)$ and $v(3)$ are viewed as multiple indicators of $\mathcal{F}$, as such $\mathcal{F}$ intervenes or moderates the relationships among the observable variables. The right-hand side path diagram (panel ii.) shows a *multiple indicator-multiple cause* (MIMIC) model. Variables $v(1)$ and $v(2)$ are associated, and each has direct effects on the latent variable $\mathcal{F}_1$, which is itself a cause of latent variable $\mathcal{F}_2$, which influences manifest variables $v(3)$ and $v(4)$. Notice that variables $v(1)$ and $v(2)$ and variables $v(3)$ and $v(4)$ are posited to be independent, given the levels of the latent variables, and that in addition to the direct effects of variables $v(1)$ and $v(2)$ on $\mathcal{F}_1$, there is an interaction effect of $v(1)$ and $v(2)$ on $\mathcal{F}_1$. Further details on this model can be found in Clogg (1981b); Madden and Dillon (1982) provide details on another type of MIMIC model in the context of an advertising experiment.

Linear logistic latent class analysis

In a series of papers Formann (1982, 1984, 1985, 1992) presents a framework for conducting latent class analysis. The framework imposes a reparameterization of the basic latent class parameters (θ_s, φ_{jrs}), in terms of real-value auxiliary w_t and z_{jrt}, where the following logistic representations are introduced:

$$\theta_s = \frac{\exp(w_s)}{\left\{\sum_{s'=1}^{S} \exp(w_s)\right\}} \tag{9.24}$$

and

$$\varphi_{jrs} = \frac{\exp(z_{jrs})}{\left[\sum_{r=1}^{R_j} \exp(z_{jrs})\right]} \qquad (9.25)$$

Notice that equations (9.24) and (9.25) restrict θ_s and φ_{jrs} to admissible interval (0,1), while leaving w_t and z_{jrs} unrestricted. The flexibility of Formann's linear logistic latent class model comes about from expressing the auxiliary parameters as functions of a set of covariates and associated sets of parameters which govern the relationship between the covariates and the auxiliary parameters. Let $\mathbf{v}$ be the vector of covariates presumed to influence the latent class sizes, and $\mathbf{q}$ be the set of covariates presumed to influence the latent class conditional response probabilities; further let η denote the fixed effect of $\mathbf{v}$ and λ denote the fixed effect of $\mathbf{q}$. In the spirit of traditional linear logistic models (Cox, 1970), we can now express the auxiliary parameters as

$$w_s = \sum_{u=1}^{U} v_{su}\eta_u \qquad (9.26)$$

and

$$z_{jrs} = \sum_{h=1}^{H} q_{jrh}\lambda_h \qquad (9.27)$$

The linear logistic latent class model can handle all of the latent class models described so far, and many more. The flexibility of this model comes about through the reparameterization that is effected. In essence, the covariates vectors $\mathbf{v}$ and $\mathbf{q}$ can be viewed as "design" vectors whose elements can be judiciously fixed to specific values to test a wide array of structural hypotheses. Formann has written a computer program for linear logistic latent class analysis, which utilizes the EM algorithm in combination with gradient methods; however, to the knowledge of these authors, the program has not, as of yet, been made available to the general research community.

5 Mixture Model Applications

In this section we review a number of finite mixture models that have appeared in the literature. It will not be possible for us to review all of the finite mixture models that have been proposed nor all of the studies in which finite mixture type models have been applied. Space constraints simply do not allow consideration of all developments published to date. Thus, we have had to be somewhat subjective in our selection. Obviously, our selection does not in any way devalue the research that we do not cover.

Analysis of brand choice data

In a 1987 paper Grover and Srinivasan introduced the concept that brand choice probabilities could be used to both segment and structure a market by decomposing brand transition matrices via latent class models. Since 1987 several other latent structure and mixture models have been proposed for analyzing brand choice data. In this section we briefly discuss two of these models, beginning with the work of Grover and Srinivasan.

Latent class analysis of two-period transition matrices The latent class methodology proposed by Grover and Srinivasan (1987) starts with a cross-classification matrix of brands purchased on two (adjacent) purchase occasions. The market is conceptualized as consisting of brand loyal segments plus (within-segment) homogeneous brand switching segments.[5] Let S_s denote the proportion of consumers in the total market belonging to the switching segments and let L_r denote the proportion of consumers in the total market who are loyal to brand r. Thus

$$1.0 = \sum_{r=1}^{R} L_r + \sum_{s=1}^{S} S_s$$

Choice probabilities are assumed to be constant over time, and unaffected by the consumer's previous purchase history; thus the model invokes the *stationarity* and *zero-order* assumptions.[6] Because of the stationarity and zero-order assumptions the probability of choosing brand r is constant, and

$$P_{(r,j)} = P_{(j,r)}$$

where $p_{(r,j)}$ denotes the probability of switching from brand j to brand r. Thus

$$S_{(r,j)} = \sum_{s=1}^{S} S_s p_{rs} p_{js} \qquad r \neq j$$

where $S_{(r,j)}$ is the number of consumers in the entire market that switch from brand j to brand r and p_{rs} gives the within-segment market share (or alternatively, the mean choice probability) of brand r. It also follows that the proportion of consumers in the total market who buy the same brand r on two occasions is given by

$$S_{(r,r)} = L_r + \sum_{s=1}^{S} S_s p_{rs}^2 \qquad \text{for } r = 1, \ldots, R$$

The aggregate market share MS_r for brand r is also found by taking a weighted average of the loyal and switching segments:

$$MS_r = L_r + \sum_{s=1}^{S} S_s p_{rs} \qquad \text{for } r = 1, \ldots, R$$

Grover and Srinivasan's loyalty and switching paradigm translates straightforwardly into a constrained latent class model. In developing the latent class representation, we will replace the j index, used previously to denote variables, by the index t which will be used here to index purchase occasions, where, in this case, $t = 1, 2$. Let the expected proportion of the population who belong to the switching segments be denoted by θ_s, $s = 1, \ldots, S$, and the within-segment conditional probabilities of purchasing brand r will be denoted by φ_{trs}. Constraints on the within-segment conditional probabilities of purchasing each brand are needed since it is assumed that

$$p_{(r,j)} = p_{(j,r)}.$$

This requires that we set

$$\varphi_{1rs} = \varphi_{2rs}$$

for each latent switching segment with the end result that we need estimate only r within-segment conditional purchase probabilities, instead of $2r$ parameters. Let θ_{L_r} denote the loyalty segments – i.e. the expected proportion of the population who are loyal to brand r. There are as many loyalty segments as there are brands. The nature of the loyalty segments requires that constraints be placed on the within-segment conditional probabilities. For each loyal segment r set

$$\varphi_{trs} = \begin{cases} 1 & \text{for } t = 1, 2 \quad r = s \\ 0 & \text{otherwise} \end{cases}$$

Table 9.9 Instant coffee cross-classification matrix

	HPDR	TCCFD	FLCR	MHCR	SDR	OTHER
HPDR	93	7	19	18	43	45
TCCFD	9	80	11	24	7	30
FLCR	19	18	82	29	14	25
HHCR	26	11	35	184	24	50
SDR	15	13	13	28	127	34
OTHER	36	25	17	37	42	263

HP = High Point
TC = Tasters Choice
FL = Folgers
MH = Maxwell House
S = Sanka
D = Decaffeninated
C = Caffeninated
FD = Freeze Dried
R = Regular

Table 9.10 Parameter restrictions (six loyalty segments and three switching segments)

(GROVER DATA 6 × 6 SWITCHING MATRIX)					
(fitting 6 loyal segments and three switching segment)					
(data GROV6.DAT)					
(date(dmy) 20-7-1991)					
This file has 117 parameters					
(initial probabilities of group 1,)					
0 0 0 0 0 0 0 0 0					
(response probs., group 1, , chain 1, indicator/wave 1)					
(class 1)	− 1	− 1	− 1	− 1	− 1	− 1
(class 2)	− 1	− 1	− 1	− 1	− 1	− 1
(class 3)	− 1	− 1	− 1	− 1	− 1	− 1
(class 4)	− 1	− 1	− 1	− 1	− 1	− 1
(class 5)	− 1	− 1	− 1	− 1	− 1	− 1
(class 6)	− 1	− 1	− 1	− 1	− 1	− 1
(class 7)	2	3	4	5	6	7
(class 8)	8	9	10	11	12	13
(class 9)	14	15	16	17	18	19
(response probs., group 1, , chain 1, indicator/wave 2)					
(class 1)	− 1	− 1	− 1	− 1	− 1	− 1
(class 2)	− 1	− 1	− 1	− 1	− 1	− 1
(class 3)	− 1	− 1	− 1	− 1	− 1	− 1
(class 4)	− 1	− 1	− 1	− 1	− 1	− 1
(class 5)	− 1	− 1	− 1	− 1	− 1	− 1
(class 6)	− 1	− 1	− 1	− 1	− 1	− 1
(class 7)	2	3	4	5	6	7
(class 8)	8	9	10	11	12	13
(class 9)	14	15	16	17	18	19

Table 9.9, adapted from Grover and Srinivasan (1987, p. 146), shows a cross-classification matrix for six varieties (five specific brands and an "all other brand" category) of instant coffee.[7] We began by considering a latent eight-class model – six latent loyalty segments and two latent switching segments. (All models were fit with use of the PANMARK computer program and all input and output tables are taken directly from this program.) The information matrix associated with this model specification was not positive definite, pointing to identification problems; more troubling, however, the parameter estimates obtained did not suggest how the model might be transformed to render it identifiable. Faced with this dilemma we decided to examine a model having three switching segments. Table 9.10 shows the restrictions for this model – in the table 0's denote free parameters, − 1's denote parameters that are fixed to specific values, and the use of integers, e.g. 2, 3, etc., denote equality constraints. The information matrix associated

Table 9.11 Parameter estimates (six loyalty segments and three switching segments)

(GROVER-SRINIVASAN DATA 6 BRAND TYPES 3 SWITCHING SEGMENTS)
(name of this file GROV6-3.Est)
(data GROV6.DAT, restr. GROV6-3.RST, start.v. GROV6-3.STV)
(date(dmy) 22-11-1992, time 13:54)
(df 12, indep.pars 23+0, LR 32.224, AIC 9769.8, BIC 9892.8)
This file contains 117 parameters
(initial probabilities of group 1.)
0.038694090 0.042237131 0.000000226 0.098789450 0.064513141 0.121486910 0.245942054 0.133287728 0.255049270

(response probs., group 1, , chain 1, indicator/wave 1)

(class 1)	1.000000000	0.000000000	0.000000000	0.000000000	0.000000000	0.000000000
(class 2)	0.000000000	1.000000000	0.000000000	0.000000000	0.000000000	0.000000000
(class 3)	0.000000000	0.000000000	1.000000000	0.000000000	0.000000000	0.000000000
(class 4)	0.000000000	0.000000000	0.000000000	1.000000000	0.000000000	0.000000000
(class 5)	0.000000000	0.000000000	0.000000000	0.000000000	1.000000000	0.000000000
(class 6)	0.000000000	0.000000000	0.000000000	0.000000000	0.000000000	1.000000000
(class 7)	0.271059365	0.000004511	0.153645034	0.141025566	0.218711529	0.215553996
(class 8)	0.021825492	0.116739345	0.595034853	0.190464433	0.008005552	0.067930326
(class 9)	0.109468913	0.171019702	0.000367322	0.197656858	0.146727563	0.374759641

(response probs., group 1, , chain 1, indicator/wave 2)

(class 1)	1.000000000	0.000000000	0.000000000	0.000000000	0.000000000	0.000000000
(class 2)	0.000000000	1.000000000	0.000000000	0.000000000	0.000000000	0.000000000
(class 3)	0.000000000	0.000000000	1.000000000	0.000000000	0.000000000	0.000000000
(class 4)	0.000000000	0.000000000	0.000000000	1.000000000	0.000000000	0.000000000
(class 5)	0.000000000	0.000000000	0.000000000	0.000000000	1.000000000	0.000000000
(class 6)	0.000000000	0.000000000	0.000000000	0.000000000	0.000000000	1.000000000
(class 7)	0.271059365	0.000004511	0.153645034	0.141025566	0.218711529	0.215553996
(class 8)	0.021825492	0.116739345	0.595034853	0.190464433	0.008005552	0.067930326
(class 9)	0.109468913	0.171019702	0.000367322	0.197656858	0.146727563	0.374759641

with this model was also not positive definite, however, the parameter estimates (see Table 9.11) did suggest potential modifications. Four parameters (one mixing proportion and three conditional within-segment (switching) probabilities) in Table 9.11 had near-zero values. Hoping that additional restrictions would render this model identifiable, we fixed these four parameters to zero and fit a latent eight-class model (five latent loyal segments and three latent switching segments). The information matrix for the modified model was positive definite. Parameter estimates are shown in Table 9.12.

Our analysis of Table 9.9 reflects the problems that applied researchers may encounter when using the latent class methodology proposed by Grover and Srinivasan. Part of the problem stems from the confounding of heterogeneity and brand loyalty – as we noted in note 5, the model which views the market in terms of loyal and switching segments is not mathematically distinguishable from a model that views the market in terms of heterogeneous brand switching segments, with no brand loyal segments. While the problems of identifiability are not insuperable, imposing additional restrictions or incorporating new data, for example, covariates, may help, they are nonetheless formidable. In general, latent class models for $I \times J$ (i.e. two-period) cross-classifications present some interesting challenges for latent class modelers.

In closing this section we should note that the situation improves in the case of multiple waves. Markov chain models (cf. Wiggins 1973), which focus on the change from one point in time to another, have been greatly advanced by the work of Poulsen (1982), who first introduced mixed Markov models and latent Markov models. These models allow feedback effects and in the latent Markov model individuals are allowed to change their latent positions. The work of Poulsen (1982) has been further advanced by Van de Pol and Langeheine (1989). The program PANMARK provides an extremely flexible framework for estimating a variety of mixed and latent Markov models.

Mixtures of multinomial logits The work of Grover and Srinivasan (1987) has spawned other approaches to segmenting and structuring markets on the basis of choice behavior. For example, Kamakura and Russell (1989) develop a model for segmenting and structuring markets based upon brand preferences and sensitivities to marketing variables. Their approach which is described below involves mixtures of product multinomials.

Kamakura and Russell develop their approach in the context of random utility theory. As is customary, suppose that the random utility, u_{ij}, that consumer i assigns to each brand, j, considered can be partitioned into a deterministic component, which depends on the characteristics of the brand, v_{ij}, and a random component, ε_{ij}; v_{iz}::

$$u_{ij} = v_{ij} + \varepsilon_{ij}$$

For simplicity, following Kamakura and Russell, express the deterministic component of this utility in terms of the intrinsic characteristic of the brand and its price:

Table 9.12 Parameter estimates (five loyalty segments and three switching segments)

(GROVER-SRINIVASAN DATA 6 BRAND TYPES 5–3 SEGMENTS WITH RESTRICTIONS)
(name of this file GROV63B.Est)
(data GROV6.DAT, restr. GROV63B.RST, start.v. GROV63B.STV)
(date(dmy) 22-11-1992, time 14:09)
(df 16, indep.pars 19+0, LR 32.224, AIC 9761.8, BIC 9863.4)
This file contains 104 parameters
(initial probabilities of group 1,)

| 0.038703529 | 0.042231182 | 0.098790814 | 0.064508827 | 0.121491674 | 0.249405218 | 0.124412897 | 0.260455860 |

(response probs., group 1, , chain 1, indicator/wave 1)

(class 1)	1.000000000	0.000000000	0.000000000	0.000000000	0.000000000	0.000000000	0.000000000
(class 2)	0.000000000	1.000000000	0.000000000	0.000000000	0.000000000	0.000000000	0.000000000
(class 3)	0.000000000	0.000000000	1.000000000	0.000000000	1.000000000	0.000000000	0.000000000
(class 4)	0.000000000	0.000000000	0.000000000	0.000000000	0.000000000	1.000000000	0.000000000
(class 5)	0.000000000	0.000000000	0.000000000	0.000000000	0.000000000	0.000000000	1.000000000
(class 6)	0.267733281	0.000000000	0.166202267	0.141326528	0.215015882	0.209722042
(class 7)	0.011700575	0.122453893	0.608785902	0.192696572	0.000000000	0.064363058
(class 8)	0.112321198	0.168744860	0.000000000	0.196808972	0.148425894	0.373699076

(response probs., group 1, , chain 1, indicator/wave 2)

(class 1)	1.000000000	0.000000000	0.000000000	0.000000000	0.000000000	0.000000000	0.000000000
(class 2)	0.000000000	1.000000000	0.000000000	0.000000000	0.000000000	0.000000000	0.000000000
(class 3)	0.000000000	0.000000000	1.000000000	0.000000000	1.000000000	0.000000000	0.000000000
(class 4)	0.000000000	0.000000000	0.000000000	0.000000000	0.000000000	1.000000000	0.000000000
(class 5)	0.000000000	0.000000000	0.000000000	0.000000000	0.000000000	0.000000000	1.000000000
(class 6)	0.267733281	0.000000000	0.166202267	0.141326528	0.215015882	0.209722042
(class 7)	0.011700575	0.122453893	0.608785902	0.192696572	0.000000000	0.064363058
(class 8)	0.112321198	0.168744860	0.000000000	0.196808972	0.148425894	0.373699076

$$u_{ij} = b_{ij} + \beta_i X_{ij} + \varepsilon_{ij} \tag{9.28}$$

where b_{ij} is the intrinsic utility/value of brand j for consumer i, and β_i is the price parameter for consumer i, and X_{ij} is the net available price of brand j for consumer i. Under the ususal assumptions of random utility theory, the conditional probability of choosing brand j is given by the multinomial logit model,

$$P_{ij} = \frac{\exp(b_{ij} + \beta_i X_{ij})}{\displaystyle\sum_{j'=1}^{J} \exp(b_{ij'} + \beta_i X_{ij'})} \tag{9.29}$$

Assume now the existence of $s = 1, 2, \ldots, S$, homogeneous segments with relative sizes θ_s, and within-segment parameters b_{js} and β_s. The unconditional probability of choosing brand j (equation (9.29)) now assumes the form

$$P_{ij} = \sum_{s=1}^{S} \theta_s P_{ijs} \tag{9.30}$$

where

$$P_{ijs} = \frac{\exp(b_{js} + \beta_s X_{ij})}{\displaystyle\sum_{j'} \exp(b_{j's} + \beta_s X_{ij})} \tag{9.31}$$

The ususal likelihood function

$$\mathcal{L} = \prod_{i=1}^{N} \prod_{j=1}^{J} (P_{ij})^{y_{ij}}$$

where

$$y_{ij} = \begin{cases} 1 & \text{if brand } j \text{ is chosen} \\ 0 & \text{otherwise} \end{cases}$$

can now be reexpressed in terms of the conditional segment parameters; viz:

$$\mathcal{L} = \prod_{i=1}^{N} \left(\sum_{s=1}^{S} \theta_s \prod_{j=1}^{J} (P_{ijs})^{y_{ij}} \right) \tag{9.32}$$

Kamakura and Russell (1989, appendix A) describe a modified Newton gradient search to find the maximum of equation (9.32).

The application described by Kamakura and Russell involves 78 weeks of retail scanner data for 585 households who purchased one of four varieties (three national brands, denoted as A, B, and C, and a composite brand representing private label and regional brands, denoted as brand P) of a nationally sold food product. In calibrating the logit model, they considered the net price (shelf price minus coupons) facing the consumer for each of the four brands at each purchase occasion. Table 9.13 taken from their reported results presents ML parameter estimates for a latent five-segment solution. The parameters correspond to the segment-level mean utilities for each brand, the segment-level price sensitivity, and the segment mixing proportions. Notice that the segments are apparently markedly different with respect to their preferences for specific brands and their price sensitivity.

Table 9.13 Parameter estimates for five-segments solution[a]

	Segment 1	Segment 2	Segment 3	Segment 4	Segment 5
Intrinsic brand utilities					
A	4.153	2.182	1.605	3.811	0.035[b]
	(0.419)	(0.293)	(0.243)	(0.430)	(0.320)
B	0.562	2.185	− 0.198	0.651	0.856
	(0.271)	(0.213)	(0.090)	(0.160)	(0.230)
C	0	0	0	0	0
	Fixed	Fixed	Fixed	Fixed	Fixed
P	− 0.825	− 1.71	− 2.963	− 1.356	1.055
	(0.343)	(0.362)	(0.189)	(0.258)	(0.217)
Price sensitivity					
β	− 1.874	− 1.436	− 3.065	− 5.424	3.66[b]
	(0.355)	(0.223)	(0.238)	(0.446)	(0.213)
Segment size					
α	− 1.019	0.975	0	− 0.452[b]	1.247
	(0.221)	(0.229)	Fixed	(0.293)	(0.249)

[a]Standard errors are in parentheses. Parameters constrained to zero are denoted as "fixed." Segment size is defined relative to all switching segments.
[b]Parameter statistically *insignificant* at the 0.05 level.
Source: Taken from Kamakura and Russell (1989, p. 384).

A mixture model for paired comparisons

One of the oldest models for the analysis of paired comparisons is the Bradley-Terry-Luce model (Bradley and Terry, 1952, Luce, 1959). The so-called BTL model parameterizes the choice proportions, π_{jk}, indicating the number of times stimulus j is preferred to stimulus k, $j = 1, \ldots, k, \ldots, J$, in terms of the directly unobservable scale values, S_j and S_k:

$$\pi_{jk} = \frac{\exp(S_j - S_k)}{[1 + \exp(S_j - S_k)]} \tag{9.33}$$

The logit of the choice proportion π_{jk}, denoted by L_{jk}, is equal to

$$L_{jk} = \ln\left[\frac{\pi_{jk}}{1 - \pi_{jk}}\right] \qquad (9.34)$$

$$= S_j - S_k$$

since

$$(1 - \pi_{jk}) = \frac{1}{[1 + \exp(S_j - S_k)]}.$$

Though the analysis of aggregated paired comparisons with the BTL model is well known, this model assumes that the sample of respondents is homogeneous; that is, there is a single vector of scale values that can adequately characterize the preferences of all individuals equally well. Recently, Dillon, Kumar and de Borrero (1993) have proposed an extended BTL model which can *simultaneously* estimate the scale values of the BTL model and capture individual differences in preference scale values as well. The extended BTL model assumes the existence of $s = 1, 2, \ldots, S$ latent segments, each characterized by a unique set of preference scale values.

Letting $\pi_{jk}^{(s)}$ be the proportion of times stimulus j is chosen over stimulus k for individuals belonging to segment s, equation (9.33) now assumes the following form:

$$\pi_{jk}^{(s)} = \frac{\exp(S_j^{(S)} - S_k^{(s)})}{[1 + \exp(S_j^{(s)} - S_k^{(s)})]} \qquad (9.35)$$

where $S_j^{(s)}$ and $S_k^{(s)}$ are the scale values associated with stimuli j and k, respectively, for those individuals belonging to segment s. Similarly, the conditional logit of the choice proportion $\pi_{jk}^{(s)}$ can be rewritten as

$$L_{jk}^{(s)} = \ln\left[\frac{\pi_{jk}^{(s)}}{1 - \pi_{jk}^{(s)}}\right] \qquad (9.36)$$

$$= S_j^{(s)} - S_k^{(s)}$$

Let us briefly sketch the procedure for obtaining ML estimates of the parameters of the extended BTL model. Without loss of generality assume that each individual in the sample is exposed to all $l (= J(J-1)/2)$ paired comparisons. The responses from the ith individual is denoted by $\mathbf{y}_i$, a 1 by l vector of ones and zeros, where each element in the vector corresponds to a specific paired comparison which is assigned the value one if the first brand in the pair is preferred to the second, and assigned the value zero otherwise. To this vector $\mathbf{y}_i$ is adjoined the vector $\mathbf{x}_i$ of measurements on a relevant set of p descriptor variables, if available.

The conditional likelihood for respondent i, given the vector of responses x_i on the set of p decriptor variables, is given by

$$\mathcal{L}(y_i, x_i) = \sum_{s=1}^{S} f^{(s)}(x_i; \beta^{(s)}) \prod_{\substack{j \ k \\ j < k}} (\pi_{jk}^{(s)})^{\delta_{ijk}} \tag{9.37}$$

where $\pi_{jk}^{(s)}$ is a function of segment-specific scale values and δ_{ijk} is an indicator function which assumes the value one if j is preferred to k by respondent i, and zero otherwise. For a sample of N individuals, the total conditional likelihood is given by

$$\mathcal{L}(\beta^{(s)}, S_j^{(s)}|y, x) = \prod_i \sum_{s=1}^{S} f^{(s)}(x_i; \beta^{(s)}) \prod_{\substack{j \ k \\ j < k}} \left[\frac{\exp(S_j^{(s)} - S_k^{(s)})}{[1 + \exp(S_j^{(s)} - S_k^{(s)})]} \right]^{\delta_{ijk}} \tag{9.38}$$

Dillon, Kumar and de Borrero (1993) describe an EM algorithm for maximizing this likelihood.

Table 9.14 Product form paired comparisons

Product form	Lotion	Cream	Stick	Aerosol spray	Pump spray
Lotion	–	167	177	175	172
Cream	33	–	167	164	155
Stick	23	33	–	131	108
Aerosol spray	25	36	69	–	63
Pump spray	28	45	92	137	–

Table 9.15 Preference values

Product form	Aggregate	Segments			
		1	2	3	4
Lotion	59.8	76.1	13.6	48.5	64.2
Cream	21.2	14.3	6.9	35.2	20.5
Stick	7.3	1.1	2.5	14.7	9.2
Aerosol spray	4.3	1.8	47.0	00	0.3
Pump spray	7.4	6.7	30.0	1.6	0.7
Segment size		33.8	14.9	24.6	26.7

To illustrate this model consider the data presented in Table 9.14, obtained from a paired comparison study involving five distinct product form types. Each of 200 respondents from five different test cities completed 10 paired comparisons. In fitting the paired comparison data, geographic region is used as a covariate. Table 9.15 presents summary results for a latent four-segment solution in terms of the preference scale value, expressed in terms of a percent, for each product form type. The latent four-segment solution reproduced the observed cell frequencies quite well ($L^2 = 3.98, p \leqslant 0.01$). First, notice from Table 9.15 that although the aggregate solution indicates that there is strong preference for lotion product forms, there are clear differences in the preferences for the different types of product forms. For example, in segment 2, representing about 15 percent of the population, there is relatively strong preference for aerosol sprays and pump sprays, whereas in segment 3, representing almost 25 percent of the population, there is strong preference for cream and stick product form types. Although not specifically shown, the analysis also revealed strong regional differences in preferences as well.

Mixtures of normal densities: a linear regression model

It is reasonable to suspect that in many marketing and consumer behavior research applications the estimation of a single set of regression coefficients depicting the relationship between a set of explanatory variables and a dependent measure may prove to be misleading due to respondent hetero-geneity. Parameter estimation for a mixture of linear regressions has been extensively investigated by Veaux (1986); more recently, DeSarbo and Cron (1988) have discussed and illustrated this model in the context of performing clusterwise linear regression.

Assume an independent sample on $i = 1, \ldots, N$ individuals drawn ran-domly from a mixture of conditional normal densities having (unknown) proportions, $\theta_1, \theta_2, \ldots, \theta_S$, and let

b_{js} = the value of the j-th regression coefficient in segment s
σ_s^2 = the residual variance within segment s.

If y_i is distributed as a finite sum or mixture of conditional univariate normal densities we can write

$$y_i \sim \sum_{s=1}^{S} \theta_s (2\pi\sigma_s^2)^{-1/2} \exp\left(\frac{-(y_i - x_i b_s)^2}{2\sigma_s^2}\right) \tag{9.39}$$

where $x_i = ((X_j))_i$ and $b_s = ((b_j))_s$. As usual, $0 \leqslant \theta_s \leqslant 1$, $\sum_s \theta_s = 1$, and $\sigma_s^2 > 0$, in order for the likelihood function to be bounded above. The loglikelihood is

$$\mathscr{L} = \sum_{i=1}^{N} \sum_{s=1}^{S} \left[\theta_s (2\pi\sigma_s^2)^{-1/2} \exp\left(\frac{-(y_i - x_i b_s)^2}{2\sigma_s^2}\right) \right] - \lambda\left(\sum_{s=1}^{S} \theta_s - 1\right) \tag{9.40}$$

The normal equations can be solved with use of either gradient (e.g. quasi-Newton) methods or by applying the EM algorithm. If the EM alogrithm is used, estimates of θ_s along with the posterior probabilities are obtained in the E-step. In the M-step, estimates of b_s and σ_s^2 would be obtained through performing what are in effect S weighted least squares regressions.

DeSarbo and Cron (1988) illustrate the use of this model in a study of factors that influence perceptions of trade show performance. A sample of 129 marketing executives were asked to rate their firm's trade show performance on eight performance factors as well as on an overall trade show performance scale. The analysis related ratings on the eight perform-ance factors to the overall rating given to the trade show. Table 9.16, adapted from their paper, describes the eight performance factors and presents summary results for the latent two-segment solution. As can be seen from the parameter estimates provided in the table, segments 1 and 2 appear to be markedly different from each other and different from the aggregate (one-segment) solution as well. Segment 1, composed of 59 marketing executives, evaluates trade shows primarily in terms of evalu-ations on non-selling factors, including servicing new customers (X_2), and enhancing corporate image and moral (X_5) and (X_7). Segment 2, on the other hand, which is composed of 70 marketing executives, evaluates trade shows primarily in terms of evaluations on selling factors, including ident-ifying new prospects (X_1), introducing new products (X_3), selling at trade shows (X_4), and new product testing (X_6).

Table 9.16 Conditional mixture maximum likelihood $S = 2$ segment solution

	Cluster 1	Cluster 2	Aggregate
INTERCEPT	4.093***	2.218***	3.03
X_1	0.126	0.242***	0.15***
X_2	0.287***	-0.164***	-0.02
X_3	-0.157**	0.206**	-0.09
X_4	-0.133***	0.074**	-0.04
X_5	0.128*	0.072	0.09
X_6	0.107	0.282***	0.18***
X_7	0.155**	-0.026	0.07
X_8	-0.124	0.023	0.04
R^2	0.73	0.76	0.85
adj.R^2	0.69	0.73	0.37
S.S.E.	20.37	12.98	0.33
I	59	70	87.67
λ_k	0.489	0.511	8.87***
σ_k	0.589	0.504	129

*$p \leqslant 0.10$
**$p \leqslant 0.05$
*$p \leqslant 0.01$
Source: adapted from DeSarbo and Cron (1988).

The basic framework developed by DeSarbo and Cron (1988) has been extended to other application areas. For example, DeSarbo, Wedel, Vriens, and Ramaswamy (1992) use this framework to develop a latent class metric conjoint analysis model which simultaneously estimates conjoint part-worths and market segment membership. Ramaswamy, DeSarbo, Reib-stein, and Robinson (1993) employ a similar mixture approach for pooling cross sections of time series observations with PIMS data in estimating marketing mix elasticities.

6 Nagging Problems in Estimating Mixture Models

It would be misleading if we contributed to the impression that the estimation of finite mixture models is not without problems. An unfortunate complication typical of mixture distributions is the fact that the likelihood need not be concave. This complication can cause two potential problems. First the ML normal equations may fail to maximize the likelihood. Such a result is generally referred to as *non-convergence*. Second, multiple maxima of the likelihood may exist. This second problem is called *local identifiability*.

Identifiability

Local identifiability means that more than one set of ML estimates may maximize the likelihood. Haberman (1977, p. 1135, theorem 3) has, for large samples, provided the conditions for the likelihood to have an unique maximum (see also Sundberg, 1974 for some related results and Yakowitz and Spragins 1968 for additional theorems which help to show which distributions yield identifiable finite mixtures); unfortunately, these results may not apply equally to all mixture models (cf. Haberman, 1977, p. 1141) and, perhaps more seriously, are extremely difficult to apply in practice.

Problems of local identifiability will depend on the particular mixture model being considered. For example, Teicher (1960) has shown that a mixture of Poisson distributions is generally identifiable. But such results are not necessarily true for other mixture distributions. In the context of latent structure analysis and specifically the latent class model, problems of local maxima have been known since McHugh (1956). Aitkin, Anderson and Hinde (1981) provide an illustration of multiple solutions in the context of fitting a latent three-class model to teaching style data; see also Haberman (1974, pp. 921–2) and Sundberg (1974, p. 53); in the context of a mixture of normal distributions, Hathaway (1983) has shown that if the maximum likelihood problem for a mixture of normal distributions is extended to consider the parameter value of the (common) standard deviation as unknown then a maximum likelihood estimate fails to exist for every sample. This fact has been also noted by others (cf. Kiefer and Wolfowitz, 1956; Day, 1969; Quandt and Ramsey, 1978; and Hosmer, 1973). Finally, in the context of mixed product multinomials, similar to the model presented by Kamakura and Russell (1989), there is little evidence to suggest that this specification is genearlizably identifiable. Generally speaking, it is very difficult to verify that a solution to the normal equations for this type of mixture is definitely a ML estimate (Haberman, 1977, p. 1135).

There is some differences in opinion as to the real problems caused by local identifiability. Some researchers (cf. Formann, 1992, p. 478) suggest that finding a local maximum of the likelihood is not a serious problem, for certain types of mixture models, especially when the EM algorithm is used to obtain ML estimates. The argument rests on the three properties of the EM algorithm discussed earlier. Because any EM sequence of parameter estimates increases the likelihood, and if the likelihood is bounded above, then at worse any EM sequence of parameter estimates ends in a stationary point of likelihood that is not a local minimum. However, if the expected matrix of second-order partial derivatives of $\mathcal{L}^*$ is negative definite at $\mathcal{P}$, then the solution corresponds to a local maximum of the likelihood, and all the parameters can be estimated. If the expected matrix of second-order partial derivatives of $\mathcal{L}^*$ is negative semidefinite at $\mathcal{P}$ then this indicates a (probable) lack of local identifiability and the model is either overparameterized or a *terminal solution* has been obtained. In the former case, one can reduce the number of components being considered and/or delete those parameters having especially large asymptotic standard deviations. In the latter case of terminal solutions one or more of the parameters tends to boundary values (e.g. 0 or 1, or possibly $\pm\infty$) and these parameters should be fixed and the model re-estimated.

Starting values

Even if a stationary value of the likelihood can be identified as a local mimimum, it must still be established as the unique or global minimum. This determination rests on whether the likelihood is unimodel. The recommended practice for determining whether the likelihood is unimodal is to perform several parameter estimation trials varying the starting values assigned to the parameters, where in principle the starting values assigned are representative of the parameter space. If the different sets of starting values yield the same solution to the likelihood equations then it is reasonable to conclude that the likelihood is unimodal. If, on the other hand, the different sets of starting values yield different local maxima, then the likelihood is multimodal. In such cases, the recommended practice is to choose the "best" maxima as the global one.

Some researchers, however, feel that the procedure described above is simply an expedient but uncertain one, and that in general mixture models are inherently plagued by statistical difficulties and operational problems. Reviewing the book by McLachlan and Basford (1988), in which these authors recommend an operational approach along the lines described above, Lindsay (1989) remarks there is no straightforward method to finding starting values for the algorithm. The authors' advice could be roughly summarized as follows: Try a number of starting values (how many? where?), let the algorithm run a long time (how long?), and select as the maximum likelihood estimator that local maximum in the interior of the parameter space with the largest likelihood. (p. 337)

The importance of "good" starting values is also underscored by the problem of when to stop the EM algorithm. The stopping criterion most frequently used for the EM algorithm is the size of the change in the likelihood or parameter estimates from one iteration to the next. Lindstrom and Bates (1988) argue that this stopping criterion "is a measure of lack of progress but not of actual convergence." Titterington *et al.* (1985, p. 90) presents evidence to suggest that different solutions are typically found in published data sets due to the fact that the EM algorithm is stopped "too early." From this discussion it is clear that researchers who follow the mixture path must present evidence on the identifiability of the solutions obtained. We would hope that in marketing applications which use mixture models there is some discussion of this problem and that evidence be presented to indicate the stability of the solution under different sets of starting values. The choice of starting values remains a problem, however. In the next section we discuss some recent advances in the area of non-parametric ML estimation which may in time provide solutions to the problems caused by starting values, as well as in deciding on how many components to retain.

Non-parametric estimation

As we discussed earlier, the conventional approach to estimating parameters of mixture models is to solve the ML equations for successive value of S, the number of components of the mixture distribution. With this approach, the number of components S is *implicitly* treated as fixed and therefore known. It is, however, useful to treat the number of components S as strictly unknown and allow ρ to vary in the set of *all* probability measures. To understand this distinction let us introduce some basic concepts related to the nonparametric maximum likelihood estimation (NPMLE) problem.

The number of φ_s that have strictly positive mass at θ_s equals the *support size* of the discrete distribution corresponding to the parameter vector $\mathcal{P}$; an alternative, but equivalent way of saying this is that the number of components, S, equals the support size of the discrete distribution. The fixed support size case occurs whenever S is treated as fixed and $\mathcal{P}$ is allowed to vary in the set Ω_s of all discrete probability measures with maximum support size S. In contrast, the *flexible support size* case occurs whenever S itself is treated as an unknown parameter and $\mathcal{P}$ is viewed as a completely unknown varying in the set Ω of *all* probability measures. In the flexible support size case, the estimated probability measure $\hat{\mathcal{P}}$ of $\mathcal{P}$

that maximizes the likelihood is known as the *nonparametric maximum likelihood estimator* of the mixing distribution (Laird, 1978).

An in-depth understanding of the motivation and properties of NPMLE is far beyond our stated intention.[8] We can, however, mention some of the key points and provide a simple example. With NPMLE a grid of parameter values, say, $\varphi_1, \ldots, \varphi_m$ are specified over which we wish to find the corresponding population proportions that maximizes the likelihood function. In general, at the start a relatively small number m of grid points should be chosen, and then expanded in specific regions to obtain more precise information concerning the number of components. The process proceeds by maximizing the likelihood over all sets of population proportions on this grid. A test function $\Phi_{\hat{\mathscr{P}}}(\varphi)$, called the directional derivative is defined such that $\hat{\mathscr{P}}$ is the NPMLE if and only if $\Phi_{\hat{\mathscr{P}}(\varphi)} \leqslant 0$ for all φ. Regardless of the gradient method used, convergence is determined by evaluating whether $\Phi_{\hat{\mathscr{P}}(\varphi)} \leqslant tolerance$ for all φ in the grid, where the tolerance is set to some small value. A *step length* parameter must also be specified which ensures that the algorithm is monotonic in the sense of increasing the likelihood at each step. Here too there are several candidates. An informative introduction to these algorithms is provided by Böhning, Schlattmann and Lindsay (1992). These authors have also made

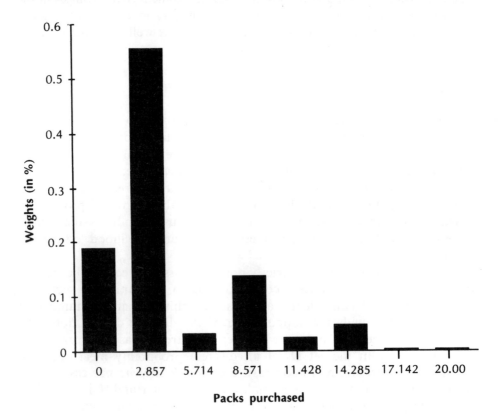

Figure 9.3 Non-parametric estimation

available a computer program, called C.A.MAN, which provides various statistical algorithms for computing NPMLE of mixing distributions of one-parameter family of densities.

To illustrate the NPMLE approach consider once again the purchase data presented in Table 9.1. Using the C.A. MAN we specified a grid of 8 equally spaced points from 0.0 to 20.0. Figure 9.3 summarizes the results. From the figure it appears that there is clear separation of three groups. Since it was unclear what is happening in the second group, we went back into C.A.MAN and worked with a finer grid consisting of 15 parameters. The results showed a solution with six support points. The support points identified by C.A.MAN were then used as starting values in program which implemented a fixed support point EM algorithm. The results of that analysis have discussed earlier and displayed in Figure 9.1.

7 Conclusions

We have attempted in this chapter to provide an integrative overview and survey of latent structure models and other related models falling under the general umbrella of finite mixture models. Because of the need to account for respondent heterogeneity, finite mixture models hold great promise. It is not surprising to not the growing number of papers appearing in the marketing literature that have proposed special variants of finite mixture models. And it is, we think, inevitable that this trend will continue. The challenges that lie ahead are, in our opinion, clear, falling squarely on the development of procedures for identifying the number of support points needed to characterize the components of the mixture distribution under investigation.

Questions

1   The truncated mixed poisson model has the form:

$$f(y_i, \mathcal{P}) = \sum_{s=1}^{S} \theta_s \frac{\exp(-\varphi_s)\, \varphi_s^{y_i}}{y_i!\{1 - \exp(-\varphi_s)]}\, y_i = \{1, 2, \ldots,\}.$$

Derive the loglikelihood function.

2   Consider the following data.

x	0	1	2	3	4	5	6	7
frequency	830	638	327	137	49	15	3	1

Fit the mixed poisson model.

3   Consider the following cross-classification taken from the 1980 Evaluation of the Section 8 Housing Assistance Program, appearing on p. 346. The questions

concerned respondents' satisfaction about (1) their house or apartment as a place to live, (2) their landlord or dwelling manager, and (3) the general ambience of their neighborhood as a place to live. Evaluate the 2-class and 3-class unrestricted latent class models.

4   Develop the constraints that would be needed in order to test the following 4-class restricted latent class model for the cross-classification table given in question 3.

(a)   In latent class 1 an item response of "fair" or "poor" to any of the residence factors is prohibited.

(b)   In latent class 2 an item response of "fair" or "poor" to any of the residence factors is prohibited.

(c)   In latent class 3 an item response of "excellent" or "poor" to any of the residence factors is prohibited.

(d)   In latent class 4 an item response of "excellent" or "good" to any of the residence factors is prohibited.

What interpretation can be given to these latent class types. Does this model provide an adequate fit to the data?

Neighborhood	Landlord	Excellent	Good	Fair	Poor
Excellent	Excellent	116	32	5	0
	Good	17	27	10	0
	Fair	3	3	7	1
	Poor	0	1	1	1
Good	Excellent	50	49	8	0
	Good	15	141	37	2
	Fair	3	12	28	4
	Poor	0	7	5	4
Fair	Excellent	7	10	6	0
	Good	3	25	26	2
	Fair	0	6	18	3
	Poor	0	2	1	4
Poor	Excellent	1	2	0	0
	Good	0	1	1	1
	Fair	0	0	1	1
	Poor	0	0	1	2

Notes

1   Actually, violation of the mean-variance property of the poisson distribution is evidence of either heterogenity or contagion.

2   Interested readers wanting more details on the general theory underlying information-theoretic based model selection criteria should consult Bozdogan (1987).

3   All parameters and standard deviations have been estimated with use of the PANMARK program.

4   Mooijaart and Heijden (1992) present evidence to suggest that the EM algorithm cannot be used to estimated parameters under specific kinds of equality constraints.

5 As discussed by Grover and Srinivasan (1987, pp. 150–3) this particular conceptualization cannot be distinguished, in a mathematical sense, from the conceptualization that views the market in terms of heterogeneous brand switching segments, with no brand loyal segments. Using this latter conceptualization, Jain, Bass and Chen (1990) propose an alternative model which provides a direct estimate for the heterogeneity parameter characterizing each of the switching segments.

6 A further implication of these assumptions is that the cross-classification of brands purchased across the two time periods must be symmetric.

7 The five specific brands considered correspond to those brands with the largest market shares.

8 Interested readers should consult Lindsay (1981, 1983a, 1983b), Böhning, Schlattmann and Lindsay (1992), and Lesperance and Kalbfleisch (1992).

References

Aitkin, M., Anderson, D. and Hinde, J. 1981: Statistical modelling of data on teaching styles. *Journal of the Royal Statistical Society*, Series A, 144, 419–61.

Akaike, H. 1974: A new look at statistical model identification. *IEEE Transactions on Automatic Control*, AC-19, 716–23.

Andersen, E. B. 1982: Latent structure analysis: a survey. *Scandinavian Journal of Statistics*, 9, 1–12.

Baker, Stuart G. 1992: A simple method for computing the observed information matrix when using the EM algorithm with categorical data. *American Statistical Association, Institute of Mathematical Statist., and Interface Foundation of North America*, 1 (1), 63–76.

Bartholomew, David J. 1987: *Latent Variable Models and Factor Analysis*, New York: Oxford University Press.

Bergan, J. R. 1983: Latent-class models in educational research. In E. W. Gordon (ed.), *Review of Research in Education 10*, Washington, DC: American Educational Research Association.

Böhning, D., Schlattmann, P., and Lindsay, B. G. 1992: Computer assisted analysis of mixtures (C.A.MAN): statistical algorithms. *Biometrics*, 48, 283–303.

Bozdogan, Hamparsum 1987: Model selection and Akaike's information criterion (AIC): The general theory and its analytical extensions. *Psychometrika*, 52, 345–70.

Bradley, R. A. and Terry, M. E. 1952: Rank analysis of incomplete block designs: The method of paired comparisons. *Biometrika*, 39, 324–45.

Bradley, R. A. and Walker, P. J. 1952: Rank analysis of incomplete block designs, I, the method of paired comparisions. *Biometrika*, 39, 324–45.

Clogg, C. C. 1977: Unrestricted and restricted maximum likelihood latent structure analysis: a manual for users. (Working Paper 1977–09), University Park: Population Issues Research Center.

Clogg, C. C. 1979: Some latent structure models for the analysis of Likert-type data. *Social Science Research*, 8, 287–301.

Clogg, C. C. 1981a: New developments in latent structure analysis. In D. J. Jackson, E. F. Borgatta (eds), *Factor Analysis and Measurement in Sociological Research*, Longon Sage.

Clogg, C. C. 1981b: Latent structure models of mobility. *American Journal of Sociology*, 86, 836–68.

Clogg, C. C. and Goodman, L. A. 1985: Simultaneous latent structure analysis in several groups. In N. B. Tuma (ed.), *Sociological Methodology*, San Francisco Jossey-Bass.

Clogg, C. C. and Sawyer, D. O. 1981: A comparison of alternative models for analyzing the scalability of response patterns. In S. Leinhardt (ed.), *Sociological Methodology*, San Francisco: Jossey-Bass.

Cox, D. R. 1970: *The Analysis of Binary Data*, London: Methuen.

Cox, D. R. and Hinkley, D. V. 1974: *Theoretical Statistics*, London: Chapman & Hall.

Dash, Joseph F., Schiffman, L. G., Berenson, Conrad 1975: Information search and store choice. *Journal of Advertising Research*, 16, 35–40.

Day, N. E. 1969: Estimating the components of a mixture of normal distributions. *Biometrika*, 56, 463–74.

Dayton, C. M. and Macready, G. B. 1976: A probabilistic model for validation behavioral hierarchies. *Psychometrika*, 41, 189–204.

Dayton, C. M. and Macready, G. B. 1980: A scaling model with response errors and intrinsically unscalable respondents. *Psychometrika*, 45, 343–56.

Dayton, C. Mitchell and Macready, George B. 1988: Concomitant-variable latent-class models. *Journal of the American Statistical Association*, vol. 83, no. 401, Theory and Methods.

Dempster, A. P., Laird, N. M. and Rubin, D. B. 1977: Maximum likelihood from incomplete data via the Em algorithm. *Journal of Royal Statistical Society*, B39, 1–38.

Dennis, J. E. and Schnabel, Robert B. 1983: *Numerical Methods for Unconstrained Optimization and Nonlinear Equations*, Englewood Cliffs, NJ: Prentice-Hall, Inc.

DeSarbo, W. S., Cron, W. L. 1988: A maximum likelihood methodology for cluster wise linear regression. *Journal of Classification*, 5, 249–82.

DeSarbo, Wayne S., Wedel M., Vriens M. and Ramaswamy V. 1992: Latent class metric conjoint analysis. *Marketing Letters*, 3 (3), 273–88.

Dillon, William R., Kumar, A. and Smith de Borrero, M. 1993: Capturing individual differences in paired comparisons: an extended BTL model incorporating descriptor variables. *Journal of Marketing Research*.

Dillon, William R. Madden, T. J. and Kumar, A. 1983: Analyzing sequential categorical data on dyadic interaction: a latent structure approach. *Psychological Bulletin*, 94, 564–83.

Dillon, William R., Madden, Thomas J., and Mulani, Narendra 1983: Scaling models for categorical variables: an application of latent structure models. *The Journal of Consumer Research, Inc.*, Vol. 10.

Dillon, William R., and Mulani, N. 1984: A probabilistic latent class model for assessing inter-judge reliability. *Multivariate Behavioral Research*, 19, 438–58.

Dillon, William R. and Mulani, Narendra 1989: LADI: A latent discriminant model for analyzing marketing research data. *Journal of Marketing Research*, 26, 15–29.

Efron, B. 1982: *The Jackknife, the Bootstrap, and Other Resampling Plans*, Philadelphia, PA: Society for Industrial and Applied Mathematics.

Eliason, S. 1987: *MLLSAPC: User's Program Guide*, working paper, Pennsylvania State University.

Everitt, B. S. 1987: *An Introduction to Optimization Methods and Their Application in Statistics*, London, New York, Chapman & Hall.

Everitt, B. S. 1988: A Monte Carlo investigation of the likelihood ratio test for number of classes in latent class analysis. *Multivariate Behavioral Research*, 23, 531–8.

Everitt, B. S. and Hand, D. J. 1981: *Finite mixture distribution*, New York: Chapman & Hall.

Feick, Lawrence F. 1987: Latent class models for the analysis of behavioral hierarchies. *Journal of Marketing Research*, 24, 174–86.

Formann, Anton K. 1982: Linear logistic latent class analysis. *Biometrical Journal*, 24, 171–90.

Formann, Anton K. 1984: *Die Latent-Class-Analysis*, Weinheim: Beltz.

Formann, Anton K. 1985: Constrained latent class models: theory and applications. *British Journal of Mathematical and Statistical Psychology*, 38, 87–111.

Formann, Anton K. 1992: Linear logistic latent class analysis for polytomous data, *American Statistical Association*, 87(418).

Gill, Philip E., Murray, Walter and Wright, Margaret H. 1989: *Practical Optimization*, Academic Press.

Goodman, L. A. 1968: The analysis of cross-classified data: independence, quasi-independence, and interactions in contingency tables with or without missing entries. *Journal of the American Statistical Association*, 65 (March), 225–6.

Goodman, L. A. 1974a: The analysis of systems of qualitative variables when some of the variables are unobservable. Part I-A modified latent structure approach, *American Journal of Sociology*, 79, 1179–259.

Goodman, L. A. 1974b: Exploratory latent structure analysis using both identifiable and unidentifiable models. *Biometrika*, 61, 215–31.

Goodman, L. A. 1975: A new model for scaling response patterns: an application of the quasi-independence concept. *Journal of the American Statistical Association*, 70, 755–68.

Grover, Rajiv and Srinivasan, V. 1987: A simultaneous approach to market segmentation and market structuring. *Journal of Marketing Research*, 24, 139–53.

Guttman, L. 1950: The basis for scalogram analysis. In S. A. Stouffer, L. Guttman, E. A. Suchman, P. F. Lazarsfeld, S. A. Star, J. A. Clausen (eds), *Measurement and prediction: Studies in social psychology in World War II (Vol. IV)*, Princeton: Princeton University Press.

Haberman, Shelby J. 1974: *The Analysis of Frequency Data*, Chicago: University of Chicago Press.

Haberman, Shelby J. 1977: Product models for frequency tables involving indirect observation. *The Annals of Statistics*, 5(6), 1124–47.

Haberman, Shelby J. 1979: Analysis of qualitative data: vol. 2. *New Developments*, New York: Academic Press.

Hartley, H. O. 1958: Maximum likelihood estimation from incomplete data. *Biometrics*, 14, 174–94.

Hartley, H. O. and Hocking, R. R. 1971: Estimating the error rates of diagnostic tests. *Biometrics*, 36, 167–71.

Hathaway, R. J. 1983: Constrained maximum likelihood estimation for a mixture of multivariate normal densities. Tech. Rep. 92, Dept. Math. Stat., University of South Carolina, Columbia, SC.

Hays, David G. and Borgatta, Edward F. 1954: An empirical comparison of restricted and general latent distance analysis. *Psychometrika*, 19(December), 271–9.

Hope, A. C. A. 1968: A simplified Monte Carlo significance test procedure. *Journal of the Royal Statistical Society*, Series B, 30, 582–98.

Hosmer, D. W. 1973: A comparison of iterative maximum-likelihood estimates of the parameters of a mixture of two normal distributions under three different types of samples. *Biometrics*, 29, 761–70.

Hosmer, D. W. 1974: Maximum likelihood estimates of the parameters of a mixture of two regression lines. *Communications in Statistics*, 3, 995–1006.

Jain, Dipak C., Fran M. Bass and Yu-Min Chen 1990: Estimation of latent class models with heterogeneous choice probabilities: an application to market structuring. *Journal of Marketing Research*, 27, 94–101.

Kamakura, Wagner A. and Russell, Gary J. 1989: A probablistic choice model for market segmentation and elasticity structure. *Journal of Marketing Research*, 26, 379–90.

Kass, Robert E. 1987: Computing observed information by finite difference. *Communication Statistics – Simulation*, 16(2), 587–99.

Kiefer, J. and Wolfowitz, J. 1956: Consistency of the maximum likelihood estimation in the presence of infinitely many incidental parameters. *Annals of Mathematical Statistics*, 27, 887–906.

Laird, N. M. 1978: Nonparametric maximum likelihood estimation of a mixing distribution. *Journal American Statistical Association*, 73, 805–11.

Langeheine, R. 1988: *New Developments in Latent Class Theory, Latent Trait and Latent Class Models*, New York: Plenum, 77–108.

Lazarsfeld, P. F. 1950: The logical and mathematical foundation of latent structure analysis. In S. A. Stouffer, L. Guttman, E. A. Suchman, P. F. Lazarsfeld, S. A. Star, J. A. Clausen (eds), *Measurement and Prediction: Studies in Social Psychology in World War II (Vol. IV)*, Princeton: Princeton University Press.

Lazarsfeld, P. F. and Henry, N. W. 1968: *Latent Structure Analysis*, Boston: Houghton Mifflin.

Lesperance, M. and Kalbfleisch, J. D. 1992: An algorithm for computing the nonparametric MLE of a mixing distribution. *Journal of the American Statistical Association*, 87, 120–6.

Lindsay, B. G. 1981: Properties of the maximum likelihood estimator of a mixing distribution. *Statistical Distributions in Scientific Work*, C. Taillie *et al.* (eds), 95–109.

Lindsay, B. G. 1983a: The geometry of mixture models, I: a general theory. *Annals of Statistics*, 11, 86–94.

Lindsay, B. G. 1983b: The geometry of mixture likelihoods, II: the exponential family. *Annals of Statistics*, 11, 783–92.

Lindsay, B. G. 1989: Review of mixture models: inference and applications to clustering by McLachlan and Basford. *Journal of the American Statistical Association*, 84, 337–8.

Lindstrom, M. J. and Bates, D. M. 1988: Newton-Raphson and EM algorithms for linear mixed-effects models for repeated-measures data. *Journal of the American Statistical Association*, 83, 1014–22.

Louis, T. A. 1982: Finding the observed information matrix when using the EM algorithm. *Journal of the Royal Statistical Society*, B44, 226–33.

Luce, R. D. 1959: *Individual Choice Behavior: A Theoretical Analysis*, New York: Wiley.

Macready, G. B. and Dayton C. M. 1977: The use of probablistic models in the assessment of mastery. *Journal of Educational Statistics*, 2, 99–120.

Madden, T. J. and Dillon, W. R. 1982: Causal analysis and latent class models: An application to a communication hierarchy of effects model. *Journal of Marketing Research*, 19, 472–90.

McHugh, R. B. 1956: Efficient estimation and local identification in latent class analysis. *Psychometrika*, 21, 331–47.

McLachlan, G. J. and Basford, K. E. 1988: *Mixture Models: Inference and Application to Clustering*, New York: Marcel Dekker.

Meilijson, Isaac 1989: A fast improvement to the EM algorithm on its own terms. *Journal of Royal Statistical Society*, B, 51, No. 1, 127–38.

Mooijaart, Ab and Van Der Heijden, Peter G. M. 1992: The EM algorithm for latent class analysis with equality constraints. *Psychometrika*, 57(2), 261–9.

Owston, Ronald D. 1979: A maximum likelihood approach to the "Test of Inclusion." *Psychometrika*, 44(December), 421–5.

Proctor, C. H. 1970: A probabilistic formulation and statistical analysis of Guttman scaling. *Psychometrika*, 35(March), 73–8.

Proctor, C. H. 1971: Reliability of a Guttman scale score. Proceedings of the Social Statistics Section, Annual Meeting of the American Statistical Association, Washington, DC: American Statistical Association.

Quandt, R. E. and Ramsey, J. B. 1978: Estimating mixtures of normal distributions and switching regressions. *Journal American Statistical Association*, 73, 730–8.

Ramaswamy V., DeSarbo, W. S., Reibstein, D. J. and Robinson, W. T. 1993: A latent pooling methodology for regression analysis with limited time series of cross sections: a PIMS application. Working paper, University of Michigan.

Schwarz, G. 1978: Estimating the dimension of a model. *Annal Statistics*, 6, 461–1.

Sundberg, R. 1974: Maximum likelihood theory for incomplete data from an exponential family. *Scandanavian Journal Statistics*, 1, 49–58.

Teicher, H. 1960: On the mixture of distributions. *Annals of Mathematical Statistics*, 31, 55–73.

Titterington, D. M., Smith, A. F. M. and Makov, U. E. 1985: *Statistical Analysis of Finitie Mixture Distributions*, New York: Wiley.

Van de Pol, F. and Langeheine, R. 1989: Mixed Markov models, Mover-Stayer models, and the EM algorithm, with an application to labour market data from the Netherlands socioeconomic panel. *Multiway Data Analysis*, 485–95.

Van de Pol, F., Langeheine, R. and de Jong, W. 1989: *PANMARK User's Manual, PANel analysis using MARKov chains*, version 1.5 Voorburg: Netherlands Central Business of Statistics.

Veaux, R. D. 1986: Parameter estimation for a mixture of linear regressions. Technical Report No. 247, Department of Statistics, Stanford University, Stanford, CA.

White, Ronald T. and Clark, R. Malcolm 1973: A test of inclusion which allows for errors of measurement. *Psychometrika*, 38(March), 77–86.

Wu, C. F. 1983: On the covergence properties of the EM algorithm. *Annals of Statistics*, 11, 95–103.

Yakowitz, S. J. and Spragins, J. D. 1968: On the identifiability of finite mixtures. *Annals of Mathematical Statistics*, 39, 209–14.

10

A Review of Recent Developments in Latent Class Regression Models

Michel Wedel and Wayne S. DeSarbo

Latent Class Mixture Models

The development of mixture models can be historically traced back to the work of Newcomb (1886) and Pearson (1894). Mixture distributions have been of considerable interest in recent years leading to a vast number of methodological and applied papers, as well as to three dedicated monographs (cf. Everitt and Hand, 1981; Titterington, Smith, and Makov, 1985; and McLachlan and Basford, 1988). In finite mixture models, it is assumed that a sample of observations arises from a (initially specified) number of underlying classes of unknown proportions. A concrete form of the density of the observations in each of the underlying classes is specified, and the purpose of the finite mixture approach is to decompose the sample into its mixture components. Specifically, we assume a set of multivariate observations on a set of n objects $\mathbf{y}_1, \ldots, \mathbf{y}_n$ as realized values of i.i.d. random variables $\mathbf{Y}$. Each $\mathbf{y}_i = ((y_{ij})), (i = 1, \ldots, n; j = 1, \ldots, J)$ is a vector of dimension J ($J = 1$ handles the univariate case), which is assumed to arise from a superpopulation which is a mixture of a finite number (S) of groups or classes, G_S $(s = 1, \ldots, S)$, in proportions $\pi_1, \ldots, \pi_S$, where it is not known in advance from which class a particular observation arises. The proportions (prior probabilities or mixture weights), π_S, satisfy the following constraints:

$$\sum_{s=1}^{S} \pi_s = 1, \qquad \pi_s > 0, \ s = 1, \ldots, S, \tag{10.1}$$

(the positivity constraints then can be relaxed to allow for negative mixture weights as in Titterington, Smith, and Makov, 1985). The conditional probability density function of $\mathbf{y}_i$ (or conditional mass function in the case of a discrete sample space), given that $\mathbf{y}_i$ comes from class s, is:

$$\mathbf{y}_i \sim f_{i|s}(\mathbf{y}_i; \boldsymbol{\theta}_s). \tag{10.2}$$

These conditional densities are usually assumed to belong to the same parametric family, although this restriction is not strictly required. The unconditional density of observation i is given by:

$$f_i(\mathbf{y}_i; \boldsymbol{\varphi}) = \sum_{s=1}^{S} \pi_s f_{i|s}(\mathbf{y}_i; \boldsymbol{\theta}_s), \qquad (10.3)$$

where $\boldsymbol{\varphi} = (\boldsymbol{\pi}, \boldsymbol{\Theta})$ denotes the vector of all unknown parameters to be estimated, and $\boldsymbol{\Theta} = (\boldsymbol{\theta}_1, \boldsymbol{\theta}_2, \ldots, \boldsymbol{\theta}_S)$. The random vector $\mathbf{y}_i$ is said to have a finite mixture distribution, with component densities $\{f_{i|s}(\mathbf{y}_i; \boldsymbol{\theta}_s)\}$ and mixing weights $\{\pi_s\}$. Note that, conditional on sample estimates of $\boldsymbol{\pi}$ and $\boldsymbol{\Theta}$, the posterior probability of observation i into class s is:

$$\alpha_{is} = \frac{\hat{\pi}_s f_{i|s}(\mathbf{y}_i; \hat{\boldsymbol{\theta}}_s)}{\displaystyle\sum_{s=1}^{S} \hat{\pi}_s f_{i|s}(\mathbf{y}_i; \hat{\boldsymbol{\theta}}_s)}. \qquad (10.4)$$

These α_{is}'s provide a "fluzzy clustering" of the observations into the S groups or classes and have often been used to classify a given sample into groups.

A large variety of parametric forms for the mixture components have been assumed in the literature, including discrete distributions such as the binomial (John, 1970a; Hasselblad, 1966), geometric (Harris, 1983), negative binomial (John, 1970a), hypergeometric (John, 1970a), poisson (John, 1970a; Hasselblad, 1969), and continuous densities such as the (univariate and multivariate) normal (Hasselblad, 1966; Wolfe, 1970), uniform (Gupta and Miyawaki, 1978), exponential (Everitt and Hand, 1981; Teicher, 1961), weibull (Mandelbaum and Harris, 1982), gamma (John, 1970b), and dirichlet (Antoniak, 1974), as well as several compound and truncated distributions. (Croon (1989), and Kamakura and Novak (1992) develop parametric mixture models for rank-ordered data.) A comprehensive overview of applications of specific parametric mixtures is provided by Titterington, Smith, and Makov (1985).

An interesting special case of mixture models is latent structure analysis which is founded upon the concept of local independence (Lazarsfeld and Henry, 1968). In latent structure analysis, the covariance between the components of the multivariate observations y_{ij} are assumed to be caused by the latent classes to which the observations belong. Within latent classes, the component mixtures are assumed to be independent:

$$f_{i|s}(\mathbf{y}_i; \boldsymbol{\theta}_s) = \prod_{j=1}^{J} f_{ij|s}(y_{ij}; \boldsymbol{\theta}_s). \qquad (10.5)$$

Lazarsfeld and Henry (1968) provided the first systematic treatment of latent structure analysis. Latent class models are subsumed under the general class of latent structure models and pertain to manifest categorical variables, the associations among which are explained by an unobserved discrete variable (see Dillon's, 1993, review in Chapter 9 for further details). In related latent trait models, associations among manifest categorical variables are explained from an underlying continuous construct (Langeheine, 1988). Both of these procedures are based on the axiom of local independence and have been extensively used in psychological test-theory (Langeheine and Rost, 1988). Goodman (1974a, b) first demonstrated how latent class models could be formulated in a general log-linear model framework, which could be estimated by maximum likelihood. Other contributions to the theory of latent structure analysis have been made by Haberman (1979), Clogg (1979), Goodman (1978, 1979), and Clogg and Goodman (1984, 1986). Textbooks dealing with this topic include those by Everitt (1984), Formann (1984), Bartholomew (1987), and Hagenaars (1990). Some recent developments can be found in the volume edited by Langeheine and Rost (1988).

Identifiability

A parametric family of mixtures is said to be identifiable if distinct values of the parameters determine distinct members of the mixture (McLachlan and Basford, 1988). Titterington, Smith, and Makov (1985) provide an overview of the identifiability of mixtures with specific component densities, demonstrating identifiability of such mixtures involving the normal, poisson, gamma, and the binomial. From a survey of the literature, they conclude that, apart from special cases with finite sample spaces or very special simple density functions (such as mixtures of uniform distributions and S-mixtures of binomial (n, p) distributions with $n < 2S - 1$), identifiability of classes of finite mixtures is generally assured. McLachlan and Basford (1988) have shown that the likelihood is invariant under interchanging of the labels of the latent classes, and propose to report only one of the possible arrangements of the classes, in order to alleviate this threat to identification. Local identification of mixture models can be established from the expected matrix of the second derivatives of the log-likelihood (Formann, 1992). Recent work on the identifiability of mixtures has been reported in Li and Sedransk (1988) and Lüxmann-Ellinghaus (1987).

Estimation

The purpose is to estimate the parameters of the finite mixture, φ, given y_{ij} and a value of S. To accomplish this, several methods can be used. Initially estimation of mixture models proceeded using the method of moments (Pearson, 1894; Charlier and Wicksell, 1924; Quandt and Ramsey, 1978), but later attention focussed on graphical techniques for detection of (univariate) mixtures (see Harding, 1948; Cassie, 1954; Bhattacharya, 1967; Fowlkes, 1979). (An overview of other estimating methods including the Bayesian, minimum distance, and recursive methods is provided by Titterington, Smith, and Makov, 1985). Hasselblad (1966, 1969) was one of the first to use maximum likelihood estimation for mixtures of two or more multivariate normals, as well as other distributions from the exponential family. As maximum likelihood has been found to be generally superior to the method of moments for the estimation of finite mixtures (Fryer and Robertson, 1972), the likelihood approach has become increasingly popular (McLachlan, 1982; Basford and McLachlan, 1985) and appears presently to be the most frequently used method (see Titterington, Smith, and Makov, 1985, for a review of its use). The likelihood for φ can be formulated as:

$$L(\varphi|\mathbf{y}) = \prod_{i=1}^{n} f_i(\mathbf{y}_i; \varphi). \qquad (10.6)$$

An estimate of φ can be obtained by maximizing the likelihood equation with respect to φ subject to the restrictions (1). This can be accomplished primarily in three ways: by using standard optimization routines such as the Newton-Raphson or Quasi Newton methods (see McHugh, 1956, 1958), the Method of Scoring (see Titterington, Smith, and Makov, 1985), or the Expectation-Maximization (EM) algorithm (Dempster, Laird, and Rubin, 1977). The Newton-Raphson and scoring methods require relatively few iterations to converge, and provide the asymptotic variances of the parameter estimates as a by-product, but convergence is not ensured. The EM can be programmed easily, iterations are computationally attractive, and convergence is ensured, but the algorithm often requires many iterations (see Titterington, Smith, and Makov, 1985; McLachlan and Basford, 1988). It is as yet unclear which of the two methods is to be preferred in general (see Langenheine, 1988; Mooijaart and van der Heijden, 1992), but the EM algorithm has apparently been some what more popular (Titterington, 1990). While most of the mixture likelihood approaches (beginning with Newcomb, 1886, and later Hasselblad 1966, 1969, and Wolfe 1970) have used iterative schemes corresponding to special cases of the EM algorithm, the formal applicability of this EM algorithm, with its attractive convergence properties, to finite mixture problems was recognized only after the developments of Dempster, Laird, and Rubin (1977), which were later supplemented by Boyles (1983), Wu (1983), and Redner and Walker (1984).

To derive the EM algorithm for latent class regression models, non-observed data, z_{is}, are introduced, indicating if observation i belongs to latent class s: $z_{is} = 1$ if i comes from latent class s and $z_{is} = 0$ otherwise. It is assumed that the z_{is} are i.i.d. multinomial, consisting of one draw on the S classes $G_1, \ldots, G_S$, with probabilities $\pi_1, \ldots, \pi_S$. With z_{is} considered as missing data, and assuming that $\mathbf{y}_1, \ldots, \mathbf{y}_n$ given $\mathbf{z}_1, \ldots, \mathbf{z}_n$ are conditionally independent, the complete log-likelihood function can be formed (Dempster, Laird, and Rubin, 1977):

$$\ln L_c(\varphi) = \sum_{i=1}^{n} \sum_{s=1}^{S} z_{is} \ln f_{i|s}(y_i; \theta_s) + \sum_{i=1}^{n} \sum_{s=1}^{S} z_{is} \ln \pi_s. \qquad (10.4)$$

This complete log-likelihood is maximized using the iterative EM-algorithm. Using some initial estimate of φ, $\varphi^{(0)}$, in the E-step the expectation of $L_c(\varphi^{(0)})$ is calculated with respect to the conditional distribution of the non-observed data z_{is}, given the observed data y_i and the provisional estimates $\varphi^{(0)}$. It can easily be seen that this expectation is obtained by replacing z_{is} in equation (10.7) by its current expected value, $E\{z_{is}|y, \varphi^{(0)}\}$, which, using Bayes' rule, can be shown to be identical to the posterior probability that y_i belongs to class s defined in equation (10.4).

In order to maximize $E\{\ln L_c(\varphi)\}$ with respect to φ in the M-step, the non-observed data z_{is} in (10.7) are replaced by their current expectations α_{is}. Maximizing $E\{\ln L_c(\varphi)\}$ with respect to π_s, subject to the constraints (in equation (10.1)) on these parameters, yields:

$$\hat{\pi}_s = \sum_{i=1}^{n} \hat{\alpha}_{is}/n. \qquad (10.8)$$

Maximizing $E\{\ln L_c(\varphi)\}$ with respect to θ_s leads to independently solving each of the S expressions:

$$\sum_{i=1}^{n} \hat{\alpha}_{is} (\partial \ln f_{i|s}(y_i; \theta_s)/\partial \theta_s) = 0, \qquad (s = 1, .., S) \qquad (10.9)$$

The E-and M-steps are alternated until no further improvement in the likelihood function is possible. Schematically, the EM algorithm may be described as follows:

1 Initialize the iteration index h, $h \leftarrow 0$; read the user specified value of S, and generate a starting partition, $\hat{\alpha}_{is}^{(0)}$. A random starting partition may be obtained or a rational start may be used.
2 Given the $\hat{\alpha}_{is}^{(h)}$, calculate M.L. estimates of the parameters of each component mixtures from equations (10.8) and (10.9)
3 Convergence test: if the change in the log-likelihood from iteration (h) to $(h + 1)$ is smaller than some positive constant, stop.
4 Increment iteration index: $h \leftarrow h + 1$, recalculate the posterior probabilities, $\alpha_{is}^{(h+1)}$, via equation (10.4) and return to step (2).

An attractive feature of the EM-algorithm is that the solution to the M-step (step (2) above) often provides closed form expressions for the parameter estimates, such as in the case of the normal density. Titterington, Smith, and Makov (1985) discuss the general form of the stationary equations for the mixture of distributions from the exponential family. A second attractive feature of the algorithm is that it provides monotone increasing values of the likelihood (Dempster, Laird and Rubin, 1977). Under mild conditions, the likelihood is bounded from above, so that convergence to at least a local optimum can be established using Jensen's inequality (cf. Titterington, Smith, and Makov, 1985). Boyles (1983) and Wu (1983) provide a discussion of the convergence properties of the EM algorithm. The problem of multiple maxima of the likelihood of mixture models is well documented (Titterington, Smith, and Makov, 1985). This problem can be minimized by performing several parameter estimations with different sets of starting values. Note, Hamilton (1991) proposed a Quasi-Bayesian approach to estimate univariate and multivariate normal mixtures, which consistently improves the maximum likelihood approach for this class of models. It eliminates the singularities associated with maximum likelihood estimation of normal mixtures, while it offers guidance for choosing among locally optimal solutions. Hamilton (1991) provides a Monte Carlo study which supports the performance of the Quasi-Bayesian over the maximum likelihood approach. The estimation equations are solved using an EM algorithm.

The preceding EM algorithm provides a general framework for estimating the various latent class regression models reviewed in the next two sections of this chapter. For these respective models (in step (2) of the algorithm), the derivatives (10.9) are taken with respect to the corresponding regression model parameters specified for each latent class. The specific estimation sub-routine employed in step (2) is dependent upon the structure of these models and the specification of the conditional densities. These issues will be further detailed in the respective sections of this chapter.

Tests for the number of classes

When applying mixture models to empirical data, the actual number of classes, S, is typically unknown. The problem of identifying the number of classes is the inference problem in mixture models with the least satisfactory statistical treatment (Titterington, 1990). Both Titterington, Smith, and Makov (1985) and McLachlan and Basford (1988) each devote an entire chapter to this topic. The problem is that the standard generalized likelihood ratio statistic to test the null-hypothesis (H_0) of S classes against the alternative hypothesis (H_1) of $S + 1$ classes is not asymptotically distributed as chisquare, because H_0 corresponds to a boundary of the parameter space for H_1, so that under H_0 the generalized likelihood ratio test statistic is not (asymptotically) a full rank quadratic form (Aitkin and Rubin, 1985; Ghosh and Sen, 1985; Li and Sedransk, 1988; Titterington, 1990).

Various tests for determining the number of classes have been proposed for special types of mixtures (see Titterington, Smith, and Makov, 1985; Anderson, 1985; Henna, 1985; Yarmal-Vuarl and Ataman, 1987). Monte Carlo test procedures have been applied to mixture problems by Aitkin, Anderson, and Hinde (1981), and McLachlan (1987). These procedures involves comparing the likelihood ratio statistic for $S + 1$ versus S classes from the real data with a distribution of that statistic obtained from K datasets containing S classes, which are generated by replacing the unknown parameters in the densities by their likelihood estimates from the original data. This procedure is computationally very cumbersome however (cf. McLachlan and Basford, 1988), while the observed rejection rates do not quite conform to the intended levels under the null-hypothesis (Titterington, 1990).

Another class of techniques for testing the number of components present are those based on information criteria in which a penalty, proportional to the number of parameters estimated, is imposed on the maximized log-likelihood:

$$C = - 2 \, ln \, L - td, \tag{10.10}$$

where t denotes the number of parameters estimated, and d is some constant. Sclove (1977) and Bozdogan and Sclove (1984) proposed the use of Akaike's Information criterion (AIC; Akaike, 1974) to determine the number of classes; with the AIC, d = 2 in equation (10.10). Two criteria related to the AIC statistic are Schwartz's (1978) Bayesian Information Criterion (BIC), where d = $ln(n)$, and Bozdogan's (1987) consistent AIC (CAIC), where d = $ln(n)$ + 1. Both of these statistics impose an additional sample size penalty on the log-likelihood, and are more conservative than the AIC statistic tending to favor more parsimonious models. They are particularly recommended when the data entail a large number of observations. That value of S is chosen for which the fit, as judged by these various criteria, is acceptable (i.e. select S which renders the minimum value). The major problem with the use of these criteria, and AIC in particular, is that they rely on the same asymptotic properties as the likelihood ratio test (Sclove, 1987), and can therefore only be used as indicative of the number of classes actually present. Recent work underway by Windham and Cutler (1991) using the estimated information matrix and the rates of convergence to estimate the number of classes appears as a promising alternative in this regard.

While the above heuristics account for overparameterization as large number of classes are derived, one must also ensure that the group centroids of the conditional densities are sufficiently separated for the solution that is selected. To assess the separation of the latent classes (for $S > 1$), an entropy measure can be utilized (see DeSarbo, Wedel, Vriens, and Ramaswamy, 1992) to examine the degree of fuzziness in latent class membership based on the estimated posterior probabilities:

$$E_S = 1 - \left[\sum_{i=1}^{n} \sum_{s=1}^{S} - \hat{\alpha}_{is} \ln \hat{\alpha}_{is} \right] / n \ln S \qquad (10.11)$$

E_S is a relative measure that is bounded between 0 and 1. A value of E_S close to zero, indicating that all the posteriors are equal for each observation, is of concern as it implies that the centroids of the conditional parametric distributions are not sufficiently well separated.

Latent Class Regression Models

There are a large number of applications in the physical and social sciences where the purpose of the analysis is the estimation of a linear model relating a dependent variable to a set of explanatory variables (see McCullagh and Nelder, 1989). In many of those applications however, the estimation of a single set of regression coefficients across all observations may be inadequate and potentially misleading if the observations arise from a number of (unknown) heterogeneous groups in which the coefficients differ. It is in these situations that latent class regression models have recently proven to be of great value. These latent class regression models, to be discussed in the sequel, are alternatively referred to as clusterwise regression models, a term originally coined by Späth (1979) for procedures that simultaneously cluster observations into a number of classes (using an exchange algorithm) and estimate regression models within each class (see also DeSarbo, Oliver, and Rangaswamy, 1990; Wedel and Kistmaker, 1989.

The literature on latent class regression models will be classified by the type of data to which the models are calibrated: normal distributed data, binary data, count data, constant sum data, or data arising from any member of the exponential family. Further, recently developed concomitant variable latent class regression models will be discussed. A taxonomy of the development of latent class regression models is provided in Table 10.1, where the order of presentation corresponds to the order in which the models are discussed by data-type below.

Latent class regression models for normal data

Work on regression mixtures was initiated by Quandt (1972), who introduced switching regression models, later extended by Hosmer (1974), and Quandt and Ramsey (1978). In switching regressions models, a linear function relating a univariate dependent variable $\mathbf{y}_i = (y_i)$ to P explanatory variables $\mathbf{x}_i = (x_{ip})$ $(i = 1, \ldots, n; p = 1, \ldots, P)$ is postulated:

$$y_i = \mathbf{x}_i \boldsymbol{\beta}_s + \varepsilon_i, \qquad (10.12)$$

Table 10.1 Applications of mixture regression models[a], [b]

Reference	Mixture type	Estimation method	Application
Normal data			
Quandt and Ramsey (1978)	Univariate normal	MD	Wage prediction
Quandt (1972)	Univariate normal	ML, NR	Housing construction
Goldfeld and Quandt (1973)	Univariate normal, hidden Markov	ML, NR	Housing construction
Cosslett and Lee (1985)	Univariate normal, hidden Markov regression	ML, NR	Cartel stability
Hamilton (1989)	Multivariate normal, hidden Markov time series	ML, NR	GNP-growth
Hamilton (1990)	Multivariate normal, hidden Markov time series	ML, EM	—
Hamilton (1991)	Multivariate normal, hidden Markov time series	QB, EM	Exchange rates
Engel and Hamilton (1990)	Multivariate normal, hidden Markov time series	ML, EM	Exchange rates
DeSarbo and Cron (1988)	Univariate normal	ML, EM	Trade show performance
Ramaswamy, DeSarbo, Reibstein and Robinson (1993)	Multivariate normal	ML, EM	Latent pooling for marketing Mix effects
DeSarbo, Wedel, Vriens and Ramaswamy (1992)	Multivariate normal	ML, EM	Metric conjoint analysis
Helsen, Jedidi, and DeSarbo (1992)	Multivariate normal	ML, EM	Country segmentation
Binary data			
Kamakura and Russell (1989)	Multinomial logit	ML, NR	Price segmentation
Kamakura (1992)	Multivariate multinomial logit	ML, NR	Value systems segmentation

Table 10.1 (*Contd.*)

Reference	Mixture type	Estimation method	Application
Bucklin and Gupta (1992)	Nested mult nomial logit	ML, NR	Purchase incidence and brand choice
Lwin and Martin (1989)	Binomial probit	ML, EM, NR	Parasite treatment resistance
De Soete and DeSarbo (1991)	Binomial probit	ML, EM	Choice of communication devices
Follmann and Lambert (1989)	Binomial logit, varying intercepts	ML, EM	Protozoan death rates
Wedel and DeSarbo (1992a)	Binomial logit	ML, EM	Paired comparison risk perception
Wedel and Leeflang (1992)	Binomial logit spline	ML, EM	Gabor Granger price experiments
Kamakura (1991)	Multinomial probit	ML, NR	External unfolding
Count data			
Wedel, DeSarbo, Bult, and Ramaswamy (1991)	Poisson	ML, EM	Direct mail address selection
Bucklin, Gupta, and Siddarth (1991)	Truncated poisson	ML, NR	Purchase frequency
Ramaswamy, Anderson, and DeSarbo (1993)	Negative Binomial	ML, EM	Purchase frequency
Constant sum data			
DeSarbo, Ramaswamy, and Chatterjee (1992)	Multivariate dirichlet	ML, EM	Multivariate constant sum conjoint analysis
Generalized linear model			
Wedel and DeSarbo (1992b)	Exponential family	ML, EM	Poisson regression coupon usage
Concomitant variable models			
Formann (1992)	Multinomial logit	ML, EM	Social mobility tables
Gupta and Chintagunta (1992)	Multinomial logit, probit and poisson	ML, NR	Scanner brand choice data

[a] ML = maximum likelihood; EM = expectation maximization algorithm; NR = Newton-Raphson algorithm; MD = minimum distance; QB = quasi-Bayes.

[b] Order of references conforms to their appearance in the text.

where the first component of x_i is a dummy variable taking the value 1, and the disturbance term ε_i is normally distributed with mean zero and variance σ^2. The parameters $\boldsymbol{\beta}_s = ((\beta_{ps}))$ take (for two "regimes") one of two unknown values for $s = 1$ and $s = 2$, depending on the unobserved "regime" that applies. The two unobserved regimes are represented by an underlying categorical variable denoting from which regime an observation arises. A two-component latent class regression model results. Goldfeld and Quandt (1973, 1976) and Cosslett and Lee (1985) develop hidden Markov switching regression models in which membership of observations in a regime is modelled by a Markov process. Hamilton (1989, 1990, 1991) and Engel and Hamilton (1990) extend the switching regression approach to time series models. The models describe discrete shifts in autoregressive parameters, where the shifts themselves are modeled by a hidden discrete-time Markov process. Whereas initially estimation was limited to small systems due to computational complexity involved in maximizing the likelihood (Hamilton, 1989), Hamilton (1990) proposed an EM algorithm that alleviates these problems by using the calculation of smoothed posterior probabilities in the E-step. In a third paper, Hamilton (1991) demonstrates advantages of the Quasi-Bayesian over the maximum likelihood approach for estimating the parameters, alleviating problems with potential singularities of the likelihood. The model was applied to the analysis of exchange rates (Engel and Hamilton, 1990; Hamilton, 1991). Titterington, Smith, and Makov (1985) review applications of switching regressions in economics.

DeSarbo and Cron (1988) first extended the stochastic switching regression models to more than two regimes. Assuming S component densities, with prior probabilities π_s ($s = 1, \ldots, S$) as above, they formulate the conditional distribution of the dependent variable, given s, as:

$$f_{i|s}(y_i; \boldsymbol{\beta}_s, \sigma_s^2) = (2\pi\sigma_s^2)^{-1/2} \exp\left\{\frac{-(y_i - x_i\boldsymbol{\beta}_s)^2}{2\sigma_s^2}\right\}, \tag{10.13}$$

which is conceptually similar to normal mixture approaches originally proposed by Wolfe (1970) and Day (1969), with the component means replaced by a linear predictor involving x_i. The unconditional distribution follows from equation (10.3), and the likelihood from (10.6). (Unless the condition $\sigma_s^2 > 0$ is imposed, the likelihood is unbounded.) To estimate the parameters φ (where φ denotes the vector of all unknown parameters), the likelihood is maximized using the EM-algorithm, the development of which is analogous to that provided for unconditional mixtures in the previous section. Estimates of the posterior probabilities in the E-step, given provisional estimates $\varphi^{(0)}$, are given by (10.4), and estimates of the prior probabilities are given by (10.8). In the M-step, closed form expressions for the estimates of the parameters $\boldsymbol{\beta}_s$ and σ_s^2 are:

$$\hat{\boldsymbol{\beta}}_s = \sum_{i=1}^{n} \hat{\alpha}_{is}(x_i' x_i)^{-1} \sum_{i=1}^{n} \hat{\alpha}_{is}(x_i' y_i), \tag{10.14}$$

$$\hat{\sigma}_s^2 = \sum_{i=1}^{n} \hat{\alpha}_{is} \, (y_i - x_i\hat{\beta}_s)^2 / \sum_{i=1}^{n} \hat{\alpha}_{is}. \tag{10.15}$$

DeSarbo and Cron provided a modest Monte Carlo analysis supporting the performance of the EM-algorithm under a variety of conditions. Whereas the above approach presents a univariate normal regression mixture, extensions to multivariate normal regression mixtures where repeated and correlated measures on each observational unit are present have also been developed (cf. Ramaswamy, DeSarbo, Reibstein, and Robinson, 1993; DeSarbo, Wedel, Vriens, and Ramaswamy, 1992; Helsen, Jedidi, and DeSarbo, 1992). Here, the conditional multivariate density of the dependent vectors $\mathbf{y}_i = ((y_{ij}))$, where j $(j = 1, \ldots, J)$ indexes replications, given S, is:

$$f_{i|s} \, (\mathbf{y}_i; \, \boldsymbol{\beta}_s, \, \boldsymbol{\Sigma}_s) = (2\pi)^{-1/2} |\boldsymbol{\Sigma}_s|^{-1/2}$$
$$\exp\left\{ -\frac{1}{2} \, (\mathbf{y}_i - x_i\boldsymbol{\beta}_s)' \, \boldsymbol{\Sigma}_s^{-1} \, (\mathbf{y}_i - x_i\boldsymbol{\beta}_s) \right\}, \tag{10.16}$$

where $\boldsymbol{\Sigma}_s$ denotes the variance–covariance matrix of $\mathbf{y}_i$ given class s. The unconditional density and likelihood are obtained from (10.3) and (10.6), estimates of the posterior and prior probabilities from (10.4) and (10.8). The EM algorithm is applied to maximize the likelihood for this model. Closed form expressions can be obtained for the parameters in the M-step as:

$$\hat{\boldsymbol{\beta}}_s = \left[\sum_{i=1}^{n} \hat{\alpha}_{is} \, (x_i' \boldsymbol{\Sigma}_s^{-1} x_i) \right]^{-1} \left[\sum_{i=1}^{n} \hat{\alpha}_{is} \, (x_i' \boldsymbol{\Sigma}_s^{-1} \mathbf{y}_i) \right], \tag{10.17}$$

$$\hat{\boldsymbol{\Sigma}}_s = \sum_{i=1}^{n} \hat{\alpha}_{is} \, (\mathbf{y}_i - x_i\hat{\boldsymbol{\beta}}_s)(\mathbf{y}_i - x_i\hat{\boldsymbol{\beta}}_s)' / \sum_{i=1}^{n} \hat{\alpha}_{is}. \tag{10.18}$$

The above multivariate normal regression mixture has been applied to the analysis of conjoint measurement data (DeSarbo, Wedel, Vriens, and Ramaswamy, 1992), as a latent pooling method for simultaneously pooling and estimating linear regression models for cross-sectional-time-series data (Ramaswamy, DeSarbo, Reibstein, and Robinson, 1993), and to the analysis of diffusion patterns of consumer durable goods within segments of countries (Helsen, Jedidi, and DeSarbo, 1992). We later provide an application of this methodology to the measurement of service quality.

Latent class regression models for binary data

A mixture regression model for a multinomially distributed dependent variable was developed by Kamakura and Russell (1989). The dependent variable constitutes consumers' choices among a set of products or brands, where $y_{ijt} = 1$ if consumer i chooses brand j at time $t(j = 1, \ldots, J;$ $t = 1, \ldots, T)$ and $y_{ijt} = 0$ otherwise. The independent variables are denoted by $x_{ijt} = (x_{ijpt})$. The model is derived from random utility theory (McFadden, 1973), whereby conditional upon class s, the stochastic utility for a specific alternative j is formulated as a linear function of explanatory variables and an error term. The assumption that the error terms of the utility are distributed i.i.d. weibull leads to a multinomial logit model for the choices within class s, with conditional probabilities:

$$p_{ijt|s} (y_{ijt}; \boldsymbol{\beta}_s) = \frac{\exp(x_{ijt}\boldsymbol{\beta}_s)}{\sum\limits_{j=1}^{J} \exp(x_{ijt}\boldsymbol{\beta}_s)} . \tag{10.19}$$

The conditional density is given by:

$$f_{i|s} (y_{ijt}; \boldsymbol{\beta}_s) = \prod_{t=1}^{T} \prod_{j=1}^{J} p_{ijt|s}^{y_{ijt}} . \tag{10.20}$$

Expressions for the unconditional density, the likelihood, and posterior probabilities follow from (10.3), (10.5), (10.4). Kamakura and Russell maximized the likelihood for the multinomial mixture logistic regression model using a Newton-Raphson algorithm. The authors apply the latent class multinomial logit to the identification of segments of consumers that differ in price-sensitivity. Kamakura (1992) extended the latent class multinomial logit to a model for multiple dependent variables, assumed to be multinomially distributed and locally independent given segment s, which are modelled from a common set of explanatory variables. This model was applied to the analysis of value systems.

Another extension of the latent class multinomial logit was recently proposed by Bucklin and Gupta (1992) who proposed a latent class nested multinomial logit which models purchase incidence and brand choice simultaneously within S choice segments and R purchase incidence segments. The unconditional choice probabilities for this model are given by:

$$p_{ijt} (y_{ijt}, d_{it}; \boldsymbol{\varphi}) = \sum_{s=1}^{S} \sum_{r=1}^{R} \pi_{rs} p_{ijt|s} (y_{ijt};\boldsymbol{\beta}_s) p_{it|r} (d_{it}; \mathbf{v}_r), \tag{10.21}$$

where the subscript t indicates time periods ($t = 1, \ldots, T$), and $d_{it} = 1$ if a category purchase was made by household i at time t, and $y_{ijt} = 1$ if brand j was chosen by household i at time t. The term $p_{ijt|s}(\bullet)$ denotes the conditional probability that brand j is chosen, given a purchase of the product category at time t and segment s. This probability is modelled as a logit function of a set of explanatory variables, analogous to equation

(10.19). Here $p_{it|r}(\bullet)$ denotes the purchase incidence probability of the product category at time t, given purchase incidence segment r. This probability is modelled as a logit function of a set of explanatory variables and parameters v_r, and an inclusive category value calculated from the brand choice model (Ben-Akiva and Lerman, 1985). The parameters of the model are estimated using a sequential procedure based on maximum likelihood. Initially households are classified into S segments on the basis of the brand choice model, and then the households are classified into R purchase incidence segments within each of the S choice segments, on the basis of the purchase incidence model. The model was applied to scanner panel data on household purchases of liquid detergents.

Lwin and Martin (1989), and De Soete and DeSarbo (1991) developed binomial mixture probit regression models for pick-any out of J data in which the conditional choice probabilities of $y_{ij} = 1$, indicating that subject i picks object j, given s, are given by:

$$p_{ijt|s}(y_{ijt}; \boldsymbol{\beta}_s) = \Phi(\mathbf{x}_{ij}\boldsymbol{\beta}_s), \qquad (10.22)$$

where $\Phi(\bullet)$ represents the cumulative normal distribution function. Follman and Lambert (1989) and Wedel and DeSarbo (1992a) propose mixtures of binomial logit regressions in which the choice probabilities are given by:

$$p_{ij|s}(y_{ijt}; \boldsymbol{\beta}_s) = \frac{\exp(\mathbf{x}_{ij}\boldsymbol{\beta}_s)}{1 + \exp(\mathbf{x}_{ij}\boldsymbol{\beta}_s)}. \qquad (10.23)$$

(In the Follman and Lambert model, only the intercepts are allowed to vary across the S classes.) The conditional distribution of y_{ij} for the mixture logit and probit regression models is:

$$f_{i|s}(y_{ij}; \boldsymbol{\beta}_s) = \prod_{j=1}^{J} p_{ij|s}(y_{ij}; \boldsymbol{\beta}_s)^{y_{ij}}(1 - p_{ij|s}(y_{ij}; \boldsymbol{\beta}_s))^{1-y_{ij}}. \qquad (10.24)$$

The unconditional distribution is given by (10.3), and the likelihood by (10.6). The above authors all use the EM-algorithm to maximize the likelihood. The estimates of the posterior probabilities in the E-step are given in (10.4). The estimates of $\boldsymbol{\beta}_s$ in the M-step are obtained from the stationary equations. These equations follow from (10.9) where the derivatives are now taken with respect to $\boldsymbol{\beta}_s$. Fisher's scoring method (De Soete and DeSarbo, 1991) or the method of iterative reweighted least-squares (Wedel and DeSarbo, 1992a) are used to solve these equations. Lwin and Martin (1989) employed a Newton-Raphson procedure to maximize the likelihood across the entire parameter space. Wedel and DeSarbo (1992a) perform a small Monte Carlo study which supports the performance of the algorithm under a variety of data conditions. The binomial mixture regression models have been applied to the analysis of the effects of a poison on the death-rate of a protozoan trypanosome (Follmann and Lambert, 1989), to the analysis of the resistance to treatment of parasites of sheep as a function of the treatment dose (Lwin and Martin, 1989), to data on consumers' choices of communication devices as a function of the attributes of such devices (De Soete and DeSarbo, 1991), and to the analysis of paired comparison choices of consumers' indicating perceived risk with respect to automobiles, as a function of the attributes of these automobiles (Wedel and DeSarbo, 1992a). Wedel and Leeflang (1992) extended the mixture binomial logit of Wedel and DeSarbo (1992a) to include regression splines, and applied their model to the analyses of consumers (binary) purchase responses to incremental price-levels in so called Gabor Granger price experiments.

Kamakura (1991) proposed a latent class multinomial probit regression model. Formulation and estimation of this model, using a Newton-Raphson procedure, is analogous to that of the Kamakura and Russell (1989) latent class multinomial logit model, with expression (10.19) replaced by a multivariate probit function. The latent class multinomial probit regression procedure was used to estimate a mixture of (external) ideal-point models on data on pairwise choices among a number of stimuli.

Latent class regression models for count data

Wedel, DeSarbo, Bult, and Ramaswamy (1991) proposed a latent class poisson regression, Bucklin, Gupta, and Siddarth (1991) a latent class truncated poisson regression, and Ramaswamy, Anderson, and DeSarbo (1993) a latent class negative binomial regression model. These models assume that the dependent variable y_{ijt} constitutes an integer count of, say, a number of products purchased by consumer i at time period t, following a poisson, a truncated poisson, or a negative binomial process respectively. Conditional upon class s, the expectation of these observations is modelled as:

$$\lambda_{it|s} = \exp\{\mathbf{x}_{it}\,\boldsymbol{\beta}_s\}. \tag{10.25}$$

The conditional densities for the poisson, truncated poisson, and negative binomial are then respectively:

$$f_{i|s}(y_{it}, t_{it}; \boldsymbol{\beta}_s) = \prod_{t=1}^{T} \frac{\exp\{-\lambda_{it|s}\,t_{it}\}(\lambda_{it|s}\,t_{it})^{y_{it}}}{y_{it}!}, \tag{10.26}$$

$$f_{i|s}(y_{it}; \boldsymbol{\beta}_s) = \prod_{t=1}^{T} \frac{\exp\{-\lambda_{it|s}\}(\lambda_{it|s})^{y_{it}}}{(1 - \exp\{-\lambda_{it|s}\})\,y_{it}!}, \tag{10.27}$$

$$f_{i|s}(y_{it}; \boldsymbol{\beta}_s) = \prod_{t=1}^{T} \frac{\Gamma(\delta + y_{it})}{y_{it}!\,\Gamma(\delta)}\left[\frac{\delta}{\delta + \lambda_{it|s}}\right]\left[\frac{\lambda_{it|s}}{\delta + \lambda_{it|s}}\right]^{y_{it}}, \tag{10.28}$$

where t_{it} denotes the length of time period t for subject i which is included as an offset in the poisson model, δ denotes the precision parameter of the NBD, and $\Gamma(\bullet)$ the gamma function. The truncated poisson accommodates non-zero positive counts, and the negative binomial accommodates heterogeneity within classes through the precision parameter. The likelihood of these models is obtained from (10.3) and (10.6), the posterior probabilities from (10.4). Whereas Bucklin, Gupta, and Siddarth (1991) use a Newton-Raphson method to maximize the likelihood over the entire parameter space, Wedel, DeSarbo, Bult, and Ramaswamy (1991), and Ramaswamy, Anderson, and DeSarbo (1993) use an EM-algorithm, the development of which follows from equations (10.7), (10.8) and (10.9), where the derivatives in (10.9) are taken with respect to β_s (respectively δ). Bucklin, Gupta, and Siddarth (1991) and Ramaswamy, Anderson, and DeSarbo (1993) apply their models to scanner data on purchase frequencies of non-durable goods, while Wedel, DeSarbo, Bult, and Ramaswamy (1991) apply their model to the selection of customers from direct mail databases.

A latent class regression model for constant sum data

For the analysis of multivariate constant-sum data, DeSarbo, Ramaswamy, and Chatterjee (1992) proposed a latent class dirichlet regression model. In this model, K dependent variables, with J replications per observational unit each, are assumed to be dirichlet, with parameters θ_{jks}, conditional upon segment s. These θ_{jks} are reparameterized in terms of a common set of explanatory variables $x_j = (x_{jp})$, and a set of coefficients $\beta_{ks} = (\beta_{kps})$:

$$\theta_{jks} = \exp\{x_j\beta_{ks}\}. \tag{10.29}$$

The conditional density, given s, is:

$$f_{i|s}(y_{ijk}; \beta_{ks}) = \prod_{j=1}^{J} \frac{\Gamma\left(\sum_{k=1}^{K}\theta_{jks}\right)}{\prod_{k=1}^{K}\Gamma(\theta_{jks})} \prod_{k=1}^{K} y_{ijk}^{\alpha_{jks}-1}. \tag{10.30}$$

The unconditional distribution and the likelihood follow from (10.3) and (10.6). The authors estimate the model using the EM-algorithm, where estimates of the posteriors in the E-step are obtained from (10.4), and in the M-step the estimates of the priors are obtained from (10.8), the estimates of β_{ks} are obtained from the stationary equations (10.9), with the derivatives taken with respect to β_{ks}. DeSarbo, Ramaswamy, and Chatterjee (1992) use a gradient based search to solve these stationary equations in the M-step. The model was applied to a conjoint study on industrial purchasing in which a sample of managers provided constant sum ratings of profiles of product-types on a set of supplier selection criteria.

A general latent class regression model for data from the exponential family

Wedel and DeSarbo (1992b) propose a generalized linear regression mixture model. This model handles many of the above existing mixture regression procedures as special cases, as well as a host of other parametric specifications in the exponential family heretofore not mentioned in the latent class regression literature. Conditional upon class s, a generalized linear model (McCullagh and Nelder, 1989) is formulated consisting of a specification of the distribution of the dependent variable, y_i, as one of the exponential family, a linear predictor, η_{is}, and a function $g(\bullet)$, which links the random and systematic components. The conditional probability density function of y_i, given class s, takes the form:

$$f_{i|s}(y_i \mid \theta_{is}, \lambda_s) = \exp\{y_i\,\theta_{is} - b(\theta_{is}))/a(\lambda_s) + c(y_i, \lambda_s)\}, \qquad (10.31)$$

for specific functions $a(\bullet)$, $b(\bullet)$ and $c(\bullet)$, where conditional upon class s, the y_i are i.i.d. with canonical parameters θ_{is} and means μ_{is}. The parameter λ_s is a dispersion parameter, and is assumed to be constant over observations in class i, while $a(\lambda_s) > 0$. The link function $g(\bullet)$ is defined as:

$$\eta_{is} = g(\mu_{is}), \qquad (10.32)$$

where the linear predictor is produced by the covariates x_i and the parameter vectors β_s in class s:

$$\eta_{is} = x_i\,\beta_s. \qquad (10.34)$$

So called canonical links occur when $\theta_{ij} = \eta_{ij}$ (respectively the identity, log, logit, inverse, and squared inverse functions for the normal, poisson, binomial, gamma, and inverse gaussian distributions; see McCullagh and Nelder, 1989). An estimate of the parameters is obtained by maximizing the likelihood equation, obtained from (10.6). The authors show that this can be done using an EM-algorithm. In the E-step, estimates of the posterior probabilities are obtained from (10.4). In the M-step, estimates of the prior probabilities are obtained from (10.8), while estimates of the regression parameters are obtained from the stationary equations (10.9), where the derivatives are taken with respect to the parameters β_s and λ_s. The stationary equations are:

$$\sum_{i=1}^{n} \hat{\alpha}_{is}^{(0)}\, V_{is}\,(y_i - \mu_{is})\,x_{ip}\,\frac{d\mu_{is}}{d\eta_{is}} = 0. \qquad (10.34)$$

Equation (10.34) is the ordinary stationary equation of a generalized linear model fitted across all observations, where observation j contributes to the estimating equations with fixed weights $\hat{\alpha}_{is}^{(0)}$. Wedel and DeSarbo propose to solve the stationary equations in the M-step, for each class s, using the iterative reweighted least squares procedure proposed by Nelder and Wedderburn (1972) for ML estimation of generalized linear models, with each observation weighted with $\hat{\alpha}_{is}^{(0)}$. The procedure was illustrated by Wedel and DeSarbo (1992b) with an application to the analysis of consumers' coupon usage.

An Application of Latent Class Regression to Conjoint Analysis: Service Quality Measurement

The early exploratory research of Parasuraman, Zeithaml, and Berry (1985) revealed that the primary criteria utilized by consumers in assessing service quality can be described by some ten separate dimensions:

1 tangibles
2 reliability
3 responsiveness
4 communication
5 credibility
6 security
7 competence
8 courtesy
9 understanding/knowing the consumer
10 access.

Table 10.2 Parasuraman, Zeithaml, and Berry (1985) determinants of service quality

---

Reliability involves consistency of performance and dependability.
It means that the firm performs the service right the first time.
It also means that the firm honors its promises. Specifically, it involves:
• accuracy in billing;
• keeping records correctly;
• performing the service at the designated time.

Responsiveness concerns the willingness or readiness of employees to provide service. It involves timeliness of service:
• mailing a transaction slip immediately;
• calling the customer back quickly;
• giving prompt service (e.g. setting up appointments quickly).

Competence means possession of the required skills and knowledge to perform the service. It involves:
• knowledge and skill of the contact personnel;

Table 10.2 (*Contd.*)

- knowledge and skill of operational support personnel;
- research capability of the organization, e.g. securities brokerage firm.

Access involves approachability and ease of contact. It means:
- the service is easily accessible by telephone (lines are not busy and they don't put you on hold);
- waiting time to receive service (e.g. at a bank) is not extensive;
- convenient hours of operation;
- convenient location of service facility.

Courtesy involves politeness, respect, consideration
- consideration for the consumer's property (e.g. no muddy shoes on the carpet);
- clean and neat appearance of public contact personnel.

Communication means keeping customers informed in language they can understand and listening to them. It may mean that the company has to adjust its language for different consumers – increasing the level of sophistication with a well-educated customer and speaking simply and plainly with a novice. It involves:
- explaining the service itself;
- explaining how much the service will cost;
- explaining the trade-offs between service and cost;
- assuring the consumer that a problem will be handled.

Credibility involves trustworthiness, believability
- company name;
- company reputation;
- personal characteristics of the contact personnel;
- the degree of hard sell involved in interactions with the customer.

Security is the freedom from danger
- physical safety (Will I get mugged at the automatic teller machine?);
- financial security (Does the company know where my stock certificate is?);
- confidentiality (Are my dealings with the company private?).

Understanding/knowing the customer involves making the effort to understand the customer's needs. It involves:
- learning the customer's specific requirements;
- providing individualized attention;
- recognizing the regular customer.

Tangibles include the physical evidence of the service: physical facilities;
- appearance of personnel;
- tools or equipment used to provide the service;
- physical representations of the service
- other customers in the service facility.

Source Taken from Parasuraman, Zeithaml, and Berry (1985).

Table 10.2 presents the actual description of these ten dimensions from these authors which serves as the essential structure of the service-quality domain from which specific items were derived for the SERVQUAL instrument.

In its present form (see Parasuraman, Zeithaml, and Berry, 1988), SERV-QUAL contains 22 pairs of Likert-type items. One set of measures, containing one item from each pair, is utilized to measure customers' expected levels of services for a particular service industry as a way of calibrating expectations. The second remaining set of measures, containing the other item from each pair, is intended to measure customers' perceived level of service provided by a specific service company as a way of calibrating perceptions. An aggregate measure of service quality is then formulated by summing the difference scores between the corresponding set of items (i.e. perceptions minus expectations).

Since this important work, several authors have criticized the use of this instrument in actual applied settings. Carman (1990) suggested that the number and type of dimensions may vary by service category. He also found problems in attempting to use the same wording across different service categories, as well as ambiguity in dealing with services that provide multiple service functions (e.g hospitals). Another valid criticism of Carman (1990) concerns the analysis of the difference scores between percep-tions and expectations collected separately in the SERVQUAL framework and his questioning of the psychometric properties of such a difference scale. Babakus and Boller (1992) have also criticized the SERVQUAL ap-proach in that the number of dimensions is likely to depend upon the service category under study. These authors also question the use of difference scores formed from subtracting expectations from perceptions. The mixed wording utilized in SERVQUAL, according to Babakus and Boller (1992), may also lead to superficial method factors in subsequent analyses. Cronin and Taylor (1992) more recently claim that the SERVQUAL instru-ment confounds the measurement of service satisfaction with service quality. In the empirical work these authors performed, the individual SERVQUAL item reliabilities and the convergent and discriminant validity of the measures were found questionable.

DeSarbo, Huff, Rolandelli, and Choi (1993) recently devised an alternat-ive measurement scheme for the measurement of perceived service quality based on conjoint analysis (Green and Rao, 1971) that can be easily modified to any service category. They propose the use of this measure-ment procedure in the general SERVQUAL framework utilizing service-specific category operationalizations of the 10 dimensions originally proposed by Parasuraman, Zeithaml, and Berry (1988) in an expectancy confirma-tion/disconfirmation response manner. The advantages of this procedure are (1) it measures true perceptions, as opposed to perceptions confounded with expectations and satisfaction as in the Parasuraman, Zeithaml and Berry approach; (2) the number, type, and operationalization of the specific dimensions (vis- à-vis the wording) are completely flexible accord-ing to the specific usage scenario; (3) estimation can be performed in an efficient manner utilizing orthogonal designs and simple OLS; (4) the proposed model can lead to interesting quality optimization models, as well as models that explore segmentation. DeSarbo et al. (1993) illustrate this approach with respect to service quality perceptions of banks and dental offices. We will briefly review their research design for service quality evaluation of banks, and apply the DeSarbo, Wedel, Vriens, and Ramaswamy (1992) latent class conjoint regression methodology to this data to explore sample heterogeneity in terms of market segments.

Study design

Based on several in-depth interviews with students and an extensive literature review (e.g. Parasuraman, Zeithaml, and Berry (1988) have previously examined banks), DeSarbo *et al.* (1993) generated tailor-made operationalizations of the original set of 10 SERVQUAL *dimensions for banks shown in Table 10.3. The authors chose to* split the tangibles factor into two separate variables for banks due to the (*a priori* determined) importance and complexity of this factor, resulting in 11 conjoint factors. In the absence of prior theory, and to reduce respondent fatigue, a 3^{11} fractional factorial design was selected for main effects-only estimation (see Addelman, 1962).

Table 10.3 SERVQUAL factors utilized in conjoint experiment

Banks	SERVQUAL dimensions
A Facility and equipment	⇐ Tangibles
B Selection and quality of financial offerings	
C Accuracy and dependability	⇐ Reliability
D Speed of service	⇐ Responsiveness
E Communication with customers	⇐ Communication
F Reputation for honesty and integrity	⇐ Credibility
G Financial strength and security	⇐ Security
H Knowledge and competence of personnel	⇐ Competence
I Politeness and courtesy of personnel	⇐ Courtesy
J Understanding of individual customer needs	⇐ Understanding
K Convenience of location and operating hours	⇐ Access

The actual design matrix, converted to dummy variables, is shown in Table 10.4. Twenty-seven profiles were used for estimation, and the last three profiles for validation. Note that the levels of each factor are coded so that "same as expected" is always represented by (0,0), while "worse than expected" is represented by (1,0), and "better than expected" is represented by (0,1). This was purposely done in order to directly estimate possible asymmetric effects between the positive and negative level states for each of the factors. The estimates for the intermediate or neutral level, "same as expected," for each factor are thus confounded with the intercept term.

After two rounds of pretesting, a questionnaire was developed for banks. Respondents were first asked to list the attributes s/he thought were important in their use of banks in an open ended framework. They were then asked to evaluate the importance of the 11 factors described in Table 10.3 on a 9-point scale. The conjoint task then followed where the 30 profiles were randomized, as well as the order of the factors. The authors then asked a battery of questions concerning the respondents' evaluations of their current bank including an overall quality assessment, ratings of their bank's performance on these 11 factors based on their previous expectations, and usage and experience levels with the particular aspects of banks. Finally, demographic questions concerning age, marital status, gender, home ownership, and level of education were included in the survey. Fifty-three students completed this bank questionnaire.

The conjoint model and aggregate OLS results

DeSarbo *et al.* (1993) focus on a standard main-effects part-worth model estimated by ordinary least squares (OLS). The response of a given respondent to the jth profile is given by:

$$y_j = \sum_{p=1}^{P} \sum_{q=1}^{Q_p} \beta_{pq} x_{jpq} + \varepsilon_j, \tag{10.35}$$

where:

$y_j =$ the perceived service quality judgment for the jth experimental profile ($j = 1, \ldots, 30$);
$\beta_{pq} =$ the part-worth of the qth level of the pth SERVQUAL factor;
$x_{jpq} =$ a dummy variable that has the value of 1 if profile j takes on the qth level of the pth SERVQUAL factor, and zero otherwise;
$Q_p =$ the number of levels of the pth SERVQUAL factor (here $Q_p = 3$ for all p)
$p =$ the number of SERVQUAL factors ($p = 11$), and
$\varepsilon_j =$ an error term.

With $J(= 30)$ profiles, the relationships in (10.35) for a given respondent can be summarized in matrix form via:

$$\mathbf{Y} = \mathbf{XB} + \mathbf{U}, \tag{10.36}$$

where:

$\mathbf{Y'} = (y_1, y_2, \ldots, y_J)$;
$\mathbf{X} =$ a $J \times K$ dummy variable matrix with a column of 1's and $q_p - 1$ columns to code a factor with q_p levels;

$$K = \sum_{p=1}^{p} Q_p - p + 1;$$

Table 10.4 3^{11} fractional factorial design with validation profiles

Profile	SERVQUAL dimension/factor										
	A	B	C	D	E	F	G	H	I	J	K
1	1	1	0	1	1	1	1	1	1	1	0
2	1	1	0	1	0	0	0	0	0	0	1
3	1	1	0	1	0	1	0	1	0	0	0
4	1	0	0	1	1	1	1	1	0	0	0
5	1	0	0	0	0	0	0	0	1	0	0
6	1	0	0	1	0	1	0	1	1	1	1
7	1	0	1	1	1	0	1	0	0	0	1
8	1	1	1	1	0	0	0	1	0	1	1
9	1	1	1	0	0	1	0	1	1	0	0
10	0	0	0	0	0	0	1	0	1	0	0
11	0	0	0	0	1	1	0	0	0	1	0
12	0	1	0	0	0	0	0	0	0	0	0
13	0	0	1	0	1	1	1	0	0	1	1
14	0	0	1	0	0	0	0	1	1	0	1
15	0	0	1	0	1	1	0	0	1	1	0
16	0	0	0	0	0	0	1	1	0	0	0
17	0	0	0	1	0	0	0	0	0	0	1
18	0	0	1	1	1	1	1	1	0	0	1
19	1	1	1	1	0	1	0	1	1	1	0
20	1	1	1	1	0	1	0	0	1	0	0

Table 10.4 (*Contd*).

		SERVQUAL dimension/factor									
Profile	A	B	C	D	E	F	G	H	I	J	K
21	0	1	0	1	0	0	1	0	0	0	0
22	1	0	1	0	1	1	1	0	0	1	1
23	1	0	1	0	0	1	0	0	1	0	0
24	1	0	1	0	1	0	1	1	0	0	1
25	1	1	0	0	0	1	0	0	1	0	0
26	1	1	0	1	0	0	0	1	0	1	0
27	1	1	0	1	1	0	1	0	0	0	1
28	0	0	1	0	0	1	0	1	0	1	1
29	1	1	0	0	0	0	0	1	1	0	0
30	1	0	1	1	1	1	1	0	1	1	1

Table 10.5   Aggregate conjoint results (OLS) for banks

		Aggregate Coefficient	Factor Importance
Intercept		4.46***	
A. Equipment:	Worse	−0.13*	0.32
	Better	0.19**	
B. Offering/	Worse	−0.44***	0.60
Office:	Better	0.16**	
C. Dependability:	Worse	−0.60***	0.85
	Better	0.25***	
D. Speed:	Worse	−0.28***	0.31
	Better	0.03	
E. Communication:	Worse	−0.01	0.16
	Better	0.15**	
F. Integrity:	Worse	−0.60***	0.80
	Better	0.20***	
G. Security:	Worse	−0.58***	0.66
	Better	0.08	
H. Competence:	Worse	−0.28***	0.28
	Better	0.00	
I. Courtesy:	Worse	−0.27***	0.36
	Better	0.09	
J. Understanding:	Worse	−0.09	0.13
	Better	0.04	
K. Access:	Worse	−0.30***	0.48
	Better	0.18***	
R^2		0.29	
F		26.06***	

*p ⩽ 0.10
**p ⩽ 0.05
***p ⩽ 0.01

$B' = (\beta_0, \beta_1, \ldots, \beta_{K-1})$;
$E' = \varepsilon_1, \varepsilon_2, \ldots, \varepsilon_J)$;

and the prime denotes transpose. The estimate of B' will be denoted $b' = (b_0, b_1, \ldots, b_{K-1})$ and is equal to $(X' X)^{-1} X' Y$, where the negative one signifies a matrix inverse. In our application, X corresponds to an orthogonal fractional factorial design (e.g. Addelman, 1962). Note that expressions (10.35) and (10.36) can be specified and estimated by respondent (individual level analysis) or over the entire sample via an aggregate or pooled analysis.

Table 10.5 presents the multiple regression results for the aggregate (over all subjects), pooled sample for banks. The table also portrays the importances for each of the SERVQUAL dimensions. (As in conjoint analysis, these importances were calculated on the basis of the range of the coefficients for the three levels within each SERVQUAL factor.) With very few exceptions, the absolute value of the coefficients in Table 10.5 for "worse than expected" levels are much greater than those for "better than expected" levels for both services across most SERVQUAL dimensions reflecting an interesting asymmetry in the responses. This implies that the costs induced by not meeting customers expectations (negative disconfirmation) may exceed the benefits of exceeding those expectations (positive disconfirmation) – a result also found by Oliver and DeSarbo (1988) and Anderson and Sullivan (1993) in a satisfaction context. Such results may also be explained through prospect theory (Kahneman and Tversky, 1979) via a risk-aversion tendency on the part of the majority of respondents. For respondents who may be characterized as seeking minimal variance (deviation from expectation) and maximal mean net benefit (expected amount of net benefit), experiencing the negative factor level (worse than expected) will both decrease the mean and increase the variance, while experiencing the positive factor level (better than expected) will increase the mean while increasing the variance. This argument implies, therefore, that the "worse than expected" levels would have a much larger impact on responses than the "better than expected" levels, as witnessed in Table 10.5. For banks, dependability and integrity are the most important SERVQUAL-based dimensions in assessing perceptions of service quality, followed by security and financial offerings.

Latent class conjoint analysis

Table 10.6 presents the various goodness-of-fit indices available in DeSarbo *et al.* (1992) latent class conjoint analysis procedure as applied to this particular bank service quality data set. As seen, the $S = 3$ latent class solution appears to have the minimum AIC value, with entropy of 0.958 suggesting sufficient centroid separation among the three multivariate normal conditional distributions.

Table 10.6 Latent class conjoint analysis results

S	LnL	Number of parameters	AIC	Entropy
1	– 1920.126	50	3940.252	0.000
2	– 1857.391	101	3916.783	0.883
3	– 1805.640	152	3915.280[a]	0.958
4	– 1769.074	203	3944.148	0.983
5	– 1705.439	254	3918.878	0.991

[a] Denotes minimum AIC.

Table 10.7 presents the part-worth regression coefficients, factor importance, and mixing proportions by latent class for the $S = 3$ solution. As with the aggregate OLS solution presented in Table 10.5, we also see the same

Table 10.7 Latent class conjoint results for S = 3 market segments

		Latent Class 1		Latent Class 2		Latent Class 3	
		Coefficient	Importance	Coefficient	Importance	Coefficient	Importance
Intercept		0.08		0.87		0.13	
A Equipment:	Worse	−0.36	0.53*	−0.54	0.63*	−0.38	0.74*
	Better	0.17		0.09		0.36	
B Offering/Office:	Worse	−0.11	0.31	−0.18	0.46	0.03	0.22
	Better	0.20		0.28		0.19	
C Dependability:	Worse	−0.44	0.58*	−1.07	1.48*	−0.38	0.73*
	Better	0.14		0.41		0.35	
D Speed:	Worse	−0.54	0.54*	0.03	0.03	−0.07	−0.21
	Better	−0.05		0.03		0.14	
E Communication:	Worse	−0.07	0.21	0.13	0.03	−0.02	0.31
	Better	0.14		0.03		0.29	
F Integrity:	Worse	−0.44	0.70*	−0.99	1.11*	−0.38	0.42
	Better	0.26		0.21		0.04	
G Security:	Worse	−0.77	0.87*	−0.67	0.89*	0.03	0.08
	Better	0.10		0.22		−0.05	
H Competence:	Worse	−0.17	0.21	−0.24	0.24	−0.52	0.55*
	Better	0.04		−0.09		0.03	
I Courtesy:	Worse	−0.25	0.25	−0.20	0.20	−0.49	0.99*
	Better	−0.01		−0.04		0.50	
J Understanding:	Worse	−0.12	0.21	−0.02	0.02	−0.13	0.13
	Better	0.09		0.00		−0.01	
K Access:	Worse	−0.40	0.56*	0.05	0.05	−0.38	0.86*
	Better	0.16		0.05		0.48	
λ		0.52		0.27		0.21	

*indicates factor importances > 0.50.

pattern of minus and plus signs for the larger derived coefficients (worse, better) across the three latent classes. However, a cursory inspection of the factor importances reveals substantial heterogeneity in the sample. Latent class one (52% of the sample) members find security and integrity as the most significant drivers of service quality, perhaps reflecting a *conservative* concern for security. Latent class two (27% of the sample) members find dependability and integrity, as the most important factors affecting their perceptions of bank service quality, perhaps reflecting a concern for *consistent performance*. Finally, latent class three (21% of the sample) members find courtesy and access as the most important factors affecting their perceptions of service quality perhaps reflecting *convenience and personal interactions*. The table also reveals the other important factors by latent class.

As in the aggregate case, the magnitude of the coefficients reflecting the "worse than" condition as uniformly larger across the three latent classes for the most part than the coefficients for the "better than" condition indicating the asymmetry in the two conditions. However, a cursory comparison of Tables 10.5 and 10.7 illustrates how an aggregate or pooled analysis can mask interesting heterogeneity in a sample of consumers which could potentially mislead the market researcher. Note, further analysis is possible here by relating the derived posterior probabilities to individual background characteristics (e.g. demographics) in order to make the derived segments more accessible.

Recent Developments

Latent class regression models are important developments of mixture models for classification for use in marketing given the importance of market segmentation. Recently, Titterington (1990) identified some recent innovative work in this field. He notes that the traditional mixture model as outlined above, implies a "hidden" multinomial, in the sense that the random variables representing class membership are assumed to be independently distributed according to an S-cell multinomial distribution, as was previously indicated. An important extension of this notion pertains to models for sequential data in which the unobserved variable $z_{is}(i = 1, \ldots, n)$ are assumed to follow a stationary Markov chain with a finite, but unknown, number of latent states S. For the hidden Markov mixture the complete-data log-likelihood can be formed based on independence of $\mathbf{Y}$ and $\mathbf{Z}$, and the EM-algorithm can be used to estimate the parameters (see Titterington, Smith and Makov, 1985). The E-step, however, requires backward and forward recursions (Levinson, Rabiner, and Sondhi, 1983; Pickett and Whiting, 1987) to estimate the conditional expectations of the unobserved data. The M-step can generally be explicitly formulated. Developments on hidden Markov models have been published by Baum and Eagon (1967), Baum *et al.* (1970), and Lindgren (1978), as well as Hamilton (1989, 1990, 1991) and Engel and Hamilton (1990). Hidden Markov models for discrete manifest data formulated in a latent class context have been proposed by Wiggins (1973), Poulsen (1982, 1990), van de Pol and de Leeuw (1986), and Bye and Schechter (1986). These models have been applied in the context of speech recognition (Levinson, Rabiner, and Sondhi, 1983), the analysis of brand-switching behavior (Poulsen, 1990), and exchange rates (Engel and Hamilton, 1990).

Hidden Markov random field (MRF) models are spatial analogues of hidden Markov chains. Here the unobserved variables indicating class membership are dependent on neighborhoods defined by cliques, and are assumed to follow a gibbs distribution. As both the E-and M-steps of the EM-algorithm for maximizing the complete log-likelihood for hidden MRF models are numerically complex, a number of other methodologies for estimation have been developed (see Titterington, 1990, for a review). MRF models have been used as models for image analysis (Geman and Geman, 1984; Besag, 1986).

The recent developments in latent class models, especially in psycho-metric applications, are numerous and a complete review is beyond the scope of this chapter. Comprehensive reviews have been given by Clogg (1981), Andersen (1982), Langeheine (1988), and Dillon (1993). DeSarbo, Manrai, and Manrai (1993) have reviewed latent class multidimensional scaling models in this handbook. Considerable interest appears to have been devoted to latent class models in which constraints are imposed upon the parameters. The models developed subsume categorical data analogs of linear structural relations models (Goodman 1974a,b; Clogg, 1981; For-mann, 1982, 1984, 1985), Scaling models (MacReady and Dayton, 1980; Rindskopf, 1983; Haertel, 1984), and mixed Markov models (Poulsen, 1982, 1990; van de Pol and Langeheine, 1989). Habermans' (1979) formula-tion appears to be the most general (Langeheine, 1988), and is equivalent to that of a log-linear model for frequencies in which unobserved variables are included. Mooijaart and van der Heijden (1992) indicate some prob-lems related to the application of the EM-algorithm for estimating con-strained latent class models.

Dayton and MacReady (1988) proposed a model that imposes a specific structure on the prior probabilities in latent class models for multivariate categorical data. They formulate a so-called submodel in which the conditional relation between external concomitant variables and prior probabilities is modelled. The model was named a concomitant variable latent class model. For L concomitant variables u_{il} ($i = 1, \ldots, n$; $1 = 1, \ldots, L$), the submodel takes the general form:

$$\pi_{is} = h\left(\sum_{l=1}^{L} \gamma_{ls} u_{il}\right), \tag{10.37}$$

for some function h ($\bullet$), which preserves the constraints on the π_{is}, such as the logistic function. Dayton and MacReady estimate the concomitant variable latent class model using the simplex method. A number of authors have recently extended the Dayton and MacReady (1988) approach to latent class regression models. Formann (1992), Gupta and Chintagunta (1992), and Kamakura, Wedel, and Agrawal (1992) propose latent class multinomial logit regression models, with conditional choice probabilities formulated as a function of explanatory variables, as in equation (10.19). Dillon, Kumar, and de Borrero (1993) recently develop a latent class extended BTL model for capturing individual differences in paired comparisons data. Prior probabilities are formulated as a function of a set of concomitant variables, as in equation (10.11), where the function $h(\bullet)$ is taken to be the logit function. Gupta and Chintagunta (1992) also develop related concomitant variable latent class regression model in which the dependent variable is assumed to follow a truncated poisson, as well as a concomitant variable latent class multinomial probit regression model. All these models simultaneously identify latent classes, estimate regression models within each class, and estimate the relationship of class membership with concomitant variables. Gupta and Chintagunta (1992) and Kamakura, Wedel, and Agrawal (1992) use a Newton-Raphson procedure to maximize the likelihood over the entire parameter space. Formann (1992) develops an EM algorithm for the estimation of the parameters which involves the solution of two independent sets of nonlinear equations in the M-step – one for the conditional probability regression parameters β_s, and one for the prior probability regression parameters, γ_{ls}. Dillon *et al.* (1993) also employ the EM-algorithm to estimate their model. Applications of these models to brand choice, and quantity purchased are provided by Gupta and Chintagunta, and Kamakura and Agrawal, while Formann presents several applications among which are the analysis of social mobility tables, and paired comparison data.

Questions

1　In the application of the latent class conjoint segmentation procedures of DeSarbo, Wedel, Vriens, and Ramaswamy (1992) to the service quality data, describe how the expectation of a preference rating y_j can be obtained.

2　Discuss the major advantages of using the latent class regression procedures such as those proposed by DeSarbo, Wedel, Vriens, and Ramaswamy (1992), Kamakura and Russell (1989), De Soete and DeSarbo (1991), Wedel and DeSarbo (1992) and DeSarbo, Ramaswamy, and Chatterjee (1992) for the analysis of metric conjoint data or conjoint choice data over the more traditionally used two-stage procedure in which in the first stage coefficients are estimated for each individual, which are in the second stage grouped by some hierarchical or non-hierarchical clustering algorithm.

3　Describe a procedure for testing the hypotheses that:

(a)　the profiles have zero-covariance within segments for the $S = 3$ segment solution of the DeSarbo, Wedel, Vriens, and Ramaswamy (1992) procedure for analyzing conjoint data;

(b)　the preference judgments have equal variances within segments, given zero covariance, for this same procedure.

References

Addelman, S. 1962: Orthogonal main-effect plans for asymmetrical factorial experiment. *Technometrics*, 4, 21–46.

Aitkin, M., Anderson, D., and Hinde, J. 1981: Statistical modelling of data on teaching style (with discussion). *Journal of the Royal Statistical Society*, A 144, 419–461.

Aitkin, M. and Rubin, D. B. 1985: Estimation and hypothesis testing in finite mixture distributions. *Journal of the Royal Statistical Society*, B 47, 67–75.

Akaike, H. 1974: A new look at statistical model identification. *IEEE Transactions on Automatic Control*, AC-19, 716–23.

Andersen, E. B. 1982: Latent structure analysis: A survey. *Scandinavian Journal of Statistics*, 9, 1–12.

Anderson, E. W. and Sullivan, M. W. 1993: Customer satisfaction and retention across firms. *Marketing Science*, forthcoming.

Anderson, J. J. 1985: Normal mixtures and the number of clusters problem. *Computational Statistics Quarterly*, 2, 3–14.

Antoniak, C. E. 1974: Mixtures of dirichlet processes with applications to bayesian nonparametric problems. *Annals of Statistics*, 2, 1152–74.

Babakus, E. and Boller, G. W. 1992: An empirical assessment of the SERVQUAL scale, *Journal of Business Research*, 24, 253–68.

Bartholomew, D. J. 1987: *Latent Variable Models and Factor Analysis*, New York: Oxford University Press.

Basford, K. E. and McLachlan, G. J. 1985: The mixture method of clustering applied to three-way data. *Journal of Classification* 2, 109–25.

Baum, L. E. and Eagon, J. A. 1967: An inequality with applications to statistical estimation for probabilistic Markov processes and to a model for ecology. *Bulletin of the American Mathematical Society*, 73, 360–3.

Baum, L. E., Petrie, T., Soules, G., and Weiss, N. 1970: A maximization technique occurring in the statistical analysis of probabilistic functions of Markov chains. *Annals of Mathematical Statistics*, 41, 164–71.

Ben-Akiva, M. and Lerman, S. R. 1985: *Discrete Choice Analysis*, London: The MIT Press.

Besag, J. E. 1986: On the statistical analysis of dirty pictures (with discussion). *Journal of the Royal Statistical Society*, B, 48, 259–302.

Bhattacharya, C. G. 1967: A simple method for resolution of a distribution into its Gaussian components. *Biometrics*, 23, 115–35.

Boyles, R. A. 1983: On the convergence of the EM algorithm. *Journal of the Royal Statistical Society*, B 45, 47–50.

Bozdogan, H. 1987: Model selection and Akaike's information criterion (AIC): The general theory and its analytical extensions. *Psychometrika*, 52, 345–70.

Bozdogan, H. and Sclove, S. L. 1984: Multi-sample cluster analysis using Akaike's information criterion. *Annals of the Institute of Statistics and Mathematics*, 36, 163–80.

Bucklin, R. E. and Gupta, S. 1992: Brand choice, purchase incidence and segmentation: An integrated approach. *Journal of Marketing Research*, 29 (May), 201–16.

Bucklin, R. E., Gupta, S., and Siddarth, S. 1991: Segmenting purchase quantity behavior: A poisson regression mixture model. Working paper, University of California, Los Angeles, USA.

Bye, B. V. and Schechter, E. S. 1986: A latent Markov model approach to the estimation of response errors in multivariate panel data. *Journal of the American Statistical Association*, 81, 375–80.

Carman, J. M. 1990: Consumer perceptions of service quality: An assessment of the SERVQUAL dimensions, *Journal of Retailing*, 66, 1, 33–55.

Cassie, R. M. 1954: Some uses of probability paper for the graphical analysis of polymodel frequency distributions. *Australian Journal of Marine and Freshwater Research*, 5, 513–22.

Charlier, C. V. L. and Wicksel, S. D. 1924: On the dissection of frequency functions. *Arkiv für Mathematik, Astronomi och Fysik*, Bd 18, 6.

Clogg, C. C. 1979: Some latent structure models for the analysis of Likert-type data. *Social Science Research*, 8, 287–301.

Clogg, C. C. 1981: New developments in latent structure analysis. In D. J. Jackson and E. F. Borgatta (eds), *Factor Analysis and Measurement in Sociological Research*, London: Sage, 215–46.

Clogg, C. C. and Goodman, L. A. 1986: Latent structure analysis of a set of multidimensional contingency tables. *Journal of the American Statistical Association*, 79, 762–71.

Clogg, C. C. and Goodman, L. A. 1986: On scaling models applied to data from several groups. *Psychometrika*, 51, 123–35.

Coslett, S. R. and Lee, L. F. 1985: Serial correlation in discrete variable models. *Journal of Econometrics*, 27, 79–97.

Cronin, J. J. and S. A. Taylor 1992: Measuring service quality: A reexamination and extension, *Journal of Marketing*, 56, 55–68.

Croon, M. 1989: Latent class models for the analysis of rankings. In De Soete, G., Feger, H., and Klauer, K. C., *New Developments in Psychological Choice Modelling*, Amsterdam: Elsevier, North-Holland.

Day, N. E. 1969: Estimating the components of a mixture of two normal distributions. *Biometrika*, 56, 463–74.

Dayton, C. M. and MacReady, G. B. 1988: Concomitant variable latent class models. *Journal of the American Statistical Association*, 83, 173–8.

De Soete, G. and DeSarbo, W. S. 1991: A latent class probit model for analyzing pick and/N data. *Journal of Classification*, 8, 45–63.

Dempster, A. P., Laird, N. M. and Rubin, R. B. 1977: Maximum likelihood from incomplete data via the EM-algorithm. *Journal of the Royal Statistical Society*, B39, 1–38.

DeSarbo, W. S. and Cron, W. L. 1988: A maximum likelihood methodology for clusterwise linear regression. *Journal of Classification* 5: 249–82.

DeSarbo, W. S., Huff, L., Rolandelli, M., and Choi, J. 1993: On the measurement of perceived service quality: A conjoint analysis approach. In R. Rust and R. Oliver (eds), *Handbook of Service Quality*, Sage Press, forthcoming.

DeSarbo, W. S., Manrai, A., and Manrai, L. 1993: Latent class multidimensional scaling: a review of recent developments in the marketing and psychometric literature. In R. Bagozzi, (ed.), *Handbook of Marketing Research*, forthcoming.

DeSarbo, W. S., Oliver, R. L., and Rangaswamy 1990: A simulated annealing methodology for cluster wise linear regression. *Psychometrika*, 54, 707–36.

DeSarbo, W. S., Ramaswamy, V., and Chatterjee, R. 1992: Latent class multivariate conjoint analysis with constant sum data. *Working Paper, University of Michigan*, Ann Arbor, MI.

DeSarbo, W. S., Ramaswamy, V., Reibstein, D. J., and Robinson, W. T. 1992: A latent pooling methodology for regression analysis with limited time series of cross sections: A PIMS data application. *Marketing Science*, forthcoming.

DeSarbo, W. S., Wedel, M., Vriens, M., and Ramaswamy, V. 1992: Latent class metric conjoint analysis. *Marketing letters*, 3, 3, 273–88.

Dillon, W. R., Kumar, A., and de Borrero, M. S. 1993: Capturing individual differences in paired comparisons: An extended BTL model incorporating descriptor variables. *Journal of Marketing Research*, 30, 42–51.

Dillon, W. R. and Kumar, A. 1994: Latent structure and other mixture models in marketing: an integrative survey and overview. In R. P. Bagozzi (ed.), *Advanced Methods of Marketing Research*, Oxford: Blackwell.

Engel, C. and Hamilton, J. D. 1990: Long swings in the dollar: Are they in the data and do markets know it? *American Economic Review*, 80, 689–13.

Everitt, B. S. 1984: *An Introduction to Latent Variable Models*, London: Chapman & Hall.

Everitt, B. S. and Hand, D. J. 1981: *Finite Mixture Distributions*, London: Chapman & Hall.

Follmann, D. A. and Lambert, D. 1989: Generalizing logistic regression by non-parametric mixing. *Journal of the American Statistical Association*, 84, 295–300.

Formann, A. K. 1982: Linear logistic latent class analysis. *Biometrical Journal*, 20, 123–6.

Formann, A. K. 1984: *Die Latent-Class-Analyse*, Weinheim: Beltz.

Formann, A. K. 1985: Constrained latent class models: theory and applications. *British Journal of Mathematical and Statistical Psychology*, 38, 87–111.

Formann, A. K. 1992: Linear logistic latent class analysis for polytomous data. *Journal of the American Statistical Association*, 87, 476–86.

Fowlkes, E. B. 1979: Some methods for studying mixtures of two normal (lognormal) distributions. *Journal of the American Statistical Association*, 74, 561–75.

Fryer, I. G. and Robertson, C. A. 1972: A comparison of some methods for estimating mixed normal distributions. *Biometrika*, 59, 639–48.

Geman, S. and Geman, D. 1984: Markov random field image models and their applications to computational vision. *Proceedings of the International Congress on Mathematics*, American Mathematical Society.

Ghosh, J. M. and Sen, P. K. 1985: On the asymptotic performance of the log-likelihood ratio statistic for the mixture model and related results. *Proceedings of the Berkely Conference, Neyman and Kiefer, II*, Wadsworth, Montery, 789–806.

Goldfeld, S. M. and Quandt, R. E. 1973: A Markov model for switching regressions. *Journal of Econometrics*, 1, 3–16.

Goldfeld, S. M. and Quandt, R. E. 1976: *Studies in Nonlinear Estimation*, Cambridge, MA: Ballinger.

Goodman, L. A. 1974a: Exploratory latent structure analysis using both identifiable and unidentifiable models. *Biometrika*, 61, 215–31.

Goodman, L. A. 1974b: The analysis of systems of qualitative variables when some variables are unobservable. Part I: A modified latent structure approach. *American Journal of Sociology*, 79, 1179–1259.

Goodman, L. A. 1978: *Analyzing Qualitative/Categorical Data: Log-linear and Latent Structure Analysis*, Cambridge: Abt books.

Goodman, L. A. 1979: On the estimation of parameters in latent structure analysis. *Psychometrika*, 44 (1), 123–8.

Green, P. E. and Rao, V. R. 1971: Conjoint measurement for quantifying judgmental data, *Journal of Marketing Research*, 8, 355–63.

Gupta, A. K. and Miyawaki, T. 1978: On a uniform mixture model. *Biometrics*, 20, 631–7.

Gupta, S. and Chintagunta, P. K. 1992: On using demographic variables to determine segment membership in logit mixture models. Working paper, Cornell University, Ithaca, NY, USA.

Haberman, S. J. 1977: Maximum likelihood estimates in exponential response models. *Annals of Statistics*, 5, 815–41.

Haberman, S. J. 1979: *Analysis of Qualitative Data: Vol. 2. New Developments*, New York: Academic Press.

Haertel 1984: An application of latent class models to assessment data. *Applied Psychological Measurement*, 8, 333–46.

Hagenaars, J. A. 1990: *Categorical Longitudinal Data*, London: Sage.

Hamilton, J. D. 1989: A new approach to the economic analysis of nonstationary time series and the business cycle. *Econometrika*, 57, 357–84.

Hamilton, J. D. 1990: Analysis of time series subject to changes in regime. *Journal of Econometrics*, 45, 39–70.

Hamilton, J. D. 1991: A Quasi-Bayesian approach to estimating parameters for mixtures of normal distributions. *Journal of Business and Economic Statistics*, 9, 27–39.

Harding, I. P. 1948: The use of probability paper for the graphical analysis of polymodel frequency distributions. *Journal of the Marine Biological Association*, UK 28, 141–53.

Harris, C. M. 1983: On mixtures of geometric and negative binomial distributions. *Communications in Statistics*, A, 12, 987–1007.

Hasselblad, V. 1966: Estimation of parameters for a mixture of normal distributions. *Technometrics*, 8, 431–44.

Hasselblad, V. 1969: Estimation of finite mixtures of distributions from the exponential family. *Journal of the American Statistical Association*, 64, 1459–71.

Helsen, K., Jedidi, K., and DeSarbo, W. S. 1992: A new approach to country segmentation utilizing multinational diffusion patterns. Working paper, University of Michigan, Ann Arbor, MI.

Henna, J. 1985: On estimating the number of constituents of a finite mixture of continuous distributions. *Annals of the Institute of Statistics and Mathemathics*, 37, 235–40.

Hosmer, D. W. 1974: Maximum likelihood estimates of the parameters of a mixture of two regression lines. *Communications in Statistics*, 3, 995–1006.

John, S. 1970a: On analyzing mixed samples. *Journal of the American Statistical Association*, 65, 755–60.

John, S. 1970b: On identifying the population of origin of each observation in a mixture of observations of two Gamma populations. *Technometrics*, 12, 565–8.

Kamakura, W. A. 1991: Estimating flexible distributions of ideal-points with external analysis of preference. *Psychometrika*, 56, 419–48.

Kamakura, W. A. 1992: A clusterwise multinomial logit model for multiple locally-independent choice sets. Working Paper, University of Pittsburgh, Pittsburgh, USA.

Kamakura, W. A. and Novak, T. P. 1992: Value-system segmentation: Exploring the meaning of LOV. *Journal of Consumer Research*, 19, 119–32.

Kamakura, W. A. and Russell, G. J. 1989: A probabilistic choice model for market segmentation and elasticity structure. *Journal of Marketing Research*, 26, 379–90.

Kamakura, W. A., Wedel, M., and Agrawal, J. 1992: Concomitant variable latent class models for the external analysis of choice data. Research Memorandum of the Institute of Economic Research, Faculty of Economics, nr. 486, University of Groningen, Groningen, Netherlands.

Langeheine, R. 1988: New developments in latent class theory. In *Latent Trait and Latent Class Models*, New York: Plenum Press, 77–108.

Langeheine, R. and Rost, J. 1988: *Latent Trait and Latent Class Models*, Plenum Press, New York.

Lazarsfeld, P. F. and Henry, N. W. 1968: *Latent Structure Analysis*, New York: Houghton Mifflin.

Levinson, S. E., Rabiner, L. R. and Sondhi, M. M. 1983: An introduction to the application of the theory of probabilistic functions of a Markov process to automatic speech recognition. *Bell Syst. Technical Journal*, 62, 1035–74.

Li, L. A. and Sedransk, N. 1988: Mixtures of distributions: a topological approach. *Annals of Statistics*, 16, 1623–34.

Lindgren, G. 1978: Markov regime models for mixed distributions and switching regressions. *Scandinavian Journal of Statistics*, 5, 81–91.

Lüxmann-Ellinghaus, U. 1987: On the identifiability of mixtures of infinitely divisible power series distributions. *Statistical and Probability Letters*, 5, 375–8.

Lwin, T. and Martin, P. J. 1989: Probits of mixtures. *Biometrics*, 45, 721–32.

McCullagh, P. and Nelder, J. A. 1989: *Generalized Linear Models*, New York: Chapman & Hall.

McFadden, D. 1973: Conditional logit analysis of qualitative choice behavior. In P. Zarembarka (ed.), *Frontiers of Econometrics*, New York: Academic Press, 105–42.

McHugh, R. B. 1956: Efficient estimation and local identification in latent class analysis. *Psychometrika*, 21, 331–47.

McHugh, R. B. 1958: Note on "Efficient estimation and local identification in latent class analysis." *Psychometrika*, 23, 273–4.

McLachlan, G. J. 1982: The classification and mixture maximum likelihood approaches to cluster analysis. In P. R. Krishnaiah and L. N. Kanal (eds), *Handbook of Statistics* (vol. 2), Amsterdam: North-Holland, 199–208.

McLachlan, G. J. 1987: On bootstrapping the likelihood ratio test statistic for the number of components in a normal mixture. *Applied Statistics*, 36, 318–24.

McLachlan, G. J. and Basford, K. E. 1988: *Mixture Models: Inference and Application to Clustering*, New York: Marcel Dekker.

MacReady, G. B. and Dayton, C. M. 1980: The nature and use of state mastery models. *Applied Psychological Measurement*, 4, 493–516.

Mandelbaum, J. and Harris, C. M. 1982: Parameter estimation under progressive censoring conditions for a finite mixture of Weibull distributions. *TIMS/studies in Management Sciences*, 19, 239–60.

Mooijaart, A. and Heijden, P. G. M. van der 1992: The EM algorithm for latent class analysis with constraints. *Psychometrika*, 57, 261–71.

Nelder, J. A. and Wedderbum, R. W. M. 1972: Generalized linear models. *Journal of the Royal Statistical Society*, A–135, 370–84.

Newcomb, S. 1886: A generalized theory of the combination of observations so as to obtain the best result. *American Journal of Mathematics*, 8, 343–66.

Oliver, R. and DeSarbo, W. S. 1988: Response determinants in satisfaction judgments, *Journal of Consumer Research*, 14, 112–31.

Parasuraman, A., Zeithaml, V. A. and Berry, L. L. 1985: A conceptual model of service quality and its implications for future research, *Journal of Marketing*, 49 (Fall 1985), 41–50.

Parasuraman, A., Zeithaml, V. A. and Berry, L. L. 1988: SERVQUAL: A multiple-item scale for measuring consumer perceptions of service quality, *Journal of Retailing*, 64(1) (Spring), 12–40.

Pearson, K. 1894: Contributions to the mathematical theory of evolution. *Philosophical Trans.*, A 185, 71–110.

Pickett, E. E. and Whiting, R. G. 1987: On the estimation of probabilistic functions of Markov chains. In *Lecture Notes in Economics and Mathematical Syst.*, No. 297, Berlin: Springer.

Pol, F. J. R. van de, and Langeheine, R. 1989: Mixed Markov latent class models. In: C. C. Clogg (ed.), *Sociological Methodology*, Oxford: Blackwell, 213–47.

Pol, F. J. R. van de, and Leeuw, J. de 1986: A latent Markov model to correct for measurement error. *Sociological Methods and Research*, 15, 118–41.

Poulsen, C. A. 1982: *Latent Structure Analysis with Choice Modelling Applications*, Aarhus: Aarhus School of Business Administration and Economics.

Poulsen, C. A. 1990: Mixed Markov and latent Markov modelling applied to brand choice behavior. *International Journal for Research in Marketing*, 7, 5–19.

Quandt, R. E. and Ramsey, J. B. 1978: Estimating mixtures of normal distributions and switching regressions. *Journal of the American Statistical Association*, 73, 730–8.

Quandt, R. E. 1972: A new approach to estimating switching regressions. *Journal of the American Statistical Association*, 67, 306–10.

Ramaswamy, V., Anderson, E. W., and DeSarbo, W. S. 1993: Clusterwise negative binomial regression for count data analysis. *Management Science*, forthcoming.

Ramaswamy, V., DeSarbo, W. S., Reibstein, D. J., and Robinson, W. T. 1993: An empirical pooling approach for estimating marketing mix elasticities. *Marketing Science*, forthcoming.

Redner, R. A. and Walker, H. F. 1984: Mixture densities, maximum likelihood and the EM algorithm. *SIAM Review*, 26, 195–239.

Rindskopf, D. 1983: A general framework for using latent class analysis to test hierarchical and Non-hierarchical learning models. *Psychometrika*, 48, 85–97.

Schwartz, G. 1978: Estimating the dimensions of a model. *Annals of Statistics*, 6, 461–4.

Sclove, S. L. 1977: Population mixture models and clustering algorithms. *Communications in Statistics*, A6, 417–34.

Sclove, S. L. 1987: Application of model-selection criteria to some problems in multivariate analysis. *Psychometrika*, 52, 333–43.

Späth, H. 1979: Algorithm 39: Clusterwise linear regression. *Computing*, 22, 367–73.

Teicher, H. 1961: Identifiability of mixtures. *Annals of Mathematical Statistics*, 32, 244–48.

Titterington, D. M. 1990: Some recent research in the analysis of mixture distributions. *Statistics*, 4, 619–41.

Titterington, D. M., Smith, A. F. M., and Makov, U. E. 1985: *Statistical Analysis of Finite Mixture Distributions*, New York: Wiley.

Wedel, M. and DeSarbo, W. S. 1992a: A latent class binomial logit methodology for the analysis of paired comparison choice data. Memorandum from Institute of Economic Research, nr. 467, Faculty of Economics, University of Groningen, Groningen, Netherlands.

Wedel, M. and DeSarbo, W. S. 1992b: A mixture likelihood approach for generalized linear models. Memorandum from Institute of Economic Research, nr 478, Faculty of Economics, University of Groningen,

Wedel, M., DeSarbo, W. S., Bult, J. R., and Ramaswamy, V. 1991: A latent class Poisson regression model for heterogeneous count data. Memorandum from Institute of Economic Research, nr. 470, Faculty of Economics, University of Groningen, Groningen, Netherlands.

Wedel, M. and Kistemaker, C. 1989: Consumer benefit segmentation using clusterwise linear regression. *International Journal of Research in Marketing*, 6, 45–59.

Wedel, M. and Leeflang, P. S. H. (1992), A pricing decision model for Gabor Granger price experiments. Memorandum from Institute of Economic Research, nr. 506, Faculty of Economics, University of Groningen, Groningen, Netherlands.

Wiggins, L. M. 1973: *Panel Analysis*, Amsterdam: Elsevier.

Windham, M. P. and Cutler, A. 1991: Information ratios for validating cluster analyses. *Conference paper, presented at the 1991 Joint Meetings of the Classification and Psychometric Societies*, Rutgers University, New York.

Wolfe, J. H. 1970: Pattern clustering by multivariate mixture analysis. *Multivariate Behavioral Research*, 5, 329–50.

Wu, C. F. J. 1983: On the convergence properties of the EM algorithm. *Annals of Statistics*, 11, 95–103.

Yarmal-Vuarl, F. and Ataman, E. 1987: Noise histogram and cluster validity for Gaussian-mixtured data. *Pattern Recognition*, 20, 385–401.

Index